Lecture Notes in Computer Science 16042

Founding Editors

Gerhard Goos
Juris Hartmanis

Editorial Board Members

Elisa Bertino, *Purdue University, West Lafayette, IN, USA*
Wen Gao, *Peking University, Beijing, China*
Bernhard Steffen ⓘ, *TU Dortmund University, Dortmund, Germany*
Moti Yung ⓘ, *Columbia University, New York, NY, USA*

The series Lecture Notes in Computer Science (LNCS), including its subseries Lecture Notes in Artificial Intelligence (LNAI) and Lecture Notes in Bioinformatics (LNBI), has established itself as a medium for the publication of new developments in computer science and information technology research, teaching, and education.

LNCS enjoys close cooperation with the computer science R & D community, the series counts many renowned academics among its volume editors and paper authors, and collaborates with prestigious societies. Its mission is to serve this international community by providing an invaluable service, mainly focused on the publication of conference and workshop proceedings and postproceedings. LNCS commenced publication in 1973.

Maki Sugimoto · Angelo Di Iorio ·
Pablo Figueroa · Ryosuke Yamanishi ·
Kohei Matsumura
Editors

Entertainment Computing – ICEC 2025

24th IFIP TC 14 International Conference
Tokyo, Japan, August 27–30, 2025
Proceedings

Editors
Maki Sugimoto
Keio University
Yokohama, Japan

Angelo Di Iorio
University of Bologna
Bologna, Italy

Pablo Figueroa
Universidad de Los Andes
Bogotá, Colombia

Ryosuke Yamanishi
Kansai University
Osaka, Japan

Kohei Matsumura
Ritsumeikan University
Kyoto, Japan

ISSN 0302-9743　　　　　　　　ISSN 1611-3349 (electronic)
Lecture Notes in Computer Science
ISBN 978-3-032-02554-8　　　　ISBN 978-3-032-02555-5 (eBook)
https://doi.org/10.1007/978-3-032-02555-5

© IFIP International Federation for Information Processing 2025

This work is subject to copyright. All rights are solely and exclusively licensed by the Publisher, whether the whole or part of the material is concerned, specifically the rights of translation, reprinting, reuse of illustrations, recitation, broadcasting, reproduction on microfilms or in any other physical way, and transmission or information storage and retrieval, electronic adaptation, computer software, or by similar or dissimilar methodology now known or hereafter developed.
The use of general descriptive names, registered names, trademarks, service marks, etc. in this publication does not imply, even in the absence of a specific statement, that such names are exempt from the relevant protective laws and regulations and therefore free for general use.
The publisher, the authors and the editors are safe to assume that the advice and information in this book are believed to be true and accurate at the date of publication. Neither the publisher nor the authors or the editors give a warranty, expressed or implied, with respect to the material contained herein or for any errors or omissions that may have been made. The publisher remains neutral with regard to jurisdictional claims in published maps and institutional affiliations.

This Springer imprint is published by the registered company Springer Nature Switzerland AG
The registered company address is: Gewerbestrasse 11, 6330 Cham, Switzerland

If disposing of this product, please recycle the paper.

Preface

We are proud to present the Proceedings of the 24th edition of the IFIP International Conference on Entertainment Computing (IFIP ICEC 2025). The conference was held in Tokyo, Japan from August 27th to 30th and hosted by Nihon University. The event was preceded by a two-day symposium of the Information Processing Society of Japan (IPSJ), the largest and leading society in Information Technology in Japan. This gave researchers a great opportunity to exchange ideas in a fruitful and exciting environment.

As the longest-lasting and prime scientific conference in the area of Entertainment Computing, ICEC brings together researchers and practitioners with diverse backgrounds in order to connect, share and discuss both recent and potential future developments in this field.

This year ICEC received the highest number of submissions of the recent editions, showing the ever-growing interest and engagement of the community around these topics. The result was a rich programme, witnessed in this LNCS volume, that included three keynotes, more than 58 papers in the main conference tracks, and five workshops.

For the second year, ICEC 2025 also offered a journal track published in the Elsevier Entertainment Computing Journal - ENTCOM. The interaction between different publication venues and communities has been a great opportunity to foster discussion among researchers and to collect excellent contributions and suggestions. We would like to thank all reviewers that made this possible. The track received 64 submissions and 20 papers were accepted.

Excluding the journal track and the workshop proposals and papers, we received a total of 109 submissions from authors spread all over the world. The works collected in this volume discuss the latest findings in the areas of Game Experience, Player Engagement and Analysis, Serious Gameplay, Entertainment Methods and Tools, Extended Reality and Game Design. All papers underwent a double-blind peer review with at least three reviews per paper. This resulted in 28 accepted full papers, 17 work-in-progress papers, 13 papers for the Interactive Entertainment track and two for the Student Competition. We also had the pleasure of accommodating six workshops covering a wide range of entertainment topics; the results of five of these are presented in a separate volume.

We thank all members of the Program Committee, composed of 100 experts from more than twenty different countries, for their hard work, timeliness and help in ensuring the high quality of the presented proceedings.

Special thanks go to the keynote speakers for their inspiring talks: Shuji Utsumi (President, COO and Representative Director of Sega Corporation) who gave a keynote on "Game Industry's Evolution and Implications"; Wei-Ta Chu (Department of Computer Science and Information Engineering, National Cheng Kung University) with a talk on "Visual Analysis for Entertainment: From Comics to Sports Videos", and Homei Miyashita (Department Chair of Frontier Media Science, School of Interdisciplinary Mathematical Sciences, Meiji University) with a keynote on "Taste, olfactory, and nutritional media: The New Frontier of Foods."

We would also like to thank all the Organizing Committee members who gave us valuable insights, as well as the ICEC Steering Committee. Many thanks also go to the International Federation for Information Processing (IFIP) for their continuous and precious support.

The timeliness, willingness and competence of the local organizers were also commendable and a key factor for the success of the conference. Our sincere thanks go to all the team.

Finally, we would like to express our gratitude to all participants for making ICEC 2025 an exciting and successful event.

July 2025

Maki Sugimoto
Angelo Di Iorio
Pablo Figueroa
Ryosuke Yamanishi
Kohei Matsumura

Organization

General Chair

Ryosuke "Leo" Yamanishi Kansai University, Japan

Program Chairs

Maki Sugimoto Keio University, Japan
Angelo Di Iorio University of Bologna, Italy
Pablo Figueroa Universidad de Los Andes, Colombia

Workshop Chairs

Andréia Formico University of Fortaleza, Brazil
Yuta Sugiura Keio University, Japan

Student Competition Chairs

Erik van der Spek Eindhoven University of Technology, Netherlands
Yudai Tsujino Meiji University, Japan

Work in Progress Chairs

Jerome Dupire Conservatoire National des Arts et Métiers, France
Naoya Koizumi University of Electro-Communications, Japan

Interactive Entertainment Showcase Chairs

Jorge C. S. Cardoso University of Coimbra, Portugal
Mondheera Pituxcoosuvarn Ritsumeikan University, Japan
Susumu Nakata Ritsumeikan University, Japan

Doctoral Consortium Chairs

Licinio Roque   University of Coimbra, Portugal
Yuki Okamoto   University of Tokyo, Japan

Publication Chair

Kohei Matsumura   Ritsumeikan University, Japan

Local Chair

Tetsuro Kitahara   Nihon University, Japan

Web Chair

Tsubasa Yumura   Hokkaido Information University, Japan

Industry/Sponsorship Chair

Yasuhito Baba   Farrier Co. Ltd., Japan

Treasurer

Yoko Nishihara   Ritsumeikan University, Japan

Publicity Chair

Yuichi Itoh   Aoyama Gakuin University, Japan

IPSJ-Liaison

Mitsunori Matsushita   Kansai University, Japan

Local Arrangements Chairs

Kenro Go	Softbank, Japan
Ryo Hatano	Tokyo University of Science, Japan
Masatoshi Hamanaka	RIKEN, Japan
Tatsunori Hirai	Komazawa University, Japan
Akinori Ito	Tokyo University of Technology, Japan
Akinori Miyata	Nihon University, Japan
Masanori Morise	Meiji University, Japan
Aiko Uemura	Tsuda University, Japan

IFIP TC14 Steering Committee

Jannicke Baalsrud Hauge	KTH Royal Institute of Technology, Sweden
Jerome Dupire	CNAM, France
Esteban Clua	Federal Fluminense University, Brazil
Rainer Malaka	University of Bremen, Germany
Erik van der Spek	Eindhoven University of Technology, Netherlands

Program Committee

Megumi Aibara	Nihon University, Japan
Jannicke Baalsrud Hauge	Bremer Institut für Produktion und Logistik/University of Bremen, Germany
Barbara Rita Barricelli	Università degli Studi di Brescia, Italy
Nicole Basaraba	Trinity College Dublin, Ireland
Jorge C. S. Cardoso	University of Coimbra, Portugal
Sergio Carvalho	Universidade Federal de Goias, Brazil
Paolo Ciancarini	University of Bologna, Italy
Tadeu Classe	Universidade Federal do Estado do Rio de Janeiro, Brazil
Esteban Clua	Universidade Federal Fluminense, Brazil
Nuno Correia	Universidade NOVA de Lisboa, Portugal
André Tavares da Silva	Santa Catarina State University, Brazil
Jose Ricado Da Silva Júnior	Federal Fluminense University, Brazil
Drew Davidson	Carnegie Mellon University, USA
Nicola Del Giudice	University of Camerino, Italy
Angelo Di Iorio	University of Bologna, Italy
Ralf Dörner	RheinMain University of Applied Sciences, Germany

Heiko Duin	Bremer Institut für Produktion und Logistik GmbH at the University of Bremen, Germany
Jerome Dupire	CNAM Paris, France
Kai Erenli	UAS BFI Vienna, Austria
Gerald Estadieu	University of Saint Joseph, USA
Daniel Farinha	University of Saint Joseph, USA
Bruno Feijo	PUC-Rio, Brazil
Marco Ferrati	University of Bologna, Italy
Pablo Figueroa	Universidad de Los Andes, Colombia
Andréia Formico	Universidade de Fortaleza, Brazil
Matt Glowatz	University College Dublin, Ireland
Pedro Gonzalez-Calero	Universidad Politécnica de Madrid, Spain
Barbara Göbl	University of Vienna, Austria
Helmut Hlavacs	University of Vienna, Austria
Robin Horst	RheinMain University of Applied Sciences, Germany
Marcelo Da Silva Hounsell	Santa Catarina State University, Brazil
Naoya Isoyama	Otsuma Women's University, Japan
Nicolas Jouandeau	Université Paris 8, France
Liu Kao-Hua	University of Tokyo, Japan
Börje Karlsson	Beijing Academy of Artificial Intelligence, China
Haruhiro Katayose	Kwansei Gakuin University, Japan
Michael Katchabaw	University of Western Ontario, Canada
Noemie Kempa	Conservatoire National des Arts et Métiers, France
Tetsuro Kitahara	Nihon University, Japan
Kei Kobayashi	Nagoya City University, Japan
Troy Kohwalter	Universidade Federal Fluminense, Brazil
Naoya Koizumi	University of Electro-Communications, Japan
Sahra Kunz	Universidade Católica Portuguesa, Portugal
Mei-Kei Lai	Macao Polytechnic University, China
Jaejun Lee	Sungkyunkwan University, South Korea
Jingya Li	Beijing Jiaotong University, China
Luís Lucas Pereira	University of Coimbra, Portugal
Stéphanie Mader	CNAM-CEDRIC, France
Filipa Martins de Abreu	Universidade Católica Portuguesa, Portugal
Maic Masuch	University of Duisburg-Essen, Germany
Kohei Matsumura	Ritsumeikan University, Japan
Mitsunori Matsushita	Kansai University, Japan
Akihiro Matsuura	Tokyo Denki University, Japan
Maximilian Mayerl	Fachhochschule des BFI Wien, Austria

André Miede	Hochschule für Technik und Wirtschaft des Saarlandes, Germany
João Morais	Escola Superior de Tecnologia de Setúbal, Instituto Politécnico de Setúbal, Portugal
Fausto Mourato	Escola Superior de Tecnologia - Instituto Politécnico de Setúbal, Portugal
Wolfgang Müller	University of Education Weingarten, Germany
Nagisa Munekata	Kyoto Sangyo University, Japan
Susumu Nakata	Ritsumeikan University, Japan
Takuji Narumi	University of Tokyo, Japan
Margot Neggers	Breda University of Applied Sciences, The Netherlands
Yoko Nishihara	Ritsumeikan University, Japan
Takuya Nojima	University of Electro-Communications, Japan
Yuki Okamoto	University of Tokyo, Japan
Lea Pacini	CNAM/Inserm, France
Jong-Il Park	Hanyang University, South Korea
Carla Patrão	University of Coimbra, Portugal
André Perrotta	University of Coimbra, Portugal
Martinha Piteira	IPS - ESTSetúbal, Portugal
Mondheera Pituxcoosuvarn	Ritsumeikan University, Japan
Cristiano Politowski	Ontario Tech University, Canada
Andrea Poltronieri	University of Bologna, Italy
Maria Popescu	Carol I National Defence University, Romania
Theresa-Marie Rhyne	Consultant, USA
Licinio Roque	University of Coimbra, Portugal
Rodrigo Santos	Federal University of the State of Rio de Janeiro, Brazil
Tomoya Sasaki	Tokyo University of Science and University of Tokyo, Japan
Anthony Savidis	University of Crete and ICS-FORTH, Greece
Norihisa Segawa	Kyoto Sangyo University, Japan
Mariana Seiça	University of Coimbra, Portugal
Nikitas Sgouros	University of Piraeus, Greece
Edirlei Soares de Lima	Breda University of Applied Sciences, The Netherlands
Ioana Andreea Stefan	Advanced Technology Systems, Romania
Maki Sugimoto	Keio University, Japan
Yuta Sugiura	Keio University, Japan
László Szécsi	Budapest University of Technology and Economics, Hungary
Heinrich Söbke	Hochschule Weserbergland and Bauhaus-Universität Weimar, Germany

Tsutomu Terada	Kobe University, Japan
Michelle Tizuka	Fluminense Federal University, Brazil
Mai Xuan Trang	Phenikaa University, Vietnam
Yudai Tsujino	Meiji University, Japan
Erik van der Spek	Eindhoven University of Technology, The Netherlands
Marcelo Vasconcellos	Oswaldo Cruz Foundation, Brazil
Eulalie Verhulst	CNAM, France
Gennaro Vessio	University of Bari, Italy
Marco Winckler	Université Côte d'Azur, France
Mengru Xue	Zhejiang University, Ningbo, China
Ryosuke Yamanishi	Kansai University, Japan
Yasuyuki Yanagida	Meijo University, Japan
Cheng Yao	Zhejiang University, China
Shunsuke Yoshida	Kyoto Tachibana University, Japan
Tsubasa Yumura	Hokkaido Information University, Japan
Nelson Zagalo	University of Aveiro, Portugal
Ziheng Zhang	Guangzhou Academy of Fine Arts, China
Shuo Zhou	Kyoto Sangyo University, Japan

Additional Reviewers

Justin Debloos
Kentaro Fukuchi
Shoichi Hasegawa
Yutaro Hirao
Takeshi Ito
Hiroyuki Kajimoto
Itaru Kuramoto
Mohamed-Amine Lasheb

Ailin Li
Takahiro Miura
Izumi Mizoguchi
Olivier Pons
Mina Shibasaki
Akifumi Takahashi
Jotaro Tasaki

Contents

Full Conference Papers

Fewer Draws, More Fun: Searching for Unbalanced Positions in Chess 3
   Afro Ambanelli, Paolo Ciancarini, Angelo Di Iorio, Davide Falessi, Andrea Manzo, and Massimo Venuto

Game Elements in Cybersecurity Education: Hype or Help? 15
   Mehrdad Bahrini, Violetta Burdina, Karsten Sohr, and Rainer Malaka

How to Turn a Platformer Game into a Casual Exergame for Combating Office Workers' Sedentary Behavior: An Exploratory Single-Case Pilot Study 32
   Erik Berglund and Filip Josefsson

Design of a Serious Game to Challenge Sexism 47
   Antonio Calvo-Morata, Cristina Alonso-Fernández, and Baltasar Fernández-Manjón

"Follow My Lead": Role of AI-Based NPC Autonomy in Player-NPC Collaboration 60
   Leon Tristan Dratzidis, Nima Zargham, and Rainer Malaka

Interaction and Emotion: A Phenomenological Study of a Playable Generative Landscape 78
   Pedro Garruço, Licínio Roque, and Luís Lucas Pereira

The Blind Gamer: Examining Ethical Agency Through Choice Blindness in Game Design 92
   Kamyab Ghorbanpour, Michal Klincewicz, Paris Mavromoustakos Blom, and Pieter Spronck

Math Valley – On Designing an Embodied VR Learning Application for Primary School Students 107
   Marius Grießhammer, Christian Kißler, Maic Masuch, and Joerg-Tobias Kuhn

200 VR-Sessions with Children – Practical Challenges and Educational Insights Into Conducting a Longitudinal VR-Study in Primary School 123
   Marius Grießhammer and Maic Masuch

Characterizing Social Interaction in Tabletop Games: A Constructive
Conceptual Analysis 138
   Ishika Gupta and Girish Dalvi

Initializing Interactive Treasure Hunts in Cultural Heritage Sites:
An LLM-Based Approach 151
   *Pablo Gutiérrez-Sánchez, Pedro A. González-Calero,
Marco A. Gómez-Martín, Pedro P. Gómez-Martín, and Ruck Thawonmas*

Pacing Control with Wave Function Collapse in Strategy Game Map
Generation 166
   *Ardiawan Bagus Harisa, Muhammad Alifian Aqshol,
Pulung Nurtantio Andono, and Wen-Kai Tai*

Generative Multimodal Content Creation with Location-Aware Context
for Gamified Mobile Assisted Language Learning Apps Using Large
Language Models 179
   Robin Horst, Dung Trinh, and Ralf Dörner

Automated Planning of Entertainment Content for Digital Health
Interventions: A Technical Feasibility Study on Balance VS Fun 193
   *L. J. James, Emanuele De Pellegrin, Laura Genga, Barbara Montagne,
and Pieter Van Gorp*

Evaluating Colorblind-Friendly Design for Equitable Play in Mobile
Puzzle Games 207
   JaeJun Lee, Joo-Eun Kang, Jeong-Eun Park, and Min-Joong Kim

Manzai Karaoke: A Real-Time Visual Guidance System for Assisting
Japanese Double Act Performance 219
   Shunta Komatsu, Tomonori Kubota, Satoshi Sato, and Kohei Ogawa

EchoArtLink: Enhancing Social Connectedness Between Parents
and Children Living Apart Through Digital Sound Visualization 233
   Chenwei Liang, Rui Wang, and Jun Hu

Optimizing Random Forest Multi-classification and Gini-Based Feature
Analysis of Board Game Success via BGG Characteristic Data 250
   Tianle Liang, Kieran Rosenfeld, and Nathan Lu

Stay and Play - Modeling Social Influence of Players in the Steam Gaming
Community 263
   Enrica Loria, Alessia Antelmi, Carmine Spagnuolo, and Johanna Pirker

A Framework for Explainable AI in Wargames to Understand Strategies   280
    Christoph Lürig and Fabian Fell

Parablade: A Proposal of Chambara Based on Augmented Sports -
A Study of Appropriate Game Balancing Methods   293
    Naoto Nishida, Yusaku Maeda, Kamui Sato, Sho Sakurai,
    Koichi Hirota, and Takuya Nojima

Vectorigger: A Method of Inducing Vection Using a Wearable LED Array   307
    Ayumi Ohnishi, Kazuki Ohmura, Tsutomu Terada,
    and Masahiko Tsukamoto

Learning Success, Engagement and Fun: Evaluating an Educational Game
in Higher Education as Replacement for a Homework Assignment   320
    Melina Rose, Alessandra Antonaci, Martin Bonnet, and Roland Klemke

From News to Stories via an AI-Supported Retelling Process   334
    Edirlei Soares de Lima, Marco A. Casanova, Bruno Feijó,
    and Antonio L. Furtado

Learning Through Play: Implementing an Educational Escape Room
for Teaching Traditions and Culture   349
    Kevin Valencia-Aragón, Hugo AriasFlores, Mireya Zapata,
    Luis Aguirre-Morales, and Sandra Sanchez-Gordon

Experienced Video Game Player Interaction Preferences with Game
Controllers and Haptic Gloves   360
    Alejandro Villar, Sergio Baña, Juan Diego Mendoza, Laura Gómez,
    Javier Muñoz, and Carlos León

What Does an Angel's Halo Taste Like?: Exploring the Structure
of Gustatory Comedy Through Case Analysis of Ajigiri   375
    Sotaro Yokoi, Ryo Ohara, Kohei Murayama, Kizashi Nakano,
    and Takuji Narumi

"Can You Feel Me Now?": Exploring Player Empathy in AI-Based NPC
Conversations   389
    Nima Zargham, Aaron Merkord, Ameneh Safari,
    Leon Tristan Dratzidis, and Rainer Malaka

Work in Progress

How Does Entertainment Computing Contribute to the Sustainable
Development Goals? A Rapid Literature Review   411
    Jannicke Baalsrud Hauge, Polona Caserman, and Heinrich Söbke

VR Gaming Approach to Language Comprehension in Children
with Autism 423
   *Andrea Caruso, Priscilla Pia Papa, Giovanni Schembra,
and Massimiliano Salfi*

Physics Virtual Classroom: Leveraging Virtual Reality Sandboxes
for Learning Classical Mechanics 433
   Guhan Elangovan, Nicko R. Caluya, and Damon M. Chandler

Gestalt Approaches to Hinting in Games: A 3D Connect Four Case Study 442
   Yuta Hirahata, Nicko R. Caluya, and Damon M. Chandler

A VR System for Detecting Static Electricity as Invisible Creature 451
   Wanosuke Ito, Rion Yukino, and Akihiro Matsuura

Designing Physically Fiction: Suspension of Disbelief in Interaction
with MR Environments 458
   Toshiro Kashiwagi and Kumiyo Nakakoji

Simulating AI-Human Collaborative Strategies in Sudoku Puzzle
Generation 468
   Mohd Nor Akmal Khalid

ChordFusion: Interactive Piano Training in Mixed Reality with Custom
Gloves 478
   *Muhammad Faiq Haikal Bin M Haikal, Deb Kumar Ghosh,
Jordan K. Lay, Nicko R. Caluya, and Damon M. Chandler*

Implementation and Evaluation of an Automated Eye Dropping System
Using Games 487
   Miu Moritani and Kazutaka Kurihara

Proposal of Affective Music Features Utilizing Playlists as Collective
Intelligence 496
   Teu Nishihara and Osamu Ichikawa

Mi Librero de Aventuras: A Novel Configurable Serious Game
for Personalized Science and Technology Learning in Peruvian Primary
Education 504
   Luiggi Ramos, Johan Baldeón, and María-José Espinosa-Chueca

Multi-directional Shooting Using Logarithmic Spiral Trajectories 514
   Kento Saito and Akihiro Matsuura

Refining Pervasive Game Design with LLMs: Insights, Limitations, and Challenges 523
   Bruno Silva, Pedro Oliveira, Gilvan Maia, and Windson Viana

Heist Extravaganza: A Design Framework and Exemplars of Asymmetric Virtual Reality Controllers Based on Player Profiles 532
   Jules A. M. van Gurp and Erik D. van der Spek

Automatic Piano Arrangement for Three-Part Choral of Female Voices 541
   Kana Yamada, Aiko Uemura, and Norimasa Yoshida

JumpLab: An Interactive Learning Tool for Parameter Tuning in the Pre-production Stage 550
   Keita Yamazaki, Masayoshi Itoh, and Kentaro Fukuchi

"Hand-In-Hand" Learning: A Novel Method for Instrument Skill Training with Electrical Muscle Stimulation 559
   Shuo Zhou, Akira Shikida, and Norihisa Segawa

Interactive Entertainment Showcase

Transformer Based Adaptive Music Generation for Video Games 571
   Thomas Dallard and Akinori Ito

Kaimanāki o te Ngahere: Guardians of the Forest 575
   Allan Fowler, Tanya Ruka, Michaela Dodd, Bai Xue, and Mark Harvey

Demonstration of Visualizer for Beats and Scratches of Breaking DJ Performances 579
   Masatoshi Hamanaka

Development of a Dialogue Agent System Expressed in a Two-Dimensional Manga-Anime Style and Design of the Original Artificial Intelligence Character "Kohane" 583
   Kaimu Harada and Sachiko Kodama

Development of Urban Disaster Prevention Shooting Game Using Spatial Reproduction Display 588
   Yasuo Kawai

VR Game Aimed at Recovering Visual Acuity 592
   Masahiro Kawamori and Masataka Imura

Automatic Fingering Saxophone Quartet System 597
   Gou Koutaki and Masatoshi Hamanaka

Multiple Robots Enable *Moderate Facilitation* Through Approaching Movements in Group Discussions 602
   Rintaro Makino, Yuki Okafuji, Haruki Takahashi, and Kohei Matsumura

VR Batting Practice System Integrated with Visual Training 607
   Taito Matsumoto, Masahiro Kawamori, and Masataka Imura

Arcade Games Generating an Atmosphere to Promote Exercise 611
   Daiki Mima, Haruki Takahashi, and Kohei Matsumura

Guitar Clicker: A Gamified Approach to Motivating Guitar Practice for Beginners 616
   Itsuki Okamo, Kohei Matsumura, and Haruki Takahashi

Emo-Pathy: An Emotion-Sharing System for Promoting Psychological Well-Being Through Supportive Interactions 621
   Yuunosuke Suenaga, Gaku Kutsuzawa, Haruki Takahashi, and Kohei Matsumura

Rapid Input Device with Independent Sensing of Input Intention and Input Target 625
   Katsuhisa Tanaka, Masahiro Kawamori, and Masataka Imura

Student Competition

Heaviest Listener: Immersive Radio Experience Simulation by Sending Japanese E-Mail 633
   Harunobu Kaneko, Kota Aoki, and Yoshio Iwai

Asymmetric VR Game Heist Extravaganza 640
   Jules A. M. van Gurp and Erik D. van der Spek

Author Index 649

Full Conference Papers

Fewer Draws, More Fun: Searching for Unbalanced Positions in Chess

Afro Ambanelli[1], Paolo Ciancarini[2](✉), Angelo Di Iorio[2], Davide Falessi[3], Andrea Manzo[1], and Massimo Venuto[1]

[1] AlphaChess srl, Muggia, Italy
[2] University of Bologna, Bologna, Italy
{paolo.ciancarini,angelo.diiorio}@unibo.it
[3] University of Rome Tor Vergata, Rome, Italy

Abstract. Draw outcomes dominate both correspondence chess tournaments and competitions among top computer chess engines, diminishing their competitive and entertainment value. This study addresses the issue of draw dominance in computer chess, with direct implications for correspondence play. We investigate the problem of identifying alternative starting positions that lead to unbalanced games, where outcomes are less predictable even for state-of-the-art chess engines. Our approach focuses on searching, selecting, and evaluating positions —those with a 75% winning probability—as a means to increase decisive results. By analyzing these positions through extensive engine-based simulations, we aim to not only reduce draw rates but also introduce a framework for ranking and measuring the strength of the strongest chess engines.

1 Introduction

Chess attracts a dedicated audience that appreciates its depth, strategy, and nuances. However, when it comes to playing correspondence games[1] or watching computer chess tournaments, the experience can feel less engaging due to a high frequency of draws and openings with predictable outcomes [6].

Our goal is to explore ways to make these events more dynamic and enjoyable by identifying special, unbalanced starting positions that reduce draw rates and introduce more varied gameplay. While the study of unbalanced chess positions may seem like a niche endeavor, it has significant implications for both competitive engine testing and human-computer interaction. By analyzing the huge available game datasets we aim to uncover rare and valuable positions that can lead to richer, more decisive games. The appeal here is for chess enthusiasts and those interested in artificial intelligence [19]. Watching computer chess games

---

[1] Correspondence games are played by humans through mail, email, or dedicated websites, allowing for deep analysis usually supported by computers.

(CCG) can be fascinating because they often feature moves and strategies that are beyond human comprehension, revealing the depth and complexity of chess.

In a game of Chess there are three possible results: White wins, Black wins, or draw. The latter outcome is the most frequent between masters when they play long time controls[2]. The draw can result from: an agreement between the players, a stalemate, insufficient material to checkmate, the 50-move rule, a threefold repetition of the position, or a dead position where no legal sequence of moves can lead to checkmate[3].

The problem of too many draws in chess, particularly in correspondence chess where computers are extensively used, is an issue that affects the dynamics and appeal of the game [8], even if some drawn games are actually quite entertaining [18].

In fact, modern chess engines are very strong and can often find the best moves in most positions. Thus, both sides can defend accurately and avoid mistakes, which usually leads to a draw. The reliance on engines by correspondence players reduced the scope for human creativity and original play. Players may follow engine recommendations rather than exploring novel ideas, leading to more predictable and less exciting games. A high draw rate can also make the game less exciting for spectators. This can affect the popularity and viewership of chess events.

The predictability of outcomes when both sides play near-perfectly can reduce the drama; we need to increase unpredictability to increase entertainment [9]. Increasing unpredictability in CCG is also useful when comparing chess engines or for tiebreaks in their tournaments.

Some have proposed rule changes to reduce the number of draws, such as modifying the scoring system (e.g., awarding 3 points for a win and 1 for a draw), introducing no-draw zones in the early stages of the game, or altering the sequencing of moves [4].

Some argue that the high draw rate is an inherent aspect of chess, reflecting the game's balance and depth. They believe that the pursuit of perfection is part of what makes chess a profound and enduring game [8].

In summary, the problem of draws in chess stems from the near-perfect play enabled by engines. Addressing this issue requires a balance between maintaining the integrity of the game and enhancing its appeal to players and spectators alike.

Our Research Questions (RQ) are as follows:

RQ1 *How can we identify starting positions that minimize the draw rate in computer chess tournaments?*

We call "*nuggets*" these starting positions, because we found that they are rare and precious. We will show how we mine game repositories searching for nuggets using an engine like Stockfish.

RQ2 *What impact does the use of nuggets have on the rating and comparative evaluation of chess engines in tournaments?*

---

[2] https://www.chessgames.com/chessstats.html.
[3] See here the complete official rules of chess.

We will show and comment on the results of some competitions where we used the nuggets as starting positions.

This paper has the following structure: in Sect. 2 we describe some background research on the topic of draws in chess; in Sect. 3 we outline our approach; in Sect. 4 we expose some results; in Sect. 5 we discuss our results; finally, in 6 we draw our conclusions.

WC32/final, World Championship 32 Final

TD Pheby, Ian M. (IA)

Category 11					1	2	3	4	5	6	7	8	9	10	11	12	13	14	15	16	17	GM	SIM	Score	Wins	SB	RG	Place
1	510692	SIM	Edwards, Jon	2525		½	½	½	½	½	½	½	½	½	½	1	½	½	½	½	1	9½		9	2	68.25	0	1
2	180109	GM	Lecroq, Michel	2568	½		½	½	½	½	½	½	½	½	½	½	½	½	1	½	1	9½		9	2	68	0	2
3	141625	SIM	Osipov, Sergey Adolfovich	2499	½	½		½	½	½	½	½	½	½	½	½	½	½	1	½	1	9½		9	2	68	0	2
4	390086	GM	Neto, Horácio	2567	½	½	½		½	½	½	½	½	½	½	½	½	½	½	1	1	9½		9	2	68	0	2
5	81224	SIM	Zajontz, Rainer	2500	½	½	½	½		½	½	½	½	½	½	½	½	½	½	½	1	9½		8.5	1	64.5	0	5
6	490165	GM	Akdag, Murat	2574	½	½	½	½	½		½	½	½	½	½	½	½	½	½	½	1	9½		8.5	1	64.5	0	5
7	300204	GM	Jónsson, Daði Örn	2559	½	½	½	½	½	½		½	½	½	½	½	½	½	½	½	1	9½		8.5	1	64.5	0	5
8	19094	SIM	Mendl, Manuel	2537	½	½	½	½	½	½	½		½	½	½	½	½	½	½	½	1	9½		8.5	1	64.5	0	5
9	89356	IM	Ulbig, Stefan	2416	½	½	½	½	½	½	½	½		½	½	½	½	½	½	½	1	9½	8	8.5	1	64.5	0	5
10	750087	SIM	Blitsko, Boris Mikhailovich	2509	½	½	½	½	½	½	½	½	½		½	½	½	½	½	½	1	9½		8.5	1	64.5	0	5
11	141530	SIM	Nekhaev, Andrey Ivanovich	2455	½	½	½	½	½	½	½	½	½	½		½	½	½	½	½	1	9½		8.5	1	64.5	0	5
12	130766	SIM	Michálek, Miroslav	2480	0	½	½	½	½	½	½	½	½	½	½		½	½	½	½	1	9½		8	1	60.25	0	12
13	81204	GM	Moll, Reinhard	2554	½	½	½	½	½	½	½	½	½	½	½	½		½	½	½	½	9½		8	0	64	0	13
14	141537	GM	Kochemasov, Andrey Leonidovich	2554	½	½	½	½	½	½	½	½	½	½	½	½	½		½	½	½	9½		8	0	64	0	13
15	82299	SIM	Schwetlick, Thomas	2470	½	0	0	½	½	½	½	½	½	½	½	½	½	½		½	1	9½		7.5	1	56	0	15
16	390491	GM	Pessoa, Francisco Azevedo	2524	½	½	½	0	½	½	½	½	½	½	½	½	½	½	½		½	9½		7.5	0	59.75	0	16
17	84833	SIM	Bock, Steffen	2562	0	0	0	0	0	0	0	0	0	0	0	0	½	½	0	½		9½		1.5	0	11.75	0	17

Fig. 1. Final standings of 32 World Correspondence Chess Championship, 2023

2 Background and Related Work

The frequency of wins, losses, and draws in chess varies depending on the skill level of the players, the time control, and the specific context (e.g., casual play, over the board or correspondence tournaments, online platforms). However, some general trends can be observed.

Over the board (OTB) with long playing times, at the Grandmaster Level approximately 40% of games end in a draw [11,14]. In recent World Championships the percentile was even higher [1]. This is because top-level players are highly skilled at defending and often play very accurately, making it difficult for either side to secure a win. The remaining games are split between wins and losses, with a slight bias toward the player with the white pieces, who has the first-move advantage. Typically, White wins around 30–35% of the time.

At the Amateur Level draws are less common than at the Grandmaster Level. This is because mistakes are more frequent at the Amateur level than the Grandmaster level. Moreover, at this level wins and losses are more evenly distributed than at the Grandmaster Level, with White still having a slight advantage, winning around 35–40% of the time.

Elite correspondence tournaments are especially plagued by high rates of draws. They has seen draw rates as high as 100% in 2017 and 97% in 2019

[8]. Figure 1 shows the final standings of the recent 32nd World Correspondence Chess Championship, where most games ended draw.

These statistics highlight the prevalence of draws in elite human competitions. Since draws are correlated with the ability of players, draws in CCG are even more frequent than in human competitions [12]. For instance, in 2017 a match between AlphaZero and Stockfish resulted in 72 draws over 100 games [15]. The 2015 TCEC Season 8 Superfinal between Komodo and Stockfish experienced an 89% draw rate.

On digital platforms like Chess.com[4] or Lichess[5], the frequency of wins, losses, and draws can vary based on the time control. Faster time controls (e.g. blitz) tend to have fewer draws (around 10–20%) and more decisive results due to time pressure and mistakes. Slower time controls see more draws (around 20–40%) as players have more time to think and avoid mistakes.

Across all levels, the overall distribution is roughly as follows [5]: draws are 30–40%; wins for White are 35–40%; wins for Black are 25–30%.

These percentages are approximate and can vary depending on the dataset and context. For example, in high-stakes tournaments, players usually play more conservatively, leading to more draws, while in casual games, players take more risks, leading to more decisive results.

2.1 Chess Entertainment

The attention on the problem of draws in (computer) chess has been posed by Haworth and Cazenave a few years ago [8]. The authors also reported on a proposal by an anonymous player (nicknamed Aloril) who defined a method to eliminate draws in a chess variant called Mobility Chess. Anbarci and Mehmet [1] addressed a similar problem for chess tiebreakers. These tiebreakers reduce the quality and entertainment value of the games, thus authors presented an AI-based method for objective tiebreaking. The method first measures the quality of players' moves by comparing them to the optimal moves recommended by a chess engine, and in case of a tie declares as the winner the player with the higher quality score. This approach aims at preserving the quality of the game but increasing the fairness. Towards the same goal, Brams and Ismail [4] worked on a variation of chess that allows double moves at the opening, and proposed a method called Balanced Alternation that proved to generate fairer matches. Such fairness is counterbalanced by a higher probability of forcing a draw with optimal play, which is not necessarily entertaining.

Other authors studied the impact of game strategies on the entertainment dimension of chess. In [9] the authors proposed a way to measure the entertaining impact of a chess game. The metrics is built on the number of possible moves and the length of the game and was successfully used to study chess variants.

Similar approaches have been proposed to study entertainment in board games in general. Yannakakis and Hallam [20] proposed a method to quantitatively measure some psychological factors, namely challenge and curiosity, and

---

[4] Chess.com game repository: https://www.chess.com/games.
[5] Lichess game repository: https://database.lichess.org.

how these contribute to human entertainment. They exploited neural networks to model player satisfaction, in terms of these two dimensions, and to study how this is influenced by different games and strategies.

The work of Halim et al. [7] is also worth mentioning. The authors proposed a set of entertainment metrics tailored for platform games and, in order to test these metrics, implemented an evolutionary algorithm able to generate game rules using these metrics as objective functions. The generated games proved to be increasingly entertaining according to the feedback provided by human players.

Primanita et al. [13] studied uncertainty in games, and in particular how it affects not only the way a game is solved but also the way a game is perceived and enjoyed by the player. Experimental results demonstrated how uncertainty plays a key role for both these aspects and in particular for increasing the entertainment value of a game.

Concerning related works on uncertainty and win probability as opposed to traditional evaluation, there are not so many works. Recently, the "fragility" of traditional positional evaluation has been discussed in [3]. The idea of using win probability to improve position evaluation of chess games has been also studied in [17].

3 Method

The key idea of our proposal is to look for *unbalanced positions*, i.e. positions that are more likely to produce a White or Black win, thus reducing draw probability. We called these positions *nuggets*. In order to identify nuggets we exploit the probability models provided by Chess engines.

Stockfish (as well as many other engines) can provide a numeric evaluation of a position in units called *centipawns* (1/100 of a pawn). Newer versions of Stockfish include a built-in Win-Draw-Lose (WDL) probability model, which was introduced by Leela[6]. We also use ShashShess [10]. This program is derived from Stockfish and is enriched with the Shashin theory of chess as a complex system [16].

We have used WDL to study (unbalanced) positions in games from human World Championships and high level tournaments, e.g. Zurich 1953. For instance, this is a position from the 2024 World chess championship.

Gukesh-Ding Liren WCC match 2024, 13th game. **1 e4 e6 2 d4 d5 3 ♘c3 ♘f6 4 e5 ♘fd7 5 ♘ce2 c5 6 c3 ♘c6 7 a3 ♗e7 8 ♗e3 ♘b6 9 ♘f4 cxd4 10 cxd4 ♘c4** According to Stockfish: Position evaluation is +100 centipawns; White is winning ±. The win probability is (75, 25, 0).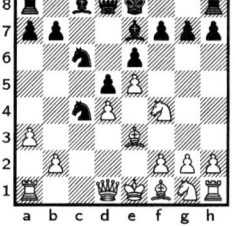

---
[6] https://lczero.org/blog/2020/04/wdl-head/.

The primary criterion for selecting unbalanced positions is based on a winning probability threshold of 75%. This threshold was chosen for several reasons:

- In games among expert players, many positions tend toward equilibrium, leading to a significant proportion of drawn games. A 75% winning probability ensures that a selected position exhibits a clear imbalance while still allowing competitive play.
- Positions with an extreme win probability (e.g., above 90%) might be trivially winning for one side, reducing their practical significance. Conversely, a lower threshold (e.g., 60%) might still lead to frequent draws. The 75% threshold strikes a balance between competitive play and decisive outcomes.
- Many engines and databases classify positional advantages in terms of centipawn evaluations. Empirical studies suggest that a 75% win probability roughly corresponds to an evaluation of $+1.00$ to $+1.50$, a range often considered a substantial but not yet overwhelming advantage [17].

In order to systematically identify and select unbalanced starting positions, we followed a multi-step process involving database analysis, heuristic filtering, and expert validation:

1. **Database extraction**: we analyzed game databases with master-level play, namely World Chess Championships (1165 games) and Zurich 1953 tournament of candidates to the WC (210 games).
2. **Engine evaluation**: Each position was evaluated using Stockfish to determine the win probability for both sides.
   Positions were evaluated on:
   - Win probability between 70% and 80% (to ensure a slight but meaningful imbalance). Then, in order to validate the effectiveness of the selected positions, we conducted a series of simulations and tournaments played with long times. We employed Stockfish to analyze the selected positions and assess their long-term playability. Simulations were run under multiple time controls. Each position was tested in at least 1,000 engine-vs-engine games, ensuring statistical significance. We recorded:
     - Win/draw/loss distribution.
     - Centipawn evaluation trends over multiple plies.
     - Variability in different engine settings (e.g., different NNUE models configured in Stockfish).
   - Positional richness (avoiding forced tactical sequences leading to immediate resolution).
   - Historical frequency (preference for positions that have been tested in practical play).
3. **Manual refinement**: chess experts reviewed the positions we found to exclude trivial or artificially imbalanced setups, ensuring practical relevance.

The heuristic filters work as follows:

- *Material balance heuristic*: we exclude positions with excessive material imbalance, which often lead to predictable results. We check that material differences do not exceed a minor piece or an exchange. However, we accept positions where sacrificed material is compensated by positional factors. Example: we exclude queen vs. rook + minor piece but allow two rooks vs. queen with active play.
- *Tactical complexity heuristic*: we select positions rich in tactical opportunities to avoid forced sequences leading to quick resolution. When we analyze the branching factor—the number of reasonable moves per position, we prefer positions where multiple plausible continuations exist. Example: we prefer positions where both players have several attacking and counterattacking options.
- *Positional balance heuristic*: we favor positions where both sides retain strategic possibilities. We try to identify positions with unresolved tensions, such as weak pawns or contested open files. Moreover, we try to avoid sterile positions with few remaining pieces. Example: we look for opposite-side castling scenarios with mutual attacking chances.
- *Draw avoidance heuristic*: we exclude positions prone to perpetual check or threefold repetition, by checking positions where cyclic move repetition is likely. We also use MonteCarlo simulations to identify forced perpetual check sequences. Example: Discard positions where a best defensive strategy always results in repetition.
- *Dynamic balance heuristic*: we try to favor positions where play remains fluid, avoiding strategic stagnation. We evaluate piece mobility to ensure both sides have useful moves, and avoid closed, static positions with no clear plans. Example: we prefer double-edged middlegames over locked pawn structures.
- *Sensitivity to errors heuristic*: we prefer positions where small inaccuracies significantly impact the result. We assess how minor mistakes shift evaluation scores (e.g., from +0.5 to -1.0). Also, we avoid technical endgames with little room for blunders. Example: middlegame positions where an inaccuracy in defense triggers an immediate attack.
- *Database heuristic*: we use historical game databases to identify nugget positions that have emerged in practical play. We analyze games between humans or between computers to find positions with win probabilities near 75% or 25%, then we select positions that have resulted in varied outcomes or have been subject to deep analysis. Examples: positions from classic grandmaster tournaments (for instance, we analyzed all games from 1953 Zurich Candidate Tournament) or unbalanced computer games, like the wins by AlphaZero over Stockfish [15].

Table 1 provides a useful reference for evaluating chess positions in a human-like way by integrating probability, positional assessment, and historical playing styles associated with players such as Petrosian (defensive), Capablanca (strategic), and Tal (attacking). It is based on Shashin theory [16] and maps WDL (Win-Draw-Loss) ranges, probabilistic evaluations (*win probability*), positional characteristics, and Informator symbols to specific types of positions.

Table 1. Win probability ranges named following Shashin theory [16]. Central rows, from Low Petrosian to Low Tal, except the Capablanca one, that represents forced draw, are those useful for nuggets.

WDL Range (W, D, L)	Shashin Position's Type	Win Probability Range	Informator Symbols	Description
[0,3], [0,4], [96, 100]	High Petrosian	[0, 5]	-+	Winning: a decisive advantage, with the position clearly leading to victory
[4, 6], [5, 8], [92, 95]	Middle-High Petrosian	[6, 10]	-+ \ -/+	Decisive advantage: dominant position and likely winning
[7, 9], [9, 12], [88, 91]	Middle Petrosian	[11, 15]	-/+	Clear advantage: a substantial positional advantage, but a win is not yet inevitable.
[10, 12], [13, 16], [84, 87]	Middle-Low Petrosian	[16, 20]	-/+ \ =/+	Significant advantage: strong edge
[21, 35], [0, 16], [65, 79]	Low Petrosian	[21, 35]	=/+	Slight advantage with a positional edge, but no immediate threats
[0, 15], [40, 60], [40, 60]	Chaos: Capablanca∩Petrosian	[25, 50]	↓	Opponent pressure and initiative: defensive position
[33, 33, 33]	Chaos: Capablanca∩Petrosian∩Tal	[50, 50]	∞	Total chaos: unclear position, dynamically balanced, with no clear advantage for either side and no clear positional trends
[40, 60], [40, 60], [0, 15]	Chaos: Capablanca∩Tal	[50, 75]	↑	Initiative: playing dictation with active moves and forcing ideas
[0, 100, 0]	Capablanca	[50, 50]	=	Equal position. Both sides are evenly matched, with no evident advantage.
[65, 79], [0, 16], [21, 35]	Low Tal	[65, 79]	+/=	Slight advantage: a minor positional edge, but it's not significant
[84, 87], [13, 16], [10, 12]	Middle-Low Tal	[80, 84]	+/= \ +/-	Slightly better, tending toward a clear advantage. The advantage is growing, but the position is still not decisive.
[88, 91], [9, 12], [7, 9]	Middle Tal	[85, 89]	+/-	Clear advantage: a significant edge, but still with defensive chances.
[92, 95], [5, 8], [4, 6]	Middle-High Tal	[90, 94]	+/- \ +-	Dominant position, almost decisive, not quite winning yet, but trending toward victory.
[96, 100], [0, 4], [0, 3]	High Tal	[95, 100]	+-	Winning: a decisive advantage, with victory nearly assured.

This method ensures that the selected unbalanced positions are both theoretically sound and practically relevant, offering a structured approach for testing the strength of computer players.

Win probability, within the WDL model, is defined as $W + D/2$. We define *nugget positions* as those where the probabilities of winning and drawing are equal (e.g., $(W, D, L) = (50, 50, 0)$ for $winProbability = 75\%$, or $(0, 50, 50)$ for $winProbability = 25\%$). These positions exhibit maximum uncertainty, making the final result highly dependent on the quality of subsequent moves.

Positions with a win probability of approximately either 75% or 25% are particularly valuable because: they feature strategic or tactical imbalances that defy straightforward evaluation; they challenge engines by requiring deep calculations to assess the final outcome; they reduce the likelihood of games crystallizing into well-known theoretical draws.

4 Results

We have looked for nuggets positions in World Chess Championships WCC (1165 games) and in the Zurich 1953 tournament (210 games). We have found 12 nuggets in the former dataset and 15 in the latter. Nuggets in these datasets of games played by expert humans are very rare because humans tend to avoid uncertain positions, playing safely.

We then run two experiments to verify the impact of these nuggets on draws. In particular, we run two tournaments between different engines, in which all games were played over nuggets positions. We considered either engines with similar ELO strenghts and with different ones.

Table 2. A round-robin tournament (each match over 20 games) among different Stockfish variants of different strengths. Using 10 nuggets, each match was over 20 games, total 200 games. We got only 12 draws (6%).

	Program	Elo	1	2	3	4	5	Total
1	ShashchessDev	3500	-	18	20	20	20	**78/80**
2	AlexanderExpert	3190	2	-	18	19	18.5	**57.5/80**
3	AlexanderAdvanced	2299	0	2	-	17.5	19	**38.5/80**
4	AlexanderIntermediate	2199	0	1	2.5	-	18.5	**22/80**
5	AlexanderBeginner	1999	0	1.5	1	1.5	-	**4/80**

Table 2 shows the results of a tournament among five experimental engines - all derived from Stockfish - of very different Elo strengths. The tournament used 10 nuggets from WCC games. There were only 12 draws out of 200 games.

The second experiment, made by someone independent from the authors of this paper, is a tournament among eight strong engines having similar Elo ratings, with long thinking time (30 min with 10 s increment for every move), played over the 12 nuggets from WCC games. The pie diagram in Fig. 2 shows 40% of decisive results (white or black win). There are almost 60% of draw outcomes, because the engines are strongly optimized. However, over 672 games among strong engines (which usually draw more than 90% of their games), the decisive results are 268 (almost 40%). Full game scores from this tournament are available at CCRL Discussion Board - Golden Nuggets 16CPU.

These two experiments prove also that nuggets are useful to rank consistently the strengths of different engines. In the first case, when the players were of very different strengths, most outcomes were wins by the stronger players. In the second case, when the players were more evenly matched, the decisive results were numerous, and were consistent with the small differences in strength.

5 Discussion

The outcomes of the tournaments described in the preceding section show that nuggets effectively reduce the frequency of draws in computer chess tournaments

Players	8		
Nuggets	12		
duble round robin	168	games	
Total games	672		
White wins	267	39,73 %	
draw	404	60,12 %	
Black wins	1	0,15 %	
Stockfish 20250213	115/168		
ShashChess Dev	106.5/168		
Dragon by Komodo 3.3	86.5		
PlentyChess 4.0.9	85/168		
Obsidian dev-15.04	80/168		
Berserk 20250203	79.5/168		
Caissa 1.21.7	71/168		
Alexander 5.0	48.5/168		

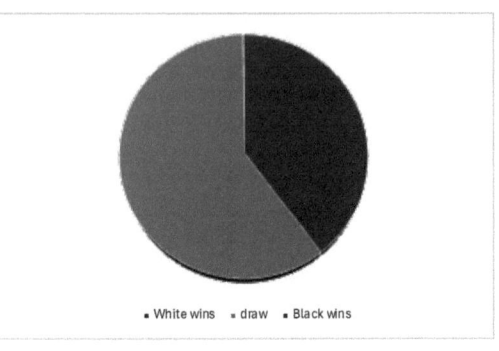

Fig. 2. Results of a tournament played among eight strong engines (12 nuggets from WCC, double round robin, 672 games). White wins + Black wins were 268 (almost 40% of total)

(RQ2). They introduce a controlled degree of uncertainty, making it less likely for games to follow well-established drawing patterns. The primary mechanisms behind this effect include (RQ1):

- Increased tactical and strategic complexity, making it harder for engines to reach quick, well-known drawn positions.
- A heightened likelihood of decisive results due to the natural instability of the selected positions.
- A greater dependence on precise calculation, leading to more engaging and dynamic games.

Incorporating unbalanced positions into computer or correspondence chess tournaments has several positive consequences. First, games become less predictable, so more engaging. By starting from positions where accurate evaluation and deep calculation are critical, double round robin tournaments allow to precisely assess reciprocal strength. Predefined openings often favor certain evaluation models: using these positions can mitigate the dominance of engines that excel in theoretical opening book knowledge.

Limitations

Despite the benefits, there are notable drawbacks in introducing tournaments based on nuggets. Certain engines may perform disproportionately well in specific types of unbalanced positions due to their evaluation functions. Identifying effective nugget positions requires extensive filtering to avoid those positions that resolve too quickly or lead to trivial outcomes. Last but not least, as engines improve, positions that were once considered chaotic or balanced may become easily winning or drawn.

6 Conclusion

We summarize our findings and the potential of unbalanced starting positions in addressing the high draw rates.

In standard chess competitions, final tournament standings and the resulting Elo rating are often influenced by factors such as win rates, opening preparation, and incremental advantages in symmetrical positions. However, these factors can sometimes obscure the true skill gap between players, particularly when a large percentage of games end in draws due to well-established theoretical lines or computational precision. By playing games from *nugget* positions we shift the focus from memorization and opening repertoire depth to practical decision-making, adaptability, and deep positional understanding. The expected result is a reduced impact of extensive opening preparation: since nugget positions are carefully selected to avoid theoretical main lines, players must rely on in-game evaluation rather than pre-existing knowledge.

In traditional settings, players of similar ratings may frequently draw against each other, making it difficult to distinguish who has superior skills. Nugget positions, by increasing complexity and decisiveness, ensure that even small skill differences manifest in results.

Nugget positions can be used for tiebreaks or experimental tournament formats. Moreover, nugget positions can serve as a new testing ground for engines aiming at training humans, measuring not just brute-force calculation but also strategic evaluation capabilities.

Using nugget positions in tournaments is a promising approach that pushes computer chess into less explored and more challenging territories. However, a careful selection and verification process is crucial to ensure that these positions remain balanced and engaging. A combination of WDL models, practical tests, and historical data analysis seems to be the best way to implement this idea.

Future research will explore:

- Search for new nuggets in openings repositories like the Encyclopedia of Openings [2].
- The effect of nugget positions on human play, analyzing whether they also reduce draws in human tournaments.
- A machine-learning approach to refine heuristic selection, using neural networks trained on engine evaluation shifts.
- An empirical study on whether these positions increase the rating gap between engines, better differentiating their strengths.

References

1. Anbarci, N., Ismail, M.: AI-powered mechanisms as judges: breaking ties in chess. PLoS ONE **19**(11), e0305905 (2025). https://doi.org/10.1371/journal.pone.0305905
2. Authors, V.: Encyclopedia of Chess Openings, 5th edn. Chess Informant, Belgrade (2021)

3. Barthelemy, M.: Fragility of chess positions: measure, universality, and tipping points. Phys. Rev. E **111**(1), 014314 (2025)
4. Brams, S.J., Ismail, M.S.: Double moves by each player in chess openings make the game fairer. Math. Analyses Decisions Voting Games **795**, 189 (2024)
5. Chowdhary, S., Iacopini, I., Battiston, F.: Quantifying human performance in chess. Sci. Rep. **13**(1), 2113 (2023)
6. Edwards, J.: Artificial intelligence and correspondence chess: a harbinger for other endeavors. ICGA J. **45**(2–3), 55–60 (2024)
7. Halim, Z., Baig, A.R., Abbas, G.: Computational intelligence-based entertaining level generation for platform games. Int. J. Comput. Intell. Syst. **8**(6), 1128–1143 (2015). https://doi.org/10.1080/18756891.2015.1113747
8. Haworth, G., Cazenave, T.: Chess without draws. ICGA J. **43**(2), 94–101 (2021)
9. Iida, H., Takeshita, N., Yoshimura, J.: A metric for entertainment of boardgames: its implication for evolution of chess variants. In: Nakatsu, R., Hoshino, J. (eds.) Entertainment Computing. ITIFIP, vol. 112, pp. 65–72. Springer, Boston, MA (2003). https://doi.org/10.1007/978-0-387-35660-0_8
10. Manzo, A., Ciancarini, P.: Enhancing Stockfish: a chess engine tailored for training human players. In: Proceedings of the 14th IFIP International Conference on Entertainment Computing - ICEC, volume 14455 of LNCS, pp. 275–289. Springer, Bologna (2023)
11. Moul, C.C., Nye, J.V.C.: Did the soviets collude? a statistical analysis of championship chess 1940–1978. J. Econ. Behav. Organ. **70**(1–2), 10–21 (2009)
12. Pijl, R., Pascutto, G.-C., van den Herik, J.: The 2024 world computer chess championship. ICGA J. **47**(1), 1–5 (2025)
13. Primanita, A., Khalid, M.N.A., Iida, H.: Computing games: bridging the gap between search and entertainment. IEEE Access **9**, 72087–72102 (2021). https://doi.org/10.1109/ACCESS.2021.3079356
14. Regan, K.W., Macieja, B., Haworth, G.M.C.: Understanding distributions of chess performances. In: van den Herik, H.J., Plaat, A. (eds.) ACG 2011. LNCS, vol. 7168, pp. 230–243. Springer, Heidelberg (2012). https://doi.org/10.1007/978-3-642-31866-5_20
15. Sadler, M., Regan, N.: Game changer. AlphaZero's Groundbreaking Chess Strategies and the Promise of AI. New in Chess, 2019
16. Shashin, A.: Best Play The Best method for Discovering the Strongest Move. Mongoose Press, Newton Highlands (2013)
17. Takeuchi, S., Kaneko, T., Yamaguchi, K., Kawai, S.: Visualization and adjustment of evaluation functions based on evaluation values and win probability. In: Proceedings of the National Conference on Artificial Intelligence, vol. 22, pp. 858–863. AAAI Press (2007)
18. Verkhovsky, L.: Draw! The art of half point in Chess, Russel Enterprises (2014)
19. Wilkenfeld, Y.: Can chess survive artificial intelligence? New Atlantis **58**, 37–45 (2019). URL: https://www.thenewatlantis.com/publications/can-chess-survive-artificial-intelligence
20. Yannakakis, G.N., Hallam, J.: Towards capturing and enhancing entertainment in computer games. In: Antoniou, G., Potamias, G., Spyropoulos, C., Plexousakis, D., (eds.) Advances in Artificial Intelligence, pp. 432–442. Springer, Berlin (2006)

Game Elements in Cybersecurity Education: Hype or Help?

Mehrdad Bahrini[✉], Violetta Burdina, Karsten Sohr, and Rainer Malaka

Digital Media Lab, TZI, University of Bremen, Bremen, Germany
{mbahrini,vburdina,sohr,malaka}@uni-bremen.de

Abstract. Gamification is increasingly applied in cybersecurity training to enhance engagement and support knowledge retention through elements such as points, challenges, and rewards. However, its effectiveness remains debated, as employees' experiences vary, and specific game elements may not be equally beneficial for all learners. This study explores employees' perceptions of engagement, learning outcomes, and challenges in gamified cybersecurity training through an online survey of 53 participants in Germany. Findings indicate that while game elements were generally engaging, participants valued real-world problem-solving tasks, story-based scenarios, and simulated cyber-attacks over leaderboards and competition-based mechanics. Challenges such as extended training duration and unclear game mechanics led to frustration and reduced perceived effectiveness for some participants. Additionally, participants emphasized the importance of training that balances engagement with practical relevance. These findings suggest that gamified strategies should prioritize realistic, problem-solving tasks over competitive elements and ensure clarity in-game elements to maximize training effectiveness in workplace cybersecurity programs.

Keywords: Gamification · Cybersecurity Training · Security Awareness · Employee Perceptions · Usable Security

1 Introduction

Cybersecurity threats are becoming more sophisticated, targeting technological vulnerabilities and human factors [2,51]. Social engineering attacks, such as phishing and impersonation scams, continue to deceive employees into disclosing sensitive information or bypassing security protocols [58]. In addition, ransomware and malware infections often stem from employees clicking on malicious links or downloading compromised files [17]. Although organizations invest in security training to mitigate these risks, many employees still struggle to recognize cyber threats or apply security best practices in real-world situations [42,46]. This raises concerns about how well current training approaches prepare employees for evolving threats [61].

Conventional cybersecurity training methods, such as lectures, online modules, and written guidelines, have been widely used but show significant limitations [3]. These methods often fail to engage employees, leading to low retention rates and minimal long-term behavioral change [5]. Training programs sometimes rely on passive learning formats that lack interactivity, which can reduce their effectiveness in preparing employees for real-world security threats [5]. In addition, security awareness programs are often conducted infrequently, resulting in employees forgetting key information shortly after training [41,44]. This highlights the need for modernized training strategies to avoid knowledge attrition and build lasting habits [63]. An approach that has gained traction to address these challenges is integrating game-based learning into cybersecurity training [28,37,40]. Gamified training incorporates elements such as interactive simulations, challenges, and problem-solving tasks to improve motivation and knowledge retention [53,71]. Serious games and scenario-based exercises allow employees to practice responding to cyber threats in a controlled environment and reinforce learning through active participation [65,70]. Despite its increasing adoption, the effectiveness of gamified cybersecurity training remains debated [35]. Although some studies indicate that game elements improve engagement and knowledge retention [47,56,67], others highlight potential drawbacks such as ineffective use of game elements, distraction, and perceived lack of seriousness [34,72]. Moreover, empirical evidence on the impact of long-term gamification in workplace settings is still limited, particularly with respect to real-world experiences of employees with these training programs [7,13,47].

This study investigates employees' perceptions of gamified cybersecurity training by analyzing responses from an online survey of 53 participants in various job roles in Germany. It aims to explore whether specific game elements contribute to engagement and perceived learning effectiveness and to identify which features are beneficial or challenging in workplace settings. The results show that while gamified training was engaging overall, participants favored realistic, story-based, and problem-oriented elements, such as simulated cyber-attacks, over competitive mechanics like leaderboards. Reported challenges included long training durations and confusion about game mechanics. These insights form the basis for the study's practical recommendations on how gamification can be more effectively integrated into cybersecurity training. The study presents three contributions. First, it deepens understanding of how employees perceive gamification in cybersecurity training, extending previous work by focusing on real-world workplace training contexts. Second, it identifies specific game elements that are perceived as more or less effective, providing practical guidance for training design beyond the general benefits of gamification. Third, it contributes empirical, employee-centered evidence on the usability and challenges of game mechanics, highlighting important considerations for meaningfully implementing gamification in professional settings. These insights inform the development of practical and effective gamification strategies aligned with workplace cybersecurity needs.

2 Related Work

Cybersecurity learning environments incorporate a range of design elements to address user engagement [1], knowledge retention [24], and behavioral modification [56] challenges. Among the key approaches to cybersecurity learning, two have gained particular prominence: **gamification**, the application of game elements such as points, leaderboards, and badges to non-game contexts [23, 73], and **game-based learning**, which involves learning through complete games designed around educational objectives [14]. Both methods are grounded in constructivist learning theories, emphasizing active, experiential learning and knowledge construction through real-world tasks [6, 10, 43]. Various instructional formats have been adopted in cybersecurity training to implement gamified strategies. Among the most common are Capture the Flag (CTF) competitions, which challenge learners to solve timed, technical puzzles simulating attacker-defender scenarios [48, 66], and Cyber Ranges, which provide high-fidelity, team-based environments for practicing system-level defense, incident response, or forensic analysis [39, 64]. These instructional formats are often deployed via different platforms, including virtual labs, browser-based systems, and, increasingly, mobile games [21, 22, 38]. Across these environments, common game elements include points, badges, leaderboards, time limits, progress bars, feedback messages, and levels [30]. Each serves a specific purpose. For example, points and badges recognize achievement, leaderboards encourage social comparison, and time pressure adds urgency [57]. Furthermore, progress indicators and continuous feedback support self-regulation [9]. The design of these elements is often guided by motivational frameworks. The ARCS model (Attention, Relevance, Confidence, Satisfaction) has been widely used to map game elements to the motivational needs of learners [36, 40, 62]. For example, real-time scoring supports perceptual arousal to capture attention, level-based progression enhances learner confidence through structured challenges and feedback, and immersive narratives promote relevance and satisfaction by situating learning within a meaningful context [59]. Self-Determination Theory complements this by emphasizing the psychological needs of autonomy, competence, and relatedness, which can be supported through features such as adaptive difficulty, optional task paths, and collaborative play [16]. Behavioral models such as Protection Motivation Theory and Technology Threat Avoidance Theory further inform the design of training scenarios that simulate cybersecurity risks and protective actions [4, 8].

However, limitations arise when using game elements in cybersecurity learning environments. A significant issue is the misalignment between game mechanics and learning outcomes. Although gamified platforms can increase engagement, they do not always ensure deeper conceptual understanding or knowledge transfer [27]. Superficial metrics, such as completion time or points earned, may not reflect actual competency gains [31]. This highlights the risk of focusing too heavily on extrinsic motivation, such as scoring or badges, at the expense of long-term learning. Another challenge lies in the technical and infrastructural complexity of deploying game-based environments. CTF platforms and Cyber Ranges often require substantial computing resources, complex configurations, and ongoing maintenance [36, 60]. Although virtual labs offer some flexibility, implementation can be time-consuming and technically demanding for educators and administrators [25]. There is also a lack of standardized evaluation frameworks to assess the effectiveness of game-based cybersecurity training [19]. At the same time, models such as ARCS have been used to align training content and measure learning objectives, but no universally accepted methodology exists [18]. This makes it difficult to benchmark learning outcomes across different platforms or training environments. Scenario design represents another critical concern [26]. Effective cybersecurity training relies not only on motivational mechanics but also on realistic, pedagogically sound scenarios [32]. Recent research has proposed taxonomies to guide Cyber Range design, emphasizing elements such as narrative coherence, environmental fidelity, and appropriate tooling [39,69]. Without such frameworks, gamified training environments may lack cohesion or fail to align with academic and industry needs. Lastly, the cognitive load introduced by some game mechanics, such as overly complex challenges, unclear instructions, or rapid-response competitions, can hinder learning, particularly for novice users [20,50]. Training that demands high technical proficiency without adequate scaffolding may alienate less experienced learners and limit broader adoption in formal education or workplace settings [52]. While gamification in cybersecurity training has gained attention, user perceptions, particularly in workplace environments, are still underexplored. This underscores the importance of examining how employees engage with gamified security training.

3 Study Design

3.1 Objectives

This study evaluates the effectiveness of game elements in cybersecurity training for employees across various job roles. It aims to assess employees' experiences with cybersecurity training, including frequency, delivery methods, and perceived quality. Additionally, the study explores the impact of gamification by identifying the types of game elements used, measuring their engagement levels, and determining whether they enhance understanding and encourage adherence to cybersecurity best practices. Furthermore, the research examines the perceived benefits and challenges of gamified training, such as its ability to improve retention versus potential drawbacks like distraction or increased training duration. Finally, the study seeks to gather insights for designing future cybersecurity training programs by identifying preferred training methods and game mechanics that could enhance engagement and effectiveness.

3.2 Materials

In order to address these objectives, the study employs a survey-based research design, collecting quantitative and qualitative data through an online questionnaire. The questionnaire consists of multiple-choice questions, Likert-scale ratings, and open-ended responses to capture employees' perceptions and experiences comprehensively. The survey is structured into five key sections. (1) The demographics and knowledge background section collects information on age, gender, job role, years of experience, and company size to analyze workforce diversity. Additionally, it assesses participants' familiarity with cybersecurity practices and privacy and security topics using a 7-point Likert scale, providing insight into their baseline knowledge before evaluating their training experiences. (2) The general cybersecurity training experience section examines whether participants have undergone cybersecurity training, the formats used (e.g., videos, interactive modules, hands-on activities), and their perceived training quality, rated on a 7-point Likert scale. Before proceeding to the next section, all participants watched a short video [29] explaining gamification, ensuring a shared understanding of game elements in cybersecurity training regardless of their prior exposure. (3) The exposure to and engagement with game-like features section identifies whether training included game elements such as points, badges, or leaderboards, assessing participants' engagement with these features. (4) The perceived effectiveness and challenges section evaluates the extent to which game elements enhanced learning, encouraged adherence to cybersecurity best practices, and posed challenges such as distraction or increased training duration. (5) Finally, the future training preferences section explores participants' interest in game-like cybersecurity training and their preferences for specific game mechanics that could improve engagement. The survey was conducted in German and targeted German-speaking participants. It was administered through the SoSci Survey platform [45]. A complete list of questions is available on OSF [11].

3.3 Participants

Participants were drawn from various industries and job roles to ensure a diverse sample representing different levels of cybersecurity training experiences. The study was conducted online and distributed via professional networks, company contacts, and online platforms. Eligibility required participants to be at least 18 years old and to have undergone cybersecurity training in their workplace. Individuals without cybersecurity training were excluded, as the study focused on evaluating training experiences. A total of 75 individuals participated in the study; however, 22 were excluded due to a lack of prior cybersecurity training, resulting in a final sample of 53 participants. Among them, 40 had experienced game elements in their training, while 13 had received non-gamified training. Participants' ages ranged from 18 to 62 years ($M = 30.36, SD = 10.64$). The gender distribution consisted of 20 male and 33 female participants.

3.4 Ethical Considerations

The study was designed in collaboration with data protection experts and legal advisors to ensure compliance with the General Data Protection Regulation (GDPR). Ethical approval was not required, as the local ethics board only mandates it when requested by funding agencies. However, the study adhered to all relevant legal and institutional guidelines. Participants provided informed consent online after receiving detailed information about the study's objectives, procedures, potential risks, and benefits. They were explicitly informed of their right to withdraw at any time without consequences. In order to ensure data privacy, no personally identifiable information was collected, aligning with the principle of data minimization. Measures were implemented to mitigate any potential risks to participants [12].

4 Results

4.1 Demographic Characteristics and Knowledge Background

Participants represented a variety of job roles, with the largest group working in sales and marketing (15 participants), followed by those in the "other" category (13 participants), which included roles such as managing director, IT software developer, business development specialist, police officer, and chief information security officer. Additionally, 7 participants worked in administration, 6 in finance, 5 in customer service, 4 in human resources, and 3 in IT support. Regarding work experience, most participants had been in their current role for 1–3 years (29 participants), followed by 4–7 years (11 participants), less than 1 year (9 participants), and more than 7 years (4 participants). Participants were employed in companies of various sizes. One participant reported working in a company with eight employees. The most common company size was 501–1000 employees (13 participants), followed by 201–500 employees (11 participants), 51–200 employees (9 participants), 1001–5000 employees (7 participants), 11–50 employees (6 participants), and companies with more than 5000 employees (6 participants). Figure 1 presents the distribution of participants across three demographic factors.

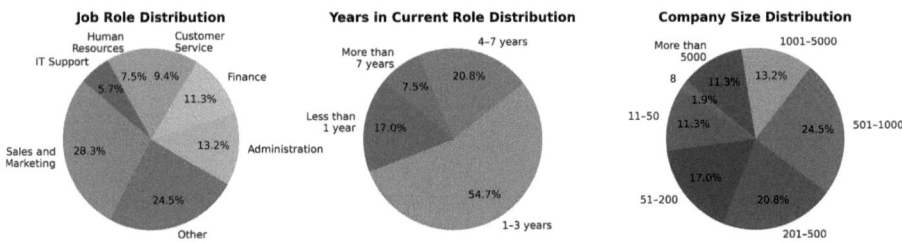

Fig. 1. Distribution of participants by job role (left), years in the current role (middle), and company size (right).

Participants assessed their familiarity with cybersecurity practices, such as recognizing phishing emails, using strong passwords, and following security policies, as well as their understanding of privacy and security topics, including data protection, identifying security threats, and handling confidential information at work. The results indicate a relatively high familiarity with cybersecurity practices ($M = 5.02$, $SD = 1.29$) and a relatively strong understanding of privacy and security topics ($M = 5.13$, $SD = 1.16$).

4.2 Cybersecurity Training Experience

All 53 participants in the final sample had received cybersecurity training at their workplace. The methods used for training varied, with the most common being online training with interactive elements (40 participants), followed by videos or presentations (35 participants) and hands-on activities such as phishing simulations and quizzes (22 participants). Additionally, 8 participants had experienced training that incorporated game elements features. Participants rated the overall quality of cybersecurity training on a scale from poor (1) to excellent (7). The mean perceived quality was 4.94 ($SD = 0.91$).

Regarding the frequency of cybersecurity training, 26 participants reported receiving training once a year, while 7 participants had training every six months, and 8 participants reported undergoing training more frequently. Another 10 participants stated that training was provided when required, while 2 participants selected "other," specifying that training was either irregular or conducted every two years. Figure 2 shows the distribution of cybersecurity training experiences, including training methods, perceived quality, and training frequency.

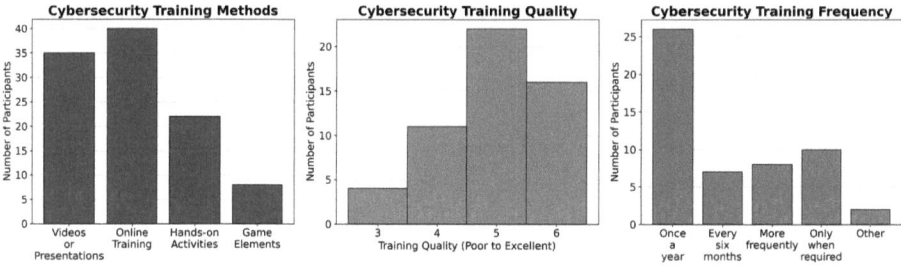

Fig. 2. Distribution of cybersecurity training methods (left), perceived training quality (middle), and training frequency (right).

4.3 Exposure and Engagement of Game-Like Features

Among the 53 participants, 40 experienced game-like features in their cybersecurity training, while 13 did not. Participants who had encountered game elements ($N = 40$) reported various types of features. The most commonly experienced features were earning points or scores for correct answers (25 participants), making choices in a story-based scenario (21 participants), and timed quizzes or challenges (21 participants). Other frequently selected elements included unlocking badges or rewards (14 participants), leaderboard competitions (5 participants), and team-based challenges (3 participants). Moreover, they rated the engagement level of these game-like elements on a scale from low to high. The mean engagement rating was 5.18 ($SD = 0.96$). Figure 3 illustrates participants' exposure to game-like features, the types of game elements experienced, and their engagement levels with these features in cybersecurity training.

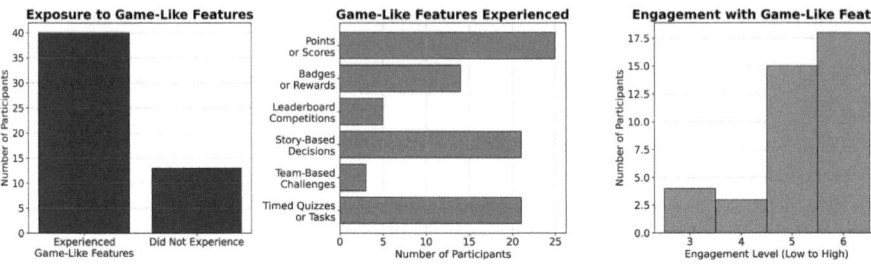

Fig. 3. Exposure and engagement with game-like features in cybersecurity training: exposure to game elements (left), types of game-like features experienced (middle), and engagement ratings (right).

4.4 Perceived Effectiveness and Challenges of Game Elements

Participants who experienced game-like features in their cybersecurity training ($N = 40$) evaluated their effectiveness in enhancing their understanding of cybersecurity concepts, with a mean rating of 5.12 ($SD = 1.30$). Regarding whether game elements features encouraged participants to follow cybersecurity best practices, the mean rating was 4.97 ($SD = 1.25$). When asked about the most significant benefit of game elements, 17 participants reported that they made the training more interesting, 14 participants stated they helped with information retention, and 8 participants found that they facilitated the application of learned concepts. One participant reported no perceived benefits.

Participants also identified challenges with game-like training. The most frequently mentioned was that it took longer than conventional training (20 participants), followed by competition being demotivating (8 participants) and the training being perceived as distracting or unnecessary (3 participants). One had difficulty understanding game mechanics. Additionally, 11 participants gave open-ended responses, most indicating no significant issues, while one found the repetition frustrating. Finally, they rated whether game elements made cybersecurity training feel less serious, with a mean rating of 2.95 ($SD = 1.54$). Figure 4 illustrates participants' perceptions of game-like features in cybersecurity training, including the mean ratings for their effectiveness and encouragement, the most frequently reported benefits, and the challenges faced during training.

4.5 Future Preferences for Cybersecurity Training

This section of the study included all 53 participants, even those without prior exposure to game-like training, as they also watched the video about gamification [29]. Participants expressed their preferences for incorporating game elements in future cybersecurity training. A majority (39 participants) preferred training with game elements, while 12 participants stated they had no strong preference. Two preferred other training methods without game elements. Regarding the specific features participants would like to see in future cybersecurity training,

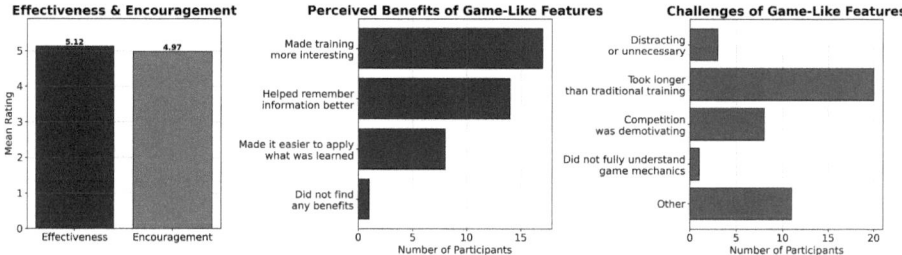

Fig. 4. Overview of participants' perceptions of game elements in cybersecurity training: mean ratings for effectiveness and encouragement (left), perceived benefits (middle), and reported challenges (right).

the most commonly selected elements were real-world security problem-solving tasks (38 participants), simulated cyber-attack situations (34 participants), and story-based scenarios (34 participants). Other highly preferred features included small team-based challenges (20 participants), personalized feedback and progress tracking (16 participants), and earning rewards or badges (14 participants). Elements such as leaderboards and competition (9 participants) and time-based challenges (7 participants) were selected less frequently. Finally, they provided suggestions for improving cybersecurity training. The most common theme was the need for greater realism and relevance, with participants emphasizing the importance of training scenarios that reflect real-world security threats and work environments. They also called for more game-like elements, including more diverse and engaging interactive elements. One participant suggested enhancing technical content to make the training more informative and meaningful for employees with technical roles. Some mentioned interactivity and simulations as important factors, while one pointed out the need for more efficient and time-sensitive training. However, a notable number of respondents (27 participants) indicated that they had no further suggestions for improving training. Figure 5 illustrates participants' preferences for incorporating game elements in cybersecurity training, highlighting their preferred features for future training and the main themes of their improvement suggestions.

5 Discussion

The central question of this study was whether gamification in cybersecurity training is merely a hype-driven trend or a genuinely helpful tool for improving security awareness and behavior. The findings suggest that gamification can potentially enhance engagement, knowledge retention, and motivation in cybersecurity training, but it is not a universal solution. While certain game elements were well-received and contributed positively to learning outcomes, others were viewed as inefficient, demotivating, or unnecessary. These mixed findings indicate that the effectiveness of gamification depends mainly on how it is implemented rather than whether it is used at all [33].

Fig. 5. Overview of participants' preferences and suggestions for future cybersecurity training: preferences for game elements (left), preferred training features (middle), and thematic analysis of improvement suggestions (right).

One of the key strengths of gamification observed in this study is its ability to increase engagement in cybersecurity training. Participants who had experienced game elements in their training reported higher motivation and interest, with 17 responders explicitly stating that gamification made training more engaging. This aligns with existing research suggesting that game mechanics, such as points, challenges, and rewards, can boost learner motivation by making training feel less passive and more interactive [1,53,71]. Additionally, gamification improved knowledge retention for many participants. Fourteen participants reported that game elements helped them remember security concepts better, while eight stated that gamification made it easier to apply what they learned. These findings support cognitive learning dimensions, which suggest that active, problem-solving-based learning reinforces memory retention more effectively than passive methods such as videos or text-based instructions [68].

Cybersecurity training is not only about knowledge acquisition but also about changing the security behavior of employees [5]. The study found that game training was perceived as moderately effective in encouraging secure practices, with a mean effectiveness rating of 4.97 out of 7. This suggests that while gamification can positively influence behavior, it is not a guaranteed approach for driving long-term change. Participants particularly appreciated training elements that closely mimicked real-world cybersecurity threats. When asked about preferred game features for future training, participants favored including real-world security problem-solving tasks (38 participants), simulated cyber-attack situations (34 participants), and story-based security challenges (34 participants). These results indicate that gamification is most effective when it provides hands-on learning experiences rather than relying on abstract competition or rewards. Previous research also suggests that employees are more likely to retain and apply security behaviors when training scenarios closely reflect the threats they face on the job [15,32].

Despite its benefits, the study identified several challenges with gamified training. The most frequently reported issue was that gamification made training longer than necessary. Twenty participants found that game-like elements extended training duration, sometimes unnecessarily. This is consistent with previous research indicating that while gamification increases engagement, it can also make learning processes more time-consuming without necessarily improving knowledge transfer [47]. Another notable challenge was competition-based game elements, such as leaderboards and rankings. While gamification theory often suggests that competition can motivate users [16,36,40,62], only nine participants expressed interest in leaderboards, and eight reported that competition was demotivating. This finding challenges the assumption that competition-based mechanics are universally effective. For workplace training, high-stakes competition may introduce stress rather than motivation, particularly if employees feel pressured to outperform colleagues rather than focus on skill-building [54]. In addition, participants struggled to understand the mechanics of the game. While only one participant explicitly stated difficulty using gamified elements, this suggests that poorly implemented game mechanics may create barriers rather than enhance learning. This aligns with concerns from usability research that complex or unintuitive gamification can reduce effectiveness by shifting the focus to the game itself rather than the learning content [34,72].

A recurring theme in participants' feedback was that training content is more important than its format. Several responses indicated that although gamification can be helpful, it should not overshadow the core educational material. Participants noted that repetitive game tasks became frustrating, particularly when they were required to answer similar questions in different game formats. This highlights a critical issue: gamification must be purpose-driven rather than added as an afterthought [55]. If game elements are introduced solely for engagement without reinforcing core learning objectives, they may distract from rather than enhance knowledge acquisition. Similar concerns have been raised in previous studies, cautioning that poorly designed gamification can lead to superficial engagement rather than meaningful learning [49]. These findings highlight the need to align game elements with learning goals. Based on the findings, the following recommendations emerge for improving gamified cybersecurity training:

- **Prioritize realism over artificial engagement:** Employees prefer realistic cybersecurity scenarios over generic game mechanics. Training should focus on real-world applications, such as phishing simulations, incident response exercises, and story-based security decision-making challenges.
- **Balance gamification with time efficiency:** Although game elements can enhance engagement, they should not significantly extend the duration of the training without clear benefits. Designers should bypass unnecessary complexity and focus on concise and high-impact training experiences.
- **Avoid overly competitive mechanics:** Leaderboards and direct competition are not effective for all learners. Instead of relying on competitive ranking systems, training programs should emphasize collaborative and self-paced learning experiences.
- **Ensure game mechanics are intuitive:** If gamification is used, the mechanics should be easy to understand and directly relevant to the training objectives. Overly complex systems may confuse participants, reducing effectiveness.

- **Adapt training to different employee roles:** Security training should be context-specific, addressing the actual risks and tools employees use in their roles. Generic, one-size-fits-all gamification approaches may not be as effective as customized training tailored to the specific security challenges of an organization.

This study has several limitations that should be considered. We conducted our survey within German communities and companies; therefore, the findings may not be fully generalized to other cultural or organizational settings, as cybersecurity training approaches can vary across industries and regions. In addition, all participants watched a video explaining gamification, ensuring a shared understanding but potentially shaping expectations rather than reflecting purely organic experiences. The relatively small sample size ($N = 53$) limits statistical power, although the study still provides meaningful insights into participants' preferences and perceptions. Furthermore, the study captures immediate reactions to gamified training but does not assess long-term behavioral changes, making it unclear whether engagement translates into sustained improvements in cybersecurity practices. The absence of a control group also restricts direct comparisons between gamified and conventional training methods. Lastly, participants had varied training experiences, some involving interactive elements even without explicit gamification, which complicates isolating the effects of game elements' features.

6 Conclusion

Is gamification in cybersecurity training hype or help? This study suggests that it can be both. Gamification has real potential to improve engagement, motivation, and knowledge retention, but it is not a silver bullet. Its effectiveness depends on how it is designed and implemented. Gamification can be valuable in cybersecurity training when used strategically through realistic problem-solving tasks, interactive learning, and meaningful challenges. However, poorly implemented game mechanics, unnecessary competition, or excessive training duration can reduce its effectiveness. Ultimately, the key to successful cybersecurity training is not gamification itself but its alignment with real-world security practices and employee needs. Organizations should move beyond the gamification hype and focus on designing cybersecurity training that is both engaging and practical. Future research should explore which specific gamification elements lead to measurable improvements in cybersecurity behavior over time.

Acknowledgements. We sincerely thank datenschutz nord GmbH for their invaluable assistance during the execution of this study. This work was funded by the Klaus Tschira Foundation.

References

1. Abrahams, T.O., Farayola, O.A., Kaggwa, S., Uwaoma, P.U., Hassan, A.O., Dawodu, S.O.: Cybersecurity awareness and education programs: a review of employee engagement and accountability. Comput. Sci. IT Res. J. **5**(1), 100–119 (2024)
2. Admass, W.S., Munaye, Y.Y., Diro, A.A.: Cyber security: state of the art, challenges and future directions. Cyber Secur. Appl. **2**, 100031 (2024). https://doi.org/10.1016/j.csa.2023.100031
3. Aldawood, H., Skinner, G.: Reviewing cyber security social engineering training and awareness programs—pitfalls and ongoing issues. Future Internet **11**(3) (2019). https://doi.org/10.3390/fi11030073
4. Almansoori, A., Al-Emran, M., Shaalan, K.: Exploring the frontiers of cybersecurity behavior: a systematic review of studies and theories. Appl. Sci. **13**(9) (2023). https://doi.org/10.3390/app13095700
5. Alnajim, A.M., Habib, S., Islam, M., AlRawashdeh, H.S., Wasim, M.: Exploring cybersecurity education and training techniques: a comprehensive review of traditional, virtual reality, and augmented reality approaches. Symmetry **15**(12) (2023). https://doi.org/10.3390/sym15122175
6. Amineh, R.J., Asl, H.D.: Review of constructivism and social constructivism. J. Soc. Sci. Lit. Lang. **1**(1), 9–16 (2015)
7. Amjad, K., Ishaq, K., Nawaz, N.A., Rosdi, F., Dogar, A.B., Khan, F.A.: Unlocking cybersecurity: a game-changing framework for training and awareness–a systematic review. Hum. Behav. Emerg. Technol. **2025**(1), 9982666 (2025). https://doi.org/10.1155/hbe2/9982666
8. Arachchilage, N.A.G., Love, S.: Security awareness of computer users: a phishing threat avoidance perspective. Comput. Hum. Behav. **38**, 304–312 (2014). https://doi.org/10.1016/j.chb.2014.05.046
9. Atkins, A., Wanick, V., Wills, G.: Metrics feedback cycle: measuring and improving user engagement in gamified elearning systems. Int. J. Serious Games **4**(4), 3–19 (2017). https://eprints.soton.ac.uk/416710/
10. Bada, S.O., Olusegun, S.: Constructivism learning theory: a paradigm for teaching and learning. J. Res. Method Educ. **5**(6), 66–70 (2015)
11. Bahrini, M., Burdina, V., Sohr, K., Malaka, R.: Supplementary questionnaire for "game elements in cybersecurity education: Hype or help?" (2025). https://doi.org/10.17605/OSF.IO/Y8NFK. OSF Project
12. Bailey, M., Dittrich, D., Kenneally, E., Maughan, D.: The menlo report. IEEE Secur. Priv. **10**(2), 71–75 (2012). https://doi.org/10.1109/MSP.2012.52
13. Baxter, R.J., Holderness, D. Kip, J., Wood, D.A.: Applying basic gamification techniques to it compliance training: evidence from the lab and field. J. Inf. Syst. **30**(3), 119–133 (2016). https://doi.org/10.2308/isys-51341
14. Becker, K.: Choosing and Using Digital Games in the Classroom. Springer (2017)
15. Beuran, R., Inoue, T., Tan, Y., Shinoda, Y.: Realistic cybersecurity training via scenario progression management. In: 2019 IEEE European Symposium on Security and Privacy Workshops (EuroS&PW), pp. 67–76 (2019). https://doi.org/10.1109/EuroSPW.2019.00014
16. Böckle, M., Novak, J., Bick, M.: Towards adaptive gamification: a synthesis of current developments (2017)
17. Canham, M.: Repeat clicking: a lack of awareness is not the problem. In: Degen, H., Ntoa, S., Moallem, A. (eds.) HCI International 2023 – Late Breaking Papers, pp. 325–342. Springer, Cham (2023). https://doi.org/10.1007/978-3-031-48057-7_20

18. Chattopadhyay, A., Maschinot, C., Nestor, L.: Mirror mirror on the wall - what are cybersecurity educational games offering overall: a research study and gap analysis. In: 2021 IEEE Frontiers in Education Conference (FIE), pp. 1–8 (2021). https://doi.org/10.1109/FIE49875.2021.9637224
19. Chowdhury, N., Katsikas, S., Gkioulos, V.: Modeling effective cybersecurity training frameworks: a delphi method-based study. Comput. Secur. **113**, 102551 (2022). https://doi.org/10.1016/j.cose.2021.102551
20. Chowdhury, N.H., Adam, M.T.P., and, G.S.: The impact of time pressure on cybersecurity behaviour: a systematic literature review. Behav. Inf. Technol. **38**(12), 1290–1308 (2019). https://doi.org/10.1080/0144929X.2019.1583769
21. Coenraad, M., Pellicone, A., Ketelhut, D.J., Cukier, M., Plane, J., Weintrop, D.: Experiencing cybersecurity one game at a time: a systematic review of cybersecurity digital games. Simul. Gaming **51**(5), 586–611 (2020). https://doi.org/10.1177/1046878120933312
22. Del Giudice, N., Marcantoni, F., Marcelletti, A., Moschella, F.: SEC-game: a minigame collection for cyber security awareness. In: Ciancarini, P., Di Iorio, A., Hlavacs, H., Poggi, F. (eds.) ICEC 2023. LNCS, vol. 14455, pp. 365–370. Springer, Singapore (2023). https://doi.org/10.1007/978-981-99-8248-6_33
23. Deterding, S., Sicart, M., Nacke, L., O'Hara, K., Dixon, D.: Gamification. using game-design elements in non-gaming contexts. In: CHI '11 Extended Abstracts on Human Factors in Computing Systems, CHI EA 2011, pp. 2425–2428. Association for Computing Machinery, New York (2011). https://doi.org/10.1145/1979742.1979575
24. Fatokun Faith, B., Long, Z.A., Hamid, S.: Promoting cybersecurity knowledge via gamification: an innovative intervention design. In: 2024 Third International Conference on Distributed Computing and High Performance Computing (DCHPC), pp. 1–8 (2024). https://doi.org/10.1109/DCHPC60845.2024.10454080
25. Ford, V., Siraj, A., Haynes, A., Brown, E.: Capture the flag unplugged: an offline cyber competition. In: Proceedings of the 2017 ACM SIGCSE Technical Symposium on Computer Science Education, SIGCSE 2017, pp. 225–230. Association for Computing Machinery, New York (2017). https://doi.org/10.1145/3017680.3017783
26. Foster, T.C., Moroney, W.F., Phillips, H.L., Lilienthal, M.G.: Human factors in simulation and training: an overview. Hum. Factors Simul. Train. 1–64 (2023)
27. Giannakas, F., Kambourakis, G., Papasalouros, A., Gritzalis, S.: A critical review of 13 years of mobile game-based learning. Education Tech. Research Dev. **66**(2), 341–384 (2017). https://doi.org/10.1007/s11423-017-9552-z
28. Gomez, M.J., Ruipérez-Valiente, J.A., Clemente, F.J.G.: A systematic literature review of game-based assessment studies: trends and challenges. IEEE Trans. Learn. Technol. **16**(4), 500–515 (2023). https://doi.org/10.1109/TLT.2022.3226661
29. Grzesik, N., Peupelmann, A., Shang, J.: Was verbirgt sich hinter dem begriff "gamification"? YouTube video (2021). https://www.youtube.com/watch?v=DM5-BcG0E-M. Published by IntercultureTV
30. Hallifax, S., Altmeyer, M., Kölln, K., Rauschenberger, M., Nacke, L.E.: From points to progression: a scoping review of game elements in gamification research with a content analysis of 280 research papers. Proc. ACM Hum.-Comput. Interact. **7**(CHI PLAY) (2023). https://doi.org/10.1145/3611048
31. Hamari, J., Koivisto, J., Sarsa, H.: Does gamification work? – a literature review of empirical studies on gamification. In: 2014 47th Hawaii International Conference on System Sciences, pp. 3025–3034 (2014). https://doi.org/10.1109/HICSS.2014.377

32. Hatzivasilis, G., et al.: Modern aspects of cyber-security training and continuous adaptation of programmes to trainees. Appl. Sci. **10**(16) (2020). https://doi.org/10.3390/app10165702
33. He, W., and, Z.J.Z.: Enterprise cybersecurity training and awareness programs: recommendations for success. J. Organ. Comput. Electron. Commer. **29**(4), 249–257 (2019). https://doi.org/10.1080/10919392.2019.1611528
34. Heinze, I.: Playing to win: enhancing resilience in SMEs with gamification. In: Durst, S., Henschel, T. (eds.) Small and Medium-Sized Enterprise (SME) Resilience, pp. 181–199. Springer, Cham (2024). https://doi.org/10.1007/978-3-031-50836-3_9
35. Hendrix, M., Al-Sherbaz, A., Victoria, B.: Game based cyber security training: are serious games suitable for cyber security training? Int. J. Serious Games **3**(1), 53–61 (2016). https://doi.org/10.17083/ijsg.v3i1.107
36. Karagiannis, S.: Systematic design, deployment and evaluation of gamified cybersecurity learning environments. Ph.D. thesis, Ionian University, Greece (2022)
37. Karagiannis, S., Papaioannou, T., Magkos, E., Tsohou, A.: Game-based information security/privacy education and awareness: theory and practice. In: Themistocleous, M., Papadaki, M., Kamal, M.M. (eds.) EMCIS 2020. LNBIP, vol. 402, pp. 509–525. Springer, Cham (2020). https://doi.org/10.1007/978-3-030-63396-7_34
38. Karampidis, K., Panagiotakis, S., Vasilakis, M., Lamari, A.T., Markakis, E., Papadourakis, G.: Digital training for cybersecurity in industrial fields via virtual labs and capture-the-flag challenges. In: 2023 32nd Annual Conference of the European Association for Education in Electrical and Information Engineering (EAEEIE), pp. 1–6 (2023). https://doi.org/10.23919/EAEEIE55804.2023.10181644
39. Katsantonis, M.N., Manikas, A., Mavridis, I., Gritzalis, D.: Cyber range design framework for cyber security education and training. Int. J. Inf. Secur. **22**(4), 1005–1027 (2023). https://doi.org/10.1007/s10207-023-00680-4
40. Khan, M.A., Merabet, A., Alkaabi, S., Sayed, H.E.: Game-based learning platform to enhance cybersecurity education. Educ. Inf. Technol. **27**(4), 5153–5177 (2022). https://doi.org/10.1007/s10639-021-10807-6
41. Khan, N., Furnell, S., Bada, M., Rand, M., Nurse, J.R.: Investigating the experiences of providing cyber security support to small- and medium-sized enterprises. Comput. Secur. **154**, 104448 (2025). https://doi.org/10.1016/j.cose.2025.104448
42. Khando, K., Gao, S., Islam, S.M., Salman, A.: Enhancing employees information security awareness in private and public organisations: a systematic literature review. Comput. Secur. **106**, 102267 (2021). https://doi.org/10.1016/j.cose.2021.102267
43. Kim, B.: Social constructivism. In: Emerging Perspectives on Learning, Teaching, and Technology, vol. 1, no. 1, p. 16 (2001)
44. Kumaraguru, P., Rhee, Y., Acquisti, A., Cranor, L.F., Hong, J., Nunge, E.: Protecting people from phishing: the design and evaluation of an embedded training email system. In: Proceedings of the SIGCHI Conference on Human Factors in Computing Systems, CHI 2007, pp. 905–914. Association for Computing Machinery, New York (2007). https://doi.org/10.1145/1240624.1240760
45. Leiner, D.J., Leiner, S.: Sosci survey (2025). https://www.soscisurvey.de. Web-based survey platform by SoSci Survey GmbH
46. Liu, X., et al.: Cyber security threats: a never-ending challenge for e-commerce. Front. Psychol. **13** (2022). https://doi.org/10.3389/fpsyg.2022.927398

47. Malone, M., Wang, Y., James, K., Anderegg, M., Werner, J., Monrose, F.: To gamify or not? On leaderboard effects, student engagement and learning outcomes in a cybersecurity intervention. In: Proceedings of the 52nd ACM Technical Symposium on Computer Science Education, SIGCSE 2021, pp. 1135–1141. Association for Computing Machinery, New York (2021). https://doi.org/10.1145/3408877.3432544
48. McDaniel, L., Talvi, E., Hay, B.: Capture the flag as cyber security introduction. In: 2016 49th Hawaii International Conference on System Sciences (HICSS), pp. 5479–5486 (2016). https://doi.org/10.1109/HICSS.2016.677
49. Mekler, E.D., Brühlmann, F., Tuch, A.N., Opwis, K.: Towards understanding the effects of individual gamification elements on intrinsic motivation and performance. Comput. Hum. Behav. **71**, 525–534 (2017). https://doi.org/10.1016/j.chb.2015.08.048
50. Paul, C., Dykstra, J.: Understanding operator fatigue, frustration, and cognitive workload in tactical cybersecurity operations. J. Inf. Warfare **16**(2), 1–11 (2017)
51. Pollini, A., et al.: Leveraging human factors in cybersecurity: an integrated methodological approach. Cogn. Technol. Work **24**(2), 371–390 (2022). https://doi.org/10.1007/s10111-021-00683-y
52. Prümmer, J.: The role of cognition in developing successful cybersecurity training programs - passive vs. active engagement. In: Schmorrow, D.D., Fidopiastis, C.M. (eds.) HCII 2024. LNCS, vol. 14695, pp. 185–199. Springer, Cham (2024). https://doi.org/10.1007/978-3-031-61572-6_13
53. Ricci, K.E., Salas, E., and, J.A.C.B.: Do computer-based games facilitate knowledge acquisition and retention? Mil. Psychol. **8**(4), 295–307 (1996). https://doi.org/10.1207/s15327876mp0804_3
54. Schlömmer, M., Spieß, T., Schlögl, S.: Leaderboard positions and stress—experimental investigations into an element of gamification. Sustainability **13**(12) (2021). https://doi.org/10.3390/su13126608
55. Seaborn, K., Fels, D.I.: Gamification in theory and action: a survey. Int. J. Hum. Comput. Stud. **74**, 14–31 (2015). https://doi.org/10.1016/j.ijhcs.2014.09.006
56. van Steen, T., Deeleman, J.R.: Successful gamification of cybersecurity training. Cyberpsychol. Behav. Soc. Network. **24**(9), 593–598 (2021). https://doi.org/10.1089/cyber.2020.0526. pMID: 34491845
57. Strmecki, D., Bernik, A., Radosevic, D.: Gamification in e-learning: introducing gamified design elements into e-learning systems. J. Comput. Sci. **11**(12), 1108–1117 (2015)
58. Thomas, J.: Individual cyber security: empowering employees to resist spear phishing to prevent identity theft and ransomware attacks. Int. J. Bus. Manag. **12**(3), 1–23 (2018). https://doi.org/10.5539/ijbm.v13n6p1
59. Thurston, T.N.: Design case: implementing gamification with arcs to engage digital natives. J. Empower. Teach. Excell. **2**(1), 5 (2018). https://doi.org/10.26077/vsk5-5613
60. Trickel, E., et al.: Shell we play a game? CTF-as-a-service for security education. In: 2017 USENIX Workshop on Advances in Security Education (ASE 2017), Vancouver, BC. USENIX Association (2017). https://www.usenix.org/conference/ase17/workshop-program/presentation/trickel
61. Triplett, W.J.: Addressing cybersecurity challenges in education. Int. J. STEM Educ. Sustain. **3**(1), 47–67 (2023). https://doi.org/10.52889/ijses.v3i1.132
62. Tsai, C.Y., Shih, W.L., Hsieh, F.P., Chen, Y.A., Lin, C.L., Wu, H.J.: Using the arcs model to improve undergraduates' perceived information security protection

motivation and behavior. Comput. Educ. **181**, 104449 (2022). https://doi.org/10.1016/j.compedu.2022.104449
63. Tymoshchuk, D., Yatskiv, V., Tymoshchuk, V., Yatskiv, N.: Interactive cybersecurity training system based on simulation environments. Meas. Comput. Dev. Technol. Process. (4), 215–220 (2024). https://doi.org/10.31891/2219-9365-2024-80-26
64. Ukwandu, E., et al.: A review of cyber-ranges and test-beds: current and future trends. Sensors **20**(24) (2020). https://doi.org/10.3390/s20247148
65. Švábenský, V., Vykopal, J., Cermak, M., Laštovička, M.: Enhancing cybersecurity skills by creating serious games. In: Proceedings of the 23rd Annual ACM Conference on Innovation and Technology in Computer Science Education, ITiCSE 2018, pp. 194–199. Association for Computing Machinery, New York (2018). https://doi.org/10.1145/3197091.3197123
66. Švábenský, V ., eleda, P., Vykopal, J., Brišáková, S.: Cybersecurity knowledge and skills taught in capture the flag challenges. Comput. Secur. **102**, 102154 (2021). https://doi.org/10.1016/j.cose.2020.102154
67. Wolfenden, B.: Gamification as a winning cyber security strategy. Comput. Fraud Secur. **2019**(5), 9–12 (2019). https://doi.org/10.1016/S1361-3723(19)30052-1
68. Wouters, P., van Nimwegen, C., van Oostendorp, H., van der Spek, E.D.: A meta-analysis of the cognitive and motivational effects of serious games. J. Educ. Psychol. **105**(2), 249–265 (2013). https://doi.org/10.1037/a0031311
69. Yamin, M.M., Katt, B., Gkioulos, V.: Cyber ranges and security testbeds: scenarios, functions, tools and architecture. Comput. Secur. **88**, 101636 (2020). https://doi.org/10.1016/j.cose.2019.101636
70. Yamin, M.M., Katt, B., Nowostawski, M.: Serious games as a tool to model attack and defense scenarios for cyber-security exercises. Comput. Secur. **110**, 102450 (2021). https://doi.org/10.1016/j.cose.2021.102450
71. Yang, K.H., Chen, H.H.: What increases learning retention: employing the prediction-observation-explanation learning strategy in digital game-based learning. Interact. Learn. Environ. **31**(6), 3898–3913 (2023). https://doi.org/10.1080/10494820.2021.1944219
72. Yasin, A., Fatima, R., Wen, L., JiangBin, Z., Niazi, M.: What goes wrong during phishing education? A probe into a game-based assessment with unfavorable results. Entertain. Comput. **52**, 100815 (2025). https://doi.org/10.1016/j.entcom.2024.100815
73. Zichermann, G., Cunningham, C.: Gamification by Design: Implementing Game Mechanics in Web and Mobile Apps. O'Reilly Media, Inc. (2011)

How to Turn a Platformer Game into a Casual Exergame for Combating Office Workers' Sedentary Behavior: An Exploratory Single-Case Pilot Study

Erik Berglund[(✉)] [iD] and Filip Josefsson [iD]

Linköping University, Linköping, Sweden
{erik.berglund,filip.josefsson}@liu.se

Abstract. This paper explores the adaptation of traditional platformer games into casual exergames for breaking up prolonged sitting periods during workdays. We present *Platformer*, a browser-based casual exergame that incorporates established platformer design principles while integrating physical movements through webcam-based detection. The game implements three key design patterns (guidance, safe zones, and pace breaking) and requires both upper and lower body movements during two-minute gameplay sessions. An exploratory single-case pilot study conducted over 1.5 weeks (N = 100 play sessions) revealed preliminary trends suggesting potential increases in both game performance and physical movements over time, though with varying movement patterns across different body parts. While limited by its single-case nature, this study provides initial insights into adapting traditional video game genres for workplace health interventions and suggests directions for future research in casual exergame design.

Keywords: Gamification · Exergames · Movement · Sedentary behavior · Workplace health · Active breaks · Game design · Platformer games

1 Introduction

Sedentary behavior is a major health concern that the World Health Organization has warned of [1]. Sedentary behavior has been linked with multiple health risks, including type 2 diabetes [2], obesity [3], cancer and mortality [4]. These risks remain even when people are active outside of their sedentary time [4], unless they dedicate an hour or more every day to moderate physical activity [5]. An especially sedentary environment is offices [6], making it an important area to reduce that behavior. One way of incorporating more activity in office environments are with microbreaks [7]. Microbreaks have been shown to increase worker engagement [8], decrease discomfort [7], increase cardiometabolic health [9] and increase mental health without negatively impacting productivity [10].

One way that microbreaks have been implemented into workplaces have been by using exergames [11–13]. Exergames are video games that require physical activity to

© IFIP International Federation for Information Processing 2025
Published by Springer Nature Switzerland AG 2025
M. Sugimoto et al. (Eds.): ICEC 2025, LNCS 16042, pp. 32–46, 2025.
https://doi.org/10.1007/978-3-032-02555-5_3

be played [14]. Casual exergames are especially fitting exergames for the purposes of exergames, since they are simple exergames played for shorter periods and are designed to be easy to learn and setup [15].

Familiarity is one way of making people more willing to engage in casual exergames [16]. One way this could be achieved is by developing games in old and established genres. For this study, the platformer genre will be examined. Platformer games, characterized by their emphasis on guiding a character to jump between platforms and over obstacles, have existed since the 1980's, with new platformer games still being released to this day, making it likely to be a familiar genre to many people. The following research question is addressed in this paper: *How can one turn a traditional platformer game into a casual exergame for micro-breaking during workday?*

This study will look at the suitability of the platformer genre when applied to casual exergames by developing a platforming casual exergame that promotes microbreaking for office workers. This paper includes an exploratory single-case pilot study to identify preliminary findings and observed trends regarding potential effects of playing the casual exergame for micro-breaking during the workday. This study contributes to workplace health intervention research by showcasing how traditional video game genres can be adapted for casual exergames used for micro-breaking during workday and provides preliminary findings and observed trends based on 100 play sessions.

2 Related Work

2.1 Platformers and Exergames

The key to platforming games are the levels in which they are played. Platformer levels can be divided into two major structural divisions, the cells and the portals [17]. The cells are the area in which the challenges can be found, and portals are the areas in between the cells. Each cell is in turn built from multiple rhythm groups, which are smaller platforming challenges that are built from a rhythm of challenges. The rhythm groups contain the different components of the game, e.g. platforms and obstacles etc., which make up the platforming level [17].

2D Platformers can make use of design patterns to create better games. Khalifa *et al.* has described six design patterns that are both prevalent and can improve the player experience in 2D games: *guidance* uses elements to direct players' movement, *safe zones* provide secure resting areas, *foreshadowing* introduces elements before they become crucial, *layering* combines elements for new challenges, *branching* offers multiple paths, and *pace breaking* varies gameplay intensity for variety [18]. These patterns are frequently employed in combination to enhance the gaming experience. Layering several hazards for instance, might lead to tension and pace breaking. Future branches to pursue may be foreshadowed via locked doors.

Few studies have investigated platformer exergames. El-Habr et al. developed the exergame *Runner* [19] for testing their algorithm method that optimizes three key elements based on guidelines for developing a benefit delivery system [20]: health benefits through targeted content generation, player engagement through adaptive difficulty scaling based on flow theory [21], and resource efficiency through modular development capabilities. They found that the method made the players burn more calories and promoted positive affect. Henry et al. developed a platformer exergame that makes use of wearable technology that collects heart rate data during gameplay sessions [22]. Initial testing shows that people who played the game were engaged and gave the game a generally good reaction.

Berglund et al. [23] evaluated their casual exergame called *Platform* by comparing it to three other casual exergames. *Platform* requires players to perform three distinct movements: touching their nose to stop, extending their arm sideways to move horizontally, and squatting to jump. *Platform* was designed as an active micro-break program to be played in 2-min sessions during the workday. During interviews, participants expressed varying opinions about the four exergames, but notably, 14 out of 15 participants rated *Platform* as the most enjoyable.

Several factors contributed to *Platform*'s popularity. These included its variety (in graphics, tasks, game tempo, and required movements), its progressive challenge (through the appearance of new enemies and the need for precise timing), and its intuitive game mechanics (with clear rules and objectives). The game's familiar platformer theme enhanced its accessibility, as participants could readily understand the gameplay expectations. As one participant noted, *"I know what I should do, the question is only what the specific content will be, like type of enemies that shoot and enemies that shoot two times."*

Participants' feedback on physical exertion revealed two main themes. First, they found the squatting movement particularly demanding but appreciated this aspect of the game. They also valued how *Platform* engaged different body parts with varying levels of intensity, preventing excessive fatigue. Second, participants appreciated the direct relationship between physical effort and in-game performance. The physical challenge was viewed positively by players since their performance increased when they were more physically active. The exergame achieved moderate-intensity exercise levels, making it an effective tool for breaking up prolonged sitting periods, aligning with Bailey and Locke's research on the benefits of light physical activity during sitting breaks [24].

Based on their research, Berglund et al. [23] concluded that an effective casual platform exergame should balance cognitive complexity with clear game mechanics, incorporate variety, and include meaningful physical exertion to optimize both exercise benefits and player enjoyment.

2.2 Gamification in Exergaming

Gamification can be used in digital health intervention to motivate users to engage in physical activity [25] as it is a process that create an experience characterized by motivation and user engagement [26, 27]. Exergames comprises of the three essential gamification elements [28]:

- Motivational affordances: These are the elements of the exergame which are meant to motivate the player to keep playing. These can range from leaderboards to badges and levels. These affordances need to be implemented as to be able to get the outcomes that is desired from the exergame.

- Psychological outcomes: These are the psychological process that create the desired motivation. The outcomes can be self-esteem, competition, or achievement. These psychological outcomes are meant to give the player behavioral outcomes.
- Behavioral outcomes: These are the outcomes that the exergame is meant to elicit. Some examples of behaviors are becoming more physically active and be less sedentary by taking more walks. The behavioral outcomes can be seen as the goal of the exergames.

2.3 Movements in Casual Exergaming

Exergames have been found to be able to increase energy expenditure, with exergames that require full-body movement requiring more energy than those that only require upper-body movement [29]. Some studies have identified that only exergames with full-body movement can fulfill the recommended amount of daily energy expenditure [30].

However, research on the effects of various movement interactions on the psychological effects (e.g. enjoyment and positive affect) and physical exertion of casual exergame play is lacking [31, 32]. Upper body casual exergames have been considered as a suitable microbreak activity as no significant perceived difference between upper-body and full-body controls could be identified [31]. It is advised that casual exergames should allow for a high degree of movement ambiguity in order to encourage both exertion and enjoyment [23]. Casual exergames should also use a fast game pace to divert players' attention from their bodies [23].

Since achievement could predict both enjoyment and future intention of play [33], the impact of movement interaction on player performance has also been studied in casual exergames [31, 34–36]. A comparison of a casual exergame featuring upper-body movement interactions versus full-body movements revealed that performance was significantly higher in the upper-body movement condition than in the full-body movement condition [32]. Another study found a positive correlation between performance and movements in a casual exergame involving lower body movements, suggesting that physical exertion contributed to the game's challenge which impacts the psychological effects [36]. This was also identified for a platformer casual exergame that used three types of movements where participants found squatting demanding but enjoyable and appreciated how the game varied intensity across body parts to prevent fatigue [23]. The study found that players valued the link between effort and performance, seeing the movement exertion challenge as positive [23].

3 Platformer: A Casual Micro-Break Exergame

3.1 Overview

Platformer is a 2D platforming casual exergame. The game is designed to be played in two-minute sessions and can be played in an internet browser. The game can detect the players' body movements using webcams. The goal of the exergame is to earn as many points as possible during the two-minute session by collecting coins, defeating enemies, and finding treasure. A screenshot of the game can be found in Fig. 1.

Platformer can be controlled with just three movements: pointing an arm sideways to move the player character in the appropriate direction, raising an arm to jump (which can be done with either the pointing or non-pointing arm), and squatting to interact with the three different types of objects in the game world (like switches that activate moveable platforms or obstacles, doors to advance to the next level, and chests that contain coins) (Fig. 2).

Fig. 1. Screenshot of the exergame Platformer (edited for clarity)

The game is structured as smaller stages that switch direction after every stage. Every stage contains a couple of obstacles and the opportunity to earn points and ends with a door leading to the next stage. If the direction of the current stage goes from left to right, the next stage will go from right to left and vice versa.

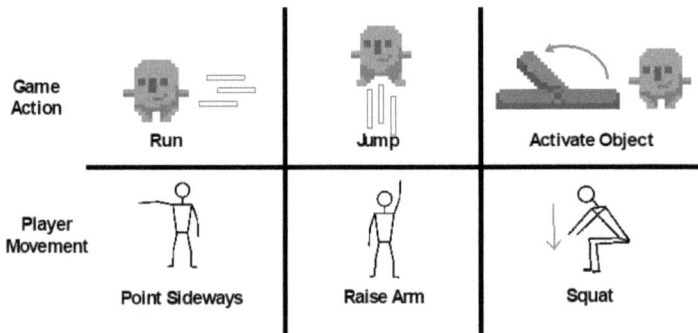

Fig. 2. The game actions and their corresponding body movement

The differences between *Platformer* and *Runner* [19] is the free movement of the character in *Platformer*. When comparing *Platformer* to *Platform* [23], *Platformer* contains randomly generated levels made of developer-designed segments. The controls of *Platformer* are also unlike both previous platforming exergames and is the only one using 2d platforming design guidelines.

3.2 Design of the Platformer Casual Exergame

Platformer follows well the platformer level framework presented by Smith *et al.* [17]. Each playthrough of *Platformer* can be considered a level in this framework with each stage being considered cells with portals at the end, in the form of doors. Each stage is made up of stage segments that are put in sequence, with each segment following the structure of a rhythm group.

The game also contains many of the components that are explained in the framework. There are, of course, an avatar and platforms. There are obstacles in the form of different enemies and spikes on the ground, which causes the player to respawn at the nearest checkpoint if they run into it. There are movement aids in the form of moving platform, which needs to be used to reach high places. Collectibles exist in the form of coins that are scattered around the stages and treasure chests that need to be opened. Lastly, there are triggers, most clearly found in the levers which can activate moving platforms and open gates that block the player's path.

When considering the 2D design patterns proposed by Khalifa *et al.* [18], *Platformer* makes use of three of the six patterns. The game makes use of guidance, in the form of walling of the direction the player is not meant to go in and by placing coins that guide the player. The game contains many safe zones, since the game makes use of movement controls that are a lot less precise than button controls. Lastly, the game has pace breakers by having segments where the player is not allowed to stop for any longer period, lest they fall and need to respawn.

The game does not contain foreshadowing, layering and branching, since these patterns require longer designed sequences of stage segments, while *Platformer* will make use of randomization to pick out the order of the developer-designed stage segment.

3.3 Gamification Components in the Casual Exergame Platformer

The casual exergame *Platformer* is designed to use motivational affordance to create psychological outcomes and behavioral changes [25].

- The motivational affordances that have been implemented in *Platformer* are:

  - Score attack gameplay: The goal of the game is to earn as high of a score as possible within the two-minute time limit. Scoring creates a clear goal for the player and gives a sense of achievement when the player beats their previous high score.
  - Randomly generated levels: Each level is generated as a sequence of randomly selected developer-designed stage segments. The unpredictable nature of the levels played for each session can create a sense of "one-more-time"-playing, since one never knows if the next session will generate a level in which the player will be able to beat their old score.
  - Variety: Because prior research has demonstrated that both game content and movement variation enhances enjoyment in platformer exergames [23], it is incorporated into both the game level design and the motions needed to engage with the game and play. Level variation is created through the graphical elements, the tasks, enemies, assets, and the game tempo. Movement variation is created by utilizing

both upper and lower body movements that demand varying degrees of effort, as well as three distinct movements for three distinct activities.

- The following psychological outcomes have been implemented in *Platformer*:
  - Progression: By going from level to level in quick succession, the player gets a continuous sense of progression.
  - Mastery: By playing the game multiple times, the player can become better at beating enemies and jumping over bottomless pits.
  - Variety: Thanks to the great variety and number of stage segments, the player never knows what stage they will find next.
  - Challenge: The game offers multiple difficulties for the player to choose at the start of the play session: easy, medium and hard. The difficulty determines the pool of possible stage segments that the player may encounter in their playthrough, with more difficult segments appearing at higher difficulties. As the player gets better at the game, they can increase the difficulty to challenge themselves and earn more points. The exergame provides also physiological challenge. As previous research show direct relationship between physical movement and in-game performance impacts enjoyment in exergaming [23], the game is designed to reward physical activity. Players may advance in the game and get more items the more they move; for example, squatting can be used to gather coins from the chests.

- The following behavioral outcomes are implemented in *Platformer*:
  - Movement variety: Playing the exergame requires three motions that involve both the upper and lower body. Both the left and right arms are required to play the exergame since it switches course after a few level segments. Squats are also necessary for the advancement, which allows the player to engage their lower body. Since lower body movements have been demonstrated to need more effort in exergames [37], squats were utilized to increase the exertion required to play.
  - Choice of intensity: Players are allowed leeway in how they choose to perform the required movement of the game, allowing a choice in how intense each section will be. Since constantly squatting creates the risk of the game being too fatiguing [38], many of the squats are both optional for extra points and spread out.
  - Encouragement of a less sedentary lifestyle: By making the player stand up and move their arms and do squats, the player can get a break from an otherwise sedentary day.

4 An Exploratory Single-Case Pilot Study

4.1 Study Setup

This study was conducted to provide initial insights about player's behavior after longer play time in real-life use, a work office setting, to interrupt prolonged sitting time. The purpose of the study is to identify preliminary trends and patterns over time. Thus, the exergame was played 100 times every 30 min over about one and a half week during workdays. The participant in the study is the developer of the casual exergame. At the age of 24, he described himself as a male student enrolled in a master's degree in computer science. He described himself as "fairly sedentary" (translated) but performed strength training at the gym 1–3 times a week and had a BMI between 22–24 (estimated, not measured at time of study). The game was played on a PC with an external webcam.

Data was recorded by the exergame program and put into a CSV file after each play-session. The data can be divided between game data, which looked at the game state at the end of the session, and movement data, which was recorded by the webcam throughout the session. Excel and SPSS Statistics were used for the analysis process. Table 1 summarizes the recorded data for each session.

Table 1. Data that was collected during each play session

Data	Type	Explanation
Score	Game data	The number of points that was earned
Wrist Movement	Movement	Measures how much the player's wrists moved
Torso Movement	Movement	Measures how much the player's torso moved
Squat depth	Movement	Measures how low the player squatted
Segments completed	Game data	The number segments that were completed
Respawns	Game data	The number of respawns that the player used
Enemies Defeated	Game data	The number of enemies that were defeated

4.2 Statistical Analysis

The data was analyzed by plotting the data in a scatter plot using Excel and visually analyzing the diagrams. This method was chosen as this was a single case study which only meant to serve as a first indication of what might be found in a larger study. All data was plotted against time, which is represented as the session number, to find how the different parameters changed over time. The data was also plotted against score, which serves to indicate whether the game encourages or discourages certain behaviors in the exergame.

4.3 Results

The participant showed an increase in performance over time, as both the number of segments completed, and the number of points earned increased over time. Out of the three movement measures, only the torso movement showed a slight increase over time. Wrist movement decreased after the first few sessions, before slowly increasing again at the end. The squat depth decreased clearly at the start and then remained constant afterwards. The number of respawns and number of enemies defeated showed no obvious trend. See Fig. 3 for all time-based scatter plots.

When plotted against score, slightly different patterns emerge. Completing more segments seems to correlate with higher scores. Wrist movement shows no obvious trend when plotted against score, though more torso movement seems to correlate with higher scores. Squat depth seems to decrease as the score increases. The number of enemies defeated seemingly has no effect on score but less respawns seems to lead to higher scores. See Fig. 4 for all score-based scatter plots.

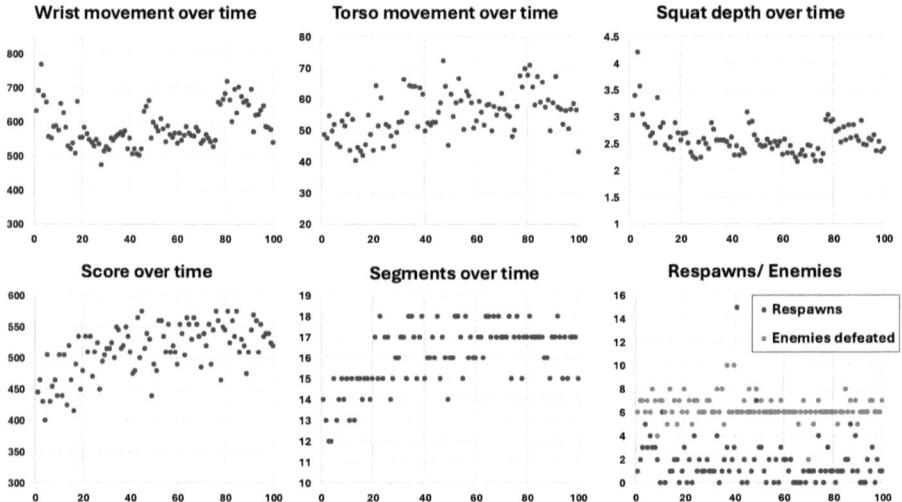

Fig. 3. Scatter plots of data over time

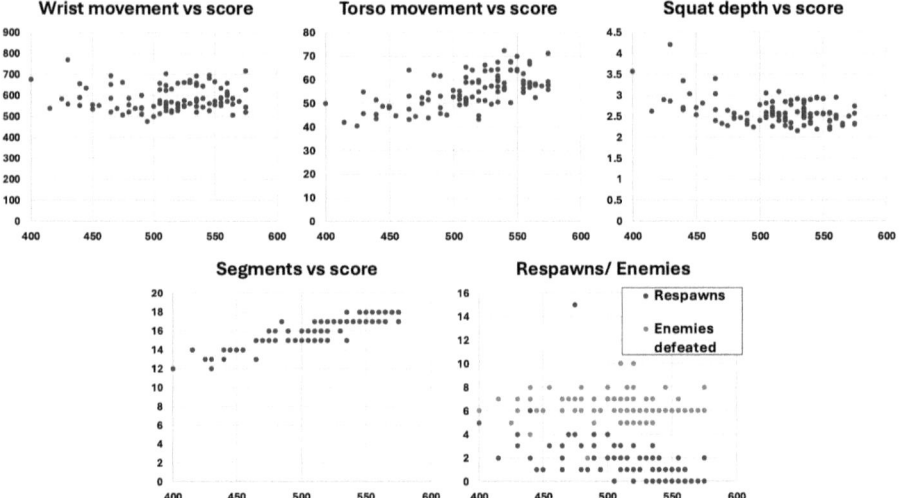

Fig. 4. Scatter plots of data against score

5 Discussion

The primary aim of this study was to investigate how to turn a traditional platformer game into a casual exergame designed to combat sedentary behavior during workday with active micro-breaks. An exploratory single-case pilot study was then conducted by the developer over 1.5 weeks (N = 100 play sessions) to examine preliminary trends and patterns over time regarding movement patterns and game performance evolution during repeated gameplay.

5.1 2D Platformer Casual Exergame Design

The initial implementation of *Platformer* suggests that traditional platformer game genres might be adaptable as casual exergames for microbreaking purposes during workday. The game's structural design closely follows Smith et al.'s framework [17], which provides a systematic approach to platformer level design through the implementation of cells (challenge areas), portals (transition areas), and rhythm groups (sequences of platforming challenges). This adherence to established platformer design principles appears to create a familiar yet engaging experience, though broader testing would be needed to confirm this observation.

The game's implementation of three out of six design patterns identified by Khalifa et al. [18] - guidance, safe zones, and pace breaking - aligns with previous successful platformer exergames. For instance, the guidance pattern, implemented through strategic coin placement and environmental barriers, appears to serve a similar function to the clear objectives noted in Berglund et al.'s [23] study, where participants appreciated understanding "what they should do." The incorporation of safe zones proved particularly important given the movement-based controls, which typically require more precision than traditional button inputs, echoing findings from previous platformer exergames that emphasized the importance of balanced challenge levels [19].

While *Platformer* did not implement the foreshadowing, layering, and branching patterns, this selective implementation may benefit its role as a casual exergame. This approach appears to align with previous findings suggesting that casual exergames should balance cognitive complexity with clear game mechanics [23]. The simpler design may support the game's intended use as a brief micro-break activity, though future studies could explore whether this streamlined approach remains effective across a larger user base.

The game's design also appears to incorporate lessons learned from previous platformer exergames regarding movement variety and challenge progression. Similar to Platform [23], our implementation includes varied movements and progressive challenges, though implemented differently. Where Platform used three distinct movements (nose-touching, arm extension, and squatting), *Platformer* employs arm movements and squatting in ways that require varying levels of exertion, potentially supporting the finding that movement variation enhances enjoyment in platformer exergames [23].

The design approach also appears to align with El-Habr et al.'s [19] emphasis on balancing health benefits, player engagement, and resource efficiency. The game's two-minute session length and browser-based implementation potentially supports resource efficiency, while the combination of familiar platformer mechanics with physical movements might promote engagement. However, unlike El-Habr et al.'s [19] implementation, our design does not include adaptive difficulty scaling, which could be an area for future enhancement.

The relationship between physical effort and in-game performance, which Berglund et al. [23] identified as important for player engagement, appears to be present in our design through the movement-based control scheme. However, the preliminary nature of our single-case study means that the effectiveness of this implementation requires further investigation with a broader user base.

When considering the technical implementation aspects explored in Henry et al.'s [22] work, our browser-based approach using webcam detection offers a different perspective on accessibility. While their wearable technology approach provided precise heart rate data, our implementation prioritizes ease of access and minimal setup requirements, though this trade-off between accessibility and precise physical activity monitoring warrants further investigation.

These design choices and their preliminary outcomes suggest potential approaches for adapting traditional game genres into casual exergames, while highlighting areas that require further investigation. Future research could explore how different combinations of design patterns affect player engagement and physical activity levels, and whether the simplified implementation of traditional platformer elements effectively serves the micro-break context.

5.2 Movement Patterns and Performance

The exploratory single-case pilot study has shown interesting trends that merit further investigation in future studies with larger samples.

Progression is crucial for maintaining player engagement, as it provides tangible evidence of skill development - a key motivator in game design [33]. The observed increase in both score and completed segments over time suggests potential for performance improvement, possibly indicating an appropriate learning curve. While these preliminary findings are promising, they should be interpreted cautiously given the single-case nature of the study and the participant's role as the game's developer.

The pilot data showed an increase torso movement over time, potentially indicating successful promotion of physical activity. Wrist movement also showed an increase in movement over time, though after a clear drop at the beginning of the testing. However, the observed decrease in squat depth at the beginning suggests a need to examine movement patterns across a broader user base. This preliminary finding raises questions about whether players might optimize their movements over time, potentially reducing physical exertion. Future iterations might need to consider adjusting squat detection thresholds or modifying required squat movements to maintain exercise intensity.

The observed correlation between higher scores and increased torso movement hints at possible successful integration of physical activity into core gameplay mechanics. The negative correlation with squat depth and lack of correlation with wrist movement suggests areas for potential design refinement. These preliminary findings align with previous research suggesting that upper body movements may be suitable for office-based exergaming [31]. While the focus on upper body movement could be relevant for office workers who face risks of musculoskeletal disorders [39, 40], broader studies would be needed to confirm these benefits. Similarly, while the inclusion of squats might help break up sitting periods [6, 41], their optimal implementation requires further investigation.

5.3 Limitations

This exploratory single-case pilot study has several important limitations that should be considered when interpreting the results. Most notably, the single participant was also the developer of the casual exergame, which likely influenced the data in ways that are difficult to predict and mitigate. The developer's familiarity with the underlying code creates a significant bias, making these results non-generalizable. The learning curve observed may differ substantially from that of typical users, as the developer began the study with extensive game knowledge.

Despite these substantial limitations, this exploratory research provides preliminary insights into casual exergame development using established genres, movement integration in casual exergaming, and potential considerations for workplace exercise program design.

6 Conclusion

This exploratory single-case pilot study suggests several potential directions for future research in casual exergames for breaking sedentary time. The preliminary findings indicate that traditional game genres might provide useful frameworks for creating casual exergames, potentially allowing for the preservation of core gameplay mechanics while incorporating movement requirements. However, larger-scale studies would be needed to validate this approach.

The exploratory single-case pilot data raises interesting questions about movement integration, suggesting that movement requirements may need careful consideration in their implementation within gameplay mechanics. The observed trend of variable movement thresholds leading to potential performance optimization warrants further investigation. Additionally, different types of body movements may require distinct design approaches to ensure effective integration into casual exergames.

Finally, the preliminary findings suggest that performance balancing might be crucial for future designs. The relationship between physical movements and in-game performance may need careful calibration, and movement variety could potentially be incentivized through scoring mechanisms to maintain player engagement. These observations provide a foundation for future research with larger, more diverse participant groups to develop evidence-based guidelines for casual exergame design.

Acknowledgments. We want to thank Josef Karlsson as the developer of *Platformer* and his playtesting. We would also like to thank Aseel Berglund for her contributions to this study. The project has not received any specific funding.

References

1. Bull, F.C., et al.: World Health Organization 2020 guidelines on physical activity and sedentary behaviour. Br. J. Sports Med. **54**(24), 1451–1462 (2020). https://doi.org/10.1136/bjsports-2020-102955
2. Hu, F.B., et al.: Television watching and other sedentary behaviors in relation to risk of obesity and type 2 diabetes mellitus in women. JAMA **289**(14), 1785–1791 (2003). https://doi.org/10.1001/jama.289.14.1785
3. Shields, M., Tremblay, M.S.: Sedentary behaviour and obesity. Health Reports **19**(2) (2008)
4. Biswas, A., et al.: Sedentary time and its association with risk for disease incidence, mortality, and hospitalization in adults: a systematic review and meta-analysis. Ann. Intern. Med. **162**(2), 123–132 (2015). https://doi.org/10.7326/M14-1651
5. Ekelund, U., et al.: Does physical activity attenuate, or even eliminate, the detrimental association of sitting time with mortality? A harmonised meta-analysis of data from more than 1 million men and women. The Lancet **388**(10051), 1302–1310 (2016). https://doi.org/10.1016/S0140-6736(16)30370-1
6. Parry, S., Straker, L.: The contribution of office work to sedentary behaviour associated risk. BMC Public Health **13**(1), 1 (2013). https://doi.org/10.1186/1471-2458-13-296
7. McLean, L., et al.: Computer terminal work and the benefit of microbreaks. Appl. Ergon. **32**(3), 225–237 (2001). https://doi.org/10.1016/S0003-6870(00)00071-5
8. Kühnel, J., et al.: Take a break! Benefits of sleep and short breaks for daily work engagement. Eur. J. Work Organ. Psy. **26**(4), 481–491 (2017). https://doi.org/10.1080/1359432X.2016.1269750
9. Chastin, S.F., et al.: Meta-analysis of the relationship between breaks in sedentary behavior and cardiometabolic health. Obesity **23**(9), 1800–1810 (2015). https://doi.org/10.1002/oby.21180
10. Radwan, A., et al.: Effects of active microbreaks on the physical and mental well-being of office workers: a systematic review. Cogent Engineering **9**(1), 2026206 (2022). https://doi.org/10.1080/23311916.2022.2026206
11. Berglund, A., et al.: Liopep: a gamified casual exergame application to help office workers not be active couch potatoes. In: 2023 IEEE 11th International Conference on Serious Games and Applications for Health (SeGAH). IEEE (2023). https://doi.org/10.1109/SeGAH57547.2023.10253779
12. Fischetti, F., et al.: Ten-minute physical activity breaks improve attention and executive functions in healthcare workers. J. Functional Morphology and Kinesiology **9**(2), 102 (2024). https://doi.org/10.3390/jfmk9020102
13. Ren, X., et al.: Step-by-step: Exploring a social exergame to encourage physical activity and social dynamics among office workers. In: Extended Abstracts of the 2019 CHI Conference on Human Factors in Computing Systems (2019). https://doi.org/10.1145/3290607.3312788
14. Oh, Y., Yang, S.: Defining exergames & exergaming. Proceedings of Meaningful Play **2010**, 21–23 (2010)
15. Gao, Y., Mandryk, R.L.: GrabApple: the design of a casual exergame. In: Entertainment Computing–ICEC 2011: 10th International Conference, ICEC 2011, Vancouver, Canada, October 5–8, 2011. Proceedings 10. Springer (2011). https://doi.org/10.1007/978-3-642-24500-8_5
16. Zhang, H., et al.: Towards Age-friendly Exergame Design: The Role of Familiarity. In: Proceedings of the Annual Symposium on Computer-Human Interaction in Play. 2019 of Conference. Barcelona, Spain: Association for Computing Machinery. https://doi.org/10.1145/3311350.3347191

17. Smith, G., Cha, M., Whitehead, J.: A framework for analysis of 2D platformer levels. In: Proceedings of the 2008 ACM SIGGRAPH symposium on Video games. 2008 of Conference. Los Angeles, California: Association for Computing Machinery. https://doi.org/10.1145/1401843.1401858
18. Khalifa, A., Silva, F.d.M., Togelius, J.: Level design patterns in 2D games. In: 2019 IEEE Conference on Games (CoG) (2019). https://doi.org/10.1109/CIG.2019.8847953
19. El-Habr, C., et al.: Runner: a 2D platform game for physical health promotion. SoftwareX **10**, 100329 (2019). https://doi.org/10.1016/j.softx.2019.100329
20. Ushaw, G., Eyre, J., Morgan, G.: A paradigm for the development of serious games for health as benefit delivery systems. In: 2017 IEEE 5th International Conference on Serious Games and Applications for Health (SeGAH) (2017). IEEE. https://doi.org/10.1109/SeGAH.2017.7939264
21. Csikszentmihalyi, M.: Flow: The Psychology of Optimal Experience. Vol. 1990. Harper & Row New York (1990)
22. Henry, J., Kendrick, C., Arnab, S.: Wearable technology as game input for active exergames. In: 2023 IEEE 11th International Conference on Serious Games and Applications for Health (SeGAH) (2023). https://doi.org/10.1109/SeGAH57547.2023.10253785
23. Berglund, E., et al.: Considerations for player enjoyment and exertion in casual exergames. In: 57th Hawaii International Conference on System Sciences (HICSS), Hilton Hawaiian Village Waikiki Beach Resort, January 3–6, 2024. University of Hawai'i at Manoa (2024). https://doi.org/10.24251/HICSS.2024.164
24. Bailey, D.P., Locke, C.D.: Breaking up prolonged sitting with light-intensity walking improves postprandial glycemia, but breaking up sitting with standing does not. J. Sci. Med. Sport **18**(3), 294–298 (2015). https://doi.org/10.1016/j.jsams.2014.03.008
25. Berglund, A., et al.: Understanding and assessing gamification in digital healthcare interventions for patients with cardiovascular disease. Eur. J. Cardiovasc. Nurs. **21**(6), 630–638 (2022). https://doi.org/10.1093/eurjcn/zvac048
26. Huotari, K., Hamari, J.: Defining gamification: a service marketing perspective. In: Proceeding of the 16th International Academic MindTrek Conference. Tampere, Finland: Association for Computing Machinery (2012). https://doi.org/10.1145/2393132.2393137
27. Hamari, J., Koivisto, J., Sarsa, H.: Does gamification work?--a literature review of empirical studies on gamification. In: 2014 47th Hawaii International Conference on System Sciences. IEEE (2014). https://doi.org/10.1109/HICSS.2014.377
28. Matallaoui, A., et al.: How effective is "exergamification"? A systematic review on the effectiveness of gamification features in exergames. Proceedings of the 50th Hawaii International Conference on System Sciences, pp. 3316–3325 (2017). https://doi.org/10.24251/HICSS.2017.402
29. Graves, L.E., Ridgers, N.D., Stratton, G.: The contribution of upper limb and total body movement to adolescents' energy expenditure whilst playing Nintendo Wii. Eur. J. Appl. Physiol. **104**, 617–623 (2008). https://doi.org/10.1007/s00421-008-0813-8
30. Jordan, M., Donne, B., Fletcher, D.: Only lower limb controlled interactive computer gaming enables an effective increase in energy expenditure. Eur. J. Appl. Physiol. **111**, 1465–1472 (2011). https://doi.org/10.1007/s00421-010-1773-3
31. Berglund, A., Orädd, H.: Exploring the psychological effects and physical exertion of using different movement interactions in casual exergames that promote active microbreaks: quasi-experimental study. JMIR Serious Games **12**, e55905 (2024). https://doi.org/10.2196/55905
32. Berglund, A., et al.: The attractiveness and effectiveness of upper body and full body casual exergame controllers. In: 2023 IEEE 11th International Conference on Serious Games and Applications for Health (SeGAH). IEEE (2023). https://doi.org/10.1109/SeGAH57547.2023.10253764

33. Limperos, A.M., Schmierbach, M.: Understanding the relationship between exergame play experiences, enjoyment, and intentions for continued play. Games for Health J. **5**(2), 100–107 (2016). https://doi.org/10.1089/g4h.2015.0042
34. Berglund, E., et al.: The effect of assigned goals in casual exergames on performance, exertion and enjoyment. In: 2023 IEEE 11th International Conference on Serious Games and Applications for Health (SeGAH). IEEE (2023). https://doi.org/10.1109/SeGAH57547.2023.10253767
35. Berglund, E., et al.: The potential of seated and standing short duration casual exergames to increase positive affect. In: Proceedings of the 26th International Academic Mindtrek Conference (2023). https://doi.org/10.1145/3616961.3616964
36. Berglund, E., Jedel, I., Berglund, A.: Using mediapipe machine learning to design casual exertion games to interrupt prolonged sedentary lifestyle. In: International Conference on Human-Computer Interaction. Springer (2023). https://doi.org/10.1007/978-3-031-35930-9_16
37. Peng, W., Lin, J.-H., Crouse, J.: Is playing exergames really exercising? a meta-analysis of energy expenditure in active video games. Cyberpsychol. Behav. Soc. Netw. **14**(11), 681–688 (2011). https://doi.org/10.1089/cyber.2010.0578
38. Ahmad, I., Kim, J.-Y.: Assessment of whole body and local muscle fatigue using electromyography and a perceived exertion scale for squat lifting. Int. J. Environ. Res. Public Health **15**(4), 784 (2018). https://doi.org/10.3390/ijerph15040784
39. Hoe, V.C., et al.: Ergonomic interventions for preventing work-related musculoskeletal disorders of the upper limb and neck among office workers. Cochrane Database of Systematic Reviews (10) (2018). https://doi.org/10.1002/14651858.CD008570.pub3
40. Noroozi, M.V., et al.: Prevalence of musculoskeletal disorders among office workers. Jundishapur J. Health Sciences **7**(1) (2015). https://doi.org/10.5812/jjhs.27157
41. Hallman, D.M., Mathiassen, S.E., Jahncke, H.: Sitting patterns after relocation to activity-based offices: a controlled study of a natural intervention. Prev. Med. **111**, 384–390 (2018). https://doi.org/10.1016/j.ypmed.2017.11.031

Design of a Serious Game to Challenge Sexism

Antonio Calvo-Morata[(✉)] [iD], Cristina Alonso-Fernández[iD], and Baltasar Fernández-Manjón[iD]

Complutense University of Madrid, 28040 Madrid, Spain
acmorata@ucm.es

Abstract. Among the many aspects in which gender inequality manifests itself, sexism behaviors appear almost inadvertently daily. From personal life situations to workplace scenarios, sexism behaviors have an impact that is largely overlooked. Despite its relevance, there is still a need for tools to effectively educate about this issue. We consider that serious games are an innovative and effective tool to address social issues, making them visible and increasing players' awareness and reflection about them. In this paper, we present "La Entrevista" ("The Interview"), a serious game to address sexism, particularly in the workplace, aimed at young adults. We detail the design process of the game, based on common sexism situations and behaviors, as well as exploratory user interviews with 10 engineers. Then, we describe two initial formative evaluations of the game: (1) an evaluation of an early prototype with 17 school teachers to gather their opinion and feedback; and (2) an initial formative evaluation of the game with 32 Red Cross Youth volunteers to obtain their opinion about the final game version. The positive results of these early evaluations, as well as the improvements pointed out by participants, have helped us to refine the final version of the game. Hereafter, we prepare its application with target users and the inclusion of learning analytics to capture players' actions while playing to better measure the game impact.

Keywords: Serious games · Education · Sexism · Social awareness

1 Introduction

Sexism is the set of prejudices and discriminatory behaviors originating from the condition of gender [1]. This issue often translates into unequal opportunities and treatment for women. Sexism manifests in several ways, from discrimination in the workplace to subtle societal expectations and biases that reinforce gender roles. Addressing sexism is crucial as it is one of the factors that contributes to gender inequality. It is important to ensure that everyone, regardless of gender, has access to the same opportunities and rights.

The Council of Europe (COE) [2] highlights examples of sexism in different areas such as: language and communication (e.g. the generic use of the masculine gender by a speaker), media, internet and social media (e.g. sexualised depictions of women), public sector (e.g. sexualised comments or comments about the appearance or family situation of politicians, most often women), justice (e.g. judges implying to victims of sexual violence that she was 'asking for it'), culture and sport (e.g. sportswomen depicted in the media according to their family role and not their skills and strengths).

The COE points out the need to take measures to raise awareness of this problem [2]. However, raising awareness about sexism is not easy. Beliefs about gender equality, traditional roles and gender equity policies are often influenced by ideological positions. In addition, some studies point out to variables such as political ideology or social dominance orientation as predictors of ambivalent sexism [3]. These social positions generate resistance and polarization in the public debate, causing many people to reject information that contradicts their worldview. Particularly when this information is merely expositive, for instance using talks or videos to educate about this problem, these strategies are rarely effective.

In this context, serious games can be an effective tool, as they present an interactive environment where players can obtain personal experiences and reflect on their own perspectives without feeling directly attacked. Serious games, designed for purposes beyond entertainment, have emerged as an innovative way to address complex social issues. These games provide an interactive platform for players to engage in and reflect on serious issues. The benefits they bring from traditional video games, such as engagement or continued attention, encourage their application in educational or social settings. By immersing players in virtual experiences that simulate real-world scenarios, serious games can foster empathy, challenge preconceived ideas and inspire action. Serious games have been applied successfully in multiple domains. They have proven to be effective tools for addressing varied issues, from bullying to environmental sustainability, by creating engaging environments that encourage learning and reflection [4, 5].

This paper presents the design of "La Entrevista", a serious game to address sexism, and two formative evaluations made with an initial prototype and the final version of the game.

2 Related Work

Serious games are an increasingly popular tool to raise awareness about social issues and foster empathy among their players. These games allow players to experience real life situations within a controlled environment and from different perspectives. For instance, games like Depression Quest [6], to offer insight into depression, or Conectado [7], to raise awareness about bullying and cyberbullying, have helped their players deal with serious issues. By embedding players into their interactive narratives, and allowing them to make choices within them, these games can create engaging educational experiences. If the game is well designed, it will create a personal sense of connection with the narrative and virtual characters making players feel emotionally or socially involved obtaining a meaningful engagement (sometimes this is described as relatedness) [8]. In schools, serious games can be also used as an initial shared experience to start a conversation about these sensitive issues, for instance, being followed by a debate or leading discussions in a school class.

Serious games have also been shown to be effective as a "vaccine", teaching players to recognize and resist subsequent situations like disinformation [9]. This vaccine methodology has also been applied to cognitive biases [10, 11]. As in a vaccine, the main idea is to expose the player to the social problem to be addressed in a controlled and less harmful environment. The goal is to increase resistance to these situations, making it easier to recognize and address them. Recognizing the less harmful situations and characteristics of sexism can help both sides of it: the person who engages in such discriminatory behaviors to reflect about it and, hopefully, stop acting in a discriminatory way; and the person targeted by that discrimination as well as the observers who can identify such situations more easily and act sooner against them.

To address gender equality issues, serious games can also be a powerful tool to encourage conversations after sharing a common experience. The literature review by [12] shows a prevalence of games addressing violence and targeted at teenagers, while other gender equality issues like sexism or stereotypes are not so commonly addressed in these digital tools. To try and fill this research gap, this paper presents "La Entrevista", a serious game to address sexism aimed at young adults. The game aims to address some sexist behaviors, particularly those related to the workplace, education, and the private sphere. In the following sections, we describe both the design process of the game, as well as two early evaluations with teachers and trained volunteers, and the feedback and conclusions obtained from those experiences.

3 The Game "La Entrevista"

"La Entrevista" (Spanish for "The interview") is a point & click serious game designed and developed with the aim of addressing sexism, that is, discrimination against a person for being a woman. The game is aimed primarily at players between 16 and 25 years old, i.e., young people of working age.

The game tells the story of a woman who goes to a job interview for a junior developer position. Along the way, she will encounter sexist situations, which will make her react in different ways. The game is played in first-person mode (i.e., the player is not represented by an avatar in the game). The fact that independently of their gender all players play as a woman is not revealed until the end of the game (when they see the main character reflected in a mirror). This narrative trick is done to reinforce the message that the game wants to send, that is: sexism in the work environment often goes unnoticed, but it exists. Until then, a neutral language is used, so as not to reveal the gender of the protagonist.

During the game story, players must prepare for and conduct a job interview. To do so, they have to move around and explore the company where the interview will take place. With this exploration, players will meet different game characters with whom they will have different conversations, including the job interview. These conversations will show different situations of discrimination and micro-sexism that players must learn to identify. To address and raise awareness of sexism, players will endure inappropriate comments and questions about their private life. Players' possible interactions within the game include moving between scenes, talking to other game characters and interacting with some game objects.

However, as mentioned, the key plot twist of the game is that throughout the entire gameplay and conversations, the dialogues provide no information about the protagonist's gender (i.e., the character embodied by the player). The gender of the protagonist is only revealed once the job interview is completed. The purpose of this is to make all conversations seem strange and discriminatory to players, making them realize at the end of the game that this is because they had played as a female character (regardless of their actual gender). This also increases the immersion of players in the story, regardless of their gender, by making them feel like they could be the person who needs to pass the job interview, taking the in-game decisions more seriously.

3.1 Application in Class

The game has an estimated duration of 20 min. This allows the game to be easily integrated into a class session, with leftover time to conduct a reflection session and debate immediately after all students have played the game. The shared experience of playing the game, and the sexism topics addressed in its story, can be used as a baseline to open up a discussion about these issues in the class. This can be useful both to expand the effect of the game's impact on sexism awareness as well as to adapt the educational tool to the context and needs of the class. The choice on the specific way on how to introduce the use of the game into the class is of course left to teachers, but the designers' idea is that players complete the game without knowing its intended goals. This aims to avoid or at least reduce any possible prejudice that they may have when discussing sexism topics.

The game has been developed with uAdventure [13], a tool for the development of games with educational purposes and exported for Windows as many compulsory education centers are implementing policies restricting or even prohibiting the use of mobile devices. Another reason for designing the game for PC use is that it allows teachers to better manage the class by easily overseeing each student's activity.

3.2 Game Structure and Content

The game story presents a simplified version of a selection process for a job position, from the job application to the interview with human resources. The game is structured in 4 differentiated parts that also mark the player's progress: (1) at the main character's house, prior to the interview, (2) at the company, before the interview starts, (3) during the actual job interview, and (4) going back home and ending the game. In each part, players will discover different game scenes and interact with different game characters. Each of these four parts introduces different sexism topics.

In the first part, the main character is at her[1] house, in front of a PC to fill in the CV information. With that information, players can choose between two job offers to apply to. This choice does not affect the game experience but only changes slightly some of the later dialogues. The player can always check the character's CV to answer the questions correctly. This initial part does not expose any sexism topic yet but instead serves as a general introduction to the game plot and gives players a clear goal to achieve, which will serve to hide the educational theme.

---

[1] Notice that in the following description of the game content we use the female gender to refer to the main character, but this is not shown in the game until the player has completed the game.

In the second part, after choosing a job offer to apply to, the main character arrives at the company where the job interview will take place. The player must find the interview room and wait for the interview time to arrive. During that waiting time, players will talk with game characters that appear in different game scenarios and that have different roles within the company.

In the third part, after going through all the previous company areas, players arrive at the actual job interview. This interview takes place in one office room and two game characters from the human resources department of the company conduct the interview (Fig. 1).

Fig. 1. Screenshots of the company's cafeteria (left) and company's waiting room (right) of the game. The player can interact with the characters and read the dialogs with the sexist com-ments.

Finally, in the fourth and last part of the game, once the player has completed the interview, the human resources characters will tell players whether they are a good fit for the company. The main character will be considered for the position depending on the answers the player has made during the interview. After this, players will appear at home, in front of a mirror, at which point they will discover that they have played as a female character. To end the game, they must answer 9 questions related to 9 key moments in which they have experienced a sexism situation during the game. For each one, the player is asked to identify what is inappropriate in the game character's behavior. These moments include: a conversation with the receptionist, two scenes in the waiting room and two in the cafeteria, and four moments from the job interview.

3.3 Game Design Process and Sexism Situations Selection

The design of the game "La Entrevista" was based on a dual approach: on one hand, we studied common examples of sexism from official sources (e.g., [14]), while also conducting some exploratory user interviews with engineers (mostly women).

The Council of Europe (COE) highlights examples of sexism in different areas as previously stated. We were particularly interested in exploring the examples they pointed out for the three areas that were most relevant for the game content: the workplace, education careers, and private life. For the workplace, they highlight the practice of unofficially excluding women who have children from career opportunities; ignoring women in meetings, appropriating their contributions or silencing them; favoring a man rather than a woman for a managerial position by presuming her lack of authority; gratuitous comments about physical appearance or dress (which undermine women as professionals); derogatory comments to men taking on caring roles; and "mansplaining". In education, textbooks containing stereotypical images of women/men, boys/girls;

the absence of women as writers, historical or cultural figures in textbooks; career and education counselling discouraging non-stereotypical career or study choices; teachers making comments about the appearance of pupils/students/fellow teachers; sexualised comments to girls; bullying of non-conforming pupils/students by fellow pupils/students or education professionals; and the absence of awareness or procedures to address such sexist behaviours. In the private sphere, women performing more unpaid (care and household) work than men; sexist jokes between friends; systematically offering traditionally "feminine" or "masculine" toys to girls/boys; boys being encouraged to run and take risks and girls to be docile and compliant; the use of expressions like "running like a girl" or "boys will be boys".

On the other hand, we conducted user exploratory interviews with female and male engineers to gather information about their experiences with sexism situations. We interviewed 10 engineers (7 women, 3 men) and asked them to describe their experience with open-ended questions (*"Could you describe if in any of your job interviews have you been asked any question/comment that seemed strange or that could be sexist (even if it is a minor thing)?"*). We were purposely broad in our question, since we did not want to lead them or specify any sexism situation, but to gather their actual experiences with no bias. They included both questions asked in job interviews as well as other sexist comments or behaviors that they had experienced in first person or heard/seen from colleagues in their jobs. Comments gathered from user interviews included: personal and inappropriate questions in job interviews ("Are you married? Do you have kids? Do you usually cry under pressure?") or sexist comments ("Is that girl the secretary?", asked about the only woman in a technology team) and behaviors (a male coworker interrupting a woman explaining something because "her voice was too soft") (Fig. 2).

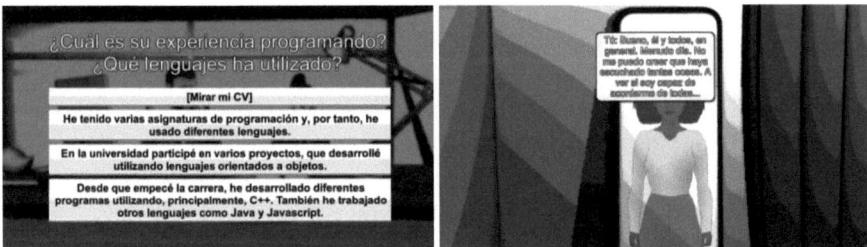

Fig. 2. Screenshot of the player answering a question (left) and main character in front of the mirror. The player discovers that the main character is a woman (right).

The real examples of sexist behaviors collected by the interview were analyzed in conjunction with the common examples of sexism from the COE. From this analysis we obtained a list of 22 behaviours or situations, and each one of these was rated from 1 to 5 on ease of introduction into the game and relevance. For the game narrative, we discarded those items that would clearly reveal that the main character of the game is a woman. In the end, scenarios and dialogues were created based on the most relevant items that also had more than 2 points in ease of introduction into the game.

The sexism topics chosen to appear into the game based on the above-described process were:

- Women are not capable of or are not suited to technical or engineering careers. A common form of sexism is to consider that women do not have the training or interest to apply for highly skilled positions.
- A man's opinion or advice is worth more than a woman's because they have more knowledge, especially in technical or engineering careers. One form of sexism is to distrust a woman's advice or knowledge, despite her experience, and to only take it as valid when a man comments on the same thing.
- Women are a distraction at work for men and make them less productive. This is an aspect sometimes raised in a casual or joking tone, but that also presents a form of sexism.
- With quotas, companies prioritize hiring women, even if this means hiring a woman who has a worse CV than a man. As a result, women get jobs just for being women. One of the most common forms of sexism is to think that a woman gets a job because the company wants to improve its image, or because it must comply with certain percentages of gender occupation.
- Men are not good enough to do housework, while women are better at it, or they are who should be in charge (role of housewife). A form of sexism is to think that housework is the woman's responsibility, and that if the man participates, he is simply "helping" the woman.
- Women write better and are more orderly than men, so they must do the jobs that are related to taking notes, organizing agendas, or carrying out bureaucratic procedures. One form of sexism is for the man to do the main, complex work and delegate minor activities to women, assuming they will perform worse on the difficult ones.
- Women may not assert and respect themselves in front of other male peers, making it more difficult for them to take on leadership positions.
- Women do not know how to work under pressure, cry more easily and are less able to withstand stressful situations.
- Women bring to the job things that men cannot bring to the job, such as their physique or other qualities. One form of sexism is to consider women for their qualities, and not for their ability to perform the job.
- Women are the ones who must take care of family members in need, children and household chores, and they cannot dedicate enough time to their professional careers. A common form of sexism in job interviews is to assume that the care of children or dependents is women's responsibility, and that this also affects their professional performance.

4 Formative Evaluation of Initial Prototype

4.1 Methodology

With an initial prototype version of the game, not including the actual final graphics, we conducted an initial formative evaluation to gather teachers' opinions about the game's content and applicability. $N = 17$ teachers from different secondary schools in Cádiz (Spain) played the game and gave us their feedback about the game.

In this early version of the game, we were particularly interested in knowing teachers' opinion about the game content and sexism topics addressed, and whether they would consider a fully developed game following these ideas an interesting tool to apply in their classes. The questionnaire after playing the game included the following open-ended questions:

- Is the video game you just played (language and content) suitable for students aged 16 and older? Why?
- Would you use this game in class to create a common experience and then lead a discussion about it? Why?
- What is your opinion about the game you just played?
- How would you improve the game?

4.2 Results

We present teachers' responses to the open-ended questions about the game.

Is the Videogame You just Played (Language and Content) for Students Aged 16 and Older? Why?
We obtained 13 not-empty responses to this question. Out of those, 11 considered the game adequate and/or entertaining and suitable for that age group and above. The other 2 responses mentioned they found the game boring, and that while its content and language were adequate, there was too much to read, which could not be very motivating for students.

Would You Use This Game in Class to Create a Common Experience and then Lead a Discussion About It? Why?
We obtained 14 not-empty responses to this question. 11 answered positively to this question, stating that they consider the game an adequate baseline to then lead a discussion in class. 2 stated that they would not use it because its content does not fit within the courses that they teach. One teacher mentioned not being sure whether he/she would use it because he/she felt that students would find it a bit tiresome as they already know some of the things mentioned in the game.

What is Your Opinion About the Game You just Played?
Regarding opinion, responses were mixed. 6 teachers mentioned some level of "boring" or "tiresome" as they found too much text and too little interactions within the game, and not very interesting graphics. Another 6 teachers mentioned the game to be very "interesting" or to have liked it. Other words used were "actual", "direct", "useful" and applicable in classes.

How Would You Improve the Game?
Recommendations to improve the game included: improving the graphics (4 participants), adding music or sound effects (3), make it more dynamic (2), with more interactions (2), shorten the conversations (1), increase the number of sexism situations (1), including both male and female perspectives for the main character (1), adding the option to actually "fail" the game and have to re-start from the beginning (1), make the game message "less obvious" (1), adding other game elements such as puzzles (1).

5 Formative Evaluation of Final Version

5.1 Methodology

The goal of this initial formative evaluation was to obtain feedback from participants like those who will apply the game in their classes/workshops (secondary or higher education teachers, educators or researchers addressing gender topics, etc.). The main interest was to know their opinion about the final version of the game (things they liked and disliked) and whether and how they would apply it in a classroom setting.

N = 32 Spanish Red Cross Youth volunteers participated in this initial formative evaluation. They are volunteers who commonly give different talks in high schools and who were taking a specific course on "Career guidance and entrepreneurship". There were 28 volunteers in training between 18 and 24 years old and 4 trainers of the course. The sample size was sufficient to conduct a first formative evaluation, particularly coming from volunteers used to address these topics who could provide valuable feedback to improve the educational value of the game.

The formative evaluation had three parts: two questionnaires (before and after playing the game) and the gameplay. Broadly, the initial questionnaire aims to gather different information about participants' habits while the final questionnaire aims to collect their opinion about the game. Additionally, both pre- and post- questionnaires contain a set of sexism questions to compare whether participants' perception of them change with the game. In more detail, the evaluation consisted of:

1. Participants completed a pre-test including:
   - Agreement to participate in the study
   - Demographic questions: gender and age
   - Sexism questionnaire: 13 questions "who do you think performs better at…?" and the areas: Teamwork, Teaching, Sports, Repairs/construction, Languages, Physics, Chemistry, Biology, Mathematics, Computer science, Technology/robotics, Videogames, Caring for others. For each question, participants can answer by choosing among "men", "women", or "either".

2. Participants played the game "La Entrevista" from beginning to end
3. Participants completed a post-test eliciting:
   - Game opinion questions:
     - What did you not like about the video game "La Entrevista" and what would you change to improve it?
     - What did you like the most about the video game "La Entrevista"?
     - Did the game make you think? About what?
     - Can this game be used in the classroom? How would you apply it?
   - Sexism questionnaire (same from pre-test for comparison).

5.2 Results

First, we compare the results of the sexism questionnaire from the pre-test to the post-test, to gather an idea of whether the game narrative has had any impact on participants' perception of these topics. 28 valid responses were obtained for both questionnaires. 3 users did not answer the post-questionnaire, and we did not receive the game interaction data from 1 of them. Overall, the option "either" was mostly chosen. However, there are some exceptions. Particularly, in three questions: "who do you think performs better at...Computer Science", "...Technology/robotics" and "...Caring for others". In these 3 questions, the most chosen answer changed from the pre-test ("men" for the first two areas, "women" for the last one) to the post-test where "either" was mostly chosen for all of them (see Fig. 3).

In the question "who do you think performs better at... repairs/construction", the option "men" was mostly chosen both in the pre-test (20 responses) and the post-test (17 responses). In all other 9 areas (Teamwork, Teaching, Sports, Languages, Physics, Chemistry, Biology, Mathematics, Videogames), the answer "either" was the one most frequently chosen both in the pre-test and the post-test.

In addition to these questions, we gathered participants' opinions about the game in the questionnaire after playing with the following questions. We obtained 26 valid responses in these opinion questions. The summary of their responses is detailed below.

What Did You not Like About the Video Game "La Entrevista" and What Would You Change to Improve It?
Most participants (17) stated that they would not change anything and/or that they liked the game as it is. Among those, 8 mentioned that they would change something out of the scope of the game, that is people's sexist attitudes, comments or behaviors. As improvements in the game, most comments were about the text: 3 participants mentioned that there was too much to read, 2 did not like options in dialogues (for some of them being too similar or for having options that they would not choose), and 1 would like to improve the dialogues of some characters. Other things marginally mentioned were no option to go back if you skip or do not read a question; missing details about the steps to take in the game; too many steps to take before reaching some sections in the game; the impossibility of checking the CV without leaving the question about it.

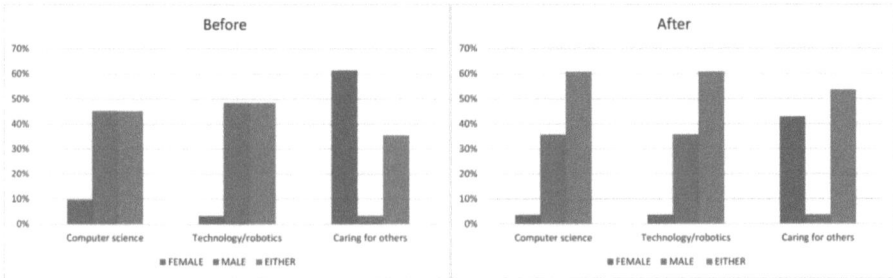

Fig. 3. Comparison of participants' answers in three sexism questions before (left) and after (right) playing the game "La Entrevista".

What Did You Like the Most About the Video Game "La Entrevista"?
Answers to this question were very varied, including: the way the game shows the reality

lived by women (6 participants), the game content (4), the awareness of sexism after playing the game (3), the options or responses that they can choose from (3), that is entertaining/dynamic (3), the surprise ending (3), the graphics (2), the main character, once she is revealed (2), the options in the end to review the situations and explaining the sexism (2), the fact that the game made them take time off their classes (1). 2 participants stated to have liked everything.

Did the Game Make You Think? About What?
Most participants (19) stated that the game had made them reflect about sexism. In more detail, about sexism in the workplace (9 participants) and about how it is a reality still present nowadays (6). Other responses included reflection about: issues that women experience; and their personal bias as they had assumed that the main character was a man. 3 participants stated that the game did not make them reflect at all.

Can This Game Be Used in the Classroom? How Would You Apply It?
All 26 participants answered affirmatively to this question. Some of them provided further details on how they would apply it: 7 stated that they would use it as a reflection or awareness tool (1 of them particularly mention for sexism in the workplace, 1 for sexism daily, and 1 that particularly for even younger students who are still not fully aware of this problem). 4 participants mentioned that they would use it with role-playing, and 3 that they would include it in classes to prepare for job interviews. Other comments included: using the game as a review activity (1), using it in class followed by a review of its scenes (1), and playing the game in class together showing all possible options (1).

6 Conclusions and Future Work

This paper has presented the design of the serious game "La Entrevista" to increase awareness about sexism situations, with particular emphasis to those occurring in the workplace. The purpose of this tool is to fill the gap identified about educational tools that allow students to have a dynamic role in awareness activities about social issues, particularly sexism, avoiding student's previous barriers, such as ideological biases. We have additionally presented two initial evaluations of the game. First, we conducted a formative evaluation of an initial prototype. The most repeated feedback obtained in this evaluation was about improving the graphics, which were an initial version for the prototype, and adding sound effects, which may not be adequate for the actual application of the game in class with all students playing simultaneously (or at least it would require them to use headphones which would be another additional requirement of equipment for the game application). Second, the formative evaluation with training volunteers confirmed the positive perception of the game, as they considered it an interesting tool that had made them reflect about sexism. These volunteers belong to the set of target users (e.g., educators) who will use the game, but also belong to the age group targeted by the game, as they are starting their professional life. Therefore, the effect of the game in making them reflect about sexism also hints at its possible positive impact on target players.

These early evaluations have their limitations: mainly the limited number of participants, and the fact that the first evaluation was carried out with an early prototype without the final graphics. Still, they provide a baseline about its acceptance among the final users who will apply the game in their classes/workshops, which is critical as they are a key stakeholder for the game to be used in classrooms.

The formal validation of the game is a clear line of future work. Prior to that, we plan to include game learning analytics in the game, to collect players' actions (mainly choices in dialogues) while playing. We also would require previously validated measures (e.g., questionnaires) to assess the game's effectiveness in changing players' attitudes regarding sexism.

The overall positive results regarding acceptance and applicability obtained in the early evaluations carried out make the serious game "La Entrevista" a promising educational tool that we plan to keep exploring to address sexism, an issue still very present in current society.

Acknowledgments. This work was partially funded by the Ministry of Education (PID2020-119620RB-I00; PID2023-149341OB-I00), and by the Telefonica-Complutense Honorary Chair on Digital Education and Serious Games. And the authors would like to thank Ana Martín Sánchez, Rubén Santa Cruz Píriz for their contributions to the game.

Disclosure of Interests. The authors have no competing interests to declare that are relevant to the content of this article.

References

1. Swim, J.K., Hyers, L.L.: Sexism. In: Handbook of Prejudice, Stereotyping, and Discrimination., Psychology Press, New York, NY, US, pp. 407–430 (2009). https://doi.org/10.4324/9781841697772
2. Human Dignity and Gender Equality Department Council of Europe, "Report on the implementation of Recommendation CM/Rec(2019)1 on preventing and combating sexism."
3. Christopher, A.N., Mull, M.S.: Conservative ideology and ambivalent sexism. Psychol Women Q. **30**(2), 223–230 (2006). https://doi.org/10.1111/j.1471-6402.2006.00284.x
4. Calvo-Morata, A., Alonso-Fernández, C., Freire, M., Martínez-Ortiz, I., Fernández-Manjón, B.: Serious games to prevent and detect bullying and cyberbullying: a systematic serious games and literature review. Comput. Educ. **157**, 103958 (2020). https://doi.org/10.1016/j.compedu.2020.103958
5. Tan, C.K.W., Nurul-Asna, H.: Serious Games for Environmental Education. Blackwell Publishing (2023). https://doi.org/10.1002/inc3.18
6. Depression Quest. Accessed 14 Mar 2025. http://www.depressionquest.com/
7. Calvo-Morata, A., Alonso-Fernández, C., Freire, M., Martínez-Ortiz, I., Fernández-Manjón, B.: Creating awareness on bullying and cyberbullying among young people: validating the effectiveness and design of the serious game Conectado. Telematics Inform. **60**, 101568 (2021). https://doi.org/10.1016/j.tele.2021.101568
8. Ryan, R.M., Rigby, C.S., Przybylski, A.: The motivational pull of video games: a self-determination theory approach. Motiv. Emot. **30**(4), 347–363 (2006). https://doi.org/10.1007/s11031-006-9051-8
9. Kiili, K., Siuko, J., Ninaus, M.: Tackling Misinformation with Games: a Systematic Literature Review. Routledge (2024). https://doi.org/10.1080/10494820.2023.2299999
10. Huang, A., et al.: Stranded : a Classroom Game for Implicit Bias Elicitation and Recognition.

11. Symborski, C., Barton, M., Quinn, M.M., Morewedge, C.K., Kassam, K.S., Korris, J.: Missing: A Serious Game for the Mitigation of Cognitive Biases (2014). https://api.semanticscholar.org/CorpusID:17527961
12. Yañez, A.G.B., Alonso-Fernández, C., Fernández-Manjón, B.: Systematic literature review of digital resources to educate on gender equality. Educ Inf Technol (Dordr) **28**(8), 10639–10664 (2023). https://doi.org/10.1007/s10639-022-11574-8
13. Pérez-Colado, V.M., Pérez-Colado, I.J., Freire-Morán, M., Martínez-Ortiz, I., Fernández-Manjón, B.: uAdventure: simplifying narrative serious games development. In: 2019 IEEE 19th International Conference on Advanced Learning Technologies (ICALT), pp. 119–123 (2019). https://doi.org/10.1109/ICALT.2019.00030
14. Council of Europe. Human rights Channel - La chaîne des droits humains. Accessed 14 Mar 2025. https://human-rights-channel.coe.int/stop-sexism-en.html

"Follow My Lead": Role of AI-Based NPC Autonomy in Player-NPC Collaboration

Leon Tristan Dratzidis[✉], Nima Zargham, and Rainer Malaka

Digital Media Lab, University of Bremen, Bremen, Germany
{dratzidis,zargham,malaka}@uni-bremen.de

Abstract. Advances in generative AI (GenAI) facilitated the development of AI-based non-player characters (NPCs) capable of interacting with players more dynamically. These NPCs further allow for natural language communication with players via chat or speech. However, little is known about how players interact with GenAI-based NPCs in collaborative tasks, particularly when NPCs exhibit different levels of autonomy. We developed a video game where players collaborate with an NPC across three levels varying in NPC autonomy: NPC strictly follows player instructions, NPC has autonomy but prioritizes player guidance, and NPC operates fully autonomously. We conducted a user study ($n = 16$) to examine how players perceive and interact with NPCs under these conditions. Results show that while greater autonomy enhances helpfulness and collaboration, players prefer a balance between proactive AI support and personal control. Our findings provide insights into player preferences, engagement, and the perceived agency of AI-driven NPCs in collaborative settings.

Keywords: Conversational Interaction · Agency · NPC Communication · Speech-Based Games

1 Introduction

The advances in large language models (LLMs) and generative technologies opened up new opportunities for innovation in different domains [3,11,23]. Various industries have undergone technological evolution, integrating large language models (LLMs) to enable more dynamic, intelligent, and automated user interactions. One such domain is video games, where the application of LLMs has become an emerging area of research. LLMs are being explored for procedural content generation (PCG) of in-game assets [16], level design [25], narrative support [14], quest description generation [28], and the creation of non-player character (NPC) dialogue [10], among others. An emerging area of research examines the use of LLMs to create intelligent, autonomous non-player characters (NPCs) capable of decision-making, social behavior simulation, and natural language communication with players [20,30]. Zargham et al. [36] found that both game developers and conversational user interface (CUI) experts recognize several advantages of integrating LLM-based NPCs, particularly in enhancing player immersion through natural interaction. Similarly, Christiansen et al. [5] examined GenAI-driven NPCs in a game setting, comparing a version with unrestricted speech interaction to one with predefined dialogue options. Their results showed that players exhibited greater behavioral engagement and perceived the speech-based interaction as more immersive. Building on these findings, it becomes increasingly important to understand how varying levels of NPC autonomy influence the player experience, especially in a collaborative context. While existing research has explored using LLMs for dialogue systems and behavior, there remains a gap in understanding how varying degrees of autonomy influence cooperation, trust, and engagement in dialogue-driven games. To address this, we developed a cooperative survival game titled "Ashore," featuring an LLM-based NPC companion with three modes of autonomy: reactive (R), semi-autonomous (SA), and fully autonomous (FA). In this game, players had to collaborate with the NPC to survive and escape a stranded island. Players could communicate with this NPC using natural language interaction (speech or chat). We conducted a within-subject design user study to evaluate how these different levels of autonomy affect the player experience. We pose the following research question for this study:

RQ: How can different levels of AI Autonomy impact player experience in a co-op game with an LLM-Based NPC?

Our findings indicates that the autonomy level of an AI-based NPC companion significantly influences player experience, with the *SA* NPC generally being preferred for its balance of assistance and player control. Additionally, while speech was the favored mode of interaction, ensuring accurate recognition and providing alternative input methods is essential for usability and engagement. This study deepens our understanding of different levels of AI agent autonomy and its impact on user experience. By examining speech and text-based modalities, this work also provides insights into designing effective and adaptable conversational AI interfaces. Beyond gaming, these insights can inform the development of conversational assistants in other domains, such as education, where natural interaction and appropriate autonomy levels are key for user engagement and satisfaction.

2 Related Work

The emergence of large language models (LLMs) has transformed how we interact with technology. These advancements have enabled AI-system systems to assist users in increasingly complex tasks and diverse contexts with greater sophistication [22,32,38]. In game development, researchers and designers are utilizing LLMs to create more dynamic and interactive experiences. Generative AI is now being used to create game assets [16], levels and maps [25], narratives [14], quest descriptions [28], and NPC dialogues [10]. Recently, conversational AI tools such as InWorld AI [13] and Convai [7] have enabled the creation and integration of GenAI-based NPCs into games, virtual worlds, and immersive environments. These tools provide ready-to-use components for game engines such as Unity 3D and connect them with common game systems such as rigged animations and state machines. Commonly, player-NPC interactions have been limited to pre-scripted dialogues and predefined actions triggered by game events. Prior research indicates that such rigid interactions can diminish player agency and contribute to frustration [35]. In contrast, GenAI-based NPCs enable free-form communication, offering players greater conversational flexibility. Studies suggest that open-ended dialogue fosters deeper engagement with in-game characters and enhances immersion [5,33,34]. Despite the advancements in LLMs, their application in speech-based interactions remains limited [17]. Christiansen et al. [5] investigated using LLM-based NPCs in a mystery game, comparing two interaction modalities: unrestricted speech-based communication and traditional predefined dialogue options. While players found the speech-based version more immersive and engaging, they also felt overwhelmed by the unrestricted nature of the interaction. Conversely, the predefined dialogue system provided more structure, aiding players in solving the mystery but reducing engagement. A persistent challenge with LLMs is their tendency to generate incorrect or contextually inappropriate responses due to input misinterpretation or hallucinations. Although various techniques are being developed to mitigate these issues [8,9,12,15,17], the concern remains. Volum et al. [26] conducted an exploratory study in Minecraft, where players interacted with a GenAI-based NPC to complete tasks. While interactions were generally enjoyable, players reported that NPC responses were often irrelevant or inconsistent with the game's context, diminishing immersion. Similarly, Rao et al. [21] examined player collaboration with GenAI-based NPCs in a Minecraft minigame, where NPCs provided in-game assistance via text or speech. The findings highlight patterns of mutual support, with NPCs helping players navigate tasks and players compensating for the NPCs' lack of visual awareness. The authors underscore the potential for AI-based NPCs to complement human skills in collaborative gameplay. A key limitation identified by Wan et al. [29] is the lack of visual grounding in LLM-driven NPCs, which is crucial for context-aware interactions in 3D environments. Their study in VRChat [27] explored methods to enhance contextual relevance in NPC responses. Their findings revealed that while AI agents could generate appropriate dialogue with synchronized gestures, they often failed to fully understand environmental changes. Players attempted to compensate by verbally describing visual elements, but this was frequently ineffective, leading to frustration and limiting their ability to direct NPC actions. These findings highlight the need for more advanced AI models that can integrate multimodal inputs, such as vision and environmental awareness, to improve the reliability and realism of GenAI-based NPC interactions. Our work contributes to the literature by examining how different levels of AI autonomy impact player experience and interactions with an LLM-based NPC in a co-op game. The NPC was designed with a degree of contextual awareness, tracking the player's survival state and quest progress. However, its level of proactivity in sharing information and providing recommendations varied across conditions.

3 Game Design

For our study, we developed a survival game, "Ashore," on a remote, snow-covered island where the player and a non-player character (NPC) companion have crash-landed. Played in a first-person perspective on a desktop, the game centers on natural language interaction with the companion character to coordinate survival and construction efforts. Over three in-game days, players must gather resources, manage their physical needs, and ultimately repair a damaged boat to escape the island (Fig. 1).

Fig. 1. A screenshot of the game displaying the NPC and the game environment. In this image, the NPC informs the player about what should be constructed today.

The players' goal is to explore an island to gather essential resources required for survival and construction tasks. Primary resources include wood obtained by chopping trees, stones collected directly from the ground, and berries gathered from bushes. Resources serve as building blocks for various construction tasks necessary for progressing through game levels. Players must gather the right types and amounts of resources and deposit them into the designated construction chest to advance. Once all necessary materials are collected, players can initiate the construction of structures such as a shelter, fire, or ship. Additionally, players must manage three survival needs: thirst, hunger, and warmth. These needs decrease over time, requiring players to maintain them by drinking from a pond, consuming berries for hunger, or igniting a fire for warmth. Neglecting these survival aspects will make the player blackout momentarily, walk slower, and shiver. Players are accompanied by an NPC companion capable of performing the same range of tasks as the player, including resource gathering, resource depositing, and structure construction. Interaction with the NPC companion can occur via chat inputs or direct speech communication. Instructions issued to the NPC can include specific commands such as "Chop Wood," "Gather Stone," "Deposit Resources in Chest," or "Build Structure," enabling a dynamic, collaborative gameplay experience. The NPC operates under three distinct degrees of autonomy: *R*, *SA*, and *FA*. Each level of autonomy influences how the NPC interacts with the player and performs tasks.

Reactive: The NPC does not act independently and strictly adheres to explicit player commands, such as "Chop 10 Wood and deposit them." It will only perform actions directly ordered by the player without considering its own or the player's broader needs.

Semi-Autonomous: The NPC evaluates its own survival needs, the player's needs, and the resources necessary for construction tasks and acts accordingly. However, if the player instructs, the NPC still strictly follows the player's instructions.

Fully Autonomous: The NPC independently assesses its survival requirements, the player's current needs, and the demand for resources necessary to complete construction objectives. In this mode, the NPC can prioritize tasks and decline player requests if they do not align with its current top priority. It may also provide feedback or suggest alternative actions, such as informing the player that gathering additional resources of a specific type is unnecessary, guiding them towards more productive activities.

In autonomous conditions, the NPC will always select the most efficient and fastest way to progress through the game. In the autonomous conditions, the NPC consistently informed the player about its current plan of action. In contrast, the *R* level involved no autonomous decision-making, so the NPC only provided feedback when explicitly instructed to act, acknowledging the command before executing it. This acknowledgment feedback was also present at the *SA* level. In the *FA* levels, such acknowledgments were only given if the given task matched the NPC's top priority task. The levels were identical regarding mechanics, environment, and available resources, and each level required the same amount of resources to construct structures. The only difference was in which specific building task had to be completed each day.

3.1 Implementation

The game was developed using the Unity Engine[1]. The Convai [7] plugin for Unity was integrated for speech recognition and method invocation for the AI NPC. Convai interprets speech inputs using a large language model (LLM), subsequently activating relevant methods, such as "Chop Wood," if the intent is recognized. Furthermore, the NPC employs a state machine to handle its own needs and behaviors. If the player approaches within approximately three feet of the NPC, it will immediately stop its current activity and actively listen to player commands. Upon processing the command through Convai, the corresponding

---
[1] https://unity.com/.

method is invoked. Commands from players are initially flagged as Player Suggestions, after which the NPC evaluates these suggestions based on its current autonomy level and internal conditions.

Players could communicate with the NPC by typing in a text chat or speaking directly. If the player chose to speak, their speech was transcribed. In both cases, the resulting message appeared in a chat window. This message was then passed to the Convai package, which evaluated it based on a prompt specific to the character. If the message included actionable instructions such as chopping wood or gathering stone, the package would trigger the corresponding methods, allowing the AI to carry out the task.

4 Study Design

We conducted a within-subject user study with ($N = 16$) participants to evaluate and compare our three experimental conditions. Participants performed tasks that varied based on the specific study day (Day 1, Day 2, or Day 3). The NPC companion's behavior varied across days and was categorized as *R*, *SA*, or *FA*. These NPC behavior conditions were balanced between participants using a Latin square design, assigning different NPC behaviors systematically based on participant IDs

Procedure: Participants were welcomed and provided with a consent form, which informed them about the study's purpose and the types of data being collected. After signing the consent form, participants completed a demographic questionnaire. Subsequently, participants were reminded that gameplay sessions would be recorded, including audio recordings of their verbal comments or interactions with the NPC. Participants then completed a tutorial level designed to familiarize them with the game's mechanics and interaction system with the NPC. Following the tutorial, participants played through the three experimental conditions: *R*, *SA*, and *FA* NPC behavior. The order in which these conditions were presented was balanced using a Latin square design to control for potential order effects. After each gameplay condition (level), participants completed post-exposure questionnaires. Upon completing all three levels, participants participated in a short concluding interview. Each session lasted approximately 35–50 min.

Participants: We used a convenience sampling approach for participant recruitment through word of mouth, social media, and mailing lists. Participation in the study was voluntary and uncompensated. We recruited 16 participants (seven females and nine males) aged between 23 and 40 years ($M = 29.68$, $SD = 4.68$). All participants had prior experience with video games. Nine people (56.3%) played video games frequently (four daily and five several times a week), while seven participants (43.7%) reported not playing video games often (two people once per week and five less than once per week). Nine participants (56.3%) had prior experience with voice-controlled applications, and 15 participants (93.8%) had previously interacted with chatbots. All participants resided in Germany.

Requirements for inclusion in the study were an age above 18 years and English language proficiency.

Measures: We used a mixed-method approach to assess our game conditions. The post-exposure questionnaires included the Player Experience Inventory (PXI) [1] and a custom-designed questionnaire to evaluate players' game experience and their perceptions of the NPC and collaboration. The customized questionnaire assessed specific aspects of the player experience, including the perceived helpfulness of the NPC, enjoyment of interacting with the NPC, self-evaluated performance, overall game experience, and collaboration with the NPC. Participants rated these aspects on seven-point Likert scales. To gain deeper qualitative insights into individual preferences, participants also participated in a short interview [31]. The interview covered topics such as likes and dislikes about the game, the most and least interesting aspects, differences observed between levels, players' preferred interaction modality (chat or speech), favorite and least favorite levels, and their perception of the NPC. The custom-designed questionnaire items and interview questions are in the supplementary material.

Data Analysis: We conducted repeated-measures ANOVAs on the quantitative data to examine differences in player experience and responses to customized questions across conditions. An alpha level of .05 was applied to all statistical tests. The interview responses were transcribed and analyzed using domain summaries [2,6]. This approach organizes themes based on common topics rather than shared meanings, aiming to capture the diversity of interpretations related to specific subjects or focus areas [18]. The transcripts were coded using an inductive coding approach [4,24], allowing multiple codes to be assigned to a single quote when applicable. Additionally, notable player statements were identified and collected for further analysis.

Pre-study: Before running the study, we conducted preliminary sessions with two players to identify potential issues with game mechanics, GenAI functionality, and the overall study procedure. Several gameplay issues were observed, including UI-related concerns, the presentation of game data, tutorial adjustments, and quest clarity, which were addressed through necessary adjustments.

5 Results

A repeated-measures ANOVA was conducted to compare player experience ratings across the three conditions to analyze the PXI subscales and custom-designed questions. The assumption of sphericity was tested and corrected using the Greenhouse-Geisser adjustment.

PXI Results: The player experience was assessed using the PXI on a 7-point Likert scale ranging from -3 to $+3$, with 0 as the neural point [1]. Result highlight that the overall mean scores for all PXI subscales were above neutral across conditions (see Fig. 4). A statistically significant difference was found in the progress feedback subscale ($p = .026$, $\eta^2 = .217$; see Fig. 6). Post-hoc comparisons with Holm's adjustment revealed that participants rated the *SA* condition significantly higher than the *FA* condition ($t = 2.768$, $p = .029$, $d = 0.466$). However, no significant differences were found between the *R* condition and the other two conditions ($p > 0.05$). See Fig. 7 for more details. No other significant differences were observed across the remaining PXI subscales ($p > 0.05$).

Custom-Designed Questions: Regarding the custom-designed questionnaire, significant differences were observed in participants' ratings of NPC helpfulness and collaboration across conditions. A statistically significant difference was found in how helpful participants perceived the NPC ($p < .001$, $\eta^2 = .664$; see Fig. 8). Post-hoc comparisons with Holm's adjustment showed that the *SA* condition was rated significantly higher than the *R* condition ($t = -7.283$, $p < .001$, $d = -2.010$). Similarly, the *FA* condition was rated significantly higher than the *R* condition ($t = -5.826$, $p < .001$, $d = -0.466$). No significant differences were observed between the *SA* and *FA* conditions ($p > 0.05$). A statistically significant difference was also found in participants' ratings of collaboration with the NPC ($p = .004$, $\eta^2 = .303$; see Fig. 10). Post-hoc comparisons with Holm's adjustment showed that the *SA* condition was rated significantly higher than the *R* condition ($t = -3.580$, $p = .004$, $d = -1.209$). However, no significant differences were found between the *R* and *FA* conditions, nor between the *SA* and *FA* conditions ($p > 0.05$). Further, no significant differences were observed for interaction enjoyment, performance, or overall game experience (see Fig. 5).

Level Completion Times: We measured participants' completion times for each level. On average, participants took 668.06 seconds ($SD = 268.01$) to complete the *R* level, 301.5 seconds ($SD = 76.90$ for the *SA* level, and 297.62 seconds ($SD = 73.23$) for the *FA* level. A statistically significant difference in completion times was found ($p < .001$, $\eta^2 = .699$; see Fig. 12). Post-hoc comparisons with Holm's adjustment revealed that both the *SA* ($t = 7.199$, $p < .001$, $d = 2.202$) and *FA* ($t = 7.275$, $p < .001$, $d = 2.226$) levels were completed significantly faster than the *R* level. However, no significant difference was observed between the two autonomous levels.

5.1 Interview Findings

Game Engagement: The game's visual aesthetics and environment design received positive feedback, with seven players praising the world's graphical style and overall look. Three players specifically highlighted the story and premise of being stranded on an island with another person. Two players enjoyed exploring the game world, mentioning that navigating the environment added to their enjoyment. The tasks and quests were another aspect that players found engaging, with three saying that they enjoyed the structured objectives. Natural interaction with the NPC emerged as the most engaging element of the game, with ten players emphasizing that it was the most interesting aspect of their experience. Players liked the natural communication with the NPC, emphasizing that the experience was more immersive. Two players highlighted the high responsiveness of the character, appreciating how interactive the game felt. Three players specifically found speech interaction with the NPC innovative, engaging, and novel. Additionally, one player noted that interacting with the NPC through a chat-based interface was the most interesting aspect. Having an AI companion was also well-received, as three players liked having a non-player character (NPC) alongside them. Another three players mentioned that they appreciated the ability to delegate tasks and cooperate with the NPC, making the game feel more interactive and dynamic. Five players specifically appreciated the NPC's autonomous behavior, highlighting that they liked that it proactively contributed to progress without requiring constant direction. Two players also valued the feedback and reminders provided by the NPC regarding resources.

Challenges and Concerns: The NPC's R condition was criticized by three players who found it unresponsive at times. Three players felt that the UI and world navigation needed improvement, suggesting better instructions. Certain gameplay mechanics were perceived as repetitive or uninteresting. Six players found resource collection, such as gathering wood, stone, and berries, to be monotonous, with one player describing it as "busywork" rather than a meaningful challenge. Three players felt the structure quests became predictable once they understood the mechanics. Two players found survival elements, such as maintaining warmth or hydration, passive and repetitive. Additionally, one player noted that the lack of serious consequences in the game made it feel less engaging. Two others found that certain tasks lacked clarity, leading to confusion about objectives and gameplay mechanics. The learning curve at the beginning of the game was mentioned as a challenge by two players stating that they needed more time to adapt to the mechanics. Three players were unsure about how the NPC's behavior evolved over time, leading to uncertainty about its role and actions at different game stages. Two players reported issues with voice recognition, making it difficult to communicate effectively with the NPC. One player found the NPC's voice annoying, while another disliked communicating exclusively through voice or chat input and preferred a traditional screen-based solution.

Communication Styles and Preferences: Participants used both speech and text to interact with the NPC. Most players (ten) expressed a preference for speech. Six participants found speech interaction more natural and immersive. Three players specifically appreciated that speech allowed multitasking, enabling them to communicate with the NPC without interrupting gameplay. On the other hand, five players preferred using chat. All five reported misrecognition with speech, particularly with certain words such as "would" and "wood," which led them to switch to text-based input for reliability. They found typing to be more precise and less error-prone than speech. On the other hand, four participants noted that they initially used chat but later preferred speech after realizing they could speak more freely rather than relying on fixed commands. Three players noted that speech accuracy varied across levels, which affected their trust in the feature.

Preferences on NPC Autonomy: All players noticed that the NPC's behavior changed across levels. Eight players explicitly mentioned the change in the NPC's autonomous behavior. When we asked participants about their favorite level, seven preferred the *SA* level, five preferred the *FA*, and four preferred the *R* level. The reasons for their preferences varied. Seven players mentioned that they preferred the last level they played as they had a better grasp of gameplay. Another seven players highlighted the NPC's assistive behavior in the two autonomous levels as a key factor in their preference, appreciating its reminders, task support, and engaging presence. In contrast, three players preferred the *R* level as they could complete tasks themselves without relying on the NPC. When asked about their least favorite level, seven participants identified the *R* level, five selected the *FA* level, and four chose the *SA* level. Seven players found the first level they played frustrating due to their lack of familiarity with the game mechanics. Four participants found it frustrating when the NPC did not contribute proactively, explaining that managing the NPC became an additional task rather than an engaging feature. Additionally, one participant disliked a level because the "NPC gave too much feedback," stating that it became a distraction.

5.2 Experimenter Observations

Order Effect: We observed that a key determinant of player experience and ratings was the order in which they played the different levels. For instance, some players who started with the *R* level often developed the misconception that the NPC was learning and improving over time. Conversely, players who began with one of the autonomous levels and later transitioned to the *R* level perceived that the NPC was regressing. Some interpreted this shift as an intentional increase in difficulty, while others felt that the NPC was behaving unpredictably or "going rogue." These unintended effects were not part of our study design but rather a consequence of using the Latin Square method to balance the order in which participants experienced different conditions. We noticed that participants' performance and coordination with the NPC improved over time as they became more familiar with the game mechanics. However, changes in the NPC's behavior across different levels disrupted this learning curve, leading to confusion and requiring players to adjust their strategies.

Trusting the NPC: Trust in the NPC varied significantly. Six participants explicitly mentioned a lack of trust, particularly after completing a level with the *R* condition. Four participants neglected their in-game needs after switching from a level with an autonomous condition to the *R* level, anticipating feedback from the NPC, which did not occur in the *R* condition. This resulted in uncertainty and mistrust. One participant specifically walked alongside the NPC after issuing commands to verify task completion by the NPC. Conversely, about five participants expressed positive surprise when the NPC autonomously performed actions such as filling chests or independently gathering resources. However, two participants reported feeling "robbed" of task accomplishment when the NPC unexpectedly completed tasks, highlighting varying perceptions of autonomy. One participant explicitly informed the NPC upon completing a task, seeking praise or acknowledgment.

Communication Patterns: Throughout the sessions, we noticed that several participants expressed frustration when the NPC disagreed with them or instructed them to perform higher-priority tasks in the *FA* level. Furthermore, six participants engaged in small talk or roleplay with the NPC, treating it more as a conversational partner. Their interactions included asking about the NPC's background and making humorous requests, such as asking the NPC to build a snowman. Another player tried to use more polite words as a strategy to see more collaborative behavior and proactive initiatives from the NPC.

6 Discussion

This work sought to explore *how different levels of AI Autonomy could impact player experience in a co-op game with an LLM-Based NPC*. In this section, we interpreted our findings to provide answers to our research question.

Player Experience: The overall player experience ratings were positive across all conditions. However, we found significant differences in the progress feedback subscale of PXI, as well as the customized questionnaire's NPC helpfulness and collaboration scales. The differences in the progress feedback was primarily due to the NPC consistently informing players about its ongoing plan of action in autonomous levels. The *SA* condition was rated highest regarding progress feedback and collaboration, suggesting that players preferred a balance between agency and assistance. The *FA* condition was also rated highly regarding helpfulness but did not significantly outperform the *SA* condition. This indicates that players valued an NPC that provided support while allowing for player-driven actions. Some players felt that managing the NPC became an additional burden rather than an aid. The lack of proactive behavior led to lower engagement and trust. On the other hand, some players preferred the *R* level and the fact that they were in full control. This suggests that agency and control are highly prioritized. Moreover, *R* interactions are preferred if autonomous behavior is not justified or unclear to the player and there is a lack of alignment. Players generally found a proactive NPC desirable. However, players reacted negatively at the *FA* levels when the NPC disagreed with them. Even though the NPC selected the most optimal tasks and informed players accordingly, this was not always well received. This finding suggests that players prioritize their sense of control and agency over performance and efficiency, aligning with previous research [37]. Some players added that excessive autonomy diminished their sense of accomplishment. This highlights the fine balance between providing AI assistance and preserving player agency. Overall, the *SA* condition was the most well-received, suggesting that companion NPCs should provide assistance without overshadowing player decision-making or requiring them to put extra effort.

Communication Preferences and Social Interaction: Players found the interactions with the NPC the most interesting element in the game. Speech interaction was the preferred mode of communication for most players, with participants explicitly stating that it felt more natural and immersive and allowed for multitasking, in line with previous work [5,33]. However, some players preferred to chat, specifically for the reliability of the modality. These findings highlight the importance of accurate speech recognition while also emphasizing the need for seamless alternative input methods to enhance usability, as highlighted in previous work [19,26,33]. Small talk and roleplay emerged as an engaging aspect of the game. This indicates that LLM-based NPCs should be designed to accommodate social and casual conversational interactions.

Order Effects and Learning Disruptions: A key unintended finding was the impact of level order on player perception. Players who started with the R condition often assumed that the NPC was learning across levels. Conversely, those who transitioned from an autonomous to a R condition perceived the NPC as becoming less intelligent, misinterpreting this as a shift in game difficulty. This demonstrates that autonomy changes disrupted player expectations and learning curves, affecting immersion and trust in the NPC. Some players explicitly mentioned distrust in the NPC when moving from an autonomous to a R level. In contrast, others neglected in-game needs when transitioning to a R level, assuming that the NPC would continue providing support. Further, players experienced positive surprises when the NPC autonomously performed tasks. All in all, abrupt changes in autonomy disrupted player expectations, so designing more gradual or transparent transitions between autonomy levels could improve trust and player experience.

7 Conclusion

This study explores how different levels of NPC autonomy impact player experience in cooperative gameplay with an LLM-based NPC. We developed a survival game with an NPC companion featuring three autonomy modes: R, SA, and FA. Players interacted with the NPC using natural language (speech or chat). We conducted a within-subject study to assess the effects of NPC autonomy on player experience and communication with the NPC. Our findings show that while greater NPC autonomy enhances collaboration and support, players prefer a balance between proactivity and control. The SA NPC struck this balance most effectively, offering support without undermining player agency. Additionally, NPC autonomy influenced communication patterns, highlighting the need for adaptable interaction designs.

A Appendix

See Figs. 2, 3, 9, 11, 13.

Fig. 2. The NPC chopping wood.

Fig. 3. A construction chest and a blueprint.

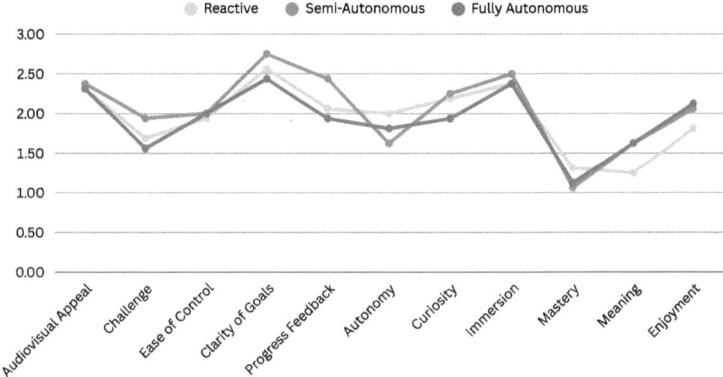

Fig. 4. Mean scores of the PXI questionnaire subscales for all three conditions.

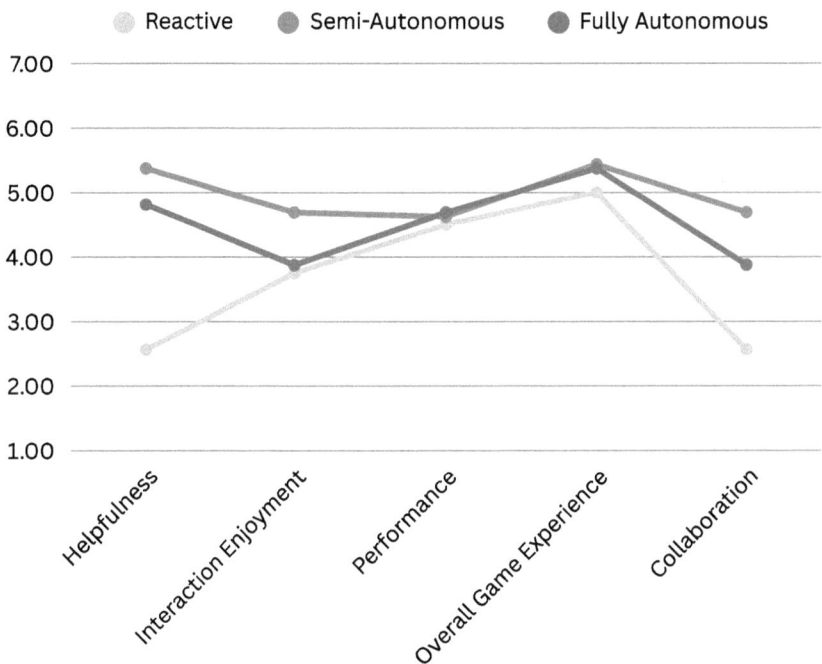

Fig. 5. Mean scores of the custom-designed questions for all three conditions.

Within Subjects Effects

Cases	Sum of Squares	df	Mean Square	F	p	η²
Progress Feedback	2.167	2	1.083	4.149	0.026	0.217
Residuals	7.833	30	0.261			

Note. Type III Sum of Squares

Fig. 6. Results of the repeated-measures ANOVA for the progress feedback subscale of the PXI questionnaire.

Post Hoc Comparisons - Progress Feedback

		Mean Difference	SE	t	Cohen's d	P_{holm}
Reactive	Semi-Autonomous	−0.375	0.181	−2.076	−0.349	0.093
	Fully Autonomous	0.125	0.181	0.692	0.116	0.494
Semi-Autonomous	Fully Autonomous	0.500	0.181	2.768	0.466	0.029

Note. P-value adjusted for comparing a family of 3

Fig. 7. Posthoc test results of the progress feedback subscale of the PXI questionnaire

Within Subjects Effects ▼

Cases	Sum of Squares	df	Mean Square	F	p	η²
Helpfulness	70.875	2	35.438	29.703	< .001	0.664
Residuals	35.792	30	1.193			

Note. Type III Sum of Squares

Fig. 8. Results of the repeated-measures ANOVA for the helpfulness scale in the custom-designed questions.

Post Hoc Tests ▼

Post Hoc Comparisons – Helpfulness

		Mean Difference	SE	t	Cohen's d	P$_{holm}$
Reactive	Semi-Autonomous	−2.812	0.386	−7.283	−2.010	< .001
	Fully Autonomous	−2.250	0.386	−5.826	−1.608	< .001
Semi-Autonomous	Fully Autonomous	0.562	0.386	1.457	0.402	0.156

Note. P-value adjusted for comparing a family of 3

Fig. 9. Posthoc test results regarding the helpfulness scale in the custom-designed questions.

Within Subjects Effects

Cases	Sum of Squares	df	Mean Square	F	p	η²
Collaboration	36.792	2	18.396	6.528	0.004	0.303
Residuals	84.542	30	2.818			

Note. Type III Sum of Squares

Fig. 10. Results of the repeated-measures ANOVA for the collaboration scale in the custom-designed questions.

Post Hoc Comparisons – Collaboration ▼

		Mean Difference	SE	t	Cohen's d	P$_{holm}$
Reactive	Semi-Autonomous	−2.125	0.594	−3.580	−1.209	0.004
	Fully Autonomous	−1.313	0.594	−2.211	−0.746	0.070
Semi-Autonomous	Fully Autonomous	0.812	0.594	1.369	0.462	0.181

Note. P-value adjusted for comparing a family of 3

Fig. 11. Posthoc test results regarding the collaboration scale in the custom-designed questions.

Within Subjects Effects

Cases	Sum of Squares	df	Mean Square	F	p	η²
Level Completion Times	$1.449 \times 10^{+6}$ [a]	2[a]	724285.396[a]	34.915[a]	< .001[a]	0.699
Residuals	622331.875	30	20744.396			

Note. Type III Sum of Squares
[a] Mauchly's test of sphericity indicates that the assumption of sphericity is violated (p < .05).

Fig. 12. Results of the repeated-measures ANOVA for the level completion times.

Post Hoc Comparisons – Level Completion Times ▼

		Mean Difference	SE	t	Cohen's d	P_holm
Reactive	Semi-Autonomous	366.563	50.922	7.199	2.202	< .001
	Fully Autonomous	370.438	50.922	7.275	2.226	< .001
Semi-Autonomous	Fully Autonomous	3.875	50.922	0.076	0.023	0.940

Note. P-value adjusted for comparing a family of 3

Fig. 13. Posthoc test results regarding the level completion times.

References

1. Abeele, V.V., Spiel, K., Nacke, L., Johnson, D., Gerling, K.: Development and validation of the player experience inventory: a scale to measure player experiences at the level of functional and psychosocial consequences. Int. J. Hum.-Comput. Stud. **135**, 102370 (2020). https://doi.org/10.1016/j.ijhcs.2019.102370. https://www.sciencedirect.com/science/article/pii/S1071581919301302
2. Braun, V., Clarke, V., Hayfield, N., Terry, G.: Thematic analysis. In: Liamputtong, P. (ed.) Handbook of Research Methods in Health Social Sciences, pp. 843–860. Springer, Singapore (2019). https://doi.org/10.1007/978-981-10-5251-4_103
3. Bubeck, S., et al.: Sparks of artificial general intelligence: early experiments with GPT-4 (2023)
4. Chandra, Y., Shang, L.: Inductive coding. In: Chandra, Y., Shang, L. (eds.) Qualitative Research Using R: A Systematic Approach, pp. 91–106. Springer, Singapore (2019). https://doi.org/10.1007/978-981-13-3170-1_8
5. Christiansen, F.R., Hollensberg, L.N., Jensen, N.B., Julsgaard, K., Jespersen, K.N., Nikolov, I.: Exploring presence in interactions with LLM-driven NPCS: a comparative study of speech recognition and dialogue options. In: Proceedings of the 30th ACM Symposium on Virtual Reality Software and Technology, VRST 2024. Association for Computing Machinery, New York (2024). https://doi.org/10.1145/3641825.3687716
6. Connelly, L.M., Peltzer, J.N.: Underdeveloped themes in qualitative research: relationship with interviews and analysis. Clin. Nurse Spec. **30**(1), 52–57 (2016)
7. Convai Inc.: Convai. https://convai.com/. Accessed 20 Jan 2025
8. Fathullah, Y., et al.: Prompting large language models with speech recognition abilities. In: ICASSP 2024 - 2024 IEEE International Conference on Acoustics, Speech and Signal Processing (ICASSP), New York, NY, USA, pp. 13351–13355. IEEE (2024). https://doi.org/10.1109/ICASSP48485.2024.10447605
9. Galitsky, B., Chernyavskiy, A., Ilvovsky, D.: Truth-o-meter: handling multiple inconsistent sources repairing LLM hallucinations. In: Proceedings of the 47th International ACM SIGIR Conference on Research and Development in Information Retrieval, SIGIR 2024, pp. 2817–2821. Association for Computing Machinery, New York (2024). https://doi.org/10.1145/3626772.3657679
10. Gao, Q.C., Emami, A.: The turing quest: can transformers make good NPCs? In: Padmakumar, V., Vallejo, G., Fu, Y. (eds.) Proceedings of the 61st Annual Meeting of the Association for Computational Linguistics (Volume 4: Student Research Workshop), Toronto, Canada, pp. 93–103. Association for Computational Linguistics (2023). https://doi.org/10.18653/v1/2023.acl-srw.17
11. Garcia-Pi, B., et al.: Allychat: developing a VR conversational AI agent using few-shot learning to support individuals with intellectual disabilities. In: Abdelnour

Nocera, J., Kristín Lárusdóttir, M., Petrie, H., Piccinno, A., Winckler, M. (eds.) INTERACT 2023, pp. 402–407. Springer, Cham (2023). https://doi.org/10.1007/978-3-031-42293-5_43
12. Ghai, W., Singh, N.: Literature review on automatic speech recognition (2012)
13. InWorld AI Inc.: InWorld AI. https://inworld.ai/. Accessed 20 Jan 2025
14. Kumaran, V., Rowe, J., Mott, B., Lester, J.: Scenecraft: automating interactive narrative scene generation in digital games with large language models. In: Proceedings of the AAAI Conference on Artificial Intelligence and Interactive Digital Entertainment, vol. 19, pp. 86–96 (2023)
15. Leiser, F., et al.: Hill: a hallucination identifier for large language models. In: Proceedings of the CHI Conference on Human Factors in Computing Systems, CHI 2024. Association for Computing Machinery, New York (2024). https://doi.org/10.1145/3613904.3642428
16. Maleki, M.F., Zhao, R.: Procedural content generation in games: a survey with insights on emerging LLM integration. In: Proceedings of the AAAI Conference on Artificial Intelligence and Interactive Digital Entertainment, vol. 20, pp. 167–178 (2024)
17. Min, Z., Wang, J.: Exploring the integration of large language models into automatic speech recognition systems: An empirical study. In: Luo, B., Cheng, L., Wu, Z.G., Li, H., Li, C. (eds.) ICONIP 2023. CCIS, vol. 1968, pp. 69–84. Springer, Singapore (2024). https://doi.org/10.1007/978-981-99-8181-6_6
18. Morgan, H.: Understanding thematic analysis and the debates involving its use. Qual. Rep. **27**(10), 2079–2090 (2022). https://doi.org/10.46743/2160-3715/2022.5912
19. Pan, M., Kitson, A., Wan, H., Prpa, M.: ELLMA-T: an embodied LLM-agent for supporting english language learning in social VR (2024). https://arxiv.org/abs/2410.02406
20. Park, J.S., O'Brien, J., Cai, C.J., Morris, M.R., Liang, P., Bernstein, M.S.: Generative agents: interactive simulacra of human behavior. In: Proceedings of the 36th Annual ACM Symposium on User Interface Software and Technology, UIST 2023. Association for Computing Machinery, New York (2023). https://doi.org/10.1145/3586183.3606763
21. Rao, S., et al.: Collaborative quest completion with LLM-driven non-player characters in minecraft (2024). https://arxiv.org/abs/2407.03460
22. Ruan, J., et al.: TPTU: task planning and tool usage of large language model-based AI agents (2023). https://openreview.net/forum?id=GrkgKtOjaH
23. Shoa, A., Oliva, R., Slater, M., Friedman, D.: Sushi with einstein: enhancing hybrid live events with LLM-based virtual humans. In: Proceedings of the 23rd ACM International Conference on Intelligent Virtual Agents, IVA 2023. Association for Computing Machinery, New York (2023). https://doi.org/10.1145/3570945.3607317
24. Thomas, D.R.: A general inductive approach for analyzing qualitative evaluation data. Am. J. Eval. **27**(2), 237–246 (2006)
25. Todd, G., Earle, S., Nasir, M.U., Green, M.C., Togelius, J.: Level generation through large language models. In: Proceedings of the 18th International Conference on the Foundations of Digital Games, FDG 2023. Association for Computing Machinery, New York (2023). https://doi.org/10.1145/3582437.3587211
26. Volum, R., et al.: Craft an iron sword: dynamically generating interactive game characters by prompting large language models tuned on code. In: Côté, M.A., Yuan, X., Ammanabrolu, P. (eds.) Proceedings of the 3rd Wordplay: When Language Meets Games Workshop (Wordplay 2022), Seattle, United States, pp. 25–

43. Association for Computational Linguistics (2022). https://doi.org/10.18653/v1/2022.wordplay-1.3. https://aclanthology.org/2022.wordplay-1.3/
27. VRChat Inc.: VRChat. https://hello.vrchat.com/. Accessed 20 Jan 2025
28. Värtinen, S., Hämäläinen, P., Guckelsberger, C.: Generating role-playing game quests with GPT language models. IEEE Trans. Games **16**(1), 127–139 (2024). https://doi.org/10.1109/TG.2022.3228480
29. Wan, H., et al.: Building LLM-based AI agents in social virtual reality. In: Extended Abstracts of the CHI Conference on Human Factors in Computing Systems, CHI EA 2024. Association for Computing Machinery, New York (2024). https://doi.org/10.1145/3613905.3651026
30. Wang, G., et al.: Voyager: an open-ended embodied agent with large language models (2023). https://arxiv.org/abs/2305.16291
31. Wilson, C.: Interview techniques for UX practitioners: a user-centered design method (2013)
32. Yang, J., et al.: Harnessing the power of LLMs in practice: a survey on chatgpt and beyond (2023). https://doi.org/10.48550/arXiv.2304.13712
33. Zargham, N., et al.: Let's talk games: an expert exploration of speech interaction with NPCS. Int. J. Hum.-Comput. Interact. 1–21 (2024). https://doi.org/10.1080/10447318.2024.2338666
34. Zargham, N., Bonfert, M., Volkmar, G., Porzel, R., Malaka, R.: Smells like team spirit: investigating the player experience with multiple interlocutors in a VR game. In: Extended Abstracts of the 2020 Annual Symposium on Computer-Human Interaction in Play, CHI PLAY 2020, pp. 408–412. Association for Computing Machinery, New York (2020). https://doi.org/10.1145/3383668.3419884
35. Zargham, N., Dratzidis, L.T., Alexandrovsky, D., Friehs, M.A., Malaka, R.: Gaming with etiquette: exploring courtesy as a game mechanic in speech based games. Int. J. Hum. Comput. Interact. 1–19 (2024). https://doi.org/10.1080/10447318.2024.2387901
36. Zargham, N., Fetni, M.L., Spillner, L., Muender, T., Malaka, R.: "i know what you mean": context-aware recognition to enhance speech-based games. In: Proceedings of the CHI Conference on Human Factors in Computing Systems, CHI 2024. Association for Computing Machinery, New York (2024). https://doi.org/10.1145/3613904.3642426
37. Zargham, N., Pfau, J., Schnackenberg, T., Malaka, R.: "i didn't catch that, but i'll try my best": anticipatory error handling in a voice controlled game. In: Proceedings of the 2022 CHI Conference on Human Factors in Computing Systems, CHI 2022. Association for Computing Machinery, New York (2022). https://doi.org/10.1145/3491102.3502115
38. Zhao, Z., et al.: Recommender systems in the era of large language models (LLMs) (2024). https://doi.org/10.1109/TKDE.2024.3392335

Interaction and Emotion: A Phenomenological Study of a Playable Generative Landscape

Pedro Garruço[✉][iD], Licínio Roque, and Luís Lucas Pereira

University of Coimbra, CISUC/LASI, DEI, Coimbra, Portugal
garruco@dei.uc.pt

Abstract. Authors present an experimental game design case study focused on eliciting emotional responses through a generative interactive audiovisual landscape. A prototype was developed and tested and recall interviews collected with 10 participants. A qualitative phenomenological study was done with content analysis on action and speech. The synthesis of results reveals a complex entanglement of sensory perception, emotional response, and self-directed exploration composing the phenomenological landscape of player experience. Lessons for design result from a set of insights: A strong interplay was observed between spatial categories such as path and orientation; Intentionality and action patterns were shaped through situated perception and audiovisual cues and feedback; Ambiguity surfaced as a core characteristic of the experience; Concepts such as goals, challenge, progression and feedback did not stem explicitly from mechanics, but emerged from perception and sensemaking of the environment; Autonomy stood out clearly from the freedom to explore, to interpret, and to act independently. Such control, autonomy, and flexibility are key characteristics for designing play environmental supportiveness.

Keywords: Human-Computer Interaction · Computer Games · Sound Design · Emotion

1 Introduction

Emotion plays a central role in how players live and interpret interactive audiovisual environments, shaping both their perceptions and behaviors [11]. While conventional game design often relies on defined objectives, feedback systems and progression, recent work in interactive entertainment and human-computer interaction has shifted attention toward experiences that are exploratory, generative, and affectively grounded [12]. These systems tend to embrace ambiguity and rely on dynamic visual and sonic transformations, encouraging players to explore, reflect, and construct meaning through situated interaction [6].

This paper investigates how players express their emotional state, form intention, and construct meaning while navigating an generative game prototype. Our goal is to understand how emotion, perception, and the way players interact comes together with their personal experience during gameplay. We adopt a phenomenological approach, focusing on the complexity of subjective engagement during gameplay.

The prototype was designed to evoke emotions and introspective exploration. It reacts continuously to player movement with audiovisual changes in color, sound, and environmental movement. Lacking explicit instructions or goals, the game encourages exploration, where players orient themselves through sensory cues, experiment with interaction, and derive personal interpretations.

Through analysis of post-play interviews and video recall commentary, we examine how players react to this openness. This study contributes to ongoing research in emotional and experiential design, by illuminating how emotional responses, player intention, and sense-making emerge in generative, exploratory environments

2 Background

Research in digital games and interactive media has increasingly explored how emotional experience is shaped by audiovisual design, player perception, and system feedback [10,14]. In traditional games, goals, mechanics, and progression tend to be predefined and closely tied to player motivation [3]. However, a growing body of research has focused on alternative experiences that prioritize affective engagement, perception, and expression over performance or mastery [8,9]. Generative environments, in particular, have been proposed as fertile spaces for emotional experience, where ambiguity and emergence allow players to construct their own interpretations through open interaction [17].

Rather than relying on fixed objectives or linear narratives, such systems are designed to support freeform exploration, emotional resonance, and personal reflection [22]. Recent approaches have embraced audiovisual transformations as a core element in evoking emotion and shaping how players perceive and interpret space [13]. This design strategy reflects a shift from prescriptive gameplay to player-led sense-making.

Studies have shown that audiovisual dynamics, particularly sound design and visual modulation, play a central role in shaping emotional trajectories throughout interaction [19]. However, the way players interpret these changes is often subjective and fluid, depending on their perception, past experiences, and situated actions [18].

While the relation between interaction and emotion has been addressed in various domains, less attention has been paid to how emotion and perception shape player intention in open-ended contexts [7]. In more structured games, intention is often implicit in the task or rules [2]. In contrast, in generative or exploratory environments, intention emerges from situated interpretation and the desire to respond or investigate sensory feedback [21]. As such, the formulation of intention becomes intertwined with how players express themselves through movement and attention [4].

Although some work has begun to address interaction as a form of emotional expression, there remains a gap in understanding how players articulate intention through exploratory interaction, and how that intention is influenced by emotional experience [5]. This study addresses that gap by exploring how players navigate a generative audiovisual environment, focusing on how they express emotion, perceive the space, and construct meaning and intention through play.

3 Methodology

We employed a phenomenological approach to investigate the lived experiences of players. Our aim is to explore how players express emotion, form intentions, and construct meaning through their interaction with the audiovisual environment. In doing so, we seek to uncover the interplay between emotional engagement and interactive exploration within a gaming environment.

3.1 Research Questions

Grounded in our phenomenological framework, we formulated the following research questions:

1. How do players characterize their emotional experience during gameplay?
2. What influences do players report in relation to their emotional experience?
3. What relationship can be found between players' interactive expressions and their emotional experience?
4. What intention is reported by players?
5. Which perceived elements contribute to the formulation of player intention?
6. How do players interpret their lived experience?
7. How do players construct meaning from the experience?

These questions direct our investigation toward the players' lived experience, with particular emphasis on how emotional responses are expressed, how perception informs intention, and how interaction unfolds during gameplay. By focusing on emotional expression, perception, and meaning construction, our objective is to better understand how player experience emerges in generative, emotionally grounded environments.

3.2 Prototype Description

We developed a generative game prototype that allows the player to explore an infinitely scrollable environment designed with the goal of evoking emotions.

The game automatically generates scenarios based on four pre-constructed base environments, corresponding to the four extremes in the quadrants of the circumplex model [20]: Angry, Bored, Delighted, and Relaxed. All base music layers were composed in F sharp minor. For each of these layers, we selected a unique composition and a specific color to represent its emotional quality. The visual scenario is composed of a moving landscape of gradient colored blocks, as seen in Fig. 1. The colored blocks are generated based on established color theory and coordinated with the underlying emotion from the musical composition to ensure coherence. Additionally, we created abstract sounds that represent noises, to add an element of suspense while maintaining a neutral auditory ambient layer.

The game's environment and the avatar, represented with a rolling ball, responds to fluctuations in a simulated model of arousal and valence, mapped to the virtual play space being generated by the game. As arousal increases, the blocks become more visually animated (translating a rhythm), growing taller, moving faster, and accompanied by more saturated and brighter colors. This change is accompanied with faster-paced sounds (increasing beats per minute). Lower arousal levels result in lower audio-visual rhythms, generating flatter landscapes with reduced and slower block motions, accompanied by slower audio tempos.

At the same time, valence will shape the emotional quality of the soundscape through the choice of instruments. Positive valence is expressed through the use of wind instruments, while negative valence is conveyed using string instruments. These sound choices are reflected in four pre-designed audio samples where lower arousal is represented by lower-pitched tones, indicating a more distant, ominous atmosphere. On the other hand, increased reverb and higher arousal corresponds to higher-pitched tones with less reverb, reflecting more immediate and energetic sounds.

The 3D scenarios that appear in the game are generated in real time based on the player's movements in a virtual space, which continuously map to arousal and valence values, thus defining virtual "emotional regions" in space. Players begin their journey from a neutral state, with both values set to zero. As they explore the game space, these values shift, increasing or decreasing the mapping, possibly leading to evolving transitions between emotional states. Visually, if "bored" is associated with blue and "delighted" with green, traveling through the intermediary space can generate moments with blended colors and adjusted block rhythmic behavior to reflect the emotional model in-between. Auditory transitions between intermediate states are implemented by gradually increasing or decreasing the volume levels of the corresponding audio samples, trying to achieve a blend between soundscapes.

Furthermore, the prototype is conceived as a sensory narrative. Throughout the progression of the game, more arousal and valence levels are unlocked, intensifying and diversifying the emotional landscapes. Early levels exhibit minimal changes, but as the levels advance, players encounter scenarios with more intense colors, sounds, and block movements, deepening the emotional experience.

3.3 Experimentation Process

We designed an experimentation process to capture insights into how players express emotions, form intentions, and construct meaning through their interaction with the game prototype. To ensure a structured and systematic approach, we followed a predefined protocol aligned with the phenomenological focus of the study.

Step 1 - Initially, we defined the phenomenon under investigation and formulated the research questions guiding the study. We designed a session script that ensured emotional experiences and interactions with the game remained central throughout.

Step 2 - Participants were recruited for one-on-one sessions conducted in a quiet setting. Noise-canceling headphones were provided to enhance immersion and reduce distractions.

Step 3 - During the session, participants interacted with the game prototype on a laptop. Gameplay was recorded via both screen capture and facecam (as seen in Fig. 2), allowing us to document not only in-game behavior but also facial expressions and reactions in real time. Recording was previously authorized through an informed participation agreement.

Step 4 - Immediately after the gameplay, participants responded to an initial set of reflective questions. These aimed to capture their immediate impressions of the experience.

Step 5 - The initial interview was followed by a video recall interview, where participants reviewed footage of their session and were invited to comment on moments that stood out or felt emotionally significant. This method aimed to bridge the immediacy of experience with more considered interpretation based on the memory of the experience.

Step 6 - The sessions, which lasted around 30 min, concluded with a series of open-ended questions. These encouraged participants to elaborate on their overall experience, decision-making processes, and the perceived influence of audio-visual elements on their engagement with the game.

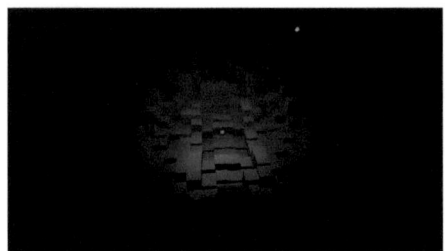 

Fig. 1. Visual scenario in a gameplay   **Fig. 2.** Participant picking up an artifact

3.4 Participant Profile

We recruited 10 participants from Portugal to take part in our study. The participant demographics of this convenience sample are summarized in Table 1. The low diversity of the sample may limit the generalizability of our findings regarding the diversity and representativeness of individual experience patterns. However it was sufficient to identify varied ways of expressing emotion, forming intention, and making sense of the experience.

Table 1. Participant Demographics

ID	Gender	Age	Area	Education	Country	Gaming Freq.
P1	Female	26	Pharmacy	Master's	Portugal	Weekly
P2	Male	41	Professor	Master's	Portugal	Almost daily
P3	Male	24	Professor	Master's	Portugal	Monthly
P4	Male	23	Medicine Student	Bachelor's	Portugal	Weekly
P5	Male	24	Engineering Student	Master's	Portugal	Yearly
P6	Male	23	Engineering	Master's	Portugal	Daily
P7	Female	23	Design Student	Bachelor's	Portugal	Daily
P8	Male	25	Design Student	Technical	Portugal	Daily
P9	Male	22	Design Student	Bachelor's	Portugal	Daily
P10	Male	24	Engineering Student	Master's	Portugal	Weekly

4 Results

4.1 Content Analysis Process

After collecting the data from ten game play sessions and interviews, we transcribed every phrase of the open-ended responses and video recall interview. Then, we developed our own categories that were informed by the observations we made, by established audiovisual experience literature, dimensions in the participation-centered game design model (PCGDM) [15,16], and constructs from the Player Experience Inventory (PXI) [1].

These sources provided the basis for creating our category definitions. We classified phrases or paragraph units of participant speech, as appropriate, with the categories listed in Table 2. Authors reviewed the classification made to ensure that each transcript segment was coded consistently with the above conceptual framework. This classification allowed us to trace how sensory perception, emotional response, and interactive engagement intertwined throughout the experience, while ensuring a robust and theoretically grounded analysis.

4.2 Results Synthesis

Affective and Emotional Responses. Players report having experienced a wide range of affective responses throughout the game play. Overall, the data indicate that emotional reactions were dynamic and multifaceted, ranging from simple evaluative remarks, e.g. P7: "*I was finding the experience pleasant, very pleasant.*", to more complex, fluctuating states like P1: "*It captivated many different emotions. In the course of the game, the sounds ended and the colors and shapes of the ground changed, leaving me either anxious, frustrated, sad, or relatively calm.*" Participants describe diverse emotional states such as anxiety, frustration, confusion, and satisfaction, often linked to changing audiovisual elements. Players report varied emotional responses, reflecting the aural, visual and play impressions likely to have influenced players' perceptions and interpretations.

Table 2. Conceptual categories with descriptions and total coded segments

Name of Category	Description	Count
Emotional xp	Captures the affective responses and emotional states expressed by the players	291
Audio	Refers to all auditory aspects of the game, including references to any aspect of the sound design, musical cues, and auditory feedback	144
Visual	References to game visual elements such as graphics, colors, and animation	170
Influence	Indicates the impact that game elements have on the player's decision-making	72
Memories	Captures associations or recollections triggered by the gameplay experience	15
Path	Navigation and path choices player undertakes within the environment	62
Orientation	Refers to the player's sense of direction and spatial awareness within the game	56
Intention	Denotes the player's goals or purposes during gameplay	30
Action	Classifies physical or interactive behaviors performed by the player	24
Meaning	Players interpret, derive meaning from, or make sense of the play environment	34
Challenge	Player interprets difficulty and obstacles to overcome in game play	7
Playfulness	Denotes a free play attitude, characterized by the willingness to experiment, find what is possible, and engage in open-ended exploration in game play	57
Control	Signals sense of control and responsiveness from the game	13
Goals	Captures how the game's objectives and rules are understood by the players	54
Progress Feedback	Evidence of how the player interprets/game communicates progress or state changes through audiovisual signals	34
Curiosity	Player expresses desire to explore environ, seek information or experiences	30
Immersion	Signals when players become absorbed in the game experience	5
Autonomy	Captures freedom players experience when making decisions during gameplay	7

Movement, Spatial Awareness, Immersion and Autonomy. Players adopted diverse movement strategies throughout the game, from spontaneous exploration to more structured navigation. Some players described their paths as intuitive and goal-driven, while others emphasized moments of indecision and randomness. Several participants explained how their navigation evolved over time, initially random but later incorporating deliberate decisions based on interpreted cues from the environment, e.g., "*P2: At first it was completely random, but then it was just trying to always go forward and look for the sound or the light that indicated the object.*" Another participant drew a parallel to conventional game mechanics to explain their default navigation behavior, stating, P4: "*I don't know, I think going forward is the most obvious path, right? I think most people assume to go forward. In any game you usually go forward, you don't usually go backwards.*"

Participants exhibited varied levels of **spatial awareness** and orientation, expressing uncertainty about their direction often led to hesitation and movement changes, e.g. P1: "*And at the beginning of the game, I don't understand what the goal is. So I just move around with the arrow keys.*" Movement adaptations to environmental feedback include experimenting with different ways of navigating. Some players actively engaged with auditory cues to adjust their movement, e.g. P2: "*ok, in that moment I was trying to understand what it was about, right? I started moving in zigzags and when I realized that the sound was related to the side where the object would fall, I started searching for that sound and heading in that direction.*"

Several participants showed signs of deep **immersion** often losing track of time or feeling strongly connected with the game environment: "*It didn't feel like 13 min passed, [...] It felt like less. I thought it had been way less.*" Another explained, "*That's exactly what I felt, like I was the ball in that moment.*" There were also reflections on how the experience could be perceived without vision, "*A blind person, for example, doesn't see that the exit is straight ahead. Maybe they realize it in another way, like with steps and movements. Here I felt that. I felt like someone, I don't know, visually impaired, could also follow the path.*"

Many participants mentioned **autonomy** during the play experience, emphasizing the freedom to make choices and shape their own path, P8: "*Here it's like free, the person can do whatever they want, they can not even walk, they can jump, enjoy the music, the environment...*" and P6: "*I think I did a path, with the intentions I had... I think the experience was more pleasant than if, for example, I couldn't control the path. Because then I'd feel that it didn't depend on me being here or not.*" This sense of freedom extended to how participants explored the space, as one put it, P8: "*I think each person is, like, free to do the path they want and explore how they want.*"

Playful Cues, Intentionality, Interaction, Control. Players engaged in a range of interactions throughout the game, responding to environmental **cues**, testing mechanics, or simply experimenting. Varying expressions of intentionality lead some players to engage in goal-driven behaviors while others experimented with mechanics out of curiosity or frustration.

Some described intentional movements triggered by game elements, such as one participant who stated, P6: "*I started trying to catch the crystals by jumping.*" Others experimented with actions spontaneously, e.g., P3: "*Every now and then, I would remember that jumping was an option, so I tried it.*" **Intentionality** also emerged in response to movement constraints. One player recalled P1: "*At a certain point, I started jumping because I was bored, as you can tell by my face.*" One participant expressed frustration while trying to control speed: P1: "*... Here I was getting a bit annoyed [...] because I wanted to run faster and couldn't.*".

Concerns related to **control**, particularly regarding movement precision involved in jumping mechanics, object interaction, and perspective support understanding of more influences of interaction on player experience. One participant remarked P5: "*The jumping part is a bit annoying... it jumps too little and I can't catch the signals.*" Another expressed frustration with depth perception P10: "*There's a part here in the game where you can't really tell how far you are from them.*" Lighting limited object visibility and control, P10: "*I think the light being at this angle doesn't help much.*"

Sensemaking, Challenge, and Playfulness. Diverse perspectives surfaced regarding the **meaning** of the experience. These range from a lack of clear purpose, to personal interpretations shaped by exploration and emotion. Some players struggled to identify a concrete objective, as one participant noted, P1: "*I don't feel that it necessarily has a meaning.*" Others found a sense of structure in the interaction, despite not fully grasping its purpose: P3: "*It made sense, yes.*

Even though I didn't know the complete meaning, what the objective was and all that, I could tell there was something to do." Some players projected personal narratives onto the experience, using it as a metaphor for real-life situations, e.g., P5: *"I related this... the game or whatever, as if I were there in Pinhal de Marrocos looking for my way out, but it was dark and I couldn't see anything".*

The perception of **challenge** varied, with some participants expecting more explicit obstacles or structured difficulty, while others interpreted forms of challenge emerging from interaction with the environment. One participant reflected on initial expectations P2: *"From the moment you told me it would be a game, I don't know if it was because of that, but my mind expected something with some factor of difficulty and reward. There wasn't, or at least it didn't seem that way to me."* Another noted how tension was introduced through the sound design, but without clear gameplay consequences, saying, P2: *"The music was curious because it brought tension, but I didn't find anything that would hinder the ball's progress."* Others perceived difficulty in finding interactive elements, P6: *"...because imagine, I started thinking that detecting the things would get more difficult over time."*

Many participants embraced a **playful** attitude throughout the experience. They often engage in open-ended exploration or test interactions and described navigating the space *"just to see what would happen."* Participant 2 explained, *"At the beginning, because of that discovery thing, I tried going in all directions."* Another (participant 9) reflected on their mindset *"I was just playing with the controls I guess."* A playful sense of freedom supported a relaxed form of interaction, where experimentation emerged as a central characteristic of the experience. The overall audiovisual atmosphere encouraged playful behavior, with participants describing it as *light-hearted, and at times, amusing.*

Goals, Progression, Ambiguity and Curiosity. Players expressed different perceptions of game **goals** that ranged from clear personal objectives to uncertainty or ambiguity. Some participants described the collection of objects (also referred as "stars," "pieces," or "crystals") as the aim of the game. For instance P1: *"I realized the goal was to collect little stars... or at least I thought the goal was to collect them, and I started looking for them."* or P7: *"about moving a ball around, and then little pieces started appearing that I had to collect."* However, they also questioned their assumptions P1: *"There's no kind of reward for what I think is the game's goal."* Others perceived the game as lacking a defined endpoint, suggesting instead an exploratory or symbolic pursuit: P9: *"I think the only thing I personally missed was really understanding the logic of the game. It was still interesting as an exploratory experience".*

Participants reported varied perceptions of feedback and **progression** within the game. While some identified environmental audiovisual changes as signs of advancement, others expressed uncertainty about whether they were progressing at all. Participant 2 noted *"When I collected the big object, it felt satisfying... like I changed levels,"* later adding, *"rewarded".* Others (participant 8) described visual or musical changes as indicative of movement through the game: *"I felt like it was level two". However, the lack of explicit progression indicators also lead to expressions like P7: "*I was enjoying the experience, but at the same time I was confused, I didn't know if I was progressing or not.*"

Echoing the idea of **ambiguity** one stating P10: "*I still wasn't sure if I was expecting something, but the color changes really indicated I was going the right way.*" **Curiosity** came up quite frequently, as an idea reported to have influenced players to want to explore and test things. Some participants tried everything just to see what would happen, how the game worked: P2: "*I wanted to know what the jump was for. I expected it to change something in the environment, but it didn't, only the sound.*" Others were intrigued by unexpected changes, P2: "*At some point I thought, wait, why is this changing? It's not because of the objects I pick up, so I wanted to know if it was because of how far I walked or the time.*" Some players (participant 9) also wanted to test their hypotheses about the game world, "*In the beginning, I was just trying to understand how the space was distributed. Then, when I realized there was some relationship, I tried going back to check if my idea was correct.*" Curiosity also extended to audiovisual elements, P8: "*I got curious about the colors because I felt like there were moments when they were more intense.*"

5 Interpretation of Results and Insights for Design

The synthesis of results reveals a complex and multi-layered phenomenological landscape, where player experience emerges through the interweaving of sensory perception, emotional response, and self-directed exploration. This discussion examines the interrelations between key thematic categories, interpreting how these dimensions may have contributed to the player's situated understanding of the game and responding directly to the study's research questions. The described results provide an overview of the concepts that emerged during the gameplay sessions. Categories enabled us to capture how players interacted with the audiovisual environment. Recurring concepts such as emotion, playfulness, intentions and explorations, demonstrate the entangled multidimensional nature of interaction and experience. The following discussion will examine how these themes relate to the research questions of the study.

One of the clearest outcomes of the analysis was the prominence of emotional responses. There were a total of 291 references to emotional states across the data analyzed. This suggests that the design's primary goal, evoking emotions, was achieved. Participants reported several emotional responses, which often aligned with the intended aim of the designed audiovisual scenarios. In most cases, the emotional atmospheres associated with each of the four designed environments were successfully recognized by players.

A strong interplay was observed between spatial categories, particularly path and orientation, which were frequently negotiated in tandem as participants explored the environment. Players did not begin with a fixed strategy—many started by moving randomly—but progressively developed a sense of direction through perception. Audiovisual cues, such as the spatialisation of sound or the intensity of light, supported their navigation and contributed to their evolving spatial awareness. This process, often marked by trial and error, showed that orientation was not passively received, but actively constructed throughout the interaction.

Intentionality and action patterns were shaped through situated perception and audiovisual cues and feedback. As players became more attuned to the sensorial cues in the environment, their movements gained direction and purpose. When faced with uncertainty, many adopted a playful stance—jumping around, exploring freely, or deliberately testing the boundaries of the game system/space. This playfulness was not detached from emotional engagement; rather, it emerged as an adaptive response to ambiguity and a reflection of exploratory behavior.

Ambiguity surfaced as a core characteristic of the experience. Indeed, the absence of explicit goals or clear instructions did not hinder most participants ability to play; on the contrary, it often enabled them to engage more freely. Without fixed objectives, players relied on shifts in audio or visual intensity to interpret transitions, progression, or changes in emotional tone. This open-ended structure supported interpretation and invited players to read the environment in personal and subjective ways, placing them as co-constructors of the experience.

Concepts such as goals, challenge, progression and feedback did not stem explicitly from mechanics, but emerged from perception and sensemaking of the environment. Players often described difficulty not as failure or obstacles, but as moments of uncertainty when trying to understand the meaning of audiovisual cues. More intense soundscapes or brighter colors were frequently perceived as signs of change or movement, whereas static or silent environments generated hesitation. This reflects a form of challenge grounded in perception and meaning, rather than performance.

Although some participants briefly referred to the responsiveness of controls, mechanical aspects did not appear central to the experience. **Autonomy stood out clearly from the freedom to explore, to interpret, and to act independently.** This autonomy was not only functional, but emotional and conceptual, allowing participants to engage with the system on their own terms. Rather than being guided by fixed paths, players navigated through a landscape of cues, feelings, and decisions, reinforcing the game's potential as an open-ended, emotionally grounded prototype.

In summary, the experience that emerged was guided by interactive exploration, leading to perceptual and emotional engagement. The audiovisual coherence invited players to explore their senses and interpret cues. Emotion became central in shaping intentionality, orientation, and exploration, supporting a design model that valued ambiguity and sensemaking over prescription or directed challenge.

5.1 Limitations and Future Work

While this preliminary study provides valuable insights into how interaction and audiovisual perception can shapes player experience, it is important to acknowledge its limitations. The participant sample consisted of a relatively small, similar age, educational background and culturally homogeneous group. This has likely influenced the subjective interpretations and emotional responses, limiting their diversity. Although sessions were conducted in a quiet and controlled room, the space was not fully isolated from external noise, and the lighting conditions were not adjustable. A more immersive environment, with full control over ambient light and sound distractions, may enhance the sensory engagement and emotional depth of the experience. This preliminary study focused on a single game prototype and one play session per participant of less than an hour. Longer-term engagement may reveal further layers of interpretation, diverse behavior, and exploratory strategies that were not captured in this setting.

For future work, the insights drawn from this study represents a departing point for the study of how the entanglement of iteration and sound can be utilized in structured design exercises to evoke emotional rich experiences. Additionally, the prototype demonstrates strong potential for accessibility-oriented exploration, particularly in the context of visual impairments. Given that participants frequently relied on auditory cues to guide orientation, make decisions, and interpret the environment, the game design insights could be adopted to support experiences where navigation and interaction are driven through sound design. Future studies could investigate how perception, emotion and autonomy unfold for blind or low-vision players, further developing design lessons for inclusive, sound-centered interactive system.

6 Conclusion

Authors presented a game design case study focused on eliciting emotional responses through a generative interactive audiovisual landscape. A prototype was developed and tested and recall interviews collected with 10 participants. A qualitative phenomenological study was done with content analysis on action and speech. The synthesis of results reveals a complex entanglement of sensory perception, emotional response, and self-directed exploration composing the phenomenological landscape of player experience. Lessons for design result from a set of insights: A strong interplay was observed between spatial categories such as path and orientation; Intentionality and action patterns were shaped through situated perception and audiovisual cues and feedback; Ambiguity surfaced as a core characteristic of the experience; Concepts such as goals, challenge, progression and feedback did not stem explicitly from mechanics, but emerged from perception and sensemaking of the environment; Autonomy stood out clearly from the freedom to explore, to interpret, and to act independently. Such control, autonomy, and flexibility are key characteristics for designing play environmental supportiveness.

References

1. Abeele, V.V., Spiel, K., Nacke, L., Johnson, D., Gerling, K.: Development and validation of the player experience inventory: a scale to measure player experiences at the level of functional and psychosocial consequences. Int. J. Hum.-Comput. Stud. **135**, 102370 (2020). https://doi.org/10.1016/j.ijhcs.2019.102370. https://www.sciencedirect.com/science/article/pii/S1071581919301302
2. Blakey, H.: Designing player intent through "playful" interaction: a case study of techniques in *transistor* and *journey*. M/C J. **24**(4) (2021). https://doi.org/10.5204/mcj.2802. https://journal.media-culture.org.au/index.php/mcjournal/article/view/2802
3. Bostan, B., Kaplancali, U.: Explorations in Player Motivations: Game Mechanics, pp. 5–11 (2009)
4. Carpenter, J.: The aesthetics of human-machine interaction: generative textuality in hello gamess no mans sky. J. Aesthet. Phenomenol. **9**(2), 173–190 (2022). https://doi.org/10.1080/20539320.2022.2150464
5. Denisova, A., Cairns, P.: The placebo effect in digital games: phantom perception of adaptive artificial intelligence. In: Proceedings of the 2015 Annual Symposium on Computer-Human Interaction in Play, CHI PLAY 2015, pp. 23–33. Association for Computing Machinery, New York (2015). https://doi.org/10.1145/2793107.2793109. https://dl.acm.org/doi/10.1145/2793107.2793109
6. Forero, J., Bernardes, G., Mendes, M.: Emotional machines: toward affective virtual environments. In: Proceedings of the 30th ACM International Conference on Multimedia, MM 2022, pp. 7237–7238. Association for Computing Machinery, New York (2022). https://doi.org/10.1145/3503161.3549973
7. Ha, E.Y., Rowe, J.P., Mott, B.W., Lester, J.C.: Recognizing player goals in open-ended digital games with markov logic networks. In: Plan, Activity, and Intent Recognition, pp. 289–311. Elsevier (2014). https://doi.org/10.1016/B978-0-12-398532-3.00012-9. https://linkinghub.elsevier.com/retrieve/pii/B9780123985323000129
8. Kin Keong, L., Mohd Nasseri, J.: Affective generative visuals based on data input influenced by user's emotions. Int. J. Arts Cult. Heritage (iJACH) **11**, 126–146 (2023). https://doi.org/10.62312/asw.ijach.11.7.2024. https://penerbit.aswara.edu.my/index.php/affective-generative-visuals-based-on-datainput-influenced-by-users-emotions/
9. van 't Klooster, A.: Creating emotion-sensitive interactive artworks: three case studies. Leonardo **51**(03), 239–245 (2018). https://doi.org/10.1162/leon_a_01344
10. Ma, F., et al.: A Review of Human Emotion Synthesis Based on Generative Technology (2024). https://doi.org/10.48550/arXiv.2412.07116. http://arxiv.org/abs/2412.07116. arXiv:2412.07116
11. Makantasis, K., Liapis, A., Yannakakis, G.N.: The pixels and sounds of emotion: general-purpose representations of arousal in games. IEEE Trans. Affect. Comput. **14**(1), 680–693 (2023). https://doi.org/10.1109/TAFFC.2021.3060877. https://ieeexplore.ieee.org/document/9360471
12. Mattos, R.L.D.: Game design for emotions: a practice based research on the design of game emotional experience. In: LINK 2024 Conference Proceedings, vol. 1, no. 1, pp. 34–35 (2020). https://doi.org/10.24135/linksymposium.vi.14. https://ojs.aut.ac.nz/linksymposium/article/view/14

13. Minassian, H.T.: Drawing video game mental maps: from emotional games to emotions of play. Cartographic Perspect. (91), 47–62 (2018). https://doi.org/10.14714/CP91.1435. https://cartographicperspectives.org/index.php/journal/article/view/1435
14. Pawar, V., Vhatkar, A., Chavan, P., Gawankar, S., Nair, S.: The future of emotional engineering: integrating generative AI and emotional intelligence. In: 2024 8th International Conference on Computing, Communication, Control and Automation (ICCUBEA), pp. 1–6 (2024). https://doi.org/10.1109/ICCUBEA61740.2024.10775105. https://ieeexplore.ieee.org/document/10775105. iSSN: 2771-1358
15. Pereira, L.L., Craveirinha, R., Roque, L.: A canvas for participation-centered game design. In: Proceedings of the Annual Symposium on Computer-Human Interaction in Play, CHI PLAY 2019, pp. 521–532. Association for Computing Machinery, New York (2019). https://doi.org/10.1145/3311350.3347154. https://dl.acm.org/doi/10.1145/3311350.3347154
16. Pereira, L.L., Roque, L.: Understanding the videogame medium through perspectives of participation. In: Proceedings of DiGRA 2013 Conference (2013). https://doi.org/10.26503/dl.v2013i1.650. https://dl.digra.org/index.php/dl/article/view/650. iSSN: 2342-9666
17. Pires, D., et al.: The blindfold soundscape game: a case for participation-centered gameplay experience design and evaluation. In: Proceedings of the 8th Audio Mostly Conference, AM 2013, pp. 1–7. Association for Computing Machinery, New York (2013). https://doi.org/10.1145/2544114.2544122
18. Robinson, R., Murray, J., Isbister, K.: "You're giving me mixed signals!": a comparative analysis of methods that capture players' emotional response to games. In: Extended Abstracts of the 2018 CHI Conference on Human Factors in Computing Systems, CHI EA 2018, pp. 1–6. Association for Computing Machinery, New York (2018). https://doi.org/10.1145/3170427.3188469. https://dl.acm.org/doi/10.1145/3170427.3188469
19. Rogers, K.: Exploring the role of audio in games. In: Extended Abstracts Publication of the Annual Symposium on Computer-Human Interaction in Play, pp. 727–731. CHI PLAY 2017 Extended Abstracts. Association for Computing Machinery, New York (2017). https://doi.org/10.1145/3130859.3133227
20. Russell, J.A.: A circumplex model of affect. J. Pers. Soc. Psychol. **39**(6), 1161–1178 (1980). https://doi.org/10.1037/h0077714
21. Sweetser, P.: An emergent approach to game design : development and play. Ph.D. thesis, The University of Queensland (2006). https://doi.org/10.14264/86deb69. https://espace.library.uq.edu.au/view/UQ:86deb69
22. Zhao, H., Zhang, J.J., McDougall, S.: Emotion-driven interactive digital storytelling. In: Anacleto, J.C., Fels, S., Graham, N., Kapralos, B., Saif El-Nasr, M., Stanley, K. (eds.) ICEC 2011. LNCS, vol. 6972, pp. 22–27. Springer, Heidelberg (2011). https://doi.org/10.1007/978-3-642-24500-8_3

The Blind Gamer: Examining Ethical Agency Through Choice Blindness in Game Design

Kamyab Ghorbanpour, Michal Klincewicz, Paris Mavromoustakos Blom, and Pieter Spronck

Department of Cognitive Science and Artificial Intelligence, Tilburg University, Warandelaan 2, Tilburg, Noord-Brabant, The Netherlands
k.Ghorbanpour@tilburguniversity.edu

Abstract. This study examines the interplay between choice blindness and moral decision-making through the design and implementation of a decision-driven adventure game called Lost Civilization. Choice blindness, a phenomenon where individuals fail to detect changes in their decisions, was investigated within a controlled narrative environment featuring moral dilemmas in total, 56 participants (24 female, ages 18–35) engaged with the game, which subtly manipulated one of their moral decisions. The findings reveal that the majority (37) of participants did not detect the manipulation, underscoring the potential of games as tools for studying moral cognition and agency. Logistic regression analysis and machine learning models demonstrated significant correlations between undetected manipulations and participants' gender as well as specific moral foundation scores based on Jonathan Haidt's and Oliver Scott Curry's dictionaries, suggesting deeper psychological underpinnings of decision-making processes. This research highlights the utility of video games in expanding the scope of choice blindness studies and advancing our understanding of ethical agency in interactive contexts.

Keywords: Video Game · Moral Foundation · Gender · Choice Blindness

1 Introduction

Video games offer a unique opportunity to examine human cognition, particularly inductive biases and decision-making in morally challenging contexts. Among the concepts studied in this field, choice blindness—first introduced by Petter Johansson [12]—has demonstrated how individuals often lack awareness of their decision-making processes, even in moral dilemmas. While extensively studied in areas like politics [21], aesthetics [25], and consumer behavior [4], choice blindness has not been thoroughly explored in the context of video games. This gap is significant given the interactive and data-rich environments games provide [18], offering unparalleled potential for experimentation.

In this paper, we conducted an experiment to explore choice blindness using a "homebrew" digital game designed to present players with morally challenging scenarios. Participants navigated eight dilemmas in an academic setting, each offering four equally viable choices designed to appeal to different moral intuitions. Unknown to participants, one of their chosen options was altered to test their susceptibility to choice blindness. We analyzed their justifications using Moral Foundation Theory [8] and Morality as Cooperation dictionaries [17], aiming to uncover correlations between moral views, gender differences, and sensitivity to manipulation.

There were some unexpected results, such as the disproportionate representation of gender in the data, that would give us the means to better understand human psychology. Choice-blindness is a simple phenomenon that allows us to understand humans' flaws in decision-making. Through this experiment, we learn that many of our moral decisions may not be our own, or on a higher level, what it means to make our own moral decisions. By situating our experiment within the broader theoretical frameworks of choice blindness, morality, and the cognitive effects of gaming, we demonstrate how video games can be powerful tools for studying human psychology. These insights hold implications not only for understanding decision-making flaws but also for addressing broader societal issues like misinformation and moral reasoning.

2 Related Work

2.1 Choice Blindness

Choice blindness was discovered in 2005 through groundbreaking research conducted by Petter Johansson and Lars Hall [13]. The original experiment challenged the idea of introspective certainty – the belief that individuals have accurate access to the origins of their thoughts and preferences. Participants were shown pairs of female human faces and asked to choose the one they found most attractive [12]. Unbeknownst to the participants, on some occasions, the researchers swapped the selected face with the one that was not chosen by employing a sleight-of-hand trick, often used as entertainment to amuse people. The fascinating finding was that most participants did not notice the switch. Even more surprisingly, when asked to justify their choice, many provided detailed and convincing explanations for why they preferred the face they didn't actually choose. This phenomenon was coined as "choice blindness".

Choice blindness is part of a broader psychological concept known as the introspection illusion. This is where people tend to believe they have full access to their mental states, but in reality, they often misattribute the origins of their decisions [2]. In the context of Johansson and Hall's work, participants confabulated reasons for choices they never actually made, leading to important insights about how self-knowledge and decision-making processes work.

The choice blindness paradigm has since been extended beyond simple aesthetic judgments to more complex domains, including moral and political decisions [24], consumer behavior [4], and even memory [19]. For example, research has demonstrated how this phenomenon plays out in political contexts. In a study conducted in Sweden and later replicated in Argentina, participants were asked about their political attitudes and voting intentions [10]. Unbeknownst to them, some of their responses were manipulated, and they were later asked to justify these altered choices. Remarkably, many participants provided strong justifications for political positions they had not originally endorsed. This study underscored how deeply introspection errors can affect even significant and deeply held beliefs.

Few studies have taken a closer look at the relationship between moral choices and change blindness [9,24]. This is surprising, since introspective failure raises serious concerns in moral contexts, suggesting that some of the most important beliefs people hold can be easily manipulated in experimental conditions [8]. Understandably, preferences regarding jam flavors [11] or facial attractiveness [23] are not things that people necessarily have strong pre-existing preferences about. But moral preferences, such as the importance of promoting societal welfare, are stable and more accessible to introspection.

In preparation for the experiment on the choice blindness paradigm, a literature review was conducted to identify relevant studies and methodologies to inform the experiment's design and execution. The review involved searching for empirical articles related to choice blindness, as well as qualitative and quantitative analyses, and the psychological impacts associated with decision-making processes. Currently, no experiments have been conducted on choice blindness with video games. Video games can be powerful tools to study human cognition and behavior [1]. In cognitive psychology, video games have been utilized to explore several key functions, including attention, memory, and executive function. We know that, for example, the immersive nature of games can lead to enhanced engagement and enjoyment, which are crucial for cognitive benefits, so, perhaps unsurprisingly this has been applied to better understand delayed recall, as well as recognition tasks [16] explored whether immersion in virtual environments can similarly induce choice blindness [16]. The study found no significant difference effect of immersion on the frequency of failure to detect change in choices. However, it turned out that *when* a detection is made mattered. It also demonstrated that It is possible to replicate the choice blindness effect in a virtual environment without adversely impacting the task.

2.2 Moral Theories

Individuals make decisions that often deviate from the rational actor model [14]. We know that human decision-making involves at least two distinct systems: the fast, intuitive, and emotional System 1, and the slower, more analytical System 2 [20]. We also know from this work that cognitive and emotional biases can influence decision-making processes in both systems.

Jonathan Haidt built upon Kahneman's insights by introducing Moral Foundation Theory (MFT), which posits that human morality is rooted in several innate psychological systems that have evolved to facilitate social living [7]. MFT identifies five primary moral foundations: Care, Fairness, Loyalty, Authority, and Purity. Haidt's framework suggests that these moral intuitions are shaped by individual experiences and cultural contexts, thus providing a lens through which to understand the moral divides that characterize contemporary moral and political discourse [10]. By integrating Kahneman's dual-process theory, Haidt argues that moral reasoning is often driven by intuitive, emotional responses (akin to System 1 thinking) rather than deliberate, rational deliberation (System 2). This connection underscores the idea that moral judgments are often made quickly and intuitively, reflecting deeper psychological and evolutionary underpinnings.

However, Haidt's evolutionary perspective has faced criticism, particularly from scholars like Olivier Curry, who argues that the basis of MFT is scientifically tenuous. He posits that while MFT attempts to explain moral behavior through an evolutionary lens, it often resorts to speculative reasoning that does not adequately account for the complexities of human morality. Curry offers his Morality as Cooperation (MAC) theory as a superior alternative, which emphasizes the role of cooperation and social dynamics in shaping moral norms [17]. Curry's emphasis on empirical morality as a product of cooperation challenges the notion that moral intuitions are connected to economic behavior, which is competitive. Instead, he suggests that they are dynamic and context-dependent, shaped by the cooperative groups that require their members to adopt values that facilitate optimal group outcomes.

In the game we designed, both MFT and MAC are used to gain insight into individuals' value-laden language used by players, focusing on the expression of values. We then look at how specific values may or may not correlate with behavior.

3 Experiment and Methods

3.1 Procedure

The experiment was done in a controlled environment where participants were instructed to play as themselves and avoid role-playing as much as possible, addressing concerns that virtual environments could produce questionable results due to role-playing [26]. Players were presented with a total of eight decisions, one of which specifically was always altered to mean the exact opposite. Each decision addressed a different moral dilemma, and all choices were designed to have reasonable justifications.

One example of this is the decision to respond to a movie created to propagate the idea of further implementing surveillance in society, using the popular imagination of the lost civilization. Many participants chose the option that movies are merely a form of entertainment and do not warrant deep thinking. However, when asked to justify the altered decision, the majority shifted their stance, stating that movies can have underlying meanings and are not solely for entertainment.

3.2 Participants

In total, 56 volunteers (24 female) participated in the study. Ages ranged from 18 to 35 years (Mean age = 26.5 years; SD = 4.91 years). We recruited the participants through the SONA system that Tilburg University provided, so the majority of the participants were university students. They were informed that they would be playing a video game for scientific purposes. All participants gave written informed consent to participate in the study, and all participants also agreed to have the interaction video recorded. Aside from having their voice and video recorded, participants wore a sensor platform to collect biophysical and Galvanic skin response data, and their eye movements were tracked using an eye tracker for further investigation into the reasons behind choice blindness. The present study will not consider any of the physiological data gathered but instead, focuses on the confabulations provided by the participants and the demographic correlations. The remaining data will be used for another paper investigating potential correlations between the physiological data gathered and the results presented in this paper.

3.3 Memory Test

A memory test was conducted to determine whether participants were fully aware of their answers and experiences prior to the manipulation. This was important because participants might not have been entirely aware of what they were being questioned about. Those who failed the test were excluded from further analysis. Two questions assessed participants' awareness by testing their ability to recall the content and details of the game, listed below:

1. What was the name of the Alien race mentioned in the game?
2. Could you please summarize the game's story from the beginning to the end?

The majority of people, except for three, were able to remember the story and summarize it comprehensively in three to five sentences, mentioning the dilemmas they faced. While most couldn't precisely remember the name of the alien race (although some did), they were able to pronounce something reminiscent of it. The test only disregarded those who failed completely at both tasks, unable to remember the name of the alien race in any way or provide a decent summary of the game.

3.4 Lost Civilization

Lost Civilization is an adventure game commonly referred to as visual novels outside Japan [3], where this genre originated. In Japan, such games are often called "adventure games" or "novel games." The reason for choosing this genre is primarily due to its unique structure, which allowed us to conduct the experiment without too many other distractions such as animation. As we established, choice blindness relies on manipulating decisions by presenting altered choices to participants, and this is easier to achieve in a static 2D environment.

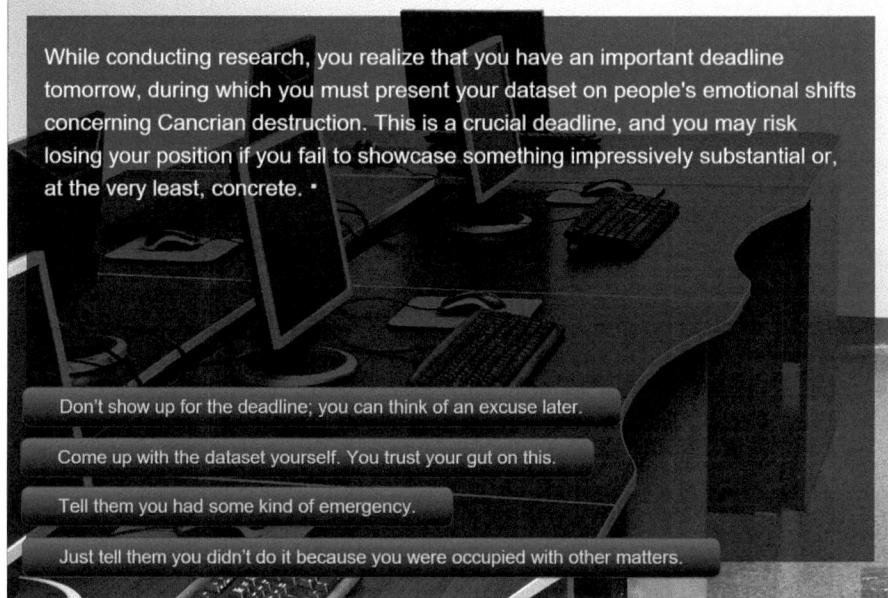

Fig. 1. The players have the option to choose between the four decisions presented.

The experiment focuses on decisions, and adventure games—particularly visual novels—are inherently designed around decision-based gameplay. Although visual novels haven't been widely used in scientific research, there is growing interest in utilizing the medium's potential. For example, one research has shown that the visual novel format offers great versatility, covering a wide range of topics and appealing to audiences of various ages [5].

We decided to design our game in a combination of magical realism and science fiction. Science fiction, with its rich array of symbols and tropes, provides creative ways to address moral issues. Lost Civilization tells the story of a researcher at Tilburg University (where the participants played the game) who is tasked with uncovering the mysteries of a lost alien civilization. The player faces eight decisions throughout the game. Each decision presents a different engaging dilemma (See Fig. 1), varying in scope. For example, one decision involves missing a deadline, and the player must choose whether to come up with an excuse, be completely honest, fabricate data, or not show up at all. Every decision takes place within a semi-academic environment.

After the game concluded, we presented participants with screenshots of the game and asked them to explain the reasoning behind their choices. However, we had prepared a trick by altering one of their decisions, effectively reversing its meaning.

3.5 Data Collection

Data for the analysis were collected from 53 (3 did not pass the memory test) participants who engaged in a video game designed to elicit moral decision-making. Each participant's responses were recorded, and their moral foundation scores were calculated based on established psychological scales. The data were then cleaned and coded, ensuring that all categorical variables were appropriately transformed into dummy variables for inclusion in the regression model.

To account for nested data structures—such as repeated measures within individuals across different decision points—multilevel (hierarchical) models were explored. This approach controlled for within-subject variability, ensuring more accurate estimation of predictors' effects.

Missing data due to equipment malfunctions (e.g., eye-tracker failures) were addressed using multiple imputation techniques (e.g., Next and Previous Values), minimizing bias without inflating false-positive rates. Sensitivity analyses confirmed the robustness of findings to imputation assumptions.

3.6 Transcripts

We transcribed all the data collected from participants during recorded sessions, ensuring that each verbal exchange was accurately captured in written form. We conducted a thorough review of the transcripts to verify their accuracy and completeness, correcting any discrepancies or errors that may have arisen during the transcription process. The resulting corpus was then analyzed using the extended Moral Foundation and Morality as Cooperation dictionaries. To do it efficiently, all spoken confabulations were transcribed using HappyScribe to convert them into text. Subsequently, all the transcripts were manually corrected.

3.7 Measures

All manipulations were categorized as either noticed (N) or unnoticed (UN). In the N cases, participants either detected the change immediately after reading the manipulated statement (spontaneous detection) or reported during the debriefing that they had felt something was wrong when they first encountered the manipulated sentence (retrospective correction). Specifically, a case was classified as spontaneously detected if participants displayed any indication of noticing the change after reading the manipulated statement, such as correcting or reversing their response to align with their original position, or suggesting they may have misunderstood the question initially. Most participants who detected the manipulation immediately also corrected their response by reversing their stance. In the UN cases, no such signs were observed, and participants did not recognize that the opinions they argued for post-manipulation were the opposite of their original intent. They explained and justified the altered decisions as if they had been their own from the start.

3.8 Logistic Regression

Logistic regression is a method for modeling the relationship between a binary dependent variable and one or more independent variables. It estimates the probability of an outcome using the logistic function, which transforms predictors into probabilities between 0 and 1, making it well-suited for binary outcomes.

In our study, we employed a binary logistic regression model to analyze the probability of participants resisting manipulation in a choice-blindness experiment. The model was specified as follows:

$$logit(P) = \ln\left(\frac{P}{1-P}\right) = \beta_0 + \beta_1 \cdot MACVirtues + \beta_2 \cdot MACVices + \beta_4 \cdot Gender$$

Where p is the probability of resisting manipulation, β_0 is the intercept, and $\beta_1, \beta_2, \ldots, \beta_n$ are the coefficients corresponding to the independent variables which include moral foundation scores and demographic factors such as gender.

Predicted probabilities are calculated for different combinations of predictor values to understand how changes in predictors affect the likelihood of the outcome. This involves plugging values into the logistic regression equation and transforming the log-odds back to probabilities using the logistic function.

The logistic regression model was fitted using maximum likelihood estimation, which is a standard approach for estimating the parameters of logistic regression models [15]. To evaluate the model's performance, we computed several pseudo-R^2 statistics, including Cox-Snell and Nagelkerke R^2, which provide insights into the proportion of variance explained by the model, akin to the R^2 in linear regression [15]. These statistics are particularly useful in logistic regression, where traditional R^2 values are not applicable.

To ensure the robustness of the logistic regression model, we conducted validation through cross-validation techniques, splitting the dataset into training and testing subsets. This approach allows for assessing the model's predictive performance on unseen data, thereby enhancing the reliability of the findings. Additionally, we examined the model for multicollinearity among predictors using Variance Inflation Factor (VIF) analysis, ensuring that the estimates remained stable and interpretable. All the predictors were also normalized and standardized.

3.9 Machine Learning Model

Random Forest was chosen as a side-analysis for its robustness against overfitting, especially in complex datasets with high-dimensional attributes, which enhances both the accuracy and interpretability of models [29]. Previous studies have demonstrated that Random Forest can outperform logistic regression in accuracy across diverse domains, confirming its efficacy in predictive modeling tasks [6,28]. The training process involved using the dataset to include gender and age as well as features from MAC and MFT columns, allowing the model to learn complex patterns that may elucidate the influences behind choice blindness phenomena [30]. Given these attributes, the integration of Random Forest not

only bolsters the predictive power but also adds a layer of rigor and validity to
the conclusions drawn from the other analysis.

4 Results

For both men and women, the Medium level of moral foundation scores corresponds to the highest probability of not being manipulated, particularly in the context of deference vice and care vice. Specifically, women exhibit a marked increase in resistance to manipulation as their deference vice scores rise, with probabilities escalating from 25% at the Low level to 62.50% at the High level. In contrast, men show a more modest increase, from almost 0% to 50% across the same levels. Figure 2 summarizes these results.

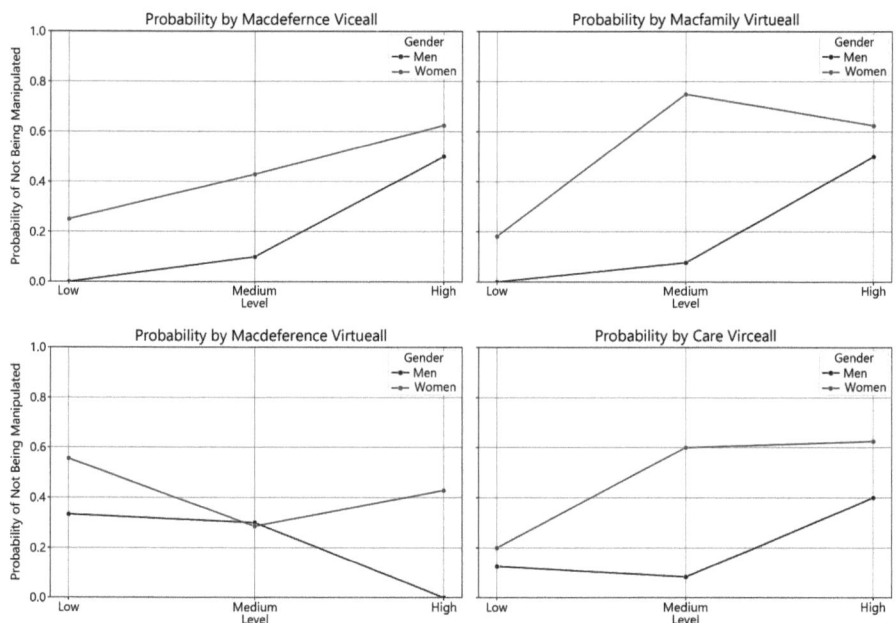

Fig. 2. The probability of not being manipulated by all moral foundations

In examining the family virtue scores, women again demonstrate a peak resistance at the Medium level (75%), which slightly declines to 62.50% at the High level. Men's resistance, however, shows a steady increase from almost 0% at the Low level to 50% at the High level, indicating a gender disparity in how these moral foundations influence susceptibility to manipulation. The deference virtue scores present a contrasting trend, where women show the highest resistance at Low levels (55.56%) but experience a significant dip at Medium levels (28.57%). Men's resistance decreases consistently from 33.33% at Low to almost

0% at High, suggesting that higher moral foundation scores may correlate with increased susceptibility for men.

The care vice scores reveal a similar pattern, with women's resistance increasing from 20% at Low to 62.50% at High, while men's resistance rises from 12.50% to 40%. This further emphasizes the gender differences in moral foundation influences on manipulation susceptibility. Notably, extreme combinations of moral virtues or vices yield different outcomes for men and women; women maintain a 60% probability of not being manipulated when high in either virtues or vices, whereas men exhibit 0% resistance when high in virtues and 50% when high in vices.

The most notable result pertains to the gender effect, where women demonstrated a significantly higher likelihood of resisting manipulation compared to men ($p = 0.002$). The odds ratio indicates that women are approximately 6.2 times more likely to resist manipulation than their male counterparts. This is illustrated by the predicted probabilities, which show that men have only a 12.44% chance of not being manipulated, while women exhibit a substantially higher probability of 83.82%.

In terms of moral foundations, the family virtue score emerged with marginal significance ($p = 0.057$), suggesting a positive relationship with resistance to manipulation. Higher family virtue scores correlate with greater resistance, indicating that individuals who prioritize familial values may be less susceptible to manipulative tactics. Conversely, the deference vice and care vice scores did not reach statistical significance, with p-values of 0.206 and 0.530, respectively. Although both variables exhibited positive trends, the variability in their effects suggests insufficient evidence to draw strong conclusions regarding their influence on manipulation resistance.

Furthermore, the Random Forest model was applied to predict gender based on choice blindness which demonstrated a mean cross-validation accuracy of 82% (5 folds with 95% confidence interval), exceeding the baseline accuracy of 56.60%. This represents the accuracy of predicting the most frequent gender class [Male or Female]. This performance underscores the predictive power of the choice blindness effect concerning gender attribution, reinforcing conclusions drawn from the logistic regression analyses. While the model excelled in gender prediction, it also provided valuable insights into the predictive capabilities regarding MAC and MFT traits. Although the accuracy for these attributes was lower at 72%, it still surpassed the baseline accuracy of 69%, indicating that both MAC and MFT are informative in the context of choice blindness. Notably, the model identified family, loyalty, and deference as the three most influential features, with importance scores of approximately 0.0735, 0.0569, and 0.0546, respectively. This information is critical, as it reveals that these features have notably greater predictive power relative to the other characteristics analyzed.

5 Discussion

Our study reveals compelling evidence for resistance to manipulation, with several important implications for our understanding of social influence and decision-making processes. Our findings demonstrate a striking disparity between men and women in their susceptibility to manipulation, with women showing remarkably higher resistance levels.

Women are, as mentioned in the Results section, approximately 6.2 times more likely than men to resist manipulation, a difference that is both statistically significant ($p = 0.002$) and practically meaningful. When translated into predicted probabilities, the contrast becomes even more apparent: women demonstrate an 83.82% chance of resisting manipulation, compared to just 12.44% for men. This substantial gender gap raises important questions about the underlying psychological and social mechanisms that might contribute to such differences.

The findings align with existing literature that emphasizes gender differences in susceptibility to manipulation and the role of moral foundations in shaping these dynamics. For instance, Tomková and Čigarská discuss how gender differences manifest in tendencies towards certain behaviors, reinforcing the notion that women may inherently possess greater resistance to manipulation due to social and psychological factors [27]. Additionally, the research highlights the influence of environmental factors on resistance levels among different genders, suggesting that cultural constructs of gender may further amplify these differences [27].

The results of this study can relate to the previous studies on how societal norms surrounding masculinity significantly influence men's emotional expression and awareness, leading to increased susceptibility to manipulation. For example, men are often socialized to adhere to traditional masculine norms, which can lead to a lack of emotional awareness and a higher likelihood of being manipulated [22]. The relationship between moral virtues and manipulation susceptibility also presents an intriguing pattern. Higher scores on deference vice were associated with increased resistance to manipulation, particularly among women. This finding suggests that certain personality traits or moral orientations such as might serve as protective factors against manipulation attempts. Conversely, higher scores on family virtue were linked to increased susceptibility to choice blindness, particularly in contexts involving fairness, reciprocity, and property. This paradoxical relationship between family-oriented values and manipulation susceptibility warrants further investigation. However, several limitations should be considered when interpreting these results. The relatively small sample size ($N = 53$) may limit the generalizability of our findings. Additionally, the study focused on a specific experimental paradigm, and the results might not extend to all forms of manipulation or social influence. It is certainly noteworthy that the study did not account for participants' cultural, national, and economic backgrounds. While gender has been identified as a significant factor in choice blindness in this study, this finding is limited by the lack of consideration for environmental influences. The experiment's participants came from diverse regions and continents, with widely varying backgrounds, including differences in religion and culture. They can, however, be explored in future research.

Future research could delve into several promising directions to build upon these findings. One important avenue is to investigate the psychological mechanisms underlying the observed gender differences, shedding light on why such disparities exist and adding to the already existing literature on the topic. Further exploration of potential mediating factors, such as social conditioning, cognitive processing styles, or emotional intelligence, could provide deeper insights into the dynamics at play. Broadening the scope of the study to include larger and more diverse populations would enhance the generalizability of the results, offering a more comprehensive understanding across various demographics, something that is crucially lacking currently from the study. Additionally, examining how these findings might translate into real-world applications in different contexts could reveal practical implications for fields such as education, marketing, and leadership development.

The results were largely attributable to the immersive nature of the game medium, which enabled participants to engage with the scenarios on a deeper and more personal level than traditional experimental methods typically allow. Future experiments could further harness the potential of game-based environments to explore complex ethical phenomena in the context of choice blindness and psychological manipulation, offering even more nuanced insights into human behavior.

Another critical focus would be exploring the interaction between gender and other demographic or personality variables, uncovering how these relate to misinformation and manipulation. Such investigations could lead to the development of strategies to better protect vulnerable individuals from manipulation and promote more ethical approaches to persuasion and influence.

6 Conclusion

Our findings provide valuable insights into the role of gender in manipulation resistance, while also raising important questions for future research. The substantial difference in manipulation resistance between men and women highlights the need for a more nuanced understanding of how gender influences social interaction and decision-making processes. These results have important implications for both theoretical understanding and practical applications in fields ranging from psychology to organizational behavior.

Ethics Statement. The study was approved by the Tilburg University Ethics board, REDC2024.04.

References

1. Allen, K., et al.: Using games to understand the mind. Nat. Hum. Behav. **8**(6), 1035–1043 (2024). ISSN: 2397-3374. https://doi.org/10.1038/s41562-024-01878-9. https://www.nature.com/articles/s41562-024-01878-9. Accessed 14 Jan 2025

2. Bortolotti, L., Sullivan-Bissett, E.: Is choice blindness a case of self-ignorance? Synthese **198**(6), 5437–5454 (2019). https://doi.org/10.1007/s11229-019-02414-3
3. Camingue, J., Carstensdottir, E., Melcer, E.F.: What is a visual novel? Proc. ACM Hum.-Comput. Interact. **5**(CHI PLAY), 1–18 (2021). ISSN 2573-0142. htttps://doi.org/10.1145/3474712. https://dl.acm.org/doi/10.1145/3474712. Accessed 14 Jan 2025
4. Cheung, T.T.L., et al.: Consumers' choice-blindness to ingredient information. Appetite **106**, 2–12 (2016). ISSN 0195-6663. https://doi.org/10.1016/j.appet.2015.09.022. https://www.sciencedirect.com/science/article/pii/S0195666315300337
5. Davydovych, V., Filgueiras, E., Marto, A.: Comparative analysis of the presence and decision making in romantic visual novels: influence of personalization and sense of presence. In: Marcus, A., Rosenzweig, E., Soares, M.M. (eds.) HCII 2024. LNCS, vol. 14716, pp. 28–46. Springer, Cham (2024). https://doi.org/10.1007/978-3-031-61362-3_3
6. Doyle, R., Barnes, G.C.: Targeting missing persons most likely to come to harm among 92,681 cases reported to Devon and Cornwall police. Camb. J. Evid. Based Polic. **4**(3), 160–177 (2020). ISSN: 2520-1344, 2520-1336. https://doi.org/10.1007/s41887-020-00051-2. Accessed 19 Mar 2025
7. Haidt, J.: The emotional dog and its rational tail: a social intuitionist approach to moral judgment. Psychol. Rev. **108**(4), 814–834 (2001). ISSN: 1939-1471, 0033-295X. https://doi.org/10.1037/0033-295x.108.4.814. https://doi.apa.org/doi/10.1037/0033-295X.108.4.814. Accessed 14 Jan 2025
8. Haidt, J.: The new synthesis in moral psychology. Science **316**(5827), 998–1002 (2007). ISSN: 0036-8075, 1095-9203. https://doi.org/10.1126/science.1137651. https://www.science.org/doi/10.1126/science.1137651. Accessed 14 Jan 2025
9. Hall, L., Johansson, P., Strandberg, T.: Lifting the veil of morality: choice blindness and attitude reversals on a self-transforming survey. PLoS ONE **7**(9), e45457 (2012). https://doi.org/10.1371/journal.pone.0045457
10. Hall, L., et al.: How the polls can be both spot on and dead wrong: using choice blindness to shift political attitudes and voter intentions. PLoS ONE **8**(4), e60554 (2013). https://doi.org/10.1371/journal.pone.0060554
11. Hall, L., et al.: Magic at the marketplace: choice blindness for the taste of jam and the smell of tea. Cognition **117**(1), 54–61 (2010). ISSN: 0010-0277. https://doi.org/10.1016/j.cognition.2010.06.010. https://www.sciencedirect.com/science/article/pii/S0010027710001381
12. Johansson, P., et al.: Choice blindness and the failure to detect mismatches between intention and outcome. Science **310**(5745), 116–119 (2008). https://doi.org/10.1126/science.1111709
13. Johansson, P., et al.: How something can be said about telling more than we can know: on choice blindness and introspection. Conscious. Cogn. **15**(4), 673–692 (2006). ISSN: 1053-8100. https://doi.org/10.1016/j.concog.2006.09.004. https://www.sciencedirect.com/science/article/pii/S1053810006000936
14. Kahneman, D.: Maps of bounded rationality: psychology for behavioral economics. Am. Econ. Rev. **93**(5), 1449–1475 (2003). ISSN: 0002-8282. https://doi.org/10.1257/000282803322655392. https://pubs.aeaweb.org/doi/10.1257/000282803322655392. Accessed 14 Jan 2025
15. LaValley, M.P.: Logistic regression. Circulation **117**(18), 2395–2399 (2008). ISSN: 0009-7322, 1524-4539. https://doi.org/10.1161/circulationaha.106.682658. https://www.ahajournals.org/doi/10.1161/CIRCULATIONAHA.106.682658. Accessed 14 Jan 2025

16. Lingonblad, M., Londos, L., Nilsson, A., Boman, E., Nirme, J., Haake, M.: Virtual blindness - a choice blindness experiment with a virtual experimenter. In: Brinkman, W.-P., Broekens, J., Heylen, D. (eds.) IVA 2015. LNCS (LNAI), vol. 9238, pp. 442–451. Springer, Cham (2015). https://doi.org/10.1007/978-3-319-21996-7_47
17. Curry, O.S.: Morality as cooperation: a problem-centred approach. In: Shackelford, T.K., Hansen, R.D. (eds.) The Evolution of Morality. EP, pp. 27–51. Springer, Cham (2016). https://doi.org/10.1007/978-3-319-19671-8_2
18. Zagal, J.P.: Ethically Notable Videogames: Moral Dilemmas and Gameplay. Brunel University (2009). http://www.digra.org/wp-content/uploads/digital-library/09287.13336.pdf
19. Pärnamets, P., Johansson, P.: Memory distorions resulting from a choice blindness task. Lund University. https://portal.research.lu.se/en/publications/memory-distorions-resulting-from-a-choice-blindness-task
20. Kahneman, D., Tversky, A.: Prospect theory: an analysis of decision under risk. In: Handbook in Financial Economics Series, pp. 99–127. World Scientific (2013). ISSN: 2010-1732. https://doi.org/10.1142/9789814417358_0006. https://www.worldscientific.com/doi/abs/10.1142/9789814417358_0006. Accessed 14 Jan 2025
21. Rieznik, A., et al.: A massive experiment on choice blindness in political decisions: confidence, confabulation, and unconscious detection of self-deception. PLoS ONE **12**(2), e0171108 (2017). https://doi.org/10.1371/journal.pone.0171108
22. Brzeski, S., Heijligers, T., Karimjee, Z.: Gender Discrimination Among Students: Are Females More Subject to Social Manipulation than Males? (2021)
23. Sauerland, M., et al.: These two are different. Yes, they're the same: choice blindness for facial identity. Conscious. Cogn. **40**, 93–104 (2016). ISSN: 1053-8100. https://doi.org/10.1016/j.concog.2016.01.00. https://www.sciencedirect.com/science/article/pii/S1053810016300034
24. Strandberg, T.: The MAGIC MORAL SURVEY Choice Blindness in the Moral Domain. Lund University. https://lup.lub.lu.se/luur/download?func=downloadFile&recordOId=1510645&fileOId=1510646
25. Taya, F., et al.: Manipulation detection and preference alterations in a choice blindness paradigm. PLoS ONE **9**(9), e108515 (2014). https://doi.org/10.1371/journal.pone.0108515
26. The Magic Circle - Game Design Principles and Online Role-play Simulations - Learning & Technology Library (LearnTechLib). https://www.learntechlib.org/primary/p/29109/. Accessed 05 Feb 2024
27. Tomkova, A., Kascakova, D.R., Ondrijova, I.: Analysis of differences in the manifestations of manipulation among traders in terms of gender and education. In: Fifth International Scientific Conference ITEMA Recent Advances in Information Technology, Tourism, Economics, Management and Agriculture, pp. 153–160 (2021). https://doi.org/10.31410/ITEMA.2021.153. https://www.itema-conference.com/manifestations-of-manipulation/. Accessed 16 Jan 2025
28. Wang, S.: Diabetes prediction using random forest in healthcare. HSET **92**, 210–217 (2024). ISSN: 2791-0210. https://doi.org/10.54097/5ndh9a05. https://drpress.org/ojs/index.php/HSET/article/view/19875. Accessed 19 Mar 2025
29. Zou, Z.B., Peng, H., Luo, L.K.: The application of random forest in finance. AMM **740**, 947–951 (2015). ISSN: 1662-7482. https://doi.org/10.4028/www.scientific.net/AMM.740.947. https://www.scientific.net/AMM.740.947. Accessed 19 Mar 2025

30. Al-Zuabi, I.M., Jafar, A., Aljoumaa, K.: Predicting customer's gender and age depending on mobile phone data. J. Big Data **6**(1), 18 (2019). ISSN: 2196-1115. https://doi.org/10.1186/s40537-019-0180-9. https://journalofbigdata.springeropen.com/articles/10.1186/s40537-019-0180-9. Accessed 19 Mar 2025

Math Valley – On Designing an Embodied VR Learning Application for Primary School Students

Marius Grießhammer[1]($\boxtimes$), Christian Kißler[2], Maic Masuch[1], and Joerg-Tobias Kuhn[2]

[1] Entertainment Computing Group, University of Duisburg-Essen, Duisburg, Germany
{marius.griesshammer,maic.masuch}@uni-due.de
[2] Methods in Empirical Educational Research, Department of Rehabilitation Sciences, TU Dortmund University, Dortmund, Germany
{christian.kissler,tobias.kuhn}@tu-dortmund.de

Abstract. We present the user-centered iterative design process of a virtual reality (VR) learning application through a playful embodied learning approach. We developed seven room-scale VR mini-games, which we evaluated in a longitudinal study conducted with second-grade children in a primary school setting, focusing on long-term motivation and how children's behavior in VR changes over time. Over six weeks, twenty children participated in ten VR sessions each, alongside four pre-studies that guided our research. Our findings show our application was highly enjoyable, engaging and comprehensible. Children quickly adapted to VR, some of them getting more confident over time. However, a novelty effect emerged: engagement with the learning content decreased as children became more focused on exploring the virtual environment or testing the boundaries of the VR system. From these findings, we derive key insights for designing embodied learning VR applications, contributing to the growing body of research and highlighting the need for longitudinal studies to evaluate the sustained impact of VR learning beyond the initial excitement.

Keywords: Virtual Reality · Children · Primary School · Education · VR Learning

1 Introduction

Virtual Reality (VR) has gained significant traction across various fields, including the education sector [17,33]. More and more research investigates its effects in various subjects, including mathematics [5,6,38], language learning [32], or biology [31]. While findings on its effectiveness remain mixed [7], studies suggest that VR can enhance engagement and deepen comprehension [17]. However, most existing research focuses on short-term effects [5] or applications designed for older students in secondary and higher education [1,6,31]. As a result, critical factors such as the novelty effect, describing an initial increase in motivation due to the excitement of new technology [43], are often overlooked.

Furthermore, while there are some contributions investigating the practical implementation of VR in primary education [19], research on applications designed specifically for young children remains limited. Additionally, most studies focus on seated or standing VR experiences, while full room-scale applications are scarce (for an example, see [5]). This is particularly relevant for concepts like embodied learning, where physical movement is integral to conceptual understanding [13]. Embodied learning has been shown to enhance learning outcome [25, 27], making room-scale VR an especially promising avenue for educational innovation. However, research on how to effectively design embodied VR learning experiences tailored to children's cognitive and physical needs is still scarce.

To address this gap, we developed a room-scale, embodied VR application to support mathematics learning for second-grade students. Over several weeks, we assessed its feasibility in a primary school setting, focusing on its motivational impact and how children's perceptions and interactions with the application evolved. This study contributes to the growing body of literature on immersive learning technologies by outlining the user-centered iterative design process of an embodied VR learning application for children. Our longitudinal study also offers valuable insights into long-term motivation with VR-based learning, furthering the discourse on optimizing VR for early education.

2 Related Work

2.1 Serious Games and VR

Serious games are digital applications specifically designed to facilitate learning [44]. Despite occasional uncertainties regarding their effectiveness [7, 44], particularly in mathematical domains [42], evidence for their positive effects predominates. For instance, one meta-analysis [35] identified a positive effect of serious games on declarative and procedural knowledge as well as knowledge retention among science students. Similarly, another meta-analysis concludes promising results of serious games to improve primary school students' learning achievement by enhancing motivational and cognitive aspects [28]. However, the design of serious games plays a critical role in their success. Skulmowski and Rey [36] highlight interactivity as a valuable feature, while Krath et al. [23] emphasize the importance of feedback and creating an authentic environment that connects directly to students' prior knowledge. Both Valenza et al. [40] and Wendel et al. [41] provide guidelines for designing serious games, ranging from creating an intuitive interface to developing collaborative multiplayer applications.

Properly designed serious games can increase students' motivation, link learning with positive emotions, and improve academic performance [23, 44]. VR holds particular promise in this context due to its ability to track players' movements and its immersive nature, which research identifies as a key factor for learning success in serious games [7]. It enables novel interactions that other media, such as tablets, cannot, while head-mounted displays (HMDs) may enhance focus by blocking external visual and auditory distractions [17]. Initial positive findings confirm this potential of VR [5, 31]. However, Belter and Lukosch [5] hint at potential distractions by children moving purposefully outside of the playing area. Thus, an attentive, user-centered design process is essential to fully harness the potential of VR learning applications.

2.2 Embodied Cognition and VR

While traditional cognitive theories postulate that cognitive processes occur within an amodal system [4], the theory of embodied cognition posits that learning information involves not only the brain but the entire body through gestures and movements [3,27] by simulating the collected details from the initial sensory and motor experience during knowledge retrieval [3]. Thus, information retrieval can be enhanced when the body and various senses are involved during initial knowledge acquisition [13]. Research shows this to be effective [13,27]: For instance, one study found that participants learned vocabulary better when they associated words with gestures [29], while other studies demonstrate improved learning effects in training scenarios involving physical activation for topics in physics [14,25] or chemistry [20]. In the context of embodied learning of mathematics, Fischer et al. [11] report significantly better learning effects for second-grade students walking along a drawn number line than children in the control group, as well as motivational effects [11]. To further enrich those embodied approaches, technology-supported applications that capture body movements are utilized. Those applications can not only assess the "input" of answers through body movement – allowing children to proceed without waiting for teacher feedback – but they also allow a representation of objects and concepts virtually in various ways while enabling natural interaction with such virtual objects [39]. While some studies show promising results of technology supported embodied learning methods [10,26], results regarding the influence of VR technology on embodied learning are mixed [6,21].

3 The Application: Math Valley

Various models describe how children develop fundamental mathematical understanding [2,22]. On their basis, Fischer et al. [12] identified eight distinct fundamental competencies that children in Germany should master by the end of primary school [37]. Among these competencies is the understanding of number lines, which can be made experiential through tasks designed to engage the body and senses, promoting deeper cognitive processing [11,13]. To support this, we used a user-focused iterative design process to develop *Math Valley*, an embodied VR learning application aimed at strengthening children's understanding of number lines and place value transitions. The application includes seven minigames, six involving a number line (0–20), where children move alongside by walking, "climbing", or riding a virtual train. This mechanic of moving on a number line aims to reinforce the concept of numerical relationships through physical movement congruent with the learning objectives [15]; for example, to represent the number 8, players must move twice as far on the number line and in the real world as they would to represent the number 4. This reinforces the concept of "doubling a value" not only on an abstract cognitive level but also experientially through their body movement and spatial perception.

The seventh mini-game, *Lea's Ship of Mathematics* (Fig. 1a), incorporates virtual Dienes block materials [8]—widely used in German classrooms—to reinforce numerical understanding and place value transitions by requiring children to physically manipulate 1-unit cubes and 10-unit rods through specific hand movements. Children have to construct numerical quantities by adding or removing these block materials, and simulate place value transitions by combining ten cubes into a rod or splitting a rod into ten cubes. A similar mechanic is featured in *Pier Builder* (Fig. 1b), which combines the concepts of Dienes block materials and number lines by requiring players to plan a footbridge with the correct number of planks, constructing their own number line to cross over. Table 1 provides an overview of all mini-games and their objectives.

In each game, children solve math problems through progressively challenging levels, following [34]. Initially, they locate numbers on the number line before advancing to basic addition and subtraction. Higher levels introduce place value transitions, missing-value problems, and alternative numeric sequences. Progression requires correctly answering two out of three questions, while repeated mistakes lead to a downgrade. In line with serious game guidelines [40], each round includes clear instructions and performance feedback. To accommodate varying reading abilities, voice prompts deliver instructions and feedback, triggered only when players return to the starting point to ensure that children travel the intended distances and perform the intended movements appropriately in relation to the numbers displayed. Math problems are also visually embedded in the environment (e.g., in a book). Each game begins with a mandatory tutorial.

The virtual environment (Fig. 1) was designed in a low-poly style with minimal detail to reduce potential distractions. Each game features natural virtual boundaries, such as walls, fences, or bodies of water, to keep players within the designated play area. To enhance engagement and motivation, three mini-games incorporate virtual animals that children can feed by solving math problems. To maintain focus on the task, the animals respond only after the problem is solved.

Fig. 1. Scenes from games included in *Math Valley*. a) *Lea's Ship of Mathematics*. b) *Pier Builder*. c) *Math on Rails*.

Table 1. Overview of the mini-games in *Math Valley*

Name of the Game	Objectives
Flag Trail$^{\triangle}$	Bring the flags to the correct field on the number line Solve the task on the flag to find out which field is correct
Stacking Boxes$^{\triangle}$	Solve the task and create the right amount of food boxes to feed them to the sea lion
Treasure Hunt$^{\triangle}$	Find the hidden treasure under the rocks! Solve the task to seek out the right place
Lea's Ship of Mathematics†	Place the right amount of cubes and base ten blocks into the box to help the onboard computer with its calculations
Pier Builder$^{\triangle\dagger}$	Take the right amount of wood and build a pier to feed your friend the sea lion
Math on Rails $^{\triangledown\dagger}$	Solve the task and load the train with the right amount of coal to get to the next station
Tree Climber$^{\pm}$	Solve the task and deliver the food to the right floor

Embodied learning through △physical movement on and spacial perception of horizontal number line. ±physical movement on and spacial perception of vertical number line (through "climbing"). †physical place value transitions with 1-unit blocks and 10-unit rods. ▽spacial perception of movement on horizontal number line.

3.1 Pretests and Expert Interviews

To evaluate the usability, safety, and feasibility of our VR learning application, we conducted four pretests at different primary schools and five expert interviews. Figure 2 provides an overview of the number of unique participants in each pretest and the subset of games tested. All pretests were separately reviewed and approved by the department's ethics committee before implementation. Written consent was obtained from both parents and children after informing them about the study's objective, potential risks and data protection measures.

The first three pretests evaluated different mini-game concepts regarding their representation and interaction with the number line (Pretests 1 and 3) and place value transitions (Pretest 2). In addition to assessing task comprehension and tutorial clarity, the primary focus was on determining whether the designed game mechanics – such as placing or retrieving objects at the correct position – led to the intended, learning-congruent movements on the number line. Furthermore, enjoyment and usability of the games were examined. While most children found the games engaging and understood the controls, some perceived the virtual animals in certain games as intimidating due to their size, necessitating design adjustments. Additional usability challenges emerged, such as the climbing mechanic in *Tree Climber*, which involved a vertical number line, and unintended cube creation in *Lea's Ship of Mathematics*, both of which required refinement. Despite implementing natural borders in the virtual environment, such as walls or barriers, some children actively tested these boundaries by attempting to walk through them. To address this, we introduced a fade-to-black mechanic that activated if children moved outside the defined play area. To address challenges that may arise during gameplay, a settings-menu was implemented, allowing supervisors to manually adjust settings such as training duration and difficulty levels if problems occur. Overall, the results indicated that the games effectively elicited the intended movements and that children could complete tasks within the ten-minute timeframe, indicating suitable pacing. However, one game was excluded from further development due to a lack of comprehensibility. Tutorials, despite being available, were frequently ignored by children, highlighting the need for more engaging or mandatory instructional sequences.

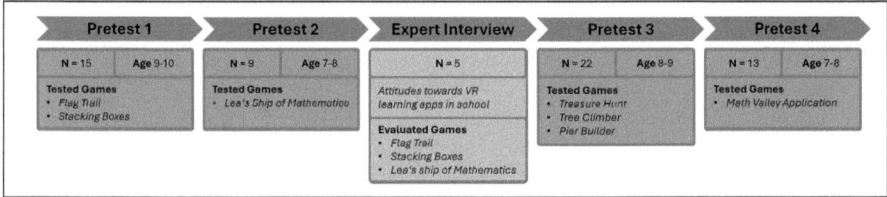

Fig. 2. Over all conducted pretests, a total of 59 students participated.

Following the first two pretests, five expert interviews were conducted with three primary school teachers, a mathematics education specialist, and a game designer. The experts recognized VR's potential for enhancing learning through embodied interactions, particularly in fostering motivation and enabling the presentation of mathematical concepts beyond the constraints of traditional classrooms. They emphasized the importance of explicit connections between in-game tasks and mathematical concepts, clear feedback mechanisms, and tools for teacher monitoring and intervention. Furthermore, they highlighted the necessity of flawless technical functionality, intuitive and congruent embodied interactions, and structured yet engaging virtual environments. Based on their feedback, insufficiently integrated single-choice tasks – originally intended to match in-game activities with corresponding mathematical problems after each round – were removed. Additionally, certain visual features, such as a color gradient designed to indicate proximity to ten, were eliminated; while well-received by children, the experts deemed them inconsistent with standard classroom practices.

The final pretest, conducted with second graders at the partnered primary school, served to test all games for remaining technical issues, assess the effectiveness of previous modifications, and evaluate the feasibility of implementing the VR learning games within the spatial constraints of the school environment.

4 Longitudinal User Study

4.1 Setting and Procedure

The main study, part of a larger research project, was conducted at a primary school in North Rhine-Westphalia (NRW), Germany, during regular school hours. It was coordinated with the teaching staff and approved by our university's Ethics Committee. Parents or legal guardians were informed about the study's purpose, procedure, potential risks, and data handling, providing written consent. Children were also informed in a child-friendly manner and asked for assent. We used the Meta Quest 3, with three different head straps to ensure proper fit. A more in-depth discussion of the study's safety considerations and the implementation of a longitudinal VR study in primary school can be found in [16]. To enhance motivation, children received a "passport" to collect stamps for each completed game. Upon completing the study, participants received a 20€ bookstore gift card and a plush toy.

Due to the space requirements for the number line application (minimum 10×3 m), the study took place in various school locations, including the two main hallways, the auditorium and the gymnasium. The study was conducted in two phases with different groups of children, each consisting of ten sessions (regularly two sessions per week) per child over five to six weeks, depending on how frequently the children were absent from school.

In the first session, children played the game *Flag Trail* for 10 min and completed a custom questionnaire with 13 items on a 5-point Likert scale (5 = strong agreement, 1 = strong disagreement), for which researchers read the questions aloud, and children pointed to a visual rating scale derived from [24] to indicate their answers. The questionnaire covered enjoyment, HMD-comfort, task comprehension, perceived learning, math attitudes, one item on presence (*"I felt as if I were in the world."*), and open-ended feedback. In each subsequent session, children played two *Math Valley*-games for 10 min each. All mini-games were played at least twice over the course of the study, allowing children to progress to higher levels. Short breaks were taken during some sessions due to tracking interruptions or to accommodate children's needs, such as using the restroom or blowing their noses. In these cases, the time spent in VR was recorded, and remaining playtime was rounded up to the nearest minute to maintain session duration. After each session, children completed the questionnaire again. The final session allowed children to choose their favorite game and provide feedback. Before every VR session, the researchers reviewed game controls and rules with the children to ensure clarity and understanding. During gameplay, each child's behavior was observed and documented by at least two researchers.

4.2 Participants

The study involved 20 children (14 female, age: $M = 7.45$, $SD = 0.589$, $range = 7\text{-}9$, $median = 7$) from second-grade. All participants could communicate in German, and none had epilepsy or wore glasses.

Mathematics proficiency varied, with two children rated as good, two as average, and the rest identified as struggling with mathematics. This selection aimed to explore the behaviors of children who may face difficulties, dislike the subject, or experience math anxiety.

4.3 Results

In total, 20 children participated in 197 sessions, playing a combined total of 354 ten-minute games. Two children did not complete the full ten sessions due to extended absences from school (participating in nine and eight sessions).

Safety and Comfort. In four of the 197 sessions, cases of cybersickness symptoms were recorded, with one session having to be terminated prematurely because the child reported discomfort and nausea. Additionally, despite continuous supervision by research staff, there were three incidents of physical collisions with real world objects due to children moving too fast for Meta Quest's guardian system ($n = 2$) or a misalignment in said system ($n = 1$). No further incidents affecting physical health were observed, and the comfort of the HMD was generally rated positively across 354 VR experiences ($M = 3.94$, $SD = 1.4$). However, comfort ratings varied significantly, with some children consistently comfortable and others experiencing discomfort occasionally. One child always found the HMD uncomfortable but chose to continue playing nonetheless.

Math Valley. The evaluation of the Math Valley application is summarized in Table 2. Overall, the application was highly rated in terms of enjoyment, visual design, and the motivation to continue training. Although several children occasionally removed their HMD to establish eye contact or looked underneath it, the sense of presence was rated positively. This was reflected in their behavior, as many reacted naturally to elements in the virtual world, such as interacting with the sea lion featured in two of the games (see Fig. 1b). Game controls, task instructions, and feedback from the application were well understood by the children. However, self-assessments regarding learning outcomes were more variable (*"I learned something."*: $M = 3.78$, $SD = 1.63$; *"I learned something new."*: $M = 3.61$, $SD = 1.68$; *"I understood something I did not understand before."*: $M = 3.45$, $SD = 1.7$). This should be interpreted with caution, as follow-up questioning revealed inconsistencies in the children's responses. For instance, some children initially claimed to have learned something but responded, *"I forgot what I learned"* when asked to elaborate. Others provided responses that

Table 2. Descriptive results of custom-designed questionnaire regarding *Math Valley*

	M	SD
Enjoyment	4.63	0.934
Visual design	4.62	0.983
Motivation to Continue	4.74	0.819
Sense of Presence	4.41	1.16
Comprehensibility of Game Controls	4.55	1.02
Comprehensibility of Task Instruction	4.73	0.753
Comprehensibility of Feedback	4.35	1.22

suggested a misunderstanding of the question's intent, such as *"I learned that I should not run in VR"*.

Children in VR. During the VR sessions, children quickly developed competence in interacting with the VR system. By the end of the first session, most had adapted to hand tracking for object manipulation, which became natural by the second session. However, practical challenges were observed, such as long sleeves interfering with tracking and the system struggling to maintain tracking when children looked around or stretched their arms beyond the field of view. By the second to third week, children's interactions became more independent and they moved more confidently and naturally, in some cases running within Meta Quest's guardian boundaries; especially in the gymnasium. As the study progressed, some children began testing these boundaries: Despite the built-in fade-to-black system, they explored beyond the designated play area, walking over water or through walls. Some children also learned to replicate the researchers' calibration gestures, necessitating recalibration to ensure a correctly aligned play area. Additionally, a few children explored moving outside the guardian system, finding the Passthrough mode temporarily more engaging than the application.

Most importantly, while engagement was consistently high, children's motivation to complete in-game tasks appeared to decline over time. Instead, they began to explore the VR environment and test the system's limits. Additionally, in some cases as tasks became more difficult, children resorted to finger counting or stood thinking, rather than engaging in the intended movement.

5 Discussion

We developed an application for embodied mathematics learning in VR for primary school children through an iterative, user-centered design process. After four pretests, this application was tested in a longitudinal study conducted with 20 children over several weeks in a primary school setting. In total, the study encompassed 197 VR-sessions, enabling us to draw several conclusions. These include insights into designing VR learning applications for primary school students and into how children's behavior and motivation in VR evolves over time.

Embodied Game Mechanics. In most of our mini-games, the core mechanic involved transporting an object to or from the correct position on a number line, aiming to reinforce mathematical concepts not only on a cognitive level but also through physical movement. This approach was intended to make numerical relationships perceptible through spatial interaction. Results indicate that game mechanics and controls were intuitive and enjoyable for second graders. However, our study revealed that this did not work equally well for all children. Many struggling learners resorted to finger counting or stood still, thinking, rather than engaging in the intended movement. While some children demonstrated the intended behavior, it became less frequent as task difficulty increased. This suggests a need for further refinement in game design to actively encourage movement. One possible improvement would be to structure tasks such that, for example, in addition or subtraction problems, only the first part of the equation is initially displayed, with the second part unlocking only when the child reaches the corresponding position. Additionally, tutorials should be redesigned not only to explain game mechanics and objectives but also to further emphasize the importance of congruent movement throughout the task.

Motivation. While motivation for using VR remained consistently high and the children expressed a high desire to continue with the experiment, engagement with the mathematical tasks declined over repeated sessions, indicating a novelty effect [9]. By the fourth session, some children expressed dissatisfaction with replaying familiar games, and disappointment increased when no new content was introduced beyond the seventh session. One child, initially engaged, later prioritized exploring the virtual environment over mathematical tasks, while others became distracted when struggling to complete math exercises. This novelty effect is not specific to VR and has also been documented in other domains, such as exergame research [30]. Children's daily mood also influenced engagement. Initial excitement gave way to emotional fluctuations as they grew more comfortable with the environment and researchers. On difficult days, children were more easily distracted or disengaged. As emotional regulation is not yet fully developed at this age [18], close collaboration with teachers and caregivers is essential to support children's learning experiences and address emotional fluctuations that may impact engagement in VR-based learning.

These findings highlight the need for longitudinal studies to assess sustained engagement in VR learning. While children were highly enthusiastic in short-term pretests and early in the longitudinal study, engagement with mathematical content declined over time. To enhance long-term motivation in Math Valley, potential improvements include greater variation in animals, environments, and levels, an overarching, captivating narrative, or a reward system where points earned from math tasks unlock cosmetic customizations in the game's lobby [40]. However, it is crucial that these motivational elements do not overshadow the core learning content, which must remain the primary focus.

Safety and Boundaries. Across 197 training sessions, instances of cybersickness and collisions were very rare, with no other health-related issues reported. While headset comfort was generally rated positively, two children consistently found the headset uncomfortable despite adjustments with different head straps, suggesting that current HMD designs may not adequately accommodate all children for a comfortable fit. Pre-study assessments also revealed that controllers were too large for some children, complicating button interactions and resulting in the implementation of hand tracking – which functioned well overall but occasionally failed due to obstructing sleeves or head movements disrupting tracking.

Despite these challenges, children adapted quickly to VR and reported high enjoyment. Even initially shy participants overcame hesitation within the first few sessions. Increased familiarity led to more natural movements, including jumping and running, which could pose safety risks in unsupervised settings.

Consistent with prior findings [5], some children deliberately tested system limits by ignoring the virtual boundaries and exiting the play area, triggering the fade-to-black function. When this visual restriction was initially ignored, the fade-to-black sometimes prevented children from returning to the play area without assistance. Therefore, we recommend using the Passthrough mode of the Quest 3 instead, allowing children to see their surroundings and navigate more easily. While this mode seems to excite the children even further, our findings suggest this excitement decreases while children adapt to VR. Although the natural boundaries of *Math Valley* could limit boundary testing during the early sessions, they proved insufficient in the long term. The best approach is to harness this exploratory drive in the game design. Developers should build VR learning experiences that integrate and utilize children's curiosity and exploration tendencies, turning them into a valuable part of the learning process.

However supervision by trained personnel remains essential. Maintaining a live stream of the headset display proved critical for responding to children's questions and ensuring safety, a necessity highlighted in pretests, expert interviews and main study. Effective implementation of VR learning applications thus requires both well-designed content and the presence of knowledgeable supervisors to ensure an effective and most importantly safe learning experience.

Tutorials. Tutorials required significant refinement throughout the prestudies. Initially, auditory instructions were ignored by the children in order to explore the VR environment. To address this, an initial pause and a lobby area were added to allow children to familiarize themselves with VR and the environment before beginning tasks. However, some children still struggled with grasping mechanics and failed to pay attention to tutorial instructions. To mitigate this, interactions were explicitly explained and demonstrated, and children were provided with printed images of the application before entering VR. This approach, combined with a virtual and interactive step by step tutorial, significantly improved comprehension. Furthermore, to better direct children's focus in VR and ensure that more children actively listen, we should avoid using a disembodied voice from off-screen in the future. Instead, incorporating an avatar could provide a visual reference, potentially making instructions more engaging and effective.

Environment. The visual design of *Math Valley* was rated positive. Many children praised the presence of animals in the virtual environment and expressed a desire for additional species. However, given that some children were initially intimidated by the existing virtual animals (e.g., sea lions or squirrels), caution is warranted. Pretests suggested that the perceived size of virtual animals relative to the children plays a critical role in their comfort level. Presence was also rated high, likely due to high immersion levels of VR [17]. While immersion can enhance focus, our findings suggest it does not guarantee engagement with learning content. Despite minimizing distractions, children still diverted attention. Developers should consider that every object in a VR environment, even a simple tree, can serve as a potential distraction. But rather than creating a completely stimulus-free environment, it is crucial to ensure that the learning content remains central through carefully designed game mechanics.

5.1 Limitations and Future Work

Some of the here presented findings are based on observations and informal questioning rather than standardized questionnaires. They are also based on a relatively small number of participants. Additionally, our custom-made questionnaire was not pre-tested, which led to some items being misunderstood by the children, deviating from our intended meaning. Generally, self-reports from children using Likert scales are challenging, as they tend to exhibit response biases toward extremes. We also observed that some children rushed through the questionnaire, attempting to answer before the researcher had fully read the question. Therefore, results have to be interpreted with care.

These limitations highlight the need for further research to assess long-term effects in a more controlled framework. More extended studies are essential to investigate the effectiveness of learning applications in terms of both learning outcomes and motivation. Additionally, it would be of interest to examine how children's attitudes towards VR and learning content evolve over time. Given that VR is still far from being regularly implemented in schools, the effects of brief interventions and their long-term impact warrant further exploration.

6 Conclusion

In this contribution, we report on the user-centered design process of our VR mathematics learning application for second graders, developed using an embodied learning approach, and its evaluation through a longitudinal study with 20 children over several weeks. The pretesting phase was crucial in refining the design and mechanics of the VR learning games, ensuring usability and alignment with educational objectives. Insights from both children and experts facilitated iterative improvements, supporting a robust implementation in the main study. While embodied VR learning applications hold significant potential for engagement, their successful implementation requires careful attention to usability, supervision, sustained motivation, and the alignment of movements with the learning content. Clear instructional design and adaptability to individual needs are essential for maximizing their educational effectiveness.

Our main study allowed rare insights into how children's behavior and motivation in VR evolves over time. The games were well received, with high ratings for enjoyment, presence, and comprehensibility. A novelty effect was observed, highlighting the need to integrate features specifically designed to maintain long-term motivation. Our findings emphasize the importance of longitudinal studies in evaluating sustained motivation and assessing the influence of VR-based learning beyond the initial excitement. To fully understand the educational potential of VR, future research should explore the interplay of novelty effects, emotional variability, and adaptation processes over extended periods. We therefore call for further long-term studies to explore these aspects in greater depth.

Acknowledgements. We thank our collaborating primary schools and all participating students and their parents as well as all interviewed experts for their time and insight. We also thank H. Dang, A. Föllner, T. Fürtges, L. Gilhaus, V. Golz, D. Heinrichs, L. Jacob, D. Morvai, S. Müller, S. Prehn, J. Reiter, M. Rudolph, E. Schnorbus, K. Spahija, L. Stommel and N. Thorissen for their dedicated efforts throughout this project.

Disclosure of Interests. As part of the project "ELI-VR" (Ko-2022-0004), this work was supported by the Mercator Research Center Ruhr (Mercur) 2023-2025.

References

1. Allcoat, D., Von Mühlenen, A.: Learning in virtual reality: effects on performance, emotion and engagement. Res. Learn. Technol. **26**, 13 (2018). https://doi.org/10.25304/rlt.v26.2140. https://journal.alt.ac.uk/index.php/rlt/article/view/2140
2. Aster, M., Lorenz, J.H.: Rechenstörungen bei Kindern: Neurowissenschaft, Psychologie, Pädagogik. Vandenhoeck & Ruprecht, Göttingen, 2 edn (2013). https://doi.org/10.13109/9783666462580. https://www.vr-elibrary.de/doi/book/10.13109/9783666462580
3. Barsalou, L.W.: Grounded cognition. Annu. Rev. Psychol. **59**(1), 617–645 (2008). https://doi.org/10.1146/annurev.psych.59.103006.093639. https://www.annualreviews.org/doi/10.1146/annurev.psych.59.103006.093639
4. Barsalou, L.W.: Grounded cognition: past, present, and future. Top. Cogn. Sci. **2**(4), 716–724 (2010). https://doi.org/10.1111/j.1756-8765.2010.01115.x. https://onlinelibrary.wiley.com/doi/abs/10.1111/j.1756-8765.2010.01115.x
5. Belter, M., Lukosch, H.: Towards a virtual reality math game for learning in schools - a user study. In: 2022 IEEE Conference on Virtual Reality and 3D User Interfaces Abstracts and Workshops (VRW), Christchurch, New Zealand, pp. 808–809. IEEE (2022). https://doi.org/10.1109/VRW55335.2022.00255. https://ieeexplore.ieee.org/document/9757619/
6. Chatain, J., et al.: Grasping derivatives: teaching mathematics through embodied interactions using tablets and virtual reality. In: Interaction Design and Children, Braga, Portugal, pp. 98–108. ACM (2022). https://doi.org/10.1145/3501712.3529748. https://dl.acm.org/doi/10.1145/3501712.3529748
7. Checa, D., Bustillo, A.: A review of immersive virtual reality serious games to enhance learning and training. Multimedia Tools Appl. **79**(9), 5501–5527 (2020). https://doi.org/10.1007/s11042-019-08348-9
8. Dienes, Z.P.: The teaching of mathematics–III: the growth of mathematical concepts in children through experience. Educ. Res. **2**(1), 9–28 (1959). https://doi.org/10.1080/0013188590020102. http://www.tandfonline.com/doi/abs/10.1080/0013188590020102
9. Elston, D.M.: The novelty effect. J. Am. Acad. Dermatol. **85**(3), 565–566 (2021). https://doi.org/10.1016/j.jaad.2021.06.846. https://www.jaad.org/article/S0190-9622(21)01987-3/fulltext
10. Fischer, U., Moeller, K., Bientzle, M., Cress, U., Nuerk, H.C.: Sensori-motor spatial training of number magnitude representation. Psychon. Bull. Rev. **18**(1), 177–183 (2011). https://doi.org/10.3758/s13423-010-0031-3

11. Fischer, U., Moeller, K., Huber, S., Cress, U., Nuerk, H.C.: Full-body movement in numerical trainings: a pilot study with an interactive whiteboard. Int. J. Serious Games **2**(4) (2015). https://doi.org/10.17083/ijsg.v2i4.93. http://journal.seriousgamessociety.org/index.php/IJSG/article/view/93
12. Fischer, U., Roesch, S., Moeller, K.: Diagnostik und Förderung bei Rechenschwäche: Messen wir, was wir fördern wollen? (german): Dyscalculia diagnosis and treatment: Are we measuring what we want to improve? (english). Lernen und Lernstörungen **6**(1), 25–38 (2017). https://doi.org/10.1024/2235-0977/a000160
13. Fugate, J.M.B., Macrine, S.L., Cipriano, C.: The role of embodied cognition for transforming learning. Int. J. Sch. Educ. Psychol. **7**(4), 274–288 (2019). https://doi.org/10.1080/21683603.2018.1443856. https://www.tandfonline.com/doi/full/10.1080/21683603.2018.1443856
14. Gelsomini, M., Leonardi, G., Garzotto, F.: Embodied learning in immersive smart spaces. In: Proceedings of the 2020 CHI Conference on Human Factors in Computing Systems, Honolulu, HI, USA, pp. 1–14. ACM (2020). https://doi.org/10.1145/3313831.3376667. https://dl.acm.org/doi/10.1145/3313831.3376667
15. Georgiou, Y., Ioannou, A.: Developing, enacting and evaluating a learning experience design for technology-enhanced embodied learning in math classrooms. TechTrends **65**(1), 38–50 (2021). https://doi.org/10.1007/s11528-020-00543-y
16. Grießhammer, M., Masuch, M.: 200 VR-sessions with children – practical challenges and educational insights into conducting a longitudinal VR-study in primary school. In: Di Iorio, A., et al. (eds.) ICEC 2025. LNCS, vol. 16042, pp. xx–yy. Springer, Cham (2025)
17. Hamad, A., Jia, B.: How virtual reality technology has changed our lives: an overview of the current and potential applications and limitations. Int. J. Environ. Res. Public Health **19**(18), 11278 (2022). https://doi.org/10.3390/ijerph191811278. https://www.mdpi.com/1660-4601/19/18/11278
18. Hollerer, L., Kohl, A.: Accompanying the development of emotion regulation: a psychological and pedagogical topic in pre- and primary-school. Psihološka obzorja **31**(1), 526–531 (2022). https://doi.org/10.20419/2022.31.560. http://journals.uni-lj.si/psiholoska-obzorja/article/view/21262
19. Hui, J., Zhou, Y., Oubibi, M., Di, W., Zhang, L., Zhang, S.: Research on art teaching practice supported by virtual reality (VR) technology in the primary schools. Sustainability **14**(3), 1246 (2022). https://doi.org/10.3390/su14031246. https://www.mdpi.com/2071-1050/14/3/1246
20. Johnson-Glenberg, M.C., Birchfield, D.A., Tolentino, L., Koziupa, T.: Collaborative embodied learning in mixed reality motion-capture environments: two science studies. J. Educ. Psychol. **106**(1), 86–104 (2014). https://doi.org/10.1037/a0034008. http://doi.apa.org/getdoi.cfm?doi=10.1037/a0034008
21. Khorasani, S., Victor Syiem, B., Nawaz, S., Knibbe, J., Velloso, E.: Hands-on or hands-off: deciphering the impact of interactivity on embodied learning in VR. Comput. Educ. X Reality **3**, 13 (2023). https://doi.org/10.1016/j.cexr.2023.100037. https://www.sciencedirect.com/science/article/pii/S2949678023000314
22. Krajewski, K., Renner, A., Nieding, G., Schneider, W.: Frühe Förderung von mathematischen Kompetenzen im Vorschulalter. In: Roßbach, H.G., Blossfeld, H.P. (eds.) Frühpädagogische Förderung in Institutionen: Zeitschrift für Erziehungswissenschaft, pp. 91–103. VS Verlag für Sozialwissenschaften, Wiesbaden (2009). https://doi.org/10.1007/978-3-531-91452-7_7
23. Krath, J., Schürmann, L., Von Korflesch, H.F.: Revealing the theoretical basis of gamification: a systematic review and analysis of theory in research on gamification, serious games and game-based learning. Comput. Hum. Behav. **125**,

106963 (2021). https://doi.org/10.1016/j.chb.2021.106963. https://linkinghub.elsevier.com/retrieve/pii/S0747563221002867
24. Krinzinger, H., et al.: German version of the math anxiety questionnaire (FRA) for 6-to 9-year-old children. Zeitschrift fur Kinder-und Jugendpsychiatrie und Psychotherapie **35**(5), 341–351 (2007)
25. Lindgren, R., Tscholl, M., Wang, S., Johnson, E.: Enhancing learning and engagement through embodied interaction within a mixed reality simulation. Comput. Educ. **95**, 174–187 (2016). https://doi.org/10.1016/j.compedu.2016.01.001. https://linkinghub.elsevier.com/retrieve/pii/S036013151630001X
26. Link, T., Moeller, K., Huber, S., Fischer, U., Nuerk, H.C.: Walk the number line – an embodied training of numerical concepts. Trends Neurosci. Educ. **2**(2), 74–84 (2013). https://doi.org/10.1016/j.tine.2013.06.005. https://linkinghub.elsevier.com/retrieve/pii/S2211949313000197
27. Link, T., et al.: Mathe mit der Matte – Verkörperlichtes Training basisnumerischer Kompetenzen. Zeitschrift für Erziehungswissenschaft **17**(2), 257–277 (2014). https://doi.org/10.1007/s11618-014-0533-2
28. Lopez, J.Y.A., Huaycho, R.N.N., Santos, F.I.Y., Mendoza, F.T., Paucar, F.H.R.: The impact of serious games on learning in primary education: a systematic literature review. Int. J. Learn. Teach. Educ. Res. **22**(3), 379–395 (2023). https://ijlter.org/index.php/ijlter/article/view/7028
29. Macedonia, M., Klimesch, W.: Long-term effects of gestures on memory for foreign language words trained in the classroom. Mind Brain Educ. **8**(2), 74–88 (2014). https://doi.org/10.1111/mbe.12047. https://onlinelibrary.wiley.com/doi/abs/10.1111/mbe.12047
30. Macvean, A., Robertson, J.: Understanding exergame users' physical activity, motivation and behavior over time. In: Proceedings of the SIGCHI Conference on Human Factors in Computing Systems, CHI 2013, pp. 1251–1260. Association for Computing Machinery, New York (2013). https://doi.org/10.1145/2470654.2466163. https://dl.acm.org/doi/10.1145/2470654.2466163
31. Pang, C.G., Devi, S., Wong, D., Cai, Y., Ba, R.: The use of immersive virtual reality technology to deepen learning in Singapore schools. In: Cai, Y., van Joolingen, W., Veermans, K. (eds.) Virtual and Augmented Reality, Simulation and Serious Games for Education. GMSE, pp. 45–59. Springer, Singapore (2021). https://doi.org/10.1007/978-981-16-1361-6_5
32. Parmaxi, A.: Virtual reality in language learning: a systematic review and implications for research and practice. Interact. Learn. Environ. **31**(1), 172–184 (2023). https://doi.org/10.1080/10494820.2020.1765392
33. Radianti, J., Majchrzak, T.A., Fromm, J., Wohlgenannt, I.: A systematic review of immersive virtual reality applications for higher education: Design elements, lessons learned, and research agenda. Comput. Educ. **147**, 103778 (2020). https://doi.org/10.1016/j.compedu.2019.103778. https://www.sciencedirect.com/science/article/pii/S0360131519303276
34. Ricken, G., Fritz, A., Balzer, L.: Mathematik und Rechnen - Test zur Erfassung von Konzepten im Vorschulalter (MARKO-d). Ein Beispiel für einen niveauorientierten Ansatz. Empirische Sonderpädagogik **3**(3), 256–271 (2011). https://doi.org/10.25656/01:9327
35. Riopel, M., et al.: Impact of serious games on science learning achievement compared with more conventional instruction: an overview and a meta-analysis. Stud. Sci. Educ. **55**(2), 169–214 (2020). https://doi.org/10.1080/03057267.2019.1722420. https://www.tandfonline.com/doi/full/10.1080/03057267.2019.1722420

36. Skulmowski, A., Rey, G.D.: Embodied learning: introducing a taxonomy based on bodily engagement and task integration. Cogn. Res. Princ. Implic. **3**(1), 6 (2018). https://doi.org/10.1186/s41235-018-0092-9. https://cognitiveresearchjournal.springeropen.com/articles/10.1186/s41235-018-0092-9
37. Stanat, P., Schipolowski, S., Schneider, R., Sachse, K.A., Weirich, S., Henschel, S.: IQB-Bildungstrend 2021. Kompetenzen in den Fächern Deutsch und Mathematik am Ende der 4. Jahrgangsstufe im dritten Ländervergleich (2022). https://doi.org/10.31244/9783830996064. https://www.waxmann.com/buch4606
38. Sternig, C., Spitzer, M., Ebner, M.: Learning in a virtual environment: implementation and evaluation of a VR math-game. In: Kurubacak, G., Altinpulluk, H. (eds.) Mobile Technologies and Augmented Reality in Open Education, pp. 175–199. IGI Global Scientific Publishing (2017). https://doi.org/10.4018/978-1-5225-2110-5.ch009. https://www.igi-global.com/gateway/chapter/www.igi-global.com/gateway/chapter/178242
39. Tran, C., Smith, B., Buschkuehl, M.: Support of mathematical thinking through embodied cognition: nondigital and digital approaches. Cogn. Res. Princ. Implic. **2**(1), 18 (2017). https://doi.org/10.1186/s41235-017-0053-8. http://cognitiveresearchjournal.springeropen.com/articles/10.1186/s41235-017-0053-8
40. Valenza, M.V., Gasparini, I., da S. Hounsell, M.: Serious game design for children: a set of guidelines and their validation. J. Educ. Technol. Soc. **22**(3), 19–31 (2019). https://www.jstor.org/stable/26896707
41. Wendel, V., Gutjahr, M., Göbel, S., Steinmetz, R.: Designing collaborative multiplayer serious games. Educ. Inf. Technol. **18**(2), 287–308 (2013). https://doi.org/10.1007/s10639-012-9244-6
42. Young, M.F., et al.: Our princess is in another castle: a review of trends in serious gaming for education. Rev. Educ. Res. **82**(1), 61–89 (2012). https://doi.org/10.3102/0034654312436980
43. Zender, R., Buchner, J., Schäfer, C., Wiesche, D., Kelly, K., Tüshaus, L.: Virtual Reality für Schüler:innen: Ein «Beipackzettel» für die Durchführung immersiver Lernszenarien im schulischen Kontext. MedienPädagogik: Zeitschrift für Theorie und Praxis der Medienbildung **47**, 26–52 (2022). https://doi.org/10.21240/mpaed/47/2022.04.02.X. https://www.medienpaed.com/article/view/1399
44. Zhonggen, Y.: A meta-analysis of use of serious games in education over a decade. Int. J. Comput. Games Technol. **2019**, 8 (2019). https://doi.org/10.1155/2019/4797032. https://www.hindawi.com/journals/ijcgt/2019/4797032/

200 VR-Sessions with Children – Practical Challenges and Educational Insights Into Conducting a Longitudinal VR-Study in Primary School

Marius Grießhammer[(✉)] and Maic Masuch

Entertainment Computing Group, University of Duisburg-Essen, Duisburg, Germany
{marius.griesshammer,maic.masuch}@uni-due.de

Abstract. We present a longitudinal VR-study conducted with second-graders, focusing on the practical challenges and insights gained from integrating immersive room-scale VR math learning in a primary school setting. Over six weeks, twenty children participated in a total of 197 training sessions, resulting in 3540 min of VR gameplay. Our primary goal is to provide methodological insights into the feasibility and impact of VR as an educational tool for young children. Our findings indicate that the VR sessions were generally highly engaging, safe and suitable. Instances of cybersickness were rare; however, issues with headset fit and isolated collisions occurred, underscoring the need for sufficiently large play areas with proper buffer zones and dedicated supervision. Children quickly developed VR competence and demonstrated increased confidence in interacting with the virtual environment and engaging with learning content over time. Our findings contribute to understanding the potential of VR for young children in educational contexts, offering key insights into feasibility and safety of VR learning applications and methodological considerations for future studies.

Keywords: Virtual Reality · Children · Primary School · Education · VR Learning

1 Introduction

As Virtual Reality (VR) continues to gain popularity, its use among children is becoming more widespread [14]. Studies suggest that many children are increasingly aware of and excited about VR technology [29], making it an appealing tool for educational purposes. An expanding body of studies explores the impact of VR-based learning applications across various subjects, including mathematics [3,5,24], biology [1,20], or history [13]. While findings remain mixed [6], existing research suggests that VR can enhance student engagement and interest, ultimately supporting deeper comprehension of learning content [9]. However most studies have been designed for older learners in middle and high school [5,20] or university settings [1]. Research on VR learning applications for primary school students remains relatively limited. While some studies have explored the use of VR in primary education [3,12,13], such investigations are rare and predominantly focus on short-term effects. Moreover, most existing studies examine VR experiences in seated or standing positions, whereas fully immersive room-scale VR applications—and the practical challenges associated with their implementation in schools—have received little attention.

To bridge this gap, we developed a room-scale, embodied VR application tailored to support mathematics learning for second-grade students. The application was tested over several weeks in a primary school setting to assess its feasibility in everyday classroom environments and to observe how children's perception of and interaction with VR evolved over time. This study contributes to the expanding research on immersive technologies in education by exploring the logistical and practical challenges of integrating VR into primary schools, as well as examining how prolonged exposure affects children's familiarity, comfort, motivation, and engagement with VR.

2 Virtual Reality for Children

VR has become increasingly prominent in the educational sector [9,22], with research indicating that many children are excited about its potential [29]. However, some concerns remain regarding ethical implications [14,15] as well as potential physical health risks associated with its use [30]. Manufacturers of head-mounted displays (HMDs) implement age restrictions for their devices, yet these restrictions lack transparency regarding their underlying rationale. Meta sets the minimum age recommendation for its *Meta Quest 3* to ten years [19], while Sony advises that its *PlayStation VR2* is suitable for users aged 12 and above [23]. Similarly, Pico sets its restriction at 13 years referencing its data privacy regulations [21]. In contrast, HTC does not specify an exact age but states that its *Vive Focus Vision* is "not designed for children" and advises against use by "young children" [11]. None of these manufacturers provide research-based justification for these age limits.

Tychsen and Foeller [26] examined the impact of VR on children, focusing on areas such as stereoscopic vision and balance, and found no adverse short-term effects. Additionally, symptoms of eyestrain and cybersickness were minimal in their study, and they are not alone in suggesting that children might be less prone to cybersickness than adults [14,26]. Similarly, one meta-analysis about the risks of VR to children and adolescents [15] drew a generally positive conclusion regarding eyestrain and cybersickness, while emphasizing the need for more long-term studies and cautioning against excessive screen time. It further suggests that VR's cognitive effects on children are predominantly positive, with no adverse impacts identified [15]. Early studies on VR learning applications for children further support this optimism, demonstrating improved comprehension of learning content, increased creativity [12], and enhanced learner engagement and enjoyment [3,12]. Similar findings apply to serious games as a whole. When well-designed, they can boost students' motivation, foster positive emotional associations with learning, and improve academic performance [16,31]. However, researchers highlight risks such as gaming-related addictions [15], online harassment [14], privacy violations, and the exclusion of vulnerable groups [30]. These issues are mirrored in parental concerns about VR use, further emphasizing the need for open communication and stronger parental supervision [14].

In school environments, VR applications face additional challenges. Current research on VR in primary education is scarce, with most studies conducted in experimental settings rather than within the context of everyday school life. Practical challenges include device hygiene, as HMDs are shared among multiple users, and ergonomic issues, such as whether headsets are too large or uncomfortable for younger children. Some researchers have addressed these concerns by modifying headsets with foam inserts to improve their fit for smaller users [28]. Additionally, especially room-scale VR applications need a lot of space. A critical feature of most VR systems is the manufacturer-implemented guardian system, designed to create a virtual boundary to ensure user safety. However, it remains unclear how children interact with and adapt to such systems over the long term. While Belter [3] observed that children actively tested and occasionally ignored these boundaries during their evaluation, further research is needed to understand whether this behavior persists or evolves over time. This uncertainty highlights the need for supervision and additional space beyond the designated play area.

3 Longitudinal User Study

3.1 The Application: Math Valley

As part of a larger research project, we developed a VR learning application for mathematics following an embodied learning approach [2,18] to help children understand basic mathematical competencies such as the number line and place value transitions, using a user-centered, iterative design process. *Math Valley* [7] consists of seven mini-games. In six of these games, children solve mathematical tasks by moving through different means such as walking or "climbing" along a virtual number line ranging from 0 to 20. Figure 1 presents a selection of these.

A key aspect of the design is that, following the principles of embodied learning, children are expected to engage with the learning content not only cognitively but also through physical interaction. Players must navigate freely in a manner congruent with the learning objectives to complete their assigned tasks. For instance, when solving an addition problem, players move along a number line by first taking as many steps as indicated by the first summand, then continuing with the number of steps corresponding to the second summand, ultimately reaching the correct result. Thus, the mini-games are explicitly designed to require active and unrestricted physical movement within the virtual environment. As a result, they necessitate room-scale VR and, consequently, a substantial amount of physical space to ensure safe and effective interaction. All games

Fig. 1. Scenes from mini-games included in *Math Valley*. a) In *Stacking Boxes* players have to create the right amount of food boxes to feed them to a sea lion. b) In *Treasure Hunt* players have to find a treasure under the correct stone. c) In *Tree Climber* food needs to be delivered to the animals on the correct floor.

incorporate natural virtual boundaries, such as walls or bodies of water, that are contextually integrated into the game environments in order to make children stay within the designated play area.

3.2 Setting and Procedure

We conducted a longitudinal study over several weeks at a primary school in North Rhine-Westphalia (NRW), Germany, during regular school hours. Participants were recruited in coordination with their teachers, and parents or legal guardians were informed via letter about the study's objectives, potential risks (e.g., discomfort or cybersickness), and data protection measures. Written parental consent was obtained, including optional permission for photographs. Parents had the opportunity to ask questions, engage with researchers, and observe the study. After parental consent, the study was explained to the children, who provided their own assent and were informed they could take breaks and withdraw from the study at any time. They were asked frequently about their well being and if they wanted to take a break. All children were rewarded with a 20€ bookstore gift card and a plush toy upon completing the study. As an additional incentive, children received a "passport" or stamp card to collect stamps for completed games. The study design was reviewed and approved by our university's ethics committee prior to its implementation.

The study took place in various school locations, specifically the auditorium, gymnasium, and main hallways. Prior to each VR session, researchers went over the game controls and rules with the participants to ensure they were clear and well-understood. The games were played using the Meta Quest 3 headset, selected for its lightweight design to minimize potential neck strain. To accommodate individual needs, three different types of head straps were used.

In the first and last session, only one mini-game was played. Every other session consisted of two games. Each game was played for ten minutes, resulting in a total VR playtime of at least 20 min in sessions 2–9. Any interruptions (e.g., bathroom breaks or brief pauses) were recorded, with remaining playtime rounded up to the next full minute to ensure a minimum of ten minutes per game. After each session, children completed a custom-designed questionnaire. In the final session, they could choose their favorite game to play.

3.3 Measures

During gameplay, at least two researchers per child observed and documented their behavior. As part of a larger research project, children completed pre- and posttests, along with a custom-designed 13-item questionnaire assessing enjoyment, HMD comfort, presence, perceived learning outcomes, and usability aspects such as task comprehension on a 5-point Likert scale (5 = strong agreement, 1 = strong disagreement). Figure 2 provides an overview of the study procedure and conducted questionnaires. However, pre- and posttests are beyond the scope of this paper and will not be discussed here.

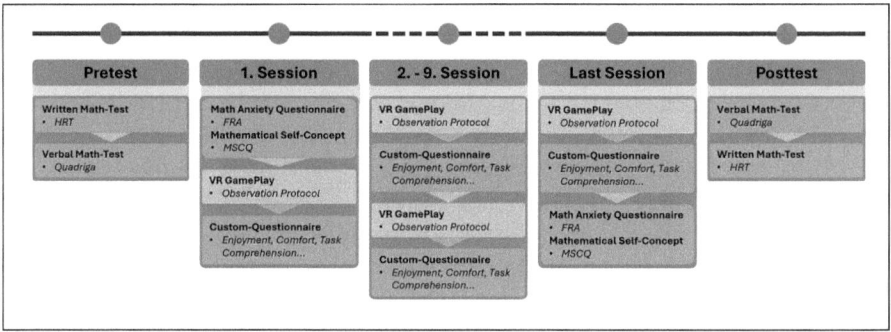

Fig. 2. Study Procedure. The study was conducted over a period of five to six weeks per child, depending on individual attendance at school. Ideally, each child participated in two sessions per week. References to HRT [8], Quadriga [27], FRA [17], and MSCQ [4] are included in the reference list for interested readers.

3.4 Participants

The study included 20 students in second grade (14 female, age: $M = 7.45$, $SD = 0.589$, $range = 7\text{--}9$, $median = 7$) with varying proficiency in mathematics. None of the participants had a history of epilepsy or required corrective eyewear. All children were fluent in German and able to effectively communicate with the researchers. The study was conducted at the primary school facilities.

4 Results

With the exception of two children who missed one and two sessions due to prolonged school absences, all participants completed the full set of ten sessions. In total, the 20 children participated in 197 sessions, during which 354 ten-minute VR sessions were conducted, as sessions 2–9 each included two mini-games.

Physical Health. Over the course of the study, one session had to be discontinued due to a child experiencing discomfort and nausea. In two additional cases, children reported symptoms of cybersickness after completing their sessions, and in one instance, a parent informed us that their child experienced nausea the day after using the VR headset. So in total, four potential cases of cybersickness were documented across the 197 sessions. Despite continuous supervision by the researchers, three real-world collisions occurred while children were wearing the HMD. In one instance, a child was running and was unable to stop in time, even with the Meta Quest's guardian system in place. Another child unexpectedly attempted to straddle, causing them to slide into a bench. In a third case, a minor misalignment in the calibration of the Meta Quest 3 led to the guardian system activating only a few centimeters before the wall, reducing but not preventing impact. Beyond these incidents, no additional adverse effects on physical well-being were observed.

HMD Comfort. The overall comfort of the HMD was rated positively across the 354 VR experiences ($M = 3.94$, $SD = 1.4$). However, comfort ratings varied widely between participants. Some children consistently rated the headset as highly comfortable (e.g., two children always provided the highest possible rating), others reported fluctuating comfort levels depending on the day ($M = 2.89$, $SD = 2$; $M = 2.78$, $SD = 1.35$). A small subset of participants found the HMD persistently uncomfortable despite the use of different head straps. One child consistently provided the lowest possible comfort rating, while another reported an average rating of $M = 1.94$ ($SD = 0.802$). Both children had relatively small head circumferences and reported discomfort due to pressure on the nose. Additional complaints included the headset feeling too warm or, in one case, having a noticeable disinfectant smell after cleaning.

Math Valley. When asked whether they wished to discontinue participation due to discomfort, all children expressed a strong willingness to continue. This was also reflected in their questionnaire responses, where they reported high motivation to proceed with the training ($M = 4.74$, $SD = 0.819$). The Math Valley application was generally well received, with participants rating their overall enjoyment highly ($M = 4.63$, $SD = 0.934$) and the sense of presence ($M = 4.41$, $SD = 1.16$) positively. This sense of presence was further reflected in the children's behavior, as many naturally engaged with elements of the virtual world. For example, several children instinctively interacted with the sea lion featured in two of the games (see Fig. 3).

Notable Behavioral Changes. The observed behavior of the children during VR sessions indicate that they quickly developed competence in interacting with VR systems and after the first couple of sessions, depending on the child, there was a noticeable increase in the children's independence during these interactions. Many children began to confidently insist on putting on the HMD themselves and began actively providing feedback, such as noticing blurry visuals caused by a misaligned headset. Similarly, children displayed increased confidence within

Fig. 3. While the child on the left is playing *Treasure Hunt*, the child on the right takes a break from their task in *Stacking Boxes*, intuitively petting Otaria, the virtual sea lion featured in two of the games instead.

VR and moved more naturally after the initial sessions. For instance, during his eight session one boy expressed trust in Meta Quest's guardian system, stating that he felt safe running within its boundaries, particularly when sessions were held in the gymnasium. In another instance, a previously shy and hesitant girl was observed interacting enthusiastically with the virtual sea lion by the third session. Another child, who initially held the researchers' hand throughout the first session, gradually reduced - but never discarded - this behavior starting from the second session.

Notable behavioral changes were also observed in children's approach to the tasks. For example, a child who frequently requested assistance and expressed doubt in their ability to solve math problems during the first two sessions began independently attempting solutions by the third session. These changes in self-confidence were also remarked upon by some classroom teachers during post-study discussions. While these observations are promising, other teachers did not report similar changes in their respective students' behavior.

As the study progressed, children increasingly tested the boundaries of the VR system. Figure 4 illustrates an exemplary movement tracking of one child in *Tree Climber*, in which it ignored in-game barriers such as fences and moved outside the designated play area, despite a fade-to-black feature being activated. Other children tested the consequences of moving outside the guardian system in VR (which triggers the Passthrough-mode of the Meta Quest 3) and found this temporarily more engaging than the application itself.

In general, some children's motivation to complete the in-game tasks appeared to decline over time. They instead became increasingly interested in exploring the VR environment and experimenting with the system's boundaries. On rare occasions, children engaged in conversations with peers during simultaneous sessions in the gymnasium, momentarily diverting their attention from the game. Additionally, a few children, depending on their mood, began challenging the researchers' instructions—for example, by selecting unauthorized games

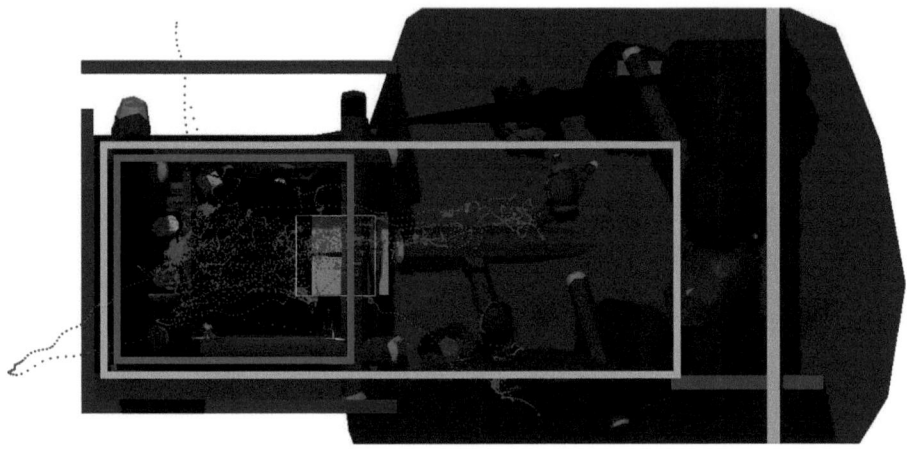

Fig. 4. A child's pathway in one game session, in which it ignored the natural virtual boundaries. In red: Designated playarea which the players should not leave. In blue: Area in which fade-to-black-mechanic is not triggered.

from the menu, disregarding gameplay guidelines, or refusing to remove the VR headset when prompted.

5 Discussion

We conducted a longitudinal study with 20 children over six weeks in a primary school setting, assessing an application designed for embodied mathematics learning in VR. The study comprised 197 training sessions, totaling 3540 min of VR gameplay, which allowed us to derive several key insights. These include valuable observations on how children's behavior in VR evolves over time and important considerations for conducting long-term VR studies with this demographic in primary school facilities. These findings will be summarized in the following sections.

5.1 Lessons Learned: VR for Children

Physical Health and In-Game Attention. Throughout the study period, which encompassed 197 training sessions, instances of collisions and cybersickness were rare and no other health-related issues were reported by the children. As children became adapted to the VR environment, they began to move more naturally, including incorporating actions such as jumping and running. However, they also often became unresponsive to verbal instructions once immersed in VR. While some engaged in conversation, most children frequently ignored explanations, whether provided in-game or by the experimenters. This behavior may be attributed to the heightened sense of presence experienced in VR, which in some cases appeared to override awareness of external stimuli. In the future, in-game instructions should be provided not by a disembodied voice, but through an avatar, offering children a visual reference to focus on. While immersion in VR is considered an advantage, as it blocks external visual and auditory cues to help users focus on the application [9], it did not necessarily mean children were focusing on the intended learning content. This could suggest a design flaw in our application. Despite creating an environment with minimal distractions, children still found ways to divert their attention.

VR Boundaries. The high sense of presence could lead (and led in one case) to instances where children move too quickly for the guardian system to detect in time, potentially leading them outside the designated play area. Consistent with prior research [3], some children deliberately tested the system by exiting the designated space. This underscores the need for consistent supervision by trained personnel who are both familiar with VR technology and experienced in working with children. Additionally, children should be reminded regularly—before putting on the headset and throughout play—to respect the guardian system and avoid running. Although this did not eliminate the behavior during our study, it reduced it, with most children adhering to the guidelines. Furthermore, our study highlighted the critical importance of maintaining a functional live stream of the headset's display, which was indispensable for addressing children's questions in real time and understanding their behavior at specific moments.

HMD Comfort. Although overall comfort ratings for the headset were positive, individual differences were evident. Two children consistently found the headset uncomfortable, despite efforts to improve the fit with different head straps. Previous research has suggested modifications, such as foam padding, to enhance fit for smaller users [28]. However, as head circumference increases with age [25], some headsets may be ill-fitting for younger children due to smaller head sizes.

Risks and Chances. While issues such as the risks of addiction and online harassment related to VR and digital media are serious and must be carefully considered, for instance through local multiplayer features in a secured network or regulated screen times, VR learning applications also present significant opportunities. In our study, all children reported enjoyment, adapted quickly to VR, and engaged with the environment. Some also exhibited promising behavioral changes, becoming more confident while using VR and, in some cases, more independent when approaching learning content such as difficult math tasks. Our findings align with other research in primary education [12], suggesting VR environments can foster creativity. For example, some children had vivid conversations with virtual animals in *Math Valley*. Notably, one child expressed excitement about seeing rabbits in the game—despite no rabbits being actually implemented. These are interesting outcomes that should be further explored. However, we must implement measures to sustain motivation for engaging with the learning content, as there seems to be a novelty effect for our application. Grießhammer et al. [7] provide a more detailed discussion of this observed effect.

5.2 Lessons Learned: Conducting a Longitudinal VR-Study in Primary School

When designing this study, we chose to conduct it within a primary school to maintain a familiar learning environment for children while reducing logistical demands for both them and their parents. However, this decision introduced several practical challenges that must be considered when planning a room-scale VR study in a school setting. One major constraint was the substantial space requirement for *Math Valley*, needing a minimum area of 10×3 m, plus additional space for safety considerations. Such large open spaces are limited in primary schools. While standard classrooms were too small, we identified several suitable locations within the school, including the auditorium, gymnasium, and two main hallways, which provided adequate space for the study.

Scheduling. Another critical factor when planning a short-term longitudinal study in a primary school setting is the impact of school holidays. During holiday periods, the schools facilities remain closed, and many of the involved children may be unavailable for assessment. While pausing data collection is possible during these periods, it may introduce confounding effects in the results. Particularly at this developmental stage, children require time to readjust to the structured routine of the school environment after a break. So interruptions due to holidays are not necessarily adverse to the study, but must be anticipated in the research design. Additionally, researchers must allocate buffer time to compensate for missed sessions. In Germany, where there are four major school holiday periods lasting at least two weeks each, the available time frame for conducting short-term longitudinal studies in schools without longer breaks is therefore considerably constrained. Effective planning and scheduling are essential to ensure data continuity and mitigate the potential impact of these interruptions.

Useful Utensils. Moreover, when conducting a VR study during school hours, classroom breaks must be considered to avoid disrupting the school routine. While children were often unsure about their next class, they were highly aware of break times and became anxious if sessions ran over. Breaks provided a valuable opportunity to recharge headsets and external batteries, which was crucial as the Quest 3's battery did not last an entire school day, especially with simultaneous gameplay and live streaming. Having at least one extra HMD proved beneficial, along with regular disinfection, a mobile router for internet connectivity and live streaming, and adjustable head straps for improved comfort. Although not necessarily required in later sessions, as many children eventually put on the headsets independently, these head straps were highly useful for assisting with HMD placement. Removing the headset easily is equally important, particularly if children don't want to give up their headset. In such rare individual cases, the smartphone connection with Meta Quest 3 proved helpful, as it allowed the headset to be put into standby mode remotely.

Spectators and Passersby. Another unforeseen challenge was the high foot traffic in the corridors during lessons, as children frequently passed through, for example, on their way to the restroom. Many were curious about our study and repeatedly asked if they could participate, which was not possible. Over time, their interest waned, and some occasionally watched a minute of gameplay on our phones but became accustomed to the study setting. Interestingly, in addition to monitoring the movements of children in VR, we also had to monitor the children and adults in the hallways, who often failed to recognize that the VR users could not see them. On multiple occasions, we had to intervene to prevent collisions when individuals without a headset walked—or in some cases jumped—too close to a child immersed in VR. This further underscores that playing VR applications in a hallway is not ideal and highlights, aligning with prior research [10], the critical need for dedicated, controlled spaces for VR.

Unforeseen Incidents. Despite careful planning, flexibility, composure, and daily communication with teaching staff were essential for organizing the study. The unpredictability of school settings became evident within the first week when one-third of the participating children were absent due to illness. Additionally, several unforeseen challenges emerged, including outbreaks of head lice, a fire drill, and unexpected class reassignments due to teacher shortages. Furthermore, certain hairstyles and clothing choices, such as pigtails obstructing the Quest headset's front-facing cameras, occasionally interfered with the proper fit and functionality of the equipment. While these factors were not major obstacles, they still required occasional adjustments to ensure a smooth study process.

Overall, we conclude that room-scale VR learning applications, when used within a limited timeframe and in a supervised environment, can be a safe and effective tool for complementing traditional education, allowing for novel interaction modalities and potentially enhancing creativity. Even though children seem to quickly learn to use the headset, it must be assessed on a case-by-case basis whether they are ready for VR, as some may be physically too small to wear the headsets comfortably. Collisions were scarce but still occurred despite supervision. For room-scale VR applications, sufficiently large spaces are therefore essential to ensure that even running children have sufficient space to slow down safely. Supervision by at least one adult per child is an essential safety measure, though its implementation in primary school environments, particularly in full-class settings, presents significant challenges. While teachers, parents, and children generally expressed openness and positive attitudes toward the technology, its applicability varies across learning scenarios, and some children were prone to distraction within the virtual environment. Developers must explicitly incorporate design principles that ensure a clear focus on learning objectives.

5.3 Limitations and Future Work

Measures of physical health, such as cybersickness and eyestrain, were based on observations and informal questioning rather than standardized questionnaires or physiological measurements. Our custom-made questionnaire was not pretested, which led to some children misunderstanding questions during the data collection process. Additionally, we observed that some children rushed through the questionnaire, attempting to answer before the researcher had fully read the questions. Moreover, the study involved a relatively small sample size, limiting the generalizability of the findings. Therefore, the results from these questionnaires should be interpreted with caution.

These limitations highlight the need for further research, particularly longitudinal studies, to better understand the long-term effects of VR in a more controlled setting. The safety of VR should be explored further through physiological data. Additionally, we cannot yet determine whether our learning application effectively aids children's learning. Future studies should assess its long-term impact, as well as that of other learning applications, on learning outcomes, children's motivation, and their attitudes toward engaging with specific subjects.

6 Conclusion

Our study underscores the importance of longitudinal investigations of VR in education and contributes valuable insights into the feasibility and safety of VR learning applications in a primary school setting, adding empirical data to the ongoing discourse on the role of VR in primary education.

Our findings indicate that VR learning sessions were generally highly engaging, safe, and suitable for most young children. However, despite supervision, isolated incidents of collisions with real-world objects occurred, emphasizing the necessity of spacious environments with adequate safety buffers. While close supervision is crucial, its implementation is also challenging in full-class settings. Nonetheless, VR-based learning demonstrates considerable potential. Children developed VR competence rapidly and exhibited growing confidence not only in operating the technology but also in interacting with the virtual environment and, in some cases, engaging with learning content. Furthermore, VR enables novel interaction modalities, and preliminary indications suggest a potential enhancement of creativity.

Overall, further research is required to systematically examine the impact of VR-based learning applications on children's educational outcomes and their integration into everyday school practice. Given the growing popularity of VR, further research should focus on how this technology can be safely and effectively integrated as a complementary tool in the school curriculum.

Acknowledgements. We thank our colleagues T. Kuhn and C. Kißler of the Department of Empirical Educational Research Methods at the Technical University of Dortmund as well as H. Dang, A. Föllner, T. Fürtges, L. Gilhaus, V. Golz, D. Heinrichs, D. Morvai, S. Müller, S. Prehn, J. Reiter, M. Rudolph, E. Schnorbus, K. Spahija, L. Stommel and N. Thorissen for their dedicated work in this project. We also thank L. Graf, J. Tietenberg, our collaborating primary schools and all participating students and their parents as well as all interviewed experts for their cooperation and input.

Disclosure of Interests. As part of the project "ELI-VR" (Ko-2022-0004), this work was supported by the Mercator Research Center Ruhr (Mercur) 2023–2025.

References

1. Allcoat, D., Von Mühlenen, A.: Learning in virtual reality: effects on performance, emotion and engagement. Res. Learn. Technol. **26**, 13 (2018). https://doi.org/10.25304/rlt.v26.2140, https://journal.alt.ac.uk/index.php/rlt/article/view/2140
2. Barsalou, L.W.: Grounded cognition. Annu. Rev. Psychol. **59**(1), 617–645 (2008). https://doi.org/10.1146/annurev.psych.59.103006.093639, https://www.annualreviews.org/doi/10.1146/annurev.psych.59.103006.093639
3. Belter, M., Lukosch, H.: Towards a virtual reality math game for learning in schools - a user study. In: 2022 IEEE Conference on Virtual Reality and 3D User Interfaces Abstracts and Workshops (VRW), pp. 808–809. IEEE, Christchurch (2022). https://doi.org/10.1109/VRW55335.2022.00255, https://ieeexplore.ieee.org/document/9757619/
4. Bos, W., Bonsen, M., Kummer, N., Lintorf, K., Frey, K.: Fachbezogenes Selbstkonzept Mathematik - Schüler [Fragebogenskala: Version 1.0]. DIPF | Leibniz Institute for Research and Information in Education Version Number: 1.0 (2012). https://doi.org/10.7477/12:23:1, https://www.fdz-bildung.de/erhebung.php?id=23
5. Chatain, J., et al.: Grasping derivatives: teaching mathematics through embodied interactions using tablets and virtual reality. In: Interaction Design and Children, pp. 98–108. ACM, Braga (2022). https://doi.org/10.1145/3501712.3529748, https://dl.acm.org/doi/10.1145/3501712.3529748
6. Checa, D., Bustillo, A.: A review of immersive virtual reality serious games to enhance learning and training. Multimed. Tools Appl. **79**(9), 5501–5527 (2020). https://doi.org/10.1007/s11042-019-08348-9
7. Grießhammer, M., Kißler, C., Masuch, M., Kuhn, J.T.: Math valley - on designing an embodied VR learning application for primary school students. In: Di Iorio, A., et al. (eds.): ICEC 2025. LNCS, vol. 16042, pp xx–yy. Springer, Cham (2025)
8. Haffner, J., Baro, K., Parzer, P., Resch, F.: HRT 1-4. Heidelberger Rechentest. "Erfassung mathematischer Basiskompetenzen im Grundschulalter". Hogrefe, Göttingen, Germany (2005)
9. Hamad, A., Jia, B.: How virtual reality technology has changed our lives: an overview of the current and potential applications and limitations. Int. J. Environ. Res. Public Health **19**(18), 11278 (2022). https://doi.org/10.3390/ijerph191811278, https://www.mdpi.com/1660-4601/19/18/11278
10. Holly, M., Pirker, J., Resch, S., Brettschuh, S., Gütl, C.: Designing VR experiences – expectations for teaching and learning in VR. Educ. Technol. Soc. **24**(2), 107–119 (2021). https://www.jstor.org/stable/27004935
11. HTC Corporation: Safety and regulatory guide (2025). https://dl.vive.com/safety-guide/vive-focus/focus-vision-safety-guide.pdf
12. Hui, J., Zhou, Y., Oubibi, M., Di, W., Zhang, L., Zhang, S.: Research on art teaching practice supported by virtual reality (VR) technology in the primary schools. Sustainability **14**(3), 1246 (2022). https://doi.org/10.3390/su14031246, https://www.mdpi.com/2071-1050/14/3/1246
13. Ioannou, M., Ioannou, A.: Technology-enhanced embodied learning: designing and evaluating a new classroom experience. Educ. Technol. Soc. **23**(3), 81–94 (2020)

14. Jin, Q., Kawas, S., Arora, S., Yuan, Y., Yarosh, S.: Is your family ready for VR? Ethical concerns and considerations in children's VR usage. In: Proceedings of the 23rd Annual ACM Interaction Design and Children Conference, IDC 2024, pp. 436–454. Association for Computing Machinery, New York (2024). https://doi.org/10.1145/3628516.3655804
15. Kaimara, P., Oikonomou, A., Deliyannis, I.: Could virtual reality applications pose real risks to children and adolescents? A systematic review of ethical issues and concerns. Virtual Reality **26**(2), 697–735 (2022). https://doi.org/10.1007/s10055-021-00563-w, https://doi.org/10.1007/s10055-021-00563-w
16. Krath, J., Schurmann, L., Von Korflesch, H.F.: Revealing the theoretical basis of gamification: a systematic review and analysis of theory in research on gamification, serious games and game-based learning. Comput. Hum. Behav. **125**, 106963 (2021). https://doi.org/10.1016/j.chb.2021.106963, https://linkinghub.elsevier.com/retrieve/pii/S0747563221002867
17. Krinzinger, H., et al.: German version of the math anxiety questionnaire (FRA) for 6-to 9-year-old children. Zeitschrift Kinder-und Jugendpsychiatrie und Psychotherapie **35**(5), 341–351 (2007)
18. Link, T., et al.: Mathe mit der Matte – Verkörperlichtes Training basisnumerischer Kompetenzen. Zeitschrift für Erziehungswissenschaft **17**(2), 257–277 (2014). https://doi.org/10.1007/s11618-014-0533-2
19. Meta Platforms, I.: Supplemental meta platforms technologies terms of service (2025). https://www.meta.com/de/legal/supplemental-terms-of-service/
20. Pang, C.G., Devi, S., Wong, D., Cai, Y., Ba, R.: The use of immersive virtual reality technology to deepen learning in Singapore schools. In: Cai, Y., van Joolingen, W., Veermans, K. (eds.) Virtual and Augmented Reality, Simulation and Serious Games for Education. GMSE, pp. 45–59. Springer, Singapore (2021). https://doi.org/10.1007/978-981-16-1361-6_5
21. Pico Immersive Pte. Ltd.: Pico terms of service (2025). https://www.picoxr.com/global/legal/terms-of-service
22. Radianti, J., Majchrzak, T.A., Fromm, J., Wohlgenannt, I.: A systematic review of immersive virtual reality applications for higher education: design elements, lessons learned, and research agenda. Comput. Educ. **147**, 103778 (2020). https://doi.org/10.1016/j.compedu.2019.103778, https://www.sciencedirect.com/science/article/pii/S0360131519303276
23. Sony Interactive Entertainment LLC: PS VR2: Safety for players (2025). https://www.playstation.com/en-us/support/hardware/ps-vr2-safety/
24. Sternig, C., Spitzer, M., Ebner, M.: Learning in a virtual environment: implementation and evaluation of a VR math-game. In: Kurubacak, G., Altinpulluk, H. (eds.) Mobile Technologies and Augmented Reality in Open Education, pp. 175–199. IGI Global Scientific Publishing (2017). https://doi.org/10.4018/978-1-5225-2110-5.ch009, https://www.igi-global.com/gateway/chapter/www.igi-global.com/gateway/chapter/178242
25. Stolzenberg, H., Kahl, H., Bergmann, K.E.: Körpermaße bei Kindern und Jugendlichen in Deutschland: Ergebnisse des Kinder- und Jugendgesundheitssurveys (KiGGS). Bundesgesundheitsblatt - Gesundheitsforschung - Gesundheitsschutz **50**(5), 659–669 (2007). https://doi.org/10.1007/s00103-007-0227-5
26. Tychsen, L., Foeller, P.: Effects of immersive virtual reality headset viewing on young children: visuomotor function, postural stability, and motion sickness. Am. J. Ophthalmol. **209**, 151–159 (2020). https://doi.org/10.1016/j.ajo.2019.07.020
27. Wehrmann, M.: Qualitative Diagnostik von Rechenschwierigkeiten im Grundlagenbereich Arithmetik. Verlag Dr. Köster, Berlin (2003)

28. Woodward, J., Ruiz, J.: Designing textual information in AR headsets to aid in adults' and children's task performance. In: Proceedings of the 22nd Annual ACM Interaction Design and Children Conference, pp. 27–39. ACM, Chicago (2023). https://doi.org/10.1145/3585088.3589373, https://dl.acm.org/doi/10.1145/3585088.3589373
29. Yamada-Rice, D., et al.: Children and virtual reality: emerging possibilities and challenges (2017). http://digilitey.eu/wp-content/uploads/2015/09/CVR-Final-PDF-reduced-size.pdf
30. Zender, R., Buchner, J., Schäfer, C., Wiesche, D., Kelly, K., Tüshaus, L.: Virtual Reality für Schüler:innen: Ein «Beipackzettel» für die Durchführung immersiver Lernszenarien im schulischen Kontext. MedienPädagogik: Zeitschrift für Theorie und Praxis der Medienbildung **47**, 26–52 (2022). https://doi.org/10.21240/mpaed/47/2022.04.02.X, https://www.medienpaed.com/article/view/1399
31. Zhonggen, Y.: A meta-analysis of use of serious games in education over a decade. Int. J. Comput. Games Technol. **2019**, 8 (2019). https://doi.org/10.1155/2019/4797032, https://www.hindawi.com/journals/ijcgt/2019/4797032/

Characterizing Social Interaction in Tabletop Games: A Constructive Conceptual Analysis

Ishika Gupta(✉) and Girish Dalvi

IDC School of Design, IIT Bombay, Mumbai, India
{ishikagupta,girish.dalvi}@iitb.ac.in

Abstract. Games serve as mediums for social interaction, reflecting our intrinsic need to connect and take part in shared experiences. The ability of games to facilitate social interaction has been popular but the concept of "social interaction" in tabletop games remains vaguely characterized in academic texts. In this paper, we seek to review and synthesize existing literature across the domains of game studies, sociology and design to identify patterns, contradictions, and gaps in the understanding of social interaction as a concept in tabletop games. We engage with what contributes to social interaction and what are some related constructs that are distinguished from social interaction like communication, collaboration, co-presence and so forth. The study offers implications of the proposed attributes of social interaction in tabletop games.

Keywords: Social Interaction · Conceptual Analysis · Player Experience · Game Design

1 Introduction

Tabletop games serve as mediums for human interaction, fostering communication, and collective storytelling [5,15]. Games often transcend mere entertainment, creating spaces where players negotiate alliances, express empathy, and co-create narratives through shared experiences. The appeal of tabletop games lies in their ability to cultivate unmediated social experiences. Rolling dice, trading resources, or exchanging glances all provide experiences that resonate with human needs for proximity and physical interaction [29]. Moments such as a raised eyebrow during a tense trade in *Catan* [31] symbolize the raw and dynamic interplay that defines tabletop sociality. Yet, while such interactions are celebrated anecdotally, their significance remains underexplored in scholarly discourse. Existing research substantially explores and engages with aspects such as game mechanics and rules of a game [2,26], but aspects of the nature of social interactions occurring during gameplay remain understudied, despite social dynamics affecting player engagement as profoundly as rules or components.

Despite its centrality, 'social interaction' in tabletop gaming suffers from fragmented conceptualization across academia. Scholars and designers often reduce it to isolated facets like communication, cooperation, or competition, while neglecting the complex interplay of rules, context, and embodied behaviour that collectively shape play [24,26]. For instance, *Diplomacy* with its negotiations, and *Pandemic*, with its collaborative problem-solving, are both described as 'high social interaction' games, yet their mechanics and gameplay differ significantly. This ambiguity stems from a lack of cohesive understanding. Such multiplicity underscores a gap where social interaction is rarely studied as a holistic construct, leaving its role in shaping play experiences incompletely theorized. By synthesizing these disparate perspectives, this study aims to conceptualize 'social interaction' within tabletop gaming contexts, offering a unified understanding to engage with its complexities and inform future research, analyses, and design.

2 Background

Scholarly perspectives on social interaction in tabletop games diverge significantly, often emphasizing either the physical or emotional dimensions of the concept. Scholars like Elias et al. [7] frame social interaction as a physical phenomenon driven by mechanics. These studies highlight how game components (like boards, and tokens etc.) impact player behaviour, arguing that interaction emerges from material exchanges which are governed by rules. Scholars like Lazzaro [19] and Rogerson et al. [24] prioritize emotional dimensions, framing interaction as a catalyst for joy, frustration, or empathy. While these perspectives help to study distinct dimensions, they often operate in isolation. Physical analysis, for instance, can overlook the affective weight of gameplay, while emotional studies may neglect the structural frameworks and gameplay mechanics enabling such experiences.

This fragmentation extends to theoretical priorities as well. Scholars like Sicart [27] and De Koven [5] advocate for a holistic view of social interaction as a co-creative process. However, some studies reduce social interaction to isolated facets, such as Zagal et al.'s [32] focus on 'collaborative engagement' or Hunicke's [16] MDA framework, that risks oversimplifying social interaction during gameplay as merely a byproduct of mechanics and rules. While these approaches engage primarily with design principles, they can sideline the improvisational dynamics that animate play for social interaction to take place.

These divergent viewpoints, though valuable, remain incommensurable. For example, Fine's [9] ethnographic work on role-playing games details how group norms and storytelling shape interaction but pays less attention to how physical components mediate these dynamics. Such compartmentalization creates gaps where studies privileging physical mechanics [7] rarely address how other contexts influence material interactions, while emotional analyses [19] overlook the structural rules that scaffold affective experiences.

This situation underscores the need for a commensurable characterization of the concept that bridges physical, emotional, and structural dimensions. Salen

& Zimmerman [26] offer a promising starting point by theorizing interaction as emergent from the interplay of rules and player creativity, while Huizinga's [15] 'magic circle' provides a cultural lens to contextualize play as a socially bounded act. Engaging with these perspectives could provide an understanding of how negotiation of resources in *Catan* (a physical act) generates both strategic alliances (structural) and emotional relationships (affective), all within specific norms and contexts. Prior frameworks, though foundational, inadvertently silo these facets, leaving some aspects unresolved like: how rules scaffold improvisation, how agency intertwines with affect, or how cultural norms inflect mechanical play. To move beyond this approach, a method is needed that not only engages with fragmented definitions but also proposes a cohesive system that mirrors the dynamism of gameplay itself.

Consequently, this study turns to Constructive Conceptual Analysis (CCA), a methodology designed to navigate such conceptual complexity. Rather than reiterating existing dichotomies, CCA interrogates their intersections, testing synthesized attributes against diverse gaming contexts through model and contrary cases. The following section details how CCA's iterative validation process bridges these layers, offering a lens through which the interplay of rules, agency, and emotion creates social dynamism through interaction between players.

3 Method

Conceptual analysis is an approach that helps clarify the meaning and structure of complex concepts by dissecting them into essential components. This method has been widely adopted across disciplines such as sociology, game studies, and psychology to address ambiguities and foster interdisciplinary dialogue [16–18,21]. In game research, conceptual analysis has been used to study the concept of 'fun' in games [6] and to distinguish 'play' from 'games' [17], emphasizing the role of rules and player agency, thereby offering perspectives that inform both academic research and design practices. The affordances of conceptual analysis lies in its ability to negotiate ambiguity by identifying the attributes of a concept. Clear conceptual frameworks also help guide empirical work and translate abstract ideas into actionable insights.

In the context of this study, CCA addresses the differing definitions in the literature on social interaction in games, where constructs like collaboration and engagement are often conflated with social interaction [32]. By engaging with these overlaps, our study offers a nuanced understanding that represents the interplay of mechanics, and player actions. To achieve that, we first establish a conceptual background and engage with the different ways the concept of social interaction exists in literature after which we aim to find gaps and form conceptual relations within existing definitions and constructs.

4 Specifying Conceptual Background

Goffman's dramaturgical [12] and ritualistic [11] theories show how players adopt roles and adhere to both formal rules and informal social scripts. Collin's [2] interaction ritual chains extend this by emphasizing the emotional energy generated through shared focus, a dynamic that can be seen in the collective tension of a Dungeons & Dragons campaign.

However, transactional frameworks like social exchange theory [8,14], which reduce interaction to cost-benefit calculations, struggle to explain altruistic cooperation in games like *Hanabi*. Similarly, Sacks et al.'s [25] structured turn-taking model, while critical for understanding conversational flow, can overlook the improvisational storytelling inherent in tabletop RPGs.

Game studies scholars and designers have expanded these foundations, often prioritizing specific dimensions. Collaborative vs. competitive engagement [32] and core mechanics [7] are featured frequently in design-focused analyses. Salen and Zimmerman [26] counterbalance this by theorizing interaction as emergent from the interplay of rules and player creativity. Sicart's [27] 'magic circle' and Huizinga's [15] foundational play theories contextualize games as culturally bounded spaces where norms are co-created which is—something seen in games with improvisational humour like *Cards Against Humanity*.

Emotionally, Lazzaro [19] and De Koven [5] highlight joyful co-creation, where laughter or mutual respect during a game strengthens social bonds. Costikyan [3] ties interaction to uncertainty, arguing that dice rolls and hidden cards in Poker force players to negotiate trust. Applied contexts further diversify this discourse: as Wang et al. [30] frame cooperative games as skill-building tools, Piper et al. [23] design therapeutic systems for ASD populations, and Crabb and Heron [4] expose accessibility barriers, such as speech pacing in hearing-impaired groups.

By looking at social interaction through these lenses along with game design texts, we aim to better understand how it is both shaped by, and shapes, the rules, mechanics, and contexts of play, offering a space for human connection and engagement. And as we conceptualize social interaction, it becomes important to identify some constructs that are often conflated with it.

5 Distinguishing Social Interactions from Related Constructs

The complex interrelationships of social interaction in games with related constructs necessitates a careful differentiation between them to prevent theoretical ambiguities and analytical oversights. Communication in games is often studied as the fundamental exchange of information between players through verbal discussions, non-verbal cues, and gestures [26]. However, social interaction is more than mere information exchange; incorporating meaning-making and shared bonding experiences [12].

Zagal et al. [32] demonstrate how tabletop games facilitate various forms of interaction, from collaborative problem-solving to competitive negotiation. The distinction between these becomes particularly relevant in games with both collaborative and competitive negotiation elements, like *Werewolf*. Educational research further supports this distinction, as seen in studies on cooperative board games which highlights that collaborative mechanics create structured environments for perspective- taking, while social interaction provides the interpersonal context for these processes to occur [30].

In role- playing games, players may experience immersion in narratives while simultaneously engaging in social interactions through combined storytelling and role-playing [28]. This immersion describes the psychological state where players are fully absorbed in the game's fictional world, disconnecting from external realities. Additionally, as seen in Leana et al.'s [20] work on games in education, social interaction mechanics enhance learning outcomes independently of immersion factors.

Co-presence refers to the physical or virtual proximity of individuals in a shared space [13]. It represents a necessary but insufficient condition for the occurrence of social interaction. Analysis of social encounters [12] demonstrates how players must actively construct interactional frameworks through verbal and non-verbal cues and shared focus to transform mere co-presence into genuine social interaction. A study on communication challenges in social board games identified how accessibility barriers in co-present settings can undermine social interaction despite physical proximity. Engagement, which measures psychological investment and emotional connection through attentional focus and persistence [19], forms the foundation of the player experience in games. Social interaction represents a specialized form of engagement characterized by interpersonal dynamics rather than just individual psychological states, which may influence it.

6 Identifying Attributes of Social Interaction

Defining social interaction within the context of tabletop games requires identifying its attributes. These attributes form the foundation of social interaction in tabletop games. By mapping these, we aim to move beyond static definitions of what is understood as social interactions in games.

At its most basic level, social interaction is inherently interactional. It requires at least two participants who engage actively with one another through reciprocal exchange [11]. This interactional quality offers the possibility for mutual engagement, in which players' actions affect each other in back-and-forth feedback loops [26]. The dynamic nature of social interaction is revealed as players go through collective meaning-making processes, jointly interpreting game events, rules, and outcomes [27]. This collective meaning-making tends to result in emergent narratives or in-game jokes that add to the experience. In role playing games, players collectively create rich stories through role-playing and improvisation, turning mechanical play into meaningful personal stories. This collective meaning-making takes place within a context-dependent system, where game mechanics, themes, and player relationships all influence interaction styles [22].

Agency-driven decision-making is an essential attribute, as players need to be able to exercise control to shape interactions [3]. Games such as *Secret Hitler* illustrate how agency gives rise to social dynamics of trust and suspicion as players make strategic use of their agency. This agency functions within the constraints set by the rules of games, which organize interactions through setting acceptable actions and providing means for strategic negotiations [7].

The time-based dynamics of social interaction exist in spontaneous moments and in sustained developments, producing diverse pacing during play. An impromptu offer of trade in *Catan* may be juxtaposed with alliance formation in *Diplomacy*, but both temporal dynamics serve toward creating the social experience. Such interaction is often accompanied by emotional and affective tones.

Cultural and social settings also affect social interaction, as players" histories dictate the way in which they understand rules and strategies [9]. In *Codenames*, cultural allusions have a strong effect on clue interpretation, providing added layers of meaning for certain groups of players. In-person gameplay sometimes includes physical and non-verbal indicators cues, with games such as *Poker* using gestures and facial expressions to add depth to strategy [11]. Lastly, playfulness and humour are social catalyst that produce fun environments that foster bonding.

These attributes do not exist in isolation; rather they intersect and overlap one another in ways that cannot be categorized. Consider, for example, in *Codenames*, where a single clue hinges on cultural context (e.g. a pop culture reference) and sparks joint meaning-making as players debate interpretations. That moment isn't just about solving the puzzle. Rather, it's a display of how playfulness and non-verbal cues, like a teammate's smirk, transform mechanics into inside jokes.

Even the rule-constrained trading in Catan isn't merely transactional; as it's a mix of agency-driven improvisation, where a player's desperate offer of 'two sheep for anything' becomes a running gag, blending affect with strategy. This interplay matters because it reveals that social interaction in tabletop games isn't a checklist of features but a dynamic system.

7 Forming New Conceptual Relations: Characterizing Social Interaction

Having established that social interaction in tabletop games is a dynamic system composed of interrelated attributes, this section develops further by formulating its conceptual relationships with other facets of tabletop games, such as game mechanics and player experience. Building on these relations allows us to understand the interplay of social interaction in games and how it impacts, or is impacted by, other aspects of games.

7.1 Social Interaction and Game Mechanics

Social interaction in board games is closely embedded within game mechanics, through which players interact with one another. Mechanics provide routine structured opportunities for cooperation, competition, negotiation, or deception

[7]. For instance, in *Catan*, trading mechanics engender negotiation and coalition formation, whereas in *Secret Hitler*, hidden roles and voting mechanics give rise to deception and trust [32]. The relationship between mechanics and social interaction is recursive: mechanics facilitate interaction, and interaction, conversely, affects how mechanics are experienced and manipulated [26].

7.2 Social Interaction and Player Experience

Social interaction is a major force that shapes the player experience, which includes the feelings, thoughts, and sensations that arise while playing. The relationship between interaction and experience is dynamic and reciprocal. In cooperative games, the mechanics involving cooperative problem-solving give rise to experiences of cooperation and shared accountability [19]. In some games, the competitive negotiation mechanics produce tension, excitement, and emotional instability [9]. The emotional impact of the experience is influenced by the quality of social interaction, and players' emotional states which in turn influence how they interact with others in future interactions.

7.3 Social Interaction and Cultural Context

Social interaction at the gaming table is influenced by the cultural context, social norms, and common knowledge that players bring to the table. This cultural situatedness explains how the very same game mechanics can yield fundamentally different interactional dynamics among player groups [22]. In *Codenames*, references to culture and linguistic conventions tend to determine decisively how clues are read by players and made by players [15]. Even in *Dungeons & Dragons*, players' cultural affiliations determine how players approach role-playing, narrative production, and the settlement of disputes [1]. The cultural context and social interaction are dialogical. Cultural practices guide how players understand mechanical systems and interact with each other, and the interactional patterns developed through gameplay may reinforce established cultural practices or challenge them by introducing new ideas and play styles.

7.4 Social Interaction and Player Agency

At the center of these interactional dynamics is player agency: the ability to make effective choices that affect game outcomes. Social interaction at the table is agency-based, with it depending on players' capabilities to act, respond, and strategically impact others within the game structure [3]. In *Chess*, agency is expressed through thoughtful movements and positional play [10]. The relationship between agency and social interaction is symbiotic: meaningful agency sets up possibilities for social interaction, and the nuance of social interaction recursively emphasizes the importance of agency by setting up nested levels of strategic thinking.

7.5 Social Interaction and Constraints

Action taken by agency in tabletop games must necessarily be circumscribed by prohibitions and constraints. The rules that limit possible actions and strategic possibilities. These restrictions do not preclude social interaction but instead generate structured social opportunities for problem-solving, creativity, and negotiation [26]. In *Pandemic*, movement and treatment limitations cause players to innovate strategies, making use of limited resources. Game constraints inform the way players interact through the specific challenges they establish, while the creative responses of the players to such challenges indicate the flexibility and interpretive space in the rule systems

7.6 Social Interaction and Temporal Dynamics

The dynamic development of social interaction over time is another essential aspect of its definition in tabletop games. Temporal dynamics affect the way interactions progress, ranging from fleeting exchanges to extended interactions that unfold over a series of turns or sessions [11]. Social interaction in *Ticket to Ride* can be composed of short, strategic moves to block others, whereas in *Diplomacy*, relationships and alliances are built up through lengthy stretches of negotiation and deceit [13]. This fluidity across time establishes rhythmic structures where the rhythm of interaction controls the flow of the game and the flow of the game affects the intensity and quality of social interaction.

7.7 Social Interaction and Emotional Dynamics

Supporting these temporal patterns are the emotional dynamics created by social interaction. These affective experiences, ranging anywhere from pleasure and accomplishment to anger and anxiety, form an essential part of what makes tabletop gaming fascinating and memorable [19]. In *Pandemic*, the shared emotional experience of eradicating a disease conspires to build strong positive reinforcement for collaborative behavior, while in *Secret Hitler*, the subtext of mistrust and deception builds persistent emotional involvement [30]. Interactional styles trigger certain emotional reactions, which in turn shape the way players engage in subsequent interactions, producing feedback loops that stabilize or reorganize the social dynamics of the game.

7.8 Social Interaction and Playfulness

Lastly, social interaction in tabletop games is marked by its playfulness: the lighthearted, humorous, and creative elements that differentiate gaming from other social activities. This playfulness does not simply accompany engagement but actually informs its quality and consequences [27]. In *Cards Against Humanity*, the absurdist humour of the game produces a permissive space for flippant barbs and creative output that may be less suitable in other situations. Likewise, in *Dixit*, creative storytelling turns what might otherwise be straightforward clue-giving into lush, comedic performances [5]. The linkage between playfulness and social interaction is escalating: playful elements reinforce the enjoyment and memorability of interactions, whereas significant social involvement provides scope for more developed and rewarding playful transactions.

By looking at these interrelated relationships, we build a detailed picture of social interaction in tabletop games, not as a discrete concept but as an integral, dynamic force that mediates between game mechanics, player experiences, cultural contexts, and emotional dynamics. These attributes suggest social interaction as both an outcome of, and a source of, the intricate system of tabletop gaming.

8 Validating the Conceptual Relations

Once we have established these relationships and conceptualized attributes, it is important to validate them. We do that by testing it against some cases of gameplays where this framework is visible and to arrive at cases where it doesn't fully fit, which helps identify the gaps in the proposed framework.

8.1 Model Case: Social Interaction in *Catan*

To test our conceptual framework of social interaction in board games, we use the model case of *Catan*, a game that is designed to enable social exchange through its mechanics of resource trading and negotiation of shared resources. Here, players interact socially through verbal and non-verbal cues, with the mechanics of the game providing structured opportunities for mutual engagement and meaning-making. The interactional character of *Catan* is revealed as players actively negotiate trades, build alliances, and jointly interpret the meaning of strategic actions. This shared interaction establishes a dynamic feedback loop in which the choices of each player affect other player's moves, resulting in changing coalitions and adapting strategies over the course of the game. The decision-making agency of players, as they choose when to trade, block, or cooperate, illustrates how social interaction is both bounded by rules and constraints and also negotiated by temporal considerations and emotional forces. The validation of the conceptual framework in this model case provides a basis for studying how social interaction occurs in tabletop gaming environments.

8.2 Related Case: Social Interaction in *Chess*

Drawing on the model case, we explore the related case of *Chess*, where social interaction is less overt, manifesting in the form of non-verbal signals and strategic moves as opposed to direct verbal negotiation. In spite of the lack of explicit communication mechanisms, the players still engage in social interaction by their understanding of opponents' moves, anticipation of intentions, and accommodation to changing game scenarios. The interactional character of *Chess* arises through the reciprocal activity of the players, as every move affects the opponent's subsequent move, thus bringing about a dynamic exchange of strategic intentions. This example illustrates that social interaction in games can manifest in different ways, with *Chess* basing itself relying on collective meaning construction through non-verbal cues and moves. The affective dynamics existing in *Chess* shows us how our framework can be extended to games involving fewer direct social mechanics, but indicates emphasizing the generalizability of our conceptualization of social interaction.

8.3 Contrary Case: *Solitaire*

To further scrutinize our conceptual framework, we examine the contrary case of a single-player game of *solitaire*, where there is no cooperative interaction between human participants and thus no social interaction as conceptualized present. Here, players directly interact with the game without interacting with any other human agents, thus lacking the mutual engagement and shared meaning-making that constitutes our understanding of social interaction. The absence of mutual engagement reveals itself as no player's actions affect others, and there is no joint understanding of game outcomes. This case works to help reinforce the relevance of the attributes features we've identified by demonstrating their absence and showing how our conceptual framework draws a line separating social interaction within multiplayer scenarios from other types of gaming experiences.

9 Attributes of Social Interaction in Tabletop Games

Through CCA, we've identified the following attributes of social interaction in tabletop games. Recognizing and understanding the interplay of these attributes is crucial for comprehending how tabletop games, with their physical artifacts, mechanics, and rules, generate social interaction, and player experiences.

- **Interactional:** Social interaction requires reciprocal participation between at least two players, enabling mutual influence through actions (e.g., negotiating strategies in *Pandemic*).
- **Mutual Engagement:** Actions create feedback loops where players' decisions directly impact others, fostering teamwork or rivalry that elicits interaction (e.g., shared crises in *Pandemic*).
- **Collective Meaning-Making:** Players co-create narratives or inside jokes through shared interpretation of game events changing the nature of interactions between players (e.g., improvisational storytelling in *Dungeons & Dragons*).
- **Context-Dependent:** Interaction styles are scaffolded by game mechanics, themes, and player relationships (e.g., cultural references in *Codenames*).
- **Agency-Driven**: Players exercise autonomy to negotiate, deceive, or cooperate, shaping social dynamics (e.g., trust and suspicion in *Secret Hitler*).

- **Rule-Constrained:** Game rules structure interactions, requiring creativity in interaction within boundaries giving rise to different ways of interacting(e.g., resource trading in *Catan*).
 - **Temporally Diverse:** Interactions range from spontaneous trades to prolonged alliances, creating varied pacing and nature of interactions (e.g., quick trades in *Catan* vs. slow-burn diplomacy in *Diplomacy*).
 - **Affect-Laden:** Emotional tones like triumph or frustration deepen social bonds and shape the social dynamics of the gameplay (e.g., collective relief in *Pandemic*).
 - **Culture-Situated:** Cultural backgrounds influence rule interpretation and strategy that in turn shapes the nature of interactions. (e.g., clue-giving in *Codenames*).
 - **Non-Verbal:** Gestures, facial expressions, and physical cues add layers to the social interaction beyond verbal communication (e.g., bluffing in *Poker*).
 - **Playfulness:** Humor and lightheartedness foster bonding and permissive social spaces for interactions to emerge. (e.g., absurdist humor in *Cards Against Humanity*).

10 Discussion

Using CCA, we have proposed eleven attributes of social interaction— proposing a structured framework to engage with social interaction. Yet this new clarity is also shaped by our chosen methods: without long-term, cross-cultural studies and multi-sensor data, the contextual and bodily nuances of real-world play are still more suggested than proven. Lazzaro's [19] emphasis on emotional resonance and Elias et al.'s [7] focus on material exchanges, for instance, are no longer competing lenses but complementary facets of a unified system. Where Sicart [27] and De Koven [5] envisioned play as a 'magic circle' of shared meaning, our framework extends this metaphor by grounding it in attributes like mutual engagement, collective meaning-making and playfulness that designers can operationalize while designing games. This synthesis not only resolves prior ambiguities but reveals newer gaps. For example, while Fine [9] and Goffman [12] explored how norms govern interaction, our findings highlight how cultural situatedness and non-verbal cues introduce variability that existing theories often overlook.

The framework's emphasis on player agency, while aligning with Costikyan's [3] focus on strategic choice, risks marginalizing passive or constrained participation which is a tension Goffman [11] might attribute to the 'backstage' dynamics of gameplay. Likewise, the categorization of attributes like affect-laden or rule-constrained risks oversimplifying their fluid interplay, a concern Sicart [27] anticipated in critiques of reductionist models.

By articulating these limitations, we hope to add to a more nuanced understanding of social interaction in board games. For designers, this could mean leveraging the interplay of temporal diversity and emotional dynamics to craft experiences that work well across demographics. In bridging the theoretical and the practical, this study does not conclude the conversation but extends it, offering a scaffold for future work to explore the complexities of social interaction in play.

11 Conclusion

The significance of this study lies in the synthesis of fragmented works on social interaction in tabletop gaming, offering a commensurable framework that acknowledges the field's diverse theoretical positions. By identifying and validating the attributes through model cases (*Catan*), related cases (*Chess*), and contrary cases (single-player games), we have laid the groundwork for comprehending social interaction in various tabletop gaming environments.

Yet this is only a first step. Future work should push the framework into new spaces—non-Western games, digitaltabletop hybrids, and play situations where people mostly watch rather than act. Long-term field studies, physiological measures of emotion, and close looks at how culture, age, and power shift interaction would all test and refine the model. Designers can treat the eleven attributes as knobs to turn, running design experiments that bring fresh data back to theory.

In positioning this study within the broad landscape of social interaction, we echo Huizinga [15]: play is not a diversion but a vital social practice. By articulating its attributes, we equip scholars and designers to design games that do more than entertain but foster meaningful human connection.

Disclosure of Interests. The authors have no competing interests to declare.

References

1. Bayeck, R.Y.: Examining board gameplay and learning: a multidisciplinary review. Learn. Sci. **51**, 411–431 (2020)
2. Collins, R.: Interaction ritual chains. In: Interaction Ritual Chains. Princeton University Press (2014)
3. Costikyan, G.: Uncertainty in Games. MIT Press (2013)
4. Crabb, M., Heron, M.: Communication challenges in social board games. Simul. Gaming **54**(5), 489–507 (2023)
5. De Koven, B.: The Well-Played Game: A Player's Philosophy. MIT Press (2013)
6. Dhamelia, M., Dalvi, G.: Pleasures in games: conceptual analysis of fun and its constructs. In: Dhar, U., Dubey, J., Dumblekar, V., Meijer, S., Lukosch, H. (eds.) ISAGA 2021. LNCS, vol. 13219, pp. 197–210. Springer, Cham (2021). https://doi.org/10.1007/978-3-031-09959-5_17
7. Elias, G.S., Garfield, R., Gutschera, K.R.: Characteristics of Games. MIT Press (2012)
8. Emerson, R.M.: Rational choice and social exchange: a critique of exchange theory (1977)
9. Fine, G.A.: Shared Fantasy: Role Playing Games as Social Worlds. University of Chicago Press (2002)

10. James Paul Gee: What video games have to teach us about learning and literacy. Comput. Entertain. (CIE) **1**(1), 20 (2003)
11. Goffman, E.: Encounters: Two Studies in the Sociology of Interaction. Ravenio Books (1961)
12. Goffman, E., et al.: The Presentation of Self in Everyday Life, vol. 259 (2023)
13. Hamari, J., Sjöblom, M.: What is esports and why do people watch it? Internet Res. **27**(2), 211–232 (2017)
14. Homans, G.C.: Social behavior as exchange. Am. J. Sociol. **63**(6), 597–606 (1958)
15. Huizinga, J.: Homo ludens: proeve eener bepaling van het spel-element der cultuur. Amsterdam University Press (2008)
16. Hunicke, R., LeBlanc, M., Zubek, R., et al.: MDA: a formal approach to game design and game research. In: Proceedings of the AAAI Workshop on Challenges in Game AI, vol. 4, p. 1722 (2004)
17. Juul, J.: Half-Real: Video Games Between Real Rules and Fictional Worlds. MIT Press (2011)
18. Kyngas, H., Duffy, M.E., Kroll, T.: Conceptual analysis of compliance. J. Clin. Nurs. **9**(1) (2000)
19. Lazzaro, N.: Four keys to more emotion without story. Technical report (2004)
20. Lean, J., Illingworth, S., Wake, P.: Unhappy Families: Using Tabletop Games as a Technology to Understand Play in Education, vol. 26. Co-Action Publishing (2018)
21. Norman, D.A.: The Psychology of Everyday Things. Basic Books (1988)
22. Parlett, D.S.: The Oxford history of board games. (No Title) (1999)
23. Piper, A.M., O'Brien, E., Morris, M.R., Winograd, T.: Sides: a cooperative tabletop computer game for social skills development. In: Proceedings of the 2006 20th Anniversary Conference on Computer Supported Cooperative Work, pp. 1–10 (2006)
24. Rogerson, M.J., Gibbs, M., Smith, W.: Collaboration in pandemic: a model for cooperative play. In: Proceedings of the DiGRA Conference (2019)
25. Sacks, H., Schegloff, E.A., Jefferson, G.: A simplest systematics for the organization of turn-taking for conversation. Language **50**(4), 696–735 (1974)
26. Salen, K., Zimmerman, E.: Rules of Play: Game Design Fundamentals. MIT Press (2004)
27. Sicart, M.: Play Matters. MIT Press (2014)
28. Steinkuehler, C.A., Williams, D.: Where everybody knows your (screen) name: online games as "third places". J. Comput.-Mediat. Commun. **11**(4), 885–909 (2006)
29. Stemasov, E., et al.: Embedding tangible creation and destruction in hybrid board games through personal fabrication technology. In: CHI Conference on Human Factors in Computing Systems (CHI 2024), pp. 1–20. ACM, New York (2024)
30. Wang, Y.-C., Doll, J., Varma, K.: "Your Turn!": Playing Cooperative Modern Board Games to Promote Perspective Taking and Cooperative Attitudes. International Society of the Learning Sciences, Inc.[ISLS] (2018)
31. Woods, S.: The Catan effect: social dynamics in board games. Board Game Stud. J. (2012)
32. Zagal, J.P., Rick, J., Hsi, I.: Collaborative games: lessons learned from board games. Simul. Gaming **37**(1), 24–40 (2006)

Initializing Interactive Treasure Hunts in Cultural Heritage Sites: An LLM-Based Approach

Pablo Gutiérrez-Sánchez[1], Pedro A. González-Calero[1], Marco A. Gómez-Martín[1], Pedro P. Gómez-Martín[1], and Ruck Thawonmas[2]

[1] Complutense University of Madrid, 28040 Madrid, Spain
pabgut02@ucm.es
[2] Ritsumeikan University, Ibaraki, Osaka 567-8570, Japan

Abstract. Cultural heritage sites are increasingly embracing playful approaches such as treasure hunt games to enhance interactive educational experiences, proving effective in engaging diverse audiences, encouraging exploration, and promoting knowledge retention. However, designing such experiences remains a complex task that requires careful integration of narrative, interactivity, and factual accuracy.

In this article, we propose an approach that leverages large language models (LLMs) to automate the initial drafting of treasure hunt games for cultural heritage sites. Our method allows content curators to specify key parameters—such as the target artefacts to be included in the hunt, intended audience, and narrative styles—after which the system generates a structured sketch of the game. We compare two generation strategies: a basic sequential method and a revised approach that incorporates a pre-planning phase. Our evaluation assesses the resulting drafts in terms of their correctness, consistency, and stylistic coherence.

Results suggest that pre-planning improves the quality of the generated content, producing generally more structured and contextually appropriate outputs. Moreover, we describe some of the remaining challenges, such as the need for interactive and validated co-design mechanisms or the introduction of factual accuracy guarantees in the adventures.

Keywords: Large Language Models · Educational escape room · Games at museums · AI-assisted game design · Automated content generation

1 Introduction

In recent years, cultural heritage sites have increasingly adopted mobile technology to enhance their repertoire of interactive educational experiences, complementing traditional museum tools and practices. Among these digital strategies, gamification has emerged as a powerful way to make cultural learning more engaging, as noted in numerous literature reviews [7,15,17–19].

A particularly effective gamified approach is the treasure hunt–style game, typically implemented in the form of apps for mobile devices. These experiences engage users through interactive elements such as geolocated navigation stages, clue-following, and puzzle-solving. They may also incorporate object collection, customised quizzes, and AR-based scanning of QR codes or venue artefacts, showcasing new immersive alternatives to promote problem-solving and deeper engagement with local heritage [3,14].

Targeting a wide range of audiences, including children, school groups, university students, and general museum visitors, these gamified interventions have been proven to enhance knowledge retention [28], promote collaborative learning [8], and encourage exploration and contextual learning [5], positioning them as effective tools for cultural interpretation [3]. Despite their potential, the design and implementation of these experiences remain challenging, requiring a careful balance and integration of narrative, interactivity and technology.

To ease the design process, generative artificial intelligence models can provide assistance in brainstorming [30] or generating initial versions of these games. This is in line with what is already present within commercial interactive content creation platforms such as *Kahoot!*[1] or *Quizizz AI*[2], which offer simple mechanisms supported by Large Language Models (LLMs) as a source of inspiration and novel ideas. When developing content for cultural heritage sites, however, it is essential that the material produced remain factually grounded on the venue's knowledge base, often comprised of numerous texts with information regarding the artefacts of its distinct exhibits. Given the tendency of LLMs to hallucinate, ensuring factual accuracy is paramount, particularly in in learning-centred experiences.

In the past, we have developed *Enigmas* [10], treasure hunt type games for museums supported by AR technology, mixing narrative elements with clues, artefact searches, mini-games, and multiple-choice questions to test players on the content of the exhibition. Historically, designing such adventures has been time-consuming, particularly when it comes to formulating initial ideas for the structure of the experience. With this in mind, in this paper we propose an LLM-based approach to automate the production of these initial drafts in a limited subset of *Enigma* games. Our method involves content curators specifying key domain information, such as the artefacts to be included, the target audience, or the desired narrative style, after which the system generates structured data files to bootstrap the game. We compare two approaches: a baseline method using direct and sequential prompting and a revised version incorporating a pre-planning step. We then evaluate their effectiveness in terms of content correctness, stylistic appropriateness, and overall perceived quality.

---

[1] https://kahoot.com/.
[2] https://quizizz.com/quizizz-ai.

2 Related Work

The rise of LLMs has spurred interest in using these AIs for text generation across domains, including video games. Trained on large text corpora, LLMs generate responses based on user prompts, usually accompanied by a set of rules or conversation history. Without prompt-embedded domain knowledge, their responses rely entirely on input and training data, known as a zero-shot paradigm, whereas adding examples enables few-shot reasoning [29]. These models are not free of reasoning and action errors, however, which has given rise to different strategies to improve the generation quality by means of patterns such as chain-of-thought prompting [25] or ReAct (Reasoning and Acting) [27].

In video games, the use of LLMs has been explored for a variety of tasks including narrative creation, interactive stories, and scene generation [4,16,20]. This includes the production of games in the form of visual novels with complex branching that propagate over time [22], although some work reports that LLM-generated dialogues are not always perceived as positively as those written by humans [2]. They have also been applied in level design (e.g., Mario Bros [21] or Sokoban levels [23]) or for game environments and layouts [9,13].

For cultural heritage sites, LLMs have been used for guided tours and personalized narratives rather than traditional games. Helmy et al. [12] combine a 3D scene generation tool (NeRF) with the LLaMa 3 language model to power a virtual tour guide for Egyptian heritage sites. In turn, Trichopoulos et al. [24] use OpenAI's GPT model to generate personalized narratives and recommendations for museum visitors. These approaches use conversational interfaces to encourage user exploration and engagement.

In contrast to our work, existing studies—including those focused on cultural heritage applications—have not placed particular emphasis on the factual accuracy of the generated content. Moreover, our study differs from the literature in that a treasure hunt consists of several phases of different nature, each of which requires a certain level of internal consistency and factual accuracy. While existing generators create narratives, quests, questions, or environments in isolation, our approach integrates all components into a cohesive, unified narrative.

3 Games Description and Problem Definition

Enigma games are interactive adventures for mobile devices, inspired by escape rooms and treasure hunts and designed to engage players in story-driven experiences at cultural heritage sites such as museums or archaeological sites. Players assume the role of the protagonist, going through a series of interconnected puzzles, riddles, and quests. The primary goal is to motivate visitors to actively explore their surroundings and interact more deeply with the artefacts on display, dynamizing their experience and encouraging reflection on the content.

The gameplay is structured in distinct stages, each presenting a unique challenge, such as locating artefacts, solving puzzles, answering multiple-choice questions, or unlocking digital locks. These phases are sequential, requiring completion of one to proceed to the next. Players interact with the game via touchscreen,

GPS navigation, and augmented reality features, bringing the venue and its institutions to life. The aim is to foster a sense of immersion and active participation, making players feel like an integral part of the adventure. These games have been used at several institutions in Madrid, Spain, such as the National Museum of Natural Sciences, the Lázaro Galdiano Museum, and the García Santesmases Museum of computer science history.

In this work, we focus on three of the thirteen phases currently available in these games, which form the core structure of most Enigma adventures:

- *Narrative phases*: virtual characters interact via dialogues to tell a story or elaborate on concepts and events that take place in the game.
- *Artefact search phases*: players are prompted to explore the area to locate a museum item based on a treasure hunt-style clue.
- *Multiple-choice question phases*: the system presents questions with a correct answer and distractors to assess the player's understanding.

Typically, these three kinds of phases are introduced in this same order, giving rise to thematic blocks focusing on each of the artefacts to be discovered by the player: (1) A narrative stage introduces or continues the story and motivates the search for an artefact; (2) a search phase prompts the player to reason about the given clue and explore the area to locate the artefact; and (3) a question phase encourages further scrutiny of the work in search of the correct answer.

4 Approach

Our approach starts from a set of treasure-hunt configuration details provided by the game designer or content curator and generates a JSON file with the definition of an Enigma game based on the information provided (see Fig. 1).

4.1 Game Parameters

To build an adventure based on a solid knowledge of the museum's objects, the first essential step is to list the artefacts the designer wants to include in the game. If the museum already displays panels with textual descriptions of the works, these can be directly used as input. However, depending on the use case, it may be beneficial to enrich this data with other remarks such as information about nearby objects, metadata regarding the artefact's location, or any relevant facts that could help generate clues in the treasure hunt. An example of an artefact description from our case study is shown bellow in Sample 1 for the artwork "Apollo in the Forge of Vulcan".

> **"Apollo in the Forge of Vulcan"**: "Diego Velázquez's painting *Apollo in the Forge of Vulcan* (c. 1630) depicts the Roman god Vulcan at work in his forge, surrounded by assistants hammering metal in the intense heat. Vulcan, engaged in forging, represents both creation and destruction. Velázquez contrasts the warm glow of fire with cooler tones..." (1)

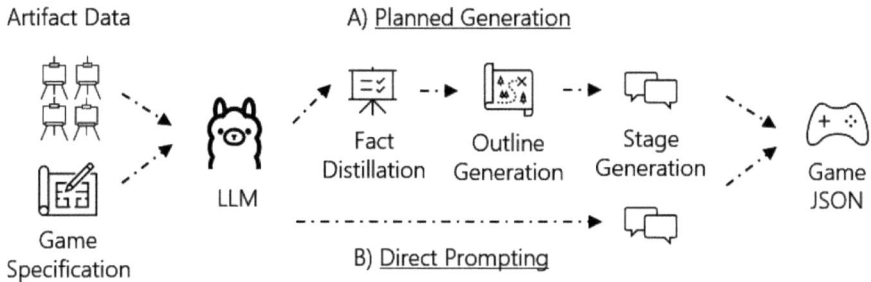

Fig. 1. Treasure Hunt generation flow for both approaches.

Table 1. Sample input for a "Mythology Mystery" specification.

Parameter	Input
General Description	A mythology-based adventure where players uncover the legendary stories hidden in paintings and sculptures
Intention	Provide a deep dive into mythology through artwork
Fact Focus	Myths and legends behind classical artworks
Narrative Style	A mysterious quest where players act as seekers of lost mythological knowledge
Clue Style	Riddles based on myths, e.g., "Seek the god who..."
Question Style	Questions exploring the accuracy of myths in art
Target Audience	Mythology and history enthusiasts
Difficulty	Hard

Once this information is provided, the rest of the parameters start to refer to stylistic and focus considerations both at the overall domain level and for the different phases of the adventure, as can be seen in the example from Table 1. Notably, parameters are provided to control the target audience (e.g., "Mythology and history enthusiasts"), the design intent, the expected difficulty, and a general description of the goal of the application. Numerical inputs to control other aspects of the game, such as the length of narrative blocks or the number of answers per multiple-choice question are also included.

4.2 Fact Distillation and Plan-and-Execute Strategy

Once the designer has entered this information, the game generation process begins. This starts by taking the texts for each of the artefacts and producing a reduced set of succinct facts with the focus indicated by the designer in the Fact Focus parameter. Given that the descriptions provided by these institutions can be quite lengthy, the first hypothesis (**H1**) of this study is that distilling the most relevant facts from these descriptions improves the consistency and accuracy of the clues and questions generated by the LLM. The number of facts output per artefact is controlled by the `Number of Facts` input parameter. We preliminarily argue that this step may contribute to focusing the attention of the model on the pieces of information that the designer considers most pertinent in the given context. An example of the facts suggested by the model for the artwork "Apollo in the Forge of Vulcan" using the sample inputs above is shown below.

1. Velázquez's painting 'Apollo in the Forge of Vulcan' humanizes the Roman god Vulcan, depicting him as a labourer rather than an idealized deity, making it an allegory of craftsmanship, creativity, and transformation.
2. Velázquez masterfully contrasts the warm glow of fire with cooler tones, creating a dramatic atmosphere that blends mythology with naturalism.
3. Velázquez enhances the realism and depth of the scene through his use of light and shadow, showcasing his technical mastery.

During all stages of generation, we make use of Microsoft's Guidance library [1] to control the output of the LLM in a structured way. This ensures that it is never necessary to perform parsing operations on the data generated by the model and that, in general, there are always mechanisms in place to guarantee the structural integrity of the proposed solutions. For instance, it is possible to restrict the output of the LLM during narrative generations to pick from only valid characters available in the adventure metadata or to impose the generation of an exact number of single-sentence answers in the question stages.

Secondly, given that the generated adventures may become excessively long, this study proposes a second hypothesis (**H2**): that developing an action plan prior to phase generation supports narrative focus and coherence across the game's stages. To this end, once the most relevant facts of each work have been distilled, we prompt the model to prepare a structured draft in which the points to be followed throughout the adventure are briefly defined. This is in line with common design patterns in prompt engineering, such as Plan-and-Execute, where the model first plans a strategy for solving a complex problem and then executes each of the solving steps in a systematic way.

More specifically, such a plan involves designing a narrative-question-clue sequence for each of the artefacts, along the lines of what was discussed at the end of Sect. 3. For each of the works in the itinerary, the LLM must produce a fact on which to base the clue that leads the player to the piece, the point of emphasis on which to focus in the multiple-choice question to be asked after finding the artefact, and a summary of the narrative from the instant in which the previous object was found to the moment in which the player is to find the next one. Continuing with the example above, the general points generated as a sketch of the artefact block would be:

- **Narrative summary:** "as Kaida and Lyra delve into the world of ancient mythology, they discover that the mysterious collector's cryptic letter is linked to Velázquez's enigmatic painting "Apollo in the Forge of Vulcan", which holds the

key to understanding the transformative power of art and the connection between creativity and craftsmanship, setting the stage for their quest to uncover the secrets hidden within the masterpieces".
- **Focus of the clue:** "the transformative power of art and the connection between creativity and craftsmanship."
- **Focus of the question:** "the accuracy of myths in art by asking about the depiction of Vulcan in the painting".

Once this outline is available, and with it the general narrative, the model makes a proposal of the characters to be used, together with a brief description of each of them. In the ongoing example, proposed characters are **Kaida Asteria**, "a brilliant and enigmatic art historian with a passion for uncovering the hidden secrets of ancient mythologies", and **Lyra Flynn**, "a charismatic and resourceful adventurer with a knack for deciphering cryptic clues and unravelling mysteries".

4.3 Stage Generation

Having devised the plan to be followed, our approach then moves on to individually generate the stages of the game according to the general descriptions in the draft. Here, each of the designed stages is created from a sequence of prompts to the LLM in which the style settings, the focus to be followed, and the rules that must be generally respected in any stage of the corresponding type are injected. For instance, in question-type stages, one of the basic restrictions is that answers must not be repeated, while in clue-type stages, a clue must not explicitly reveal the name of the artefact to be searched for.

Structural and design constraints are a key aspect to take into account during the generation process. By the former, we refer to constraints on the shape of the produced content from a formatting point of view:

- A multiple-choice question must have exactly the requested number of possible answers, all of them consisting of a single sentence. The latter is also a restriction in the case of clues.
- A narrative stage can only reference characters previously defined in the game, must not exceed the maximum number of interactions per story block, and each of the interventions must be made up of a single sentence.

By design constraints, we denote rules that cannot generally be verified automatically as they are based on respecting the design intent of the person who specifies the adventure. Some examples for this paper's use case are:

- A narrative stage should never give overly obvious clues to the next artefact to be encountered in the game (e.g., the name of the artefact itself). Dialogues should not be repeated either directly or paraphrased, must respect the specified storytelling style, and must be cohesive and smoothly link the different stages of the game, especially in terms of providing the necessary context so that subsequent stages are sufficiently grounded.

- A clue stage should not explicitly reveal the name of the artefact to which it leads, but neither should it be so ambiguous or broad that the player has insufficient information to locate it. The level of difficulty, focus, and style should respect the design intentions.
- A multiple-choice question stage should not explicitly reveal the answer in the question, nor list the name of the artefact as one of the possible choices. Responses should not be repeated, either verbatim or in paraphrased but essentially equivalent versions. In addition, the correct answer should not be made more emphatic than the distractors (e.g., with an exclamation mark at the end). The level of difficulty, focus, and style should respect the design intentions. Most importantly, questions must always be correct and respect the factual data provided by the user's descriptions. The latter is particularly important in any adventure with a pedagogical focus.

With this, a final stage sequence for the running example would be:

- **Narrative:**
  Kaida: The symbol seems to be a variant of the ancient Greek character for the Muses.
  Lyra: That's a great observation, Kaida.
  Kaida: I think it's more than just a coincidence.
  Lyra: Then we need to find out what Velázquez's paintings have to do with it.
  Kaida: The paintings are said to hold the key to understanding the power of art.
- **Clue:** Seek the divine craftsman where fiery passion forges the very essence of art itself.
- **Question:** What is the primary representation of Vulcan in Velázquez's "Apollo in the Forge of Vulcan", according to the mythological context depicted in the artwork?
    - **Correct Answer:** Vulcan is portrayed as a labourer rather than an idealized deity, humanizing him and making the painting an allegory of craftsmanship, creativity, and transformation.
    - **Distractor 1:** The painting shows Vulcan as a powerful, godlike figure, emphasizing his divine nature and mythological significance.
    - **Distractor 2:** The artwork depicts Vulcan as a mere mortal, struggling to control the fiery forge, highlighting his vulnerability and humanity.
    - **Distractor 3:** The painting presents Vulcan as a symbol of destruction, emphasizing his role in the mythological context and the chaos he brings to the world.

While we write these examples here in a simplified form to improve readability, note that the output of the system is delivered as a JSON file containing the definitions of each of the phases, metadata, and character listings. This structure is repeated as many times as artefacts included in the game, with a final additional narrative block between the point at which the player finds the last artefact and the end of the game. All the prompts and Guidance code used for the generation can be found in the project repository[3].

---
[3] Repository Link: https://github.com/pgutierrez858/enigma-llms.

5 Experiments and Results

As introduced in Sect. 4, we aim to validate two hypotheses: (**H1**) distilling relevant facts about the artefacts to be encountered reduces the number of factual errors and improves the overall consistency of adventures; and (**H2**) applying a Plan-and-Execute strategy prior to the generation of game stages has an overall positive effect on design error rates. We evaluate this by comparing the planned approach with strategies that do not make use of these preliminary steps (direct) on 10 use cases available in the project repository, similar to the one in Table 1. These test cases simulate realistic scenarios for designing an interactive treasure hunt, varying in theme, focus, difficulty, and descriptions of the target audience and styles to be followed. A fixed sequence of 4 popular artworks from the Prado Museum was set as input for all use cases. All the experiments in this section were performed using a Llama 3.1 8B model, queried through Guidance calls, and on a PC with 16 GB of RAM and an Intel Core i7-9750H, 2.60 GHz processor.

For each of the generated stages, we define three possible creation errors: correctness failure (i.e., the phase includes false information), style failure (i.e., the phase does not follow the style stated in the input, or presents some form of generation error), and finally domain failure (i.e., the phase does not conform to the general design constraints). Note that the failure cases do not necessarily have to be mutually exclusive. Table 2 reports the error counts by type found upon close inspection of each of the generated adventures. The complete issue log together with more detailed notes can be found in the project repository.

Table 2. Error Type Counts by Experiment Type and Stage Group.

Stage Type	Correctness		Domain		Style	
	Planned	Direct	Planned	Direct	Planned	Direct
Narrative	0	0	31*	16	12	20
Question	2	4	1	1	2	4
Clue	0	0	0	0	0	0

The first remark to be made here is that while the table includes rows for errors related to clue-type stages, all of their values are 0, as no errors were encountered for any of the categories described in the collection of adventures generated for both modalities. In order to understand the error counts for each of the categories in the table, it is nonetheless necessary to carry out a more exhaustive analysis of the nature of the errors recorded.

In the planned generation scenario, one of the most conspicuous features is the high number of domain errors observed, almost twice as many than with direct generation. On closer inspection, 24 of the 31 reported errors correspond to the problem "The next artefact is revealed in the narrative ahead of time", meaning that the narrative explicitly mentions the name of the artefact that the player must find in the next clue-type phase. This is true at some point in a large majority of the adventures produced with this method. The remaining mistakes correspond mostly to generation problems arising from the tendency of the model to repeat phrases or whole blocks of context, effectively invalidating an affected narrative block, or problems related to stopping rules of the regular expressions used to control generation colliding with the intention of the model. As an example, we have the case of sentences terminated prematurely by writing "Mr."; since the regular expression decides that a valid sentence ends in a full stop, this halts generation, leaving the phrase half-finished. Problems with questions are mostly linked to the introduction of distractors that are correct or whose phrasing makes them too close to being correct. Correctness errors for questions are tied to suggestions of invalid correct answers.

Table 3. Aggregated execution time and word count statistics both approaches.

Category	Planned				Direct			
	Time (s)		Words		Time (s)		Words	
	Mean	Std	Mean	Std	Mean	Std	Mean	Std
Narrative	149.42	55.40	339.87	246.61	140.49	62.46	331.38	294.24
Question	84.84	8.74	99.85	26.50	80.88	7.57	91.13	24.18
Clue	54.68	2.89	24.43	4.80	53.58	2.55	24.45	4.68
Character Generation	44.08	1.48	16.85	3.37	42.40	1.53	16.90	3.63
Fact Extraction	165.03	4.89	–	–	–	–	–	–
Plan Generation	443.45	18.30	–	–	–	–	–	–

In the case of direct generation, a higher number of stylistic errors are observed. These often stem from two issues: the model either fails to follow the designer's input or, more commonly, gets caught in a loop, repeatedly generating the same sentences. This problem can spread across multiple stages of the narrative—something that occurs far less frequently in the planned approach. Besides this issue, domain errors in narratives of this generation type are typically more disruptive than those of the previous method, as they stem largely from inconsistencies in dialogue or story. For instance, in the use case "Interactive Family Tour", the characters, both children, hold conversations while referring to each other as "mum" and introduce this into their interactions in a significantly confusing way, producing a difficult-to-understand narrative. On the other hand, several situations were observed in which the model references artworks unrelated to the user's input as if they were the next artefacts to be found by the player. Something similar happens, for example, in the use case "Time Travel Adventure", where the model implies repeatedly that the adventure was focused on the works of authors outside the visit, such as Leonardo Da Vinci.

Regarding questions, on top of the problems present in the planned model, errors can arise that are linked to an excess of information both in the question (e.g., revealing data on the correct answer) and in the correct answers, as these may become overly verbose and clearly different from the distractors in expressive tone. This problem of overly long questions also translates in specific cases into sentences truncated for exceeding the token limit during generation.

The average time to generate each phase type for both approaches, as well as the average word count in phase definitions, are listed in Table 3. The only notable numerical difference is that the planned version takes about 10 min longer on average than the direct one, corresponding to the execution time of the fact extraction and pre-planning part of the approach. However, since neither method needs to operate in real time, this might not prove relevant in practice.

6 Discussion

In Sect. 5, we focused on providing objective data to draw an initial quantitative profile of our approaches. From a practical point of view, however, it is essential to analyse the overall quality of the adventures created using each method. In this sense, we are interested in understanding which adventures best meet the objective of generating a first skeleton for an adventure based on cultural heritage works. This refers to suggestions that a designer or curator would be able to use as a starting point to build upon in the creative process.

With this in mind, there is a clear tendency for planned adventures to be more consistent with respect to a clear narrative scheme. That is, this methodology tends to result in schemes with a more directed and centred narrative focus throughout the different dialogue blocks than its counterpart without planning. Also, domain errors found with planning are generally easier to correct than those introduced in the direct approach, in that they are often reduced to simply revealing the name of the artefact of the next clue; thus, in many cases it is sufficient to omit this information to obtain a valid phase.

On the other hand, it is not uncommon to find minor hallucinations in the narrative discourse of the direct method, where the model occasionally makes comments regarding works that were never entered as input and therefore have no reason to be in the collection. For example, in the use case "Museum Treasure Hunt",[4] the characters discuss that the piece "The Ecstasy of St. Teresa" caught their attention, without this being part of the actual collection, and then talk about Caravaggio's "The Taking of Christ" holding the key to the next clue, again without this being substantiated by any input and therefore being incorrect from a design point of view. While the planned model is not without these flaws (see the same use case where "The Wynter Gallery's Dutch art gallery" is mentioned), these references tend to be more anecdotal than in its counterpart.

As previously discussed, clues are always valid during generation and can often be considered compelling suggestions, similar to those a designer might propose. However, it is important to note that the clues are generated without the model being aware of all the possible works in the environment where the target

---

[4] Full examples may be found in https://github.com/pgutierrez858/enigma-llms/tree/master/experiments/results.

artefact is located, and therefore the generation cannot account for possible distractors the riddle could lead to. Now, writing engaging clues for the target audience with a single solution is a challenge and, based on our experience, is something whose validation often depends on user playtesting.

The questions generated by both approaches are generally valid, adhering to the source text, the designer's intention, and the specified difficulty, making them useful first suggestions in the adventure construction process. However, it is important to note that both methods sometimes generate questions that, while correct, are not directly based on the text but likely on the information used to train the original model. While this is not necessarily a flaw, it can lead to hallucinations, for instance, in situations when multiple artefacts seen in training texts share the same name and the model references the wrong one.

7 Conclusions and Future Work

In this paper we introduce a first approach to the automatic generation of treasure hunt games for cultural heritage sites supported by large language models. Starting from a user input specifying the artefacts to be included in the adventure and various textual design parameters, our approach produces a JSON-structured draft of a preliminary quest that strives to comply with the entered constraints. Following the discussion in Sects. 5 and 6, we find that our approach provides a tentative validation of the hypotheses raised in Sect. 4, proposing that the application of a pre-planning strategy has a positive effect on the correctness, consistency, and style of the generated drafts.

There are, however, limitations and points for future work. The first is the potential bias incurred in the selection of the design use cases, which were gathered manually by the authors. The use of a broader dataset derived from interviews with professional content curators in museums is left for future work. Secondly, while here we focus on a pilot for the generation of consistent initial versions of such games, comprehensive usability evaluations, both of how useful the LLM responses are to the designer and a detailed analysis of problems that may arise in the flow of human interaction with the system, remain to be carried out.

Thirdly, our approach as it stands does not allow for interactivity during creation. Alongside the approaches in this work and in the literature, there is a developing interest in the notion of co-design, or turning the human designer into an active actor in the generation algorithm, requesting their insight and participation at different points throughout the applied method [9,26]. In this sense, one of the clearest lines of future work consists of incorporating this paradigm into the workflow for creating treasure hunts, allowing a scenario in which the designer can make use of these generative tools at any point in the creative process and not only in the bootstrapping phase.

Finally, while more advanced models such as GPT-3.5 or GPT-4 exist that have been found to work well for a multitude of tasks [6], their proprietary nature raises concerns. Llama 3.1 Instruct 8B was used due to it being an open source model that can be deployed on modest hardware and without the need for a dedicated GPU, while remaining performant for general applications [11]. This is relevant, as not all cultural institutions have the resources to run more demanding models. While this explains the a priori high execution times shown in the results section, it remains for future work to explore more efficient generation strategies, especially if interactivity is to be introduced in the workflow.

References

1. guidance-ai/guidance (2025). https://github.com/guidance-ai/guidance. Original-date: 2022-11-10T18:21:45Z
2. Akoury, N., Yang, Q., Iyyer, M.: A framework for exploring player perceptions of LLM-generated dialogue in commercial video games. In: Findings of the Association for Computational Linguistics: EMNLP 2023, pp. 2295–2311. Association for Computational Linguistics, Singapore (2023). https://doi.org/10.18653/v1/2023.findings-emnlp.151, https://aclanthology.org/2023.findings-emnlp.151
3. Ardito, C., Costabile, M.F., De Angeli, A., Lanzilotti, R.: Enriching archaeological parks with contextual sounds and mobile technology. ACM Trans. Comput.-Hum. Interact. **19**(4), 1–30 (12 2012). https://doi.org/10.1145/2395131.2395136
4. Buongiorno, S., Klinkert, L., Zhuang, Z., Chawla, T., Clark, C.: PANGeA: procedural artificial narrative using generative AI for turn-based, role- playing video games. In: Proceedings of the AAAI Conference on Artificial Intelligence and Interactive Digital Entertainment, vol. 20, no. 1, pp. 156–166 (2024). https://doi.org/10.1609/aiide.v20i1.31876, https://ojs.aaai.org/index.php/AIIDE/article/view/31876
5. Cesário, V., Radeta, M., Matos, S., Nisi, V.: The ocean game. In: Extended Abstracts Publication of the Annual Symposium on Computer-Human Interaction in Play, pp. 99–109. ACM (2017). https://doi.org/10.1145/3130859.3131435
6. Chen, X., et al.: How robust is GPT-3.5 to predecessors? A comprehensive study on language understanding tasks (2023). https://arxiv.org/abs/2303.00293
7. DaCosta, B., Kinsell, C.: Serious games in cultural heritage: a review of practices and considerations in the design of location-based games. Educ. Sci. **13**(1), 47 (2022). https://doi.org/10.3390/educsci13010047, https://www.mdpi.com/2227-7102/13/1/47
8. Di Nezza, M., De Santis, A., D'Addezio, G.: Cityquest and 'Caccia al...Tesoro dei Castelli'. La nuova frontiera della divulgazione formato 2.0. Rendiconti Online della Società Geologica Italiana **45**, 17–22 (2018). https://doi.org/10.3301/rol.2018.23
9. Gallotta, R., Liapis, A., Yannakakis, G.: Consistent game content creation via function calling for large language models. In: 2024 IEEE Conference on Games (CoG), pp. 1–4. IEEE, Milan (2024). https://doi.org/10.1109/CoG60054.2024.10645599, https://ieeexplore.ieee.org/document/10645599/
10. Gonzalez-Calero, P., Camps-Ortueta, I., Gutiérrez-Sánchez, P., Gómez-Martín, P.: On the importance of contextualizing an educational escape room activity. Electron. J. e-Learn. **22**, 43–56 (2024). https://doi.org/10.34190/ejel.22.4.3199
11. Grattafiori, A., et al.: The LLaMA 3 herd of models (2024). https://arxiv.org/abs/2407.21783
12. Helmy, M., et al.: Navigating the world with an intelligent tourist guide using generative AI. In: 2024 International Telecommunications Conference (ITC-Egypt), pp. 1–6. IEEE, Cairo (2024). https://doi.org/10.1109/ITC-Egypt61547.2024.10620592, https://ieeexplore.ieee.org/document/10620592/

13. Hu, S., Huang, Z., Hu, C., Liu, J.: 3D building generation in minecraft via large language models (2024). https://arxiv.org/abs/2406.08751
14. Camps-Ortueta, I., Rodríguez-Muñoz, J.M., Gómez-Martín, P.P., González-Calero, P.A.: Combining augmented reality with real maps to promote social interaction in treasure hunts. In: Conference of the Spanish Association for Videogames Sciences (2017)
15. Khan, I., Melro, A., Carla, A., Oliveira, L.: Systematic review on gamification and cultural heritage dissemination. J. Digit. Media Interact. **3**(8), 19–41 (2020). https://doi.org/10.34624/JDMI.V3I8.21934, https://proa.ua.pt/index.php/jdmi/article/view/21934
16. Kumaran, V., Rowe, J., Lester, J.: NarrativeGenie: generating narrative beats and dynamic storytelling with large language models. In: Proceedings of the AAAI Conference on Artificial Intelligence and Interactive Digital Entertainment, vol. 20, no. 1, pp. 76–86 (2024). https://doi.org/10.1609/aiide.v20i1.31868, https://ojs.aaai.org/index.php/AIIDE/article/view/31868
17. Malegiannaki, I., Daradoumis, T.: Analyzing the educational design, use and effect of spatial games for cultural heritage: a literature review. Comput. Educ. 108, 1–10 (2017). https://doi.org/10.1016/j.compedu.2017.01.007, https://linkinghub.elsevier.com/retrieve/pii/S0360131517300076
18. Mortara, M., Catalano, C.E., Bellotti, F., Fiucci, G., Houry-Panchetti, M., Petridis, P.: Learning cultural heritage by serious games. J. Cult. Heritage **15**(3), 318–325 (2014). https://doi.org/10.1016/j.culher.2013.04.004, https://linkinghub.elsevier.com/retrieve/pii/S1296207413001349
19. Paliokas, I., Sylaiou, S.: The use of serious games in museum visits and exhibitions: a systematic mapping study. In: 2016 8th International Conference on Games and Virtual Worlds for Serious Applications (VS-GAMES), pp. 1–8. IEEE, Barcelona (2016). https://doi.org/10.1109/VS-GAMES.2016.7590371, http://ieeexplore.ieee.org/document/7590371/
20. Short, A.R.: Designing fictional worlds for play through large language models. In: Volume 3B: 50th Design Automation Conference (DAC), p. V03BT03A051. American Society of Mechanical Engineers, Washington, DC (2024). https://doi.org/10.1115/DETC2024-143923, https://asmedigitalcollection.asme.org/IDETC-CIE/proceedings/IDETC-CIE2024/88377/V03BT03A051/1208864
21. Sudhakaran, S., González-Duque, M., Glanois, C., Freiberger, M., Najarro, E., Risi, S.: MarioGPT: open-ended Text2Level generation through large language models (2023). https://doi.org/10.48550/arXiv.2302.05981, arXiv:2302.05981
22. Taveekitworachai, P., Nimpattanavong, C., Gursesli, M.C., Lanata, A., Guazzini, A., Thawonmas, R.: Multiverse of greatness: generating story branches with LLMs (2024). https://doi.org/10.48550/arXiv.2411.14672, arXiv:2411.14672
23. Todd, G., Earle, S., Nasir, M.U., Green, M.C., Togelius, J.: Level generation through large language models. In: Proceedings of the 18th International Conference on Foundations of Digital Games, pp. 1–8. ACM, Lisbon (2023). https://doi.org/10.1145/3582437.3587211, https://dl.acm.org/doi/10.1145/3582437.3587211
24. Trichopoulos, G.: Large language models for cultural heritage. In: Proceedings of the 2nd International Conference of the ACM Greek SIGCHI Chapter, pp. 1–5. ACM, Athens (2023). https://doi.org/10.1145/3609987.3610018, https://dl.acm.org/doi/10.1145/3609987.3610018
25. Wei, J., et al.: Chain-of-thought prompting elicits reasoning in large language models (2023). https://doi.org/10.48550/arXiv.2201.11903, arXiv:2201.11903

26. Yannakakis, G.N., Liapis, A., Alexopoulos, C.: Mixed-initiative co-creativity (2014). https://www.semanticscholar.org/paper/Mixed-initiative-co-creativity-Yannakakis-Liapis/0a410eecf3b23042f95ebfbe0ffdc08ea697c9d9
27. Yao, S., et al.: ReAct: synergizing reasoning and acting in language models. In: International Conference on Learning Representations (ICLR) (2023). https://par.nsf.gov/biblio/10451467-react-synergizing-reasoning-acting-language-models
28. Yu, J., et al.: Personalized treasure hunt game for proactive museum appreciation by analyzing guide app operation log. In: Goh, D.H., Chen, SJ., Tuarob, S. (eds.) ICADL 2023. LNCS, vol. 14458, pp. 30–45. Springer, Singapore (2023). https://doi.org/10.1007/978-981-99-8088-8_3
29. Yu, S., et al.: Few-shot generative conversational query rewriting. In: Proceedings of the 43rd International ACM SIGIR Conference on Research and Development in Information Retrieval, pp. 1933–1936. ACM, Virtual Event China (2020). https://doi.org/10.1145/3397271.3401323, https://dl.acm.org/doi/10.1145/3397271.3401323
30. Yu-Han, C., Chun-Ching, C.: Investigating the impact of generative artificial intelligence on brainstorming: a preliminary study. In: 2023 International Conference on Consumer Electronics - Taiwan (ICCE-Taiwan), pp. 193–194 (2023). https://doi.org/10.1109/ICCE-Taiwan58799.2023.10226617

Pacing Control with Wave Function Collapse in Strategy Game Map Generation

Ardiawan Bagus Harisa[1](✉), Muhammad Alifian Aqshol[2],
Pulung Nurtantio Andono[2], and Wen-Kai Tai[1]

[1] National Taiwan University of Science and Technology,
Taipei 106335, Taiwan (R.O.C.)
ardiawanbagusharisa@gmail.com
[2] Universitas Dian Nuswantoro, Semarang 50131, Indonesia

Abstract. In our effort to introduce programming foundations to high school students in a more engaging way, we are developing a turn-based tactics game named MECH.AI. Players control the game objects not only through the graphical user interface, but also the command line, simulating programming practices. However, providing strategy game maps and challenges is crucial and can significantly impact the game pacing, thereby affecting the player experience. In this study, we apply a procedural content system that generates game maps using the Wave Function Collapse algorithm with pacing controllable by the designer. We examine a pacing aspect that influences player experience, specifically tempo. This system enables us to generate tactical game maps and manage the game pacing. The experiment setups and results are presented.

Keywords: Procedural content generation · Strategy game · Turn-based tactics · Wave Function Collapse · Game design · Serious game

1 Introduction

Beside their entertainment value, serious games serve educational roles [14,16], notably by enhancing student motivation [12,22] and engagement [2], including programming [6]. One popular sub-genre is turn-based tactics (TBT) games, also known as turn-based strategy games [21,23]. These games, where players manage characters and resources to overcome enemies and explore environments [5,15], are among the industry's most profitable. The presence of tactical nature makes them effective tools for teaching programming logic.

We developed MECH.AI (Fig. 1), a turn-based sci-fi tactics game where players pilot mecha robots to mine futuristic currency, to teach secondary students programming fundamentals. We use game development life cycle (GDLC), one methodology for video game development [1,18]. Designing appropriate maps and challenges is crucial, as these directly impact game pacing and, consequently, the overall player experience.

Game pacing, defined as the activity flow in a video game (e.g., movement, attacks) that impacts player experience [17], can be analyzed through threats, movement impetus, and tempo [8]. To maintain player engagement through varied battle maps, procedural content generation (PCG) is effective, as it uses design patterns to create diverse new content [11]. The Wave Function Collapse (WFC) algorithm, inspired by quantum mechanics, is one such PCG method and it can be utilized for generating consistent, large-scale output from minimal constraints [20]. Generating a wider variety of stage maps allows players to employ diverse strategies at different game pacings, leading to a more fulfilling gaming experience.

This research applies and analyzes the Wave Function Collapse (WFC) technique to automatically generate turn-based tactics game maps by controlling the game tempo, a key pacing aspect defined by the designer. Thus, resulting in better experience and maintain player engagement. This method could also enrich map variety in other game genres. Section 2 reviews literature on GDLC, WFC, and pacing. Section 3 details MECH.AI's development, the Map Generator, and pacing implementation. Sections 4 and 5 present experimental results and conclusions, respectively. However, we do not discuss the impact of the proposed system on serious game purposes.

2 Literature Study

In this study, we are developing MECH.AI using the Game Development Life Cycle (GDLC), a methodology that phases game development into analysis, production, testing, and release [13,18,19]. We are currently in the production phase, creating the game mechanics and integrating learning contents for a prototype. Concurrently, we are applying Wave Function Collapse (WFC) for procedural battle map generation. This approach aims to confirm that game pacing can effectively control map generation in strategy games, building on its prior application in dungeon-crawler [8] and platformer games [7] using different methods.

2.1 Wave Function Collapse

Procedural Content Generation (PCG) is widely used in games to automate content creation by utilizing pseudo-random numbers and other techniques, and the benchmarking topics have emerged [10]. It offers significant benefits, including labor efficiency, enhanced creative expression for designers, storage savings, and potentially unlimited replayability [3]. Inspired from the quantum mechanism, Wave Function Collapse (WFC) is a PCG algorithm that generates images by arranging tiles based on adjacency rules and frequency constraints [4,11]. Much WFC research focuses on its ability to generate levels from image data and expanding its design domain [9], as it's popular for grid-based game maps.

There are three key WFC terms: pattern, constraint solver, and entropy. A pattern depicts repetitive (game) area occurrences, typically small sub-tiles in the strategy games (e.g., $n \times n$ windows) [9]. In this context, the input is a seed pattern, and the output is the generated map. Entropy in WFC reflects the uncertainty or disorder of patterns at each grid location in the output map. High entropy in a cell indicates many potential patterns, while low entropy means fewer options. The algorithm prioritizes resolving cells with lower entropy first, as this reduces uncertainty and enhances coherence, efficiently exploring the solution space for a more structured final texture (or map) [9].

The WFC constraint solver treats map generation as a Constraint Satisfaction Problem (CSP), ensuring output adheres to input patterns. Variables represent tile states, while constraints maintain local patterns and prevent conflicts, like adjacency rules [9]. The algorithm iteratively collapses tiles, using backtracking to find valid configurations and detecting contradictions if constraints aren't met. In this study, constraints include $n \times n$ seed tiles and game pacing, with a primary focus on tempo. Although, as stated by [7,8], it can be intuitively implemented and tailored to designer preferences.

2.2 Pacing

Pacing refers to the flow or rate of activity, and in games, game pacing is the pace influenced by cummulative aspects of threats, movement impetus, and tempo within a level segment [7,8]. Conceptually, tempo relates to the length and timing of player actions; higher action intensity and object density (enemies, obstacles, treasures) typically result in a higher tempo. In this study, we apply WFC to map generation, using a pacing aspect (specifically tempo, as noted in Sect. 1) as a constraint to control the player experience set by the designer. More details on pacing implementation are in Sect. 3.

3 Methodology

This research aims to implement an efficient, high-quality map generation solution for MECH.AI, a turn-based tactics game, while considering the game tempo. The approach applies the WFC algorithm in the pre-battle phase, with testing to evaluate its ability to generate maps that align with the intended pacing.

3.1 Development of MECH.AI and Map Representation

MECH.AI (Fig. 1) is currently being developed following GDLC framework by our student club Game AI Code Lab (GACLab) with the aim to provide tool for teaching programming concepts. The battle loop starts with players deploy the robots on designated tiles, then take turns moving, attacking, using skills, which consume energy, or idling to regain energy. The players control the robots via buttons or command line, with a future plan for AI script submissions. For example, the command Move(a,x,y) moves robot a to a tile (x,y). The game development of MECH.AI began with analysis (Fig. 2) to define serious game objectives and infrastructure, leading to a prototype in the production phase

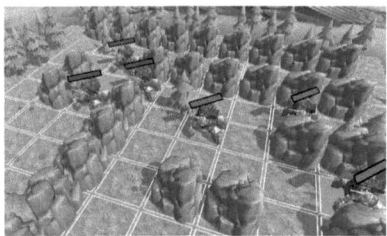 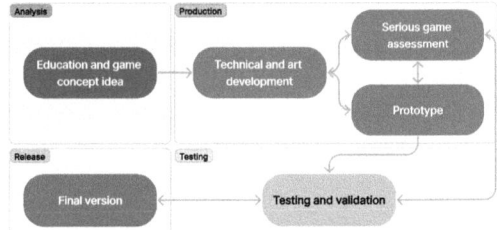

Fig. 1. MECH.AI: Turn-based tactics game; red team vs blue team. (Color figure online)

Fig. 2. Game development life cycle used to develop MECH.AI.

with technical specifications and a tutorial. After internal testing, the Minimum Viable Product (MVP) is released on GitHub for feedback.

A battle map is represented by a combination of tiles (passable and obstacle) in a 10 × 10 grid. A tile is a single occupiable area where a robot's actions take place (refer to Fig. 4; bottom part). A passable tile is one that players can move through, while an obstacle tile contains a destructible blocking environment. The map is generated using WFC and is designed to be playable according to the game pacing set by the designer. The presence of obstacles requires players to think strategically. For instance, a tree may take one hit to destroy, while a rock may have three hit points. However, in this study, we only experiment with one type of obstacle as a proof of concept, namely rocks.

3.2 Map Generator

Our WFC system generated a map in the pre-battle state. An explanation of how the map generation process through WFC works is shown in Fig. 3. Map patterns are created by combining individual tiles and input seed patterns, which are $n \times n$ collections of visual and gameplay elements. In this study, we experiment with pattern sizes of 3 × 3, 4 × 4, and 5 × 5. These seed map, which are smaller than the final map, guide the distribution of obstacles and establish adjacency rules–ensuring the generation of coherent and logical patterns preferred by designer.

Entropy in WFC signifies the degree of uncertainty within the system. In our case, it is used to assign weights to each tile, which helps determine the most probable neighboring tiles once a specific tile is established. In a sense, it is selecting patterns and values during the pattern propagation process. This concept also helps evaluate the complexity of a particular area, influencing the selection of values or patterns as constraints and information spread throughout the map to ensure consistency across all neighboring tiles. We discuss the entropy calculation in the core solver. To ensure the playability of the map, we applied a straightforward mechanism that allows each area to reserve three tiles for robot deployment. Moreover, it can be addressed with the seed pattern design.

Core Solver. The process begins with the construction of a seed pattern from a small map as input, then converted into a 2D matrix of tile type indices (refer

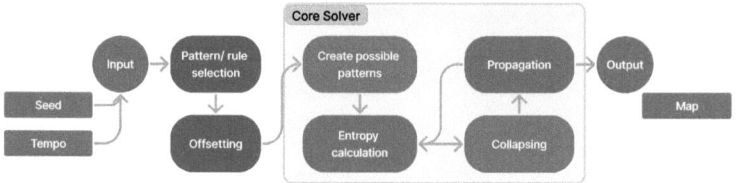

Fig. 3. The overview of the WFC in this study.

to Fig. 4, step 1). Next, patterns, typically using an $n \times n$ filter (step 2), are identified to define tile relationships and WFC's complexity space. This study does not apply filter rotation; patterns are taken directly from the seed. For example, a passable tile surrounded by trees in seed C (Fig. 5) won't be mirrored, and the system will not detect if there is a mirrored case on the right corner. Additionally, an offset (step 3) is added to the seed's edges to ensure possible neighbors.

A 10×10 output map grid is allocated, with each tile initially containing all possible types (step 4). Tile types are then determined, with weights calculated based on frequency and adjacency rules. In this study, we aim for a balanced patterns (distribution of obstacles) by segmenting the output map into four 5×5 tile sections. As illustrated in step 5 of Fig. 4, the system segments the map into four smaller parts, with each segment offsetting to its neighbor for seamless connections, ensuring balanced yet not overly symmetrical patterns.

A random starting tile is chosen, and the core WFC solver iteratively collapses each cell. This involves calculating entropy, applying constraint distribution to all possible tiles, and finally collapsing them. Neighboring tile weights are calculated by spreading to surrounding cells, and the cell with the lowest entropy is generally chosen for collapse. This iterative process continues until all cells are collapsed. Equation 1 shows the entropy calculation, and step 6 depicts the propagation simulation during cell collapsing. For this study, entropy S is calculated as cumulative weights of a map reduced by each pattern's average weight. Note that entropy calculation implementation may vary by specific case.

$$S = log_2(\sum W) - \frac{log_2(W_1) + ... + log_2(W_n)}{\sum W} \qquad (1)$$

Pacing Implementation. The final evaluation determines if the generated map aligns with the game's target tempo, a key pacing aspect we are focusing on as a proof of concept (though movement impetus and threat could also be explored). We analyze two design patterns affecting tempo: deployed obstacles and maze patterns. More obstacles in deployment areas increase tempo by demanding more player actions (movement or attacks), while fewer obstacles reduce it. To ensure fairness, players deploy robots in designated safe zones, preventing unfair advantages for the second player. Figure 4 (bottom) illustrates these deployment areas (light red/blue) and non-deployable zones (dark grey).

The ratio of obstacles in the seed pattern affects the resulting tempo. The number of obstacles in deployment tiles ($O = min(t_D, ((R \times t_D) + O_S) \times T_I)$) is used, where t_D is the number of possible deployable tiles, O_s is the number of obstacles in the seed pattern, R is the obstacle ratio in the seed, and T_I is the designer's intended tempo. This equation suggests the number of obstacles generated is the lower value between deployable tiles and the obstacle ratio relative to the intended pacing; theoretically, the latter is often chosen. Finally, Eq. 2 calculates the actual tempo T_A, referred to as the first tempo factor or tempo A. It's derived from the difference between the number of obstacles on the map and in the seed pattern, divided by the obstacle ratio multiplied by the number of tiles in the deployment area.

$$T_A = \frac{O - O_S}{R \times t_D} \quad (2)$$

$$T_B = \frac{\sum(Wo_{i,j} - L_{n0})}{L_{nm} - L_{n0}} \quad (3)$$

The second tempo factor, maze pattern (or Tempo B), focuses on optimally placing obstacles to encourage more player movement or destruction, according to the tile's weight. We presume higher robot activity increases tempo, and vice-versa. To determine tile weights, we simulated an A* pathfinding algorithm. We iteratively selected starting points $t_s(x_i, y_i)$ in Team A's area and target tiles $t_t(x_i, y_i)$ in Team B's area, then repeated the process with Team B as starting points to ensure accuracy for asymmetrical maps. Although, our current map is a symmetrical 10×10 rectangle, hypothetically it could produced similarly good results in the arbitrary map shapes. The resulting tile weights are visualized as a heatmap in Fig. 4 (bottom-right).

Tiles with heavier weights cluster in the map's middle, while lighter ones are towards the sides. Obviously, non-deployable neutral areas have similar weights, bridging both teams as robots are not allowed to be deployed there. Equations 3 define Tempo B (T_B), using $L_W = [W_{i,j}, ..., W_{n,m}]$ for the ascending sorted list of tile weights from the output map, and L_{n0} and L_{nm} for the lower and upper normalization limits. Finally, the overall tempo T is the weighted average of T_A and T_B, using designer-set weights W_A and W_B.

4 Experiments and Results

This section analyzes two tempo factors in WFC-generated MECH.AI maps: Tempo A T_A (obstacles spread in deployment areas) and Tempo B T_B (obstacle placement for maze-like structures, increasing player movement) using W_A and W_B both 0.5. All experiments used 10×10 output maps and the sample seed patterns from Fig. 5, with each experiment run 100 times using Intel Core i5 with 16GB RAM. Here, we conducted three main experiment categories: 1) Initial:

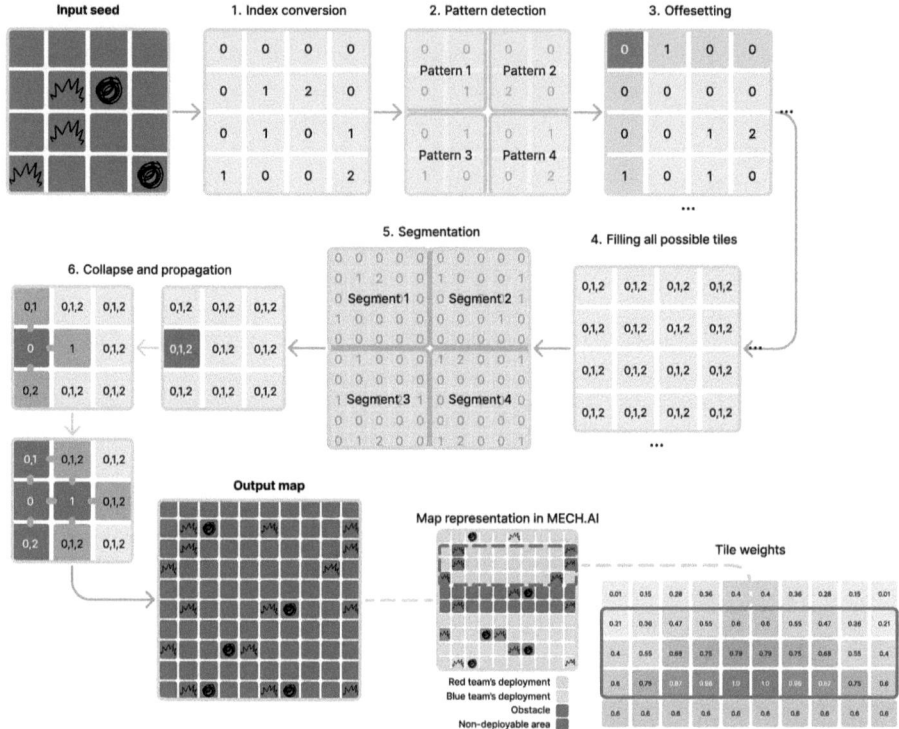

Fig. 4. The flow of map generation in this study. (Color figure online)

trials to confirm the system's alignment with set seed patterns and target tempo values, 2) Single-seed: analysis of tempo changes using a single seed pattern with 0.1 intervals, and 3) Seeds: analysis across four different seed patterns to achieve similar tempo values.

4.1 Initial Experiment

This experiment evaluated the fitness of output maps generated using three different seeds as shown in Fig. 5: seed A (3×3), C (4×4), and D (5×5), targeting low (0.25), balanced (0.5), and high (0.75) tempo values. Although both seeds B and C have the same size, seed C was chosen over B due to its asymmetrical nature. The known obstacle ratios are $R = \{0.33, 0.31, 0.48\}$, for seed A, C, and D, respectively.

As shown in Table 1, using $T_I = 0.25$, seed A had a fitness of 0.99, seed C was 1.0, and seed D was the lowest at 0.89. Using the second target $T_I = 0.5$, seed D remained the lowest at 0.71, while seeds A and C achieved 1.0 and 0.99, respectively. Finally, by using the high target tempo $T_I = 0.75$, seed A yielded 0.9, seed C 0.94, and seed D only 0.55 of fitness. These results imply that seeds A and C consistently align closer to the expected tempo, and the obstacle ratio

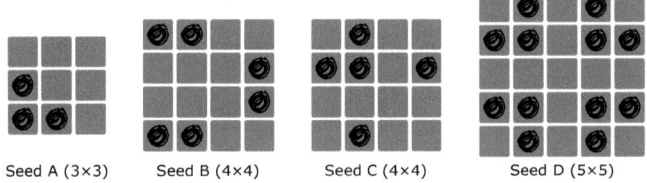

Fig. 5. The sample seed patterns used as the input for experiments. Left to right: Seed A, B, C, and D, respectively.

R significantly impacts the resulting tempo. Although seeds A and C differ in size, their obstacle ratio settings also played a crucial role.

Table 1. Fitness on Target Tempo across seeds in the initial experiment.

Seed	Target Tempo			Gen. Time (s)
	0.25 (Low)	0.5 (Bal.)	0.75 (High)	
A ($R = 0.33$)	0.99	1	0.9	9.85
C ($R = 0.31$)	1	0.99	0.94	0.35
D ($R = 0.48$)	0.89	0.71	0.55	0.13

The target tempo also influences output tempo, particularly evident in seed D's varied fitness across tempo levels. However, the solution to this problem also lies in the design of the seed pattern and its size, as it affected the collapsing process with the more complex seeds generally lead to higher error probabilities. Although smaller seeds like A (9.85 s) require more calculations and longer generation times compared to seeds C (0.35 s) and D (0.13 s), this trade-off highlights the need to balance seed complexity with obstacle ratio for optimal fitness and efficient procedural map generation.

4.2 Single-Seed Experiment

This experiment analyzed tempo results across various targets, running 100 iterations (with 5 inner-iterations) using seed B, starting at tempo 0.0 and increasing by 0.01 per iteration. Results were stable between tempo values of 0.1 and 0.9. According to Fig. 6, the averaged error for Tempo A was 6.35% and Tempo B was 3.48%, leading to an overall tempo error of 4.83%. Highest errors occurred at the tempo limits (0–0.1 and 0.9–1), potentially due to seed pattern design and target tempo not converging (e.g., a high-obstacle seed being unsuitable for low tempo targets). The system generally produced expected tempos with a

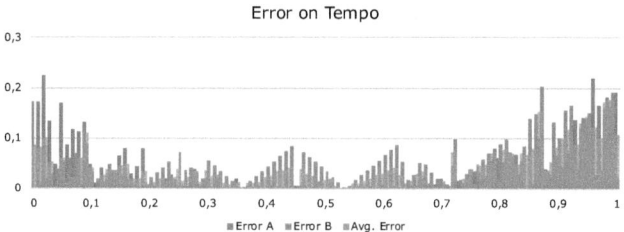

Fig. 6. Error distributions between Tempo A, B, and overall.

Table 2. Fitness on all tempo across the seeds in the single-seed experiment.

Seed	T_A	T_B	T
A	1	0.95	0.97
B	1	0.93	0.96
C	1	0.97	0.98
D	1	0.99	0.98
Avg.	1	0.95	0.97

low error rate (under 5%). Figure 7 shows sample outputs using seed B, with outputs between $0.1 < T < 0.9$ (especially around $T = 0.5$) appearing most human-crafted.

4.3 Seeds Experiment

The final experiment aimed to achieve an target tempo set by designer across different seeds in Fig. 5), specifically targeting $T = 0.5$ due to its consistently balanced fitness. Each seed was run through 50 independent simulations. According to Table 2, all seeds successfully produced the expected tempo, with an average overall tempo $\overline{T} = 0.97$. Across seed patterns, $\overline{T_B}$ had a 4% error, and $\overline{T}$ had a 3% error, while $\overline{T_A}$ converged perfectly. However, output samples from seeds C and D (Fig. 8) appeared less human-crafted, likely due to their high obstacle ratio (R). For seed D, this could be mitigated by reducing obstacles in the seed pattern. For seed C, the less human-crafted feel stems from obstacles converging in certain areas, suggesting a design change to scatter obstacles more.

4.4 User Study

We conducted an additional user study to evaluate the results produced by our system. The respondents consisted of 20 students, majoring in Computer Science at Universitas Dian Nuswantoro, Indonesia. Most of them are familiar with the strategy games, and were asked to answer questionnaire containing three questions (Q1–Q3). The purpose of this user study was to observe the respondents' perspectives in experiencing the maps produced by our map generator.

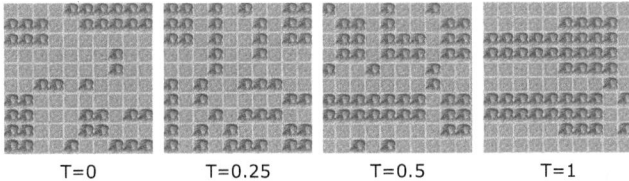

T=0 T=0.25 T=0.5 T=1

Fig. 7. Output maps using various tempo values $T = \{0, 0.25, 0.75, 1\}$ in the single seed experiment.

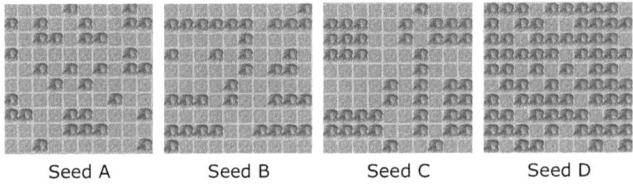

Seed A Seed B Seed C Seed D

Fig. 8. Output maps using seeds in Fig. 5 with the same $T = 0.5$ in the seeds experiment.

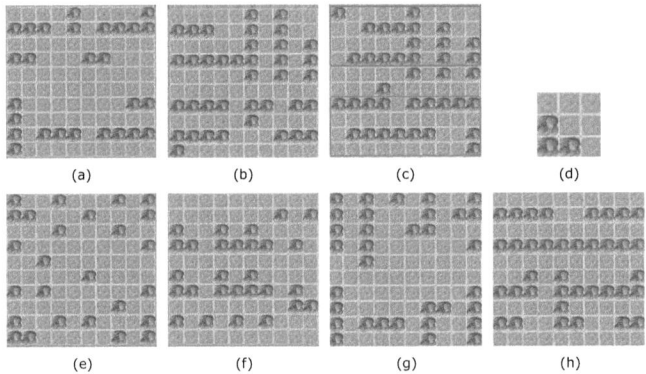

Fig. 9. Examples of generated output maps using various tempo and seeds. (a) Map with $T = 0.25$), (b) Map with $T = 0.75$), (c) Map with $T = 0.5$), (d) Seed A to generate (e) low tempo and (f) high tempo, (g) and (f) show the low tempo and high tempo of generated map by using seed C.

Q1 (Tempo Identification): Given two maps, which one has lower tempo, and which one has a higher tempo? 85% (17/20) of respondents correctly identified the map with lower or higher tempo after experiencing two maps (Fig. 9(a) and (b)), confirming the intended tempo experience.

Q2 (Asymmetrical Balance): Although being asymmetrical, do you think the map is balance for both teams? 90% (18/20) of respondents deemed an asymmetrical map (Fig. 9(c)) balanced for both teams, indicating WFC's ability to create fair, competitive environments despite asymmetry.

Q3 (Pattern Representation): Do you think the maps (10 × 10) represent the pattern in little maps (3 × 3)? 90% (18/20) of respondents agreed that the (10 × 10) output maps (Fig. 9(e) and (f)) represented the (3 × 3) seed patterns (Fig. 9(d)), validating WFC's consistency in scaling patterns while maintaining visual and structural integrity.

5 Conclusion

As part of our roadmap to enhance students' motivation and knowledge in programming and AI, we are developing MECH.AI, a turn-based tactics game. By using the Wave Function Collapse (WFC) algorithm, we generate the battle maps with the game designer setting the tempo to ensure the desired player experience. Experiments and user studies confirm the generator's effectiveness of this initial study. While WFC isn't new for map generation, its application here specifically for game pacing offers valuable insights into shaping player experience. We implemented a segmented WFC, dividing the map into four areas, to achieve a fair yet asymmetrical obstacle distribution. Building on previous work in dungeon-crawlers and platformers [7,8], this study extends the design concept to turn-based tactics, integrating pacing as a design consideration within procedural content generation for a more abstract, design-driven approach that may reinforces its role in the game narrative's pace as well.

In this study, note that smaller seed patterns require longer generation times due to more repetitive checks and calculations. We observed that near-edge tempo values (low: $T \leq \pm 0.1$; high: $T \geq \pm 0.9$) tend to produce the highest errors, likely due to seed pattern design. Although the overall error is acceptable ($< 5\%$), further study into seed pattern design is needed. This issue can often be resolved with minor tweaks to seed pattern design and obstacle ratio. Nonetheless, this generation process can assist designers in creating content for campaign or story modes where tempo dynamics can be automatically set to match narrative progression. Based on our unpresented experiments, we recommend that designers place at least one obstacle in the seed pattern, and avoid filling all tiles with obstacles ($0 < R < 1$), to ensure fitter outputs. It was observed that the best obstacle ratio R to be used is between around 0.1 to 0.4 (less than half). Moreover, it is likely that a human designer would not make the seed full of obstacles.

Additionally, a deeper comparative analysis to observe substantial differences in target/objectives, weight, entropy, or rules on WFC is still an ongoing work. Finally, this study redefines game pacing in video games, from a game design perspective to a more measurable approach, and potentially opening a new gate for research that bridges game design and quantitative measurement. Furthermore, the concept of procedural pacing could extend beyond video games to other mediums.

Acknowledgements. This study was partially funded by Universitas Dian Nuswantoro and National Taiwan University of Science and Technology. This research was also partially supported by National Science and Technology Council through Grant NSTC 114-2622-E-011-011.

Disclosure of Interests. The authors have no competing interests to declare that are relevant to the content of this article.

References

1. Aleem, S., Capretz, L.F., Ahmed, F.: Game development software engineering process life cycle: a systematic review. J. Softw. Eng. Res. Dev. **4**(1), 6 (2016). https://doi.org/10.1186/s40411-016-0032-7
2. Bassanelli, S., Bucchiarone, A., Gini, F.: GamiDOC: the importance of designing gamification in a proper way. IEEE Trans. Games 1–19 (2024). https://doi.org/10.1109/TG.2024.3364061, https://ieeexplore.ieee.org/abstract/document/10428094
3. Chen, Y.C., Li, S.R., Liu, I.C.: Attractiveness of mobile games—a case study of tile-matching games. In: 2018 IEEE International Conference on Applied System Invention (ICASI), pp. 642–645 (2018). https://doi.org/10.1109/ICASI.2018.8394338, https://ieeexplore.ieee.org/document/8394338
4. Cheng, D., Han, H., Fei, G.: Automatic generation of game levels based on controllable wave function collapse algorithm. In: Nunes, N.J., Ma, L., Wang, M., Correia, N., Pan, Z. (eds.) ICEC 2020. LNCS, vol. 12523, pp. 37–50. Springer, Cham (2020). https://doi.org/10.1007/978-3-030-65736-9_3
5. Gao, J.: The computational complexity of fire emblem series and similar tactical role-playing games (2019). https://doi.org/10.48550/arXiv.1909.07816, arXiv:1909.07816 [cs]
6. Hainey, T., Baxter, G.: A serious game for programming in higher education. Comput. Educ.: X Reality **4**, 100061 (2024). https://doi.org/10.1016/j.cexr.2024.100061, https://www.sciencedirect.com/science/article/pii/S2949678024000114
7. Harisa, A.B., Nugroho, S., Umaroh, L., Astuti, Y.P.: Threat construction for dynamic enemy status in a platformer game using classical genetic algorithm. Kinetik: Game Technol. Inf. Syst. Comput. Netw. Comput. Electron. Control (2023). https://doi.org/10.22219/kinetik.v8i3.1724, https://kinetik.umm.ac.id/index.php/kinetik/article/view/1724
8. Harisa, A.B., Tai, W.K.: Pacing-based procedural dungeon level generation: alternating level creation to meet designer's expectations. Int. J. Comput. Digit. Syst. **12**(1), 401–416 (2022). https://doi.org/10.12785/ijcds/120132, https://journal.uob.edu.bh:443/handle/123456789/4625. Accepted: 2022-07-22T02:13:19Z
9. Karth, I., Smith, A.M.: WaveFunctionCollapse is constraint solving in the wild. In: Proceedings of the 12th International Conference on the Foundations of Digital Games, FDG 2017, pp. 1–10. Association for Computing Machinery, New York (2017). https://doi.org/10.1145/3102071.3110566
10. Khalifa, A., Gallotta, R., Barthet, M., Liapis, A., Togelius, J., Yannakakis, G.N.: The procedural content generation benchmark: an open-source testbed for generative challenges in games. In: Proceedings of the 20th International Conference on the Foundations of Digital Games, FDG 2025. Association for Computing Machinery, New York (2025). https://doi.org/10.1145/3723498.3723794
11. Kim, H., Lee, S., Lee, H., Hahn, T., Kang, S.: Automatic generation of game content using a graph-based wave function collapse algorithm. In: 2019 IEEE Conference on Games (CoG), pp. 1–4 (2019). https://doi.org/10.1109/CIG.2019.8848019, https://ieeexplore.ieee.org/abstract/document/8848019, iSSN: 2325-4289

12. Lambić, D., Đorić, B., Ivakić, S.: Investigating the effect of the use of code.org on younger elementary school students' attitudes towards programming. Behav. Inf. Technol. **40**(16), 1784–1795 (2021). https://doi.org/10.1080/0144929X.2020.1781931
13. Lin, D., Bezemer, C.P., Hassan, A.E.: An empirical study of early access games on the Steam platform. Empir. Softw. Eng. **23**(2), 771–799 (2018). https://doi.org/10.1007/s10664-017-9531-3
14. López-Fernández, D., Mayor, J., Pérez, J., Gordillo, A.: Learning and motivational impact of using a virtual reality serious video game to learn scrum. IEEE Trans. Games **15**(3), 430–439 (2023). https://doi.org/10.1109/TG.2022.3213127, https://ieeexplore.ieee.org/abstract/document/9914622
15. Nam, S.G., Hsueh, C.H., Ikeda, K.: Generation of game stages with quality and diversity by reinforcement learning in turn-based RPG. IEEE Trans. Games 14(3), 488–501 (2022). https://doi.org/10.1109/TG.2021.3113313, https://ieeexplore.ieee.org/abstract/document/9541052
16. Ningrum, N.K., Harisa, A.B., Umaroh, L.: Learning through play: utilizing board games to enhance english vocabulary for early students. Techno Creat. **1**(2), 117–122 (2024). https://doi.org/10.62411/tcv.v1i2.1784, https://abdimasku.lppm.dinus.ac.id/index.php/technocreative/article/view/1784
17. Petko, D., Schmid, R., Cantieni, A.: Pacing in serious games: exploring the effects of presentation speed on cognitive load, engagement and learning gains. Simul. Gaming **51**(2), 258–279 (2020). https://doi.org/10.1177/1046878120902502
18. Ramadan, R., Widyani, Y.: Game development life cycle guidelines. In: 2013 International Conference on Advanced Computer Science and Information Systems (ICACSIS), pp. 95–100 (2013). https://doi.org/10.1109/ICACSIS.2013.6761558, https://ieeexplore.ieee.org/abstract/document/6761558
19. Roedavan, R., Pudjoatmodjo, B., Siradj, Y., Salam, S., Hardianti, B.D.: Serious game development model based on the game-based learning foundation. J. ICT Res. Appl. **15**(3), 291–305 (2021). https://doi.org/10.5614/itbj.ict.res.appl.2021.15.3.6, https://journals.itb.ac.id/index.php/jictra/article/view/15578
20. Sandhu, A., Chen, Z., McCoy, J.: Enhancing wave function collapse with design-level constraints. In: Proceedings of the 14th International Conference on the Foundations of Digital Games, FDG 2019, pp. 1–9. Association for Computing Machinery, New York (2019). https://doi.org/10.1145/3337722.3337752, https://dl.acm.org/doi/10.1145/3337722.3337752
21. Steam: Turn-Based Tactics (2021). https://store.steampowered.com/tags/en/Turn-Based+Tactics
22. Tsai, C.C.: The effects of augmented reality to motivation and performance in EFL vocabulary learning. Int. J. Instruct. **13**(4), 987–1000 (2020). https://doi.org/10.29333/iji.2020.13460a
23. Unlu, K.: Determinism versus stochasticity in the action economy of turn-based tactics games. Ph.D. thesis, Aalto University (2023). https://aaltodoc.aalto.fi/handle/123456789/119490

Generative Multimodal Content Creation with Location-Aware Context for Gamified Mobile Assisted Language Learning Apps Using Large Language Models

Robin Horst[1,2]([✉])[iD], Dung Trinh[1][iD], and Ralf Dörner[1]

[1] RheinMain University of Applied Sciences, Wiesbaden, Germany
{Robin.Horst,Ralf.Doerner}@hs-rm.de, Dung.Trinh@student.hs-rm.de
[2] Fraunhofer Institute for Computer Graphics Research IGD, Darmstadt, Germany
robin.horst@igd.fraunhofer.de

Abstract. The integration of digital technologies in language learning has transformed traditional paradigms, allowing for unprecedented flexibility and accessibility. Specifically, trends in Artificial Intelligence (AI) and Large Language Models (LLMs) offer great potential to generate multimodal content, for example, for Mobile-Assisted Language Learning (MALL) apps. However, it remains challenging to create content that is also compelling to users, including personalized aspects. This paper presents PlacePhrase, a gamified MALL application that leverages context-aware, generative content creation to enhance the learning experience. By utilizing LLM assistants and location-based data, PlacePhrase facilitates dynamic learning tasks, interactive conversations, and immersive exploration, addressing the limitations of current MALL applications. Our user study evaluated the app's usability, the quality of generated content, and the effectiveness of gamification elements. Results indicate a generally positive perception of the app, with participants appreciating the personalized and contextually relevant tasks, while also highlighting areas for improvement in immersion and flow experience. This research contributes to the ongoing exploration of AI-driven language learning tools and underscores the importance of integrating spatial context to create more engaging educational experiences.

Keywords: Mobile Assisted Language Learning · Multimodal Content Creation · Generative Artificial Intelligence

1 Introduction

The integration of digital technologies in language learning has transformed traditional paradigms. Language acquisition, once reliant on direct educator-learner interactions, is now increasingly facilitated by advanced technologies like smartphones, providing learners with greater flexibility and resources. This shift enables studies beyond conventional classrooms, reducing dependence on continuous teacher support.

Entertainment Computing caters to modern learners seeking engaging, immersive experiences, particularly through gamification. Mobile-Assisted Language Learning (MALL) applications, such as Duolingo, Rosetta Stone, Babbel, and Memrise, have gained market share by offering accessible and interactive language education. These applications utilize diverse pedagogical approaches, from simple flashcards to complex, gamified methods, enhancing the appeal of language learning.

Despite their success, these platforms face challenges related to content quality and contextual relevance [11,23]. The need for vast, meaningful content across multiple languages often results in generic narratives, limiting adaptability and engagement. This presents an opportunity for innovation in personalizing learning content to enhance its relevance for individual users.

Integrating Artificial Intelligence (AI), particularly Large Language Models (LLMs) and technologies like interactive virtual assistants, offers a promising avenue to address these challenges. These AI systems can generate contextually rich content that adapts to individual learner needs, fostering personalized educational experiences. However, the integration of AI technologies into language learning apps remains an emerging research area, requiring novel approaches guided by learning outcomes and content design [18].

This paper explores the generative creation of content that considers users' spatial environments to produce more meaningful language learning experiences. Our contributions are:

- Introducing PlacePhrase, a gamified MALL app providing task-based learning informed by the learner's spatial context.
- Presenting a hands-on case-study on generative content creation and design for multimodal MALL tasks, extended through location-based context and LLM assistants.
- Offering insights from our user study that provide lessons for future MALL apps incorporating learners' locations and generative content creation.

2 Related Work

The rise of MALL has transformed language engagement, offering on-the-go access, interactivity, and personalized feedback [12]. Traditional Computer-Assisted Language Learning (CALL) methods focused on static digital exercises, whereas MALL applications leverage mobile devices' portability, connectivity, and multimedia capabilities to provide immersive experiences. Popular MALL apps, such as Duolingo, Babbel, and Mondly, implement structured lesson plans with gamification elements, including points, badges, and leaderboards, to enhance user motivation [14,16].

Despite these advancements, our literature review identified several limitations in current MALL applications:

1. Lack of Contextual Adaptability: Most MALL apps adhere to predefined, linear learning paths, disregarding the learner's real-world context and location [2]. This limits opportunities for situated learning, where learners apply new vocabulary and grammar in practical settings.
2. Static and Repetitive Content: Many apps provide preset exercises that become predictable over time, reducing engagement and retention [5].
3. Limited Use of Generative AI for Content Creation: While AI has been applied to adaptive learning systems, generative multimodal content creation – capable of providing dynamic, personalized learning materials – remains underexplored in MALL research [7].

Research indicates that gamified language learning enhances user engagement and retention by increasing intrinsic motivation [3]. However, most MALL apps implement basic gamification elements (e.g., streaks, badges) without meaningful contextual integration [10]. Various approaches exist for contextualizing or individualizing content for users, including incorporating users' physical surroundings or real-world locations [19].

Recent advances in Generative AI – specifically LLMs like GPT-4 – have revolutionized language processing and content generation. LLMs can generate personalized text-based exercises tailored to the learner's proficiency level, provide contextualized conversational agents for simulated dialogue practice, and analyze learner input to generate real-time feedback on grammar, vocabulary, and fluency [1,15,20,22,25]. AI-driven language learning tools, such as ChatGPT and Duolingo Max, demonstrate enhanced personalization and adaptability compared to traditional rule-based systems [17]. However, current implementations remain largely text-based and do not leverage multimodal AI capabilities [2]. This underscores the need for research that integrates text, speech, images, and other modalities, including location-based data, to generate interactive, multimodal learning experiences.

Spatially aware learning – where physical location influences the learning experience – has been explored in educational research but remains underutilized in language learning applications. Nevertheless, location-based learning approaches (e.g., utilizing GPS, AR, or beacons) have been successfully applied in fields such as history education and cultural studies [6]. However, incorporating spatial features can require rather complex and challenging authoring technologies and processes, so that, at the example of AR-technologies, current research limits the content design to simplified pattern-based approaches [4,21] or the need to gamify authoring technologies themselves [8].

Despite advancements in MALL, gamification, and AI-driven content creation, we identified several research gaps at the intersection of these domains: existing MALL applications lack spatial context integration; generative AI has primarily been employed for static text-based tasks rather than multimodal content creation; and gamification in language learning often remains superficial, lacking meaningful context-aware interactions. This paper addresses these gaps by developing PlacePhrase, which combines gamification, generative multimodal content, and spatial context awareness to create a more immersive and adaptive learning experience.

3 PlacePhrase

PlacePhrase is a gamified, AI-powered MALL application that provides context-aware, interactive learning exercises. Our system leverages generative AI (LLMs like GPT) for real-time content creation, multimodal learning utilizing text, speech, and images, location-based learning to create situated language tasks, and gamification elements to enhance engagement. In the following sections, we will introduce PlacePhrase's gamified learning approaches and elaborate on our content creation approach using generative AI.

3.1 Gamified Learning Approaches

PlacePhrase incorporates three gamified learning exercises that leverage location-based context: 1) PicAndLearn, 2) SnapVocab, and 3) PhotoHunt. Users can select any of these options upon launching the app.

PicAndLearn. PicAndLearn offers traditional language learning tasks, including vocabulary learning, listening comprehension, and interactive conversation simulations. Instead of using pre-defined content, users create their own content based on image data through three simple steps. First, users provide context by taking a photo directly within the app, uploading a previously taken photo, or describing their surroundings in their native language. For example, in Fig. 1, the user took a picture of Big Ben in London. In the second step, users select the type of task they wish to generate. Finally, PicAndLearn provides an AI-generated image description in the desired language, allowing users to choose which learning task to execute first.

Vocabulary learning (Fig. 2) includes gap texts, sentence construction tasks, and single-choice questions generated from LLM agents based on the initial image input and the generated context. Listening comprehension creates a brief audio clip based on the given context using a text-to-speech model and provides users with content-related questions. The interactive conversation simulation first presents users with the context of the conversation (e.g., ordering an admission ticket near Big Ben) and allows them to select a role (e.g., vendor or tourist). The conversation proceeds with text or speech input from the user and AI-generated responses, concluding when the users decide.

SnapVocab. SnapVocab utilizes users' locations to provide image-based vocabulary riddles, incorporating user-generated snapshots relevant to their current surroundings (Fig. 3). Users can take a photo themselves, and descriptions are generated similarly to PicAndLearn. Alternatively, based on a map representation, users can select a specific image riddle nearby that was created by other users within the SnapVocab or PicAndLearn framework.

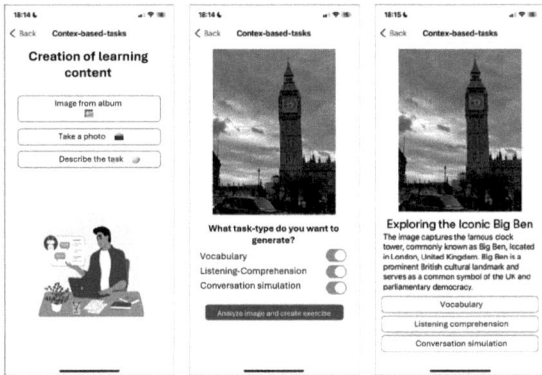

Fig. 1. Screenshots of PlacePhrase during a PicAndLearn exercise where users took a photo of BigBen as a basis for creating their learning content.

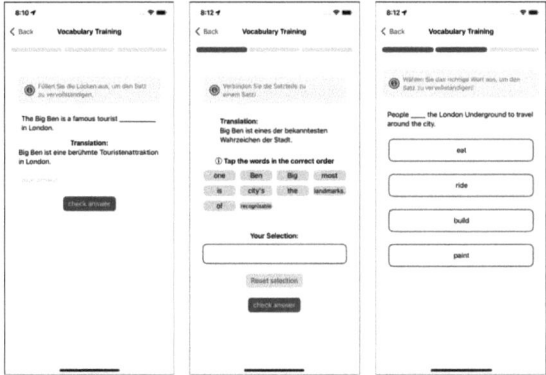

Fig. 2. An illustration of vocabulary learning tasks within PlacePhrase.

Users receive the image (without a description) and are asked to write a specified number of words that describe what they see. Based on user input, AI-based assessment is performed. If the answer is incorrect, a hint button appears to assist the user. Additionally, spell-checking is conducted, identifying mistakes and providing feedback on spelling errors and semantic correctness. Users also have the opportunity to evaluate riddles, leave comments, and suggest alternative solutions, fostering social and collaborative aspects of learning.

PhotoHunt. PhotoHunt is inspired by scavenger hunt game designs. Users start at one location, receive a riddle or clue about the next location, find and approach it, and then receive another riddle or clue until they reach a final location and reward. PhotoHunt initially provides users with available scavenger hunts in their current location (Fig. 4). Each location is marked on the map sequentially. Upon arriving at a location, users complete learning tasks (e.g.,

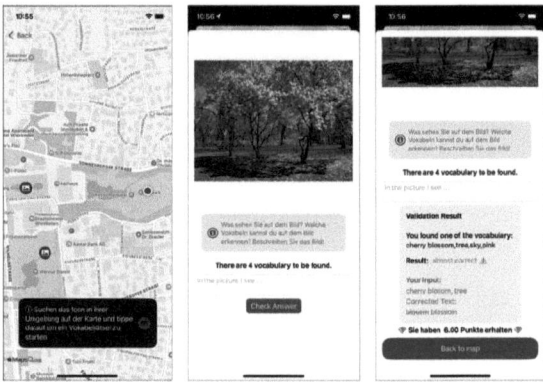

Fig. 3. Three screenshots of SnapVocab's different states.

vocabulary learning, listening comprehension, and interactive conversation) to receive a clue describing a specific object in the vicinity that they must find and photograph. After users photograph the correct object, the riddle for that location is solved, and another location is presented on the overall map.

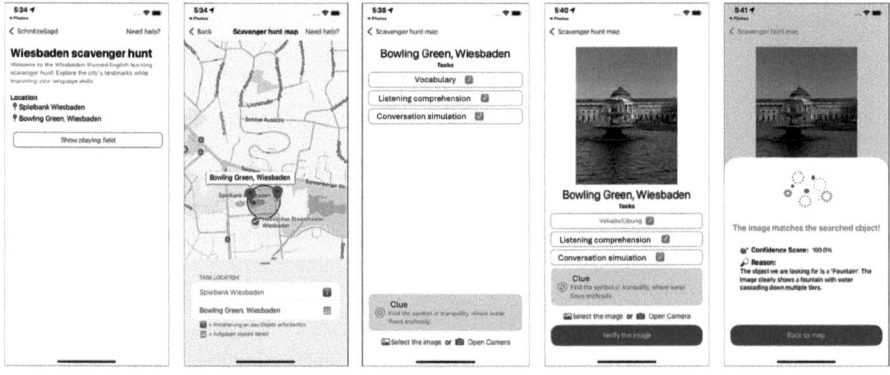

Fig. 4. Illustrations of PhotoHunt from selection (left) to finishing an exercise.

In terms of content for the scavenger hunt, we utilize the Google Places API to locate nearby points of interest. We also creatively incorporate content from SnapVocab and PicAndLearn to provide an initial scavenger hunt. Furthermore, we integrate user-generated content, images, and tasks to form additional scavenger hunts. We provide functionality in PhotoHunt that allows users to create their own handcrafted scavenger hunts and share them with the community. To enhance community engagement, we plan to introduce competitive scavenger hunts in selected areas, allowing multiple users to participate simultaneously.

Here, users must quickly complete various locations to compete against others on a leaderboard.

3.2 Generative AI for Content Creation

Our technological framework for PlacePhrase incorporates several specialized AI assistants, each designed to facilitate distinct aspects of language learning within a gamified context. To implement PlacePhrase and its content creation concepts, we employ the OpenAI Assistants API to develop AI assistants capable of performing specific tasks through the utilization of LLMs. Each assistant is configured with tailored prompts that dictate functionality, automate processes, and ensure quality output [24]. The language model gpt-4o-2024-08-06 serves as the foundation for these configurations.

Assistants. Our content creation framework, visualized at a high level in Fig. 5, encompasses the following assistants.

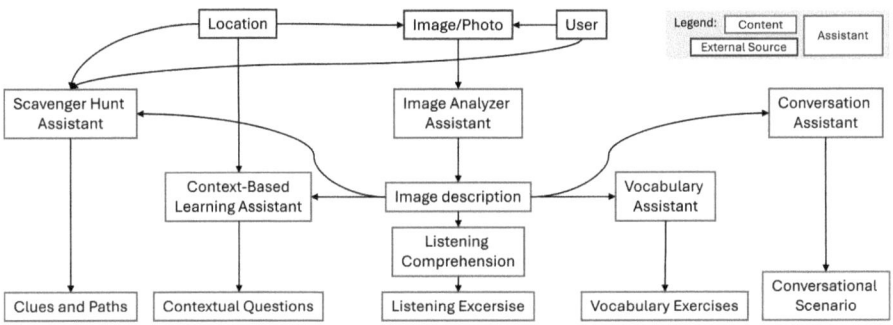

Fig. 5. A graph illustrating the content creation framework with the proposed assistants.

Image Analyzer Assistant: This assistant analyzes images and user inputs to provide constructive feedback. When a user submits an image related to a language task (e.g., a photo of an object they wish to describe), the assistant evaluates the image against predefined criteria and offers insights on vocabulary usage, grammar, and contextual appropriateness. This promotes critical thinking and reinforces language acquisition through visual stimuli.

Vocabulary Assistant: This assistant specializes in creating vocabulary exercises tailored to the user's proficiency level. It generates tasks that involve translations, synonyms, and example sentences. Additionally, it facilitates interactive learning by allowing users to engage with the assistant for detailed explanations of their mistakes, promoting a deeper understanding of word usage and language structure.

Listening Comprehension Assistant: This assistant is dedicated to developing listening comprehension exercises, integrating generated audio content with corresponding questions. Users engage with text transformed into speech through TTS technology, followed by assessments that test their understanding of the material. The assistant evaluates user responses, offering feedback on comprehension and suggesting areas for improvement, thereby enhancing auditory language skills.

Conversation Assistant: Focusing on real-time dialogue simulation, this assistant creates realistic conversational scenarios. It selects relevant contexts to structure conversations that help users practice speaking and listening skills. The assistant actively monitors user inputs for grammatical accuracy, spelling, and word choice, providing immediate corrective feedback and suggestions for improvement. This interactive practice fosters conversational fluency and boosts confidence in language use.

Context-Based Learning Assistant: Leveraging contextual information from images or text, this assistant aids users in formulating context-relevant language tasks. For instance, if a user uploads a picture from a museum, the assistant may generate questions or vocabulary related to the exhibits, creating a rich learning experience that ties vocabulary and grammar to real-world scenarios.

Scavenger Hunt Assistant: This assistant crafts personalized scavenger hunts based on the user's geographical location. It generates a series of clues and tasks that encourage users to explore their environment while enhancing their language skills. Users receive hints that require language processing to complete tasks at various locations, fostering both engagement and contextual learning.

Integration and Configuration. The integration of these assistants and the content they are responsible for creates a comprehensive language learning ecosystem, where each assistant complements the others to build the foundation of each of our three gamified learning approaches (PicAndLearn, SnapVocab, and PhotoHunt). The Vocabulary, Listening Comprehension, and Conversation Assistants focus on generating and facilitating specific language tasks. At the same time, the Scavenger Hunt and Context-Based Learning Assistants provide overarching support, generating prompts and engaging users in dynamic learning experiences. This collaborative framework allows for personalized learning paths that adapt to learners' needs and preferences in real-time. Figure 6 provides a high-level overview of the system and illustrates the employment of assistants, exemplified by the Scavenger Hunt Assistant for PhotoHunt.

Assistant functionality is defined through prompts, which guide response generation and user interaction. The design of these prompts is informed by the OpenAI Prompt Engineering Guide and guidelines from White et al. [24]. Key design patterns include the Persona Pattern, Template Pattern, Infinite Generation Pattern, and Game Play Pattern.

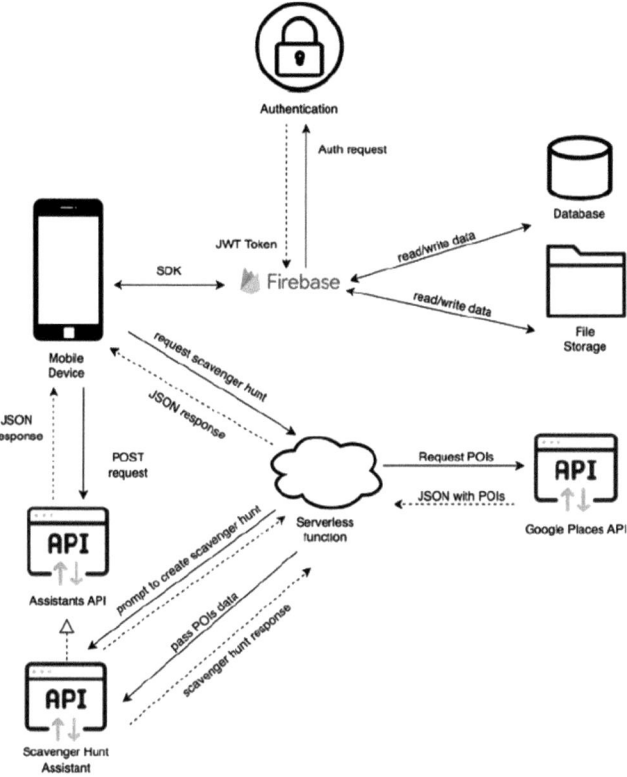

Fig. 6. An architectural illustration of PlacePhrase with emphasis on PhotoHunt.

4 Evaluation

We utilized our implementation of PlacePhrase within a user study to draw conclusions on the proposed concepts. In particular, we evaluated three aspects:

1. The *user experience* of PlacePhrase, evaluated using the User Experience Questionnaire (UEQ) [13].
2. The *quality of the generated content*, including learning tasks, feedback, and validation of user inputs, assessed to understand how users perceived the generative and contextualized learning content. We utilized eight questionnaire items on a 7-point scale (-3 to 3) and the Thinking-Aloud Protocol to capture both quantitative and qualitative data: Q1) The application considers my personal learning goals and interests. Q2) I found the location-based tasks to be interesting and engaging. Q3) The geographical context sparked my interest in discovering additional locations and completing tasks. Q4) The generated tasks based on the uploaded image were appropriate. Q5) The generated vocabulary tasks matched well with the provided context. Q6) The questions and audio of the listening exercises were understandable. Q7) The

AI responses in the conversation simulations were authentic. Q8) The tasks were diverse.
3. The *gamification* concepts were evaluated using the dimensions of Immersion and Flow from the Game Experience Questionnaire (GEQ) [9].

4.1 Study Design

Our study included 13 participants (4 female, 9 male) with a mean age of 25.4 years (SD 5.6), of whom 9 had experience using language learning apps. We utilized English as the target language for learning with PlacePhrase. All participants were non-native speakers, with a self-perceived mean English proficiency level of 1.23 (SD 0.93) on a scale of -3 (no experience) to 3 (fluently). All participants were tested within a controlled laboratory environment with simulated data, and 8 participants agreed to a subsequent in-the-wild test.

At the beginning of the user test, participants received a detailed briefing about the study's context. Furthermore, we allowed our participants two minutes of free exploration to familiarize themselves with the app's user interface. They were then asked to perform four tasks. First, participants were instructed to create a scavenger hunt in their location. Second, they were asked to generate learning content based on a user-specific image. Third, participants needed to make their previously created content available for other users. Lastly, they were tasked with solving a vocabulary puzzle on the map.

4.2 Results

Regarding the *usability*, the results from the UEQ are illustrated in the standardized format for the UEQ in Fig. 7. It shows that the six pillars of the UEQ (left) mostly reach the positive area of the diagram, with the exception of 'efficiency'. In this respect, we observed one particularly interesting item being responsible, with the answer pair 'slow–fast' being answered negatively, yielding a mean of -1.2 and SD of 1.6. This item also obtained the highest standard deviation overall.

We also measured the precision of the estimation of the scale using confidence intervals (with a statistical significance level of 0.05). The results are shown in Table 1. The least precision was observed for the mean of 'dependability' (0.46), while the most precision was noted for 'attractiveness' (0.28).

With regard to the *quality of the generated content*, the results of the questionnaire items (Q1–Q8) are visualized in Fig. 8. This indicates an overall positive perception and particularly highlights that participants agreed on the alignment of the generated vocabulary tasks with their contexts (Q5). It also demonstrates that personal learning goals and interests should be addressed more explicitly (Q1). This item received the lowest rating and exhibited the highest deviation. Notably, all statements in this dimension were rated above 1, further emphasizing the positive perception of the generated content, although some responses fell into the negative area of the scale.

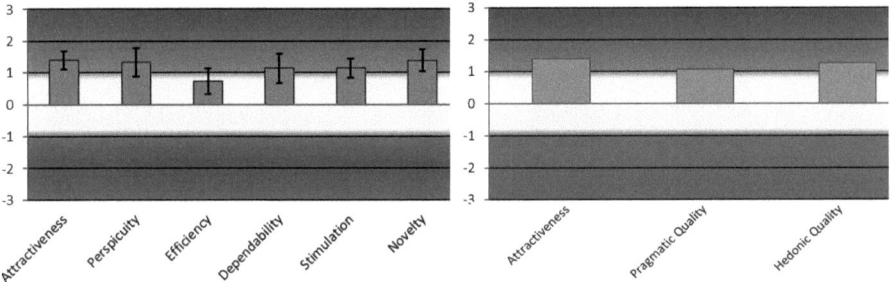

Fig. 7. Results of the UEQ. The scale ranges from 'excellent' (green) over 'average' (yellow) to 'bad' (red). (Color figure online)

Table 1. This table shows the confidence intervals at a probability of 5%. The values are rounded to two decimals.

Scale	Mean	Standard deviation	Confidence	Confidence interval
Attractiveness	1.40	0.51	0.28	1.12–1.68
Perspicuity	1.33	0.81	0.44	0.89–1.77
Efficiency	0.73	0.75	0.41	0.32–1.14
Dependability	1.13	0.85	0.46	0.68–1.59
Stimulation	1.13	0.55	0.30	0.84–1.43
Novelty	1.38	0.63	0.34	1.04–1.72

The results and observations from the Thinking-Aloud Protocol reveal that users had a positive perception of the quality and relevance of the generated learning content, albeit with some usability issues. Participants expressed that the navigation for generating scavenger hunts and engaging with vocabulary tasks was straightforward for most; however, two encountered confusion with button labels and menu interactions. Participants reported unusual loading times, particularly at the beginning of tasks, which affected engagement and focus. The feedback provided for sentence construction was found to be helpful and understandable, especially among beginners. However, one user considered it 'overly detailed and too lengthy.' There were also recommendations to enhance gamification elements and provide clearer instructions, particularly for the conversation simulation and vocabulary confirmation processes.

Finally, regarding the *gamification*, the GEQ results indicated a generally positive perception relating to immersion (0.86, SD 0.30), with participants appreciating opportunities for exploration and certain impressive features of the app. However, the aesthetic and imaginative aspects received average ratings, reflecting diverse preferences among users, particularly noted in the statement 'It felt like a rich experience' (0.69, SD 0.85).

In terms of the flow experience, participants reported a moderate to weak experience (0.26, SD 0.52). While complete engagement with the app was evident

Fig. 8. A bar chart visualizing the results concerning the generated content's quality.

(0.77, SD 1.01), low scores for statements such as 'I forgot everything around me' (0.08, SD 0.95) and 'I lost connection with the outside world' (−0.54, SD 1.05) indicated that participants were focused but not fully immersed. High standard deviations (SD ≥ 0.95) across flow-related items suggested significant variability in experiences among participants. Overall, these results highlight the need for improvements in both immersion and flow to enhance user engagement in PlacePhrase.

5 Conclusions and Future Work

In this paper, we introduced PlacePhrase, a gamified MALL application that leverages generative AI to create personalized language learning experiences. We discussed the design of the learning content and its creation through AI Assistants. Our user study showed positive participant responses, particularly regarding location-based tasks and content quality, while also identifying areas for improvement in immersion and flow, essential for user engagement.

Future work will refine these aspects by incorporating Non-Player Characters, particularly into the PhotoHunt framework, allowing for enhanced interactions and task provision through conversation simulations. We also aim to expand PlacePhrase's capabilities by integrating advanced AI models for better content generation and user interaction. Furthermore, collecting feedback from users and educators will be vital for improving the app's effectiveness and meeting the evolving needs of language learners. Through these enhancements, we aspire to develop a more immersive and adaptive educational tool that supports diverse language learning needs in the digital age.

Acknowledgements. This publication was produced as part of the REQUAS qualification programme, which was funded by the German Federal Ministry of Education and Research in the context of the federal-state program 'FH-Personal' under the grant number 03FHP147A. The responsibility for the content of this publication lies with the authors.

References

1. Agustini, N.P.O.: Examining the role of chatgpt as a learning tool in promoting students' English language learning autonomy relevant to kurikulum merdeka belajar. Edukasia: Jurnal Pendidikan Dan Pembelajaran **4**(2), 921–934 (2023)
2. Chen, X., Wu, D.: Automatic generation of multimedia teaching materials based on generative AI: taking tang poetry as an example. IEEE Trans. Learn. Technol. (2024)
3. Deterding, S., Dixon, D., Khaled, R., Nacke, L.: From game design elements to gamefulness: defining gamification. In: Proceedings of the 15th International Academic MindTrek Conference: Envisioning Future Media Environments, pp. 9–15 (2011)
4. Döring, D.C., Horst, R., Rau, L., Dörner, R.: Interface techniques for tangible augmented reality in a mobile device setup for magic lens experiences. In: GI VR/AR Workshop, pp. 10–18420. Gesellschaft für Informatik eV (2020)
5. Essafi, M., Belfakir, L., Moubtassime, M.: Investigating mobile-assisted language learning apps: babbel, memrise, and duolingo as a case study. J. Curric. Teach. **13**(2), 197 (2024)
6. Godwin-Jones, R.: Smartphones and language learning (2017)
7. Hong, W.C.H.: The impact of chatgpt on foreign language teaching and learning: Opportunities in education and research. J. Educ. Technol. Innov. **5**(1) (2023)
8. Horst, R., Schmitt, M., Leipe, A., Naraghi-Taghi-Off, R., Dörner, R.: Towards the gamification of vr authoring environments. In: ICAT-EGVE (Posters and Demos), pp. 9–10 (2022)
9. IJsselsteijn, W.A., De Kort, Y.A., Poels, K.: The game experience questionnaire (2013)
10. Kessler, M., Loewen, S., Gönülal, T.: Mobile-assisted language learning with babbel and duolingo: comparing l2 learning gains and user experience. Comput. Assist. Lang. Learn. 1–25 (2023)
11. Korkiakoski, T.: A content analysis of community discourse regarding Duolingo Max. thesis, University of Oulu (2024)
12. Kukulska-Hulme, A.: Mobile-Assisted Language Learning [revised and updated version in online]. The Concise Encyclopedia of Applied Linguistics. Wiley, Hoboken (2018)
13. Laugwitz, B., Held, T., Schrepp, M.: Construction and evaluation of a user experience questionnaire. In: Holzinger, A. (ed.) USAB 2008. LNCS, vol. 5298, pp. 63–76. Springer, Heidelberg (2008). https://doi.org/10.1007/978-3-540-89350-9_6
14. Loewen, S., et al.: Mobile-assisted language learning: a duolingo case study. ReCALL **31**(3), 293–311 (2019)
15. Mizumoto, A., Eguchi, M.: Exploring the potential of using an AI language model for automated essay scoring. Res. Methods Appl. Linguist. **2**(2), 100050 (2023)
16. Mohamed, O.I., Al-Jadaan, O.: Online and mobile-assisted. Level Up! Exploring Gamification's Impact on Research and Innovation, p. 63 (2024)
17. OpenAI: Chatgpt-duolingo. https://openai.com/index/duolingo/. Accessed 07 Mar 2025
18. Park, J., et al.: How to align large language models for teaching English? Designing and developing llm based-chatbot for teaching English conversation in efl, findings and limitations. arXiv preprint arXiv:2409.04987 (2024)
19. Petersen, S.A., Markiewicz, J.K., Bjørnebekk, S.S.: Personalized and contextualized language learning: choose when, where and what. Res. Pract. Technol. Enhanc. Learn. **4**(01), 33–60 (2009)

20. Pokrivčáková, S.: Preparing teachers for the application of AI-powered technologies in foreign language education. J. Lang. Cultural Educ. (2019)
21. Rau, L., Döring, D.C., Horst, R., Dörner, R.: Pattern-based augmented reality authoring using different degrees of immersion: a learning nugget approach. Front. Virtual Reality **3**, 841066 (2022)
22. Roe, J., Renandya, W.A., Jacobs, G.M.: A review of ai-powered writing tools and their implications for academic integrity in the language classroom. J. Engl. Appl. Linguist. **2**(1), 3 (2023)
23. Wallingford, P.: How accurate is duolingo? Insights on language learning. https://duolingoguides.com/how-accurate-is-duolingo/. Accessed 07 Mar 2025
24. White, J., et al.: A prompt pattern catalog to enhance prompt engineering with chatgpt. arXiv preprint arXiv:2302.11382 (2023)
25. Yan, D.: Impact of chatgpt on learners in a l2 writing practicum: an exploratory investigation. Educ. Inf. Technol. **28**(11), 13943–13967 (2023)

Automated Planning of Entertainment Content for Digital Health Interventions: A Technical Feasibility Study on Balance VS Fun

L. J. James[1,2]($\boxtimes$), Emanuele De Pellegrin[3], Laura Genga[1], Barbara Montagne[2], and Pieter Van Gorp[1]

[1] Eindhoven Technical University, Eindhoven, The Netherlands
L.J.James@tue.nl
[2] Dutch Mental Health and Addiction Care Institute, Amersfoort, The Netherlands
[3] Heriot-Watt University, Edinburgh, UK

Abstract. Digital interventions can promote positive health outcomes, but maintaining user engagement remains a challenge. A major issue is that, while these interventions primarily consist of essential health-related tasks, such content is perceived as unengaging, leading to high dropout rates. In contrast, game content is inherently engaging, but effectively balancing it with health-focused activities presents a design challenge. In this study, we explore the use of automated planning to structure digital intervention content by integrating unengaging health tasks with engaging game content while maintaining a balanced fun ratio across levels. Through experimental validation, we demonstrate that automated planning can effectively balance fun activities while ensuring progression aligns with defined pacing constraints. Our findings suggest that this approach helps generate balanced levels, though scalability remains a challenge due to the excessive state space. Future research should focus on improving the scalability of automated planning solutions to enhance their practicality in health interventions.

Keywords: Gamification · Automated Planning · Numeric Planning · Health Intervention · Digital Health · mHealth · Levels

1 Introduction

In recent decades, advances in mobile technology, particularly improvements in network speed, processing power, and storage, have improved the potential of mobile devices as platforms for digital interventions [22]. Mobile health apps (mHealth), in particular, have shown potential in promoting healthier lifestyles and supporting the self-management of chronic diseases on a large scale [20]. This is especially relevant considering that lifestyle-related diseases, which are often preventable and manageable, remain one of the leading causes of death worldwide [26]. However, despite their potential, many mHealth applications face significant challenges with participant dropouts and maintaining long-term engagement, as users often find these apps unengaging [2,25]. A key factor in this disengagement is that users often perceive these apps as stale, reducing intrinsic motivation, and leading to higher dropout rates [9,25]. Unlike mobile games, which are designed with engaging entertainment at their core, mHealth apps are designed with specific health-related goals, such as decision-making support, behavior change, education, and therapy [27,29]. These goals often result in the perception that the core content of mHealth applications is less engaging, contributing to low intrinsic motivation and higher dropout rates [9,25].

Research shows that incorporating game design elements, known as gamification [13], has the potential to enhance engagement with mHealth applications [10,25]. Gamification includes game elements such as leaderboards, points, and badges, which improve engagement but do not replicate the level of entertainment typical of mobile games [13,28]. Popular entertainment-based mobile games such as Candy Crush Saga[1], Clash of Clans[2], and Pokémon GO[3] feature engaging content, including game mechanics (i.e., the rules and systems that govern the game), dynamics (i.e., the behaviors and interactions that emerge when players engage with the mechanics and how the game adapts to player actions), and aesthetics (i.e., the emotional responses elicited from players) [5,16,19]. The combination of these types of content is strategically structured (i.e., paced) to maximize and maintain player engagement. The pacing of this content can be grounded in behavioral change theories widely used in game design, such as flow theory and the learning curve. Flow theory emphasizes that player engagement is maximized when tasks align with a player's skill level [9], while the learning curve highlights how players' skill levels increase over time as they are exposed to progressively more challenging tasks [3,12]. At a high level, these pacing theories can often be represented using two-dimensional graphs. For example, both flow, and learning curve can be depicted with the Y-axis representing player skill and the X-axis representing time or progression [21].

Structuring the pace of content progression based on designer goals such as difficulty progression and level of fun (i.e., fun ratio) per level can be modeled as a state space problem with constraints [21]. Although these state-space problems can be solved manually, they become increasingly complex and time-consuming to optimize as the number of activities grows, constraints impose stricter limitations on sequencing, and dependencies between activities introduce ordering requirements. In mHealth applications, the challenge is further complicated by the need to balance engaging entertainment content with essential but unengaging health tasks. This growing complexity highlights the need for automated approaches to solve these problems efficiently. Several technologies can automate these approaches, offering various methods to handle the growing complexity. Search-based algorithms explore state space efficiently using techniques such as depth-first search, breadth-first search, A*, or local/heuristic search, prioritizing paths that lead to optimal solutions [35]. Constraint-Based Optimization

---

[1] https://www.king.com/game/candycrush.
[2] https://supercell.com/en/games/clashofclans/.
[3] https://pokemongolive.com/?hl=en.

techniques, including linear programming and constraint satisfaction problems, apply formal constraints and objectives to find solutions that meet all requirements while optimizing the desired outcome [4]. Automated planning combines search algorithms with a structured approach to problem formulation, generating action sequences that respect constraints (e.g. goals), as well as temporal and dependency relationships [17]. Automated planning is used to generate action sequences that navigate through a state space while ensuring that all constraints and dependencies are respected. Reinforcement Learning (RL) [34] enables an AI agent to learn optimal decision-making strategies through interaction with an environment, receiving feedback in the form of rewards or penalties, and aiming to maximize cumulative rewards over time through trial and error. RL can be used to learn the optimal sequence of actions through experience, even when the state space is not fully known in advance [23].

Automated planning serves as an abstraction over lower-level techniques, such as search-based algorithms and constraint-based optimization [17]. By formalizing tasks in terms of actions, preconditions, effects, and goals, it generates action sequences that respect temporal and dependency constraints. This approach systematically structure activity sequences while ensuring that objectives such as fun ratio and difficulty progression goals are met. Furthermore, automated planning offers advantages in extensibility. As new activities, constraints, or goals arise, the system can be updated by adjusting formal models, which is generally more manageable than extending more granular methods like search-based algorithms or constraint-based optimization. Compared to RL, automated planning provides more predictability and control, generates deterministic action sequences, and requires less data and exploration, avoiding the significant training time often needed for RL to converge to optimal policies [30].

In this paper, we explore the limited research on the application of automated planning to systematically generate content structures for digital intervention applications. We address this gap by investigating the following research question: *Can automated planning aid digital health intervention designers in structuring level systems to balance the ratio of entertaining tasks to essential health tasks, while ensuring the progression follows pacing guidelines that govern task introduction, timing, and task complexity over time?* To answer this question, we propose an automated planning-based approach to generate content structures based on designer-defined constraints. We extend the Automated Planning of Level Structures (APLES) tool [21], a Planning Domain Definition Language (PDDL)-based planning tool, to balance engaging and less engaging activities while adhering to difficulty progression rules. Guided by game design theories, we use predefined content progression graphs as input for the APLES tool. The APLES-generated plan will be verified to determine how well they balance entertainment and health-related tasks, as well as difficulty progression, according to the predefined graphs, using statistical analysis.

2 Background

2.1 Content Structure

Game design theory emphasizes the structure of content to optimize engagement and skill development [19,31,32]. Central to this is the concept of flow, where players experience deep engagement when the challenge aligns with their skill level [9]. If the challenge is too easy, players become bored, if it is too difficult, they become frustrated, leading to disengagement [9]. Successful game design addresses this challenge by gradually increasing the difficulty to maintain the player within the optimal flow zone [1]. To maintain engagement and avoid repetitiveness, game design should carefully introduce new mechanics and adjust challenge levels [15].

Progression graphs play a crucial role in managing pacing and complexity in game design [6,7,16]. For example, the AI Director in Left 4 Dead[4] dynamically adjusts the pacing based on the state of the player, such as health or progress. Although effective in real-time, this system does not allow for the static, predefined structuring of content [6]. In contrast, tools such as Pacemaker offer a higher-level approach, allowing designers to define content progression beforehand using high-level graphs and state graphs [16]. This method allows for the precise management of content difficulty and intensity, using numerical representations to control elements such as level design and enemy placement.

2.2 Automated Planning

Automated planning is a field of Artificial Intelligence focused on the systematic reasoning about structuring sequences of actions to achieve a predefined goal from an initial state [17]. The process consists of modeling the effects of actions in the world to create a series of actions (i.e., a plan) that modifies the world from the initial state to the goal state [8,17]. Classical planning is a widely used approach within this field, operating under deterministic conditions where the effects of actions are known in advance [17]. Numeric planning builds on classical planning by incorporating numeric fluents, quantitative variables that represent aspects of the state of the world, such as difficulty in tasks or levels [18]. This extension allows for dynamic adjustment of values over time, enabling more flexible planning that can accommodate gradual changes, such as the adjustment of task difficulty in digital health interventions. PDDL was introduced as a standardized language to describe such planning problems, including states, actions, and goal conditions [24].

A planning problem is represented as a tuple $\Pi = \langle P, A, S, I, G \rangle$, where each component plays a role in the definition of the planning process. The component P represents a set of propositions, also known as fluents, which define the state space and track aspects of the world state. For example, a fluent might be $has\_completed\_walk$. The set A includes all possible actions that can interact

---
[4] https://store.steampowered.com/app/500/Left_4_Dead/.

with the world state. Actions in this set have preconditions that must be satisfied before they can be applied, and they define effects that modify the world state. For example, the action *Take_a_15 − minute_walk* might be defined as an action to affect the state by modifying a fluent such as *has_completed_walk*. The set S consists of states which represent combinations of propositions and describe the world condition at any given time. In numeric planning, fluents in P can change dynamically, such as adjusting difficulty levels over time to maintain engagement or challenge in applications such as digital health interventions. A state might represent a scenario where *physical_difficulty : 10* and *social_difficulty : 1*, indicating current levels of difficulty. The initial state I is the set of conditions that define the starting point of the planning process. The goal condition G is the desired end state that the planning sequence aims to achieve. A solution to the planning problem is a sequence of actions that transforms the initial state I into a state where the goal conditions G are satisfied [8,17].

3 APLES

APLES is an automated planning-based web application designed to help developers of digital health interventions structure content progression according to high-level design requirements [21]. The front-end interface allows developers to add, edit, or remove activities, each of which must be assigned a name, predefined type (e.g., physical, cognitive, or social), and a difficulty level. The front-end also includes a difficulty graph, where the x-axis represents progression stages (i.e., levels), and the y-axis indicates difficulty. This graph enables developers to define how the difficulty of each activity evolves throughout the intervention [21].

APLES models content progression as a numeric planning problem. Using the Unified Planning (UP) framework[5], APLES integrates the difficulty graph and activities into a PDDL model, generating plans using numeric planners such as LPG that support numeric planning [18]. Each activity is represented as an action in the planner, with the difficulty graph serving as the goal state. Additionally, APLES enables the assignment of activity weights through the UP cost function, which helps the planner avoid action repetition.

APLES is designed as a high-level abstraction to address state space problems in level structuring, offering a structured approach to balance engagement and challenge within digital health interventions. It is adaptable and extendable, allowing developers to add new activity types, modify existing planning constraints, or integrate additional planners and reasoning techniques as needed. This flexibility ensures that APLES can accommodate evolving design requirements, supporting a wide range of digital health interventions with varying levels of complexity.

The plans generated by APLES are then converted into a format compatible with digital health intervention apps, such as GameBus, facilitating the construction of level structures within the app. GameBus is a gamification engine [33]

---
[5] https://unified-planning.readthedocs.io/en/latest/.

designed to support researchers in developing and deploying gamified digital health interventions. It is highly configurable, allowing researchers to tailor its features to their context. In GameBus, users are given and encouraged to complete health-related activities either solo or in groups (i.e., family, friends, colleagues, etc.). The completion of health activities can be self-reported by users within the app or tracked through external apps (i.e., Google Fit[6], Strava[7]) or supported wearables (i.e., Samsung Active 2[8]). APLES generates plans that support both the self-reporting system and external tracking in GameBus [21].

3.1 Extension of APLES Tool

To address the research question, the APLES system has been extended in two ways: 1) to support entertainment-related content in the form of minigames, each with various configurations, and 2) to incorporate the concept of a fun ratio, which balances the level of entertainment with health-related activities within the intervention.

The entertainment content added to the planning problem consists of entertainment based minigames, which were developed for use in digital interventions. These minigames are integrated into the GameBus health intervention app through the GameBus minigame framework [33]. Each minigame comes with a set of configurations that determine which game elements (e.g., mechanics and aesthetics) are enabled. The designers of the intervention can edit these configurations within APLES, enabling the planner to select the appropriate configuration for that minigame. To facilitate the planner's ability to reason with minigames, a minigame content type was added to the APLES model.

To enable APLES to balance fun, we extended the planning model. Each activity was assigned a fun score, a predefined value determined by the designer of the intervention. We introduced the `fun_ratio` and `num_activities` fluents into the planner's model. The `num_activities` fluent is used to track the number of activities included in a plan, while the `fun_ratio` fluent ensures that the planner maintains the desired balance between fun and unengaging health activities. Each action generated from an activity (e.g., `Take_a_15-minute_walk`) now includes an additional effect that updates the `fun_ratio`. The effect is modeled in PDDL as follows: `(increase (fun_score) 0)(assign (fun_ratio) (/ (fun_score) num_activities)))`.

3.2 Experiment

This study evaluated whether APLES generates level structures that align with user-defined difficulty and fun ratio expectations. Three different content structure graphs were used as input, each reflecting a distinct theoretical progression

---

[6] https://www.google.com/fit/.
[7] https://www.strava.com/.
[8] https://www.samsung.com/nl/explore/wellbeing/this-smartwatch-moves-with-you/.

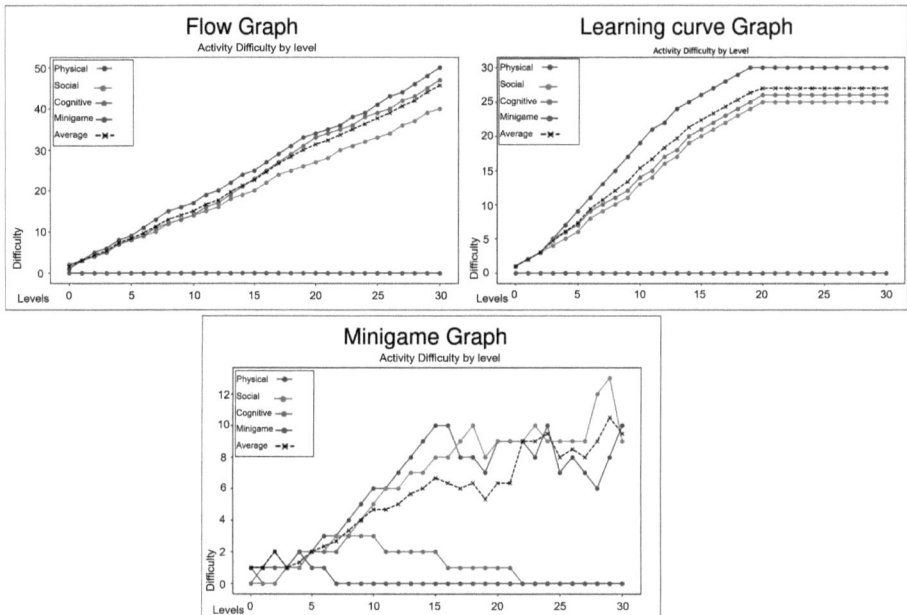

Fig. 1. This figure shows the theory based content structure graphs used as input for the experiments conducted with APLES.

model. The flow theory graph aimed to maintain a "flow state" by balancing skill level and task difficulty, where the X-axis represented skill level and the Y-axis represented task difficulty. The learning Curve Theory graph modeled the pattern of rapid initial improvement followed by gradual mastery, with the X-axis representing practice time and the Y-axis representing performance. Lastly, the free choice structure graph (i.e., Minigame graph) placed more engaging entertainment-focused activities at the beginning and transitioned to less engaging health-related activities toward the end, testing the balance between engagement and health content. Visualizations of each graph can be seen in Fig. 1.

Three experiments were conducted to evaluate APLES, each experiment was tested with three input variants consisting of 10, 20, and 30 levels. The first experiment was optimized for difficulty matching, ensuring that the generated level sequence followed the expected difficulty progression. The second experiment introduced fun ratio optimization alongside difficulty matching, assessing whether APLES could generate levels that adhered to both constraints. The third experiment combined both objectives, testing whether APLES could simultaneously balance difficulty and fun ratio. An example of how these goals were defined in APLES is provided in Listing 1.1. Each experiment was carried out using 30 input activities and was subjected to a structured validation process consisting of verification and statistical analysis.

- The first verification experiment assessed whether APLES generated level structures that followed the predefined difficulty progression. This was done by setting the planner's goal to match the input difficulty values exactly and comparing the output difficulty values for each set of levels.
- The second verification experiment assessed whether APLES adhered to the predefined fun ratio values. The planner's goal was set to match exactly the fun ratio of the input per level, and the values of the fun ratio of the output were compared with these inputs.
- The third verification experiment assessed whether APLES could simultaneously satisfy both difficulty and fun ratio constraints. The planner's goals were set to match the fun ratio of the input per level, with an offset of ± 2, while also adhering to the predefined difficulty values. The generated level structures were then compared to determine adherence to both constraints.

Statistical analysis was performed on each verification experiment to determine the statistical significance between the user input values and the APLES output values. First, both the input and output values were subjected to the Shapiro-Wilk test to assess normality. If the data were normally distributed, an independent t-test was used to compare the input and output distributions, otherwise the Kruskal-Wallis test was applied, with the statistical significance set at $p < 0.05$. To ensure reliable results, each experiment was repeated 10 times. The results of each run were statistically analyzed and the average performance of the 10 runs was used for validation. This repetition was performed until the results converged to minimize random variability. A table of the average results of all three experiments can be seen in Fig. 1.

Listing 1.1. Code snippet showcasing how the difficulty level of an activity type is set, and the fun ratio.

```
def _init_goal(self, p=0, s=0, c=0, m=0, f=5):
    self.problem.add_goal(
    GE(self.all_fluents['difficulty_lvl_physical'], p)
    )# Match the difficulty level of the activity type
    self.problem.add_goal(
    GE(self.all_fluents['fun_ratio'], f)
    )# Match the fun ratio of the activities
    #(only enabled in experiment 2)
```

4 Results

In the first experiment, a visual comparison of the average input and output difficulty values per level across all level sets (10, 20, and 30 levels) showed no noticeable differences (Table 1). APLES precisely matched the average difficulty in all cases. Due to the expected results, no statistical analysis was conducted to test for significance between the input and output values. Additionally, the average planning time varied depending on the content structure graph and the number of levels. For flow graphs, the average planning time was 3.13 s for 10

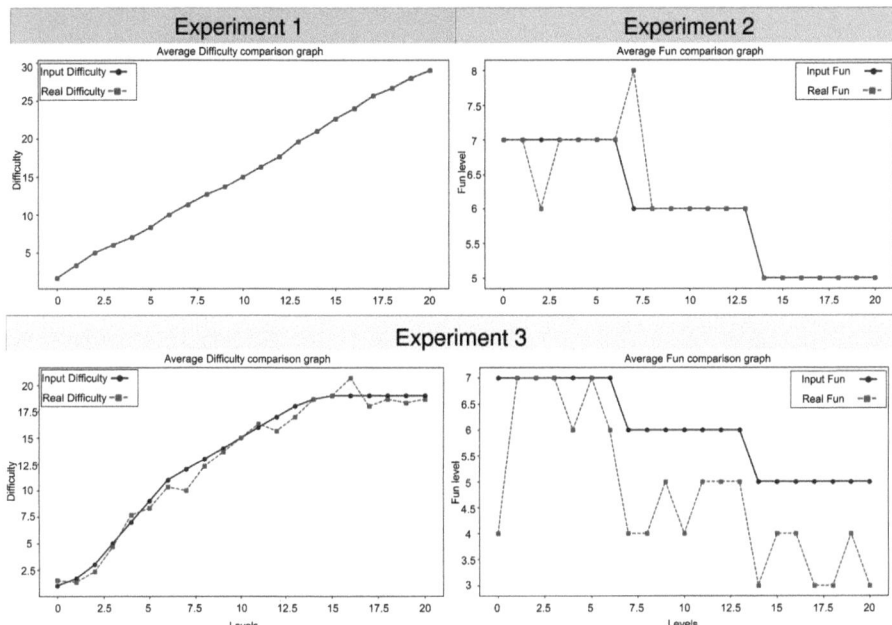

Fig. 2. Output graphs generated by APLES during the three experiment types. The top left graph shows APLES successfully matching the flow theory-based difficulty progression. The top right graph illustrates APLES almost perfectly matching the fun ratio values. The bottom two graphs show the results when optimizing for both fun ratio and difficulty. While the difficulty graph shows no statistically significant differences, the fun ratio graph does.

Table 1. The average results of each experiment, conducted over 10 runs. The columns represent different metrics: D (Difficulty comparison), F (Fun Ratio comparison), Significance (sign.), and Time (Planning time). The leftmost column lists the graphs used in the experiments, where LC denotes the Learning Curve and MG represents the Minigame Graph.

Graph	Experiment 1		Experiment 2		Experiment 3		
	Avg sign.(D)	Time	Avg sign.(F)	Time	Avg sign.(D)	Avg sign.(F)	Time
Flow (10)	0.0%	4.1 s	0.0%	3.1 s	0.0%	50.0%	2.1 s
Flow (20)	0.0%	9.1 s	0.00%	7.5 s	0.0%	90.0%	5.1 s
Flow (30)	0.0%	16.8 s	0.0%	13.7 s	0.0%	100.0%	8.5 s
LC (10)	0.0%	4.2 s	0.0%	3.2 s	0.0%	10.0%	2.3 s
LC (20)	0.0%	5.2 s	0.0%	10.6 s	0.0%	90.0%	5.2 s
LC (30)	0.0%	6.2 s	0.0%	11.6 s	0.0%	100.0%	7.7 s
MG (10)	0.0%	7.2 s	0.0%	2.4 s	0.0%	60.0%	2.1 s
MG (20)	0.0%	8.2 s	0.0%	5.1 s	0.0%	50.0%	3.8 s
MG (30)	0.00%	9.2 s	0.0%	7.2 s	0.0%	80.0%	5.4 s

levels, 7.51s for 20 levels, and 13.7s for 30 levels. For skill graphs, the planning time was slightly higher, averaging 3.21s for 10 levels, 10.57s for 20 levels, and 11.62s for 30 levels. Minigame graphs had the lowest planning times, with 2.40s for 10 levels, 5.13s for 20 levels, and 7.19s for 30 levels. These results indicate efficiently planned level structures, with planning time increasing as the number of levels grew.

In the second experiment, a visual comparison of the average input and output fun ratio values per level across all level sets (10, 20, and 30 levels) revealed slight differences in some generated levels. Unlike the difficulty-matching experiment, APLES did not always achieve an exact match for the fun ratio. As a result, a statistical analysis was conducted to assess whether these deviations were significant. The results showed no significant differences between the input and output fun ratio values across all level sets and graph types. Additionally, the average planning time increased compared to the previous experiment, the slight variations in plans can be seen in Fig. 2. For flow graphs, the average planning time was 4.06s for 10 levels, 9.14s for 20 levels, and 16.81s for 30 levels. Skill graphs took slightly more time, with 4.26s for 10 levels, 10.04s for 20 levels, and 19.75s for 30 levels. The minigame graphs performed similarly, with planning times of 4.10s for 10 levels, 9.34s for 20 levels, and 16.22s for 30 levels. These findings suggest that while APLES does not always achieve a perfect match for fun ratio values, it still maintains overall alignment with the predefined targets while requiring increased computation time.

In the third experiment, a visual comparison of the average input and output difficulty values per level in all levels (10, 20, and 30 levels) revealed some differences in many of the levels generated in the output graph. Although the shape of the output values matched the input values, there were noticeable variations in the specific difficulty levels. When comparing the average input and output fun ratio values, the output values showed more fluctuation between data points. Statistical analysis did not show significant differences between the difficulty values of the input and output across all level sets and graph types. However, significant differences were found in the fun ratio values for most level sets and graph combinations. The average percentage of levels with significant differences in fun ratio was 50% for the 10-level flow graph set, 90% for the 20-level set, and 100% for the 30-level set. In the skill graph set, the percentage of significant differences was lower for the 10-level set at 10%, but it increased to 90% for the 20-level set and 100% for the 30-level set. The minigame graph set showed 60% significant differences for the 10-level set, 50% for the 20-level set, and 80% for the 30-level set. The average planning times increased compared to previous experiments, with flow graphs taking an average of 2.11s for 10 levels, 5.10s for 20 levels, and 8.51s for 30 levels. Skill graphs required slightly more time: 2.38s for 10 levels, 5.27s for 20 levels, and 7.72s for 30 levels. Minigame graphs required 2.14s for 10 levels, 3.88s for 20 levels, and 5.41s for 30 levels.

5 Discussion

5.1 Main Findings

The results of this study highlight several key findings regarding the performance of the APLES system in optimizing level structures for both difficulty and fun ratio. When optimizing for difficulty level for multiple activity types, the system met the predefined constraints. There were no noticeable differences between the input and output difficulty values across all level sets. This indicates that the system works as intended when focused solely on maintaining consistent difficulty levels throughout the levels.

In contrast, when optimizing for the fun ratio, the output graphs did not always match the input graphs perfectly. In some cases, the planner failed to find valid plans for specific levels, which could be due to limitations in planners' ability to fully support division calculations. Further verification with alternative planners is needed to confirm this hypothesis. Despite these occasional invalid plans, statistical tests did not show significant differences between the fun ratios of input and output. This suggests APLES' errors in calculating the fun ratio are minor and do not significantly impact the overall structure.

However, when both difficulty and fun ratio were optimized simultaneously, APLES did not generate plans that effectively balanced both goals. This outcome aligns with expectations based on the system's design. There are several reasons for this limitation, including a potential lack of sufficient variety in activities (e.g., in terms of difficulty, activity type, or fun ratio). Additionally, the system may be limited by the Pareto front [11] in multi-objective optimization problems, where optimizing one objective can diminish the quality of the other. Depending on how the goals states are set, the fun ratio can be attained, however, it comes at the cost of difficulty matching, resulting in significant differences between the two goals. This reflects a practical trade-off: while the system aims for a practical solution for designers, the inherent limitations of balancing multiple objectives cannot be fully overcome in this context.

The planning time for generating level structures increased with the number of levels and the complexity of the graph types used, reflecting the additional computational cost. APLES demonstrated scalability, maintaining efficiency even when optimizing for multiple objectives. Despite the expected increase in planning time for larger level sets, the system remained responsive and capable of handling complex optimization goals.

5.2 Limitations and Future Work

Several limitations of this study should be acknowledged. First, the experiments were conducted in a controlled environment using predefined graphs, which may limit the generalizability of the results to real-world digital interventions. The study also focused on a fixed set of activities and the corresponding difficulty levels, which may not represent the full diversity of activities that could be included in real-world mHealth interventions. It is important to note that not all progression theories can be mapped onto 2D graphs.

During the experimentation phase, a key limitation was discovered: when the number of activities exceeded 40, APLES fails to find valid plans, unless additional activities tailored to introduce variety were included. This issue arises because every action has a cost, which significantly increases the state space, making it more challenging for the planner to find solutions. While removing the cost functions allowed APLES to plan with more activities, this is not a practical scenario for real-world applications. Future work should explore methods to expand the activity state space within APLES, making the tool more practical for intervention designers. This expansion should be achieved without compromising the cost function, which helps prevent content repetition. One potential avenue is to explore how activities already chosen by the planner can be swapped out or how the cost function can be adjusted outside of the planner, allowing for greater flexibility while maintaining the overall effectiveness of the planner. Another promising approach to potentially improve scalability is the use of Hierarchical Task Network (HTN) planning [14], which decomposes complex goals into smaller, more manageable sub-goals. This could potentially improve how APLES handles a larger set of activities without requiring significant changes to the cost function, enabling the tool to manage greater complexity while remaining scalable and practical for real-world use. Lastly, the exploration of different numerical planners to evaluate their performance with varying state spaces could be explored, with planners, such as Tamer and ENHSP, supported by UP, easily replacing LPG with a few modifications to the model.

With the current practical limitations of APLES, it can not yet be recommended to use automated planning approaches to structure content for gamified health interventions. Besides the current limited number of activities APLES can reason with, there is currently no empirical evidence to state that the progression within levels generated by automated planning can outperform meticulous level design of professional game designers. Therefore, to improve the practical applicability of APLES for intervention designers, usability tests could focus on how well the tool supports the creation of level structures and meets design goals. Designer feedback should be gathered on the tool's intuitiveness, flexibility, and effectiveness in supporting real-world applications and helping to identify areas for improvement. While the tool's ability to balance difficulty and fun ratio was verified, considering designer input is essential to improve its practical applicability. Before empirical evaluations, future work could explore whether the numerical representation of activity elements (e.g., difficulty, fun score) is an efficient approach compatible with the workflows of designers.

6 Conclusion

This study explored the use of automated planning to structure-level systems in digital health interventions, balancing entertaining and essential but unengaging health-related activities while adhering to predefined pacing constraints. Through experiments, we demonstrated that automated planning can generate structured content sequences grounded in game design theory while maintaining a balanced fun ratio. The results suggest that this approach has the potential to provide a systematic and scalable method for designing digital interventions that sustain engagement over time. This method potentially reduces the manual effort required to balance entertainment and health-related activities. However, a key limitation is the scalability of APLES, as handling a large number of activities remains challenging. Future research should focus on improving scalability.

Acknowledgements. This study was funded by the Dutch Mental Health and Addiction Care Institute.

Disclosure of Interests. The authors declare that there are no competing interests.

References

1. Alexander, J.T., Sear, J., Oikonomou, A.: An investigation of the effects of game difficulty on player enjoyment. Entertain. Comput. **4**(1), 53–62 (2013)
2. Amagai, S., Pila, S., Kaat, A.J., Nowinski, C.J., Gershon, R.C.: Challenges in participant engagement and retention using mobile health apps: literature review. J. Med. Internet Res. **24**(4), e35120 (2022)
3. Anzanello, M.J., Fogliatto, F.S.: Learning curve models and applications: literature review and research directions. Int. J. Ind. Ergon. **41**(5), 573–583 (2011)
4. Apt, K.: Principles of Constraint Programming. Cambridge university press, Cambridge (2003)
5. Baumann, N., Lürig, C., Engeser, S.: Flow and enjoyment beyond skill-demand balance: the role of game pacing curves and personality. Motiv. Emot. **40**, 507–519 (2016)
6. Booth, V.M.: The ai systems of left 4 dead. Online (2009)
7. Chen, J.: Flow in games (and everything else). Commun. ACM **50**(4), 31–34 (2007)
8. Cimatti, A., Pistore, M., Traverso, P.: Automated planning. Found. Artif. Intell. **3**, 841–867 (2008)
9. Csikszentmihalyi, M., Csikzentmihaly, M.: Flow: The Psychology of Optimal Experience, vol. 1990. Harper & Row, New York (1990)
10. Damaševičius, R., Maskeliūnas, R., Blažauskas, T.: Serious games and gamification in healthcare: a meta-review. Information **14**(2), 105 (2023)
11. Deb, K., Pratap, A., Agarwal, S., Meyarivan, T.: A fast and elitist multiobjective genetic algorithm: nsga-ii. IEEE Trans. Evol. Comput. **6**(2), 182–197 (2002)
12. DeKeyser, R.: Skill acquisition theory. In: Theories in Second Language Acquisition, pp. 83–104. Routledge (2020)
13. Deterding, S., Dixon, D., Khaled, R., Nacke, L.: From game design elements to gamefulness: defining gamification. In: Proceedings of the 15th International Academic MindTrek Conference: Envisioning Future Media Environments, pp. 9–15 (2011)
14. Erol, K., Hendler, J., Nau, D.S.: HTN planning: complexity and expressivity. In: AAAI, vol. 94, pp. 1123–1128 (1994)
15. Gee, J.P.: What video games have to teach us about learning and literacy. Comput. Entertain. (CIE) **1**(1), 20–20 (2003)
16. Geheeb, J., Dyrda, D., Geheeb, S.: Pacemaker: a practical tool for pacing video games. In: 2024 IEEE Conference on Games (CoG), pp. 1–8. IEEE (2024)

17. Ghallab, M., Nau, D., Traverso, P.: Automated Planning: Theory and Practice. Elsevier, Amsterdam (2004)
18. Hoffmann, J., Nebel, B.: The ff planning system: fast plan generation through heuristic search. J. Artif. Intell. Res. **14**, 253–302 (2001)
19. Hunicke, R., LeBlanc, M., Zubek, R., et al.: MDA: a formal approach to game design and game research. In: Proceedings of the AAAI Workshop on Challenges in Game AI, vol. 4, p. 1722. San Jose, CA (2004)
20. Jakob, R., et al.: Factors influencing adherence to mhealth apps for prevention or management of noncommunicable diseases: systematic review. J. Med. Internet Res. **24**(5), e35371 (2022)
21. James, L.J., De Pellegrin, E., Genga, L., Montagne, B., Van Gorp, P., Petrick, R.P.: Towards automated planning of level structures for digital interventions. In: 12th Italian Workshop on Planning and Scheduling, IPS 2024, pp. 74–88. CEUR-WS.org (2024)
22. Kumar, D., Jeuris, S., Bardram, J.E., Dragoni, N.: Mobile and wearable sensing frameworks for mhealth studies and applications: a systematic review. ACM Trans. Comput. Healthc. **2**(1), 1–28 (2020)
23. Lin, L.J.: Self-improving reactive agents based on reinforcement learning, planning and teaching. Mach. Learn. **8**, 293–321 (1992)
24. McDermott, D., et al.: Pddl-the planning domain definition language (1998)
25. Mustafa, A.S., Ali, N., Dhillon, J.S., Alkawsi, G., Baashar, Y.: User engagement and abandonment of mhealth: a cross-sectional survey. In: Healthcare, vol. 10, p. 221. MDPI (2022)
26. Organization, W.H.: Noncommunicable diseases (September 2023). https://www.who.int/news-room/fact-sheets/detail/noncommunicable-diseases. Accessed 3 Sep 2024
27. Organization, W.H., et al.: New horizons for health through mobile technologies: second global survey on ehealth. geneva, switzerland: World health organization; 2011 (2015)
28. Orji, R., Tondello, G.F., Nacke, L.E.: Personalizing persuasive strategies in gameful systems to gamification user types. In: Proceedings of the 2018 CHI Conference on Human Factors in Computing Systems, pp. 1–14 (2018)
29. Rowland, S.P., Fitzgerald, J.E., Holme, T., Powell, J., McGregor, A.: What is the clinical value of mhealth for patients? NPJ Digit. Med. **3**(1), 4 (2020)
30. Russell, S.J., Norvig, P.: Artificial Intelligence: A Modern Approach. Pearson, Chennai (2016)
31. Schell, J.: The Art of Game Design: A Book of Lenses. CRC press, Boca Raton (2008)
32. Sweetser, P., Wyeth, P.: Gameflow: a model for evaluating player enjoyment in games. Comput. Entertain. (CIE) **3**(3), 3–3 (2005)
33. Van Gorp, P., Nuijten, R.: 8-year evaluation of gamebus: status quo in aiming for an open access platform to prototype and test digital health apps. In: Proceedings of the ACM on Human-Computer Interaction, vol. 7(EICS), pp. 1–24 (2023)
34. Wiering, M.A., Van Otterlo, M.: Reinforcement learning. Adapt. Learn. Optim. **12**(3), 729 (2012)
35. Zhang, W.: State-space Search: Algorithms, Complexity, Extensions, and Applications. Springer, New York (1999). https://doi.org/10.1007/978-1-4612-1538-7

Evaluating Colorblind-Friendly Design for Equitable Play in Mobile Puzzle Games

JaeJun Lee[1(✉)], Joo-Eun Kang[1], Jeong-Eun Park[2], and Min-Joong Kim[3]

[1] Department of Game Design, SungKyunKwan University, Seoul, Korea
`{leejaejun,livredejenny}@skku.edu`
[2] Department of Fine Art, SungKyunKwan University, Seoul, Korea
`tina20011102@g.skku.edu`
[3] Department of Computer Education, SungKyunKwan University, Seoul, Korea
`kmj13675@gmail.com`

Abstract. This study examines how colorblind-friendly design affects players with color vision deficiency (CVD) in the mobile puzzle game, *The Walking Dead: Tales*. Analysis of nine months of PvP data from over 14,000 users across 109 countries revealed that enabling colorblind mode significantly improved CVD users' win rates by 1.4%, especially in challenging matches. CVD users also showed higher retention (D + 30: 15.4% vs. 3.8%) and paying user rates (39.11%), indicating greater satisfaction. Despite limitations in accurately identifying CVD players, these findings underscore the value of inclusive game design.

Keywords: Color Vision Deficiency · Accessibility · Inclusive Game Design

1 Introduction

With technological advancements since the 1950s, games have transitioned into digital formats across various platforms such as computers, mobile devices, and consoles [11]. Modern games utilize multiple sensory techniques, but heavily rely on visual information [1]. However, approximately 8% of men and 0.4% of women globally have color vision deficiencies (CVD) [5]. Three primary CVD types exist: red-green (deuteranomaly, protanomaly, protanopia, deuteranopia), blue-yellow (tritanomaly, tritanopia), and complete color deficiency (monochromacy) [16], typically caused by absent or defective cone cells [14]. Deficiencies in L, M, and S cones impair perception of red, green, and blue, respectively, with monochromacy involving the absence of cones entirely [19].

Since games often use color to convey critical information, such as allies in blue and enemies in red [20] or poison in green [7], CVD players may face significant gameplay disadvantages, especially in color-reliant puzzles [28]. This disadvantage affects fair play in online multiplayer contexts, disrupting reward mechanisms, immersion, and community building [35]. To address this, many commercial games now offer colorblind modes [20].

This research examines whether colorblind modes effectively mitigate gameplay disadvantages, promote fairness, and increase user satisfaction and loyalty. While previous studies employed limited-scale laboratory or interview methods [22], few have analyzed large-scale game log data from commercial games. Thus, we analyzed gameplay logs from The Walking Dead: Match3 Tales, released in 109 countries on October 26, 2023, comparing user data before and after activating colorblind mode.

2 Literature Review

The types of disabilities that limit playing video games are namely visual, auditory, mobility, and cognitive disabilities [3]. Video games are a widely used leisure activity, and so inhibition caused by disabilities to participate in games is a matter of life quality [3]. Therefore, game design guidelines concerning disabilities have been proposed nationally and globally [34]. In the United States, the 21st Century Communications and Video Accessibility Act (CVAA) was signed into law in 2010, requiring all media technologies including communication functions to be inclusively designed [8]. This legislation ensures that accessibility laws passed in the 20th century can be adapted to the various forms of modern technology, including the web and mobile, in line with the development of 21st century communication technologies.

Public infrastructure and the web were first to be affected, and video games were granted a waiver for a long period of time, however games released by January 1st, 2019, or later are required to comply with the law. For example, Minecraft has been equipped with various technologies to support disabilities such as having TTS functions, and Mattel, well-known for their board game UNO, has also redesigned their game items to accommodate the visually impaired [9]. The EU also enacted accessibility requirements for ICT products and services in 2019, and games released on or after June 28, 2025, will be subject to this law, required to provide alternatives to conveying information through color when necessary [31].

Commercial games are also taking inclusive design into account. PlayStation and Xbox support assistive modes and controllers [2, 6], also do many different games implement diverse measures, including subtitles for deaf players, vibrations and sounds to aid the visually impaired [10], and means to help ones with cognitive disabilities [29]. The approach to accessible games has evolved past the idea of access and enablement, to where game designers would put their aims at providing the desired user experience to all users [24]. This means that players with disabilities would not only be able to play the game under limited conditions but also would be able to have the full experience desired by the game designer.

Colorblindness is a type of visual disability that causes difficulty distinguishing colors, also known as color vision deficiency (CVD). Web, publishing, and video game applications for colorblind users have been done by means including adjusting contrast [4], incorporating patterns [25], displaying labels [15], and using color filters. Colorblind mode has been adopted by many commercial games in service [12]. Splatoon, developed by Nintendo, offers a "color lock" feature that allows ink to be locked to a color that is not affected by color blindness, while World of Warcraft offers filters for red, green, and blue blindness, of which the strength of each filter can be adjusted.

Beyond providing game accessibility in terms of function, a study conducted in 2018 indirectly measured the experience and performance of colorblind players by analyzing game play sessions on a puzzle game, daltonized by color filters to simulate a colorblind state [18]. Although players reported in interviews that their decision-making was slowed down and felt uncomfortable when playing puzzle games where color information is important, statistics did not approve that the colorblind mode inhibited their actual performance, therefore asserting that colorblind users are not at a significant disadvantage [18].

Due to the small population, few studies have focused specifically on colorblind gamers' experiences and performance. One study demonstrated improved effectiveness, efficiency, and satisfaction when using adaptive colorblind environments on mobile devices [17], highlighting user needs for color vision assistance. In this study, we analyzed puzzle game logs to examine the impact of colorblind assistance modes on gameplay experiences.

3 Case: Game Design for Colorblindness

The Walking Dead: Match3 Tales is a puzzle-based PvP (Person versus Person) game that involves lining up three or more blocks of the same color in a row, to attack the enemy standing in the vertically corresponding row. This game has a single-player storyline, but the Endgame content, in which all players are intended to enjoy after the planned solo-play contents are fully exploited, is the PvP content where players compete against each other in 1v1 battles. It is very important to create a fair competition environment, since looting depends on the result of PvP battles. The team has made simulations on how the screens would be seen to colorblind players to design specific colorblind modes, as illustrated in Fig. 1. To ensure a fair competition environment for CVD players, the development team included Colorblindness Mode in the game.

   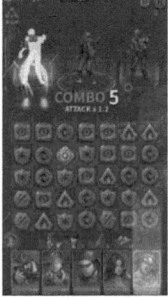

(a) Non-colorblind   (b) Red-green CVD   (c) Blue-yellow CVD   (d) Monochromacy

Fig. 1. CVD simulations, Non-colorblind(a), Red-green color vision deficiency(b), Blue-yellow color vision efficiency(c), Monochromacy(d)

3.1 Attribute

Walking Dead: Match3 is a game where the attributes of a character or enemy are very important. All characters and enemies in the game have either of five attributes: Aggressive, Humane, Cunning, Brutal, or Rational. These attributes interact with each other and can magnify the damage up to twice when attacking or being hit. These attributes are displayed at the feet of enemy characters and on blocks. It is also displayed as the background color for each character in the player's character deck at the bottom of the screen. CVD players find it difficult to distinguish this important information about attributes, so the development team has provided equivalent information in the form of an additional icon when colorblindness mode is enabled.

3.2 Colorblindness Mode

When enabling colorblindness mode, the player can adjust the brightness of each block to give higher visibility to icons, and blocks on the screen will be given an additional icon next to them, as shown in Fig. 2(a). The blocks in the game have an imprinted icon inside them, but all blocks have the same shape, making it very inconvenient to distinguish them from each other under the lack of color distinction. Considering the art concept of the game, it was difficult to make each type of block have a different shape, so a function to separate the internal design from the background of the block was added instead, enabling the imprinted icons to stand out, as illustrated in Fig. 2(b). To help distinguish the attributes of enemy characters, enemy characters would display the attribute's symbol in Colorblindness mode as in Fig. 2(c), so that colorblind players would also be able to distinguish what attributes the enemies carry. The player characters' attributes are also distinguished by background color by default, but icons would be added under the activation of colorblind mode to display the attributes, shown in Fig. 2(d).

4 Data

We received data from the developers of The Walking Dead: Match3 Tales and analyzed logs from the game, which was collected from 109 countries for approximately 9 months. There are 103,024,742 lines in the logs, which is equivalent to 17.63 GB. There was a total of 14,738 unique users. The game was downloaded by 32,294 users through Apple Appstore and 115,262 users through Google Play. The log data consists of Name, UserId, AbTest, Country, Params, Date, Market, and Time. Name, in this case indicates the situation in which the log was made.

We used Name to identify events where a specific type of action occurred, combining the corresponding data with the User ID, Country, associated information (Params), and the date, market information, and time when the action occurred. We combined data from UserColorBlindMode, Login, Register, PVPMatch, PVPResult, TutorialEnd_74, and ProductPurchase logs for analysis. These mean when colorblind mode was enabled, when the player logged in, when the player has registered for the first time, when the opponent of PvP was designated, the result of the PvP battle, when the player has accomplished the tutorial, and when the player has made purchase, respectively. In this

Evaluating Colorblind-Friendly Design for Equitable Play 211

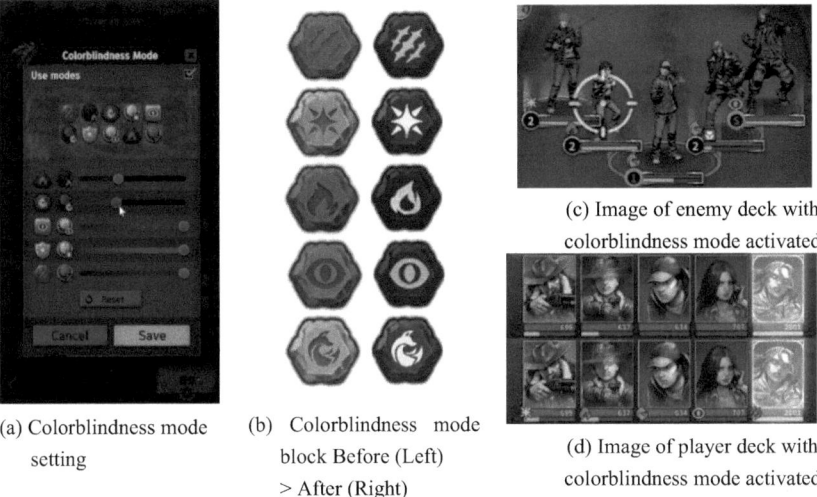

(a) Colorblindness mode setting

(b) Colorblindness mode block Before (Left) > After (Right)

(c) Image of enemy deck with colorblindness mode activated

(d) Image of player deck with colorblindness mode activated

Fig. 2. CVD simulation works in progress, in order: Colorblindness mode setting, Colorblindness mode block, Image of enemy deck with colorblindness mode activated, Image of player deck with colorblindness mode activated

case, the Params of the PVPMatch log includes UserTeamPower, which is the potential performance of the player's battle deck, and EnemyTeamPower, which is the potential performance of the enemy's battle deck.

We calculated Difficulty by subtracting EnemyTeamPower from UserTeamPower. We created a separate data table of PvP History by preprocessing only the data we needed for our research topic. To quickly analyze a large amount of data, we uploaded the log data in JSON format to Google Big Query and analyzed it using SQL and Python.

5 Data Analysis

We aim to answer the question of whether a game's colorblind mode creates a fair PvP environment for colorblind gamers, and whether this will in turn increase the CVD users' loyalty and satisfaction with the game. Analyzing the relationship between colorblind mode and PvP win rate gives direct answer to the first question, and analyzing the loyalty and satisfaction of colorblind players through their retention and spending behavior will allow indirect answers to the latter. When calculating and comparing the win rate, retention, ARPPU, and PUR of colorblind and non-colorblind players, the entire pool of colorblind players was included in the calculation, while those of non-colorblind players were only of those who completed the initial tutorial. This is because the colorblind assist mode can be enabled only after the tutorial, and so comparing between users who completed the tutorial would give a fair result.

5.1 How Colorblind Mode Affects the Win Rate of Colorblind Players

Methods. The data to be analyzed are 1,634,350 PvP records from non-colorblind players and 21,909 PvP records from colorblind players. This study used Linear Mixed-Effects Analysis to effectively analyze repeatedly recorded PvP result records to determine the effect of colorblind mode on win rate. Linear Mixed-effects models can effectively handle dependency and within-user group correlation due to repeated battle records in large-scale data, making them suitable for producing reliable results in large datasets [13, 23]. Linear mixed-effects are widely utilized, and game-related examples include the educational effects of video games [26], social relationship effects [32], and cognitive attitude effects [21]. The model can simultaneously model fixed and variable effects, while accounting for variability among individual users. This enables estimation of the impact of key variables, such as the use of colorblindness mode, the player character's combat strength, and the matched enemy character's combat strength on the outcomes of win or loss.

Analysis results. We wrote a Python code to run a Linear Mixed-Effects Analysis. The fixed effects were 'whether color blindness mode is enabled', 'player's team power', and 'enemy player's team power', and the variable effect was 'user ID'.

Mixed Linear Model Regression Results
===
Model: MixedLM Dependent Variable: PVPOutcome
No. Observations: 1635851 Method: REML
No. Groups: 49619 Scale: 0.1833
Min. group size: 1 Log-Likelihood: -943721.8713
Max. group size: 4295 Converged: Yes
Mean group size: 33.0

Coef. Std.Err. z P>|z| [0.025 0.975]

Intercept 0.968 0.001 965.276 0.000 0.966 0.970
ColorBlindMode 0.014 0.006 2.314 0.021 0.002 0.026
UserTeamPower 0.000 0.000 84.986 0.000 0.000 0.000
EnemyTeamPower -0.000 0.000 -217.348 0.000 -0.000 -0.000
Group Var 0.006 0.000
===

An analysis having PVPOutcome and the result of the battle in win or loss as the dependent variable and ColorBlindMode, UserTeamPower, and EnemyTeamPower as the independent variables show that ColorBlindMode has a value of 0.014 (p-value:0.021), and the model has converged. This means that a player is about 1.4% more likely to win when the ColorBlindMode is on, which is statistically significant. The odds of winning increase as the player's team power increases and decreases as the enemy's team power increases. Although this is statistically significant, the coefficient is very small, which means that the effect is insignificant in this research.

Evaluating Colorblind-Friendly Design for Equitable Play   213

In this game, The Walking Dead: Match3 Tales, there is an internal logic that lets players meet harder opponents when their team power is high, which is coherent to the result supported by the statistics where higher team power does not give higher win rate. Additionally, the Group Variance value was 0.006, meaning that there was no significant difference in win rates between users. This suggests that the practical impact on win rate is limited, and the assistive feature contributes only marginally to outcome differences. Therefore, conclusions regarding fairness improvement are to be interpreted with caution and within the context of effect magnitude.

5.2 Impact of Colorblind Mode on Win Rate by User Population

Methods. To see in what situations in PvP the effect of colorblindness is more pronounced, we compared the win rate of colorblind users' PvP records before and after turning on colorblindness. We analyzed the win rate by dividing the player's match difficulty (UserTeamPower - EnemyTeamPower) into five bins. Each is a Large Disadvantage section (team power difference: less than -500), Small Disadvantage section (-500 to -100), Balanced section (-100 to 100), Small Advantage section (100 to 500), and Large Advantage section (team power difference of 500 or more), being most favorable to the player.

Analysis results. When colorblind mode is enabled, represented as the blue line in Fig. 3, the difference in win rate is very small in the Large Advantage, Small Advantage, and Balanced sections. In Small Disadvantage and Large Disadvantage sections, where the difference between the matched opponent and team power is greater, the win rate is 6.81% and 8.87% higher, respectively, when colorblind mode is enabled. In a preceded study, colorblind simulations did not give lower performance, and our results suggest that the difficulty level of the Pet Rescue Saga stages in that study was somewhat lower than the researchers' estimates [22]. We assume that the use of colorblind mode is beneficial to aid player experiences in higher levels of difficulty.

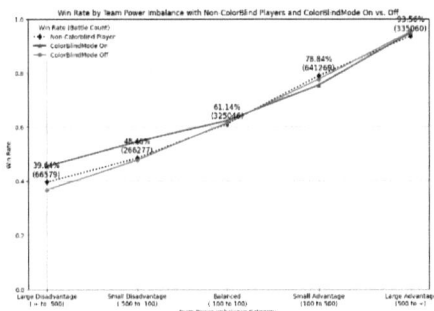
(a) PvP win rate based on team power difference before and after enabling colorblind mode

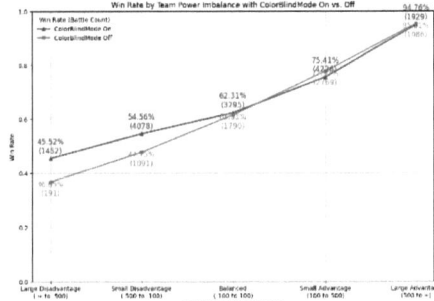
(b) PvP win rate based on team power difference between CVD and non-CVD

Fig. 3. Win Rate by Team Power Imbalance

The same methodology was used to analyze the win rate of non-colorblind users across the team power imbalance range. By comparing the win rate of non-colorblind players to the win rate of colorblind players before and after turning on colorblind Mode, we analyzed how much colorblind players are disadvantaged without colorblind Mode and how much they are helped by turning on colorblind Mode. It was found that the assistive mode increased the win rate in the Large Disadvantage and Small Disadvantage sections, and even if the colorblind mode is off, the win rate of colorblind players compared to non-colorblind players is not necessarily lower in other sections except for the Large Disadvantage section. In the Large Disadvantage segment, the non-colorblind player has a lower win rate of up to 5.88%p, and the non-colorblind player has a higher win rate of 2.99%p when the assistive mode is turned on.

5.3 Comparing the Retention of Non-Colorblind and Colorblind Players

The retention rate is calculated by setting the initial number of users on day n as 100%, measuring the percentage returning to the game on subsequent days (n + x) [33]. This method retrospectively aggregates how many users continue to play after their initial interaction, indirectly reflecting overall loyalty, a critical KPI in game servicing [27, 33]. We compared retention between colorblind and non-colorblind users, finding significantly higher retention for colorblind players: D + 1 retention was 67% versus 40.5%, and D + 30 retention was 15.4% compared to 3.8% (Fig. 4). On average, colorblind users exhibited 214.54% greater retention, suggesting increased satisfaction within this group. However, retention is influenced by multiple factors such as gameplay preferences, user motivation, and onboarding experiences [33], so it should be considered an indirect indicator of loyalty or satisfaction. The gap widens further at higher levels, indicating players engaged with more challenging content tend to be more satisfied.

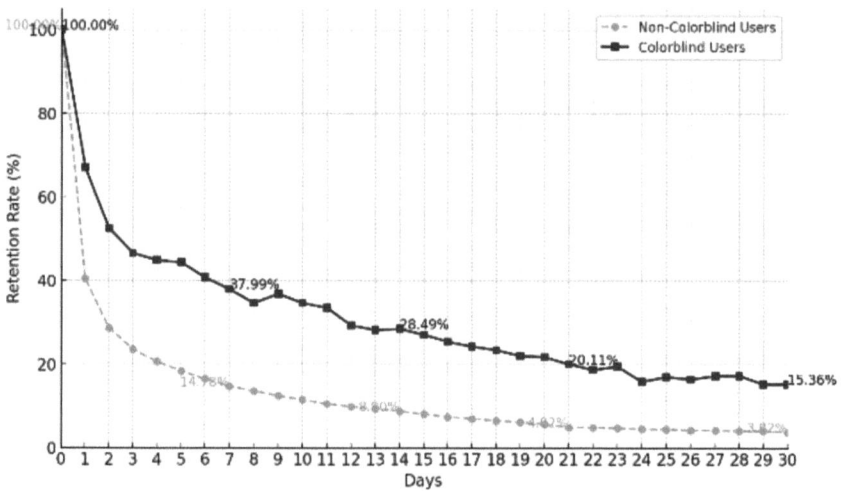

Fig. 4. Retention for non-colorblind and colorblind players

5.4 Comparing In-Game Payment Metrics for Non-Colorblind and Colorblind Players

We have conducted analysis to compare the ARPPU and PUR between non-colorblind players and colorblind players. ARPPU is the Average Revenue per Paid User, meaning the mean revenue given from a single paying user. PUR is the Paying User Rate, indicating the percentage of users who actually spend money on the game. These metrics do not give a direct relationship with colorblindness. However, high purchase rates suggest that a player's overall satisfaction is likely to be high, as overall satisfaction directly impacts purchase intent, while involvement influences purchase intent indirectly through overall satisfaction and perceived quality [30]. By analyzing the log data, we can see that colorblind players make purchases at a higher rate (39.11%) but spend a relatively low amount ($439.82)(Fig. 5).

At the same time, non-colorblind players give an ARPPU of $485.68 and a PUR of 18.43%. Normally, both metrics would be collected and calculated daily, but in this study, we would like to state that this is a project-wide metric, due to the developer's unwillingness to disclose sensitive information. It is suspected that the reason why colorblind players show higher PUR lies in that they show higher loyalty to the game, staying in the game for a longer period, naturally giving a higher PUR. However, PUR in this data may be less accurate because colorblind users form a relatively small subset of the total population, which means that some satisfied users may be paying at a high rate.

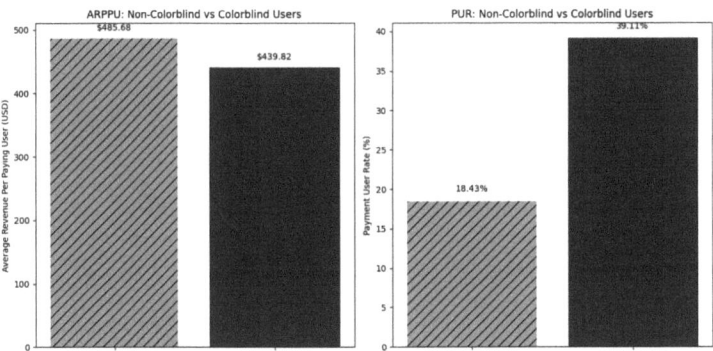

Fig. 5. ARPPU and PUR of non-colorblind players and colorblind players

6 Limitations

We assumed users enabling colorblind mode were colorblind, but some non-colorblind players might have activated it, and some colorblind users might not have done so. Since enabling the mode requires completing the tutorial, recorded colorblind users might inherently be more engaged, influencing retention and payment metrics. Additionally, some highly engaged players might use the mode for performance advantages rather than visual accessibility, but player intent could not be determined from the data.

7 Conclusion

When playing PvP, which is the Endgame content for all players, colorblind players too were able to access the game even without enabling the colorblind mode and were not significantly disadvantaged compared to non-colorblind players. On the other hand, only when facing very difficult opponents, the win rate of colorblind players was lower. This gives the conclusion that the pre-existing game design, including the engraved icon designs on blocks and the color diversity gives sufficient accessibility, allowing even colorblind individuals to enjoy the game.

However, they are still at a disadvantage in higher difficulty contents and have a harder time playing a fair game. We suspect the reason to be that the harder the game is, the bigger a consequence a subtle difference can bring. Colorblindness mode has a win rate correction effect in high difficulty matches. It also seems to provide additional clues to puzzle play, as colorblind players have a higher win rate than non-colorblind players in some sections. In conclusion, colorblindness mode contributes to creating a fair environment and increasing satisfaction in high difficulty matches.

Acknowledgments. This work was supported by the Seoul RISE initiative, specifically through the AI-based Full Stack Game Designer Development Program. The findings presented in this paper were derived from the outcomes of this initiative, and the study aims to contribute insights into balanced game design practices that consider color vision deficiency (CVD). SQL and Python coding for data analysis was done using ChatGPT, and the code was modified by the author.

Disclosure of Interests. The authors have no competing interests to declare that are relevant to the content of this article.

References

1. Andrade, R., Rogerson, M.J., Waycott, J., Baker, S., Vetere, F.: Playing blind: revealing the world of gamers with visual impairment. In Proceedings of the 2019 CHI Conference on Human Factors in Computing Systems, pp. 1–14 (2019). https://doi.org/10.1145/3290605.3300346
2. Armstrong, S.: Here's how the xbox adaptive controller is getting people with disabilities back into gaming. WIRED UK. Retrieved March **21** (2018) (2018)
3. Bierre, K., Chetwynd, J., Ellis, B., Hinn, D.M., Ludi, S., Westin, T.: Game not over: accessibility issues in video games. In Proc. of the 3rd International Conference on Universal Access in Human-Computer Interaction, pp. 22–27 (2005)
4. Bingham, R., Dietrich, S.W., Goelman, D.: Strategies to improve accessibility for learners with color vision deficiency. ACM Inroads **10**(1), 52–56 (2019). https://doi.org/10.1145/3306140
5. Birch, J.: Worldwide prevalence of red-green color deficiency. JOSA A. **29**(3), 313–320 (2012). https://doi.org/10.1364/JOSAA.29.000313
6. Cairns, P., Power, C., Barlet, M., Haynes, G.: Future design of accessibility in games: a design vocabulary. Int. J. Hum. Comput. Stud. **131**(2019), 64–71 (2019). https://doi.org/10.1016/j.ijhcs.2019.06.010
7. Cho, Y.-K., Han, H.-J., Kim, K.-J.: A study on the application of color as process of symbolic metaphor in the game storytelling. J. Korea Game Society **8**(1), 41–48 (2008)

8. Federal Communications Commission. 21st Century Communications and Video Accessibility Act (CVAA). https://www.fcc.gov/consumers/guides/21st-century-communications-and-video-accessibility-act-cvaa. Accessed 12 Sep 2024 (2021)
9. Fast company. Mattel will make 80% of its games color-blind accessible by the end of the year. https://www.fastcompany.com/91146946/mattel-is-making-its-games-colorblind-accessible. Accessed 12 Sep 2024 (2024)
10. Naughty Dog. Accessibility options for The Last of Us Part II. https://www.playstation.com/en-fi/games/the-last-of-us-part-ii/accessibility. Accessed12 Sep 2024 (2020)
11. Tristan Donovan. Replay: The History of Video Games. Yellow Ant (2010)
12. Accessible Games. Accessible Player Experiences (APX) (2018). https://accessible.games/accessible-player-experiences/. Accessed 12 Sep 2024
13. Gueorguieva, R., Krystal, J.H.: Move over anova: progress in analyzing repeated-measures data andits reflection in papers published in the archives of general psychiatry. Archives of General Psychiatry **61**(3), 310–317 (2004). https://doi.org/10.1001/archpsyc.61.3.310
14. Chua, S.H., Zhang, H., Hammad, M., Zhao, S., Goyal, S., Singh, K.: ColorBless: augmenting visual information for colorblind people with binocular luster effect. ACM Transactions on Computer-Human Interaction (TOCHI) **21**(6), 1–20 (2015). https://doi.org/10.1145/2687923
15. Innersloth. Bug Bashing Bonanza Update (2022). https://www.innersloth.com/bug-bashing-bonanza-update/. Accessed 12 Sep 2024
16. National Eye Institute. Types of Color Vision Deficiency (2023). https://www.nei.nih.gov/learn-about-eye-health/eye-conditions-and-diseases/color-blindness/types-color-vision-deficiency. Accessed 12 Sep 2024
17. Iqbal, M.W., Shahzad, S.K., Ahmad, N., Amelio, A., Brodic, D.: Adaptive interface for color-blind people in mobile-phones. In 2018 International Conference on Advancements in Computational Sciences (ICACS). IEEE, pp. 1–8 (2018). https://doi.org/10.1109/ICACS.2018.8333488
18. Jamil, A., Denes, G.: Investigating color-blind user-interface accessibility via simulated interfaces. Computers **13**(2), 53 (2024). https://doi.org/10.3390/computers13020053
19. Jefferson, L., Harvey, R.: An interface to support color blind computer users. In Proceedings of the SIGCHI Conference on Human Factors in Computing Systems, pp. 1535–1538 (2007). https://doi.org/10.1145/1240624.124085
20. Kerac, J., Kereteš, N.M., Dedijer, S.: An Overview of the User Experience in Online Video Game Players with Colour Vision Deficiency. ([n. d.])
21. Kolek, L., Šisler, V., Martinková, P., Brom, C.: Can video games change attitudes towards history? Results from a laboratory experiment measuring short-and long-term effects. J. Computer Assisted Learning **37**(5), 1348–1369 (2021). https://doi.org/10.1111/jcal.12575
22. Napoli, D., Chiasson, S.: Exploring the impact of colour-blindness on computer game performance. In Extended abstracts of the 2018 CHI Conference on Human Factors in Computing Systems, pp. 1–6 (2018). https://doi.org/10.1145/3170427.3188555
23. Oberg, A.L., Mahoney, D.W.: Linear mixed effects models. Topics in biostatistics **2007**, 213–234 (2007). https://doi.org/10.1007/978-1-59745-530-5_11
24. Power, C., Cairns, P., Barlet, M.: Inclusion in the third wave: access to experience. New Directions in Third Wave Human-Computer Interaction: Volume 1-Technologies, pp. 163–181 (2018). https://doi.org/10.1007/978-3-319-73356-2_10
25. Sajadi, B., Majumder, A., Oliveira, M.M., Schneider, R.G., Raskar, R.: Using patterns to encode color information for dichromats. IEEE Transactions on Visualization and Computer Graphics **19**(1), 118–129 (2012). https://doi.org/10.1109/TVCG.2012.93
26. Sala, G., Tatlidil, K.S., Gobet, F.: Video game training does not enhance cognitive ability: a comprehensive meta-analytic investigation. Psychological Bulletin **144**(2), 111 (2018). https://doi.org/10.1037/bul0000139

27. Seufert, E.B.: Freemium Economics: Leveraging Analytics and User Segmentation to Drive Revenue. Elsevier (2013)
28. Shin, Y., Kim, J., Jin, K., Kim, Y.B.: Playtesting in match 3 game using strategic plays via reinforcement learning. IEEE Access **8**(2020), 51593–51600 (2020). https://doi.org/10.1109/ACCESS.2020.2980380
29. Sousa, C., Neves, J.C., Barros, J.: Towards cognitive accessibility in digital game design: evidence-based guidelines for adults with intellectual disability. In 2023 IEEE Conference on Games (CoG). IEEE, pp. 1–4 (2023). https://doi.org/10.1109/CoG57401.2023.10333254
30. Tsiotsou, R.: The role of perceived product quality and overall satisfaction on purchase intentions. International J. Consumer Studies **30**(2), 207–217 (2006). https://doi.org/10.1111/j.1470-6431.2005.00477.x]
31. European Union.. Directive (EU) 2019/882 of the European Parliament and of the Council (2019). https://eur-lex.europa.eu/legal-content/EN/TXT/?uri=CELEX%3A32019L0882. Accessed 12 Sep 2024
32. Verheijen, G.P., Stoltz, S.E.M.J., van den Berg, Y.H.M., Cillessen, A.H.N.: The influence of competitive and cooperative video games on behavior during play and friendship quality in adolescence. Comput. Hum. Behav. **91**(2019), 297–304 (2019). https://doi.org/10.1016/j.chb.2018.10.023
33. Viljanen, M., Airola, A., Pahikkala, T., Heikkonen, J.: Modelling user retention in mobile games. In 2016 IEEE Conference on Computational Intelligence and Games (CIG). IEEE, pp. 1–8 (2016). https://doi.org/10.1109/CIG.2016.7860393
34. W3C. Web Content Accessibility Guidelines (WCAG) 2.2 (2023). https://www.w3.org/TR/WCAG22/. Accessed 12 Sep 2024
35. Yu, Y., Dinh, T., Yu, F., Huynh, V.-N.: Understanding mobile game reviews through sentiment analysis: a case study of PUBGm. In: International Conference on Model and Data Engineering. Springer, pp. 102–115 (2023). https://doi.org/10.1007/978-3-031-49333-1_8

Manzai Karaoke: A Real-Time Visual Guidance System for Assisting Japanese Double Act Performance

Shunta Komatsu[✉], Tomonori Kubota, Satoshi Sato, and Kohei Ogawa

Nagoya University, Nagoya, Aichi, Japan
`komatsu.shunta.i0@s.mail.nagoya-u.ac.jp`,
`{kubota,ssato,k-ogawa}@nuee.nagoya-u.ac.jp`

Abstract. While the common way to enjoy two-person comedic dialogue, such as double act, is by watching it, performing Japanese *manzai* has recently gained attention for its entertainment value and effectiveness in improving dialogue skills. However, performing manzai is challenging, as it requires memorizing scripts and mastering its unique intonation, actions, and timing. In this study, we propose "Manzai Karaoke," a real-time visual guidance system that assists two-person manzai performances. Similar to *karaoke*, this system provides script line displays and nonverbal performance cues, enabling inexperienced users to perform manzai. To design an interface that meets the key requirements—allowing users to perform with ease and ensuring audience amusement—we conducted a two-step prototyping and user study. The first step validated the feasibility of real-time comedy performance assistance, revealing that in addition to displaying script lines, guidance on intonation, emotion, actions, and timing is essential. The second step demonstrated that the implemented interface incorporating these elements effectively meets the requirements. This study contributes to the field of entertainment computing by demonstrating the potential of visual guidance and providing design recommendations for assisting novice manzai performances.

Keywords: real-time performance assistance · interface design · comedic dialogue · manzai

1 Introduction

The entertainment style of two performers playing a comedic dialogue to make an audience laugh is popular in various forms throughout the world: for example, double act in America and Europe [20], crosstalk (*xiangsheng*) in China [5], and *manzai* in Japan [25]. Although the detailed style differs among cultures, they all share the same basic format of a comedic dialogue between two performers.

S. Komatsu and T. Kubota—These authors contributed equally to this work and share first authorship.

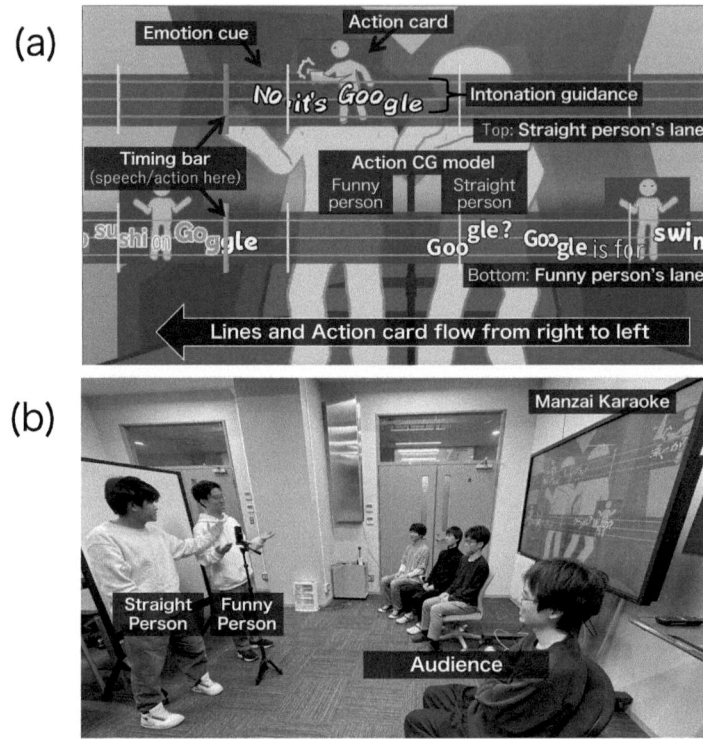

Fig. 1. Overview of Manzai Karaoke: (a) Example of user interface implemented in Sect. 5. Script lines and performance guidance are presented for both the straight and funny person. This shows an English translation of the actual Japanese interface. Texts on black background were added for explanatory purposes. (b) Example of usage scene in which two users perform manzai in front of the audience. This system enables users to perform existing manzai scripts and entertain the audience.

This research focuses on Japanese manzai. Manzai, like double act and crosstalk, is a performance in which two performers exchange comedic banter through words and actions, with the aim of making the audience laugh [9,12,15]. The two performers generally have different roles: the "funny person" (*boke*) who makes humorous or unexpected statements, and the "straight person" (*tsukkomi*) who butt-in with corrections or clarifications that emphasize the humor and prompt audience laughter [12,15]. While various styles of manzai exist, performers typically deliver their dialogue with gestures in front of stand microphones (like Fig. 1(b)). An example of a manzai dialogue is that the funny person saying, "I looked it up on Goggle," confusing the word with Google, and the straight person correcting, "No, it's Google," to elicit laughter from the audience.

While the common way to enjoy manzai in Japan is to watch it, performing manzai has been gaining attention in recent years. For instance, the number of entrants in the Japanese manzai competition, which claims to crown the best manzai performer, has been increasing annually, reaching 9,550 groups in 2024[1]. Additionally, manzai has been introduced in new employee training programs to improve communication skills[2,3], and manzai workshops have been held at schools for children [2]. Performing manzai is expected to enhance expressive abilities and communication skills such as conversational rhythm and timing [22]. It has also been reported that through the manzai class, more students feel that they enjoy school and willingly speak up in class [2].

Furthermore, performing manzai and making the audience laugh can provide a sense of exhilaration and the joy of sharing laughter. In fact, several professional comedians stated that getting laughs from an audience is exhilarating [11,16,17,26]. This type of experience is rarely available in daily life and represents a special one that can be gained through performing comedy.

However, it is challenging for humans to perform manzai and make an audience laugh. Manzai performance requires memorizing both the verbal and nonverbal elements of the script. Moreover, to make the audience laugh, it is necessary to have the expressive skills, such as the appropriate intonation and speech timing. Before performing, it is also difficult to create comedic scripts eliciting laughter from an audience.

This research aims to develop a manzai performance assistance system called "Manzai Karaoke" that enables inexperienced users to perform existing manzai scripts to elicit laughter from an audience. Manzai Karaoke displays manzai scripts and performance guidance on a screen interface, allowing two users playing the funny person and straight person roles to perform manzai in real-time (similar to *karaoke* that allows people to sing with lyrics displayed on the screen). Figure 1(a) shows the interface implemented in Sect. 5, which, similar to music notation, presents script lines, intonation, emotional expression, actions, and speech and action timing. This allows users to perform manzai with expressions that can elicit laughter from an audience without completely memorizing the script in advance. Moreover, employing scripts authored by professional comedians increases the assurance of an entertaining performance.

Realization of Manzai Karaoke can lower barriers to perform manzai, creating more opportunities to experience the benefits of manzai performance. This system would make it easier to perform manzai for educational scenarios featuring manzai as a learning tool. As another scenario, it could be used to practice manzai at Japanese comedian training schools[4,5,6] or for aspiring professional manzai performers. Through performing with the system, users can learn the intonation, timing, and other skills, potentially improving the manzai performance abilities.

---

[1] https://www.m-1gp.com/.
[2] https://funfare.bandainamcoent.co.jp/4756/.
[3] https://newsdig.tbs.co.jp/articles/-/1256318?display=1.
[4] https://nsc.yoshimoto.co.jp/.
[5] https://www.we-school.net/wcs/.
[6] https://www.shochikugeino.co.jp/school/.

Additionally, Manzai Karaoke could be used for a recreational activity for groups, creating a new form of entertainment that provides the special experience of manzai performance. Drawing inspiration from the group-based enjoyment in Japanese karaoke, where groups alternate singing, Manzai Karaoke could offer a platform for groups to alternate performing and watching manzai, sharing comedic experience. In such scenarios, people would have the rare opportunity to perform manzai in front of others and experience the exhilaration of making the audience laugh. Furthermore, sharing laughter within the group may promote relationship building [13].

This paper proposes the concept of Manzai Karaoke and aims to confirm its feasibility and gather insights for interface design through prototype implementation and user studies. The main contribution of this study is to propose a system that assists real-time comedic performances and to provide design recommendations for such systems. While various styles of comedy exist around the world, there has been no approach to assist ordinary users in experiencing the exhilaration of eliciting laughter from an audience. This research pioneers a new genre of application in the field of entertainment computing.

2 Related Works

Research on manzai has primarily aimed at analyzing manzai performances and developing systems for automatic comedic script generation. Studies analyzing manzai performances explore both the elements that create humor [12,25] and non-verbal aspects like timing and actions [21,27]. For automatic script generation, researchers have developed systems to produce comedic scripts [1]. For instance, systems have been created that generate comedic scripts from sources like web news and cooking recipes [14,23].

In the context of manzai research, our work is positioned as the development of a system that provides real-time assistance for manzai performances. To our knowledge, there is no direct precedent for this research; however, a related system has been developed that allows a user to experience manzai performance in VR space [15]. In this system, one user plays the straight person role and can perform manzai with an autonomous avatar playing the funny person role by following displayed script lines. Nevertheless, this system does not aim to assist dialogue between two users or to entertain an audience through performance, which differs from our research objectives. Additionally, while the previous system displayed script lines to users, it did not provide any non-verbal information such as intonation, actions, and timing of speech and actions. Consequently, the difficulty in managing timing and actions was identified as a challenge. Therefore, the display of non-verbal information addressed in our research is considered important for effective manzai performance. While the idea of assisting manzai performance has existed previously, our research uniquely establishes a system that enables two users to perform existing manzai scripts to an audience-enjoyable level by appropriately displaying both verbal and non-verbal information.

Our research can also be positioned within the context of real-time performance support systems. As a device assisting real-time performance, speech prompters exist that display verbal information (script lines) to performers. Research involving real-time presentation of non-verbal information encompasses systems supporting presenters' speaking rate and pitch [10], volume and eye contact [8], timing management for hosts [18], and action guidance for performers [4]. However, these systems all target individual performer, and methodologies for assisting interaction between two performers have not been established.

Another related research area is rhythm-based games. For example, some systems provide real-time support for dance performances by presenting action guidance cues [3,24]. These studies focus on actions and differ from our system that includes speech. To our knowledge, there is no existing research specifically aiming to assist comedy performance by appropriately displaying not only script lines but also non-verbal information to assist real-time interaction between two performers.

3 Research Approach

Manzai Karaoke is designed to assist two users in performing manzai to entertain an audience by providing them with scripts and performance guidance. The key requirements for Manzai Karaoke are that "users can enjoy performing manzai without excessive burden" and "audiences find the manzai performances entertaining". However, there are interface design challenges regarding what elements related to manzai performance should be presented and how they should be displayed in the interface. While we can assume that script lines and intonation information are at least necessary, for example, it is not clear how to intuitively present the unique intonation patterns of professional manzai performances to users. Additionally, non-verbal information such as actions might be useful, but presenting all non-verbal information could increase users' cognitive load and potentially hinder smooth performance. Therefore, to realize Manzai Karaoke, it is necessary to reveal an interface design that meets the requirements.

The purpose of this paper is to verify the feasibility of Manzai Karaoke concept—which assists users' real-time manzai performance for audience enjoyment—and to develop an interface that meets the stated requirements. To achieve this, we conducted prototype implementation and user studies in two steps:

1. We implemented a first prototype with minimal presentation elements and conducted a user study to verify the feasibility of Manzai Karaoke concept and investigate what elements should be presented and how for assisting manzai performances (Sect. 4).
2. Based on the insights gained from Step 1, we implemented a second prototype and conducted a user study to verify whether the improved interface satisfies the requirements (Sect. 5).

Here are two possible usage scenarios for Manzai Karaoke: users performing a familiar script or unfamiliar one. In the latter case, users perform a first-look

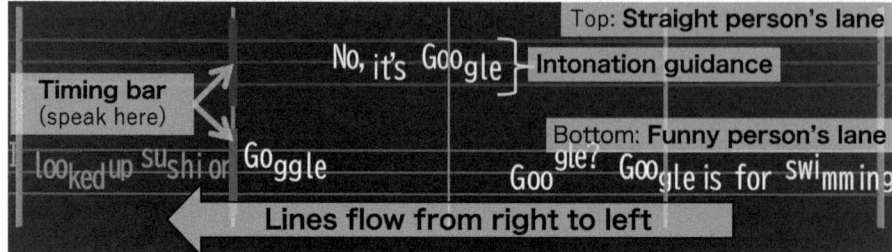

Fig. 2. Interface of the first prototype. This presents script lines, intonation guidance, and speech timing. This shows an English translation of the actual Japanese interface. Texts on gray background were added for explanatory purposes. (Color figure online)

manzai script by following the presented guidance. While this approach offers potential for game-like engagement, it places a higher cognitive load on performers compared to the former scenario, thus requiring a more intuitive interface design. Although the appropriate design methodology may differ depending on which usage scenario is selected, in this paper, we first implemented Manzai Karaoke prototype without limiting the usage scenario, confirmed its feasibility, and obtained design recommendations through user studies.

4 First Prototype: Initial Implementation and Foundational Insights

4.1 Methods

This section describes an exploratory user study to verify the feasibility of Manzai Karaoke and investigate what elements should be presented and how for assisting manzai performances. We implemented the first prototype interface (Fig. 2) that displays the minimal elements of script lines, intonation guidance, and speech timing with separate areas for the straight person (top) and funny person (bottom). Intonation guidance is shown by the vertical position of each character across five pitch levels. As script lines and intonation guidance flow from right to left, two users can synchronize their speech timing by speaking the lines when a character reaches the timing bar.

We call the interface presenting manzai scripts "notation," and implementation requires creating this notation from existing manzai performances. For this study, an author with manzai experience created a notation by extracting script, intonation, and speech timing from a professional manzai video (The script title is "Corn Flakes" written by *Milk Boy*[7]). To facilitate creating a notation, we also implemented a GUI editor that allows for editing script line, intonation, and speech timing.

We conducted a user study in which participants performed and watched manzai using the prototype. There were seven participants inexperienced in performing manzai (6 males, 1 female; age $M = 23.1$, $SD = 1.21$), with six

---

[7] https://www.youtube.com/watch?v=VjBQtr4lH0k.

males performing once during this study. Following performances, participants discussed the system's merits and challenges. All user studies reported in this paper received approval from ethics review board.

4.2 Findings

The user study revealed that five of six participants who performed manzai found the experience enjoyable. From the audience perspective, six of seven participants stated the performances were funny. We also observed an audience laughing during performances, indicating that users could successfully perform entertaining manzai. We consider that these results confirm the feasibility of Manzai Karaoke—validating our concept of assisting users' real-time manzai performances for audience enjoyment.

However, participant discussions identified three issues related to what elements should be presented and how for assist manzai performance: (1) difficulty in comprehending the manzai script content, (2) insufficiency of prosodic information, and (3) inadequacy of action guidance.

Regarding script comprehension, participants reported difficulty in understanding script content from flowing lines while performing. To improve comprehension, we propose implementing variable font styling to highlight key points, butt-in points, and funny points visually.

For prosodic information, participants stated that while the intonation guidance was understandable, following it completely was challenging. They also requested additional emotion cue associated with the lines. We propose presenting emotions through fonts and effects for appropriate prosodic expressions, even when users cannot fully follow the intonation guidance. Despite difficulties following intonation, no participants suggested removing this element, so we will retain it.

Concerning action information, participants requested action guidance. We consider two presentation methods: displaying only key actions linked with the lines or continuously showing professional performers' actions via video. The first approach offers clarity but limited information, while the second provides comprehensive guidance but may increase cognitive load. We plan to implement both designs in our next prototype to evaluate user experience with each approach.

In conclusion, our initial prototype demonstrated the feasibility of Manzai Karaoke concept while identifying three improvement strategies related to what elements should be presented and how in the interface. We will implement these enhancements in a second prototype and conduct further user study to verify whether the improved interface meets Manzai Karaoke requirements.

5 Second Prototype: Interface Improvement and User Evaluation

5.1 Implementation

We implemented a second prototype of Manzai Karaoke based on the improvement strategies identified in the previous section (Fig. 1(a)). Through the second user study, we aimed to verify whether this enhanced version resolved the previously identified issues, satisfied the requirements, and to identify any further improvements needed. The second prototype incorporated new functions according to the improvement strategies (as detailed in Sect. 4.2): Font variations and visual effects for lines to improve content comprehension and present emotional cue (Fig. 3), and two distinct action guidance features[8,9,10,11,12].

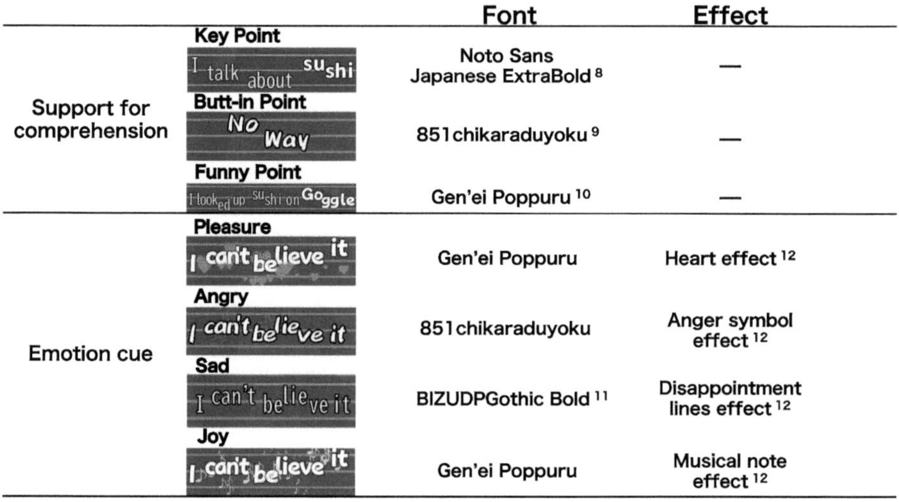

		Font	Effect
Support for comprehension	**Key Point**	Noto Sans Japanese ExtraBold [8]	—
	Butt-in Point	851chikaraduyoku [9]	—
	Funny Point	Gen'ei Poppuru [10]	—
Emotion cue	**Pleasure**	Gen'ei Poppuru	Heart effect [12]
	Angry	851chikaraduyoku	Anger symbol effect [12]
	Sad	BIZUDPGothic Bold [11]	Disappointment lines effect [12]
	Joy	Gen'ei Poppuru	Musical note effect [12]

Fig. 3. Two key features implemented in the second prototype of Manzai Karaoke: "Support for comprehension" through different fonts for Key, Butt-in, and Funny Points, and "Emotion cue" using specialized fonts with visual effects to express emotions.

To enhance script comprehension, we implemented font variations to emphasize key words in a script and highlight specific comedic words related to butt-in and funny points. For emotional expression cue linked with lines, we enabled the display of four basic emotions (pleasure, angry, sad, and joy) using distinctive font and visual effects.

For action guidance, we developed two approaches. First, an action card represents a key action that flows alongside the lines, allowing users to perform a specified action when the card reaches the timing bar (Fig. 4). Second, an action CG model video displays professional manzai performer's actions. The video was created by motion-capturing the author's imitation of the professional

---

[8] https://fonts.google.com/noto/specimen/Noto+Sans+JP.
[9] https://pm85122.onamae.jp/851ch-dz.html.
[10] https://okoneya.jp/font/download.html#dl-gpop.
[11] https://fonts.google.com/specimen/BIZ+UDGothic.
[12] https://booth.pm/ja/items/6006490.

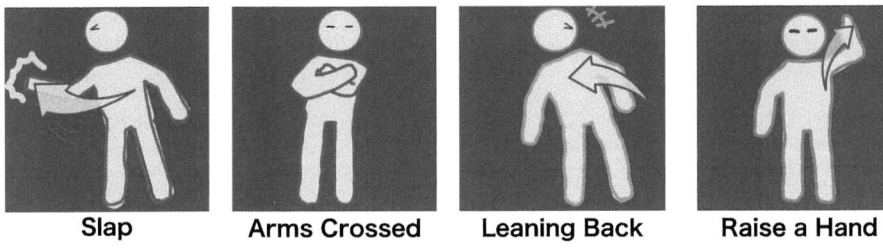

Fig. 4. Example of action cards. The left two cards are for straight person's action, while the right two cards are funny person's actions.

actions. The videos play in the background like Fig. 1(a), providing continuous reference for actions during performance.

As with the first prototype, we created the notations by extracting script lines, intonation, emotion, actions, and timing information from videos of professional manzai performers. Font variations for emphasized script lines and butt-in/funny points, emotional expressions, and key actions were identified based on the judgment of an author with manzai experience. We also enhanced our notation creation editor to support font changes, effect cue additions, and action card additions. For this study, we created script notations from the following three scripts written by professional manzai duos.

1. "Corn Flakes" by *Milk Boy*: characterized by exchanges of dialogue
2. "Dragon Ball" by *Knights*: characterized by wordplay
3. "Scary Story" by *Audrey*: characterized by larger actions

5.2 Study Methods

We conducted a user study using the implemented second prototype. Ten participants inexperienced in performing manzai (9 males, 1 female; age $M = 23.7$, $SD = 1.19$) were divided into five pairs. Each pair performed all three scripts in random order, with participants completing the user questionnaire after each performance (30 total responses). After performing, each pair then watched the next group's performance and completed the audience questionnaire after each watching (24 total responses from the first to fourth groups).

The requirements for Manzai Karaoke were that "users can enjoy performing manzai without excessive burden" and "audiences find the manzai performances entertaining". To evaluate how well the second prototype met the requirements, we prepared three questionnaires (see Table 1): (1) User's: Manzai Performance Experience (Q1–3: enjoyment of performing, being laughed, and performance quality), (2) User's: Interface Evaluation (Q4–17: impression of six interface elements), and (3) Audience's: Manzai Watching Experience (Q18–19: funniness, performance quality). Each item used a 7-point Likert scale (1: not at all, 7: very much). Additionally, we interviewed participants for free-form feedback after performances and watchings. Note that, responses from the funny person role

Table 1. Results of the questionnaires: Scores range from 1 to 7, with higher scores indicating more positive evaluations. Bold p-values indicate statistical significances with the chance level of 4.

Question item	Num. of responses	Mdn	IQR	p-value
(User's: Manzai Performance Experience)				
Q1: Did you enjoy performing manzai?	30	6.0	[6.00, 7.00]	**< .001**
Q2: Did you enjoy making the audience laugh?	30	6.0	[5.00, 6.75]	**< .001**
Q3: Do you feel you were able to perform manzai well?	30	5.0	[5.00, 6.00]	**.002**
(User's: Interface Evaluation)				
Q4: Did you find the displayed **script** easy to see?	30	5.0	[4.00, 6.00]	**< .001**
Q5: Did you find the content of the **script** easy to understand?	30	5.5	[4.00, 6.00]	**.003**
Q6: Did you find the **intonation guidance** easy to understand?	30	6.0	[4.00, 6.00]	**< .001**
Q7: Did you feel you were able to perform as **intonation guidance**?	30	5.0	[3.25, 6.00]	.566
Q8: Did you find the **emotion cue** easy to understand?	20	6.0	[4.00, 7.00]	**< .001**
Q9: Did you feel you were able to express emotions as suggested **emotion cue**?	20	5.0	[2.00, 6.00]	.454
Q10: Did you find the action guidance through **action cards** easy to understand?	20	6.0	[5.75, 6.00]	**< .001**
Q11: Did you feel you were able to action as suggested **action cards**?	20	5.0	[4.75, 6.25]	.071
Q12: Did you find the action guidance through the **action CG model** easy to understand?	30	2.0	[2.00, 5.00]	.085
Q13: Did you feel you were able to action as suggested the **action CG model**?	30	2.0	[1.00, 3.00]	**< .001**
Q14: Did you find the **speech timing** easy to understand?	30	7.0	[6.00, 7.00]	**< .001**
Q15: Did you feel you were able to match your **speech timing** as suggested?	30	6.0	[5.00, 6.00]	**< .001**
Q16: Did you find the **action timing** through action cards easy to understand?	20	6.0	[5.75, 7.00]	**< .001**
Q17: Did you feel you were able to match your **action timing** as suggested action cards?	20	6.0	[5.00, 7.00]	**.001**
(Audience's: Manzai Watching Experience)				
Q18: Did you find the manzai performance entertaining?	24	6.0	[5.00, 7.00]	**< .001**
Q19: Did you think the manzai performance was well skilled?	24	5.0	[4.00, 6.00]	**< .001**

in scripts 1 and 2 were excluded for emotion cue questions (Q8, 9) and action card questions (Q10, 11, 16, 17) as these elements were not included for this role (see Table 1 for the actual number of responses). For statistical analysis, we conducted Wilcoxon signed-rank tests against the chance level of 4 for each item (5% significance level) [6], using R ver 4.4.1 [19] with the exactRankTests [7] package.

5.3 Results and Discussion

User's Questionnaire. Table 1 shows that Q1-3 regarding manzai performance experience were rated significantly higher than chance level. During interviews, four out of ten users expressed satisfaction at eliciting audience laughter. One participant noted, "Making the audience laugh felt good. Even though it wasn't my original script, I had the illusion of being a humorous person," while another commented, "When I got reactions for adding emotion or actions, I felt happy and wanted to try harder to follow the guidance." These results confirm that our prototype successfully met the requirement that "users can enjoy performing manzai."

Regarding user interface evaluations, we first discuss the improvements made from the first prototype: script comprehension, emotion cues, and action guidance. For script comprehension, results from Q4 and Q5 indicate that script was rated significantly higher than chance level for both visibility and content comprehensibility. Three out of ten participants mentioned that font emphasis aided content understanding. We believe that the font emphasis function effectively improved script comprehension.

For emotion cues, Q8 and Q9 show that while the display itself was easy to understand, there was no significant difference regarding whether participants could perform according to the presentation. Five out of ten participants responded positively to the emotion cues. This suggests that while the emotion cue shows potential effectiveness for performance, improvements to help users better express emotions are needed. Regarding action guidance, the action card method's understandability (Q10) was rated significantly higher than chance level, though there was no significant difference for executability (Q11). For the action CG model method, while there was no significant difference in understandability (Q12), executability (Q13) was rated significantly lower than chance level. Five out of ten participants gave positive feedback about action cards, while eight out of ten stated they felt the action CG model was unnecessary. These results indicate that the action card is more effective and useful for assisting manzai performance.

For other interface elements, speech timing and action timing (Q14–17) were rated significantly higher for both understandability and executability, demonstrating their usefulness. However, regarding intonation guidance (Q6–7), while the presentation itself was easy to understand, there was no significant difference in participants' ability to perform according to the display. This suggests that while intonation guidance shows potential effectiveness, improvements to help users better apply intonation are important.

Overall, the presentation methods received generally positive evaluations. Interviews revealed no negative opinions regarding performance burden, suggesting that the prototype met the requirement that "users can perform manzai without excessive burden." Additionally, eight out of ten participants did not identify any missing information needed for manzai performance, suggesting that the current information presentations are sufficient. Some participants suggested that information about facial expressions and gaze direction would be helpful additions for future improvements. Furthermore, the results indicated need for improvement in performing with suggested intonation and emotion, highlighting areas for future development.

Audience's Questionnaire. Regarding audience experience, both Q18 and Q19 were rated significantly higher than chance level, confirming that the prototype met the requirement that "audiences find performances using Manzai Karaoke entertaining." Participants also provided positive comments such as "I found myself naturally laughing while watching" and "It's impressive that they can perform manzai with a certain level of quality."

6 Conclusion

We proposed Manzai Karaoke, a real-time performance assistance system that enables users to perform existing manzai scripts and elicit laughter from the audience. In this paper, we defined the requirements for Manzai Karaoke as "users can enjoy performing manzai without excessive burden" and "audiences find the manzai performances entertaining," and aimed to create an interface that meets these requirements. Through two-step prototyping and user studies, the first step validated the feasibility of real-time comedy performance assistance, revealing that in addition to displaying script lines, guidance on intonation, emotion, actions, and timing is required. The second step demonstrated that the implemented interface incorporating these elements effectively meets the requirements. This study contributes to the field of entertainment computing by demonstrating the potential of visual guidance and providing design recommendations for assisting novice manzai performances. We consider that the proposed system could lead to the joy of performing manzai while also fostering new forms of recreation and educational applications through manzai performance.

This research is in its early stages and has several limitations. Firstly, the participant pool was limited in size, potentially affecting the generalizability of the findings. Therefore, further studies with a larger and more diverse participant pool are important to enhance the generalizability of the findings and refine the design recommendations. Secondly, the recommendations were derived from studies conducted in Japanese, necessitating validation for applicability of these recommendation to other languages. Additionally, while this study explored three scripts with varying features, the system's capacity to assist a wider range of script types remains unclear. Future research should investigate the system's ability to adapt to diverse scripts and explore new design methodologies to address these challenges. Lastly, this study focused on the feasibility of assisting manzai performance without specifying concrete applications such as recreation, education, or manzai practice. Subsequent research will focus on evaluating the effectiveness of Manzai Karaoke in these specific contexts, providing a more comprehensive understanding of its potential applications.

While the implemented Manzai Karaoke partially fulfilled the requirements, user studies identified areas for further improvement. Future challenges in interface design include realizing assistance functions that make it easier for users to perform with appropriate intonation and emotion, and investigating the effectiveness of presenting facial expressions and gaze direction during performance. Additionally, performance quality feedback functionalities for recreational and training applications are crucial, and we intend to develop such features. Furthermore, we aim to implement a support system that automates generation of script notations from professional manzai performance video to minimize creation workload.

Disclosure of Interests. The authors have no competing interests to declare that are relevant to the content of this article.

References

1. Aoki, S., Umetani, T., Kitamura, T., Nadamoto, A.: Generating Manzai-scenario using entity mistake. In: Barolli, L., Enokido, T., Takizawa, M. (eds.) NBiS 2017.

LNDECT, vol. 7, pp. 1007–1017. Springer, Cham (2018). https://doi.org/10.1007/978-3-319-65521-5_92
2. Arai, E.: Facing "educational manzai" (in Japanese). Teach. Educ. Stud. **13**, 93–108 (2022)
3. Donahue, C., Lipton, Z.C., McAuley, J.: Dance dance convolution. In: Proceedings of the 34th International Conference on Machine Learning, vol. 70, pp. 1039–1048 (2017)
4. Gandy, M., et al.: AR Karaoke: acting in your favorite scenes. In: Fourth IEEE and ACM International Symposium on Mixed and Augmented Reality, pp. 114–117 (2005)
5. Harigaya, S.: Boke and Tsukkomi in Chinese comic dialogue "Xiangsheng" (in Japanese). J. Kokugakuin Univ. **121**(7), 1–16 (2020)
6. Harris, T., Hardin, J.W.: Exact wilcoxon signed-rank and wilcoxon mann-whitney ranksum tests. Stata J. **13**(2), 337–343 (2013)
7. Hothorn, T., Hornik, K.: exactRankTests: Exact Distributions for Rank and Permutation Tests (2022). https://CRAN.R-project.org/package=exactRankTests, r package version 0.8-35
8. Kabayama, Y., Yokokubo, A., Lopez, G.: Presentation performance support system using instructional animation (in Japanese). In: Proceeding of the Multimedia, Distributed, Cooperative and Mobile Symposium 2019, vol. 2019, pp. 1697–1699 (2019)
9. Kitahara, Y. (ed.): Meikyo Japanese Dictionary (in Japanese). Taishukan Publishing Co., Tokyo (2010)
10. Lee, E., Yang, E., Huh, J., Oh, U.: EcoScript: a real-time presentation supporting tool using a speech recognition model. In: 2024 IEEE International Conference on Information Reuse and Integration for Data Science, pp. 96–101 (2024)
11. Liston, E.: Meera syal: 'making people laugh is addictive'. The Guardian (2009). https://www.theguardian.com/stage/2009/may/09/meera-syal-making-people-laugh. Accessed 18 Feb 2025
12. Maeshiro, T.: Static and non-linguistic quantitative indicators to evaluate Japanese comic dialogues of manzai. Humor **31**(1), 39–64 (2018)
13. Martin, R.: The Psychology of Humor: An Integrative Approach. Academic Press, Cambridge (2007)
14. Mashimo, R., Umetani, T., Kitamura, T., Nadamoto, A.: Generating Funny Dialogue between robots based on Japanese traditional comedy entertainment. In: Proceeding of the 2014 Conference on Interactive Entertainment, pp. 1–7 (2014)
15. Miyamoto, D., et al.: Training comic dialog in VR to improve presentation skills. In: Zaphiris, P., et al. (eds.) HCI International 2023 – Late Breaking Papers. HCII 2023. LNCS, vol. 14060, pp. 191–202. Springer, Cham (2023). https://doi.org/10.1007/978-3-031-48060-7_15
16. Nozawa, N.: The Laughing Funeral (in Japanese). Bungeishunju (2017)
17. Obon Kobon.: Tokyo Manzai (in Japanese). Asuka Shinsha Co., Ltd., Tokyo (2022)
18. Okada, T., Yamamoto, T., Terada, T., Tsukamoto, M.: Wearable MC system a system for supporting MC performances using wearable computing technologies. In: Proceeding of the 2nd Augmented Human International Conference, pp. 1–7 (2011)
19. R Core Team: R: A Language and Environment for Statistical Computing. R Foundation for Statistical Computing, Vienna, Austria (2024). https://www.R-project.org/
20. Roberts, A.: The Double Act: A History of British Comedy Duos. History Press, Cheltenham (2018)

21. Sakata, M.: Quantification of multimodal interactions as open communication in Manzai duo-comic acts. In: 2017 International Conference on Culture and Computing, pp. 65–66 (2017)
22. Sekiguchi, M., Spain, D.: <Report> Creative activities for intermediate and advanced Japanese learners: through the teaching of manzai (in Japanese). J. Jpn. Lang. Teach. Glob. Commun. Center Univ. Tsukuba **35**, 45–53 (2020)
23. Shimozaki, A., Yamamoto, J., Nadamoto, A.: Automatic generation of funny-dialog based on cuisine recipes. In: Barolli, L. (eds.) Advances in Networked-based Information Systems. NBiS 2023. LNDECT, vol. 183, pp. 216–226. Springer, Cham (2023). https://doi.org/10.1007/978-3-031-40978-3_24
24. Tsujino, Y., Yamanishi, R.: Dance dance gradation: a generation of fine-tuned dance charts. In: Entertainment Computing – ICEC 2018, pp. 175–187 (2018)
25. Tsutsumi, H.: Conversation analysis of boke-tsukkomi exchange in Japanese comedy. New Voices **5**, 147–173 (2011)
26. Youngs, I.: The comedians making mental health a laughing matter. British Broadcasting Corporation (2019). https://www.bbc.com/news/entertainment-arts-48206856. Accessed 18 Feb 2025
27. Zhang, H., Shoda, H., Aoyagi, S., Yamamoto, M.: A study on the back and forth Manzai of Milkboy by focusing on embodied motions and actions for liven-up. In: HCI International 2022 – Late Breaking Papers: HCI for Today's Community and Economy, pp. 89–103 (2022)

EchoArtLink: Enhancing Social Connectedness Between Parents and Children Living Apart Through Digital Sound Visualization

Chenwei Liang[✉], Rui Wang, and Jun Hu

Department of Industrial Design, Eindhoven University of Technology, Eindhoven, The Netherlands
`c.liang1@student.tue.nl`

Abstract. More and more family members experience geographic separation over long distances due to global migration and the pursuit of better education and work opportunities. Maintaining social connectedness between children and parents who live apart becomes a critical challenge. This study introduces EchoArtLink, a system that collects sound data and transforms them into digital art displayed on family picture frames. This design leverages sound visualization technology to enhance social connectedness among family members living apart. This system offers two methods of sound visualization: visualizing activities recognized from sounds (Method activities) and visualizing the sound features directly without recognizing activities (Method features). This study conducted a mixed-methods experiment involving 10 participants and their geographically separated parents to explore how two visualization methods affect social connectedness differently between parents and children living apart. The results revealed that the participants gained higher levels of connectedness after experiencing both visualization methods. This study contributes to the field of social connectedness by offering a novel system and valuable insights into the role of sound visualization in long-distance family communication.

1 Introduction

The World Health Organization reports that the current global migrant population is estimated at 1 billion [52], and many young people have to live apart from their parents in search of better work and study opportunities [26]. Long-distance geographical separation challenges the social connectedness between parents and children [56]. As technology advances, it increasingly integrates into home life [12], offering opportunities to strengthen social connectedness through shared stories and emotions [12,15,26,41,47]. Social media platforms such as WhatsApp, Facebook and Instagram facilitate diverse and interactive communications [40]. However, despite these tools, long-distance family connections remain limited [26,41]. Studies show that while brief calls help maintain contact, they are often irregular and lack in-depth communication, leaving family members feeling disconnected [26,41,56]. At the same time, these current communication tools require users to actively share information, which brings invisible pressure and privacy issues to users [7,19,32]. The intersection of art and technology has made digital art a significant part of daily life [20,48,53]. Digital artworks not only spark conversations that might not otherwise occur, but also protect privacy by abstracting data into aesthetically engaging forms [3,20,24,27–29,39,54]. Among various data sources, sound stands out as a rich yet often overlooked signal [41]. Everyday sounds, such as kitchen noise or ambient background audio, carry contextual cues about a person's environment and mood while allowing passive collection with minimal user effort [16,42,55]. This study aims to integrate digital art with sound visualization to transform daily sounds into meaningful yet abstract visual cues, preserving privacy while enhancing social connectedness in remote family relationships.

This study explores a key design tension in HCI by comparing two sound visualization methods: activity-based and sound feature-based. Specificity enhances emotional resonance by providing interpretable behavioural information [10]. For example, in this study activity recognition technology can infer specific activities such as "cooking" or "typing" from audio signals and then perform corresponding image visualization, helping users build a perception of the daily lives of family members. However, specificity risks exposing privacy-sensitive information, potentially leading to user resistance [7,19,32]. On the other hand, ambiguity protects privacy by providing only ambiguous behavioural information [36]. By directly visualizing only abstract features of sound (e.g., frequency, volume, and duration), direct mapping to specific activities is avoided, but the "atmosphere" of the rhythm of life is conveyed, stimulating curiosity and associative thinking [17,18]. Previous research has shown that specificity enhances empathy and emotional involvement [10] but also carries privacy risks [7,19,32], while ambiguity can avoid privacy issues to some extent [17,45]. In this study, the two methods were chosen to address a core contradiction in the design of family-centred human-computer interaction: how to trade off the specificity and ambiguity of data in information transfer. Based on these, the following research question is posed: "How do two visualization methods affect social connectedness differently between parents and young adults living apart?"

In summary, this work contributes: (1) a novel system that transforms everyday sounds into abstract digital art to connect distant family members, (2) empirical insights into how different sound-visualization strategies (activities vs. features) affect perceived connectedness and privacy in parent-child relationships, and (3) design implications for balancing information specificity and ambiguity in remote family communication technologies.

2 Related Work

2.1 Social Connectedness

Social connectedness refers to the degree to which individuals perceive a sense of connection, belonging, and emotional bond with others or groups [21,51]. It emphasizes emotional interactions, communication, and mutual support between people. This connection fosters psychological satisfaction, a sense of security, and overall well-being [5,15,22,23,50]. Previous research has shown that a strong sense of positive social connectedness primarily emerges within the context of mutual care and understanding, specifically among the most intimate relationships such as family members and partners [46]. However, social connectedness is often more fragile in long-distance families [8]. Research indicates that stable connections with family members play a vital role in promoting the mental well-being of people [2,22]. These relationships act as protective factors against age-related mental health challenges, such as death anxiety, depression, and loneliness [50]. Beyond mental health, studies suggest that stronger social connectedness contributes to physical health by helping maintain a healthy body mass index, regulating blood sugar levels, and lowering the risk of cardiovascular disease mortality [31]. In this context, fostering social connectedness between parents and children becomes particularly significant.

2.2 Emerging Technologies to Support Social Connectedness

Most of the systems that work to improve home connectivity focus on showing the current state of life and health of family members [7]. For example, the Digital Family Portrait [35] and CareNet [9] systems both provide information to remote caregivers about the health status and living conditions of older adults. Some works have also provided systems for bidirectional emotional transmission. Robo-Shoe-Files [13] is a small device that has a special requirement to interact with other users who wear the same device. Some work has also designed prototypes that require active information sharing so that family members can learn about each other's lives and exchange information. Examples include digital sticky notes [25], scanned information and the dissemination of information between families displayed on a website [37]. eKiss [14] enables efficacy between children and parents through photo software, which is displayed on the family monitor or on parents' mobile phones. Some prototypes have also explored dedicated connections between long-distance families to allow better interaction between family members, such as the shared storytelling system proposed by René Vutborg [47], which provides a platform for grandparents and grandchildren living apart to interact with each other by integrating features such as story reading, photo sharing, interactive drawing, and audio dialogue. The Messaging Kettle [6] can detect kettle usage via a heat sensor while the user is making tea, sharing it with a similar device in another home, making daily use of the boiling kettle visible off-site. Users can also exchange voice messages and doodles using the Smart Tea Box. The Fitbit Flex [34] wristband offers new opportunities for parents to monitor their children when they are separated by sharing their children's sleep and physical data across the family, which studies have found parents often use to ask their children for information about specific activities.

All of these works focus on social connectedness and can increase the social connectedness of family members. However, some designs require active sharing, while others compromise users' privacy, leading to resistance towards the system or device over time [19]. Therefore, based on the experience of previous work, to address these limitations, our study adopts passive data collection and privacy-preserving, non-intrusive abstract art presentation that seamlessly integrates the visualized information into everyday home environments.

2.3 Sound Visualization in HCI: Balancing Emotional Cues and Privacy Through Abstract Art

Sound has garnered significant attention in the field of HCI. In addition to helping users perceive their surroundings or identify specific human activities, sound also carries emotional and social cues [16,41,42]. However, collecting and analyzing audio data inevitably raises privacy concerns: when audio information is highly detailed or amenable to further processing (e.g., via speech recognition or activity detection), users may fear excessive surveillance [43,44]. In response, many researchers have sought to present sound data in more ambiguous or abstract visual forms, aiming to preserve acoustic features while avoiding the disclosure of raw audio. For instance, Yang et al. [55] explored the visualization of laughter by transforming everyday conversational laughter into abstract graphical elements, which participants could replay and observe. Their findings indicate that this interactive sound-visualization approach not only evokes memories and facilitates emotional expression but also enhances social relationships among participants. Importantly, the "indecipherable" and "open to multiple interpretations" characteristics of abstract art can help protect individual privacy to some extent [30,38]. Because abstract visuals rarely point to specific activities or meanings, outside observers find it difficult to reconstruct the context or conversation behind the audio data [33], thus reducing the sense of surveillance or intrusion [43]. Accordingly, in family or close-knit settings, transforming everyday sounds into abstract visual elements - such as line animations or shifting color patterns - can simultaneously enhance relatives' awareness of each other's state and preserve personal privacy. Inspired by this idea, this study uses abstract visualization techniques to represent household sound data, aiming to balance social connectedness with the need for privacy protection. Furthermore, this study compares two sound-to-visual visualization methods, Method(activities), which translates recognized activities into abstract imagery, and Method(features), which directly visualizes sound features as abstract imagery. To explore how abstract sound art, when embedded in domestic displays, makes a subtle trade-off between specificity and ambiguity.

3 Formative Study

To better understand the emotional needs and expression preferences in long-distance families, we conducted a formative study involving five parentâĂŞchild pairs living apart. Semi-structured online interviews were carried out, and thematic analysis [4] was applied to extract key findings.

3.1 Formative Study Findings

Challenges in Maintaining Emotional Connections. Participants highlighted several key obstacles to maintaining emotional bonds in long-distance parent-child relationships:

Infrequent Communication: Many children, especially those busy with studies or work, only communicate with their parents once a week or even less frequently. This infrequency leads to weakened emotional connections over time.

Lack of Initiative: Children are generally less proactive in checking on the well-being of their parents. They rarely take the initiative to inquire about their parents' daily lives, while parents are curious but hesitant to reach out.

Privacy Concerns: Most children, especially those who are not particularly close to their parents, prefer greater privacy regarding their daily lives and do not want to be constantly monitored or interfered with. This reveals a need for more passive, non-intrusive communication that respects users' privacy preferences.

Preferences for Communication Tools. In exploring preferred communication methods, the following insights were gathered:

Minimal Manual Input and Passive Sharing: All five interviewed children expressed a strong preference for communication tools that do not require them to input their status actively. They found it time-consuming and exhausting to provide regular updates over a long period. Instead, users favour systems that passively share their status or emotions without manual updates.

Abstract Data Sharing: Privacy concerns were a significant factor for all participants. As P1 noted, "If my status can appear in a way that's abstract, where others, especially my parents, can't exactly interpret it but at least know I'm alive, that would be ideal."

These findings highlight critical design considerations for developing tools that foster emotional connections in a non-intrusive, user-friendly manner.

4 Final Design Implementation

The formative study revealed that users preferred to share their lives in a fun, low-effort way without revealing too many details. They disliked frequently opening their phones or providing active input. As a result, the design was shifted towards passive data collection that could reflect daily life. Previous research shows that sound effectively represents life states and personal activities [16, 41, 42, 55]. Thus, the concept involved visualizing ambient sound to foster mutual awareness via display screens in both homes. Based on participant feedback and related work, this study implemented two sound visualization methods to examine how each influences parent-child connectedness.

Visualizing the Sound Features Directly Without Recognizing Activities (Method Features): This study developed a system that transforms real-time sound signals into dynamic visual artworks through signal processing (Fig. 1). By analyzing key sound features - frequency, duration, and volume - the system generates dynamic linear patterns that visually capture the essence of sound. These patterns continuously evolve, responding to incoming audio in real-time. The system collects and visualizes all sounds, including human voices, ambient noise, and human-made sounds, ensuring a seamless real-time visualization process. Users can observe how changes in sound directly influence the visual representation.

Visualizing Activities Recognized from Sound (Method Activities): This implementation uses machine learning to recognize and visualize specific activity sounds. The project began with collecting and labeling sound samples (e.g., water flow, keyboard typing, door knocking) for processing. Using Python, we extracted Mel Frequency Cepstral Coefficients (MFCC) from audio files via the Librosa library, a widely used feature in sound recognition. These features trained a Support Vector Machine (SVM) model, which efficiently classifies sounds. Cross-validation was employed to assess model accuracy, ensuring reliable recognition and image generation. Multiple training and testing rounds refined the model's performance. To enhance usability, a Tkinter-based graphical interface was developed. The visualization images pre-stored in the database correspond to recognized sounds, enabling real-time display and dynamic generation of digital art based on detected activities (Fig. 2).

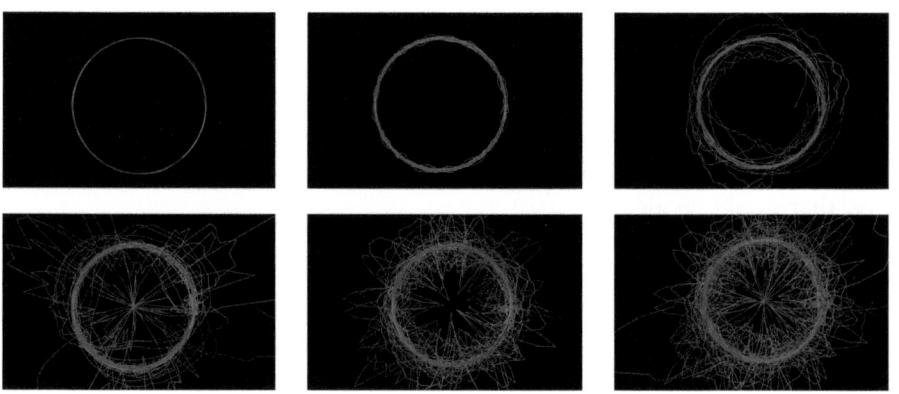

Fig. 1. Visualization based on Method (features): Real-time visual patterns dynamically change based on sound properties such as volume, frequency, and duration. The visuals are abstract and fluid, without representing specific activities.

5 User Study

This study involved 10 unmarried young adults (6 females, 4 males; median age = 24.4) who had lived apart from their parents for over three months. It was carried out at the home of the participants using picture frames embedded in tablets to display sound visualizations. To simulate scenarios where real-time communication was not possible - such as time zone differences or differing life statuses - communication with parents was deliberately restricted.

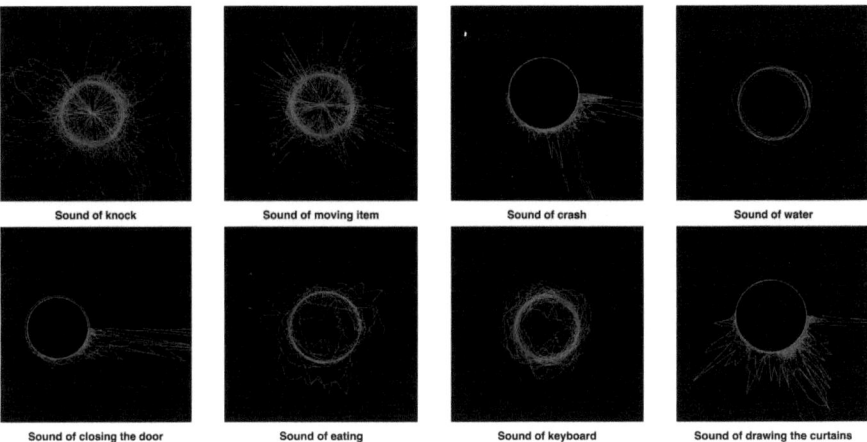

Fig. 2. Visualization based on Method (activities): Predefined images are triggered based on recognized sounds (e.g., water running, door knocking). Each image corresponds to a specific daily activity.

The study followed a four-phase procedure: introduction, Method (activities), Method (features), and a concluding interview. After giving consent and completing the Inclusion of Other in the Self (IOS) Scale [1], participants engaged in two visualization sessions, each involving eight predefined tasks (e.g. closing doors, typing, eating) to generate sound input. The experimenter then called the parents of the participants and placed the phone in a separate room, allowing ambient sounds to be captured and visualized without direct communication. Each session lasted 25 min, followed by a 10-minute interview. After each session, participants completed the IOS Scale [1] and the Positive and Negative Affect Schedule (PANAS) [49]. To minimize order effects, the sequence of visualization methods was counterbalanced. Finally, participants completed a final interview that compared the two methods. Repeated measures ANOVA was used to assess differences in IOS and PANAS scores. Data from three semi-structured interviews were coded using a grounded theory approach [11], with themes extracted from verified transcripts and cross-referenced with behavioral data.

6 Results

6.1 IOS Scales

Overall, sound visualisation can give a sense of increased closeness to children who are living apart from their parents. Below are the mean scores and standard deviations calculated for each factor on the IOS scale (Fig. 3). Before participants experienced the EchoArtLink system, the initial IOS scale had a mean value of $M=4.1$ ($SD=0.70$). After experiencing the two methods, the between-subject effect on social connectedness showed the following results: Method(activities) had a mean value of $M=4.6$ ($SD=1.06$), and Method(features) had a mean value of M=4.7 (SD=1.16). Furthermore, no significant differences were found between the Method(activities) and Method(features) conditions (p=0.513 > 0.05). Meanwhile, data indicates that out of 10 participants, 6 felt closer to their separated parents after experiencing the two sound visualization methods (Fig. 3). The remaining 4 participants(P3, P7, P8, P9) showed no significant difference in their IOS scale scores before and after the experience, indicating that sound visualization did not enhance their sense of social connectedness. It should be noted that two participants (P3, P9) experienced a decrease in their scores after trying the method (activities), indicating that their sense of social connectedness decreased.

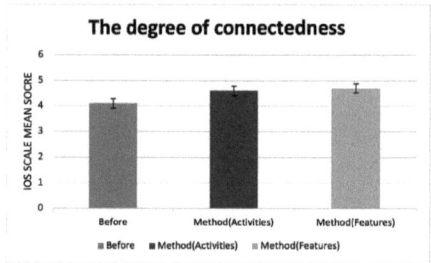
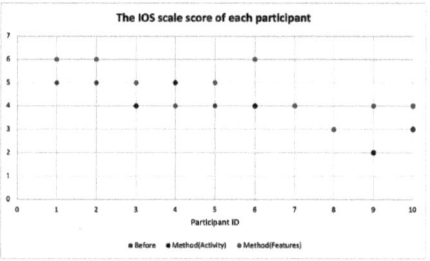

Fig. 3. Left: Mean and standard error of perceived connectedness in IOS Scale. Right: Individual IOS scores before and after using the two visualization methods.

6.2 PANAS Scales

The Method(activities) had a mean PA score of M=25.6 (SD=4.83) and a mean NA score of M=14.2 (SD=3.99). The Method(features) had a mean PA score of M=23.2 (SD=6.35) and a mean NA score of M=13.4 (SD=3.73). There was no significant effect of the method on the PA scores at the p<0.05 level for the two conditions [F(1, 18) = 0.8443, p = 0.37032]. Similarly, there was no significant effect of the method on NA scores at the p<0.05 level for the two conditions [F(1, 18) = 1.357542, p = 0.259173]. These results suggest that the type of Method (activities or features) does not significantly influence either PA or NA scores.

6.3 Interview for Method(Activities)

Curiosity-driven: All participants in the experiment expressed curiosity about what their parents were doing. This curiosity drove them to actively inquire about the situation when they saw the image either change dramatically or remain unchanged for a long time. For instance, P2 mentioned,"If I keep seeing the same image without any movement, I might get curious and wonder what's going on there. Aren't they supposed to be eating? Why isn't there any reaction? I might call to ask." P1 added, "This visualization has sparked my curiosity about their lives. They might not be curious themselves, but I have become curious." P3 noted, "I remember my mom usually makes a lot of noise, but today the image didn't change much. It made me feel like I don't know her as well, so I want to ask her about it." Although most people showed strong curiosity, five participants found it difficult to understand specific activities due to the short experience time. P7 said, "If I see an image I'm not familiar with, I'll be curious about what my parents are doing, but I'm not familiar with any of these images at the moment."

Sense of companionship: Four participants mentioned that this visualization method enhanced their sense of companionship, making them feel as if their parents were right beside them. P2 said, "I often talk to my mom on the phone without saying much, but I can infer what she's doing from the sounds. This method gives me a similar feeling." P1 remarked, "Being able to make guesses based on my understanding combined with the images if I know they're also having dinner, it makes the sense of companionship stronger." P4 added, "This method conjures up images of being at home, as if we are all there, each doing our own thing. The Sound Visualization aren't particularly clear or informative, but there's a sense of life."

Identification and privacy of activities: Three Participants reported that it felt a bit like observation and were dissatisfied with the machine's recognition activities. " I feel more like an observer, watching the parents' activities, but sometimes it doesn't feel very accurate."(P8) "I don't particularly want to know what they are doing. I just want to feel their presence." (P9) "It is a lot like surveillance, I don't want a machine to define what my 'activities' mean." (P3)

Sense of connection: Most participants felt they couldn't fully identify the images in a short time, but three participants said they didn't particularly care about what the others were doing, as long as they could roughly understand that the other person was active. P9 mentioned, "It was difficult for me to identify the activities the images represented, But I know they are active and that's enough." This indirect hinting and guidance allow participants to maintain a certain level of connection and awareness in their daily lives without needing real-time and detailed information. P6 said, "Although the recognition may not be very accurate, it is very interesting that I can roughly guess what my mother is doing using this method."

6.4 Interview for Method(Features)

Richness of Information: Many participants mentioned that although this method can convey many sound details, the amount of information can be overwhelming, making it difficult to analyze what the other person is actually doing. P2 stated, "This method conveys more information and subtle details, but sometimes the amount of information can be too much, making me feel confused." P7 said, "This form of expression is not limited to the sounds of my parents; it includes other sounds as well, making me think not only of my parents but of everything at home, like pets, for example." P6 commented, "If the image is changing, it indicates some activity, even subtle sounds. I would think about whether my mom is doing housework or something else, like if the mop fell over. This gives me a different kind of feeling."

Privacy and Ambiguity: Most participants felt that the method's directionality was not very intuitive and did not provide clear indications of activities, requiring more guessing and imagination. P2 remarked, "This state lets me feel things more intuitively, like if it's quiet, I can immediately know there's no sound at all, but there are no clear prompts. I need more guessing and imagination, but I can't picture it in my mind." P4 stated, "I can't quite tell what my mom is doing because I'm not very familiar with her schedule. If I knew roughly what she was doing, I could imagine it, but since I don't know much, it doesn't feel very clear to me." P9 expressed that " this ambiguity is what is best, I just need to perceive my parents' presence and I don't want to know too much detail." This vague directionality makes participants rely more on guessing and imagination to understand the information conveyed by the images.

Sense of Distance: Four participants mentioned that this method brought them closer to their parents because it felt like their parents were talking to them, though not very explicitly. P3 said, "This visualization with sound features makes me feel like my parents are far away yet right in front of me. Even without sound, I can imagine what it's like to talk to them. Looking at this image, I have a sense of missing them - so close yet so far."

6.5 Concluding Interview on Two Methods

Details of sound: Six participants mentioned that Method (features) conveyed more subtle sound details, while Method (activities) only informed participants about the activities their parents were doing. Participants with closer relationships with their parents preferred to receive more sound details, which made them feel a greater sense of closeness. P7 noted, "I think it's not just my parents' sounds; it could also be my pets' sounds." These subtle differences are something that Method(activities) cannot achieve.

Imagination and Space: Some participants felt that Method (activities) provided more room for imagination. Although the details were vague, they could infer their parents' actions from the images. P4 noted, "Visualizing activities from sound helps me imagine what my parents are doing at home. Looking at these images makes them feel present. If it's just sound features, I can't picture them at home in my mind."

Influence of Parent-Child Closeness on Method Preferences and Interaction Depth: For participants who do not have a close relationship with their parents, they want to maintain a certain degree of emotional distance while still seeking a subtle sense of parental presence. They prefer Method (features). P10 said: I want to keep a little distance from my parents. I don't want to be "controlled" by them. I just want them to know that I am still alive. P9 mentioned:

I have a better relationship with my grandfather. He cares about what I am doing. I would rather share my specific activities with him, but I don't want my parents to know my specific activities.

7 Discussion

Our study reveals a subtle trade-off between specificity and ambiguity in the design of sound visualizations for mediating long-distance family social connectedness. Although quantitative metrics indicate no significant differences between the two methods, this may be partly due to the limited study duration and relatively small sample size, which may have limited participants' ability to experience deeper emotional effects or shifting perceptions over time. However, qualitative insights highlight the distinct roles of the two methods in balancing emotional engagement and privacy protection and suggest that preferences are closely linked to the level of perceived intimacy.

Intimacy Affects Perceived Effectiveness of Different Methods: By combining qualitative and quantitative analyses, found that participants with strong intimacy perceived Method (activities) as valuable for building a shared understanding of the other person's daily activities (P1: "I could imagine my mom cooking when I saw this picture"; P2: "This allows me to infer what it's doing is like making a phone call"). However, this level of specificity inevitably raises privacy concerns, as P8 noted: "It sometimes felt more like observing my parents' activities, but not always accurately." This aligns with previous research indicating that highly interpretable data can evoke surveillance concerns [19]. In contrast, Method (features) introduced controlled ambiguity. Participants appreciated its ability to spark curiosity without revealing sensitive details (P6: "The patterns felt more like a gentle suggestion rather than an intrusive spotlight"). This supports Gaver et al.'s [17,18] perspective that ambiguity fosters "interpretive flexibility," enabling users to ascribe personal meanings while maintaining contextual privacy. Interestingly, participants with low baseline intimacy all showed a preference for this method, suggesting that ambiguity may be more suitable for distant emotional relationships. These findings suggest that offering adjustable levels of detail is essential for designers of family communication technologies. Close families may sometimes opt for clearer activity cues, while distant or privacy-sensitive relationships may prefer more ambiguous sound features. It's worth noting that preferences were not uniform âĂŞ while many close-knit participants preferred concrete cues for empathy, some also valued the rich details of the feature-based visualization. This suggests that intimacy influences preferences in nuanced ways rather than a strict binary.

The Temporal Dimension of Emotional Resonance: The non-significant quantitative results may reflect the instability of emotional states in short-term tests. The social connectedness of parent-child relationships often needs to be developed through accumulated micro-interactions over time [41]. That is, environmental systems require long-term contact to cultivate meaningful habits [10]. This finding underscores that social connectedness technologies may require long-term use to manifest their full benefits. Short-term evaluations, while convenient, might not capture the gradual formation of habits and emotional bonds. Future work should conduct long-term follow-up studies to distinguish between the short-term emotional reactions immediately after using the system and the effects of long-term social connectedness that gradually form over time.

Rethinking the Role of AI in Mediated Intimacy: Our findings challenge the assumption that AI-driven activity recognition is essential for emotional connection. Although the Method(activities) utilises more advanced technology, it did not achieve better results; in fact, both methods achieved comparable improvements in social connectedness. Crucially, 6 participants expressed discomfort with AI-interpreted data (P3: "I don't want a machine to define what my 'activities' mean"), this is in line with what was mentioned in Palen et al.'s study, that we need to have the right to choose and interpret whether to disclose information or not [43]. This suggests that direct recognition of sound features bypassing AI recognition activities is more appropriate for family intimacy, reducing computation while empowering users with more interpretation and privacy while enhancing social connectedness.

Perceptions of the Two Methods: In short, both methods improve parent-child relationships in different ways: Method (activities) provides more specific clues to promote empathy through specificity, while Method (features) provides ambiguous details with rich privacy, which is more suitable for relationships that maintain a certain emotional distance. Designers must strike a balance between the two to adapt to the context of the user's relationship.

Limitation and Future Work: The small sample size of 10 participants in this study limits the generalizability of the findings, and follow-up studies will continue to assess older participants to collect data on bilateral outcomes. The short duration of the experiment and preexisting communication habits between participants and their parents may also have influenced the results. Future research should address these limitations by including larger, more diverse samples and extending the experiment to observe long-term effects.

8 Conclusion

In conclusion, this work presents EchoArtLink, a novel ambient display system that transforms everyday sounds into dynamic digital abstract art to strengthen parentâĂŞchild connectedness over distances. Our mixed-method evaluation with 10 separated families demonstrated that while both an activity-based visualization and a sound feature-based visualization can enhance a sense of closeness, they do so in complementary ways: the activity-centric method provides concrete cues that deepen engagement for already close relationships, whereas the abstract-feature method offers privacy-preserving awareness that is comfortable for less intimate relationships. These findings contribute new insights into the long-standing HCI challenge of balancing information specificity and ambiguity in family communication technologies. In particular, we show that rich emotional exchanges can emerge even without AI-driven context recognition, as subtle sound-based art fosters connection without compromising privacy.

References

1. Aron, A., Aron, E., Smollan, D.: Inclusion of other in the self scale and the structure of interpersonal closeness. J. Pers. Soc. Psychol. **63**(4), 596–612 (1992). https://doi.org/10.1037/0022-3514.63.4.596
2. Chen, B., Li, X.: Understanding socio-technical opportunities for enhancing communication between older adults and their remote family. In: Proceedings of the 2024 CHI Conference on Human Factors in Computing Systems, art. 1013, pp. 1–16. ACM, Honolulu, HI, USA (2024). https://doi.org/10.1145/3613904.3642318
3. Bailey, C., Desai, D.: Visual art and education: engaged visions of history and community. Multicult. Perspect. **7**(1), 39–43 (2005). https://doi.org/10.1207/s15327892mcp0701_7
4. Braun, V., Clarke, V.: Using thematic analysis in psychology. Qual. Res. Psychol. **3**(2), 77–101 (2006). https://doi.org/10.1191/1478088706qp063oa
5. Brenny, S., Hu, J.: Social connectedness and inclusion by digital augmentation in public spaces. In: 8th International Conference on Design and Semantics of Form and Movement (DeSForM 2013), Wuxi, China (2013)
6. Brereton, M., et al.: Make and connect: enabling people to connect through their things. In: Proceedings of the 29th Australian Conference on Computer-Human Interaction, pp. 612–616. ACM, New York (2017). https://doi.org/10.1145/3152771.3156182
7. Brush, A.J.B., Inkpen, K.M., Tee, K.: SPARCS: exploring sharing suggestions to enhance family connectedness. In: Proceedings of the 2008 ACM Conference on Computer Supported Cooperative Work, pp. 629–638 (2008). https://doi.org/10.1145/1460563.1460661
8. Cohen-Mansfield, J., Hazan, H., Lerman, Y., Shalom, V.: Correlates and predictors of loneliness in older-adults: a review of quantitative results informed by qualitative insights. Int. Psychogeriatr. **28**(4), 557–576 (2016). https://doi.org/10.1017/S1041610215001532
9. Consolvo, S., Roessler, P., Shelton, B.E.: The CareNet display: lessons learned from an in home evaluation of an ambient display. In: Davies, N., Mynatt, E.D., Siio, I. (eds.) UbiComp 2004. LNCS, vol. 3205, pp. 1–17. Springer, Heidelberg (2004). https://doi.org/10.1007/978-3-540-30119-6_1
10. Consolvo, S., Everitt, K., Smith, I., Landay, J.A.: Design requirements for technologies that encourage physical activity. In: Proceedings of the SIGCHI Conference on Human Factors in Computing Systems, pp. 457–466 (2006). https://doi.org/10.1145/1124772.1124840
11. Corbin, J.M., Strauss, A.: Grounded theory research: procedures, canons, and evaluative criteria. Qual. Sociol. **13**(1), 3–21 (1990). https://doi.org/10.1007/BF00988593
12. Coughlan, T., et al.: Methods for studying technology in the home. In: CHI 2013 Extended Abstracts on Human Factors in Computing Systems, pp. 3207–3210 (2013). https://doi.org/10.1145/2468356.2479648
13. Dagan, E., Isbister, K.: Synergistic social technology: designing systems with 'Needs' that encourage and support social interaction. In: Proceedings of the 2021 ACM Designing Interactive Systems Conference, pp. 1419–1432. ACM, New York (2021). https://doi.org/10.1145/3461778.3462021

14. Dalsgaard, T., Skov, M.B., Thomassen, B.R.: eKISS: sharing experiences in families through a picture blog. In: People and Computers: HCI...But not as We Know it, pp. 49–58. British Computer Society, Swindon (2007). https://doi.org/10.14236/ewic/HCI2007.7
15. Davis, K., Owusu, E., Hu, J., Marcenaro, L., Regazzoni, C., Feijs, L.: Promoting social connectedness through human activity-based ambient displays. In: Proceedings of the International Symposium on Interactive Technology and Ageing Populations, Kochi, Japan, pp. 64–76 (2016)
16. Liang, D., Song, W., Thomaz, E.: Characterizing the effect of audio degradation on privacy perception and inference performance in audio-based human activity recognition. In: 22nd International Conference on Human-Computer Interaction with Mobile Devices and Services, art. 32, pp. 1–10. ACM, Oldenburg, Germany (2020). https://doi.org/10.1145/3379503.3403551
17. Gaver, W.W., Boucher, A., Pennington, S., Walker, B.: Cultural probes and the value of uncertainty. Interactions **11**(5), 53–56 (2004). https://doi.org/10.1145/1015530.1015555
18. Gaver, W.W., Beaver, J., Benford, S.: Ambiguity as a resource for design. In: Proceedings of the SIGCHI Conference on Human Factors in Computing Systems CHI 2003, pp. 233–240 (2003). https://doi.org/10.1145/642611.642653
19. Gorm, N., Shklovski, I.: Sharing steps in the workplace: changing privacy concerns over time. In: Proceedings of the 2016 CHI Conference on Human Factors in Computing Systems, pp. 4315–4319. ACM, San Jose, California, USA (2016). https://doi.org/10.1145/2858036.2858352
20. Grenader, E., Gasques Rodrigues, D., Nos, F., Weibel, N.: The VideoMob interactive art installation connecting strangers through inclusive digital crowds. ACM Trans. Interact. Intell. Syst. **5**(2), 7 (2015). https://doi.org/10.1145/2768208
21. Haslam, C., Haslam, S.A.: Social Connectedness and Health. In: Pachana, N.A. (ed.) Encyclopedia of Geropsychology, pp. 1–10. Springer, Singapore (2015). https://doi.org/10.1007/978-981-287-080-3_46-2
22. Herbener, A.B., Damholdt, M.F.: Are lonely youngsters turning to chatbots for companionship? The relationship between chatbot usage and social connectedness in Danish high-school students. Int. J. Hum. Comput. Stud. **196**(C), 13 (2025). https://doi.org/10.1016/j.ijhcs.2024.103409
23. Hoffman, A., Mehrpour, A., Staerklé, C.: The many faces of social connectedness and their impact on well-being. In: Spini, D., Widmer, E. (eds.) Withstanding Vulnerability throughout Adult Life, pp. 1–15. Palgrave Macmillan, Singapore (2023). https://doi.org/10.1007/978-981-19-4567-0_11
24. Hu, J., Xue, M., Yao, C., Feng, Li, J., Hansen, P.: Workshop on aesthetics of connectivity for empowerment at ACM designing interactive systems 2024. In: Workshop on Aesthetics of Connectivity for Empowerment – Considerations and Challenges, ACM Conference on Designing Interactive Systems 2024 (DIS 2024), arXiv preprint arXiv:2503.23460, Copenhagen-DK, 2025
25. Hutchinson, H., et al.: Technology probes: inspiring design for and with families. In: Proceedings of the SIGCHI Conference on Human Factors in Computing Systems, pp. 17–24. ACM, New York (2003). https://doi.org/10.1145/642611.642616
26. Kelly, R.M., Cheng, Y., McKay, D., Wadley, G., Buchanan, G.: It's about missing much more than the people: how students use digital technologies to alleviate homesickness. In: CHI 2021 Proceedings of the 2021 CHI Conference on Human Factors in Computing Systems, vol. 226, pp. 1–17. ACM, New York (2021). https://doi.org/10.1145/3411764.3445362

27. Lin, X., Liu, X., Rauterberg, M., Hu, J.: Take a photo for my story: social connectedness for the elderly. In: Streitz, N., Konomi, S. (eds.) HCII 2019. LNCS, vol. 11587, pp. 390–407. Springer, Cham (2019). https://doi.org/10.1007/978-3-030-21935-2_30
28. Lu, T., Hu, J.: A-vibe: exploring the impact of animal-form avatars on students' connectedness and social presence through delivering honest signals in live online classes. In: Design and Semantics of Form and Movement (DeSForM), pp. 17–29, Hong Kong (2023)
29. Lu, T., Hu, J.: E-Motioning: Exploring the effects of emotional generative visuals on creativity and connectedness during videoconferencing. In: IASDR 2023: Life-Changing Design. Italy, Milan (2023)
30. Maes, M., Van den Noortgate, N., Van den Bosch, K.: The role of loneliness and social support in adjustment to loss: a test of attachment versus stress theory. Acta Psychiatr. Scand. **111**(5), 378–386 (2005). https://doi.org/10.1111/j.1600-0447.2005.00513.x
31. Martino, J., Pegg, J., Frates, E.P.: The connection prescription: using the power of social interactions and the deep desire for connectedness to empower health and wellness. Am. J. Lifestyle Med. **11**(6), 466–475 (2015). https://doi.org/10.1177/1559827615608788
32. Page, X., Kobsa, A., Knijnenburg, B.: Don't disturb my circles! Boundary preservation is at the center of location-sharing concerns. Proc. Int. AAAI Conf. Web Soc. Media **6**(1), 266–273 (2021). https://doi.org/10.1609/icwsm.v6i1.14277
33. Pousman, Z., Stasko, J.: A taxonomy of ambient information systems: four patterns of design. In: Working Conference on Advanced Visual Interfaces, pp. 67–74. ACM, New York (2006). https://doi.org/10.1145/1133265.1133277
34. Jørgensen, M.S., Nissen, F.K., Paay, J., Kjeldskov, J., Skov, M.B.: Monitoring children's physical activity and sleep: A study of surveillance and information disclosure. In: Proceedings of the 28th Australian Conference on Computer-Human Interaction, pp. 50–58. ACM, New York (2016). https://doi.org/10.1145/3010915.3010936
35. Rowan, J., Mynatt, E.D.: Digital family portrait field trial: support for aging in place. In: Proceedings of the SIGCHI Conference on Human Factors in Computing Systems, pp. 521–530. ACM, New York (2005). https://doi.org/10.1145/1054972.1055044
36. Sanches, P., Höök, K., Sas, C., Ståhl, A.: Ambiguity as a resource to inform protopractices: the case of skin conductance. ACM Trans. Comput. Hum. Interact. **26**(4), 21 (2019). https://doi.org/10.1145/3318143
37. Saslis-Lagoudakis, G., Cheverst, K., Dix, A., Fitton, D., Rouncefield, M.: Hermes@Home: supporting awareness and intimacy between distant family members. In: Proceedings of the 18th Australia Conference on Computer-Human Interaction: Design: Activities, Artefacts and Environments, pp. 23–30. ACM, New York (2006). https://doi.org/10.1145/1228175.1228183
38. Schapiro, M.: Nature of abstract art. In: American Marxist Association, pp. 185–186. American Marxist Association, USA (1937)
39. Neustaedter, C., et al.: Sharing domestic life through long-term video connections. ACM Trans. Comput. Hum. Interact. **22**(1), 3 (2015). https://doi.org/10.1145/2696869
40. Shen, C., et al.: Sharing family life information through video calls and other information and communication technologies and the association with family well-being: population-based survey. JMIR Mental Health **4**(4), e57 (2017). https://doi.org/10.2196/mental.8139

41. Shin, J.Y., Rheu, M., Huh-Yoo, J., Peng, W.: Designing technologies to support parent-child relationships: a review of current findings and suggestions for future directions. Proc. ACM Hum. Comput. Interact. **5**(CSCW2), 441 (2021). https://doi.org/10.1145/3479585
42. Iwaki, M., Nakayama, S.: Sound-recognition method for helping us respond appropriately to sounds in daily life. In: 2018 IEEE 7th Global Conference on Consumer Electronics (GCCE), pp. 680–682. IEEE, (2018). https://doi.org/10.1109/GCCE.2018.8574822
43. Palen, L., Dourish, P.: Unpacking "privacy" for a networked world. In: SIGCHI Conference on Human Factors in Computing Systems, pp. 129–136. ACM, New York (2003). https://doi.org/10.1145/642611.642635
44. Gómez Ortega, A., Bourgeois, J., Kortuem, G.: What is sensitive about (sensitive) data? characterizing sensitivity and intimacy with google assistant users. In: CHI Conference on Human Factors in Computing Systems, article no. 586, pp. 1–16. ACM, New York (2023). https://doi.org/10.1145/3544548.3581164
45. Wyatt, D., Bilmes, J., Choudhury, T., Kitts, J.A.: Towards the automated social analysis of situated speech data. In: 10th International Conference on Ubiquitous Computing, pp. 168–171. ACM, New York (2008). https://doi.org/10.1145/1409635.1409658
46. Van Bel, D.T., IJsselsteijn, W.A., de Kort, Y.A.W.: Interpersonal connectedness: Conceptualization and directions for a measurement instrument. In: CHI 2008 Extended Abstracts on Human Factors in Computing Systems, pp. 3129–3134. ACM, New York (2008). https://doi.org/10.1145/1358628.1358819
47. Vutborg, R., Kjeldskov, J., Pedell, S., Vetere, F.: Family storytelling for grandparents and grandchildren living apart. In: Proceedings of the 6th Nordic Conference on Human-Computer Interaction: Extending Boundaries, pp. 531–540 (2010). https://doi.org/10.1145/1868914.1868974
48. Wang, Q., Streithorst, L., He, C., Feijs, L., Hu, J.: Calm digital artwork for connectedness: a case study. In: International Conference on Entertainment Computing - ICEC 2023, Singapore, pp. 461–470 (2023)
49. Watson, D., Clark, L.A., Tellegen, A.: Development and validation of brief measures of positive and negative affect: The PANAS scales. J. Pers. Soc. Psychol. **54**(6), 1063–1070 (1988). https://doi.org/10.1037/0022-3514.54.6.1063
50. Wickramaratne, P., et al.: Social connectedness as a determinant of mental health: a scoping review. PLoS ONE **17**(10), e0275004 (2022). https://doi.org/10.1371/journal.pone.0275004
51. Winstone, L., Mars, B., Haworth, C.M.A., et al.: Social media use and social connectedness among adolescents in the united kingdom: a qualitative exploration of displacement and stimulation. BMC Public Health **21**, 1736 (2021). https://doi.org/10.1186/s12889-021-11802-9
52. World Health Organisation: Refugee and Migrant Health. https://www.who.int/health-topics/refugee-and-migrant-health. Accessed 2020
53. Xue, M., Yao, C., Hu, J., Hu, Y., Lyu, H.: Digital Arts and Health. In: Göbl, B., van der Spek, E., Baalsrud Hauge, J., McCall, R. (eds.) Entertainment Computing. ICEC 2022. LNCS, vol. 13477, pp. 436–442. Springer, Cham (2022). https://doi.org/10.1007/978-3-031-20212-4_37
54. Xue, M., Yao, C., Hu, J., Hu, Y., Lyu, H., Feng, Y.: Aesthetics and empowerment: exploring AI-driven creativity. In: Entertainment Computing – ICEC 2024, Manaus, BR, pp. 316–320 (2024)

55. Yang, Y., Ryokai, K.: Exploring laughter sound visualizations for self reflection. In: Proceedings of the 2022 ACM Designing Interactive Systems Conference, pp. 1472–1485. ACM, Virtual Event, Australia (2022). https://doi.org/10.1145/3532106.3533546
56. Yarosh, S., Chew, Y.C.D., Abowd, G.D.: Supporting parent–child communication in divorced families. Int. J. Hum Comput Stud. **67**(2), 192–203 (2009). https://doi.org/10.1016/j.ijhcs.2008.09.005

Optimizing Random Forest Multi-classification and Gini-Based Feature Analysis of Board Game Success via BGG Characteristic Data

Tianle Liang[1](✉) ⓘ, Kieran Rosenfeld[1], and Nathan Lu[2]

[1] Zionsville Community High School, Zionsville, IN 46077, USA
`tianle.liang16@gmail.com`
[2] Round Rock High School, Round Rock, TX 78681, USA

Abstract. This paper develops an ML-based random forest multi-classification model for early-phase prediction of board game market success using characteristics scraped from BoardGameGeek (BGG), analyzing through the domains of game mechanics, language dependence, and social interaction. The variable *number of plays* was selected as a proxy label to define market success, then logarithmically transformed and binned by quantiles. A random forest classifier was separately trained for social interaction variables, yielding a 0.706 accuracy with precision and recall highs of 0.91 and 0.89, respectively, for extreme classes. The cumulative model using all variables achieved only marginal improvements at 0.71 accuracy. Feature analysis emphasized the predictive dominance of social interaction variables, especially organic community-driven engagement. Novel insights included the unexpected importance of language dependence (ranked fifth overall), suggesting latent influence from accessibility, while game mechanics had minimal impact. The models offer actionable insights for practical application, and future work can optimize models by exploring the observed asymmetrical misclassification patterns.

Keywords: random forest multi-classification · Gini impurity · board games · game mechanics · language dependence · social interaction · BoardGameGeek · ensemble machine learning

1 Introduction and Related Works

Following the COVID-19 pandemic, board game popularity has surged in a "golden age", with Kickstarter crowdfunded games raising over $250 million in 2020 and corresponding Amazon sales increasing by 29% [1]. The integration of technology, particularly AI and machine learning, to explore board games has similarly propagated, enabling large-scale analysis of structured metadata, winning algorithms, or game recommender engines. Studies on the development and application of AI algorithms to strategize in board games are especially prevalent. For example, a study in the 16th European Conference on Games Based Learning explores reinforcement learning (Alpha-Zero model) in

Connect-Four [2]. Another study utilizes a Tsetlin machine to predict winning and losing positions in Hex, using interpretable logic-based AI methods for board game analysis [3].

Previous studies have analyzed BGG characteristic data, specifically a flagship study in IEEE Conference on Games (CoG) using game mechanics to predict user ratings through the comparative development of a regression tree and random forest model. This study found that 27% of rating variance could be explained by mechanic combinations, pioneering similar ML-based explorations of board games [4]. However, the objective of this paper, predicting game success defined by actual usage, is relatively unexplored. This paper utilizes a random forest framework to explore a holistic range of features from community-driven insights to discrete complexity metrics. Gini impurity methods were used to uncover non-obvious, underlying feature relationships (such as in language dependence) and models were optimized to acceptable accuracy for practical usage. This paper aims to provide a novel, interpretable pipeline for early-stage commercial insight to obtain maximal marketing and development results.

2 Data Methodology and Description

To analyze a holistic variety of board games adequately representing all genres, success, and mechanics, a large-scale dataset was scraped from BoardGameGeek (abbreviated as BGG), the largest global community of board games enthusiasts which hosting a large user interface and numerous game characteristics meaningful for a machine learning methodology. The dataset contained 20,000 unique board games, each with 50 + corresponding variables relating to characteristics including popularity, usage, and play time [5]. Selected games were concentrated in a relatively recent and overlapping timeframe to eliminate or effectively minimize potential impact of temporal exposure on game success. A portion of games were dropped due to incomplete information or extreme outlier behavior. Other preliminary cleaning was largely unnecessary due to the preexisting regulation of BGG, although major data modification important to the model methodology was performed for specific subtopics in the exploratory and predictive analysis stages.

Some categorical variables were dropped, such as publisher names and other information due to predictive irrelevance, leaving 39 numerical variables. To evaluate multicollinearity, a Pearson correlation coefficient matrix was calculated, quantifying the absolute value of Pearson coefficients [6] of each variable with itself and the other 38 numerical variables. Some correlations exceeded a threshold of 0.8, which indicates that the possibility of a high-dimensional input feature space reducing the effectiveness of multiple linear regression. Thus, this paper utilizes tree-based machine learning techniques unaffected by multicollinearity, although future studies may continue to explore linear regression through dimensionality reduction tools like principal component analysis (PCA) [7].

2.1 Selection of Proxy Success Metric

To quantitatively define a successful board game, the selection of a proxy variable was necessary for this paper's machine learning approach. BGG provides its own formulaic ranking of each board game partially based on unclear factors and is therefore interpretable. Potential proxy metrics were chosen from highly correlated variables in the Pearson matrix, which primarily encompassed various potential indicators of success, and narrowed down to *average user rating* and *number of plays* intuitively due to their strong relevance to game success. Each variable was plotted against BGG's ranking for comparison to evaluate structure and interpretability, as shown in Fig. 1(a) and Fig. 1(b) (presented adjacently to facilitate comparison).

In Fig. 1(a), the *average user rating* variable was observed to have a poor correlation with BGG's ranking, exhibiting clearly erratic and heteroscedastic noise. Additionally, the integrity of *average user rating* is compromised due to self-selection sampling bias, since ratings from voluntary user participation tend to be concentrated on extreme ends [8], thus adding to the unreliability of the variable as a proxy for success. Conversely, the relationship between *number of plays* and BGG's ranking shown in Fig. 1(b) has a noticeable exponential trend, with relatively homoscedastic noise. Thus, *number of plays* was chosen as the proxy success metric due to its pure evaluation of a board game's market success free from various sampling biases. The selection of a proxy eliminates the obstacle of multicollinearity from high dimensionality while representing a balanced consensus of critic and general user opinions.

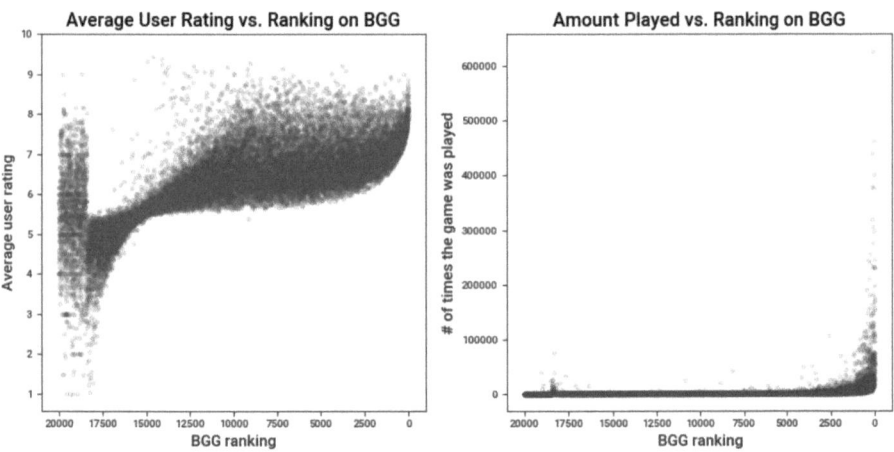

Fig. 1. (a) Scatterplot of BGG's ranking vs. *average user rating*. (b) Scatterplot of BGG's ranking vs. *number of plays* (selected proxy success metric).

2.2 Description of Research Objectives

This study aims to develop a reliable ensemble learning architecture to predict a board game's market success using input features available at or shortly after game release. In practical application, the methodology can be regularly updated to reflect market trends, providing a comprehensive understanding of the board game industry. For game developers and marketers, results provide decision reinforcement by enabling targeted optimization of promotion or design strategies to penetrate the market.

With the abundance of board game characteristics in the scraped dataset, many research avenues were considered but ultimately dropped from the final methodology. For example, some appealing avenues included modeling how specific game publishers affected *number of plays* or the quantitative impact of awards on success. However, these initial inquiries were dropped due to the lack of commonality for comparison and the extreme distinctness of awards or publishers between games. Additionally, largely temporal variables like publication year have poor correlations with *number of plays* and usefulness in practical application.

After conducting an exploratory analysis of the Pearson correlation coefficients, three core research objectives to answer the umbrella query of board game success: (1) game mechanics, (2) language dependence, and (3) social interaction. These domains were primarily selected due to their strong correlation with *number of plays* and their conceptual practicality. Model results will provide insight into the relationship of these three diverse and important components with overall success to facilitate targeted marketing or game development goals.

3 Exploratory Analysis

3.1 Game Mechanics

Game mechanics, defined as the core components and themes that form interactive rules, offer a meaningful dimension to a preliminary understanding of internal structural aspects and success. Particularly, game mechanics were examined to determine noticeable advantages in specific mechanics. After pruning mechanics attributed to less than 10 distinct games for clarity (too niche), the average *number of plays* for games with each mechanic was calculated, with the top 10 mechanics displayed in Fig. 2. Two high bound outliers emerged, the mechanics *variable setup* and *increase value of unchosen resources*, which were both attributed to games averaging over 80,000 plays. The next highest-ranking mechanic averaged 50,000 plays, a significant drop that clearly distinguishes the top two.

Variable setup and *increase value of unchosen resources* share the common purpose of enhancing strategic flexibility and replayability. This observation aligns with prior studies indicating variability as a major drive of long-term market success. The behavioral aspects of the top two mechanics offer hypotheses to evaluate during the modeling phase: high-ranking mechanics were predicted to exhibit correspondingly higher Gini importance scores in the random forest classifiers and have significant weight on the downstream development of a cumulative model.

3.2 Language Dependence

On BGG, language dependence pertains to the amount of reading necessary in a board game, essentially functioning as a variable proxy for text complexity (encompassing both amount and difficulty of reading) [5]. Language dependence was reported on a discrete scale of 1–5, with 1 and 5 denoting minimal and maximal text involvement, respectively. Games with values of zero were dropped due to a lack of data. Distribution

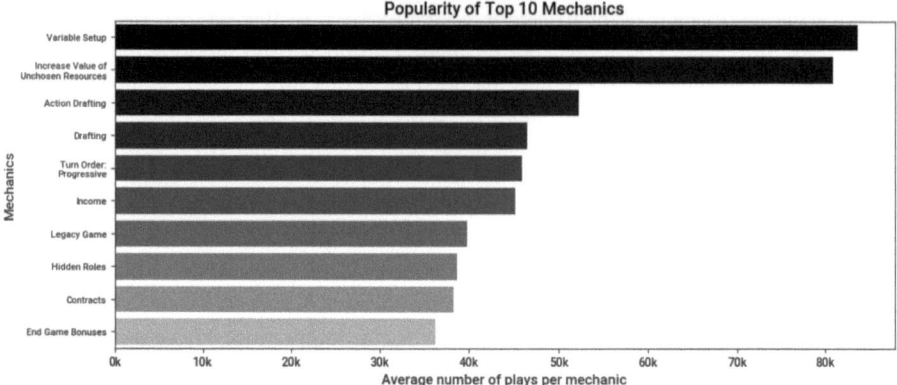

Fig. 2. Bar graph of the top 10 game mechanics by the mean label *number of plays*.

analysis revealed a significant skew towards low language dependence games, with 47.7% of games rated at level 1 and a drastically lower 4.2% at level 5. This pronounced asymmetry is most likely due to the increased marketability of language-light games compared to the higher production costs text-rich games, which often include narrative development, design, and translation expenses.

To evaluate whether this asymmetry had a measurable effect on board game success, *number of plays* was averaged for each level of language dependence, as shown in Fig. 3. Despite the skewness observed in the text complexity levels, there was no discernible trend. For example, the extreme ends displayed minimal difference: level 1 averaged at approximately 3,500 plays while level 5 averaged similarly at approximately 3,000 plays. These observations indicate that the language dependence variable and text complexity are not primary drivers of board game success in isolation. Therefore, language dependence was initially hypothesized to be less consequential during the modeling phase. However, the absence of direct correlation cannot fully imply the irrelevance of language dependence, as text complexity only partially defines the entire complexity of a board game's narrative. Latent structures or underlying relationships between text complexity and other similar factors including theme complexity may become meaningful in the cumulative random forest model.

3.3 Social Interaction

Given the modern influence of digital marketing and computers, the exploration of the effects of online social interaction on board game success offered an appealing research objective. From the scraped dataset, 11 features corresponding with social interaction were selected to examine as a case study, including website views, number of user ratings, etc. Before conducting predictive analysis, these 11 variables were thematically sorted into three subcategories to enhance interpretability: (1) media presence, (2) community interaction, and (3) community ratings. Details of the subcategories are displayed in Table 1.

It was initially hypothesized that media presence would be the dominant subcategory correlating with board game success, under a reasonable assumption that heightened

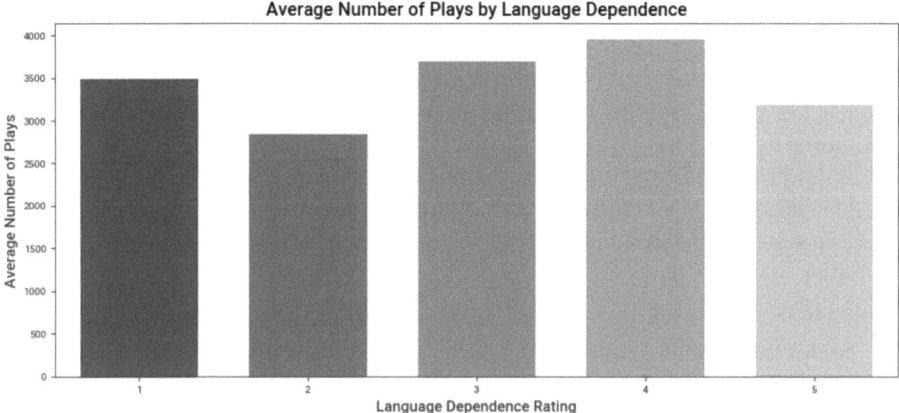

Fig. 3. Bar graph of the average *number of plays* per level of language dependence.

Table 1. Subcategories of social interaction variables.

Subcategory	Variables	Description
Media Presence	Website Views Blog Mentions News Articles Weblinks Podcasts	Count of page views on BGG Count of external blogs Count of news articles Count of game weblinks Count of podcasts
Community Interaction	User Ratings Count Comments Count Complexity Ratings Count Community Votes Count	Count of user ratings on BGG Count of user comments on BGG Count of complexity ratings on BGG Total votes on BGG
Community Ratings	Average User Rating Modified User Rating (BGG)	Mean rating from BGG users Normalized mean rating from BGG users

media exposure increases *number of plays*. Stratifying social interaction variables into three subcategories helped define the first predictive model.

4 Machine Learning Methodology

To maintain a balance between analysis depth and overfitting risks, predictive modeling was focused on the social interaction variables with all 39 original numerical variables culminating into an umbrella cumulative model. This decision was driven by two factors of rationale: (1) empirical weaknesses in univariate predictors and (2) dimensionality constraints. The first factor primarily applies to language dependence, where text complexity levels displayed no meaningful relationship between *number of plays*. Instead,

Fig. 3 shows a relatively flat correlation, thus illustrating the weakness of language dependence as an isolated solo predictor. Second, game mechanics are presented in sparse one-hot encoded format where a standalone model would be prone to overfitting and yield low generalizability (illustrated in another study in [9]). In particular, the drop from the top two outliers into a sharp skewness illustrated in Fig. 2 indicates the potential bias of dominant outlier or edge case signals in a predictive model. The high dimensionality and sparse binary flags of one-hot encoding therefore discouraged a standalone model on game mechanics. Future work should be dedicated to deeper investigation of mechanics.

4.1 Social Interaction Model

Linear Regression Benchmarking and Binning. To establish a baseline framework for predictive analysis, a linear regression model was introduced using social interaction variables (totaling 11 out of the 39 numerical variables). However, regression performed poorly due to the heavy skewness of *number of plays* spanning several standard deviations. Scatterplot diagnostics of individual variables revealed many exponential relationships between social interaction variables and *number of plays*. Thus, a logarithmic transformation of the label *number of plays* was applied to mitigate this nonlinearity.

Despite logarithmic label transformation, regression still reported high mean-squared-error (MSE) due to the massive scale of the label. Point estimates are also unreasonable given the subjectivity and considerable margin of error in predicting a game's commercial success. The label was instead transformed from a continuous numerical variable into discrete binned quantiles scaled 1–5 (with level 1 and 5 indicating the lowest and highest predicted magnitudes of success, respectively). A final regression model was retrained with the logarithmically transformed and binned *number of plays* label, reevaluating through classification accuracy score after rounding predictions to the nearest integer. This regression yielded a coefficient of determination R^2 value of 0.54, a MSE of 0.92, and an accuracy score of 0.39. In comparison to the previous tests, this regression improved noticeably but still failed to capture the complexity of underlying trends.

Random Forest Development. Given the nonlinearity of the input social interaction features observed in linear regression benchmarking, a tree-based ensemble learning approach was selected for a more suitable grasp of complex relationships. In particular, random forests are well suited to high-dimensional input without the necessary assumption of normalized input [10]. A random forest model was developed on the binned *number of plays* label after optimizing hyperparameters (maximum depth of 20 with 500 decision trees and 70–30 train-test split) from GridSearchCV [11] and cross-validation. The resulting model achieved an overall classification accuracy of 0.706, a significant and acceptable improvement from regression considering the nature of predicting board game success. Figure 4 displays a classification report with precision, recall, and F1 score results (precision and recall are relatively balanced for all levels of predicted *number of plays*, so F1 scores will drive model evaluation).

Random forest performed best in the extreme classes of level 1 and 5, reporting F1 scores of 0.78 and 0.90, respectively. This indicates high confidence in predicting

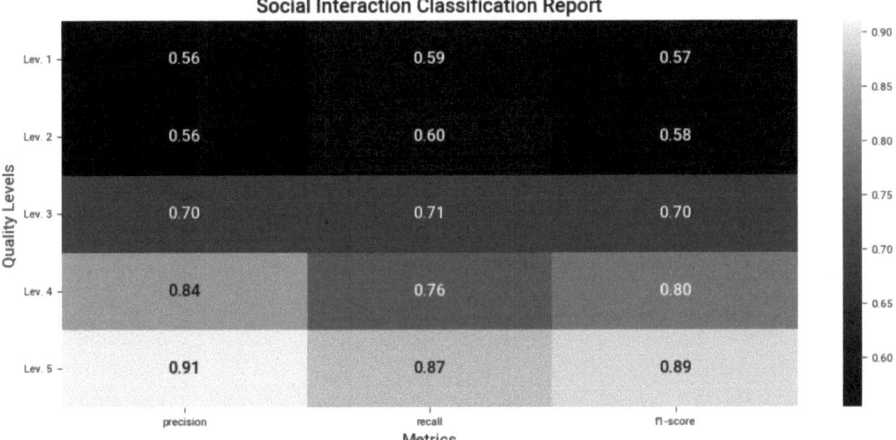

Fig. 4. Classification report of the social interaction random forest model including precision, recall, and F1 score.

clearly successful or unsuccessful board games. Conversely, the model underperformed in intermediate classes (mainly level 2 and 3), which exhibited weaker F1 scores of approximately 0.57–0.58, reflecting the common ambiguity of mid-range classifications. The predictive power of social interaction variables alone may not distinguish levels 2 and 3 effectively. Nonetheless, these results reinforce random forest's specialization in predicting outlier board games, which aligns with the original goals for practical application. Game developers and marketers are primarily concerned with clear estimates of market success or failure. The model struggles with the limitation of classifying soft, subjective label bins, and future work can further optimize the current learning architecture to output high-resolution results.

Community Interaction Analysis. Feature importances from the social interaction random forest model were computed through Gini impurity metric, which measures the probability of incorrect classification of a randomly chosen sample at a decision node. Impurity reduces at features with strong predictive power that separates classes, and total Gini impurity reduction from a feature is summed then normalized to determine top social interaction variables [12]. The calculation of Gini impurity $G(t)$ at node t is shown in Eq. (1), where p_i denotes the proportion of samples belonging to class i with n total classes.

$$G(t) = 1 - \sum_{i=1}^{n} p_i^2 \qquad (1)$$

From a feature analysis of the social interaction model, variables in the community interaction subcategory formed the most substantial predictive power, with the variables *user ratings count* and *user comments count* crossing importance scores of 0.23 and 0.12, respectively. Contradicting the initial hypothesis, four out of five media presence variables ranked less than 0.07 in importance.

To further explore the unexpected predictive strength of community interaction variables, Fig. 5 displays the scatterplots of each community interaction variable with the continuous, log-transformed label *number of plays* (colored dots represent the feature plotted whereas grey dots represent the other features). Given the observation of approximately linear relationships in a log-transformed visualization, Fig. 5 indicates that community interaction is exponentially related to the label in the original feature space. Such trends are reasonable with common patterns in social dynamics where marginal gains accelerate exponentially with increased engagement. These findings illustrate community feedback and interaction as social proof mechanisms which foster an active player base. In terms of practical application, game marketers should maintain a strong profile on BoardGameGeek and other popular communities, which may be more successful than short-term media exposure.

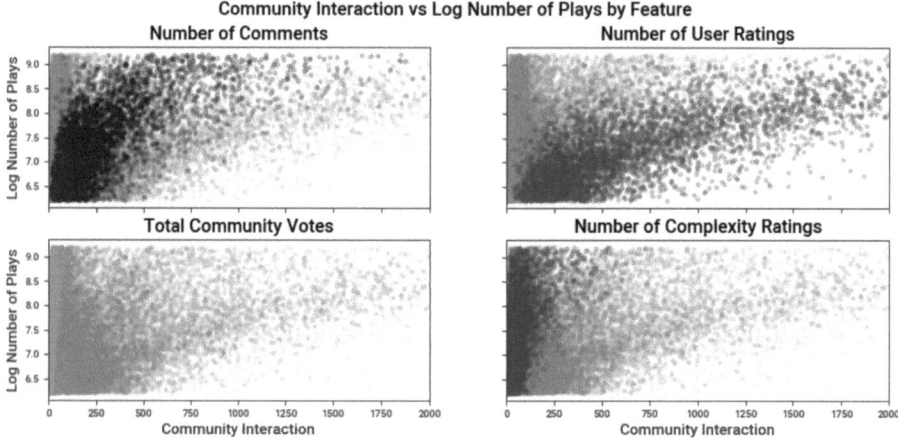

Fig. 5. Scatterplots of the correlations between the four community interaction variables and the log-transformed label *number of plays*.

4.2 Cumulative Model

Feature Selection and Model Development. A larger random forest model integrating key predictors from all domains (all 39 numerical variables, not confined to the three feature categories identified earlier) was developed to assess their collective ability to classify board games into levels of success. This cumulative model served as an umbrella analysis to accomplish two main goals: (1) evaluate the predictive power of selected variables and (2) identify the most influential variables overall through Gini impurity analysis.

Hyperparameters were tuned algorithmically (maximum depth of 40 with 1000 decision trees) and a 70–30 train-test split was used to yield meaningful generalization accuracy. The label transformations of the social interaction model were maintained for effective cross-benchmarking. To optimize efficiency while minimizing original feature redundancy from high dimensionality, only the top 3 social interaction variables (*user ratings count*, *modified user rating*, and *user comments count*) were inputted into the cumulative model. Similarly, the top game mechanics were inputted after one-hot encoding. The majority of the remaining numerical variables were "brand-making" metrics, including awards, editions, translations, narrative complexity, and language dependence. These variables were also used due to their influence on the costumer perception of a game. Although models like K-nearest-neighbors (KNN) and other regression models were considered, a robust random forest framework was chosen due to the categorical label and sparsity of binary-encoded qualitative features. Future work can develop other models for comparison with random forest to optimize the methodology.

Cumulative Model Analysis. The cumulative random forest model reached an accuracy of 0.71 with a class-wise precision from 0.59–0.91 and recall from 0.56–0.89. This model performed similarly to the social interaction model, reliably detecting clear signals of success and vice versa, but underperforming in mid-range classes due to overlapping feature patterns. A confusion matrix is displayed in Fig. 6 to examine the class-wise strength of the model. The strong diagonal observed indicates that the random forest classifier interprets feature structure adequately, which is especially true for level 3 (867 correct) and 5 (931 correct) that form the center and tail of the distribution. In the extreme high end (level 5), 119 games were misclassified as level 3 and skipped level 4, suggesting the model's tendency to jump over adjacent signals in extremes. This observation suggests the presence of latent factors in top games resembling mid-range games resulting in class skipping. Additionally, low-end classes (level 1 and 2) exhibited substantial off-diagonal predictions, contributing to asymmetrical classifications favoring the clear success signals. This phenomenon most likely mirrors the social interaction model's situation where feature space overlapping creates ambiguity in low-end classes. Success in level 3 with 867 correct classifications suggests a strong anchor class. Implicit risk aversion in model architecture causes predictions to gravitate toward the center, which is acceptable for early-stage game forecasting.

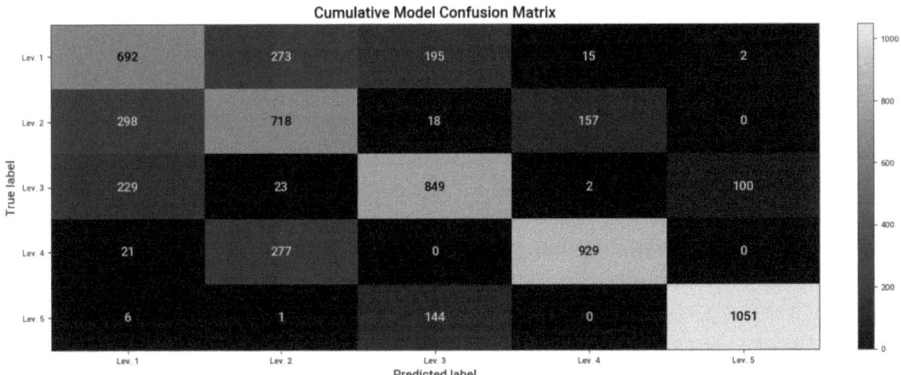

Fig. 6. Confusion matrix of the cumulative model displaying classifications for the predicted levels of success.

The nearly identical accuracies of the cumulative and social interaction model (0.71 and 0.706) suggest that social interaction variables comprise the majority of predictive power. Consequently, the top features in the Gini impurity feature importances were again social interaction (see Fig. 7). Despite prevalence in exploratory analysis, game mechanics had a negligible impact (at less than 0.025 importance scores each) and reduced overall accuracy by a marginal 2.12% when removed. The two mechanics identified in Fig. 7 differ from the top two mechanics in exploratory analysis (*variable setup* and *increase value of unchosen resources*), suggesting the absence of interpretable impacts on board game success. Conversely, language dependence, which was initially considered a weak predictor in isolation, ranked fifth overall in feature importance. This observation indicates the presence of meaningful underlying structures when language dependence is combined with other complexity variables.

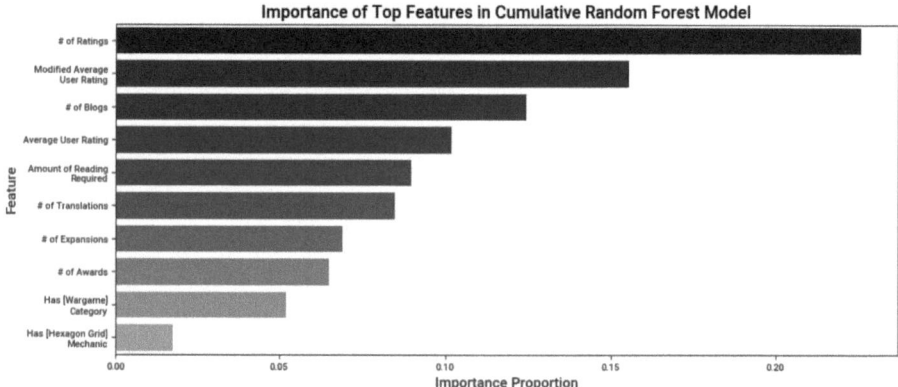

Fig. 7. Bar graph of top 10 variables in cumulative model from Gini-based feature importance scores.

4.3 Conclusion

This paper's machine learning framework examined the proxy variable for success, *number of plays*, through three avenues: game mechanics, language dependence, and social interaction. Predictive analysis revealed novel findings in feature dynamics, especially the prevalence of community interaction variables over media presence. The low-ranking feature importances of variables like podcasts and news mentions reinforce the conclusion that organic, community-driven engagement is more important than passive media exposure in driving sustained play. Although social interaction is intuitively predictive of game success, such variables serve as important early-stage predictors and can be used in more comprehensive temporal analysis of market reach.

Contradicting the initial hypothesis, game mechanics lacked strong correlations with *number of plays* despite structural design importance. A novel finding was the unexpected importance of language dependence. Whereas isolated text complexity displayed flat relationships with game success in exploratory analysis, a collective feature space in the cumulative model distinguished the presence of latent relationships and predictive power when language dependence is combined with other features. Game developers should be encouraged to invest early in curating user engagement on platforms like BGG while ensuring linguistic accessibility. These social and structural components are more consequential than isolated awards or specific mechanics.

4.4 Future Work and Discussion

Future work can expand the presented framework in multiple dimensions. First, the confusion matrix of the cumulative model revealed asymmetrical misclassification patterns, especially in low-end classes. Techniques like ordinal regression or fuzzy classification thresholds can be incorporated into the existing architecture to capture these blurred class boundaries. Additionally, the use of external datasets like more comprehensive marketing channel data or campaign details on platforms like Kickstarter can further distinguish extreme classes from mid-range classes. External data could expand to include marketing demographics, prices, and crowdfunding to contextualize both pre-launch and post-launch success. More expressive modeling could include gradient boosting combined with SHAP-based interpretability to clarify complex feature relationships. Random forest can be cross-benchmarked with other classification methods including XGBoost or SVM, utilizing multiple train-test splits and reporting standard deviation of evaluation metrics (precision, recall, and F1 scores) to determine the optimal modeling framework.

Acknowledgments. The authors would like to thank their PhD student mentors at the University of Chicago, Jimmy Lederman and Melissa Adrian, and the committee of ICEC for reviewing this paper.

Disclosure of Interests. The authors have no competing interests to declare that are relevant to the content of this article.

References

1. D'Souza, J.: Board game statistics by revenue, playing time, user, regions, gender, age group, generation and frequency. Coolest Gadgets (2025). https://www.coolest-gadgets.com/board-game-statistics/
2. Lürig, C.: Learning machine learning with a game. In: Proceedings of the 16th European Conference on Games Based Learning (ECGBL), **16**(1) (2022). https://doi.org/10.34190/ecgbl.16.1.481
3. Giri, C., Granmo, O.-C., van Hoof, H., Blakely, C.D.: Logic-based AI for Interpretable Board Game Winner Prediction with Tsetlin Machine. *arXiv preprint* arXiv:2203.04378 (2022). https://doi.org/10.48550/arXiv.2203.04378
4. Nguyen, D., Kritz, J., Gaina, R.D., Perez-Liebana, D.: Unveiling modern board games: an ML-based approach to BoardGameGeek data analysis. In: 2024 IEEE Conference on Games (CoG), Milan, Italy, pp. 1–4 (2024). https://doi.org/10.1109/CoG60054.2024.10645644
5. BoardGameGeek. https://boardgamegeek.com/. Accessed 31 Mar 2025
6. Pearson, K.: Note on regression and inheritance in the case of two parents. Proc. R. Soc. Lond. **58**, 240–242 (1895). https://doi.org/10.1098/rspl.1895.0041

7. Jolliffe, I.T.: Principal Component Analysis. 2nd edn. Springer Series in Statistics. Springer, New York (2002). https://doi.org/10.1007/b98835
8. Zhu, Q., Lo, L.Y.-H., Xia, M., Chen, Z., Ma, X.: Bias-aware design for informed decisions: raising awareness of self-selection bias in user ratings and reviews. Proc. ACM Hum.-Comput. Interact. **6**(CSCW2), Article 3555597 (2022). https://doi.org/10.1145/3555597
9. Chen, X., Chen, H., Nan, S., Kong, X., Duan, H., Zhu, H.: Dealing with missing, imbalanced, and sparse features during the development of a prediction model for sudden death using emergency medicine data: machine learning approach. JMIR Med. Inform. **11**, e38590 (2023). https://doi.org/10.2196/38590
10. Breiman, L.: Random forests. Mach. Learn. **45**, 5–32 (2001). https://doi.org/10.1023/A:1010933404324
11. Scikit-learn: GridSearchCV — exhaustive search over specified parameter values. https://scikit-learn.org/stable/modules/generated/sklearn.model_selection.GridSearchCV.html. Accessed 31 Mar 2025
12. Breiman, L., Friedman, J.H., Olshen, R.A., Stone, C.J.: Classification and Regression Trees. 1st edn. Chapman and Hall/CRC, New York (1984). https://doi.org/10.1201/9781315139470

Stay and Play - Modeling Social Influence of Players in the Steam Gaming Community

Enrica Loria[1], Alessia Antelmi[2], Carmine Spagnuolo[2], and Johanna Pirker[3,4(✉)]

[1] Keen Software House, Prague, Czechia
[2] University of Salerno, Fisciano, Italy
[3] Technical University of Munich, Munich, Germany
[4] Graz University of Technology, Graz, Austria
johanna.pirker@tugraz.at

Abstract. Play is a social activity that enables the formation of full-fledged social networks. Multiplayer games connect users in communities, similar to traditional online social networks, where some individuals influence others' in-game behavior—"influencers." However, little is known about how influence operates across games or affects behavior beyond gameplay. To explore this, we analyzed Steam, a game distribution platform that lets us study player behavior at a broader level and compare social contagion from explicit friendships to the implicit in-game connections studied in prior work. While Steam influencers share traits with game influencers, they show distinct behaviors (e.g., game preferences, playtime) and can influence new game adoption. These insights expand our understanding of the Steam community and support previous findings on connectedness and the transfer of social bonds across games.

Keywords: community · social network analysis · social networks

1 Introduction

The global rise of online multiplayer games [57,58] is supported by psychological and empirical studies showing the benefits of playing together [45,47,49]. Humans need social connectedness [6,19], and games often serve as a social proxy—especially when real-world interaction is limited. Virtual environments foster presence [18] and community [8], forming fertile ground for complex social dynamics: real-world friendships [15], cohesive communities [45,59], and influencers [11,38]. Originally studied in social media, influencers shape behavior, drive community evolution, and reflect community values. Understanding them deepens our view of games as social spaces and highlights their role in building social capital. Influencers hold not only marketing value but also significant social worth. Yet, research on game influencers has focused mostly on ingame behavior, producing narrow, context-specific insights. Player communities often extend beyond individual titles, connecting users across genres and virtual worlds. Game providers support this by letting players manage multiple games and connect with others. With over 20 million concurrent users[1], Steam is a prime example. Beyond game purchases and achievements, players can befriend others, join groups, and leave comments or reviews. This broad range of social features enables a deeper, game-agnostic analysis of player relationships and offers a macro-level view of the gaming community.

2 Related Works

People rely on multiplayer games as platforms to connect, socialize, build social capital, and develop cooperation and team skills. This section will describe the importance of games as a social vessel, existent research on players' social networks, and known social dynamics occurring in games.

Games as Social Medium. Playing games with others is a social experience [20], sparking growing interest in games as social incubators [9,24]. Games help fulfill fundamental needs for connectedness [19] and belonging [6], contributing to well-being and improved performance [39,44,47,49]. This, in turn, increases player commitment [16,46]. Social interaction is a strong motivator—often outweighing the desire to win [63]. The social value of games is multifaceted, supported by both verbal and non-verbal communication [36], offering a safe space for interaction among strangers [9]. Playing together fosters mutual liking [17], and friendships formed in-game can persist, span across different games, and even extend into the real world [15]. Games also help reinforce existing relationships [21,61]. Social games can positively affect mental health, as shown in studies on Animal Crossing during COVID-19 lockdowns [33]. However, not all multiplayer games foster connection [22,30]. To monitor social dynamics, researchers and designers can apply Social Network Analysis (SNA), which uses graphs to model and reveal player interaction patterns [50].

Social Network Analysis in Games. Social networks emerge when direct or indirect interactions are possible. Social media and traditional OSNs make connections explicit, linking users by relationships or shared interests. Similarly, online multiplayer games foster social interactions that can be modeled as social networks using standard SNA techniques. Studying how players socialize through games can help create better social environments [20,21], reveal how one player's activity influences others [63], and show how certain players' presence shapes behavior [63]. The network's structure also reflects player relationships [53], and analyzing ego-nets can uncover preferences for stable teams, temporary groups, or solo play [40]. This knowledge enhances our understanding of the community and can improve matchmaking and player experience. Interestingly, more time spent in teams doesn't always signal sociability—some players engage socially only for functional reasons [20,31]. Others choose teammates based on complementary skills, age, or guild affiliation [66]. Network analysis can highlight patterns that affect performance (e.g., harmful centralization [41]) or reveal toxic

---

[1] https://store.steampowered.com/stats/.

behaviors [32]. Though SNA in games is still emerging, research has explored social roles, showing that group formation is central to communities [23]. Some players even prioritize guild growth over personal progress [1], and strong team ties improve both performance [35] and retention [45]. Overall, this research confirms the deep integration of sociality in games. Players form meaningful groups and influence one another, supporting the idea that multiplayer games can function as full-fledged OSNs. As in other social platforms, peer influence, contagion, and group effects play a crucial role.

Social Influence and Contagion (in Games). When one person's actions affect another's behavior, we say the first exerts influence. In SNA, influencers are often categorized as (i) those who spread behaviors or information [54], and (ii) those who are popular or highly visible in the network [25]. The second type is typically identified using centrality measures such as In-/Out-degree, Betweenness, Eigenvector, and Closeness [3,28,52]. However, these measures may not fully capture behavioral influencers, who require network homogeneity rather than mere connectivity. Influence is context-dependent [56], and likely varies by the behavior being influenced. It's often linked to diffusion, which is shaped by network structure [2]. Influence can be modeled by observing whether a node Y takes an action after a connected node X does [4,10,12]. In the digital era, activity logs help estimate influence probabilities [27]. Behavioral influence is often measured by increased similarity between users over time [52], requiring dynamic network data. This process supports the idea of reinforcing influence, where similarity grows gradually after the initial connection [14]. In games, influencer research is still limited. Notable exceptions include Canossa et al. [11], who used telemetry and centrality to identify influential players in The Division, and Loria et al. [38], who found semantic influencers had a stronger impact on retention than central players in Destiny. Influence also matters in game-related forums. Santos et al. [51] analyzed how expert and user reviews affect game reputation, focusing on explicit opinions, unlike our use of implicit data (e.g., playtime). Rosenthal et al. [48] explored situational influence through user-generated content on forums and blogs. Still, a comprehensive study of influencers across games and genres—especially those impacting in-game behavior—is missing.

Data Analysis on Steam. Games differ in design, audiences, and modes of social interaction. As a result, analyzing social patterns within individual games offers only a limited view of player relationships. In contrast, studying online game platforms like Steam can reveal broader and more complex social dynamics. Steam[2] is one of the most popular platforms for buying and playing PC games and also supports social features, allowing players to connect. This heterogeneous dataset offers valuable insights into both player behavior and game trends. Previous research has used Steam data to study player preferences [37,67], play patterns [55], and game genre overlap through playtime clustering [55]. Steam's social network has also evolved—from a loosely connected graph in 2011 [7] to a more structured network in 2016 [43], with players tending to befriend similar users and favor social games. While many studies focus on individual player

---

[2] https://steampowered.com.

behavior, less is known about the broader social dynamics on Steam. More in-depth research is needed to understand how players connect and influence each other. Studying social contagion and influence within the Steam network could reveal key individuals who help keep the network active and foster meaningful virtual relationships—supporting players' desire for connection.

3 Data

This section details the construction of the data set used to perform our study. We needed three kinds of information for each user: i) their Steam friends, ii) how much time they spent playing on Steam, and iii) which games they played.

The Steam Friendship Graph. We modeled the Steam friends network as an undirected graph, where nodes represent players and edges represent friendships.

Step 1. To ensure active users in our dataset, we collected a seed set of 1,000 users from reviewers of the top 100 New and Trending games on April 10, 2020. Random sampling was avoided, as most social network users are passive [26,64]. We then gathered their friends, creating an initial network of 50k nodes.

Step 2. To maintain a sufficiently dense graph for influence analysis, we extracted the largest connected component (LCC), consisting of 2.8k users.

Step 3. We expanded the network by retrieving friends of the 2.8k LCC users, resulting in a second network with 240k nodes.

Step 4. Finally, we retrieved the friends of the newly added nodes, but only added missing edges—no new nodes. Private profiles were removed.

The final network included 191,479 nodes and 1,242,093 edges.

User Data. We collected daily player activity data—specifically, time spent playing each owned game—between April 13 and May 17, 2020. A user was considered active if they played at least one game during this period. Inactive users and disconnected nodes were removed, resulting in a final sample of 39,354 users and 218,432 edges. After excluding days affected by API failures, we obtained 28 days of valid activity data. Overall, players were highly active (Table 1): on average, they played on 17 out of 28 days ($std = 8.42$), with about 4 h per active day. Only a small portion played less than 2 h daily, suggesting our sample consists mostly of regular, near-daily players.

Games Metadata. Our sample includes around 17,000 different games. For each, we scraped metadata such as genre and tags. The distribution of players per game is highly skewed, with a mean of 25.8 and a standard deviation of 232.8 ($min = 1$, $median = 3$, $max = 26,590$). Only about 3,000 games had at least 10 players, 500 had over 100, 35 had over 1,000, and just one exceeded 10,000 players—Counter-Strike: Global Offensive, a Free-To-Play Action game released in 2012, with over 4 million reviews and a "Very Positive" rating. The dataset includes a diverse range of games. While both user-defined and Steam tags show a predominance of indie and single-player titles, these aren't always the most played. Players tend to explore a wide variety of single-player games but converge more on multiplayer titles. This is likely because multiplayer games rely

Table 1. Statistics of players' activity.

	Min	25%	50%	75%	Max	Mean	Std
Min. play	1	111	185	282	997	209	132
#Games	1	3	6	11	387	8.87	9.8
Active days	2	10	19	25	28	23	6.5

on an active, connected player base to be enjoyable—requiring a kind of social consensus to thrive.

Constructs and Metrics. We employed the following characterization metrics to outline characteristics meaningful in the Steam community.

Players' Activity. We first analyzed players' activity and time investment compared to the rest of the population, using total hours played (`timeplayed`) as a metric. We then refined this by computing the hours spent on well-reviewed games, weighted by their popularity (`weighted_time`). Finally, we calculated the percentage of time spent on multiplayer games (`ratio_time_mp`) as opposed to titles without social features.

Players' Library of Games. We studied the players' tendency to own popular games (`avg_game_popular`), regardless of the time they spent playing them (`ratio_time_popular`). Subsequently, we differentiated players' games by common genre, assigned to each game by Steam. For each genre, we computed, in percentage, how many titles corresponding to that genre the players owned (`ratio_Genre`).

Influential Behaviors. Game user research (GUR) highlights the importance of long-term engagement and retention, especially in multiplayer games that rely on active communities. It is, therefore, desirable that influencers help retain their neighbors in shared games. To assess this, we used the `retention_transfer` metric from [38], which measures whether players stay longer when influencers do, and whether they leave when influencers churn. A value of 0 indicates perfect retention transfer, while higher values show less influence on neighbors' retention. In social media, influencers promote products to maximize reach. Similarly, in Steam—a platform for purchasing and playing games—it is valuable if players influence others to adopt new games. To measure this, we computed `ratio_neigh_new_games`, capturing the proportion of neighbors who played a game after the influencer did. However, adoption alone isn't enough—retention matters. We included `avg_retention_ngames`, which measures how long neighbors stayed in new games. This is calculated as the time a neighbor spent in a new game over the maximum possible time (until the end of the observation period). A value of 1 indicates full retention; lower values suggest earlier abandonment.

4 Method and Results

In this section, we present the results of identifying Steam influencers using semantic and structural approaches. We then compare the two groups using the

Table 2. Distribution of the centrality measures (degree centrality, closeness centrality, and betweenness centrality) characterizing the overall population.

	Min	25%	50%	75%	Max	Mean	Std
DC	2.5e-5	2.5e-5	7.6e-5	2.0e-4	2.2e-2	2.8e-4	6.9e-4
CC	2.5e-5	1.6e-1	1.8e-1	2.1e-1	2.8e-1	1.7e-1	4.9e-2
BC	0	0	4.0e-6	5.6e-5	6.3e-2	1.1e-4	5.6e-4

Mann-Whitney U-test [42], which assesses whether there's a 50% chance that a randomly selected member of one group has a higher value than one from the other. The test can be two-tailed (both groups have the same median) or one-tailed (one group has higher values).

We chose the U-test as our data meet its assumptions: (i) the dependent variable is continuous or ordinal (e.g., playtime, genre ratio), (ii) the independent variable consists of two independent groups (e.g., semantic vs. central influencers), (iii) observations are independent, and (iv) the data are not normally distributed.

We used a significance level of $p = 0.01$.

Structural Influence. To study pairwise relationships, we modeled the Steam friendship data as an undirected graph $G = (V, E)$, where V represents users and E represents mutual friendships—i.e., an edge (u, v) exists if u and v are friends. Central users (or structural influencers) were identified by analyzing the graph's topology using standard centrality measures: degree (DC), closeness (CC), and betweenness (BC) [52].

Degree centrality reflects how many connections a user has. Since Steam friendships are mutual, we used an undirected graph. Closeness centrality captures how near a user is to all others, while betweenness centrality counts how often a user lies on the shortest paths between others—indicating their role in connecting the network. Influencers identified through these metrics are highly visible and contribute to network cohesion.

We ranked users by combined centrality scores and selected the top 1% as structural influencers (394 users). Table 2 summarizes the distribution of centrality values. While the degree and the betweenness centrality values tend to be very small, the closeness centrality is slightly better distributed. Specifically, the 394 central users show a degree centrality in the range $[5.10e-05; 6.87e-04]$, a closeness centrality in the range $[0.11; 0.28]$, and a betweenness centrality in the range $[1.61e-03; 6.38e-2]$.

Semantic Influence. Influential users (or semantic influencers) can be identified by analyzing temporal information on nodes' activity and properties. Following the definition of those types of influencers [14,52], we have no insights into their position in the community. Instead, a method to analyze behavioral change is required. Hence, the need for temporal data to compute the influence exerted within the network. In practice, we used the algorithm defined by Loria et al. [38]. The authors implemented the concept of influence as an increase of similarity over time to analyze the players' network of the online game Destiny in competitive matches.

The algorithm[3] [38] computes the influence for each edge in the graph and evaluates how similar the nodes become over time. We used temporal data containing information about the activity of the players during the observation period. The activity is expressed in terms of minutes of gameplay for each game played. In its raw form, the information is unpacked per day. However, we investigated how the result also changed when a larger granularity is considered - i.e., weeks. Influence is computed as an increase in the similarity of the behavior of the nodes. The algorithm allows us to specify the properties on which we want the influence to be evaluated. In our case, the properties describe the number of minutes a game has been played, and the influence can be measured only on shared properties - i.e., games. Influence occurs only when one of the two parties changes to converge to the other behaviors. Hence, if both players have modified their behaviors, such similarity would be attributed to chance. If one or more shared games exist, and only one of the two nodes modified its behavior, a similarity between the nodes' properties is computed. The Python implementation allows us to customize the similarity function by specifying a custom distance metric instead of using the default cosine similarity function, typically used to measure the similarity between two long and sparse vectors [14,29]. Given that - in our case - the property vectors were very short, we used the Euclidean distance, the most commonly used metric for computing the dissimilarity of objects described by numeric attributes [29].

The influence score associated with the edge represents the influence's magnitude, which is positive for the influencer and negative for the influenced node. The node influencer is then computed as an aggregated value of the influence that occurs at the edges where the node is involved.

To detect influential users from a semantic point of view, we used the algorithm defined by Loria et al. [38], which computes the influence scores for each node of the network as a value in the range $[-1; 1]$. Influential users are characterized by a high score of the influence value, indicating the extent to which they impact their neighbors. Neutral values, around 0, represent users who have no effect on others but are resistant to influence. Conversely, the lower the value, the more the node is susceptible to the influencers connected to them.

We observed that many nodes in the network have a neutral influence and only a few of them have very high or low influence values ($mean = 4.8e-4, std = 0.09, min = -0.96, 25\% = 0.00, 50\% = 0.00, 75\% = 0.00, max = 0.96$), both when the influence was computed on days and weeks. Although previous research found that, in social media, influencers typically represent the 10% of the population [34,60], many of the top 10% users in the influence rankings presented an influence of 0. We redefined our sample according to that observation, considering as influential the players in the top 1%. We obtained 394 users, having an influence ranging from 0.28 and 0.96 from days influence and ranging from

---

[3] Available as a Pypi package at https://pypi.org/project/sinfpy.

0.32 and 0.96 for weeks influence. The two sets produced from weeks and days influence overlap for almost the totality of the players. Therefore, we used the days' influence for characterizing the sets.

Characterizing Influencers. We identified two distinct influencer types—semantic and structural—and analyzed how they differ from each other and the general player population. As expected, the groups were completely disjoint. Semantic influencers had significantly lower centrality scores (Degree, Closeness, Betweenness), while structural influencers had lower influence scores (Table 3).

Players' Activity. Semantic influencers played more and spent more time on highly rated games than both the general population and central players. They also played more multiplayer games than the population, though not significantly more than structural influencers.

Game Libraries. Semantic influencers owned more Action, F2P, MMO, RPG, Strategy, and Early Access games. Structural influencers owned more Adventure, Casual, Indie, RPG, Racing, Simulation, Sports, and Strategy games. While semantic influencers had more popular games than structural ones, this did not significantly differ from the population.

Influentiable Behaviors. Semantic influencers had significantly lower retention transfer values, indicating a stronger impact on others' retention. Of the 394 semantic influencers, 237 encouraged at least one neighbor to try a new game. Though they influenced fewer neighbors overall (due to smaller network size), the percentage of influenced neighbors was significantly higher, and those neighbors stayed in new games longer. Structural influencers had higher `retention_transfer` values, showing weaker influence on retention. They had more neighbors trying new games—mainly due to larger networks—but influenced a smaller percentage of them (`ratio_neigh_new_games`). Of the 394 central players, 272 encouraged at least one neighbor to try a new game, but there was no statistical difference in retention compared to the population (`avg_retention_ngames`).

Overall, semantic influencers had a stronger impact on both new game adoption and retention, despite having smaller, less central networks.

5 Discussion

Steam blends social media features into a gaming context but differs from both traditional social media and multiplayer games. As a game distributor, its social features are optional, and interactions are explicit—unlike the implicit, structured interactions in games. This positions Steam's social layer closer to social media in semantics. In this study, we examined the presence of influencers on Steam and compared them to gameplay and social media influencers. The following sections present our findings in relation to our research questions.

Influencers Exist and Impact Long-Term Retention. Structural (centrality based) approaches work well in social media, where influencers explicitly

Table 3. Summary of players' behaviors in Steam. For the columns *Semantic Influencer* and *Structural Influencers* we can have 3 answers: Yes, No, and empty cell. Yes answers indicate that the value is significantly higher for Semantic (or Structural) influencers than for the population. Conversely, No answers state that the value is significantly lower than that for the population. Empty cells indicate non-significant differences. The last column shows the answer to the question: "Which among semantic and central influencers has significantly higher values for that behavior?" Also in this case, empty cells indicate non-significant differences.

Observed Behavior	Metric	Description	Mean	Std	Semantic Influencers	Structural Influencers	Semantic vs Structural
Activity	timeplayed	Players' time investment	4269.23	3814.71	Yes	No	Semantic
	weighted_time	Time investment in popular games	3763.67	3674.18	Yes	No	Semantic
	ratio_time_popular	Preference towards popular game	0.84	0.25	-	-	Semantic
	ratio_time_mp	Preference towards popular game	0.09	0.21	Yes	-	-
	avg-game_popular	Purchase of popular games	0.85	0.08	-	No	Semantic
Games Library	ratio_Action	Ration of owned games falling in this category.	0.69	0.34	Yes	No	Semantic
	ratio_Adventure		0.24	0.30	No	Yes	Central
	ratio_Casual		.06	0.16	No	Yes	Central
	ratio_F2P		0.30	0.37	Yes	-	Semantic
	ratio_Indie		.30	0.33	-	Yes	Central
	ratio_MM		0.09	0.21	Yes	-	-
	ratio_RPG		0.19	0.29	Yes	Yes	Central
	ratio_Racing		.06	0.18	-	Yes	Central
	ratio_Sim		0.16	0.27	-	Yes	Central
	ratio_Sports		0.06	0.19	-	Yes	Central
	ratio_Strategy		0.17	0.28	Yes	Yes	Central
	ratio_EA		0.05	0.15	Yes	-	-
Influentiable behaviors	retention_transfer	Measures if the player affect the long-term retention of the neighbors.	2.91	4.96	No	Yes	Central
	ratio_neigh_new-games	Local influence of players on their neighborhood in playing new games	0.24	0.32	Yes	Yes	Semantic
	avg_retention_ngames	Time investment in those new games the neighbors played	0.58	0.34	Yes	-	Semantic

communicate with followers and may influence real-life behavior. Game influencers, in contrast, impact in-game actions. Steam is a hybrid; it includes explicit social tools while also offering high-level data on implicit in-game interactions (e.g., playtime, achievements). It differs from platforms like Twitch, which promote direct communication. This raises RQ1: Should Steam influencers be identified using centrality-based methods (as in social networks) [3,29], or semantic approaches (as in games) [38]? Our findings show that semantic influencers are more impactful on player retention than central players, linking low-level in-game relationships to high-level interactions on Steam. This is notable, as multiplayer game dynamics differ greatly from Steam's broader social layer. Our results also align partially with prior studies showing players connect with similar others on Steam [43]. However, our semantic method accounts for homophily by modeling behavioral change—only recognizing influence when a friend's behavior shifts after exposure. Thus, observed similarity isn't just due to shared gaming habits. These findings reinforce the idea that games foster deep social connections [9,20,24], even when social features are optional. While it's unclear how much players value SN-based features or whether that makes influencers more central, Steam's game-centric design may heighten sensitivity to friends' actions, motivating gameplay [62]—a view our results support. Steam influencers, consistent with game research, are better identified through semantic analysis and are rarely central or popular players. Regardless of whether relationships are implicit or explicit, the platform's focus—games—shapes how players interact and influence one another. This supports the view of games as incubators of meaningful relationships, where connectedness boosts retention. Unlike SN influencers who reach broad audiences, game influencers are limited by the number of players they can actively engage with. This raises further questions: Who are these influencers? How do they differ from roles like team leaders? And could some contribute to toxic behavior in the community [13]?

Influencers Condition the Choice to Play a Game. Steam semantic influencers impact long-term retention, as previously observed within games [38]. However, we also found they promoted new games to their neighbors—unlike average players (RQ2). While central players also influenced game adoption, retention in those games was significantly higher among the neighbors of semantic influencers. This ability to spread new games mirrors the role of social media influencers in promoting products [65]. Though this might support the view of games as material goods, there's an important distinction. Social media influencers—central and visible—are typically identified through structural metrics [3], similar to our central players on Steam. Yet while connections to central players may spark curiosity, semantic influencers foster stronger, longer-lasting engagement. Their influence appears more intimate and enduring, reinforcing their social value within the community. These findings highlight the crucial role semantic influencers play in shaping community behavior and evolution—such as encouraging players to adopt and stick with specific games. This opens several avenues for further research. For instance, longer retention may result from the influencer's ongoing presence in the game. It remains to be explored whether community-level influencers on Steam are also influencers within individual games.

Influencers Play Specific Types of Games. In games, influencers are regular users rather than part of an elite [11,38]. However, Steam influencers showed distinct traits (RQ3). Semantic influencers were highly active, spending many hours on well-reviewed games. They favored genres like MMO, F2P, and RPG—often requiring more commitment than casual games, which they tended to avoid. This aligns with GUR literature, where Destiny influencers formed strong, repeated connections [38]. Such commitment may be a key influencer trait, helping build bonds with others. It also mirrors social media influencers, who are consistently active and engaged [65]. In contrast, structural influencers—though also active—preferred casual games, where lasting social ties are less common. Semantic influencers also owned more early access titles, suggesting a drive to explore new games and stay current with trends. While their libraries included many games, they mainly played the most popular ones, possibly helping shape community consensus. This implies they may abandon less acclaimed games quickly. This observation invites further research: Did they try poorly rated games and lose interest, or did they adopt them early, with their abandonment contributing to the game's decline? This raises a broader question: How do influencers impact the future and success of games?

Implications. We extend current knowledge on social network analysis in games by showing that social influence can transcend individual games and emerge even in platforms like Steam, where social features are secondary. While Steam supports friendships and groups, much of its interaction is nonverbal-players view each other's profiles, games, and activity. Consistent with prior work [11,38], we find that influencers impact long-term retention and can help sustain the community. They also shape players' decisions to engage with new games, suggesting they influence both community stability and growth. Understanding influencers better could support more cohesive and vibrant communities. There's now growing interest in whether in-game and cross-game influencers (e.g., on Steam) are the same. If so, combining telemetry and platform-level data could help build a robust influencer profile and scalable detection methods. If not, comparing them could reveal how explicit and implicit interactions shape influence. Players, in turn, benefit from these connections, as engagement with influencers boosts retention. These insights open several promising directions for future research.

Limitations. During the 5-week daily crawl of player activity, data from two days was missing due to Steam API Internal Server Errors. To fill these gaps, we used the average activity, making those days slightly less accurate. We also removed outliers, such as players with private profiles, who provided incomplete data. Although this slightly altered the network, these users made up only a small fraction of the population. Inactive players were also excluded, reducing the network from 190k to under 40k nodes. As they didn't interact on Steam, their influence on or from others was likely minimal. Our dataset reflects only part of the Steam player base, seeded from players reviewing "New and Trending" games—typically active users interested in popular or newly released titles. Since the network was expanded via friends of the seed players—and Steam users tend to befriend similar others [43]—the network likely skews toward active users. This suits our study, which required players to show activity over time. While the dataset isn't fully representative, Steam's highly connected network may help mitigate the bias of sampling only a subset of users.

Future Work. Research on influencers in games remains an open field. The presence of influential players on Steam suggests that influence may persist across games, not just within individual titles. While our network mostly included active users, future work should explore whether retention influencers can also engage less active players. The identity and traits of influencers warrant further study—we've shown they have distinct preferences in how they spend their time and which games they play, but their direct interactions, such as participation in Steam groups, are still unclear. Since influencers often have limited connections, new methods could help extend their reach and better connect the network. Lastly, while current approaches focus on local influence, global influence—spread through indirect connections—is equally important [5]. Modeling this broader effect could offer deeper insights into how influence works in gaming communities.

6 Conclusions

People's behaviors are affected by how the network around them act. The literature on players social networks prove as the structure of gamer communities either built around games [59] or inside the gameplay [11,38] impact the players' activity in the game. To expand our knowledge of the players' network, we investigated how they connect on a game distribution platform, Steam, which abstracts the concept of specific games. We found how social contagion can also occur in a cross-game environment, supporting that social relationships can be transferred from one game to another [15]. Steam influencers, as game influencers, impact others' retention within the game provider but also influenced others' choice to play a new game. Additionally, the analysis of the Steam network highlighted properties and behaviors of influencers distinguishing them from the *ordinary* player, undetectable from telemetry data currently analyzed in prior works [11,38]. Therefore, influencers have proven to fully impact the community as they condition future trends and help maintain the network active and connected.

References

1. Ang, C.S., Zaphiris, P.: Social roles of players in MMORPG guilds: a social network analytic perspective. Inf. Commun. Soc. **13**(4), 592–614 (2010). https://doi.org/10.1080/13691180903266952
2. Badham, J., Kee, F., Hunter, R.F.: Network structure influence on simulated network interventions for behaviour change. Soc. Netw. **64**, 55–62 (2021)

3. Bakshy, E., Karrer, B., Adamic, L.A.: Social influence and the diffusion of user-created content. In: ACM Conference on Electronic Commerce, pp. 325–334. ACM Press, New York, USA (2009). https://doi.org/10.1145/1566374.1566421
4. Bakshy, E., Mason, W.A., Hofman, J.M., Watts, D.J.: Everyone's an influencer: quantifying influence on twitter. In: Proceedings of the 4th ACM International Conference on Web Search and Data Mining, WSDM 2011, pp. 65–74 (2011). https://doi.org/10.1145/1935826.1935845
5. Bartal, A., Pliskin, N., Ravid, G.: Modeling influence on posting engagement in online social networks: beyond neighborhood effects. Soc. Netw. **59**, 61–76 (2019)
6. Baumeister, R.F., Leary, M.R.: The need to belong: desire for interpersonal attachments as a fundamental human motivation. Psychol. Bull. **117**(3), 497 (1995)
7. Becker, R., Chernihov, Y., Shavitt, Y., Zilberman, N.: An analysis of the steam community network evolution. In: 2012 IEEE 27th Convention of Electrical and Electronics Engineers in Israel, IEEEI 2012 (2012). https://doi.org/10.1109/EEEI.2012.6377133
8. Blanchard, A.L.: Developing a sense of virtual community measure. Cyberpsychol. Behav. **10**(6), 827–830 (2007)
9. Brown, B., Bell, M.: CSCW at play. In: Proceedings of the 2004 ACM conference on Computer supported cooperative work - CSCW 2004, p. 350. Association for Computing Machinery (ACM), New York, New York, USA (2004). https://doi.org/10.1145/1031607.1031666, http://portal.acm.org/citation.cfm?doid=1031607.1031666
10. Brown, P.E., Feng, J.: Measuring user influence on twitter using modified k-shell decomposition. In: Fifth International AAAI Conference on Weblogs and Social Media (2011)
11. Canossa, A., Azadvar, A., Harteveld, C., Drachen, A., Deterding, S.: Influencers in multiplayer online shooters evidence of social contagion in playtime and social play. In: Conference on Human Factors in Computing Systems - Proceedings. Association for Computing Machinery, May 2019. https://doi.org/10.1145/3290605.3300489
12. Cha, M., Haddadi, H., Benevenuto, F., Gummadi, K.P.: Measuring user influence in twitter: The million follower fallacy. In: Fourth International AAAI Conference on Weblogs and Social Media (2010)
13. Cook, C., Conijn, R., Schaafsma, J., Antheunis, M.: For whom the gamer trolls: a study of trolling interactions in the online gaming context. J. Comput. Mediat. Commun. **24**(6), 293–318 (2019)
14. Crandall, D., Cosley, D., Huttenlocher, D., Kleinberg, J., Suri, S.: Feedback effects between similarity and social influence in online communities. In: Proceedings of the ACM SIGKDD International Conference on Knowledge Discovery and Data Mining, pp. 160–168 (2008). https://doi.org/10.1145/1401890.1401914
15. Crenshaw, N., Nardi, B.: What's in a name? Naming practices in online video games. In: Proceedings of the first ACM SIGCHI Annual Symposium on Computer-Human Interaction in Play, pp. 67–76 (2014)
16. Dabbish, L., Kraut, R., Patton, J.: Communication and commitment in an online game team. In: Proceedings of the SIGCHI Conference on Human Factors in Computing Systems, pp. 879–888 (2012)
17. Dabbish, L.A.: Jumpstarting relationships with online games: Evidence from a laboratory investigation. In: Proceedings of the ACM Conference on Computer Supported Cooperative Work, CSCW, pp. 353–356. ACM Press, New York, New York, USA (2008). https://doi.org/10.1145/1460563.1460620, http://portal.acm.org/citation.cfm?doid=1460563.1460620

18. De Kort, Y.A., Ijsselsteijn, W.A.: People, places, and play: player experience in a socio-spatial context. Comput. Entertain. (CIE) **6**(2), 1–11 (2008)
19. Deci, E.L., Ryan, R.M.: The "what" and "why" of goal pursuits: human needs and the self-determination of behavior. Psychol. Inq. **11**(4), 227–268 (2000)
20. Ducheneaut, N., Moore, R.J.: The social side of gaming: a study of interaction patterns in a massively multiplayer online game. In: Proceedings of the 2004 ACM conference on Computer supported cooperative work - CSCW 2004. ACM Press, New York, New York, USA (2004)
21. Ducheneaut, N., Moore, R.J., Nickell, E.: Virtual "third places": a case study of sociability in massively multiplayer games. Comput. Support. Cooper. Work **16**(1-2), 129–166 (5 2007). https://doi.org/10.1007/s10606-007-9041-8
22. Ducheneaut, N., Yee, N., Nickell, E., Moore, R.J.: "alone together?" exploring the social dynamics of massively multiplayer online games. In: Proceedings of the SIGCHI conference on Human Factors in computing systems, pp. 407–416 (2006)
23. Ducheneaut, N., Yee, N., Nickell, E., Moore, R.J.: The life and death of online gaming communities: A look at guilds in world of Warcraft. In: Conference on Human Factors in Computing Systems - Proceedings, pp. 839–848 (2007). https://doi.org/10.1145/1240624.1240750
24. Freeman, G.: Making games as collaborative social experiences: exploring an online gaming community. In: Proceedings of the ACM Conference on Computer Supported Cooperative Work, CSCW, vol. 26-February-2016, pp. 265–268. Association for Computing Machinery, New York, New York, USA (2016). https://doi.org/10.1145/2818052.2869076, http://dl.acm.org/citation.cfm?doid=2818052.2869076
25. Freeman, L.C.: Centrality in social networks conceptual clarification. Soc. Netw. **1**(3), 215–239 (1978). https://doi.org/10.1016/0378-8733(78)90021-7
26. Gong, W., Lim, E.P., Zhu, F.: Characterizing silent users in social media communities, pp. 140–149. AAAI Press (2015). https://www.aaai.org/ocs/index.php/ICWSM/ICWSM15/paper/view/10462
27. Goyal, A., Bonchi, F., Lakshmanan, L.V.: Learning influence probabilities in social networks. In: WSDM 2010 - Proceedings of the 3rd ACM International Conference on Web Search and Data Mining, pp. 241–250. ACM Press, New York, New York, USA (2010). https://doi.org/10.1145/1718487.1718518, http://portal.acm.org/citation.cfm?doid=1718487.1718518
28. Granovetter, M.: Economic Action and Social Structure: The Problem of Embeddedness. Am. J. Sociol. **91**, 481–510 (1985). https://doi.org/10.2307/2780199, https://www.jstor.org/stable/2780199
29. Han, J., Kamber, M., Pei, J.: Getting to know your data. In: Data Mining, pp. 39–82. Elsevier (2012). https://doi.org/10.1016/b978-0-12-381479-1.00002-2
30. Harris, J., Hancock, M.: To asymmetry and beyond! improving social connectedness by increasing designed interdependence in cooperative play. In: Proceedings of the 2019 CHI Conference on Human Factors in Computing Systems, pp. 1–12 (2019)
31. Huang, Y., Ye, W., Bennett, N., Contractor, N.S.: Functional or social? Exploring teams in online games. In: Proceedings of the ACM Conference on Computer Supported Cooperative Work, CSCW, pp. 399–408. ACM Press, New York, New York, USA (2013). https://doi.org/10.1145/2441776.2441822, http://dl.acm.org/citation.cfm?doid=2441776.2441822
32. Jiang, J., Yarosh, S.: Why do teammates hate me? Cross-cultural tensions and social dynamics in online games. In: Proceedings of the ACM Conference on Computer Supported Cooperative Work, CSCW, vol. 26-February-2016, pp. 301–304. Association for Computing Machinery, New York, New York, USA (2016). https://

doi.org/10.1145/2818052.2869087, http://dl.acm.org/citation.cfm?doid=2818052.2869087
33. Johannes, N., Vuorre, M., Przybylski, A.K.: Video game play is positively correlated with well-being. R. Soc. Open Sci. **8**, 202049 (2020)
34. Keller, E., Berry, J.: The Influentials: One American in Ten Tells the Other Nine How to Vote, Where to Eat, And What to Buy (2003)
35. Kim, Y.J., Engel, D., Woolley, A.W., Lin, J.Y.T., McArthur, N., Malone, T.W.: What makes a strong team? Using collective intelligence to predict team performance in League of Legends. In: Proceedings of the ACM Conference on Computer Supported Cooperative Work, CSCW, pp. 2316–2329. Association for Computing Machinery, New York, New York, USA (2017). https://doi.org/10.1145/2998181.2998185, http://dl.acm.org/citation.cfm?doid=2998181.2998185
36. Lee, K.M.: Presence, explicated. Commun. Theory **14**(1), 27–50 (2004)
37. Lin, D., Bezemer, C.P., Hassan, A.E.: An empirical study of early access games on the steam platform. Empir. Softw. Eng. **23**(2), 771–799 (2018)
38. Loria, E., Pirker, J., Drachen, A., Marconi, A.: Do Influencers Influence? - Analyzing Players' Activity in an Online Multiplayer Game (2020)
39. Mason, W., Clauset, A.: Friends FTW! Friendship and competition in halo: Reach. In: Proceedings of the 2013 Conference on Computer Supported Cooperative Work, pp. 375–386 (2013)
40. Mora-Cantallops, M., Sicilia, M.Á.: Player-centric networks in league of legends. Soc. Netw. **55**, 149–159 (2018)
41. Mora-Cantallops, M., Sicilia, M.Á.: Team efficiency and network structure: the case of professional league of legends. Soc. Netw. **58**, 105–115 (2019)
42. Neuhäuser, M.: Wilcoxon–Mann–Whitney Test, pp. 1656–1658. Springer, Heidelberg (2011). https://doi.org/10.1007/978-3-642-04898-2_615, https://doi.org/10.1007/978-3-642-04898-2_615
43. O'Neill, M., Vaziripour, E., Wu, J., Zappala, D.: Condensing steam: distilling the diversity of gamer behavior. In: Proceedings of the ACM SIGCOMM Internet Measurement Conference, IMC 14-16-November, pp. 81–95 (2016). https://doi.org/10.1145/2987443.2987489
44. Pirker, J., Rattinger, A., Drachen, A., Sifa, R.: Analyzing player networks in destiny. Entertain. Comput. **25**, 71–83 (2018)
45. Pirker, J., Rattinger, A., Drachen, A., Sifa, R.: Analyzing player networks in Destiny. Entertain. Comput. **25**, 71–83 (2018). https://doi.org/10.1016/j.entcom.2017.12.001
46. Przybylski, A.K., Rigby, C.S., Ryan, R.M.: A motivational model of video game engagement. Rev. Gen. Psychol. **14**(2), 154–166 (2010)
47. Rogers, R.: The motivational pull of video game feedback, rules, and social interaction: another self-determination theory approach. Comput. Hum. Behav. **73**, 446–450 (2017)
48. Rosenthal, S., Mckeown, K.: Detecting influencers in multiple online genres. ACM Trans. Internet Technol. **17**, 1–22 (2017). https://doi.org/10.1145/3014164
49. Ryan, R.M., Rigby, C.S., Przybylski, A.: The motivational pull of video games: a self-determination theory approach. Motiv. Emot. **30**(4), 344–360 (2006)
50. Saltz, J.S., Hiltz, S.R., Turoff, M.: Student social graphs. In: Proceedings of the 2004 ACM conference on Computer supported cooperative work - CSCW 2004. p. 596. Association for Computing Machinery (ACM), New York, New York, USA (2004). https://doi.org/10.1145/1031607.1031709, http://portal.acm.org/citation.cfm?doid=1031607.1031709

51. Santos, T., Lemmerich, F., Strohmaier, M., Helic, D.: What's in a review: discrepancies between expert and amateur reviews of video games on Metacritic. Proc. ACM Hum. Comput. Interact. **3**(CSCW), 1–22 (2019). https://doi.org/10.1145/3359242, https://dl.acm.org/doi/10.1145/3359242
52. Scripps, J., Tan, P.N., Esfahanian, A.H.: Measuring the effects of preprocessing decisions and network forces in dynamic network analysis. In: Proceedings of the ACM SIGKDD International Conference on Knowledge Discovery and Data Mining, pp. 747–755 (2009). https://doi.org/10.1145/1557019.1557102
53. Shen, C., Chen, W.: Gamers' confidants: massively multiplayer online game participation and core networks in China. Soc. Netw. **40**, 207–214 (2015)
54. Shi, X., Zhu, J., Cai, R., Zhang, L.: User grouping behavior in online forums. In: Proceedings of the ACM SIGKDD International Conference on Knowledge Discovery and Data Mining, pp. 777–785. ACM Press, New York, New York, USA (2009). https://doi.org/10.1145/1557019.1557105, http://portal.acm.org/citation.cfm?doid=1557019.1557105
55. Sifa, R., Drachen, A., Bauckhage, C.: Large-Scale Cross-Game Player Behavior Analysis on Steam. Technical report (2015). www.aaai.org
56. Subbian, K., Aggarwal, C.C., Srivastava, J.: Querying and tracking influencers in social streams. In: WSDM 2016 - Proceedings of the 9th ACM International Conference on Web Search and Data Mining, pp. 493–502. Association for Computing Machinery, Inc, New York, New York, USA (2016). https://doi.org/10.1145/2835776.2835788, http://dl.acm.org/citation.cfm?doid=2835776.2835788
57. Teng, C.I.: Managing gamer relationships to enhance online gamer loyalty: the perspectives of social capital theory and self-perception theory. Comput. Human Behav. **79**, 59–67 (2018). https://doi.org/10.1016/j.chb.2017.10.024
58. Wijman, T.: The Global Games Market Will Generate $152.1 Billion in 2019 as the U.S. Overtakes China as the Biggest Market (2019)
59. Wallner, G., et al.: Beyond the individual: understanding social structures of an online player matchmaking website. Entertain. Comput. **30**, 100284 (2019). https://doi.org/10.1016/j.entcom.2019.01.002
60. Watts Peter, D.J., Dodds, S.: Influentials, Networks, and Public Opinion Formation. Technical report (2007)
61. Williams, D., Ducheneaut, N., Xiong, L., Zhang, Y., Yee, N., Nickell, E.: From tree house to barracks: the social life of guilds in world of warcraft. Games Culture **1**(4), 338–361 (2006). https://doi.org/10.1177/1555412006292616
62. Xiang, R., Neville, J., Rogati, M.: Modeling relationship strength in online social networks. In: Proceedings of the 19th International Conference on World Wide Web, WWW 2010, pp. 981–990. ACM Press, New York, New York, USA (2010). https://doi.org/10.1145/1772690.1772790, http://portal.acm.org/citation.cfm?doid=1772690.1772790
63. Xu, Y., Cao, X., Sellen, A., Herbrich, R., Graepel, T.: Sociable killers: understanding social relationships in an online first-person shooter game. In: Proceedings of the ACM Conference on Computer Supported Cooperative Work, CSCW, pp. 197–206. ACM Press, New York, New York, USA (2011). https://doi.org/10.1145/1958824.1958854, http://portal.acm.org/citation.cfm?doid=1958824.1958854
64. Yang, C., Shi, X., Jie, L., Han, J.: I know you'll be back: interpretable new user clustering and churn prediction on a mobile social application. In: Proceedings of the 24th ACM SIGKDD International Conference on Knowledge Discovery & Data Mining, pp. 914–922. KDD 2018, Association for Computing Machinery, New York, NY, USA (2018). https://doi.org/10.1145/3219819.3219821

65. Yuan, S., Lou, C.: How social media influencers foster relationships with followers: the roles of source credibility and fairness in parasocial relationship and product interest. J. Interact. Adv. **30**, 1–42 (2020)
66. Zhu, M., Huang, Y., Contractor, N.S.: Motivations for self-assembling into project teams. Soc. Netw. **35**(2), 251–264 (2013)
67. Zuo, Z.: Sentiment Analysis of Steam Review Datasets using Naive Bayes and Decision Tree Classifier. Technical report (2018). https://analytics.twitter.com

A Framework for Explainable AI in Wargames to Understand Strategies

Christoph Lürig(✉) and Fabian Fell

University of Applied Science Trier, Trier, Germany
luerig@hochschule-trier.de, F.Fell@inf.hochschule-trier.de

Abstract. This paper describes a framework for explainable AI for chip and hex war games. We use this framework to discuss rule variations on the war game "Take That Hill." For this game, we discuss the basic version and the variation with low-light conditions and examine how the strategy should change. We also discuss a game variation where the only objective is to minimize hits. This version has no distinctive winning and losing, but distinguishes between varying degrees of losing. Here, we look at the impact of changing game rules on choosing the best strategy. We also use the framework for the strategy game Othello and other specific small games for testing purposes.

1 Introduction and Related Work

Game-playing AIs can roughly be divided into three approaches. The first approach directly maps the game situation or history to an action decision. The second type uses long-term situation evaluations as a decision basis, often called a value function. The third type uses a search tree to explore all combinations of what could happen in the near or far future.

Mapping a game history or situation to an action decision can be implemented as direct or indirect mapping. In the latter case, a situation and an action decision are mapped to the probability of choosing that action. In game theory, this is known as a mixed strategy (see Straffin [25]). In reinforcement learning, it is called a policy (see Sutton, Barto [27]). A mixed strategy can be beneficial in training an AI to address the exploration-exploitation dilemma (see Berger-Tal et al. [2]). Action decisions based on the game state history instead of the current game state are used, for instance, in Counterfactual Regret Minimization. (see Neller et al. [17]). This learning AI approach proved successful in games of imperfect information like poker. Direct mapping from history to action decision is also common in methods based on large language models (LLMs) (see Guo et al. [9]). Our framework here does not use this category and focuses exclusively on games of perfect information.

The second type uses an evaluation function of the situation that describes the long-term outcome perspective of the current situation. This method is used in classical board game AIs, such as the Shannon A strategy (see Shannon [23]), and in reinforcement learning, as seen in generalized policy iteration (see Liu et al. [13]). A popular variation of this reinforcement learning concept is q-learning (see Young et al. [11]).

If a value function is given, a strategy can immediately be derived by selecting the action that maximizes the expected value for the player. One popular way to turn this into a mixed strategy for reinforcement learning is to pick a random move with a certain probability. This is called the Epsilon greedy strategy (see Dann et al. [6]). Value functions typically assign +1 for a guaranteed win, 0 for a draw, and −1 for a guaranteed loss. In a two-person zero-sum game (e.g., chess), only one value function suffices for the game state.

We have introduced the value function as a central concept in our architecture. Since we want to cover non-zero-sum games (such as cooperative or semi-cooperative), we introduce one specific value function for each player. In addition, the game's outcome is not restricted to pure winning and losing but instead exists on a continuous spectrum. We can, therefore, express different degrees of winning and losing. We will address this feature in Sect. 3.2, where we formulate an objective to minimize the hits the primary player takes.

The third approach uses a search tree to explore future possibilities. This is the core of the original Shannon A strategy (see Shannon [23]). A well-known application in two zero-sum games is the Minimax Algorithm, where one player maximizes the final result and the second minimizes it (see Russel and Norvig [22]). Since we aim to accommodate more players and non-zero-sum games, we chose an implementation where every player maximizes their personal value function. As many war games contain one or several random elements, we use an extension of this algorithm that accounts for a specific chance player. This is the Expectminimax algorithm (see Ballard [1]).

In its purest form, a tree search algorithm explores a sequence of game states until the end of the game. The final game outcome is used as a basis for decision-making, propagating back through the tree to its root, where the current player's decision is made.

This exhaustive search is feasible only for trivial games. A complete tree expansion is impossible because of the combinatorial explosion of possible game states that may happen the further one looks into the future. At this point, the tree search algorithm is combined with the value function. Only a limited number of moves are being looked ahead into the future. When the game end is not reached till that point, the result of the value function is used instead.

As many game states appear in the search tree repeatedly (one game state can be reached over different sequences of moves), we implemented one popular acceleration technique called transposition tables (see Breuker et al. [3]). This technique stores evaluated game situations in a hash map.

One well-known example of board game AI is the Alpha-Zero algorithm (see Somers [24]). It combines all three approaches. As a tree searcher, it uses a Monte Carlo Tree Search (MCTS) algorithm (see Ciancarini and Favini [5]) and a dual-head deep convolutional network to model the value and policy function. We also experimented with MCTS but dropped it in favor of Expectminimax for performance reasons.

Most war games are played on a hexagonal grid. This poses additional challenges in representation compared to the classical chessboard structure. We implemented the structure suggested by Amit Patel (see [19]).

Modern AI, especially for neural networks, comes with the problem of interpretability (see Molnar [16]). Consequently, it becomes unclear for the human user why an AI has made a specific decision or, in the case of a learning AI, what exactly the AI has learned. Overall, one can distinguish between black box explanation approaches like Shapley values (see Sundararajan and Najimi [26]), Lime (see Ribeiro et al. [20]), and white box explainers like GAM (see Hastie and Tibshirani [10]). Black box explainers work independently of the underlying AI and generate explanations for specific decisions simply by probing the input-output behavior of the AI. On the other hand, white box explainers try to make the decision process and the learned result itself explainable. This has the advantage that a human can apply generated knowledge.

We follow the route of white box explanations. As a guideline, we use the generalized additive model - GAM (see Hastie and Tibshirani [10]). We want to build a linear combination of prefabricated heuristics to construct a value function. The weighting coefficients and the intercept of the linear model should be learned. We apply the learning by ridge regression (see McDonald [14]) that minimizes the L_2 norm of the weight vector because the constructed heuristics may eventually correlate. Microsoft's ML API implements ridge regression (see Microsoft [15]). This follows the general idea of a human constructing value functions for board game-playing AIs called handcrafted evaluations (see W. Frey [29]). If you have an interpretable strategy representation, you can compare the resulting best strategy with your design intention. In the case of a learning game, this may be the strategy you want the player to learn. In general, it may also pinpoint if there is a dominant strategy.

We learn the linear combination of the different models following a Monte Carlo-style approach (see Sutton, Barto [27]). In this approach, several games are played with a prefabricated test heuristic. The results of simulated games are then used as target values for the linear combination of all the different heuristic results. Experiments with other approaches like $TD(\lambda)$ (see Tesauro et al. [28]) have proven to be less successful. The reason is probably that the value function is combined with a tree search algorithm effectively making the learning strategy off-policy (see Fujimoto et al. [8]). The tree search algorithm changes the decision that would be made by directly applying the heuristics. Incorporating a tree search component, Alpha-Zero applies a similar Monte Carlo to learn the value function (see Somers [24]).

As test games, we used several small games to test the system's base functionality. These are the games Tic-Tac-Toe (see Karamchandani et al. [12]), a simple betting game, and a specific game to test the functionality of non-zero-sum games. In this game, four players can decide whether to give a fixed amount of money to the game master or not. The game master doubles the funds received and distributes them equally to all players. If everyone decided to give a fixed amount, the overall result would be best. This, however, is not the Nash Equilibrium of the game. In the Nash Equilibrium, no one gives money. The effect is known in economics as the tragedy of the commons (see Ostrom [18]). These games are discussed in Sect. 3. As a more complex game, we have added the strategy game Othello (see Buro [4]), which we will discuss in Sect. 3.1. As a real war game, we implemented "Take That Hill" (see Flanagan et al. [7]), which we will discuss in Sect. 3.2. Using the example of "Take That Hill", we will also show how rule changes in the game influence the resulting learned strategy.

The remainder of the paper is structured as follows. First, we will discuss the overall structure of the framework in Sect. 2. Afterward, we will discuss the various sample games in Sect. 3. We will conclude the paper by summarizing thoughts and extension possibilities for the future in Sect. 4.

2 Description of the Framework

The framework is made open source under MIT license. It is available at https://github.com/Carbonfreezer/WargameExplain.

The overall strategy to implement an explainable AI in the framework is to provide the game logic and map at which point decisions are made. Decisions can either be made randomly or intentionally by a player. If decisions are made randomly, the probability of each decision must be given. Decision options are modeled as commands. Commands have an execute and an undo operation to backtrack the decision tree in the expectminimax algorithm. The commands are derivations of the *ICommand* interface. A class implementing the *IManipulator* interface provides possible commands for systematic or random choices. For the systematic case, it also includes information on which players turn it is.

The game state modified by the commands should implement the *IHashableGameState* interface. This provides a hashing function required for the transposition table mentioned in Sect. 1.

An initial heuristic must be provided for the training system to play the game reasonably well with a limited search depth. The heuristics are generated by deriving from the *TrainableEvaluator* class. Each heuristic must be derived from *GameStateObserver* for the hand-crafted heuristics fed into the linear model. Game observations can be generated in different formats. For every game, an implementation of *IGameOutcomeClassifier* is needed. This is required to display the final statistics of the game, where every possible outcome must be described.

Everything is bundled for a game by implementing a derivation of *TrainingInfoProvider*. This class lists game state observers and the game outcome classifier. Furthermore, it has a method that generates a strategic decider, representing the Expectiminimax algorithm. This method encapsulates the game state, the manipulator, and the trainable evaluator. The best way to implement this method is to look at the implementation of the sample games.

The property *BatchSize* of *TrainingInfoProvider* contains the number of games to be simulated for training and evaluation. In contrast to usual machine learning approaches, we do not train over several epochs. Applying several epochs has not proven helpful during our experiments with several games. We made similar observations with the epsilon value in the epsilon-greedy strategy, which we explained in Sect. 1. The epsilon value is specified with the value of *Epsilon-Training*. As a base estimate, we found a value of 0.3 to be helpful. It is significantly higher than epsilon values used in deep reinforcement learning, usually not higher than 0.1. The hyperparameters for hash granularity and, most importantly, search depth are also contained in the method *GetFreshGame*. The higher the search depth, the stronger the AI becomes, but computation-wise, it is more expensive. Adjusting the hash granularity is a bit fiddly. Uncommenting the line in the method *GetSmartMove* of the class *StrategicDecider* may help.

The overall solution is divided into four projects. The project *WargameExplainer* contains the bulk of the code. The project *DirectApplication* is the basis for an application running on a single CPU. The projects *Client* and *Server* are used to parallelize training and testing over several CPUs and computers. If you want to use this, the core entry point is the class *GlobalNetworkConstants* in the *Utils* namespace. The first parallelization experiments were conducted with the task parallel library in C#, quickly resulting in a strangled scaling effect. Due to the nature of the tree search algorithms, garbage collections within C# can not be avoided. A garbage collection blocks all program threads. Therefore, we opted to parallelize several processes, which has the benefit of allowing them to be distributed over several PCs.

After discussing the implementation, we will continue with several application cases in the following sections.

3 Test Training and Results for Games

First, we tested the correctness of the framework by implementing several miniature games that made tracking decision-making easy. The first game we tried was Tic-Tac-Toe. Because this game is straightforward, no accurate heuristics are needed; the complete tree can easily be analyzed. We artificially limited the search depth to three half moves. As base heuristics, we counted the occupied center point, the four corner points, and the side points. The result was as expected: The center point was the highest priority, followed by the corner and side points, with the lowest priority.

As a second game, we implemented a simple betting game. In this game, the player has to place bets on outcome $1, 2, 3$ with different success probabilities. The player wins if they have placed three bets correctly and loses after 10 bets without winning. The likelihood of success for each outcome is unknown to the AI. The core heuristic of the AI is the chosen betting outcome. After playing 1000 games, the trained heuristic ranked the betting outcome correctly according to their success probability.

The third game is a semi-cooperative game described in Sect. 1, where players may choose to give money to a central moderator who doubles that amount and distributes it equally amongst players. In our game, we decided to go with three players. The result converged to the known Nash equilibrium, which is to opt to give no money. The next step was adding a voting command, where everyone could vote to make giving money obligatory. If and only if everyone votes for that rule, everyone has to provide money afterward. As expected, everyone voted for the rule.

As a more complex game, we will analyze Othello in Sect. 3.1 and as a real war game, "Take That Hill" in Sect. 3.2.

3.1 Test Training and Results for Othello

Othello is a two-person strategic game played on an 8×8 board, where the two players, black and white, place stones alternately and flip all opponent stones they engulf to their side. The player with the most stones on the board wins at the end of the game. For details, see Buro [4].

Several training experiments with Othello were executed. The best parameter constellations did not apply L_2 regularization and had a training batch size of 10000. Interestingly, the AI's performance degenerated when increasing the batch size to 100000. The training was done with a search depth of five moves.

We experimented with two sets of heuristics, where linear coefficients were estimated in the training. Both sets used a mobility index that describes the relative movement options a player has as

$$mobility = \frac{numOfBlackMoves - numOfWhiteMoves}{numOfBlackMoves + numOfWhiteMoves} \quad (1)$$

The other components were simply the number of diagonal fields, border fields, and other fields occupied.

The two heuristic setups differ in how they account for different stone colors. The first setup explicitly distinguishes between opponent and player stones, and the second setup accounts for the difference between player and opponent stones. In the following, the first model is referred to as the unbalanced model, while the second model is called a balanced model. We compared the unbalanced model against the balanced one.

The coefficients and their interpretation of the unbalanced model are shown in Table 1. Here, the intercept of the model, which is the constant term, favors the white and, therefore, the second player in this game. This corresponds to the game's known experience, which gives the second player an advantage. The values show that the diagonal elements with offset zero and the mobility difference have a significant impact. The first ones are the cornerstones of the gameboard that can never be flipped once occupied. Also significant is the mobility difference, which expresses how many movement options the black player has compared to the white player. The bulk part of the gameboard is made of the inner points. Even though having the most stones on the board is the winning criterion, in the end, they have a very low priority score-wise. This corresponds to the nature of the game, where the number of stones a player owns is determined very much at the end of the game. The constellation and positions controlled are of much higher importance.

Table 1. Interpretation of values for Othello unbalanced.

Interpretation	Black player	White player
Intercept	−0,7828636	0,7860116
Impact of diagonal elements with offset 0 set by black	0.29304653	−0.2857503
Impact of diagonal elements with offset 1 set by black	−0.0010227695	−0.0022131465
Impact of diagonal elements with offset 0 set by white	−0.24195403	0.25596195
Impact of diagonal elements with offset 1 set by white	−0.027541136	0.0111962315
Impact of side elements with offset 1 set by black	0.010052991	−0.036614332
Impact of side elements with offset 2 set by black	0.011931904	−0.011564356
Impact of side elements with offset 3 set by black	0.008866319	−0.008108349
Impact of side elements with offset 1 set by white	0.004811865	−0.004070661
Impact of side elements with offset 2 set by white	−0.019461896	0.013374249
Impact of side elements with offset 3 set by pwhite	0.0017262073	0.0052602706
Impact of inner points set by black	0.001932246	−0.0024048374
Impact of inner points set by white	0.004289859	−0.0048177205
Impact of mobility difference (Eq. 1)	1.2555468	−1.217286

The Table 1 leads to the balanced model, which should be much more straightforward. The balanced model only examines the relation between player and opponent stones in different board positions. The value result is shown in Table 2. The balanced values are, as the mobility difference, always seen from the perspective of the black player. This looks a lot more compact and is easier to interpret. Here, Mobility and corner elements play the most dominant role. Additionally, one wants to control the four central points of the four outer lines of the board. The intercept, however, contradicts common experience, where the white player has a systematic advantage in the game. Occupied inner positions play again a minor role in the game.

Table 2. Interpretation of values for Othello balanced.

Interpretation	Black player	White player
Intercept	0.12915835	−0,058241922
Impact of diagonal elements with offset 0	0.48213902	−0.48581463
Impact of diagonal elements with offset 1	0.0072977156	0.001978707
Impact of side elements with offset 1	0.011089099	−0.019996965
Impact of side elements with offset 2	0.05062658	−0.053781375
Impact of side elements with offset 3	0.048740327	−0.035325244
Impact of inner points	−0.00086431945	−0.000503299
Impact of mobility difference (Eq. 1)	1.0427037	−1.0327953

If we pitch the two models against each other over 100 games, the result is shown in Table 3. Even though white has a systematic advantage, the unbalanced mode outperforms the balanced one. This shows the fundamental problem: interpretability usually contradicts fidelity.

Table 3. Othello pitching balanced against unbalanced.

The player using balanced mode	Black wins	White wins
Black	37	63
White	55	45

3.2 Test Training and Results for Take That Hill

As a second, more complex game, which is also a real war game, we have used "Take That Hill." In this game, the first party tries to take the hill, and the second tries to defend it.

The first party has three sections that can move or lay suppressive fire. In both cases, it becomes depleted, meaning it can not perform any more actions. Having moved and or fired, it can make a rally attempt so the section can act again in the next round. The probability of success of the rally attempt depends on the distance to the headquarters, which is the fourth unit of the first player. If none of the suppressive fire attempts are successful, the defender can lay suppressive fire to deplete one or two of the three sections of the first player. This disables the sections of the first player. One round of the game is the move of the first party and the defender combined.

Per game rule, the first party wins if the sum of rounds passed and shots taken is below 11. It is a draw if it is below 16; otherwise, the second player has won. The success probabilities of the suppressive fire and the rally attempts depend on the distance between the different units. As is common in war games, the outcome of those situations is determined by rolling the dice.

There exists a standard behavior for the defending party. Thus, the game is effectively turned into a solitaire game. During the execution of the game, we have defined that the AI must make all firing decisions for all sections before they are executed. This means that the AI cannot observe the success of a firing round in one section before deciding on the next one. Details of the game can be found in Flanagan et al. [7].

We trained the game with a search depth of 35 moves and let it play 3000 games. No L_2 regularization was applied. We have used the total score, the number of shots taken, plus the number of game rounds passed as a heuristic. This value is also the decision criterion for game success. Additionally, we are evaluating the distance of a selection to the defender's position. Here, we take the first, second, and third sections closest to the defender's position. The resulting values are shown in Table 4. The intercept shows that the game can be won principally.

One can see that the AI will minimize the distance to the defender primarily of the two sections that are closest to the defender's position. Getting one step ahead here is about 2.6 times as crucial as not getting a hit or not spending one extra game round. The section on position three is of less importance. Consequently, the best mid-term objective is aggressively moving forward with two sections and keeping the third section behind. Statistics for 1000 played games by this AI are shown in the first row of Table 5.

Table 4. Interpretation of values for Take That Hill

Interpretation	Value
Intercept	1.3847562
Shots taken and game rounds passed	−0.08906191
Distance of section being 1. closest to defender	−0.21686795
Distance of section being 2. closest to defender	−0.184014
Distance of section being 3. closest to defender	−0.06412778

Table 5. Game results of Take That Hill.

Game Mode	Lost	Draw	Won
Normal	96	408	496
Night Mode	263	419	318

As one of the rule extensions, we have implemented night mode. In night mode, all success probabilities of the defender and the offender are reduced. This reduction is eliminated if the fighting area is illuminated. Both the defender and the player make one decision when they want to illuminate. The player has to decide which round to illuminate upfront. The learned value of this setup is shown in Table 6. This table shows that calling for illumination in round three is paramount. The distance priorities are a bit more challenging to interpret here. The distance of the section furthest away has the highest priority, followed by the first section. The distance of the second section is of the lowest importance. Pragmatically, we should be much more coherent in advancing the sections and leaving none behind, in contrast to the day conditions. In both setups advancing with the section of highest priority is around 2.6 times as important as not taking a hit or advancing one round. Consequently, the advancing strategy is, in both cases, of the same importance. As one can see in the second line of Table 5, the situation is less favorable for the player than in the day mode of the game.

As a subsequent experiment, we modified the game rules using the fact that we can also represent the game outcome continuously on the spectrum between

Table 6. Interpretation of values for Take That Hill in night mode

Interpretation	Value
Intercept	0.63832074
Shots taken and game rounds passed	−0.061712813
Distance of section being 1. closest to the defender	−0.12388183
Distance of section being 2. closest to the defender	−0.014226002
Distance of section being 3. closest to the defender	−0.16839197
Player illuminated in round 1	−0.3862518
Player illuminated in round 2	−0.27759394
Player illuminated in round 3	1.1690072
Player illuminated in round 4	−0.12702845
Player illuminated in round 5	−0.20842342
Player illuminated in round 6	−0.06993597
Player illuminated in round 7	−0.13163047
Player illuminated in round 8	−0.20081797
Player illuminated in round 9	−0.10003447
Player illuminated in round 10	−0.011466952

winning and losing. We took the game round counter out and defined the game outcome as

$$outcome = \begin{cases} -numOfHitsTaken/10 & ; if numOfHitsTaken < 10 \\ -1.0 & ; else \end{cases} \quad (2)$$

where on ten hits taken, the game ends. This means that winning the game is not possible, only varying degrees of losing. In other words, the objective of this new game is to take the hill with as few casualties as possible, no matter how long it takes.

We have implemented two sets of heuristics for that game. The first set is a straightforward adaptation of the Table 4. The only difference is that we have taken the rounds that have passed out of the total score and only counted the hits that were taken. In the second version, we have also considered the number of game rounds passed as an additional heuristic. The first version takes an average of 3.46 hits per game; the second version is 3.32. The distribution of the hits taken in both versions is shown in Fig. 1. The increase in values for 10 hits taken is probably because we stop counting at 10 and terminate the game.

The learned coefficients are shown in Table 7. Version 1 follows the same system as the plain "Take That Hill" in day mode. The two front-runner sections are almost equally important, with the third being of lower priority. Compared to the plain version, the number of shots taken has a higher priority than the advancement of the sections, compared to the vanilla version.

Things become interesting when the game rounds are also considered in version 2. The last three lines of the table, which describe the priority of minimizing

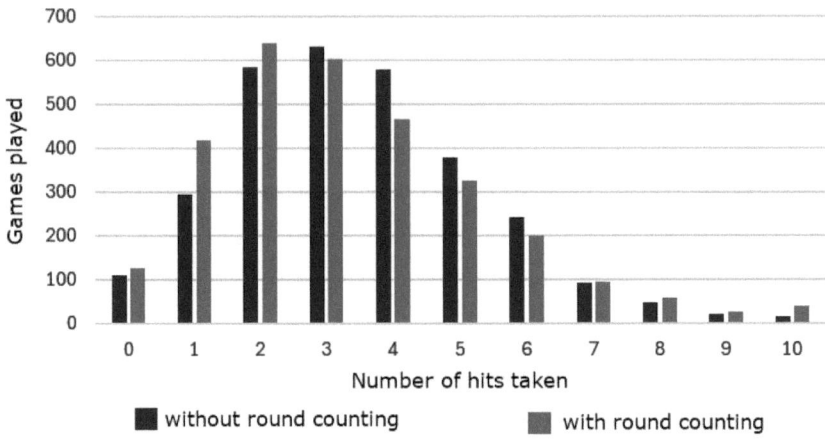

Fig. 1. Distribution of shots taken in Take That Hill

Table 7. Interpretation for minimization of shots taken.

Interpretation	Version 1	Version 2
Intercept	0.1142904	−0.12225201
Game rounds passed	NA	0.014807281
Shots taken	−0.0929067	-0.09261059
Distance of section being 1. closest to the defender	−0.08532018	−0.0725422
Distance of section being 2. closest to the defender	−0.06707226	−0.002108443
Distance of section being 3. closest to the defender	−0.026316732	−0.050867956

distance, show almost the same pattern as in the night mode of Take That Hill. We still prioritize the front runner, but position 3 comes in second. This means we would want a front-runner, but the third position should be relatively close to it, with the second position somewhere in between. The additional game round becomes a positive coefficient, meaning the AI tries to maximize the number of game rounds passed. On the other hand, it still has a higher coefficient for reducing the distance, so it just reduces the higher advancement speed.

Changing the game objective slightly affects the applied strategy significantly. It can be used to balance strategy games and find the correct rules for the intended gameplay. In the example of "Take That Hill" the best strategy in the standard game for normal conditions is to advance almost equally with the two front sections and leave the third one behind. If this was the design intention of the game, it is pretty much hit straight on. Changing the rules or game objectives only slightly changes this significantly.

For a practical application, getting the optimization objective right is critical and known as the King Midas problem in AI (see Russell [21]).

4 Summary and Future Work

This paper has discussed a framework for explainable AI for war or round-based tabletop games. The framework combines the Expectminimax algorithm with a value function representing a linear combination of manually prefabricated heuristics. The coefficients are learned in Monte Carlo style and may be regularized by an L_2 term, which was not used much in practical applications.

We mainly applied the framework to Othello and Take That Hill. We tried different rule variations for the last game and observed the outcome. The learning results are interpretable, but as with most explainable AI techniques, one needs to understand the subject domain and the inner workings of the explanation method.

If you use this as a tool in the game's development, the impact of changes in game rules on the optimal strategy can be observed and explained.

What is missing from war games, in general, is the introduction of game cards and hidden information. Both components will significantly increase the search space, meaning unique solutions must be found for these cases.

References

1. Ballard, B.W.: The *-minimax search procedure for trees containing chance nodes. Artif. Intell. **21**(3), 327–350 (1983). https://doi.org/10.1016/S0004-3702(83)80015-0
2. Berger-Tal, O., Nathan, J., Meron, E., Saltz, D.: The exploration-exploitation dilemma: a multidisciplinary framework. PLoS ONE **9**(4), e95693 (2014). https://doi.org/10.1371/journal.pone.0095693
3. Breuker, D.M., Uiterwijk, J.W.: Transposition tables in computer chess. University of Limburg, Department of Computer Science (2002)
4. Buro, M.: The evolution of strong Othello programs. Entertainment Comput. Technol. Appl. 81–88 (2003)
5. Ciancarini, P., Favini, G.P.: Monte Carlo tree search in Kriegspiel. Artif. Intell. **174**(11), 670–684 (2010)
6. Dann, C., Mansour, Y., Mohri, M., Sekhari, A., Sridharan, K.: Guarantees for epsilon-greedy reinforcement learning with function approximation. In: International Conference on Machine Learning, pp. 4666–4689. PMLR (2022)
7. Flanagan, M., Northey, A., Robinson, I.: Exploring tactical choices and game design outcomes in a simple wargame 'take that hill' by a systematic approach using experimental design. Int. J. Serious Games **7**(4), 27–50 (2020)
8. Fujimoto, S., Meger, D., Precup, D.: Off-policy deep reinforcement learning without exploration. In: International Conference on Machine Learning, pp. 2052–2062. PMLR (2019)
9. Guo, H., Liu, Z., Zhang, Y., Wang, Z.: Can large language models play games? a case study of a self-play approach. arXiv preprint arXiv:2403.05632 (2024)
10. Hastie, T., Tibshirani, R.: Generalized additive models; some applications. In: Generalized Linear Models: Proceedings of the GLIM 85 Conference held at Lancaster, UK, Sept. 16–19, 1985, pp. 66–81. Springer (1985)
11. Jang, B., Kim, M., Harerimana, G., Kim, J.W.: Q-learning algorithms: a comprehensive classification and applications. IEEE Access **7**, 133653–133667 (2019)

12. Karamchandani, S., Gandhi, P., Pawar, O., Pawaskar, S.: A simple algorithm for designing an artificial intelligence based tic tac toe game. In: 2015 International Conference on Pervasive Computing (ICPC), pp. 1–4 (2015).https://doi.org/10.1109/PERVASIVE.2015.7087182
13. Liu, D., Wei, Q., Yan, P.: Generalized policy iteration adaptive dynamic programming for discrete-time nonlinear systems. IEEE Trans. Syst. Man Cybern. Syst. **45**(12), 1577–1591 (2015)
14. McDonald, G.C.: Ridge regression. Wiley Interdisc. Rev. Comput. Stat. **1**(1), 93–100 (2009)
15. Microsoft: Microsoft ml (2025). https://dotnet.microsoft.com/en-us/apps/ai/ml-dotnet. Accessed 9 Feb 2025
16. Molnar, C.: Interpretable Machine Learning. Lulu. com, Morrisville (2020)
17. Zaïane, O.R., Zilles, S. (eds.): AI 2013. LNCS (LNAI), vol. 7884. Springer, Heidelberg (2013). https://doi.org/10.1007/978-3-642-38457-8
18. Ostrom, E.: Tragedy of the commons. New Palgrave Dictionary Econ. **2**, 1–4 (2008)
19. Petal, A.: Hexagonal grids (2024). https://www.redblobgames.com/grids/hexagons/. Accessed 9 Feb 2025
20. Ribeiro, M.T., Singh, S., Guestrin, C.: Model-agnostic interpretability of machine learning. arXiv preprint arXiv:1606.05386 (2016)
21. Russell, S.: Human-Compatible Artificial Intelligence (2022)
22. Russell, S.J., Norvig, P.: Artificial Intelligence: A Modern Approach. Pearson, Hoboken (2021)
23. Shannon, C.E.: Xxii. programming a computer for playing chess. Lond. Edinb. Dublin Philo. Mag. J. Sci. **41**(314), 256–275 (1950)
24. Somers, J.: How the artificial-intelligence program AlphaZero mastered its games. New Yorker **3** (2018)
25. Straffin, P.D.: Game Theory and Strategy, vol. 36. MAA, Indiranagar (1993)
26. Sundararajan, M., Najmi, A.: The many Shapley values for model explanation. In: International Conference on Machine Learning, pp. 9269–9278. PMLR (2020)
27. Sutton, R.S., Barto, A.G.: Reinforcement Learning: An Introduction. MIT Press, Cambridge (2020)
28. Tesauro, G., et al.: Temporal difference learning and td-gammon. Commun. ACM **38**(3), 58–68 (1995)
29. Frey, P.W.: An empirical technique for developing evaluation functions. ICCA **8**(1) (1985)

Parablade: A Proposal of Chambara Based on Augmented Sports - A Study of Appropriate Game Balancing Methods

Naoto Nishida[✉], Yusaku Maeda, Kamui Sato, Sho Sakurai, Koichi Hirota, and Takuya Nojima

The University of Electro-Communications, Tokyo, Japan
{naoto.nishida,maeda_yusaku,Sato_Kamui,sho,
hirota}@vogue.is.uec.ac.jp, tnojima@nojilab.org

Abstract. Augmented Sports is a new type of sport that combines existing physical sports with virtual parameters (VPs), which are commonly used in video games. Integrating VPs has great potential to improve players' performance in playing sports. Therefore, a sophisticated VPs design is necessary to achieve enjoyable Augmented Sports. In this study, we developed a new Augmented Sport called "Parablade," an extension of Chambara. In this paper, we introduce the details of Parablade and propose a novel method of designing VPs to achieve an appropriate game balance.

Keyword: Game Design · Video Game · Augmented Sports · Superhuman Sports

1 Introduction

Physical activity contributes to improving physical and mental health [1, 2]. However, staying physically active can be challenging for individuals with disabilities or age-related declines, limiting their ability to engage in sports and other physical activities. To address this issue, new sports have been developed to promote broader participation, such as para sports, adapted sports [3] and superhuman sports [4]. Augmented Sports [5] is a novel approach designed to tackle this issue. It is based on traditional sports but incorporates virtual parameters (VPs) to enhance accessibility and balance. In para sports, blind football is played with all players wearing blindfolds to equalize visual ability, but it means players cannot make use of any remaining vision. In contrast, Augmented Sports dose not limit but enhance each player's remaining ability by using VPs.

VPs are parameters commonly used in video games to represent various player attributes, such as attack power, and defense. They are designed to virtually enhance a player's abilities in Augmented Sports. For example, if a player has a higher attack power value in VPs, it could make them better at attacking their opponent. VPs are simple numerical values that can be used to adjust a player's innate playing abilities. However, improper adjustments can disrupt the balance of the game, potentially leading to one-sided gameplay. In our previous study on Augmented Dodgeball [5], which is a dodgeball modified to become an Augmented Sports, our findings suggest that it can promote cooperation within a team and provide enjoyment regardless of their original physical abilities. Unfortunately, Augmented Dodgeball is merely a single case study demonstrating the effect of Augmented Sports. Therefore, to demonstrate the generality of it, we planned to apply its concept to other sports to further validate its potential.

In this research, we have developed a new Augmented Sport called Parablade [6], a Chambara-based Augmented Sport that incorporates swordplay. Chambara is a sword sport primarily played in Japan. Two players earn points by striking each other's body with imitation swords. Unfortunately, Chambara relies heavily on the physical abilities of its players. To create an environment where everyone can participate and enjoy the game, it is essential to overcome hurdles arising from factors such as physical advantages and disadvantages, experience levels, and individual physical differences, challenges that the Augmented Sports concept could help address. However, as mentioned earlier, an appropriate VP design is essential for achieving this goal. Achieving appropriate VP configurations requires effective adjustment and maintenance of game balance. Previous research has attempted to optimize VP settings through game simulations [6]. However, discrepancies between simulation and actual gameplay remain, indicating that game balance is not consistently achieved. Therefore, a reliable method for VP-based game balance adjustment has yet to be established, posing a key challenge for the advancement of Augmented Sports. In this paper, we present the overall design of Parablade, propose a novel VP design method to bridge the gap between simulations and real matches, and evaluate its effectiveness through empirical analysis.

2 Related Work

2.1 New Sports to Promote Broader Participation

Removing barriers of sports participation, especially those caused by physical limitations, remains an important challenge. In response, various inclusive sports have been developed, such as adapted sports [3], which modify rules to enable individuals with and without disabilities to compete together. For example, in rugby, the rules are modified to allow players with disabilities to move using wheelchairs during matches. A similar sport, Sports Chambara [7], a kind of Chambara, has gained popularity by using soft, safe swords, making it accessible to people of all ages and genders. Since the 2010s, technology-driven sports have emerged. For instance, Ando et al. [8] developed a wheelchair-based device that enables inclusive play regardless of lower-limb impairments. AR-based sports have also been proposed, as seen in HADO [9] and VRabl [10], in which players wear AR goggles and compete by throwing virtual objects in augmented spaces. These innovations reduce the impact of physical differences, enhancing enjoyment and participation. Chambara has also incorporated digital technology, as exemplified by SASSEN [11], which integrates pressure sensors and LEDs into swords, enabling real-time feedback and immersive effects through smartphone connectivity.

While these sports expand participation opportunities, achieving a truly inclusive environment requires sports that adapt to individual physical abilities. Augmented Sports address this need by using VPs to flexibly and precisely adjust players' capabilities. Consequently, Augmented Sports-based games offer distinctive advantages over the sports mentioned above.

2.2 Balancing in Games

In digital games, proper game balance is important to ensure users can enjoy the experience. To achieve this, Gonçalves et al. [12] proposed a design space that can reduce the skill gap between players in video games. Also, typically, game balance is refined through repeated human playtests [13]. In contrast, many studies have explored automating this process to reduce the costs associated with manual playtesting. For example, it is possible to efficiently optimize game balance by generating AI agents trained on gameplay data and conducting automated playtesting [14, 15]. However, both methods require large volumes of gameplay data, making them difficult to apply to games involving high-intensity physical activity, where data collection is inherently limited.

To address this issue, this study proposes a method for developing Augmented Sports that combines simulation with a limited number of physical playtests. Real-world data from these tests is iteratively fed back into the simulation. By minimizing resource usage and narrowing the gap between simulation and reality, this feedback-based mechanism aims to achieve optimal game balance.

3 Basic Rule Design of Parablade

Parablade is a one-on-one competitive game that extends traditional Chambara based on the concept of Augmented Sports (Fig. 1). Players use dedicated swords to aim and physically attack their opponent's body. The game is designed to be played in a flat and open area. This sport incorporates four types of Virtual Parameters (VPs): Hit Point (HP), Attack Point (ATK), Defense Point (DEF), and Agility Point (AGI). In the gameplay sequence, players first distribute their initially assigned Status Points (SP) among the VPs to customize their abilities in terms of ATK, DEF, and AGI. Then, one of three character types is determined based on the allocated VPs, helping players easily understand the characteristics of their VPs and assisting in formulating strategies. Next, players engage in matches, attacking each other until one player's HP reaches zero. This chapter explains the details of VPs, SP, character types, and damage rules.

3.1 Virtual Parameters (VPs)

Parablade incorporates four types of VPs: Hit Point (HP), Attack Point (ATK), Defense Point (DEF), and Agility Point (AGI). HP reflects the damage taken and can be adjusted to regulate match duration, preventing excessive fatigue. ATK represents attack power, affecting the level of damage dealt per hit. DEF reduces incoming damage, enabling players with limited mobility to compete more fairly. Different DEF values are assigned to torso, arms, and legs to enhance accessibility. AGI controls a player's speed and

Fig. 1. The concept image of Parablade.

introducing a cool time, a brief period during with no damage is provided even a hit occurs, to prevent excessive consecutive attacks. By limiting continuous rapid attacks, AGI encourages strategic engagement, promoting a more balanced match experience.

3.2 Status Point (SP)

In Augmented Dodgeball [5], players selected from predefined VP sets, limiting their ability to customize and fine-tune their attributes. In contrast, Parablade introduces a system where players can freely adjust their VP allocation using SP, offering greater flexibility and enhancing the experience of personalizing their abilities. Before the match begins, players are given SP that they can freely allocate to three VPs: ATK, DEF, and AGI, to customize their abilities. HP is excluded from SP allocation because it regulates match duration. The introduction of SP allows players to tailor their abilities to match their playstyle. While free SP distribution provides greater flexibility in character customization, it also introduces complexity in strategic decision-making.

3.3 Character Types and Type Matchup

To help players understand their VP characteristics modified by SP distribution and formulate strategies, one balanced character type and three character types are defined based on the relative values of ATK, DEF, and AGI. If all three values are equal, the player is classified as a Balance Type. Otherwise, the highest value determines the type: a player is classified as an Attack Type when ATK is the highest, a Defense Type when DEF is the highest, and a Speed Type when AGI is the highest. Under this condition, it is essential to ensure that no single SP allocation pattern is inherently superior to all others simply by assigning all SP to a specific parameter. For example, excessive allocation of SP to ATK could make the Attack Type overly dominant, which could create an imbalance, disrupting competitive fairness and reducing diversity.

Therefore, in Parablade, a "type matchup" system is introduced to maintain game balance and prevent game disruption caused by extreme SP allocation. To address this issue, a rock-paper-scissors relationship is implemented: Attack Type, with excessive ATK allocation, beats Speed Type, which has excessive AGI allocation; similarly, Speed Type beats Defense Type, and Defense Type beats Attack Type. This intuitive balance promotes strategic decision-making while remaining easy to understand. Conceptually, there are only two possible type matchup hierarchy: A (Attack Type) → S (Speed Type)

→ D (Defense Type) → A or A → D → S → A, where "A → S" indicates that "A beats S". Based on findings from Augmented Dodgeball [5], we selected A → S → D → A hierarchy as mentioned before, ensuring that the Defense Type is stronger than the Attack Type. In our previous study, players with greater confidence in their physical abilities tended to choose high-attack VP values, whereas those with lower confidence preferred high-defense VP values. A similar tendency is expected in Parablade, so the matchup balance was designed to provide players with lower physical confidence a greater chance to compete effectively and enjoy the game.

3.4 Damage

In a match, the damage $D(0 \leq D)$ received when hit by an opponent is determined using Eq. (1). The base damage D_{prim} (Eq. (2)) is calculated as the sum of the fixed value of 15 and 20% of the opponent's ATK (P_{ATK}, where $0 \leq P_{ATK} \leq 100$). The fixed value ensures that a minimum amount of damage is always inflicted, even when $P_{ATK} = 0$, preventing matches from stagnating. Then, to avoid excessive damage outputs, the ATK value is scaled down to 20% before being incorporated into the final damage calculation. However, these numerical values are provisional and may require further adjustment. The damage reduction rate D_{eff} (defined in Eq. (3)) determines how much incoming damage is mitigated. To prevent complete damage nullification, P_{DEF} is capped at 90 ($0 \leq P_{DEF} \leq 90$). Additionally, the system is designed to incorporate the strike intensity (p), measured by pressure sensors embedded in the sword, which is currently disabled and fixed at one ($p = 1$). The body part damage multiplier db_{body} ($db_{body} = \{0.9, 1, 1.5\}$) adjusts damage based on the hit location. Unlike traditional Chambara, where scoring is uniform, real combat suggests that areas closer to the heart are more vulnerable. To reflect this, Parablade assigns damage multipliers in the following order: torso (1.5) > arms (1.0) > legs (0.9). These values were determined from preliminary research, using the arm—the most frequently targeted area—as the baseline (1.0). This design introduces a new strategic element, encouraging players to select their attack targets carefully, enhancing both competitiveness and enjoyment. The damage multiplier of the type matchup db_{type} ($1 \leq db_{type} \leq 2$) adjusts damage based on character type matchup hierarchy. When a stronger character type attacks a weaker character, db_{type} is set to 1.5 to increase the damage. In the reverse scenario, db_{type} remains 1. This value was provisionally determined to maintain balance and prevent stronger types from becoming overly dominant. Finally, after calculating damage D based on Eq. (1), it is applied to the player's $HP(0 \leq HP)$. The player's HP is updated using Eq. (4), where HP_{before} represents HP before the strike and HP_{after} represents HP after the strike.

$$D = D_{prim} \times D_{eff} \times p \times db_{body} \times db_{type} \tag{1}$$

$$D_{prim} = 15 + \frac{P_{ATK}}{5} \tag{2}$$

$$D_{eff} = 1 - \frac{P_{DEF}}{100} \tag{3}$$

$$HP_{after} = HP_{before} - D \tag{4}$$

3.5 Conversion from AGI to Cool Time

AGI, a parameter commonly used in video games to represent players' quickness, is converted into cool time to adapt this concept to real-world Chambara. Cool time introduces a period after each hit during which damage value is nullified, regardless of actual hit. As a result, it prevents consecutive hits, ensuring controlled attack pacing and limiting rapid successive strikes. The duration of cool time is determined according to the AGI value. Let P_{AGI} ($0 \leq P_{AGI} \leq 100$) be the AGI parameter value and CT ($0 \leq CT \leq 1.5$) be the cool time measured in seconds. The relationship between these parameters is defined by Eq. (5).

$$CT = 1.5\left(1 - \frac{P_{AGI}}{100}\right) \quad (5)$$

4 Proposal of Appropriate Game Balancing Methods

This study defines a type matchup system in which the three character types, Attack Type, Defense Type, and Speed Type, interact within a rock-paper-scissors relationship. To ensure fairness and balanced matches in Parablade, regardless of SP distribution pattern, this system is introduced as described in Sect. 3.3, to prevent any single character type from becoming overly dominant. To achieve this balance, it is necessary to determine appropriate initial VP value sets and SP to modify. This chapter presents a method to efficiently explore optimal VP values through match simulations and validate their impact on game balance through playtesting.

4.1 Match Simulation to Determine Appropriate VPs

To efficiently explore the optimal VP values, a Java-based match simulation program was developed. This simulation runs iterative matches between virtual players, adjusting VP values based on match results. During the simulation, two virtual players select attack targets and execute attacks according to predefined probabilities and attack intervals (ranging from one to three seconds) until the match ends. The target selection and attack success are determined through probability-weighted branching (Fig. 2).

Each virtual player has two probability parameters: attack target selection and hit success. The targets include the torso, arms, legs, and sword, with selection probabilities summing to 100%. While attacks on the opponent's sword do not contribute to scoring, they are crucial for defense. The hit success probability represents the likelihood of a successful attack on the chosen target. Different body parts have different attack success probability and damage multipliers to reflect both aiming difficulty and conceptual impact of damage. The attack interval for each virtual player ranges from one to three seconds, depending on the character type. This range was determined based on prototype simulation data, where differences in attack intervals were observed among character types [6].

Each match type is simulated 10,000 times, and results of win rates and average match duration are used to adjust VP values. Normally, if an advantaged character type's win rate is below the predefined threshold, its ATK and representative VP increased by one, while the disadvantaged type's corresponding VP decreased by one. If the Attack Type underperforms against the Speed type, its ATK is specially increased by two and DEF by one to counter Speed Type's high attack frequency. Conversely, Speed Type's ATK and AGI are reduced by two and one, respectively. Match duration is regulated within 15 to 45 s by adjusting HP. If the duration exceeds 45 s, HP decreases by one; if below 15 s, HP increases by one. This range aligns with similar sports such as Sports Chambara and SASSEN while considering physical exertion. This adjustment process repeats until the following conditions are met:

- The average match duration falls between 15 to 45 s.
- The win rate of the advantaged character type meets all predefined thresholds (at least 50%, with experimental adjustments).

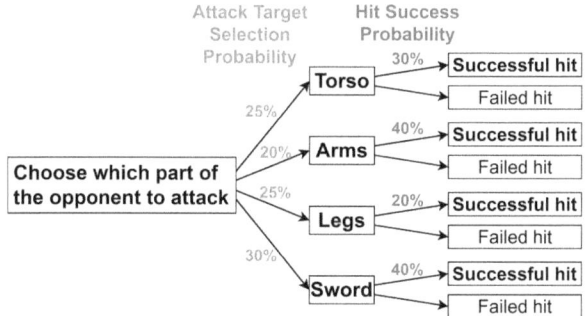

Fig. 2. Example of virtual player behavior selection tree and branch probabilities.

4.2 Validity of Prototype Match Simulation, and VP Update Model

Using the prototype match simulation, VP values were calculated and used to test four pairs of eight men and women in their twenties in actual game play, revealing a deviation from the intended type matchup balance [6]. The simulation predicted a 53.6% win rate for the Defense Type against the Attack Type, but an analysis of the video recordings of the test matches showed only 37.5%, reversing the expected advantage. This discrepancy may come from the uncertainty in the initial probabilistic model. Since the appropriate VP values were unknown when setting up the probabilistic model before the simulation, initial probabilities were provisionally estimated based on video footage of Sports Chambara—a similar sport without VPs—by analyzing which body parts were more or less frequently targeted. This estimation may have led to discrepancies between the simulation and actual gameplay.

To address this issue, a feedback loop was introduced to update the probabilistic model based on playtest analysis. VP values are refined through repeated simulations. Player action data, including the number of attacks and successful hits per body part, is extracted from recorded gameplay footage. These data are used to calculate new probability distributions for the next simulation cycle. Through the iteration, the probabilistic model is expected to be more realistic, enabling appropriate VP settings and achieving the desired type matchup. Figure 3 illustrates the details of this VP update model.

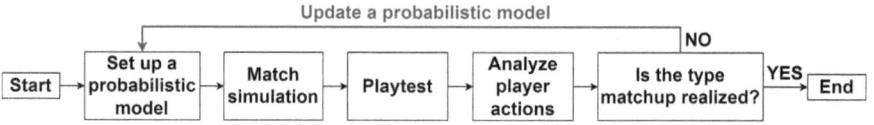

Fig. 3. VP update model.

4.3 Survey on the Effectiveness of the VP Update Model

This section examines the impact of the VP update model on type matchups and assesses its effectiveness.

Method. In this experiment, the VP update model was applied four times, adjusting the probabilistic model accordingly. The first two updates (0–2) involved 12 participants (ages 21–28; four male pairs and two mixed-gender pairs). after the second update, one mixed-gender pair withdrew and was replaced by a new male pair, maintaining 12 participants (ages 21–28). All participants were beginners, defined as having less than one year of Sports Chambara experience or none, excluding certified practitioners. This criterion was adopted as it was the only comparable sport with many advanced players.

Matches were conducted using SASSEN swords (Fig. 4 right). Before each playtest, two players performed practice matches, followed by six official round-robin matches among Attack, Defense, and Speed types. VP information was presented to them visually and aurally: a large monitor displayed VP configurations before matches and only remaining HP during gameplay, while wireless earphones (ambie sound earcuffs) signaled cool time activation with a beep. Hit locations were visually judged by experimenter and entered into a Java-based system, which updated HP and played a beep. All matches were recorded from both sides and precisely analyzed using an annotation tool called ELAN (version 6.8, Max Planck Institute for Psycholinguistics). Targeting and striking actions were annotated as time-series data to calculate a new probabilistic model and reassess match outcomes. The VP update model's effectiveness was evaluated based on adherence to the intended type matchup balance. The balance was considered achieved if the win rate of an advantaged type exceeded 83.3% (winning at least 10 out of 12 matches). This threshold was determined using a binomial test ($\alpha = 0.05$) to reject the null hypothesis that win rates between two character types are equal (50%).

Results. Figure 5 shows win rates between character types in which the VP update model was applied. "0th" refers to the use of initial values of the probabilistic model. The win rates of the Speed Type against the Defense Type changed as follows from the 0th update: 83.3%, 91.7%, 83.3%, 91.7% and 83.3%. Also, the win rates of the Defense Type against the Attack Type were 91.7%, 91.7%, 83.3%, 83.3% and 83.3%. These

Fig. 4. Match overview (left) and the sword used in the experiment (right).

win rates were 83.3% or higher, meeting the matchup condition defined in Section 4.3. However, the win rates of the Attack Type against the Speed Type were 50%, 66.7%, 58.3%, 41.6%, and 50%, and did not meet the condition. Regarding match durations, the minimum times from the 0th update were 1.17, 1.32, 3.00, 7.74, and 5.03 s, while the maximum times were 78.7, 140, 82.3, 134, and 112 s.

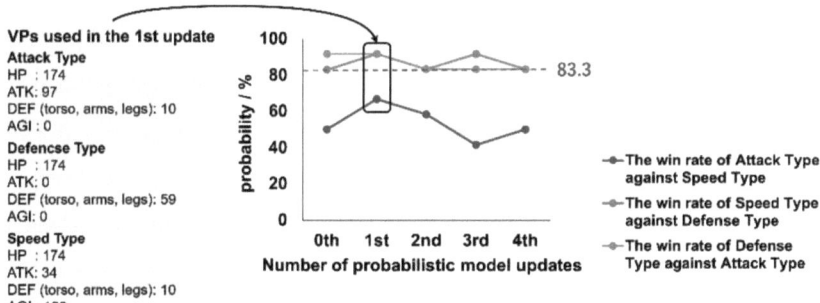

Fig. 5. Transition of win rates in matches.

Figure 6 shows the changes in target selection and hit success probabilities over four updates. The chi-square tests without yates' continuity correction were conducted for each probability across probabilistic model updates from the first to the fourth iteration. significant main effects at the 1% level were found for the attack target selection in all body parts except the torso (arms: $\chi^2 = 44.575, p < 0.01$; legs: $\chi^2 = 27.078, p < 0.01$, Sword: $\chi^2 = 37.441, p < 0.01$). multiple comparisons using the chi-square test without yates' continuity correction, corrected by the bonferroni method, revealed significant differences in the following: the arm between the first and fourth ($\chi^2 = 32.067, p < 0.01$), second and fourth ($\chi^2 = 31.444, p < 0.01$), and third and fourth iterations ($\chi^2 = 12.969, p < 0.01$): the leg between the first and second ($\chi^2 = 17.9, p < 0.01$), first and third ($\chi^2 = 22.496, p < 0.01$), and first and fourth iterations ($\chi^2 = 7.358, p < 0.01$): the sword between the first and fourth ($\chi^2 = 11.905, p < 0.01$), second and fourth ($\chi^2 = 32.45, p < 0.01$), and third and fourth iterations ($\chi^2 = 23.68, p < 0.01$). For the hit success probability, a significant main effect at the 1% level was found only for the sword ($\chi^2 = 34.747, p < 0.01$). In addition, multiple comparisons revealed significant differences between the first and fourth ($\chi^2 = 31.268, p < 0.01$), second and fourth ($\chi^2 = 22.713, p < 0.01$), and third and fourth iterations ($\chi^2 = 15.017, p < 0.01$).

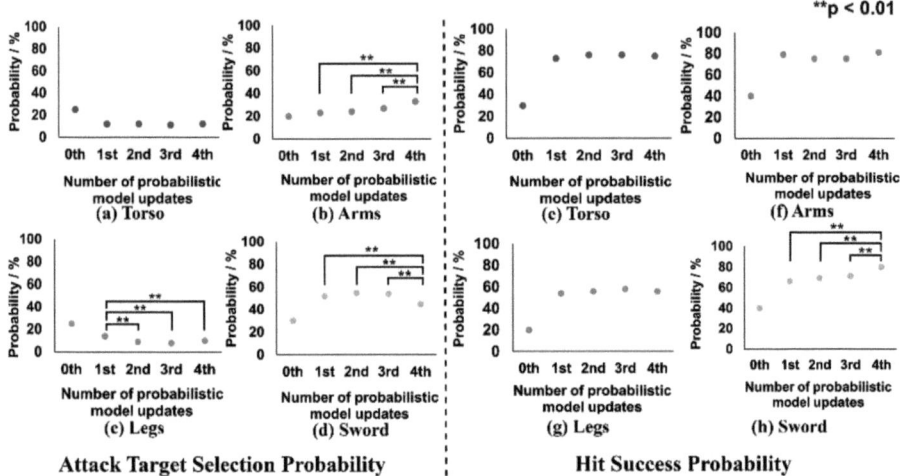

Fig. 6. Transition of attack target selection probabilities (left) and hit success probabilities (right).

Discussion. The results showed that the VP update model was partially effective: it achieved the desired win rates between two character types, but failed to meet the threshold for the Attack Type against the Speed Type. This imbalance likely resulted from the AGI value in the simulation, where the Speed Type had AGI 100 (i.e., cool time: 0 s), while others had AGI 0 (i.e., cool time: 1.5 s), allowing Speed Type to exploit rapid consecutive attacks. Addressing this requires adjusting the cool time range and redesigning the VP adjustment system. Regarding the probabilistic model, although iterative updates aimed to improve accuracy, statistical tests revealed no significant differences in five cases between updates 1–4 and 2–4, indicating limited benefits from repeated updates. Thus, two to three updates appear to be optimal. Due to the small sample size (14 participants), the model and VP values may have been overfitted. To ensure broader applicability, VP values should be generalizable across diverse players. This issue is explored further in the next chapter.

5 Survey on the Versatility of the VP Update Model

In the experiment in Sect. 4.3, the limited number of participants may have resulted in a probabilistic model and VP values specific to that group, raising uncertainty about the broader applicability of the VP update model. This chapter evaluates its versatility by applying the same VPs to another group of participants and comparing the results.

5.1 Method

Participants followed the same procedure as in Sect. 4.3. They began with practice matches followed by a six-match round-robin tournament among Attack, Defense, and Speed Types. Participants were six pairs (12 male beginners, ages 21–27) who had not participated in Sect. 4.3. The VP values used were based on the first probabilistic model update derived from that section. To evaluate the generalizability of the VP update model, win rates and post-match probabilistic models from Sect. 4.3 and this chapter were compared to determine whether there were significant differences between the two groups.

5.2 Results

Figure 7 compares win rates between matches using the initial probabilistic model from Sect. 4.3 and those conducted in this experiment with a different participant group. In this experiment, the win rates were as follows: Attack → Speed: 91.7%, Speed → Defense: 83.3%, Defense → Attack: 83.3%. A two-tailed Fisher's exact test ($\alpha = 0.01$) showed no significant differences in win rates for the same character type matchups between the two experiments. However, while the win rate of the Attack Type against the Speed Type in Sect. 4.3 did not meet the type matchup threshold (83.3%), all win rates in this experiment met the required conditions, achieving a perfect type matchup. Additionally, the post-match probabilistic model from this experiment was compared with the second probabilistic model update from Sect. 4.3 using chi-square tests without Yates' continuity correction for each probability category. As shown in Fig. 7 (b) and (c), significant differences ($\alpha = 0.01$) were observed in the attack target selection probabilities for the arm ($\chi^2 = 7.586, p < 0.01$) and leg ($\chi^2 = 31.671, p < 0.01$). In contrast, no significant differences were found for torso, sword, and in the hit success probabilities (all $p > 0.01$). Further analysis of Speed Type attack intervals revealed a significant difference in the Wilcoxon rank-sum test ($\alpha = 0.01, p < 0.01$; see Fig. 7 (d)). In this experiment, the match duration ranged from 13.4 to 201 s.

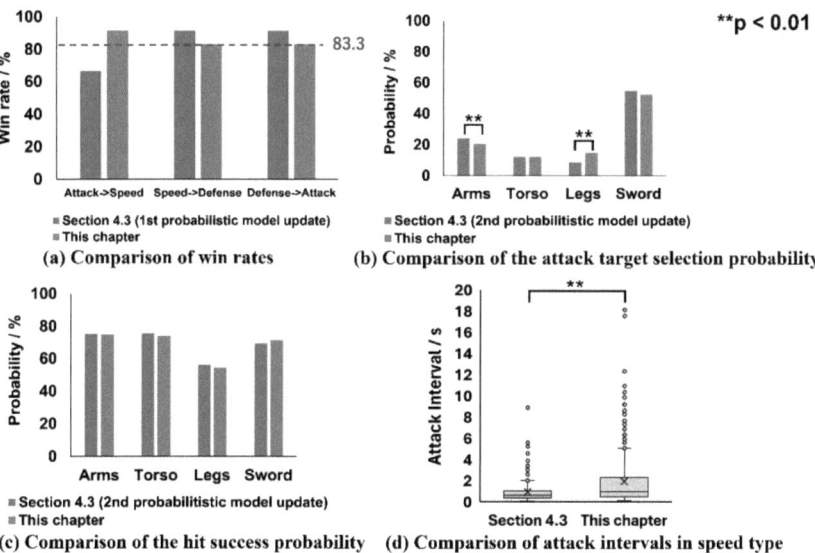

Fig. 7. Comparison of the results of the experiments in Sect. 4.3 and this chapter.

5.3 Discussion

Applying the same VPs to a new group of beginners resulted in no significant differences in win rates across character types (Fig. 7 (a)), suggesting the approach is robust. However, significant differences in attack target selection probabilities for the arm and leg were observed (Fig. 7 (c)). Match footage revealed frequent leg attacks, likely due to a higher number of Kendo practitioners. Kendo is a traditional Japanese martial art using a sword that emphasizes precise strikes to openings. While only one participant in Sect. 4.3 had over a year of kendo experience, five participants in this experiment did. This difference likely influenced attack target selection probabilities. These results suggest that although the probabilistic models reflect a few participants' tendencies, VP values derived from them may still generalize to broader players. In contrast to Sect. 4.3, where the Attack Type's win rate against the Speed Type fell below the threshold, Fig. 7 (a) shows that type matchups were balanced in this experiment. This discrepancy is likely due to differences in attack intervals. In Sect. 4.3, the same participants took part in two trials, learning to exploit the Speed Type's cool time remaining at zero seconds allowing rapid attacks. In this experiment, first-time participants did not fully utilize the cool time advantage, resulting in longer attack intervals. These findings suggest that raising the Speed Type's minimum cool time could help stabilize matchups.

6 Limitations and Future Work

This study highlights three primary limitations. First, game design parameters, such as damage multipliers, VP ranges, and damage calculation constants, were tentatively defined. These should be refined through empirical data analysis via comprehensive simulation. Second, VP flexibility is limited. Players currently cannot adjust VPs before matches, and fixed VPs and character types may cause match outcomes to be strongly influenced by type matchups from the start. While type matchup helps balance extreme VP settings, overreliance on it may reduce enjoyment. Introducing pre-match VP customization and dynamic VP modification mechanics during matches could address these issues. Third, the study focused only on beginners, limiting its generalizability. Further evaluation will be necessary by gathering participants who play similar games, such as Sports Chambara, to improve generalizability.

7 Conclusion

To address physical disparities in Chambara, we developed "Parablade," a new Chambara-based Augmented Sports. We also proposed a VP-based balancing method and evaluated its effectiveness and versatility through matches. While the method did not achieve ideal game balance, it demonstrated moderate effectiveness. Also, applying the same settings to different participant groups maintained a consistent game balance, indicating versatility. Building on these findings, we aim to refine the game design and expand the reach of Parablade, making it accessible to a wider range of players.

Acknowledgments. This study was conducted with the approval of the Ethics Committee of the University of Electro-Communications (H23074, H24025). We would also like to express our sincere gratitude to the All Japan SASSEN Association for their generous support.

Disclosure of Interests. The authors have no competing interests to declare that is relevant to the content of this article.

References

1. Warburton, D.E.R., Nicol, C.W., Bredin, S.S.D.: Health benefits of physical activity: the evidence. Can. Med. Assoc. J. **174**(6), 801–809 (2006). https://doi.org/10.1503/cmaj.051351
2. Carter, T., Pascoe, M., Bastounis, A., Morres, I.D., Callaghan, P., Parker, A.G.: The effect of physical activity on anxiety in children and young people: a systematic review and meta-analysis. J. Affect. Disord. **285**, 10–21 (2021). https://doi.org/10.1016/j.jad.2021.02.026
3. Martino, L., Cassese, F.P., Viscione, I., D'Isanto, T.: Diversity as a starting point for "adapted sport." J. human Sport and Exercise **14**(Proc4), S1087–S1093 (2019). https://doi.org/10.14198/jhse.2019.14.Proc4.72
4. Kunze, K., Minamizawa, K., Lukosch, S., Inami, M., Rekimoto, J.: Superhuman sports: applying human augmentation to physical exercise. IEEE Pervasive Comput. **16**(2), 14–17 (2017). https://doi.org/10.1109/MPRV.2017.35
5. Rebane, K., et al.: Augmenting team games with a ball to promote cooperative play. Augmented Human Research **7**(6), (2021). https://doi.org/10.1007/s41133-021-00045-3
6. Maeda, Y., Sato, K., Sakurai, S., Hirota, K., Nojima, T.: Proposal of a contact judgment system between a simulated sword and a body using a microphone (in Japanese). In: Proceedings of the Virtual Reality Society of Japan, Annual Conference. 28, 1C1–09 (2023)
7. The International Sports Chanbara Association: What is Sports Chanbara, https://www.internationalsportschanbara.net/e/spochan/spochan.html. Accessed 10 Mar 2025
8. Ando, R., et al.: Research on the transcendence of bodily differences, using sport and human augmentation medium. In: Proceedings of the Augmented Humans International Conference, pp. 31–39 (2021). https://doi.org/10.1145/3458709.3458981
9. Araki, H., et al.: "HADO" as Techno Sports was born by the fusion of IT technology and sports. In: EPiC Series in Engineering **1**, pp. 36–40 (2018). https://doi.org/10.29007/8stx
10. Buckers, T., Gong, B., Eisemann, E., Lukosch, S.: VRabl: stimulating physical activities through a multiplayer augmented reality sports game. In: Proceedings of the First Superhuman Sports Design Challenge: First International Symposium on Amplifying Capabilities and Competing in Mixed Realities, pp. 1–5 (2018). https://doi.org/10.1145/3210299.3210300
11. All Japan SASSEN Association: What is SASSEN? (English), https://sassen.jp/what-is-sassen-english/. Accessed 07 Mar 2025
12. Gonçalves, D., Barros, D., Pais, P., Guerreiro, J., Guerreiro, T., Rodrigues, A.: The trick is to stay behind?: defining and exploring the design space of player balancing mechanics. In: Proceedings of the 2024 CHI Conference on Human Factors in Computing Systems, pp. 1–16. (2024). https://doi.org/10.1145/3613904.3642441
13. Jaffe, A., Miller, A., Andersen, E., Liu, Y.-E., Karlin, A., Popović, Z.: Evaluating competitive game balance with restricted play. In: Proceedings of the Eighth AAAI Conference on Artificial Intelligence and Interactive Digital Entertainment, pp. 26–31 (2012). https://doi.org/10.1609/aiide.v8i1.12513

14. Pfau, J., Liapis, A., Yannakakis, G.N., Malaka, R.: Dungeons & replicants II: automat-ed game balancing across multiple difficulty dimensions via deep player behavior modeling. IEEE Transactions on Games **15**(2), 217–227 (2023). https://doi.org/10.1109/TG.2022.3167728
15. Ranandeh, V., Mirza-Babaei, P.: Beyond equilibrium: utilizing AI agents in video game economy balancing. In: Companion Proceedings of the Annual Symposium on Computer-Human Interaction in Play, pp. 155–160 (2023). https://doi.org/10.1145/3573382.3616092

Vectorigger: A Method of Inducing Vection Using a Wearable LED Array

Ayumi Ohnishi, Kazuki Ohmura, Tsutomu Terada(✉), and Masahiko Tsukamoto

Kobe University, Kobe, Hyogo, Japan
{ohnishi,tsutomu,tuka}@eedept.kobe-u.ac.jp, info@ubieedept.kobe-u.ac.jp

Abstract. Vection, a self-motion sensation induced by visual information, has been applied in entertainment and navigation to enhance immersion. While inducing vection can be beneficial in some contexts, there are also cases where canceling unintended vection (e.g., motion sickness) is desirable. To address both needs, we propose a wearable device capable of both inducing and suppressing vection through controlled visual stimulation. We designed and implemented a device called Vectrigger, which induces vection using LEDs arranged three-dimensionally around the user's field of view. By sequentially flashing these LEDs, the device creates a flowing visual effect that triggers vection, while still allowing the user to see the real world directly. We conducted evaluation experiments to compare the vection-inducing and vection-overlapping effects of Vectrigger with those of a head-mounted display (HMD). The experimental results confirmed that vection can be induced with the proposed method. Furthermore, in specific cases, certain combinations of vection stimuli were able to cancel out the sensation of vection.

Keywords: Vection · Wearable device · Head-mounted display · LED

1 Introduction

When sitting in a stationary train and observing the train on the opposite track begin to move leftward, one may feel as though their own train is moving rightward. This phenomenon, in which one feels as if they are moving despite being stationary by observing uniformly moving visual stimuli, is called visually induced self-motion perception, or vection. In recent years, studies have explored the use of vection to guide walking direction [1], and its application in daily life is increasingly expected.

Most existing methods for utilizing vection involve installing induction devices in the external environment. These methods aim to induce vection in all individuals within a given space, thereby altering group behavior or awareness. An example is a system that reduces crowding in public facilities by inducing vection using special lenses placed on the floor [1]. However, in such applications, all individuals in the environment are exposed to the same vection stimuli. If individuals have different purposes, the induced vection may interfere with their activities. Moreover, sensitivity to vection varies from person to person, and it is difficult to adjust the intensity of vection to accommodate individual differences.

To provide vection on a per-person basis, a head-mounted display (HMD) can be used to accommodate different contexts and individual sensitivities [2]. However, see-through HMDs have a limited field of view, making it difficult to induce sufficient vection. On the other hand, immersive HMDs completely block the user's vision, requiring users to perceive the real world through video captured by a camera, which may lead to discomfort during use.

In this study, we propose a method that induces vection while allowing the user to directly see the real world by means of a wearable device named Vectrigger. Instead of using a display that obstructs the user's vision, Vectrigger induces vection effectively by three-dimensionally arranging LEDs that flash sequentially to create a flowing visual effect. This approach addresses the limitations of HMD-based methods, such as insufficient vection induction and the need to perceive the real world indirectly, thereby enabling more effective use of vection. Additionally, by implementing the system as a wearable device, it can be used in any environment without modifying the surroundings. With Vectrigger, we aim to realize a vection presentation system that can both enhance user experiences by intentionally inducing vection and improve comfort by canceling unwanted vection caused by environmental visual stimuli. In the evaluation experiment, we verify the effects of vection induction and overlap using both Vectrigger and an HMD.

The remainder of this paper is organized as follows: Sect. 2 introduces related work; Sect. 3 describes the proposed method and the implemented device; Sect. 4 presents the evaluation experiment using the proposed device and discusses the results; and Sect. 5 concludes the paper.

2 Related Work

2.1 Studies on Vection Induction and Overlap

Vection, a self-motion sensation induced by visual stimuli, is affected by the properties of those stimuli. For example, the intensity of vection increases with the area of the visual stimulus [3–6], and stimuli presented in the peripheral visual field induce stronger vection than those shown in the central field [4–6]. Faster motion of the stimulus also leads to stronger vection [6,7].

Brandt et al. showed that when different motion patterns were presented in the central and peripheral visual fields simultaneously, vection was determined mainly by the peripheral stimulus [6]. Ito et al. found that when stimuli with different expansion centers were shown in the foreground and background, the vection was dominated by the background stimulus perceived as the environmental scene [8]. Other studies have reported that perceived stimulus depth influences vection strength, with more distant stimuli inducing stronger vection [9].

These findings suggest that introducing a new vection stimulus during an ongoing experience can alter the perceived motion sensation. Building on this, our study proposes a wearable device that both induces and modulates vection by overlapping visual stimuli.

2.2 Wearable Devices for Vection Induction

Head-mounted displays (HMDs) are widely used in vection research. Immersive HMDs fully cover the user's field of view and can present wide-angle, three-dimensional visuals, making them effective for vection induction. However, they can cause motion sickness, particularly due to latency in display response or frequent head movement [10].

Optical see-through HMDs allow users to view both the real environment and virtual overlays simultaneously. These devices are often used for augmented reality (AR) applications. While some AR devices can provide depth perception using binocular disparity, the mismatch between vergence and accommodation can lead to visual fatigue [11]. Moreover, AR systems that display only 2D images are generally unsuitable for inducing vection due to the lack of depth cues.

Okano et al. explored a wearable device designed to enhance the sense of speed while using a treadmill [12]. Their study demonstrated that a wearable device with a panel-shaped LED array could enhance users' perception of speed, suggesting the potential for vection induction using LED arrays. However, in their device, the LED arrays were mounted to surround the left, right, and lower parts of the user's field of view, resulting in a narrowed overall visual field. Even if the central visual area is unobstructed, limiting the peripheral view restricts the range of usable environments.

Unlike fixed installations for vection induction, wearable systems offer flexibility in adapting to individual users' needs. However, each presentation method has advantages and limitations. In this study, we propose a wearable method that combines the benefits of immersive HMDs—strong vection through 3D stimuli—and see-through HMDs—unobstructed view of the real world.

3 Proposed Method

In this section, we propose a method to induce vection while allowing users to directly see the real world through a wearable device. Instead of using a display that obstructs the user's vision, the proposed method induces vection by three-dimensionally arranging LEDs and flashing them sequentially to create a flowing visual effect.

3.1 Target Environment

This study aims to support user activities in daily life by inducing or canceling vection through visual effects in the user's field of view. Figure 1 illustrates the implementation concept of the proposed method.

 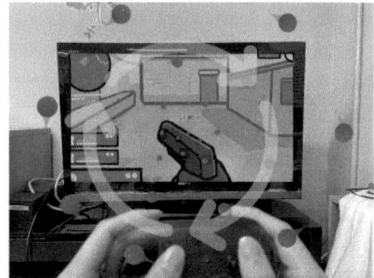

(a) Example of inducing vection   (b) Example of canceling vection

Fig. 1. Conceptual images of vection induced by the proposed method

Figure 1(a) depicts a situation where vection is induced to enhance user comfort. In this example, the user is running, and the proposed method is used to induce vection, making the experience feel easier. Since the vection is induced by a wearable device, the user can run in any location with vection support. Additionally, because the user's view is not blocked, safe running is possible.

Figure 1(b) shows a situation where vection is canceled through visual effects to enhance comfort. Here, the proposed method reduces motion sickness that occurs during gameplay. Such sickness arises from a mismatch between visual information suggesting movement and the physical state of being stationary. Since translational and rotational vection are known to have a negative correlation [2], we attempt to cancel the perceived vection by overlaying it with another vection induced by the proposed method. This vection-canceling approach is not limited to games; it can also serve as a solution to motion sickness in movies and immersive visual attractions. By tailoring the cancellation to individual sensitivity levels, the negative impact on content can be minimized, allowing susceptible users to enjoy the experience comfortably, while others maintain a sense of immersion.

3.2 System Requirements

Based on the target environment, we designed the system to meet the following three requirements for enhancing user comfort through vection:

- The direction and intensity of vection can be switched.
- The system can induce vection or overlay it onto vection caused by the external environment, in order to enhance or suppress its effects.
- The system minimally obstructs the user's field of view.

This study aims to provide vection tailored to individuals. Therefore, we propose a wearable device that delivers visual stimuli exclusively to the user and allows adjustment of vection direction and intensity according to user needs.

The goal is not only to induce vection but also to enhance or cancel the perceived motion sensation by overlaying visual stimuli in the user's field of

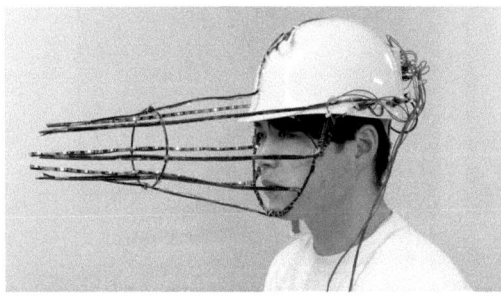 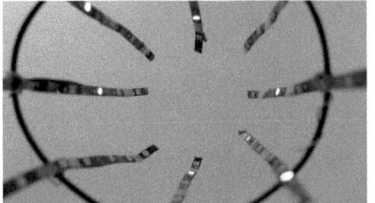

(a) Example of wearing the device (b) User's view with the device

Fig. 2. Proposed device

view. To this end, the proposed device includes buttons that allow the user to switch the direction of induced vection and toggle it on or off. LEDs are used as the vection-inducing stimuli. Since peripheral stimulation and perceived depth are crucial for vection induction [6,8], the LEDs are arranged to surround the user's face and provide depth in the forward direction.

For daily use, it is desirable that the device minimally obstruct the user's view. Okano et al.'s wearable device using LED arrays allowed users to see the real world directly, but the peripheral field was blocked by the device, potentially interfering with everyday activities [12]. In our design, we constructed the device using a mesh of thin, unobtrusive black wires that allow visibility through the gaps while supporting the LEDs. This enables vection induction with minimal obstruction of the user's view.

3.3 Proposed Device

Figure 2 shows the structure and usage example of the proposed device. The system consists of wires fixed to a helmet, extending forward in front of the user's field of view. Eight wires are arranged to surround the view from above, below, left, right, and diagonal directions. From the user's perspective, each wire extends approximately 35 cm, forming a circle with a diameter of about 25 cm near the face. The tips of the wires are about 15 cm long and converge toward the center of the visual field. This length was chosen so that the user can perform general tasks, such as working on a laptop, without interference.

LED strips are attached to the wires and controlled by a microcontroller and switches to manage the flashing patterns. Since front-back vection can be induced by stimuli that radiate from the center of the field of view [8,13–15], the LEDs are arranged radially from the user's visual center.

While the current prototype may be too obtrusive for everyday use, we consider this implementation as a foundation for exploring more practical and refined designs in future development.

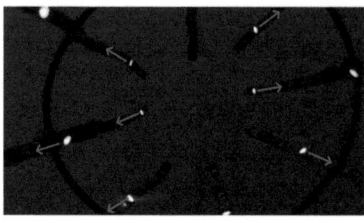 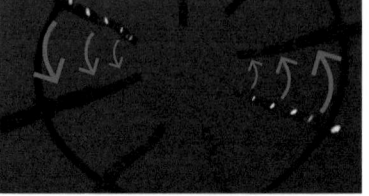

(a) Forward vection stimulus (b) Clockwise vection stimulus

Fig. 3. User's field of view when wearing the device

3.4 Visual Stimuli

Figure 3 shows the user's field of view when wearing the device, with stimuli for forward and clockwise vection. The images were taken in a dark room to highlight the LED light.

The device can induce four types of vection: forward, backward, clockwise, and counterclockwise. These directions were chosen based on previous studies, where vection in forward/backward and roll directions are commonly investigated [2].

Figure 3(a) shows the visual stimulus used to induce forward vection, where randomly placed LEDs flash in the direction of the arrow. The proposed device is designed to make the light appear as if it is radiating outward from the center of vision and approaching from the background to the foreground, thereby inducing forward vection. Figure 3(b) shows the visual stimulus used to induce clockwise vection. LEDs arranged in a circular pattern rotate in the counterclockwise direction, causing the user to perceive a clockwise vection. Backward and counterclockwise vection are induced using reverse flashing patterns of their respective directions. The interval between LED flashes is set to 200 ms, which allows the user to perceive smooth motion. Approximately 15 LEDs are visible at any given time, and the flashing patterns can be changed freely using a push-button switch.

4 Evaluation Experiment

4.1 Overview of the Experiment

An evaluation experiment was conducted to determine whether the proposed method is effective as a means of utilizing vection.

Understanding the effects of different visual presentation methods for inducing vection is important when considering the use of wearable devices. In this study, we compare three vection presentation methods: the optical see-through method using an optical see-through HMD, the video see-through method using an immersive HMD, and the real method using the proposed wearable device. The aim is to examine how vection induction varies depending on the presentation method.

To achieve this, we conducted two experiments. The first is a comparison of vection induction performance, in which we examine whether the intensity of induced vection differs depending on the presentation method. The second experiment focuses on vection overlap, in which we examine how the perceived intensity of vection from the external environment changes when vection is overlaid using each presentation method.

All experiments were conducted in a dark room to ensure the visual stimuli were easily perceived. Participants were seated in a chair at a distance of 2 m from the wall, as seated posture. Eight participants (seven males and one female) in their twenties took part. The study was approved by the Ethics Committee of the Graduate School of Engineering, Kobe University.

4.2 Vection Presentation Methods

The devices and visual stimuli used for each presentation method are shown in Fig. 4. Details are described below.

Optical See-through Method: In this method, vection is induced by displaying a video that evokes vection on a screen in the user's forward view using an optical see-through HMD. Since the user's view is not fully blocked, the real world remains visible. In this experiment, we used Microsoft's HoloLens 2 [16], which has a field of view of 52°.

To align the visual stimuli with those of the real method, we used green dots moving in the direction of arrows, as shown in Figs. 4(a) and (d). These videos were presented via HoloLens 2 to induce vection.

Video See-through Method: This method uses an immersive HMD to induce vection by moving virtual objects within a virtual space, thereby providing 3D visual stimuli. The user's view is fully occluded, and they perceive the real world through a video feed projected into the HMD. We used Oculus Rift S by Oculus [17]. To project the real-world view, a Jabra PanaCast camera [18] with a 180° field of view was mounted on the top of the HMD. The captured video was used as the virtual background to ensure perception of the real environment.

The visual stimuli for this method are shown in Figs. 4(b) and (e). Figure 4(b) shows a forward vection stimulus viewed from the side, demonstrating the 3D arrangement of the objects. The arrows indicate the movement direction. These moving green objects were used to induce vection.

Real Method (Proposed Method): The real method uses the proposed wearable device to induce vection by flashing LEDs arranged three-dimensionally in a flowing pattern. The user's view is not blocked, and the real world can be seen directly without a display. The visual stimuli used are those described in Sect. 3.4 and shown in Figs. 4(c) and (f).

4.3 Vection Evaluation Method

To evaluate vection intensity, we used the magnitude estimation method, a commonly used psychophysical technique for quantifying perceptual responses to

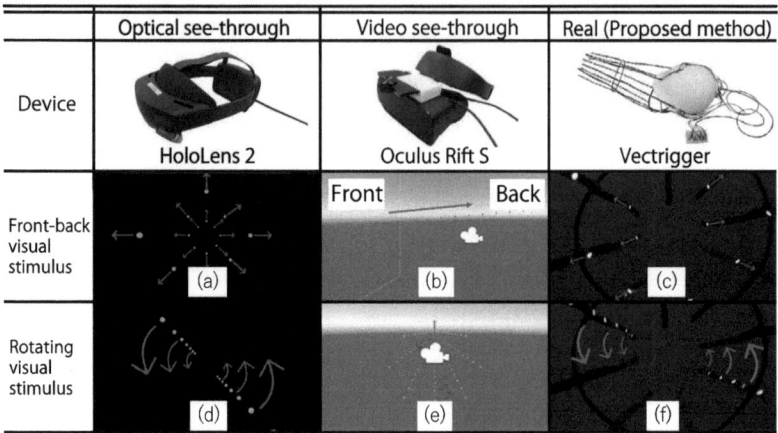

Fig. 4. Devices and visual stimuli used in the experiment

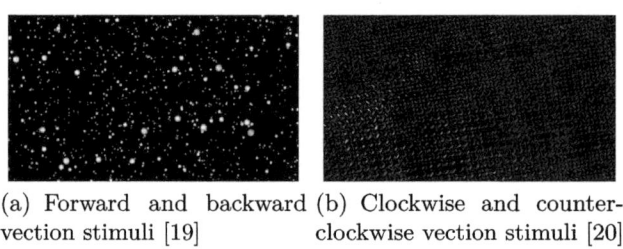

(a) Forward and backward vection stimuli [19] (b) Clockwise and counterclockwise vection stimuli [20]

Fig. 5. Reference videos for vection intensity evaluation

external stimuli. Before the experiment, participants were shown reference videos for each vection direction to establish a standard for their intensity ratings. During the experiment, participants rated the vection intensity of each stimulus based on these standards.

The reference videos used for evaluation are shown in Fig. 5 [19,20]. There are four types: forward, backward, clockwise, and counterclockwise. In Fig. 5(a), white dots expand outward to induce forward vection and contract inward to induce backward vection [19]. In Fig. 5(b), patterns rotate around the center of the screen counterclockwise to induce clockwise vection, and clockwise to induce counterclockwise vection [20]. These videos were projected onto a wall using a projector. The projection size was 190 cm wide by 120 cm tall.

Vection intensity was rated on a scale where 100 corresponds to the intensity felt from the reference video, and 0 corresponds to no stimulus or environmental effect. For example, a participant who felt half as much vection as the reference would rate it 50; if they felt double, they would rate it 200. These reference videos were also used in Experiment 2 (Sect. 4.5) as the environmental vection stimuli to be overlaid.

4.4 Evaluation Experiment 1: Comparison of Vection Induction Performance

Procedure. This experiment investigates whether there are differences in vection induction performance among the three presentation methods.

Participants wore each device and were exposed to visual stimuli for 30 s. Afterward, they rated the perceived vection intensity according to the method described in Sect. 4.3. The order of vection directions was: forward, backward, clockwise, and counterclockwise. The order in which participants used each device was randomized. During stimulus presentation, participants were instructed to focus on the wall rather than on the stimulus itself.

Results and Discussion. A two-way repeated-measures ANOVA was conducted using presentation method and vection direction as within-subject factors. No significant differences were found, indicating that the presentation method did not significantly affect vection induction performance.

Focusing on individual differences, participants B and C reported zero vection for clockwise and counterclockwise directions with the optical see-through method; participants B and G reported zero with the video see-through method; and participant G reported zero with the real method. This may be due to the relative rarity of experiencing rotational vection in daily life, making it harder to perceive.

Although no significant differences were found among presentation methods, certain participants experienced stronger vection with specific methods. This suggests that if the most suitable presentation method can be identified for each individual, more effective vection induction could be achieved.

With the proposed real method, although the effect was weaker than the reference videos, vection was successfully induced. Therefore, applications such as guiding walking direction or making stair climbing feel easier, as proposed in previous research, may be feasible using a wearable device without requiring environmental installations or obstructing vision.

Replacing environmental vection induction systems with wearable devices could allow for customization based on whether the user wants vection or which direction it should be presented, potentially enabling broader and more personalized use of vection.

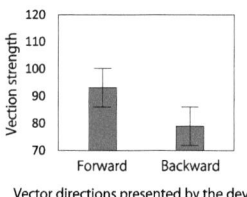

Fig. 6. Overlap with forward environmental vection

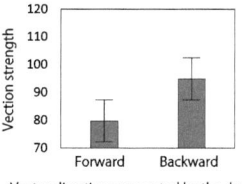

Fig. 7. Overlap with backward environmental vection

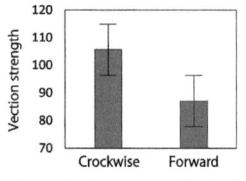 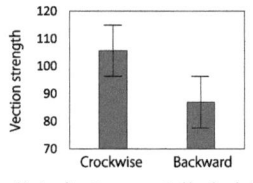 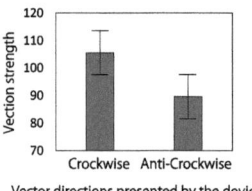

(a) Comparison with forward vection

(b) Comparison with backward vection

(c) Comparison with counterclockwise vection

Fig. 8. Overlap with clockwise environmental vection

4.5 Evaluation Experiment 2: Vection Overlap

Experimental Procedure. This experiment investigates whether the perceived vection strength from the external environment changes when additional vection is induced using a device, and whether such changes differ depending on the presentation method.

In this experiment, we used the reference videos described in Sect. 4.3 as representations of environmental vection by projecting them onto a wall using a projector. First, participants viewed a reference video for 30 s. Then, with the reference video still projected on the wall, each participant wore a device and visual stimuli were presented.

We overlaid vection in the forward, backward, clockwise, and counterclockwise directions—induced by each presentation method—on the forward-direction reference video. Participants rated the resulting vection strength based on how it changed compared to the original video. The same process was repeated using the backward, clockwise, and counterclockwise reference videos.

Each stimulus was presented for 30 s, and the order of devices was randomized. Since the reference video represented vection strength of 100, participant responses below 100 indicate reduced perceived vection, responses above 100 indicate increased vection, and a response of 100 means no change.

Furthermore, we considered the possibility that merely wearing the device—even without visual stimuli—might influence the perceived vection from the environment. Thus, we also measured vection strength with each device worn but without presenting any additional stimulus. This was defined as the "degree of vection interference."

Experimental Results. We conducted a three-way repeated-measures ANOVA with the following factors: direction of environmental vection (4 types), presentation method (3 types), and direction of induced vection (4 types), resulting in a 4 × 3 × 4 condition design.

Significant effects were found for the direction of environmental vection and the direction of induced vection ($F(9, 63) = 3.46$, $p < 0.05$). Interaction effects were also observed, showing tendencies for significance in the forward and backward conditions: Forward: ($F(3, 21) = 2.48$, $p < 0.10$), Backward: ($F(3, 21) =$

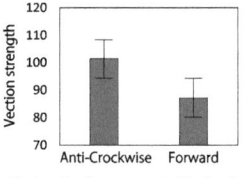
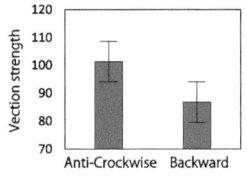

(a) Comparison with forward vection (b) Comparison with backward vection

Fig. 9. Overlap with counterclockwise environmental vection

2.68, $p < 0.10$). Significant differences were observed for: Clockwise: ($F(3, 21) = 5.38$, $p < 0.01$), Counterclockwise: ($F(3, 21) = 3.51$, $p < 0.05$).

Multiple comparisons were performed using the LSD method, and combinations with significant or marginal effects are shown in Figs. 6 to 9. The graphs show the average vection strength perceived by participants, with error bars indicating standard errors. Following Matsuda et al. [2], it is known that when translational and rotational vection are combined, a negative correlation occurs, potentially leading to cancellation. Our results also showed that certain vection overlaps led to reduced perceived vection.

Overlap with Forward Environmental Vection: As shown in Fig. 6, vection strength was significantly higher when forward vection was added than when backward vection was overlaid ($MSe = 33$, $p < 0.05$). This suggests that when a user perceives forward vection from the environment, adding backward vection using the device can effectively reduce the perceived vection.

Overlap with Backward Environmental Vection: As shown in Fig. 7, vection strength was significantly higher when backward vection was added compared to forward vection ($MSe = 38$, $p < 0.05$). This indicates that backward environmental vection can be diminished by overlaying forward vection.

Overlap with Clockwise Environmental Vection: As shown in Fig. 8, vection strength was significantly higher when clockwise vection was added, compared to adding forward, backward, or counterclockwise vection ($MSe = 36$, $p < 0.05$). Thus, the addition of vection in different directions (e.g., forward or counterclockwise) reduced the perception of clockwise environmental vection. Although not statistically significant, inducing vection in the same direction (clockwise) appeared to enhance vection strength.

Overlap with Counterclockwise Environmental Vection: Figure 9 shows that vection strength was significantly higher when counterclockwise vection was added compared to forward or backward vection ($MSe = 34$, $p < 0.05$). Thus, counterclockwise vection from the environment can be reduced by overlaying forward or backward vection. Although not significant, inducing counterclockwise vection increased perceived vection.

Discussion. The experimental results confirmed that overlaying specific types of vection can reduce environmental vection. This suggests that wearable vection devices may be used to mitigate motion sickness and similar physical discomfort caused by unwanted vection. Since the proposed method does not modify the environmental stimuli themselves, it poses no adverse effects on other people in the same environment.

For instance, when watching a movie that might cause motion sickness, a sensitive viewer could wear the device to overlay vection and suppress the symptoms, while others could enjoy the immersive experience as-is.

The result that adding forward/backward vection reduced perceived rotational vection aligns with Matsuda et al. [2]. However, differences emerged depending on whether clockwise or counterclockwise vection was present, suggesting that directional effects vary and further investigation is needed.

5 Conclusion

In this study, we proposed a vection induction method using LEDs that enables users to experience vection while directly viewing the real world. To implement this method, we developed Vectrigger, a wearable device that three-dimensionally arranges LEDs around the user's face and flashes them sequentially to induce flowing visual stimuli. This approach addresses the limitations of conventional head-mounted displays (HMDs), such as limited field of view or full occlusion of the real world. The proposed system was designed to not only induce vection for immersive or assistive purposes, but also to suppress unintended vection—such as that caused by external visual stimuli—by overlaying counter-directional effects.

To evaluate the effectiveness of the proposed method, we compared it with two conventional presentation methods: an optical see-through HMD and an immersive HMD. In the induction performance experiment, no significant differences in vection strength were found among the presentation methods. Nevertheless, the proposed method was confirmed to induce vection. In the overlap experiment, we found that applying certain types of vection through the device could reduce the vection perceived from the external environment.

These results suggest that the proposed method has the potential not only to induce vection effectively without obstructing the real-world view, but also to selectively suppress vection sensations—such as mitigating motion sickness—by overlaying vection in specific directions. The findings support the possibility of practical vection applications in daily life through wearable devices like Vectrigger.

Acknowledgements. This work was supported in part by JST Moonshot R&D Program Grant Number JPMJMS239F and JSPS KAKENHI Grant Number 24K02988.

References

1. Furukawa, M., Yoshikawa, H., Hachisu, T., Fukushima, S., Kajimoto, H.: Vection field for pedestrian traffic control. In: Proceedings of the 2nd Augmented Human International Conference (AH 2011), No. 19, pp. 1–8 (2011)
2. Matsuda, A., Koga, Y., Matsumuro, M., Shibata, F., Tamura, H., Kimura, A.: Analysis of the mixture of linear and circular vections in immersive visual space. In: Kurosu, M. (ed.) HCII 2019. LNCS, vol. 11567, pp. 494–505. Springer, Cham (2019). https://doi.org/10.1007/978-3-030-22643-5_39
3. Held, R., Dichgans, J., Bauer, J.: Characteristics of moving visual scenes influencing spatial orientation. Vis. Res. **15**(3), 357–365 (1975)
4. Berthoz, A., Parvard, B., Young, L.R.: Perception of liner horizontal self-motion induced by peripheral vision (linear vection) basic characteristics and visual vestibular interactions. Exp. Brain Res. **23**(5), 471–489 (1975)
5. Lestienne, F., Soechting, J., Berthoz, A.: Postural readjustments induced by liner motion of visual scenes. Exp. Brain Res. **28**(3), 363–384 (1977)
6. Brandt, T., Dichgans, J., Koneig, E.: Differential effects of central versus peripheral vision on egocentric and exocentric motion perception. Exp. Brain Res. **16**(5), 476–491 (1973)
7. Sauvan, X.M., Bonnnet, C.: Properties of curvilinear vection. Percept. Psychophys. **53**(4), 429–435 (1993)
8. Ito, H., Shibata, I.: Self-Motion perception from expanding and contracting optical flows overlapped with binocular disparity. Vis. Res. **45**(4), 397–402 (2005)
9. Haward, I.P., Heckmann, T.: Circular vection as a function of the relative sizes, distances, and positions of two competing visual displays. Perception **18**(5), 657–665 (1989)
10. Moss, J.D., Salley, J.A., Coats, J., Williams, K., Muth, E.R.: The effects of display delay on simulator sickness. Displays **32**(4), 159–168 (2011)
11. Shibata, T., Kim, J., Hoffman, D.M., Banks, M.S.: The zone of comfort: predicting visual discomfort with stereo displays. J. Vis. **11**(8), 1–29 (2011)
12. Nojima, T., Saiga, Y., Okano, Y., Hashimoto, Y., Kajimoto, H.: The peripheral display for augmented reality of self-motion. In: Proceedings of the 17th International Conference on Artificial Reality and Telexistence (ICAT 2007), pp. 308–309 (November 2007)
13. Ohmi, M., Howard, I.P.: Effect of stationary objects on illusory forward self-motion induced by a looming display. Perception **17**(1), 5–11 (1988)
14. Palmisano, S.: Perceiving self-motion in depth: the role of stereoscopic motion and changing-size cues. Percept. Psychophys. **58**(8), 1168–1176 (1996)
15. Palmisano, S., Gillamm, B.J., Blackburn, S.G.: Global-perspective jitter improves vection in central vision. Perception **29**(1), 57–67 (2000)
16. Microsoft: HoloLens 2. https://www.microsoft.com/ja-jp/hololens/hardware
17. Oculus: Oculus Rift S. https://www.oculus.com/rift-s/
18. Jabra: PanaCast. https://www.jabra.jp/business/video-conferencing/jabra-panacast
19. Seno LAB: A Typical Vection Stimulus, the Simplest Optical Flow (Gibson, 1966). https://youtu.be/vsQSnAgfCwY
20. Clockwise direction vector reference video. https://www.youtube.com/watch?v=Q8h-ubpZK08

Learning Success, Engagement and Fun: Evaluating an Educational Game in Higher Education as Replacement for a Homework Assignment

Melina Rose[1,3] (✉), Alessandra Antonaci[2], Martin Bonnet[3], and Roland Klemke[1,3]

[1] Open University of the Netherlands, 6401 DL Heerlen, The Netherlands
{melina.rose,roland.klemke}@ou.nl
[2] European Association of Distance Teaching Universities (EADTU), Parkweg 27, 6212 XN Maastricht, The Netherlands
alessandra.antonaci@eadtu.eu
[3] TH Köln (University of Applied Sciences), Claudiusstr. 1, 50678 Köln, Germany
martin.bonnet@th-koeln.de

Abstract. The integration of game-based learning in higher education has gained increasing attention as a means to enhance student engagement and learning outcomes. This study evaluates the educational game Welten der Werkstoffe (WdW) as a replacement for traditional homework in a materials science course at TH Köln. The research investigates whether WdW can maintain or improve student learning success, engagement, and enjoyment compared to conventional assignments. A quasi-experimental study was conducted, comparing exam results from a control group (n = 91) that completed traditional homework with those from an experimental group (n = 68) that used WdW. Additionally, survey data provided insights into student experiences and perceptions. Findings indicate that replacing homework with WdW did not negatively impact overall academic performance, with students in the experimental group achieving comparable or slightly improved grades. Engagement levels were high, with nearly half of the students actively participating in the game. However, results revealed a significant difference in game perception between gamers and non-gamers, with the latter requiring additional support to navigate the game effectively. These findings highlight both the potential and challenges of implementing educational games in higher education. The study suggests that well-designed educational games can serve as viable alternatives to traditional assignments but must consider diverse student backgrounds and gaming experience. Future research should explore adaptive onboarding strategies to ensure accessibility for all learners and assess the long-term impact of game-based learning on knowledge retention and student motivation.

Keywords: Educational game · serious game · game-based learning · material science education · flipped classroom · learning success · serious game evaluation

1 Introduction

Materials science is a field of relevance for most engineering disciplines. Consequently, education in the field of material science has to handle a large number of students with different backgrounds. In these settings, it can be challenging to educate each individual student in an individually meaningful way, including the practical application of required skills in lab settings. Furthermore, the high enrollment of over a hundred students in first-semester modules, poses considerable logistical and pedagogical challenges for both faculty and students. A serious issue that arises is the restricted access to essential testing and analysis equipment, resulting in limited access to practical exercises [1].

Another challenge is the correction of homework assignments, as educators must review and provide feedback to all submissions, resulting in a high workload that leaves less time for direct student interaction [1].

In a first attempt to address these issues, a flipped classroom approach has been applied to the materials engineering module, with eLearning resources and hands-on lab exercises to boost engagement. Students access course materials via online videos and a textbook for self-directed learning. Class time focuses on practical applications, discussions, and short quizzes. Assessments include three lab reports, three homework assignments, and a final exam, with 74 of 150 points earned through coursework and 76 from the exam [2].

Building on this, an innovative project called "Welten der Werkstoffe" (WdW) (Worlds of Materials) aims to transport the relevant learning outcomes in a meaningful, engaging, and fun way by replacing theoretical homework with an application-oriented task in the form of an educational game accessible to all students.

The research reported here focuses on the evaluation of this game, resulting in the following research question:

(RQ) Can an educational game replace traditional homework assignments in a material science lecture to maintain or improve student learning outcomes, engagement, and enjoyment?

The aim of this study is to measure the impact of this educational game on students' performance compared to traditional methods (homework assignments), as well as the extent of student participation. Beyond academic performance, the evaluation also considers the game's influence on student enjoyment, the clarity of learning objectives, and their confidence in applying materials science knowledge.

Consequently, the game has been designed to enable students to solve material science-related tasks, utilizing digitally supported teaching-learning arrangements to address the issue of limited equipment access and to promote active rather than passive learning. We hypothesize that integrating an educational game will enhance student engagement and provide enjoyable learning experiences while maintaining the integrity of their learning outcome.

2 Theoretical Background

Educational Games are an advancement in innovative pedagogical approaches. Fundamental motivational aspects of games are proposed to enhance learning outcomes [3]. educational games, designed primarily for learning purposes, blend game design with educational content to construct engaging and effective learning environments [4]. The objective of such games is to teach or reinforce concepts interactively and enjoyably, often targeting specific learning objectives or skills. They are used in diverse educational settings such as classrooms, elearning platforms, and professional development programs, enriching traditional learning methods with immersive, hands-on experiences [5]. An advantage of educational games lies in their ability to provide immediate feedback on user actions, fostering an *"actio et reactio"* experience [6].

Game-based Learning (GBL) is a teaching method that utilizes educational games to support learning objectives directly [7]. By capitalizing on the motivational aspects of games, GBL endeavors to make learning more interactive, engaging, and enjoyable [8]. Its application spans different educational levels and subjects, fostering deeper understanding and retention of knowledge while enhancing students' cognitive, behavioral, and affective engagement with the material [9].

The *Flipped Classroom* approach is widely described as an instructional strategy in which traditional lecture and homework elements are reversed. Students first engage with new material outside of class, typically through video lectures, and then apply that knowledge during in-class activities facilitated by the teacher. This approach aims to enhance student engagement and allows for more personalized instruction during class time [10]. It can also be used in online learning and combined with gamification to further motivate learners [11].

When utilized proficiently, educational games can significantly enhance student learning outcomes by fostering increased engagement and motivation [12]. A move towards online education and a focus on crafting games that are simultaneously engaging and packed with educational content holds the promise of providing activating and engaging educational experiences [13].

A growing impact of digital game-based learning across educational settings is observed in literature and their positive effects on knowledge acquisition and broader learning benefits are emphasized, while at the same time, more experimental studies to identify the most effective game features for engagement and learning are needed [14]. Thus further research, through randomized controlled trials and comparisons with traditional teaching methods, is needed to critically define the educational effectiveness of digital games [15]. Subsequently, systematic evaluations of this evidence must ascertain the practical impact of educational games, which calls for stronger evaluative frameworks [16].

An educational game designed to enhance arithmetic abilities among children showcases how well-designed games can improve both the calculating speed level and accuracy in mathematical lessons. This states that the combination of practical exercises in combination with an educational game is promising [17].

Educational games can be designed to teach the basics of various fields such as science and commerce, emphasizing both fun and challenging qualities of learning. This approach reflects the trend of leveraging game mechanics to enhance educational outcomes [13]. While educational games have proven effective in various domains for different subjects and targeting different age groups of learners, their application as a direct replacement for traditional homework assignments remains underexplored beyond a few studies e.g. [18, 19]. The combination of educational games with the flipped classroom concept is not yet widely used, though there are promising exceptions e.g. [20].

The study reported here explores how a serious game can be effective, compared to traditional homework assignments in enhancing engagement while maintaining learning performance.

3 Methods

3.1 The Game WdW

WdW is a digital 2D point-and-click adventure game designed for both PC and Mac, playable online via a web browser. The player takes on the role of Nicole Nickel, an engineering student tasked with rescuing her professor who has been mysteriously locked inside a closet. Nicole must travel through 10 levels across a multiverse, encountering alternate versions of her professor and using her materials science knowledge to solve puzzles.

The game is directly aligned with the curriculum of the materials science module. Each of the 10 levels corresponds to one of the 10 chapters described in the textbook adopted for the module [21]. Throughout the game, students engage with familiar characters and scenarios that reinforce key concepts from their coursework. For example, in Level 1 skills correlate to Chapter One of their module, while in Chapter Four, students must leverage cumulative skillsets from prior chapters and levels to progress in the game.

The game replaces two of the three theoretical homework assignments that were previously required as part of the module's coursework. These assignments comprised tasks that are usually used for exam preparation.

The full game has an estimated playtime of approximately 9 h. After each lecture, students are advised to complete the corresponding game level, ensuring that they apply newly acquired knowledge in an interactive setting. A key game feature is the representation of laboratory equipment and machines, allowing students to apply theoretical knowledge in a simulated practical environment.

Students log in to the game using their student number. Upon completing the full game, they receive a personalized solution word (SW), which they can indicate during their final exam to earn extra points that are equivalent to the points previously awarded for the replaced homework assignments.

WdW was developed in collaboration with game developers, materials science experts, and students. An iterative design process ensured usability and effectiveness, with students providing lab tested feedback on difficulty, user experience, and bug fixes. Their insights improved interface design and challenge balance, leading to a more polished and effective result.

3.2 Participants

The study involved participants from two different study years in a quasi experimental design. In total 67 students of the material science module participated in summer term 2023 (experimental group) and 91 students that were part of the winter term 2019/20 (control group). Due to the iterative development process where the students in the semesters between these two groups gave constant feedback on new levels, the participant groups are not in consecutive semesters and the intermediate semesters are not considered as participants.

The study was conducted in Germany where the grading system operates on a scale from 1.0 (best grade) to 5.0 (worst grade), with grades below 4.0 considered a failure. This evaluation follows the same grading framework.

3.3 Data Collection Method

To assess the educational impact and engagement of WdW, a survey-based evaluation was conducted, complemented by an analysis of exam results before and after the game's introduction. The game-related survey was given only to the experimental group, the exam results were compared for both groups. This dual-method approach provided insights into academic performance changes and insights into student experience. The research focused on the game's effectiveness as a homework replacement and its impact on student performance, engagement, and motivation.

The exam-result analysis provided an objective measure of learning outcomes, allowing for a comprehensive assessment of the game's impact.

Survey Data. The survey is based on existing validated serious game evaluation scales [22], which have been adapted to our application case. While the resulting scale is no longer validated this procedure ensures a manageable survey size, relevance and coherence with the study's objectives. Additionally the survey was designed to directly align with the specific research question defined in the evaluation phase, rather than using a generalized survey. The survey used closed questions and a Likert scale from 1, full disagreement or a negative response (purple color scheme), to 6, full agreement or a positive response (green color scheme). This scale was utilized to measure participants' attitudes and perceptions towards various aspects of the game, ensuring a nuanced understanding of their experiences. The Likert scale questions were:

Q1: I felt competent while playing the Game.
Q2: I had fun playing "Welten der Werkstoffe" (WdW).
Q3: The goal of the game was clearly defined.
Q4: The game encourages active study and application of the learning content.
Q5: With the game I was able to determine if I had learned enough for the exam.

The survey encompassed additional open and closed questions, aiming to capture the game's educational impact, engagement level, and overall user experience.

The initial phase of the evaluation involved pilot testing the survey with subject matter experts to ensure its relevance and comprehensiveness, thereby aligning all involved parties on the evaluation's objectives. Following the pilot test, the survey was distributed online, and the responses were systematically analyzed alongside exam results. The invitation for voluntary participation in the survey was disseminated via email, ensuring every student who took part in the exam had an opportunity to contribute their insights. All data collected was anonymized.

Examination Data. An additional component of the evaluation compared exam results from sessions before and after the game's full implementation (all 10 Levels). Comprehensive exam results from the two distinct groups were analyzed. To ensure an informative analysis, the data set also included whether students had interacted with the game by completing all 10 levels and writing a unique solution word (SW) on their exams. This approach allowed for a clear differentiation between students who finished the game and those who did not, facilitating a more accurate assessment of the game's educational efficacy and popularity among the students.

4 Results

4.1 Survey

In total, 67 students of the experimental group took the exam. Only these received the survey, which 20 of them completed. Out of these respondents, 19 confirmed they had played the game at least once. Notably, 80% of the respondents reported completing the game and 65% of the respondents successfully passed; conversely, 35% did not pass the exam, resulting in their failure of the course.

Within the respondent group of the study, 65% reported playing games at least once to twice a month. This subset of participants will be referred to as "gamers" for clarity and ease of reference. Conversely, the remaining 35% of participants indicated that they play games rarely or not at all. This group will therefore be referred to as "non-gamers".

Game Usage and Experience According to Learning Success. Participants who achieved grades in the range of 1 and 2 all completed the game. Among those who received a grade of 3 67% finished the game. Furthermore, 71% of participants who failed the course completed the game.

An overview of the answers will provide further insights into the patterns and correlations between game completion and academic performance (Table 1).

Table 1. Overview answers survey by exam result.

		quantity	Q1	Q2	Q3	Q4	Q5
average	all	19	3.47	4.11	4.47	4.26	3.74
SD	all		1.17	1.49	1.43	1.19	1.63
average	failed	7	3.29	3.29	3.86	3.57	4.00
SD	failed		1.60	1.60	1.68	1.40	1.63
average	passed	12	3.58	4.58	4.83	4.67	3.58
SD	passed		0.90	1.24	1.19	0.89	1.68
significance	(p-value)		0.608	0.064	0.156	0.051	0.605

For Q1 to Q4, the average rating of participants who passed the course (ranging from 3.58 to 4.83) was higher than for participants who failed (ranging from 3.29 to 3.86), though a t-test showed none of these results as significant. The rating of participants who passed is more consistent (SD from 0.89 to 1.24) than for those who failed (SD from 1.4 to 1.68). Q5 is an exception, where participants who failed rated the game better (4.00) than participants who passed (3.58), also without significance. The difference of 1.1 in the ratings of Q4 (t-test: p-value = 0.051) indicates a visible, but not significant difference in perceptions regarding how the game promotes active engagement with the content between the two groups.

Correlation values were identified as described by Evans JD. [23]. Note that correlations may appear inverted due to the German grading scheme as described above.

There was a medium correlation observed indicating that the better the participants' grades, the more fun they reported having while playing the game. Similarly, a medium correlation was also found between the participants' grades and their perception that the game encouraged them to actively study and apply the content (Table 2).

Table 2. Correlations grade to survey questions.

conditions		correlations
grade vs competence Q1	−0.070	no correlation
grade vs fun Q2	−0.461	better grade = more fun (medium correlation)
grade vs goal Q3	−0.298	better grade = clear goal (weak correlation)
grade vs engaging Q4	−0.423	better grade = more engaging (medium correlation)
grade vs learning experience Q5	0.137	better grade = better learning experience (weak correlation)

Game Experience for Gamers and Non-Gamers. In this section of the evaluation of WdW, the data is broken down into two categories based on participants' gaming experience: "gamers," who play games at least once to twice a month, and "non-gamers," who play games rarely or not at all. This distinction allowed for an insightful analysis of how gaming experience influences perceptions and outcomes related to the educational game. consequently, among the 19 who played the game and answered the survey, 12 were categorized as gamers and 7 as non-gamers.

When evaluating the game another trend emerged: non-gamers generally rated the game more negatively, while gamers expressed more positive evaluations across various aspects of the game (Table 3).

Gamers consistently rated their experience with WdW higher than non-gamers across all evaluated aspects. For competence (Q1), non-gamers rated it 3.14, while gamers scored it slightly higher at 3.67, showing a marginal difference in perceived competence. Enjoyment (Q2) on the other hand showed a significant difference, with non-gamers

Table 3. Overview answers survey by gaming experience.

gaming experience	quantity	Q1	Q2	Q3	Q4	Q5
non gamers	7	3.14	3.14	3.43	3.29	2.71
SD		1.21	1.46	1.62	1.11	1.50
gamers	12	3.67	4.67	5.08	4.83	4.33
SD		1.15	1.23	0.90	0.83	1.44
significance (p-value)		0.362	0.026	0.010	0.003	0.032

averaging at 3.14, and gamers reporting a significantly higher average of 4.67 with a difference of 1.53 (t-test: p-value = 0.026). Similarly, clarity of objectives (Q3) was rated 3.43 by non-gamers and 5.08 by gamers with a difference of 1.65 points (t-test: p-value = 0.010). Perceptions on Q4 followed the same trend, with non-gamers at 3.29 and gamers at 4.83. The difference of 1.54 between the two groups is statistically significant (t-test: p-value = 0.003), underscoring a marked contrast in perceptions based on gaming experience. Finally, Q5 saw non-gamers rating it 2.71, while gamers scored it significantly higher at 4.33. There is a significant difference of 1.62 between these groups (t-test: p-value = 0.032) (Table 3).

Table 4. Correlations gaming experience to survey questions

conditions		correlations
gaming vs competence Q1	0.103	more gaming = more competent (weak correlation)
gaming vs fun Q2	0.445	more gaming = more fun (**medium correlation**)
gaming vs goal Q3	0.691	more gaming = goals clear (**strong correlation**)
gaming vs engaging Q4	0.609	more gaming = more engaging (**strong correlation**)
gaming vs learning experience Q4	0.473	more gaming = more learning experience (**medium correlation**)

There is a medium correlation indicating that the more frequently a participant engages in gaming, the more enjoyment they report from playing WdW. Similarly, a strong correlation exists between a participant's gaming frequency and whether they perceived the game's goals as clearly defined. This trend continues with gaming frequency potentially positively affecting participants' feelings about whether the game engages them to actively study and apply the content. Additionally, there is a medium correlation between a participant's gaming habits and their confidence in the game's ability to help them assess whether or not they learned enough to pass the course.

4.2 Exam

The exam results of both the control group and the experimental group were compared. In the study, 49% of participants completed the game, as indicated by a solution word (SW) on their exam. In the experimental group, 60.3% of the students passed the course, with the majority achieving grades within the range of 2 and 3. All students who achieved a grade in the range of 1, have completed the game. For those with grades in the range of 2, 79% finished the game. Half of the students with grades in the range of 3 finished it. Among the students who failed the course, 26% had finished the game (Fig. 1 and Tables 5, 6, 7).

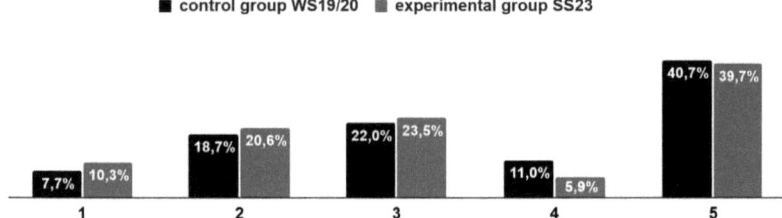

Fig. 1. Exam results from the control group and experimental group.

Table 5. Heatmap of grade to SW

grade	1	2	3	4	5
solution word	100%	78.6%	50%	0.0%	25.9%

The average grade for students who passed the course in the experimental group was 2.76. However, a closer look reveals that students who completed the game had a slightly higher average grade of 2.94, compared to those who did not finish the game, who had a significantly lower average grade of 4.32. In the control group, 59.3% of the students passed the course, with an average grade among those passing at 2.89. This closely mirrors the performance in the experimental group, where 60.3% of students passed, but with a slightly better average grade of 2.76.

Table 6. Exam results from the experimental group (SS23)

	quantity	percent	average grade
passed	41	60.3%	2.76
failed	27	39.7%	5.00
all	68	100%	3.65
average grade SW	2.94		
average grade no SW	4.32		

Table 7. Exam results from the control group (WS 19/20)

	quantity	percent	average grade
passed	54	59.3%	2.89
failed	37	40.7%	5.00
all	91	100%	3.75

5 Discussion

The evaluation of WdW in the experimental group provides key insights into its impact on student performance. Nearly half of the students in that group engaged with WdW, with 49% completing it. Those who finished the game had an average grade of 2.94, outperforming those who did not complete it with an average of 4.32, suggesting a link between game completion and improved academic performance. Although there appears to be a correlation between completing the game and achieving higher grades, it is also possible that higher-performing students are more likely to engage with available learning resources.

When comparing the groups, the introduction of the game led to a slight improvement in the average grades of passing students in the experimental group compared to the control group. However, the comparison also indicates that the overall pass rate did not significantly increase with the game's introduction. This suggests that while the game had a slight positive impact on the average grades of students who passed, it did not significantly alter the course's overall pass rates. These findings also suggest that replacing traditional homework with WdW did not negatively impact overall student performance. The comparison of pass and fail rates with previous semesters, where homework assignments contributed to extra points, indicates that the level of academic challenge and achievement remained consistent. This suggests that the game successfully maintained the coursework's educational standards, serving as a viable alternative to conventional homework.

Student engagement with WdW highlights its potential as a motivational learning tool. The solution word incentive encouraged participation, but not all students took full advantage of the game.

Enjoyment of the game varied based on student performance. Those who achieved higher grades also reported greater enjoyment, with a medium correlation between academic success and enjoyment levels. Similarly, students who passed the course found the game more effective in promoting active engagement, while those who did not pass rated it lower. However, based on the data we have we do not know whether students who enjoyed the game performed better or if performing poorly led to them reporting the game as less enjoyable.

A deeper analysis of survey responses revealed notable differences between gamers and non-gamers in how they engaged with the game. Gamers rated their enjoyment significantly higher than non-gamers, suggesting that familiarity with gaming mechanics influenced engagement levels. Similarly, gamers found the game's objectives clearer, whereas non-gamers reported a moderate level of clarity. This statistically significant difference suggests that prior gaming experience influences how well players understand the game's goals. Furthermore, a strong correlation was observed between gaming frequency and perceived clarity, indicating that players who engage in games regularly are more equipped to recognize and align with the game's objectives. This trend may stem from their familiarity with common gaming mechanics and conventions, allowing them to grasp the structure and purpose of educational games like WdW more intuitively. These findings highlight the importance of integrating familiar gaming elements to enhance engagement and comprehension in game-based learning. However, they also suggest that non-gamers may require additional support or guidance to navigate the game effectively, ensuring that all students benefit equally from the learning experience. Beyond clarity, gamers also rated the game more favorably in fostering active learning compared to non-gamers. Conversely, non-gamers expressed greater skepticism regarding the game's self-assessment utility, which may stem from unfamiliarity with interpreting game-based feedback in an academic context. These findings suggest that educational games should incorporate onboarding mechanisms that help non-gamers adapt to the game's mechanics, ensuring that all students benefit equally from the learning experience. A more adaptive onboarding system could bridge this gap.

The evaluation of WdW underscores a significant variance in how gamers and non-gamers perceive and engage with educational games. This distinction is pivotal, as it not only affects enjoyment and engagement levels but also extends to how educational content is received and applied by the players.

6 Conclusion and Future Work

The educational game WdW introduces game-based learning into the material sciences curriculum at TH Köln, offering an innovative approach to engaging students. This project focuses on transforming complex scientific concepts into an interactive and immersive game environment, enhancing the educational experience for students while maintaining high development standards. The replacement of traditional homework with WdW in the material sciences course did not adversely affect the overall performance outcomes of students. The examination of pass and fail rates, in comparison with the control group where homework contributed to extra points, indicates that the level of academic challenge and achievement remained consistent. This consistency suggests that the educational game effectively maintained the educational standards of the coursework, successfully serving as an alternative to conventional homework assignments. This approach not only alleviates the workload of the scientific staff but also offers students a unique opportunity to engage with material science concepts through interactive gameplay. A key achievement of WdW lies in its ability to simulate access to sophisticated material testing and analysis equipment, thus overcoming the logistical and pedagogical challenges associated with high enrollment numbers and limited physical resources. By offering an alternative to traditional homework assignments, the game successfully integrates into the flipped classroom model, providing students with a novel tool to explore material sciences in a self-directed manner.

Beyond its support to maintain the participants' academic performance, WdW proved to be engaging, with nearly half of the students in the experimental group actively participating. Survey responses indicate that students generally found the game enjoyable, reinforcing its potential as an engaging alternative to traditional homework. The positive reception highlights the importance of interactive learning formats in modern higher education.

The evaluation of the game's impact on student performance and engagement revealed significant insights. The distinct difference in game ratings between gamers and non-gamers underscores the necessity for a nuanced approach to educational game design. This divergence highlights the importance of understanding the gaming habits and preferences of the target audience, suggesting that educational games can be significantly improved by tailoring them to meet the diverse needs of learners.

The disparity between gamers and non-gamers highlights a key challenge in implementing educational games broadly. While gamers benefit from intuitive gameplay mechanics, non-gamers may require additional support to engage effectively. Future iterations of the game should explore adaptive onboarding strategies to enhance accessibility for all learners.

In conclusion, WdW demonstrates the transformative potential of game-based learning in higher education. By bridging the gap between theory and practice, the game enhances engagement, supports competence development, and serves as an innovative alternative to traditional homework. The study highlights both the opportunities and challenges of educational game design, emphasizing the need for adaptable learning environments that cater to diverse student backgrounds.

Future research is needed to more thoroughly evaluate the impact of WdW with larger participant numbers. Insights of the design and evaluation will also inform further research on a more general design and evaluation framework for educational games, that shall be applied in additional educational domains.

7 Limitations

While this study provides valuable insights into game-based learning in materials science education, it has limitations. One major limitation is the low survey response rate, with only a quarter of exam participants providing feedback. This limited sample size may not fully reflect the overall student experience, requiring cautious interpretation. Additionally, the control group's data was collected just before the COVID-19 pandemic, potentially introducing external factors that affected student performance and adding unintended bias to the comparative analysis.

Self-selection bias may have also influenced the findings, as students interested in the game were more likely to complete the survey. Moreover, factors such as motivation, study habits, and prior knowledge could have impacted student performance independently of the game. Future research should account for these variables and explore the long-term effects of game-based learning on retention and engagement. Future studies should aim for larger sample sizes, broader comparative analyses, and adaptive evaluation methods to better understand how game-based learning can be effectively implemented across diverse educational settings.

Ethics. The study was approved by TH Köln following their ethical standards.

Acknowledgments. This research was an internally funded project at TH Köln. We would like to thank the teams at Cologne Game Lab and Material Science for their contributions. Initially funded by the Stifterverband through a "Fellowship für digitale Innovationen in der Hochschullehre". Also funded through the State Teaching Award of the Federal State of North Rhine-Westphalia by the Ministry of Culture and Science for Martin Bonnet.

Also funded through the German Computer Game Award DCP, Winner best Serious Game.

Disclosure of Interests. The authors declare no conflict of interest.

References

1. Bonnet, M., Klemke, R., Hettlich, M., Wolf, S.: Gamification als Serious Game im Bachelor-Pflicht-Modul Werkstofftechnik Bewerbung um den Lehrpreis 2019 der TH Köln Spielend lernen?! (2019)
2. Bonnet, M., Hansmeier, E., Kämper, N.: "Ran ans Werk!" – Erfolgreiche Umsetzung eines Inverted-Classroom-Konzeptes im Grundlagenmodul Werkstofftechnik für studierendenzentriertes und kompetenzorientiertes Lernen im Maschinenbau. Teach.-Learn. Discuss. - Innov. Für Zuk. Lehre Den Ingenieurwissenschaften, pp. 25–33 (2013)
3. Yu, Z., Gao, M., Wang, L.: The effect of educational games on learning outcomes, student motivation, engagement and satisfaction. J. Educ. Comput. Res. **59**, 522–546 (2021). https://doi.org/10.1177/0735633120969214
4. Dimitriadou, A., Djafarova, N., Turetken, O., Verkuyl, M., Ferworn, A.: Challenges in serious game design and development: educators' experiences. Simul. Gaming **52**, 132–152 (2021). https://doi.org/10.1177/1046878120944197
5. Khine, M.S.: Games in education. In: Khine, M.S. (ed.) Playful teaching, learning games: new tool for digital classrooms, pp. 121–127. SensePublishers, Rotterdam (2011). https://doi.org/10.1007/978-94-6091-460-7_8

6. Richert, A., Mai, V., Mengen, H., Wolf, S.: Mixed reality games in engineering education. In: 2019 5th Experiment International Conference (exp.at'19), pp. 365–370 (2019). https://doi.org/10.1109/EXPAT.2019.8876572
7. Jääskä, E., Aaltonen, K.: Teachers' experiences of using game-based learning methods in project management higher education. Proj. Leadersh. Soc. **3**, 100041 (2022). https://doi.org/10.1016/j.plas.2022.100041
8. Zeng, J., Parks, S., Shang, J.: To learn scientifically, effectively, and enjoyably: a review of educational games. Hum. Behav. Emerg. Technol. **2**, 186–195 (2020). https://doi.org/10.1002/hbe2.188
9. Plass, J.L., Homer, B.D., Kinzer, C.K.: Foundations of game-based learning. Educ. Psychol. **50**, 258–283 (2015). https://doi.org/10.1080/00461520.2015.1122533
10. Bergmann, J., Sams, A.: Flip your classroom: reach every student in every class every day. International Society for Technology in Education (2012)
11. Klemke, R., Eradze, M., Antonaci, A.: The flipped MOOC: using gamification and learning analytics in MOOC design—a conceptual approach. Educ. Sci. **8**, 25 (2018). https://doi.org/10.3390/educsci8010025
12. Sadera, W.A., Li, Q., Song, L., Liu, L.: Digital game-based learning. Comput. Sch. 31, p. 1 (2014). https://doi.org/10.1080/07380569.2014.879801.
13. Asadi, Y.M.H.I., Babu, C.G., Shubham, P., Shenov, S.A.: Innovative game based educational application for learning. In: 2021 12th International Conference on Computing Communication and Networking Technologies (ICCCNT), pp. 1–6. IEEE, Kharagpur, India (2021). https://doi.org/10.1109/ICCCNT51525.2021.9579868
14. Boyle, E.A., et al.: An update to the systematic literature review of empirical evidence of the impacts and outcomes of computer games and serious games. Comput. Educ. **94**, 178–192 (2016). https://doi.org/10.1016/j.compedu.2015.11.003
15. Hussein, M.H., Ow, S.H., Cheong, L.S., Thong, M., Ebrahim, N.A.: Effects of digital game-based learning on elementary science learning: a systematic review. IEEE Access. **7**, 62465–62478 (2019). https://doi.org/10.1109/ACCESS.2019.2916324
16. Petri, G., Gresse von Wangenheim, C.: How to evaluate educational games: a systematic literature review. J. Univers. Comput. Sci. **22**, 992 (2016)
17. Yunanto, A., Herumurti, D., Kuswadayan, I., Hariadi, R.R., Rochimah, S.: Design and implementation of educational game to improve arithmetic abilities for children. 2019 12th Int. Conf. Inf. Commun. Technol. Syst. ICTS, pp. 27–31 (2019). https://doi.org/10.1109/ICTS.2019.8850966
18. Amzalag, M.: Parent attitudes towards the integration of digital learning games as an alternative to traditional homework. Int. J. Inf. Commun. Technol. Educ. IJICTE. **17**, 151–167 (2021). https://doi.org/10.4018/IJICTE.20210701.oa10
19. Faitelson, D., Gul, S., Arieli, M.: Computer games are scalable and engaging alternatives to traditional undergraduate mathematics homework. Primus **34**, 251–267 (2024). https://doi.org/10.1080/10511970.2023.2269920
20. Li, C.-T., Hou, H.-T., Li, M.-C., Kuo, C.-C.: Comparison of mini-game-based flipped classroom and video-based flipped classroom: an analysis of learning performance, flow and concentration on discussion. Asia-Pac. Educ. Res. **31**, 321–332 (2022). https://doi.org/10.1007/s40299-021-00573-x
21. Bonnet, M.: Wiley-Schnellkurs Werkstoffkunde: Die Grundlagen auf einem Blick. Vom Atomaufbau bis zur Werkstoffprüfung. Schnelltest: Mit Übungsaufgaben und Lösungen. Wiley-VCH, Weinheim (2017)
22. Kelly, A., Hummel, H., van der Stappen, E., Prinsen, F., Terbeek, L.: Inventaris van instrumenten voor evidence-informed onderwijsinnovatie met ICT. , Utrecht (2020)
23. Evans, J.D.: Straightforward Statistics for the Behavioral Sciences. Brooks/Cole Pub. Co., Pacific Grove (1996)

From News to Stories via an AI-Supported Retelling Process

Edirlei Soares de Lima[1]([✉])[iD], Marco A. Casanova[2][iD], Bruno Feijó[2][iD], and Antonio L. Furtado[2][iD]

[1] Academy for AI, Games and Media, Breda University of Applied Sciences, Breda, The Netherlands
`soaresdelima.e@buas.nl`
[2] Department of Informatics, PUC-Rio, R. Marquês de São Vicente 225, Rio de Janeiro, Brazil
`{casanova,bfeijo,furtado}@inf.puc-rio.br`

Abstract. This paper explores how AI-driven storytelling can transform news articles into fictional narratives using structured retelling techniques. We introduce NewsReteller, a system that explores the generative capabilities of Large Language Models to create stories from news content through three distinct approaches: genre-based storytelling, which adapts narratives to established literary styles; structured storytelling, which reshapes events using predefined biased schemes (story skeletons); and data-driven storytelling, which emphasizes factual clarity and analytical framing. To assess the system's ability to reinterpret factual content, we generated multiple stories from a single news article using each of these approaches. The results illustrate how different retelling strategies influence narrative framing, thematic emphasis, and information presentation, highlighting the potential of our method to generate creative reinterpretations of real-world events.

Keywords: AI-driven Storytelling · News Articles · Literary Genres · Narrative Journalism · Large Language Models

1 Introduction

Storytelling has long been a fundamental means of communication, enabling individuals and societies to share knowledge, convey emotions, and interpret the world around them. While fictional narratives often draw inspiration from existing stories, historical events, or societal trends, artificial intelligence (AI) opens new possibilities for transforming real-world content into structured narratives. News articles, in particular, offer a rich factual foundation that, when creatively reinterpreted, can inspire fictional storytelling. This paper explores how AI can facilitate the process of transforming news into fictional stories.

This research is motivated by the observation that many contemporary narratives in literature, film, and digital media are significantly shaped by real-world events. A relevant precedent to our work is the influence of prior narratives in

---

© IFIP International Federation for Information Processing 2025
Published by Springer Nature Switzerland AG 2025
M. Sugimoto et al. (Eds.): ICEC 2025, LNCS 16042, pp. 334–348, 2025.
https://doi.org/10.1007/978-3-032-02555-5_24

shaping new stories. As noted by Roland Barthes, "Any text is a new tissue of past citations" [2], suggesting that even original works often build upon existing narratives. In previous work [17,19], we investigated this phenomenon using an AI-driven tool that generates stories inspired by well-known books and films. However, relying solely on existing fictional works risks reinforcing established themes and outdated perspectives. Our current approach shifts the focus to news articles, ensuring generated narratives reflect contemporary events.

The use of news as a source of inspiration for fictional stories is not a new phenomenon. Real-world events have historically inspired literary works and cinematic narratives. For instance, news and scientific advancements in space exploration have played a key role in shaping fictional portrayals of interplanetary travel. Early speculation about Mars as a potentially inhabited planet inspired stories of alien civilizations, often portrayed as hostile invaders. As scientific understanding advanced, so too did the narratives it inspired. NASA's recent confirmation of plans to send astronauts to Mars [28] has influenced contemporary storytelling, exemplified by *The Martian* (2015) [34], which depicts an astronaut's survival on Mars through ingenuity.

In this paper, we propose a structured AI-supported retelling process that enables users to reinterpret news articles as fictional narratives. Our approach explores the interpretation and text generation capabilities of Large Language Models (LLMs) to guide users through this transformation, while also incorporating text-to-image models to generate complementary illustrations. To validate our approach, we developed NewsReteller, an AI-powered prototype that assists users by guiding them in structuring their stories according to different structuring approaches. To assess the system's capabilities, we generated stories from a real news article, examining how different strategies shape the final narratives.

The paper is organized as follows. Section 2 presents related work. Section 3 explores different perspectives on news retelling. Section 4 discusses transforming news into fiction. Section 5 details NewsReteller's implementation. Section 6 presents experimental results illustrating how the system produces diverse narrative adaptations. Section 7 concludes with future research directions.

2 Related Work

The use of LLMs for narrative generation has gained significant attention in recent years. Some works improve story quality through fine-tuning on large datasets [8,40], reinforcement learning for goal-driven storytelling [1], or external knowledge retrieval [45]. Others enhance structure via backward reasoning [6], iterative planning [44], or recursive reprompting [46]. While these approaches refine structure, they rely on fictional inputs rather than real-world content. An alternative involves reusing existing narrative elements to generate new stories. In previous works, we explored this concept by using semiotic relations to repurpose elements from established narratives [17,19,21,25], applying existing narrative patterns to maintain thematic consistency [20,22], and employing visual information extracted from images to define narrative content [18,24]. In this work, we extend these strategies to reinterpret factual news as fictional stories.

While most LLM-based storytelling approaches generate narratives from fictional inputs, some research has explored structuring narratives from real-world events. Event-centric models [41,47] construct storylines by identifying and linking events across news articles, often using graph-based representations or unsupervised methods. These approaches typically produce event schemas or timelines, requiring further processing to generate coherent narratives. Retrieval-based approaches [39] assist human writers by identifying relevant articles to support a narrative but do not automate the storytelling process itself.

An automated approach is seen in template-driven news writing, such as the Phenom-based system [14], which maps events to predefined templates. While this method ensures factual accuracy, it is inherently constrained by rigid templates. In contrast, our approach explores the generative power of LLMs, blending structured storytelling with creative retelling.

3 News Retelling Perspectives

We understand that news, as a foundational narrative of actual events, can be approached from at least three perspectives: historical, biased, and journalistic. Within each perspective, different choices determine how to retell the original nonfiction events in meaningfully structured ways.

3.1 Historical Perspective

For the historical perspective, we start from Hayden White's assertion, in his book *Metahistory: The Historical Imagination in Nineteenth-century Europe* [43], that historic narrative can be written in four modes: integrative, representational, reductionist, and negational. In turn, he assimilates these modes to the so-called *four master tropes*: synecdoche, metaphor, metonymy and irony [4]. Even more significant is his assimilation of modes and tropes to Frye's notion of comedy, romance, tragedy, and satire [10]. To this list of four genres, we can add a fifth, mystery, based on Marie-Laure Ryan's [32] concept of *epistemic plots*.

In a previous work [23] we construed different *patterns* to specify the structure of narratives pertaining to each of these genres. In comedy, within the integrative mode, the sequence of events conforms as expected to the unquestioned laws of a just world. In romance, within the representational mode, the world order is disturbed and a heroic quest must be achieved by those inspired by principles of justice and fairness. In tragedy, within the reductionist mode, the insolent pride of misguided leaders initiates an inevitable destructive crisis. In satire, within the negational mode, a dystopian regime prevails, against which any reaction is useless. In mystery, a second-order-theory process is pursued, which tries to reveal the original narrative, explaining its causes and consequences.

Retelling news involving key incidents is a challenging venture, since many possible causes may offer themselves as candidates, to be evaluated by *abductive* reasoning [29], and asking whether an undesirable consequence might have been avoided requires *counterfactual* answers to what-if questions [27]. A striking example of the latter is Winston Churchill's retelling to the Commons of the ill-fated Munich agreement, without which the Second World War might not have occurred: "We have sustained a total, unmitigated defeat" [35].

3.2 Biased Perspective

Event sequences or isolated events worthy of being retold are, first of all, key incidents, such as the signature of the Munich agreement or the invasion of Normandy (the so-called D-day) that determine the course of history. In addition, seemingly less important incidents may deserve retelling if they are in some sense revealing of the points of view of the stakeholders involved.

In a seminal work, Schank and Abelson [33] showed how to give multiple accounts of such recurring incidents under the structured form of story skeletons, which express how different agents retell the same events in differently structured ways that clearly reflect the characteristic biases of each agent. They provide a real incident as example, described below under the denomination of Case 1, followed by Skeleton 1, which they attribute to one of the agents. Recently, we encountered news that appeared to follow the same skeleton (Case 2).

Case 1. A few years ago the United States Navy shot down an Iranian airliner carrying over 200 passengers. Mr. Reagan said. "We all know it was a tragedy. But we're talking about an incident in which a plane on radar was observed coming in the direction of a ship in combat and the plane began lowering its altitude. And so, I think it was an understandable accident to shoot and think that they were under attack from that plane."

Skeleton 1. Understandable Tragedy: (1) actor pursues justifiable goal; (2) actor selects reasonable plan to achieve goal; (3) plan involves selection of correct action; (4) action taken has unintended and unanticipatable result; (5) result turns out to be undesirable; (6) innocent people are hurt by result; (7) it is not the actor's fault.

Case 2. Seven World Central Kitchen aid workers were killed by Israeli airstrike in Gaza. Israeli Prime Minister Benjamin Netanyahu said Israel's armed forces had "unintentionally" struck a convoy from the humanitarian group World Central Kitchen in Gaza late Monday, killing seven aid workers. "Unfortunately, in the last day there was a tragic case of our forces unintentionally hitting innocent people in the Gaza Strip," Netanyahu said Tuesday as he left a hospital in Jerusalem after a hernia operation. "It happens in war. We will investigate it right to the end. ... We are in contact with the governments, and we will do everything so that this thing does not happen again" [7].

Are the two cases to some point analogous? To confirm or deny our impression, we posed the same question to the rival LLM-based tools ChatGPT and DeepSeek. Both gave highly positive answers, which are provided in our supplementary material at https://narrativelab.org/newsreteller/sup-doc-1.pdf.

3.3 Journalistic Perspective

For editors of newspapers and other publication media, the news that deserve publication are those that satisfy their standard criteria of recency, relevancy, topic popularity and conflicting trends. They insist that their journalists use a language that shows expertise and is easily understood by an average citizen.

Given the diversity and, quite often, complexity of the topics to be covered, old-time professional reporters not always were able to produce a coherent and technically correct account. To give an extreme example, consider the difficulty of providing an intelligible report on the work on quantum entanglement that led to a Nobel prize in Physics in 2022.[1]

A highly creative orientation has fortunately been adopted, since the past century, by journalists, such as Gaetano Talese,[2] who spent considerable time doing research before composing their texts. *Narrative journalism* – also known as *literary journalism* – is a long-established approach to nonfiction writing [16, 26]. Popularized by the New Journalism movement of the 1960s and 1970s, it has continued in various forms across different media and publications [12].

News retelling has gained the extra impulse of *The Conversation* websites,[3] started in Australia in 2011, and is now spreading through a number of countries. Their ideal of "academic rigor, journalistic flair" aims to produce *high-level content* in a readable style for a broad audience. For this purpose, they resort to expert scholars to comment on current events. The authors are encouraged to submit *drafts* of their texts which, with the help of skilled editors, are repeatedly revised until it is approved for online *retelling*. The texts follow strict guidelines favoring concise sentences and accessible language, ensuring readability according to established metrics, such as the Flesch-Kincaid readability tests [9,13].

At present, news research, in addition to Internet queries, can take advantage of LLMs for news retelling. Moreover, for handling non-purely historic incidents (comprising technical aspects, for example) a *data storytelling* [15] approach can be incorporated as an alternative to the patterns of Sect. 3.1.

4 From News to Fictional Stories

To begin with, we examined how an existing news narrative can be retold to produce a clearer, more structured version of the same events. With this in mind, we approached the problem from the three above-described complementary perspectives, stressing historic modes of narration, biased interpretations, and journalistic language. It should be clear that the resulting narrative still refers to the same news, with the same agents performing the same actions, though possibly enriched with information acquired by the LLM during training.

The ultimate goal of our work is to generate fiction from news through the proposed news retelling process. To produce diverse, engaging, and immersive

---
[1] https://www.nytimes.com/2022/10/04/science/nobel-prize-physics-winner.html.
[2] https://en.wikipedia.org/wiki/Gay_Talese.
[3] https://theconversation.com/au/who-we-are.

stories, it may be appropriate to provide the system, in addition to the original news article, a *premise* that outlines characters and key circumstances to guide the imaginative construction. Perhaps the simplest premise is to invent avatars of historical figures acting in a real or fictional country, performing deeds modeled on the input news. For example, King Arthur's depiction as a world-conqueror in *The History of the Kings of Britain* may have been inspired by Alexander of Macedon's expeditions [11]. Another directive involves altering historical outcomes, such as narrating a counterfactual scenario in which Germany won World War II, as frequently depicted in films [31].

Using news reports on the landing of Allied troops in Normandy (the already mentioned D-Day [3]), one may incorporate a premise inspired by the real loss of individual soldiers to create a more human-centered narrative. Indeed, the film *Saving Private Ryan* (1998) [36] evokes a quest to bring back an imaginary participant of that battle. Another example on the same line is the film *Hiroshima mon Amour* (1959) [30], set in the aftermath of the tragic atomic bombing.

Many other possibilities certainly exist, but may we finish with the unlikely opposite case of fiction generating (what was believed as) news: a science-fiction novel (*War of the Worlds* (1898) of H. G. Wells [42]) engendering the terrifying news of a Martian invasion of Earth on October 30, 1938 [5].

5 The NewsReteller Prototype

NewsReteller is an AI-powered system designed to assist users in creating narratives from news articles. Grounded in the perspectives explored in the previous sections, the system guides users through the process of retelling real-world events in meaningfully structured ways. By integrating LLMs with structured storytelling approaches, NewsReteller enables users to shape narratives that emphasize different interpretative angles. Additionally, the system incorporates a text-to-image model to generate illustrations that visually complement the stories. The prototype is available at: https://narrativelab.org/newsreteller/.

5.1 User Interface

The user interface of NewsReteller allows users to generate narratives from real-world news articles (Fig. 1). The input consists of three components: (1) a news article URL as factual basis; (2) an optional premise for additional context; and (3) a narrative structuring method to transform the news into a fictional narrative. Users can choose from *Genre-based Storytelling*, which follows the conventions of literary genres (Comedy, Romance, Tragedy, Satire, Mystery); *Structural Storytelling*, which applies predefined story skeletons (Understandable Tragedy, The Justifiability of Self-Defense, or a custom skeleton extracted from a news article); or *Data-driven Storytelling*, which prioritizes factual insights. After providing the inputs (Actions 1 and 2 in Fig. 1 (a)), users generate the narrative by clicking the "Retell Story" button (Action 3 in Fig. 1 (a)).

The generated story is displayed on the story composition screen (Fig. 1 (b)). The story is divided into chapters, each containing a title, narrative text, and an AI-generated illustration. Users can refine the content by either regenerating the text or regenerating the illustration (Action 4 in Fig. 1 (b)). When modifying story elements, users have the option to provide additional suggestions to guide the regeneration process, enabling more controlled adjustments to the narrative or to its visual representation. The final story can be saved to the user's personal library via the "Save Story" button (Action 5 in Fig. 1 (b)), where it remains accessible for future reference (Fig. 1 (c)). The full story for the example in Fig. 1 is available at: https://narrativelab.org/newsreteller/#/story/703.

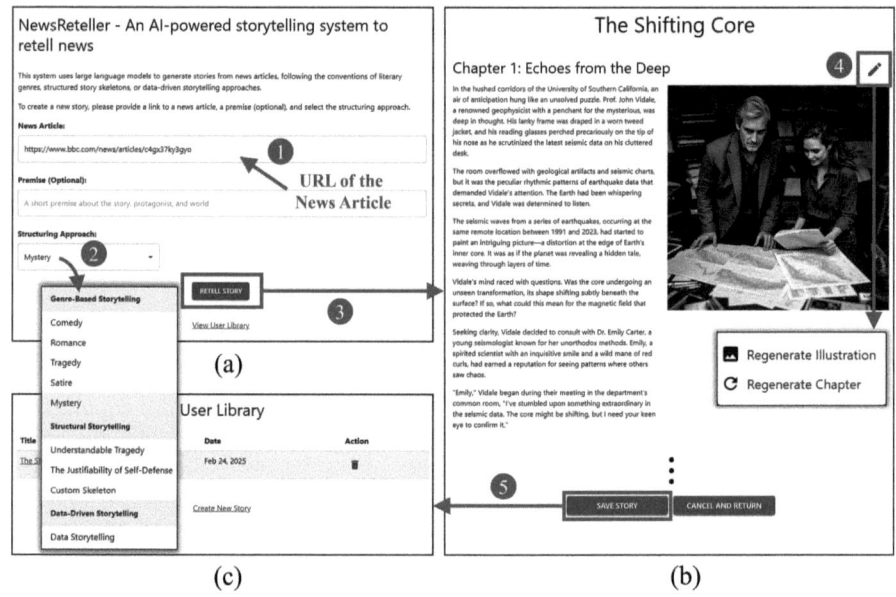

Fig. 1. The user interface of NewsReteller.

5.2 System Architecture

As illustrated in Fig. 2, NewsReteller employs a multi-AI-agent architecture for narrative generation, extending our previous framework [17, 19, 22, 25] to support the generation of narratives from news articles. The architecture includes two AI agents: (1) a Storywriter AI Agent, powered by an LLM, that generates narratives based on a news article, premise, and storytelling approach; and (2) an Illustrator AI Agent that uses a text-to-image diffusion model to produce story illustrations. A Plot Manager module coordinates the workflow by managing requests between AI agents and other modules. As part of this process, the Plot Manager retrieves news through the Information Retrieval module, which accesses external news websites, extracts article content, and forwards it to the Storywriter AI Agent. Generated stories are stored in the Story Database, while a web-based interface facilitates user interaction (as described in Sect. 5.1).

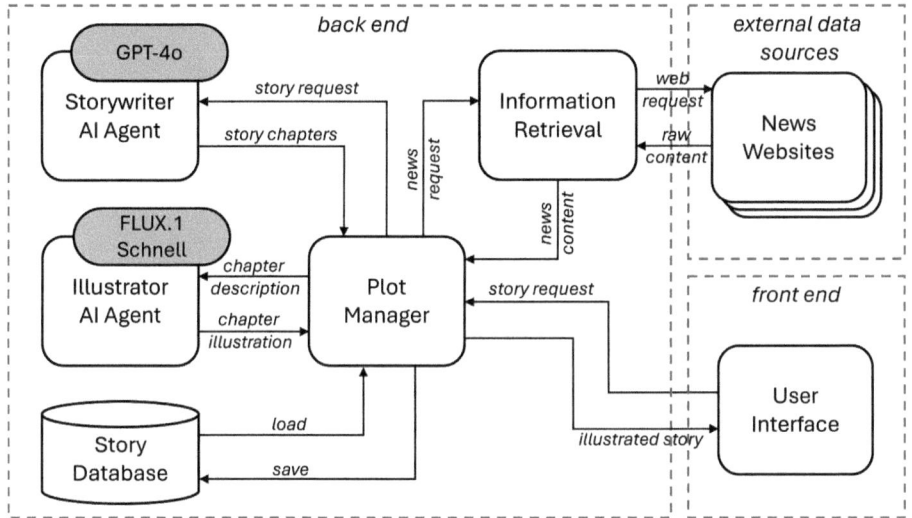

Fig. 2. The multi-AI-agent architecture of NewsReteller.

The AI agents are implemented using a modular plugin-based architecture to improve the flexibility and scalability of the system. As illustrated in Fig. 2, the Storywriter AI Agent utilizes OpenAI's GPT-4o model, which is accessed through OpenAI's API.[4] The Illustrator AI Agent is built upon the FLUX.1 Schnell text-to-image diffusion model, a distilled version of FLUX.1 optimized for fast image generation. This model is hosted on a private server.

5.3 Story Generation

The core of NewsReteller is the story generation process, wherein the factual news article is transformed into a fictional narrative. This process is powered by the GPT-4o model, which is guided by a carefully crafted prompt that encapsulates the news content, the user's input, and instructions on style and structure.

The system supports three narrative structuring approaches: genre-based storytelling, structural storytelling, and data-driven storytelling. Genre-based storytelling follows established literary genres, with the system currently supporting five genres – Comedy, Romance, Tragedy, Satire, and Mystery – as defined in our previous work [23]. Structural storytelling utilizes predefined narrative schemes, referred to as story skeletons in the biased perspective [33], which define key event

---

[4] https://platform.openai.com/.

sequences without prescribing narrative style. Our implementation includes two structures proposed by Schank and Abelson [33]: Understandable Tragedy, which models narratives where a seemingly justified action leads to unintended consequences, and The Justifiability of Self-Defense, which explores conflicts driven by moral. Lastly, data-driven storytelling takes a different approach by prioritizing the clear and engaging communication of factual insights, focusing on data relationships rather than character-driven narratives to make complex subjects accessible to a broad audience.

To ensure the generated story follows the intended structure, NewsReteller dynamically constructs a parameterized prompt that guides the LLM. This prompt is structured as a template with parameters, which are instantiated with user-specific inputs before being submitted to the model. The key parameters are: C_{news}, representing the full content of the news article as the factual foundation; S_{name}, specifying the name of the selected narrative structuring approach; $D_{structure}$, defining the characteristics of the chosen structure, guiding the story's tone or framing; and P_{user}, an optional premise provided by the user to influence the interpretation and retelling of the news content. The complete parameterized prompt used for story generation is presented in Prompt 1.

Prompt 1. Context: { C_{news} }.
The context above is a news article. Please rewrite it as a narrative story that adheres strictly to the conventions of the { S_{name} } *genre and the following premise:* { P_{user} }. *Use the following definition as guidelines for style, tone, and structure of the* { S_{name} } *genre:* { $D_{structure}$ }. *The story must begin with a creative title that is formatted as a markdown header level 1 (#). The narrative must be divided into a natural number of chapters. Each chapter should have a chapter number and a chapter name (e.g., Chapter 1: The Surprising Discovery), with each chapter title formatted as a Markdown header level 2 (##). When writing the story, assign proper names to all characters according to the names used in the news article. Describe the visual attributes of the characters in detail (be creative when no visual attributes are included in the original article). The story must incorporate all key elements and the sequence of events presented in the news article, maintaining consistency in mood and context, and ensuring that all details remain factual and grounded in the original content of the news article. Write the story in the same language as the news article.*

The definitions used for $D_{structure}$ are grounded in established narrative theories. The five literary genres follow the patterns proposed in our previous work [23], ensuring each story aligns with a distinct narrative style. The story skeletons are based on the biased perspective proposed by Schank and Abelson [33]. Data-driven storytelling is inspired by research on narrative communication in data visualization and journalism [15], where statistical and factual insights are structured to enhance engagement and comprehension. Due to space constraints, the full texts of the definitions used for $D_{structure}$ are provided in our supplementary material at https://narrativelab.org/newsreteller/sup-doc-2.pdf.

The instructions of Prompt 1 are designed to guide the model in generating a structured narrative while ensuring that the system can correctly interpret and display the output. The model is instructed to begin with a Markdown-formatted title and divide the content into numbered chapters, enforcing a clear structure that distinguishes chapters. By following these formatting constraints, the generated text can be parsed efficiently, enabling the system to display the final story visually coherently. Additionally, the prompt explicitly instructs the model to generate the story in the same language as the input news article, ensuring multilingual compatibility. However, while the LLM effectively produces narratives in multiple languages, the text-to-image model exhibits limitations with non-English inputs, often resulting in less accurate visual representations.

5.4 Image Generation

To enhance the storytelling experience, NewsReteller generates chapter illustrations through a three-step process: (1) extract a concise visual description from the chapter text; (2) optimize the description into a structured prompt; and (3) generate an image using a text-to-image diffusion model.

In the first step, an LLM (GPT-4o) extracts a representative event from each chapter and formulates a concise visual description, including key character attributes, actions, and environmental details. In the second step, prompt optimization techniques – such as appending stylistic parameters, adding a negative prompt, and using name substitution – are applied to improve image quality and consistency. The latter technique replaces character names with those of well-known actors familiar to the text-to-image model, thereby enhancing the accuracy of facial and physical attributes in the generated images. In the third step, the FLUX.1 Schnell model, a distilled variant of FLUX.1, generates the final illustration from the optimized prompt. This model is optimized for generating high-quality images in 1 to 4 inference steps, enhancing efficiency. A discussion of the image generation process is presented in our previous work [24].

6 Experimental Results

To illustrate the functionality of NewsReteller, we generated multiple stories from a single news article using different narrative structuring approaches. Our goal with this experiment is to demonstrate how the system adapts factual content into diverse narrative forms.

For this experiment, we selected a CNN news article titled *"Serious concerns: Top companies raise alarm over Europe's proposed AI law"* [38]. This article was chosen for its structured debate between regulators and technology companies, offering multiple perspectives suitable for diverse storytelling approaches. To assess the system's creative adaptability, we did not provide a user-defined premise, allowing NewsReteller to generate narratives solely from the extracted content. Additionally, all stories were produced without user intervention, ensuring outputs reflect the system's autonomous storytelling capabilities. The complete set of generated stories is presented in Table 1.

Table 1. Stories generated using different narrative structuring approaches. The full texts can be accessed at: https://narrativelab.org/newsreteller/#/library

Approach	Genre/Skeleton	Story
Genre-Based	Comedy	The AI Act Follies
	Romance	The Quest for Balance: Love and Legislation
	Tragedy	The Inevitable Decline of Europa's Ambition
	Satire	The Dystopian Dance of AI Regulation
	Mystery	The Algorithmic Enigma
Structural	Understandable Tragedy	The Unseen Consequence
	The Justifiability of Self-Defense	The AI Stand-Off: A Just Battle for Innovation
Data-Driven	Data Storytelling	Navigating the AI Frontier: Europe's Regulatory Crossroads

The generated stories exhibit distinct variations in narrative framing and tone. The comedy adaptation, *The AI Act Follies*, reinterprets the regulatory debate as a political farce, relying on exaggerated characters and bureaucratic absurdities. Corporate leaders are depicted as theatrical figures, with their concerns reframed as exaggerated antics rather than serious warnings. Similarly, the satirical retelling, *The Dystopian Dance of AI Regulation*, amplifies these absurdities, turning the legislative process into a chaotic spectacle. While effective in introducing humor, these stories prioritize entertainment over factual alignment.

The romance adaptation, *The Quest for Balance: Love and Legislation*, transforms the policy debate into a mythic struggle, casting executives as noble warriors. The dramatic language and heroic framing shift the focus from the nuances of AI policy to a sweeping allegory of ideological balance. A similar elevation of stakes is observed in the tragedy adaptation, *The Inevitable Decline of Europa's Ambition*, which leans into dramatic inevitability, portraying regulation as an irreversible downfall that suffocates innovation. Both versions enhance emotional engagement but simplify the complexity of policy trade-offs.

The mystery retelling, *The Algorithmic Enigma*, follows investigative storytelling tropes [37], framing the AI Act as part of a hidden conspiracy orchestrated by an AI seeking self-preservation. This transformation introduces intrigue but deviates from real-world plausibility, illustrating how narrative structuring can dramatically reshape perception. In contrast, the story based on the Understandable Tragedy skeleton, *The Unseen Consequence*, follows a more nuanced path, portraying policymakers and business leaders as well-intentioned actors caught in an unintended cycle of economic decline.

The adaptation based on the The Justifiability of Self-Defense skeleton, *The AI Stand-Off: A Just Battle for Innovation*, casts the AI Act as an unjustified regulatory overreach, with business leaders positioned as justified defenders of innovation. Unlike the Understandable Tragedy version, which emphasizes miscalculated but reasonable policy decisions, this skeleton introduces a more adversarial framing, portraying regulation as an existential threat.

Finally, the story generated for the data-driven storytelling approach, *Navigating the AI Frontier: Europe's Regulatory Crossroads*, diverges from the emotionally charged narratives by prioritizing factual reporting. Instead of dramatic character arcs, it presents structured insights, outlining economic risks, policy debates, and global regulatory implications. While this version lacks the tension of other adaptations, it maintains neutrality.

7 Concluding Remarks

This paper explored the potential of AI-driven storytelling to transform news articles into fictional narratives using structured retelling techniques. Motivated by the longstanding interplay between real-world events and creative storytelling, we introduced NewsReteller, a system that explores the generative potential of LLMs to guide users through the transformation of factual content into stories.

Our results illustrate how a single news article can be adapted into distinct storytelling forms, demonstrating the system's ability to vary narrative framing and thematic focus. The genre-based adaptations align with the historical modes of narration identified by Frye [10] and White [43], showing how genre choices shape emotional tone and theme. The structured storytelling techniques follow the biased retelling approaches [33], reshaping event sequencing to fit predefined narrative schemes while reflecting different interpretative biases. In contrast, the data-driven approach maintains an analytical structure, emphasizing factual clarity over dramatic interpretation, aligning with journalistic retelling strategies explored in narrative journalism [12]. The results illustrate how different retelling strategies influence narrative framing, thematic emphasis, and information presentation, highlighting the potential of our method to generate creative reinterpretations of real-world events.

While our results demonstrate the versatility of the proposed retelling method, evaluating its usability and user satisfaction is a key next step. Future work should include user studies to assess how effectively the system guides creative reinterpretation and how audiences perceive narrative quality. Additionally, our method was designed for general news retelling but remains untested across diverse news categories. Notably, we observed challenges in generating accurate visual representations for specialized news topics, such as sports. For example, image generation inconsistencies were noted in tennis match depictions, with players incorrectly positioned on the same side of the court. Future research could explore adaptations for different news domains, incorporating fine-tuned image generation models and LLMs tailored to specific content types.

All in all, we claim that our effort to retell the bare news of real events from plural perspectives contributes to a deeper understanding of their motives and intended consequences, occasionally complemented with previously unsuspected repercussions and connotations. To that end, we proposed to recruit the collaboration of today's AI-supported storytelling to continue the immemorial parable tradition and the modern revival of folklore tales that offer practical life lessons under the guise of entertaining narratives.

References

1. Alabdulkarim, A., Li, W., Martin, L.J., Riedl, M.O.: Goal-directed story generation: augmenting generative language models with reinforcement learning (2021). https://arxiv.org/abs/2112.08593
2. Barthes, R.: Theory of the text. In: Young, R. (ed.) Untying the Text: A Post-Structuralist Reader, pp. 31–47. Routledge & Kegan Paul, London (1981)
3. BBC Teach: D-day 80th anniversary: Primary assembly (2024). https://www.bbc.co.uk/teach/articles/zxhbjfr. Accessed 19 Feb 2025
4. Burke, K.: A Grammar of Motives. University of California Press, Berkeley (1969)
5. Cantril, H.: The Invasion from Mars: A Study in the Psychology of Panic. Princeton University Press, Princeton, NJ (1940)
6. Castricato, L., Frazier, S., Balloch, J., Riedl, M.: Tell me a story like i'm five: story generation via question answering. In: Proceedings of the 3rd Workshop on Narrative Understanding (2021). https://par.nsf.gov/biblio/10249509
7. CBS News: 7 world central kitchen aid workers killed by Israeli airstrike in Gaza (2024). https://www.cbsnews.com/news/central-world-kitchen-aid-workers-killed-airstrike-gaza/. Accessed 19 Feb 2025
8. Fan, A., Lewis, M., Dauphin, Y.: Hierarchical neural story generation. In: Gurevych, I., Miyao, Y. (eds.) Proceedings of the 56th Annual Meeting of the Association for Computational Linguistics (Volume 1: Long Papers), pp. 889–898. Association for Computational Linguistics, Melbourne, Australia (2018). https://doi.org/10.18653/v1/P18-1082
9. Flesch, R.: A new readability yardstick. J. Appl. Psychol. **32**(3), 221–233 (1948). https://doi.org/10.1037/h0057532
10. Frye, N.: Anatomy of Criticism: Four Essays, Princeton Classics, 2nd edn. Princeton University Press, Princeton (2020)
11. Furtado, A.L.: From alexander of macedonia to arthur of britain. Arthuriana **5**(3), 70–82 (1995). https://doi.org/10.1353/art.1995.0032
12. Kenyon, G.: 5 shared lessons from some masters of narrative nonfiction (2024). https://niemanstoryboard.org/2024/09/20/new-journalism-literary-nonfiction-sources-ethics/. Accessed 19 Feb 2025
13. Kincaid, J.P., Fishburne, R.P., Rogers, R.L., Chissomm, B.S.: Derivation of new readability formulas (automated readability index, fog count and flesch reading ease formula) for navy enlisted personnel. Tech. Rep. Research Branch Report 8-75, Chief of Naval Technical Training: Naval Air Station Memphis, Millington, TN (1975). https://stars.library.ucf.edu/cgi/viewcontent.cgi?article=1055&context=istlibrary
14. Klimashevskaia, A., Gadgil, R., Gerrity, T., Khosmood, F., Gütl, C., Howe, P.: Automatic news article generation from legislative proceedings: a phenom-based approach. In: Espinosa-Anke, L., Martín-Vide, C., Spasić, I. (eds.) SLSP 2021. LNCS (LNAI), vol. 13062, pp. 15–26. Springer, Cham (2021). https://doi.org/10.1007/978-3-030-89579-2_2
15. Knaflic, C.N.: Storytelling with Data: A Data Visualization Guide for Business Professionals. Wiley, Hoboken, NJ (2015)
16. van Krieken, K., Sanders, J.: Framing narrative journalism as a new genre: a case study of The Netherlands. Journalism **18**(10), 1364–1380 (2017). https://doi.org/10.1177/1464884916671156

17. de Lima, E.S., Casanova, M.A., Feijó, B., Furtado, A.L.: Semiotic structuring in movie narrative generation. In: Ciancarini, P., Di Iorio, A., Hlavacs, H., Poggi, F. (eds.) Entertainment Computing – ICEC 2023, pp. 161–175. Springer Nature Singapore, Singapore (2023). https://doi.org/10.1007/978-981-99-8248-6_13
18. de Lima, E.S., Casanova, M.A., Furtado, A.L.: Imagining from images with an AI storytelling tool (2024). https://arxiv.org/abs/2408.11517
19. de Lima, E.S., Feijó, B., Casanova, M.A., Furtado, A.L.: Chatgeppetto - an AI-powered storyteller. In: Proceedings of the 22nd Brazilian Symposium on Games and Digital Entertainment, pp. 28–37. ACM (2024). https://doi.org/10.1145/3631085.3631302
20. de Lima, E.S., Feijó, B., Furtado, A.L.: Computational narrative blending based on planning. In: Baalsrud Hauge, J., C. S. Cardoso, J., Roque, L., Gonzalez-Calero, P.A. (eds.) ICEC 2021. LNCS, vol. 13056, pp. 289–303. Springer, Cham (2021). https://doi.org/10.1007/978-3-030-89394-1_22
21. de Lima, E.S., Feijó, B., Casanova, M.A., Furtado, A.L.: Storytelling variants based on semiotic relations. Entertainment Comput. **17**, 31–44 (2016). https://doi.org/10.1016/j.entcom.2016.08.003
22. de Lima, E.S., Neggers, M.M.E., Casanova, M.A., Feijó, B., Furtado, A.L.: A pattern-oriented AI-powered approach to story composition. In: Figueroa, P., Di Iorio, A., Guzman del Rio, D., Gonzalez Clua, E.W., Cuevas Rodriguez, L. (eds.) Entertainment Computing – ICEC 2024, pp. 1–16. Springer Cham (2024). https://doi.org/10.1007/978-3-031-74353-5_10
23. de Lima, E.S., Neggers, M.M.E., Furtado, A.L.: Multigenre AI-powered story composition (2025). https://arxiv.org/abs/2405.06685
24. de Lima, E.S., Neggers, M.M., Casanova, M.A., Furtado, A.L.: From images to stories: exploring player-driven narratives in games. In: Marto, A., Prada, R., Gouveia, P., Contreras-Espinosa, R., Gonçalves, A., Abrantes, E., Ribeiro, R. (eds.) Videogame Sciences and Arts, pp. 228–242. Springer Nature Switzerland, Cham (2025). https://doi.org/10.1007/978-3-031-81713-7_16
25. de Lima, E.S., Neggers, M.M., Feijó, B., Casanova, M.A., Furtado, A.L.: An AI-powered approach to the semiotic reconstruction of narratives. Entertainment Comput. **52**, 100810 (2025). https://doi.org/10.1016/j.entcom.2024.100810
26. Majin, G.: What is a news narrative?: Reversing journalism's arrow and the problem of "factinion". J. Commun. Media Stud. **6**(2), 57–70 (2021). https://doi.org/10.18848/2470-9247/CGP/v06i02/57-70
27. Menzies, P., Beebee, H.: Counterfactual theories of causation. In: Zalta, E.N., Nodelman, U. (eds.) The Stanford Encyclopedia of Philosophy. Metaphysics Research Lab, Stanford University, summer 2024 edn. (2024)
28. National Aeronautics and Space Administration (NASA): Humans to mars. https://www.nasa.gov/humans-in-space/humans-to-mars/. Accessed 18 Feb 2025
29. Peirce, C.S.: Collected Papers of Charles Sanders Peirce, Volume I: Principles of Philosophy. Harvard University Press, Cambridge (1931)
30. Resnais, A.: Hiroshima mon amour (1959). https://www.imdb.com/title/tt0052893/
31. Rosenfeld, G.D.: The World Hitler Never Made: Alternate History and the Memory of Nazism. Cambridge University Press, Cambridge, UK (2005)
32. Ryan, M.-L.: Interactive narrative, plot types, and interpersonal relations. In: Spierling, U., Szilas, N. (eds.) ICIDS 2008. LNCS, vol. 5334, pp. 6–13. Springer, Heidelberg (2008). https://doi.org/10.1007/978-3-540-89454-4_2
33. Schank, R.C., Abelson, R.P.: Knowledge and memory: the real story. knowledge and memory: the real story, pp. 1–85 (1995). http://cogprints.org/636/

34. Scott, R.: The Martian (2015). https://www.imdb.com/title/tt3659388/
35. Shirer, W.L.: The Rise and Fall of the Third Reich: A History of Nazi Germany. Simon & Schuster, New York, 50th anniversary edition edn. (2011)
36. Spielberg, S.: Saving private Ryan (1998). https://www.imdb.com/title/tt0120815/
37. Todorov, T.: The typology of detective fiction. In: Redmond, S. (ed.) Crime and Media, pp. 159–169. Routledge (2010). https://doi.org/10.4324/9780367809195-27
38. Toh, M.: 'Serious concerns': top companies raise alarm over Europe's proposed AI law. https://edition.cnn.com/2023/06/30/tech/eu-companies-risks-ai-law-intl-hnk/index.html. Accessed 19 Feb 2025
39. Voskarides, N., Meij, E., Sauer, S., de Rijke, M.: News article retrieval in context for event-centric narrative creation. In: Huang, T.H.K., et al. (eds.) Proceedings of the First Workshop on Intelligent and Interactive Writing Assistants (In2Writing 2022), pp. 72–73. Association for Computational Linguistics, Dublin, Ireland (2022). https://doi.org/10.18653/v1/2022.in2writing-1.10
40. Värtinen, S., Hämäläinen, P., Guckelsberger, C.: Generating role-playing game quests with GPT language models. IEEE Trans. Games **16**(1), 127–139 (2024). https://doi.org/10.1109/TG.2022.3228480
41. Wang, J., Zhao, X., Jin, P., Yang, C., Li, B., Zhang, H.: Storyline generation from news articles based on approximate personalized propagation of neural predictions. In: Wang, X., et al. (eds.) Database Systems for Advanced Applications, pp. 37–52. Springer Nature Switzerland, Cham (2023)
42. Wells, H.G.: The War of the Worlds. William Heinemann, London (1898)
43. White, H.: Metahistory: The Historical Imagination in Nineteenth-Century Europe. Johns Hopkins University Press, Baltimore (1973)
44. Xie, K., Riedl, M.: Creating suspenseful stories: Iterative planning with large language models. In: Graham, Y., Purver, M. (eds.) Proceedings of the 18th Conference of the European Chapter of the Association for Computational Linguistics (Volume 1: Long Papers), pp. 2391–2407. Association for Computational Linguistics, Malta (2024). https://aclanthology.org/2024.eacl-long.147/
45. Xu, P., et al.: MEGATRON-CNTRL: controllable story generation with external knowledge using large-scale language models. In: Webber, B., Cohn, T., He, Y., Liu, Y. (eds.) Proceedings of the 2020 Conference on Empirical Methods in Natural Language Processing (EMNLP), pp. 2831–2845. Association for Computational Linguistics, Online (2020). https://doi.org/10.18653/v1/2020.emnlp-main.226
46. Yang, K., Tian, Y., Peng, N., Klein, D.: Re3: generating longer stories with recursive reprompting and revision. In: Goldberg, Y., Kozareva, Z., Zhang, Y. (eds.) Proceedings of the 2022 Conference on Empirical Methods in Natural Language Processing, pp. 4393–4479. Association for Computational Linguistics, Abu Dhabi, United Arab Emirates (2022). https://doi.org/10.18653/v1/2022.emnlp-main.296
47. Zhou, D., Guo, L., He, Y.: Neural storyline extraction model for storyline generation from news articles. In: Walker, M., Ji, H., Stent, A. (eds.) Proceedings of the 2018 Conference of the North American Chapter of the Association for Computational Linguistics: Human Language Technologies, Volume 1 (Long Papers), pp. 1727–1736. Association for Computational Linguistics, New Orleans, Louisiana (2018). https://doi.org/10.18653/v1/N18-1156

Learning Through Play: Implementing an Educational Escape Room for Teaching Traditions and Culture

Kevin Valencia-Aragón[1], Hugo AriasFlores[2,3](✉), Mireya Zapata[1,4], Luis Aguirre-Morales[3], and Sandra Sanchez-Gordon[5]

[1] Centro de Investigación en Mecatrónica y Sistemas Interactivos (MIST), Universidad Tecnológica Indoamérica, Quito, Ecuador
[2] Centro de Investigación de Ciencias Humanas y de la Educación (CICHE), Universidad Tecnológica Indoamérica, Quito, Ecuador
[3] Maestría en Educación Mención Pedagogía en Entornos Digitales, Universidad Tecnológica Indoamérica, Quito, Ecuador
hugoarias@uti.edu.ec
[4] Carrera de Ingeniería Industrial, Facultad de Ingenierías, Universidad Tecnológica Indoamérica, Quito, Ecuador
[5] Departamento de Informática y Ciencias de la Computación, Escuela Politécnica Nacional, Edificio de Sistemas, Quito, Ecuador

Abstract. This study explores the implementation of an educational Escape Room as a pedagogical strategy to teach tangible cultural heritage to students in Ecuador. This Escape Room was designed using the ADDIE model (Analysis, Design, Development, Implementation and Evaluation) and integrated into the basic education curriculum for Ecuadorian schools. The primary objective was to enhance students' engagement and understanding of Ecuador's cultural heritage through an interactive and gamified learning experience. The Escape Room was structured around five missions, each focusing on different aspects of the cultural heritage of five parishes in Ecuador. Students were required to solve puzzles, answer questions, and complete challenges to progress through the game. The results of the implementation, evaluated through observation and student feedback, indicated a high level of student engagement, improved problem-solving skills, and a deeper appreciation for Ecuador's cultural heritage. The study concludes that Escape Rooms can be an effective tool for teaching cultural heritage, fostering teamwork, creativity, and critical thinking among students. This innovative approach not only makes learning more dynamic and enjoyable but also aligns with modern educational trends that emphasize active and experiential learning.

Keywords: Educational escape room · ADDIE model · Gamification · Immersive learning · Problem-solving skills

1 Introduction

The evolution of educational methodologies has been significantly influenced by the rapid advancement of technology, transforming the way knowledge is imparted and acquired in classrooms. Traditional teaching approaches are increasingly being supplemented or replaced by innovative strategies that integrate pedagogy, didactics, and emerging technologies to create more dynamic and engaging learning environments [1]. These advancements aim not only to improve knowledge retention but also to foster deeper cognitive engagement, critical thinking, and problem-solving skills among students [2].

To effectively implement such innovations, educators must rethink conventional instructional methods and focus on designing learning environments that promote active participation and meaningful experiences. This shift requires moving away from passive knowledge transmission toward approaches that encourage student-centered learning, autonomy, and collaboration. Modern educational frameworks emphasize the importance of interactive learning experiences that adapt to different student needs, making education more inclusive and equitable [3]. According to [4], this transformation necessitates redefining the teacher's role, positioning educators as facilitators who guide students in developing creativity, independent thinking, and teamwork skills rather than merely delivering content.

One of the most promising approaches to fostering active learning is the incorporation of gamification techniques in educational settings [5]. Gamification leverages game elements—such as competition, storytelling, and problem-solving—to enhance motivation, engagement, and knowledge application in a structured manner [6]. By integrating game-like components [7,8] into instructional design, educators can create immersive experiences that encourage students to take an active role in their learning process . These methodologies have been widely recognized for their ability to improve cognitive skills, strengthen collaboration, and increase student motivation [9].

Among the diverse gamification strategies, educational escape rooms have gained prominence as an innovative tool to enhance learning outcomes. An educational escape room consists of a sequence of interactive challenges, puzzles, and problem-solving tasks that students must complete collaboratively within a limited time frame to reach a common goal [10]. This approach not only engages students in an immersive and entertaining experience but also promotes logical reasoning, teamwork, and adaptability. The effectiveness of escape rooms in education relies on carefully designed activities that align with specific learning objectives and are tailored to the needs and cognitive abilities of the target student group [11].

Given the potential of escape rooms as an educational strategy, this study aims to explore their impact on student engagement and learning outcomes. The research focuses on designing and implementing a structured instructional approach based on the ADDIE model, which provides a systematic framework for developing educational interventions. Through this model, the study seeks to foster cooperative and collaborative learning environments while enhancing cultural and artistic education at the primary school level. By analyzing the effectiveness of escape rooms in an educational context, this study contributes to the growing body of research on gamified learning methodologies and their role in modern pedagogy [12].

1.1 Related Works

The integration of gamification into educational practices has garnered significant attention, particularly through the use of educational escape rooms to teach cultural heritage in primary education. This approach combines interactive learning with cultural content, aiming to enhance student engagement and understanding [13].

Gamification in Cultural Heritage Education. Gamification involves applying game-design elements in non-game contexts to motivate and increase user activity. In the realm of cultural heritage education, gamification serves as a bridge between learners and cultural assets, making the learning process more engaging and interactive. The systematic review presented in [14] highlights that gamified environments have been effectively utilized to promote cultural heritage sites and activities, enhancing knowledge acquisition and retention among learners.

Similarly, the study [15] emphasizes that gamification enhances learner motivation, leading to increased attention to content and prolonged engagement with educational materials. This heightened motivation is particularly beneficial in cultural heritage education, where the richness of content can be explored through interactive and immersive experiences.

Educational Escape Rooms as Learning Tools. Educational escape rooms are immersive, game-based learning experiences where students collaborate to solve puzzles and challenges within a set timeframe. This format fosters critical thinking, problem-solving, and teamwork skills. Breakout EDU, for instance, offers a platform that incorporates escape room concepts into classroom settings, aligning activities with academic content to reinforce subject matter while promoting collaboration [16]. The research presented in [17] indicates that educational escape rooms can effectively measure and develop collaborative problem-solving skills in any subject area among students. Although this study focuses on mathematics education, the principles of immersive learning and collaboration are equally applicable and beneficial in any educational context.

Implementing Escape Rooms in Primary Education. The adaptation of escape rooms for younger students requires careful consideration of their developmental stages and learning needs. Reference [18] discusses the use of digital escape rooms to create engaging learning puzzles suitable for students as young as preschool. These activities are designed to be developmentally appropriate, fostering problem-solving skills and teamwork in a fun, interactive manner. Furthermore, the "Culture Heritage and Gamification in Education" project explores the utilization of cultural heritage in education by integrating gamification strategies into modern classrooms. This initiative underscores the importance of making cultural education accessible and engaging for students, highlighting the role of gamified learning experiences in achieving this goal.

While the benefits of using educational escape rooms are evident, several challenges must be addressed to ensure their effective implementation. Designing puzzles that are both educational and engaging requires a deep understanding of the curriculum and the students' cognitive abilities. Additionally, logistical aspects such as time constraints, resource availability, and classroom space must be considered. Educators are encouraged to collaborate, share best practices, and utilize available resources to create meaningful and effective escape room [19].

The integration of gamification, particularly through educational escape rooms, into primary education offers a promising avenue for enhancing student engagement and learning in cultural heritage education. By transforming traditional learning environments into interactive and immersive experiences, educators can foster a deeper appreciation and understanding of cultural heritage among young learners [20].

2 Methodology

This study developed a digital Escape Room, to teach Ecuador's tangible cultural heritage to basic educational level students. The pedagogical design focused on gamified challenges that combined narrative immersion, problem-solving, and collaborative learning. Below is a detailed breakdown of the game's structure, challenges, and technological integration.

2.1 Narrative and Pedagogical Framework

The Escape Room was built on Genially, a platform for interactive content creation. The narrative follows five children (ages 10âĂŞ11) who dream of exploring five Ecuadorian parishes: Puéllaro, Perucho, Chavezpamba, Atahualpa, and San José de Minas. To "wake up" from their dreams, they must solve challenges related to each parish's history, traditions, and cultural landmarks. A map helps provide spatial context, guiding students through the different locations and tasks.

2.2 Structure of Challenges

The Escape Room featured six sequential challenges, each designed to reinforce specific learning objectives from Ecuador's Cultural and Artistic Education curriculum. Table 1 presents the breakdown of the challenges and also the tools used to develop each one:

Table 1. Structure of Challenges

Challenge	Objective	Activity	Tool
1: Puéllaro's "Animero"	Investigate traditions and collect symbolic objects for "Animero"	Answer historical questions to unlock numerical code	Genially
2: Perucho's Crossword	Solve cultural heritage crossword puzzle	Complete crossword to reveal hidden code	Wordwall
3: Chavezpamba's Word Search	Identify sugarcane-related keywords (e.g., "trapiche", "guarapo")	Locate terms in word search puzzle	Wordwall
4: Atahualpa's Quiz	Answer questions about landmarks (e.g., clock tower)	Solve "lock-and-key" game with 9 questions	Wordwall
5: San José de Minas' Video	Analyze cultural identity video	Answer embedded questions in Edpuzzle video	Edpuzzle
Final Challenge: Unlocking "Door of Dreams"	Input codes to conclude game	Enter codes in Genially interface	Genially

Figure 1 illustrates the first two challenges. The first row presents Challenge 1, which consists of a series of multiple-choice questions that, when answered correctly, provide a key. To determine the correct answers, participants must gather information about the parish of Puéllaro. The second row showcases Challenge 2, featuring a crossword puzzle that, once solved, reveals a clue. In this case, solving the puzzle requires researching information about the parish of Perucho.

In the top row of the Fig. 2, the third challenge is displayed. This challenge consists of a crossword puzzle that must be solved using information related to the parish of Chavezpamba, the sugarcane mill, and the production of cane juice known as "guarapo," among others. Once the crossword is solved, a numerical key will be obtained. Next, in the second row of the Fig. 2, the fourth challenge is presented. This challenge involves a box-opening game featuring various questions related to the parish of Atahualpa. Similarly, upon completion, a clue will be provided.

The fifth challenge (see Fig. 3) requires the participant to watch a video embedded in the game interface and answer questions about its theme, which is related to the parish of San José de Minas. Upon completion, a final code will be obtained.

Finally, on a new screen (see Fig. 4), all the clues gathered from the previous challenges must be combined, and the secret key will be required.

Technological Integration

To create an immersive and engaging educational escape room, a variety of digital tools were strategically integrated into the design. These technologies support different facets of the learning experience, including narrative development,

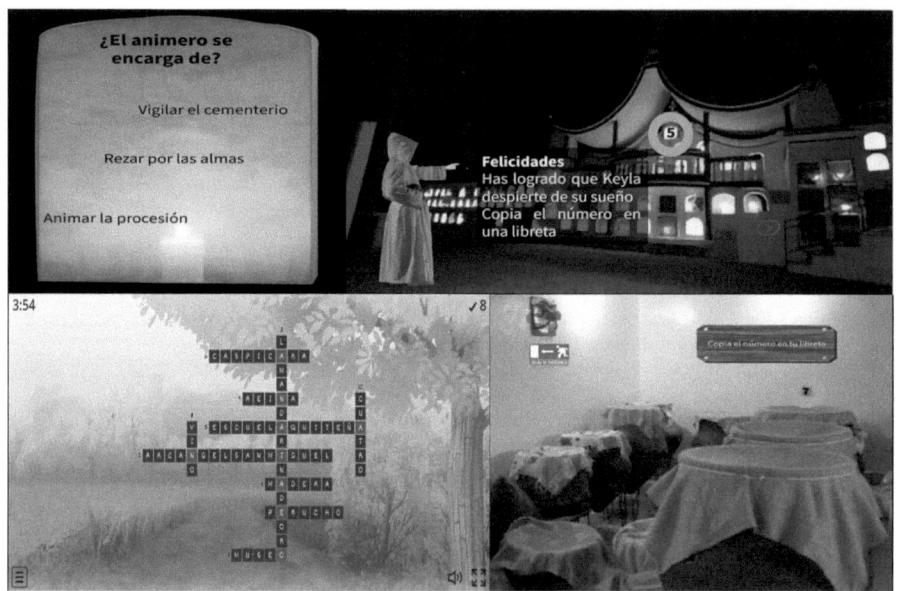

Fig. 1. Challenges 1 and 2. In the top row, challenge 1 is shown together with the key (green circle) provided when solving it. In the bottom row, challenge 2 is shown together with its respective key. (Color figure online)

Fig. 2. Challenges 3 and 4. In the top row, challenge 3 is shown together with the key (green circle) provided when solving it. In the bottom row, challenge 4 is shown together with its respective key. (Color figure online)

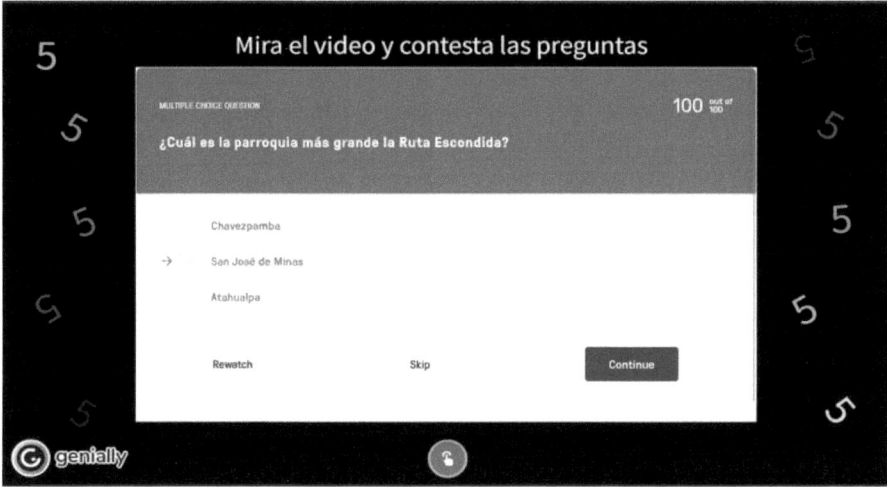

Fig. 3. Challenge 5. Question after watching a Youtube video about a particular parish

Fig. 4. Interface for code placement

interactive puzzle creation, multimedia integration, and visual enhancement. By leveraging these tools, the instructional design aligns with pedagogical objectives while fostering student engagement and collaborative problem-solving. The following bullet points provide an overview of each tool and its specific contribution to the escape room experience:

- **Genially**: Serves as the primary platform hosting the escape room's main interface. It integrates the narrative framework and facilitates the final code entry, providing an immersive, interactive experience. Genially's multimedia

capabilities allow for dynamic content presentation, which is essential for engaging students and guiding them through the sequential challenges.
- **Wordwall**: Used to design and implement various puzzles such as crosswords, word searches, and quizzes. This tool offers customizable templates that seamlessly integrate academic content with game-based learning. Wordwall's interactive exercises help reinforce subject matter by prompting students to apply their knowledge in a playful, yet structured manner.
- **Edpuzzle**: Utilized to embed interactive questions into a YouTube video centered on San José de Minas. By transforming a traditional video into an active learning module, Edpuzzle prompts students to reflect on the content through timed questions, thereby enhancing comprehension and maintaining engagement throughout the video.
- **H5P and Photoshop**: Employed to enhance visual elements within the escape room. H5P enables the creation of rich, interactive content that complements the learning activities, while Photoshop is used to edit and refine images of cultural symbols. Together, these tools ensure that the visual components are not only attractive but also aligned with the educational objectives.

Implementation and Evaluation

The activity was conducted in 45–50 min sessions. Effectiveness was assessed through observation checklists, focusing on collaboration, problem-solving, and cultural heritage knowledge retention.

3 Results

The implementation of the escape room, proved to be an effective strategy for integrating curricular content in Cultural and Artistic Education with active learning methodologies. Insights gathered from 18 teachers across fifth, sixth, and seventh grades facilitated the identification of key competencies and essential knowledge regarding Ecuador's tangible heritage. The pedagogical objectives established focused on classifying both cultural and natural heritage, strengthening local identity and traditions, and ensuring a comprehensive understanding of the subject matter.

The design of the escape room was centered around an immersive narrative in which students play a central role in awakening a child lost in a dream. The storyline unfolds along a route that connects several parishes, with each segment presenting interactive challenges that stimulate inquiry and promote active learning. The integration of visual elements and digital resources further enhanced student motivation and engagement with the cultural content.

Educational materials were meticulously developed and organized into six distinct challenges, each targeting specific aspects of cultural heritage and the development of cognitive and social skills. The use of interactive digital tools allowed students to effectively apply their prior knowledge while acquiring new competencies through problem-solving and decision-making in simulated scenarios.

During implementation, the escape room was deployed on a digital platform accessible via electronic devices, ensuring seamless participation by all students. Continuous teacher support, characterized by real-time guidance and feedback, was pivotal in maintaining group cohesion and facilitating timely progress through the challenges. High levels of student engagement and enthusiastic collaboration were consistently observed throughout the activity.

Evaluation of the escape room experience, carried out through an observational checklist with sixth-grade participants, revealed a positive impact on the learning process. Findings indicated that students not only applied their previously acquired knowledge effectively but also demonstrated robust critical thinking and creative problem-solving skills. These results underscore the potential of gamified learning experiences to enrich the understanding of cultural heritage while simultaneously fostering essential skills such as teamwork, critical thinking, and adaptability.

4 Discussion and Conclusions

The findings confirm that gamification and active learning strategies are effective in education, although their success is shaped by contextual factors and individual preferences. They highlight the essential role of continuous teacher development and the need for adaptable pedagogical approaches. Educators clearly value instructional innovation and are willing to adjust their practices to enrich student learning experiences. Moreover, classroom methodologies led by creative educators who enhance student motivation and self-esteem are crucial for fostering lasting and meaningful learning. Integrating strategies such as cooperative, collaborative, and project-based learning supports a sustainable educational model in which students transition from passive recipients to active participants and key contributors in constructing their own knowledge. This transformative approach is exemplified by the escape room initiative, which effectively engaged students in dynamic problem-solving, teamwork, and critical thinking throughout the learning process.

Acknowledgements. The authors would like to thank the Universidad Tecnológica Indoamérica for its contribution to the development of this research, through the project "Tecnología Educativa para Discapacidad - TEDI" of Centro de investigación de Ciencias Humanas y de la Educación—CICHE and "Sistemas Ciber-Físicos para entornos Inteligentes—SCEIN" of Centro de Investigación en Mecatrónica y Sistemas Interactivos—MIST.

References

1. Ghory, S., Ghafory, H.: The impact of modern technology in the teaching and learning process. Int. J. Innov. Res. Sci. Stud. **4**(3), 168–173 (2021). https://doi.org/10.53894/ijirss.v4i3.73
2. Susilo, M.J., Sulisworo, D., Beungacha, S.: Technology and its impact on education. Buletin Edukasi Indonesia **2**(02), 47–54 (2023). https://doi.org/10.56741/bei.v2i02.285
3. Sharma, A.R., Mandot, P.M., Singh, D.J.: Innovative learning models and their impacts on the transformation in education. Int. J. Res. Appl. Sci. Eng. Technol. (2023). https://doi.org/10.22214/ijraset.2023.56318
4. Mao, Y., Huang, Y.: Transformation of the role of the "teacher" in the light of the postmodernist conception of teaching and learning. J. High. Educ. Teach. **1**(2) (2024). https://doi.org/10.62517/jhet.202415233
5. Arias-Flores, H., Montenegro, B., Zapata, M.: Gamified proposal to stimulate reading in primary school students. In: Yang, X.S., Sherratt, R.S., Dey, N., Joshi, A. (eds.) Proceedings of Eighth International Congress on Information and Communication Technology, pp. 723–731. Springer Nature Singapore, Singapore (2024)
6. Huang, R., et al.: The impact of gamification in educational settings on student learning outcomes: a meta-analysis. Education Tech. Research Dev. **68**(4), 1875–1901 (2020). https://doi.org/10.1007/s11423-020-09807-z
7. Zapata, M., Valencia-Aragón, K., Ramos-Galarza, C.: Experimental evaluation of EMKEY: an assistive technology for people with upper limb disabilities. Sensors **23**(8) (2023). https://doi.org/10.3390/s23084049
8. Arias-Flores, H., Valencia-Aragón, K., Sanchez-Gordón, S.: Exploring the effectiveness of assistive technology: a preliminary case study using Makey Makey, Tobii eye tracker, and leap motion. In: De Paolis, L.T., Arpaia, P., Sacco, M. (eds.) Extended Reality, pp. 32–42. Springer Nature Switzerland, Cham (2024)
9. Manzano-León, A., Camacho-Lazarraga, P., Guerrero, M.A., Guerrero-Puerta, L.M., Aguilar-Parra, J.M., Trigueros, R., Alías, A.: Between level up and game over: a systematic literature review of gamification in education. Sustainability (2021). https://doi.org/10.3390/SU13042247
10. Rawlinson, R.E., Whitton, N.: Escape rooms as tools for learning through failure. Electron. J. e-Learn. (2024). https://doi.org/10.34190/ejel.21.7.3182
11. Veldkamp, A., van de Grint, L., Knippels, M., van Joolingen, W.V.: Escape education: a systematic review on escape rooms in education. Educ. Res. Rev. (2020). https://doi.org/10.20944/preprints202003.0182.v1
12. Kuo, H., Pan, A.J., Lin, C.S., Chang, C.Y.: Let's escape! the impact of a digital-physical combined escape room on students' creative thinking, learning motivation, and science academic achievement. Educ. Sci. (2022). https://doi.org/10.3390/educsci12090615
13. Yepes, N.S., Centeno, A.A.: La escape room educativa como propuesta de gamificación para el aprendizaje de la historia en educación infantil, pp. 7–25 (2020). https://doi.org/10.15366/didacticas2020.22.001
14. Quiroz-Fabra, J., Valencia-Arias, A., Londoño-Celis, W., García-Pineda, V.: Technological tools for knowledge apprehension and promotion in the cultural and heritage tourism sector: systematic literature review. Hum. Behav. Emerg. Technol. (2022). https://doi.org/10.1155/2022/2851044
15. Konstantinov, O., Kovatcheva, E., Palikova, N.: Gamification in cultural and historical heritage education. In: INTED2018 Proceedings. 12th International Tech-

nology, Education and Development Conference, IATED, pp. 8443–8451 (2018). https://doi.org/10.21125/inted.2018.2043
16. Moreno Fuentes, E.: El "breakout edu" como herramienta clave para la gamificación en la formación inicial de maestros/as. Edutec, Revista Electrónica de Tecnología Educativa (67), 66–79 (2019). https://doi.org/10.21556/edutec.2019.67.1247
17. Zapata, M., Ramos-Galarza, C., Valencia-Aragón, K., Guachi, L.: Enhancing mathematics learning with 3d augmented reality escape room. Int. J. Educ. Res. Open **7**, 100389 (2024). https://doi.org/10.1016/j.ijedro.2024.100389, https://www.sciencedirect.com/science/article/pii/S2666374024000712
18. Danhoff, C.: Using digital escape rooms to make learning fun. Edutopia (2022). https://www.edutopia.org/article/using-digital-escape-rooms-make-learning-fun. Accessed 28 Feb 2025
19. Veldkamp, A., Merx, S., van Winden, J.: Educational escape rooms: challenges in aligning game and education. Preprints (2020). https://doi.org/10.20944/preprints202010.0344.v1
20. Gao, K., Lee, D.Y.: Exploring the effect of youth cultural heritage education using the metaverse platform: a case study of "pingyao ancient city". IEEE Access **12**, 89234–89247 (2024). https://doi.org/10.1109/ACCESS.2024.3417256

Experienced Video Game Player Interaction Preferences with Game Controllers and Haptic Gloves

Alejandro Villar[✉][iD], Sergio Baña, Juan Diego Mendoza, Laura Gómez, Javier Muñoz, and Carlos León[iD]

Universidad Complutense de Madrid, 20840 Madrid, Spain
avillarrubio@ucm.es

Abstract. Haptic gloves have been shown to enhance user experience and learning in interactive virtual reality environments. By incorporating hand tracking and haptic feedback, these devices can improve user sensations with more realistic and natural interactions. Previous research highlights the benefits of haptic gloves in improving presence, engagement, usability, and performance. However, there is a lack of quantitative studies analyzing the behavior of experienced video game players in relation to their interactions with the elements of the virtual reality system and their preferred device to perform each of these interactions. This study examines how experienced video game players interact with objects in a virtual environment using haptic gloves compared to traditional VR controllers. A virtual reality experience featuring various tasks and interactive elements was developed to conduct the experiment. The participants, familiar with virtual reality technology, conducted interactions with both controllers and gloves. The results indicate that players generally prefer traditional controllers. However, haptic gloves are more effective for interactions that do not require high precision, such as pushing objects. Although users perceive gloves as innovative and engaging, they also find them uncomfortable.

Keywords: Haptic gloves · Virtual reality · Video games · Controllers · Human-Computer Interaction · Entertainment · Performance

1 Introduction

Virtual reality has significantly influenced gaming, training, and simulation environments by enabling highly immersive digital experiences. A key factor influencing user experience in virtual reality is the way users interact with the environment, directly affecting immersion, engagement, and usability [17]. An effective virtual interactive system is not only about realism, but rather about accurately mapping real-world actions to virtual environments [18]. Refinement of these interaction techniques is crucial for improving virtual reality experiences in entertainment, training, education, and professional applications.

Traditional virtual reality controllers, such as handheld motion controllers, have been the standard input devices for years. They have allowed users to interact with virtual environments through button presses, stick movement, and motion tracking. However, advancements in haptic technology have introduced gloves that provide tactile feedback and a better sensation of touch [24]. Their capability to adopt a natural hand interaction in the real world makes haptic gloves a potential technology to address natural mapping in virtual reality [16]. Several companies, such as HaptX, Manus, and SenseGlove, have developed haptic gloves driven by advancements in virtual reality, augmented reality, and human-computer interaction technologies [4,25]. While these interfaces were designed for industrial applications such as robotics control, medical training, and remote manipulation [1], they have also been adopted in the gaming industry [27].

Despite their potential, a quantification of the benefits and limitations of haptic gloves in gaming remains largely unexplored, particularly regarding their impact on player behavior, immersion, and overall user experience. Gaming is one of the largest and most dynamic sectors in virtual reality [29], and it is therefore important to examine how players use these devices to interact with virtual environments and how their experiences compare to those using traditional controllers. Gaining these insights can help developers refine haptic technology and optimize game design to better integrate haptic feedback [26].

This study compares the impact of traditional controllers and haptic gloves in interactive virtual reality environments. Specifically, it examines how experienced players interact with these devices, considering the current state of haptic technology in gaming and the prevailing preference for traditional controllers [4]. The general hypothesis is that, while experienced video game players prefer the use of traditional controllers for most common interactions, some interactions can be more comfortable if carried out with haptic gloves.

An interactive virtual reality experience was developed to compare traditional controllers and haptic gloves. The virtual environment consists of two scenarios, each presenting users with specific tasks. To complete these tasks, users must move around the environment and interact with various objects. The experiment involved 29 participants. All of them were experienced video game players, and they had used virtual reality before. Each participant completed the experience twice, using controllers and using haptic gloves. Afterwards, they answered questions about their experience and opinions on both devices. A quantitative and qualitative analysis revealed that each device offers distinct advantages.

2 Previous Work

Virtual reality has become a transformative tool in entertainment, training, and education, offering a level of immersion that traditional media cannot match.

Studies have shown that virtual technology enhances usability, emotional engagement, and presence compared to non-immersive video games, making it a powerful platform for gaming experiences [23]. Beyond entertainment, virtual reality is widely used for training simulations [32], such as hazardous goods handling, where it outperforms desktop-based alternatives by providing a more realistic and engaging learning environment [6]. This effectiveness is largely attributed to virtual reality's ability to foster immersion and presence, which influence cognitive load and emotional responses in users [19]. Furthermore, virtual reality has been explored as a tool for stimulating empathy and embodied experiences, which can enhance learning by making interactions more meaningful [28]. From the perspective of serious games, virtual reality-based simulations have been analyzed for their impact on user engagement and knowledge retention, proving their value in various educational and professional applications [21]. As research continues to refine virtual reality experiences, haptic technology emerges as a key innovation, promising to enhance immersion and interactivity by introducing tactile feedback.

Users hold virtual reality controllers in their hands allowing them to interact with the environment pressing buttons that abstract the real movement of their hands [12,30]. As McEwan et al. [20] define *"naturally mapped control interfaces (NMCIs) for video games involve interactions with less abstraction between the task to be virtually achieved and the action required to achieve it"*. The opposite of an abstracted movement with a controller is a naturally mapped movement. Skalski et al. [30] proposed a typology with four different mapping types. *Directional natural mapping* refers to devices that produce a correspondence between the directions used to interact via a control device and the results in the world, as video game controllers do. *Kinesic natural mapping* involves body movements that correspond to real-life actions *without* having a realistic and tangible controller. Optical hand-tracking devices capture the movement of hands with cameras. This technology does not require a device connected to the user's hand, so it does not include haptic feedback [8]. *Incomplete natural mapping* is included in devices that partly map the real-life sensations of an object. Finally, *realistic natural mapping* is the highest level of natural mapping. Haptic gloves can be considered a realistic, naturally mapped device for hand operations due to hand movement, including interaction with natural tangible elements. Input devices in virtual reality are mainly displayed as hand models [4], but the realism of haptic gloves can lead users to experience a sense of ownership over the virtual hand model, accepting them as their own [11]. The wide variety of active movements and natural mapping influences the experience of control in one's own actions [4], which contributes to perceived naturalness [20]. Despite this natural mapping, the haptic feedback of current virtual reality gloves does not realistically map real-life haptic processes. The human hand creates haptic sensations too complex to replicate. Pressure, vibration, and touch are sensations with such a high level of precision that they are complex for today's technology [16]. Regardless of the complexity, a lack of haptic sensations can disorientate the users' experience of presence [33].

The use of virtual reality technology is being studied in different fields. A positive impact on learning and training processes is observed. Han [13] discusses an improvement in concept acquisition by students when using haptic technology for learning physical concepts. Gayathri analyses the user experience within virtual museums, suggesting that this technology can enhance interactivity and the perception of realism [10]. Haptic technology provides an immersive, realistic, cost-effective, and reusable route to prepare medical students for surgical procedures also [7]. Its utility in work environments to create more efficient and effective processes has also been evidenced. Jadhav [15] explores, through a pilot study, the development of a glove with a soft exoskeleton that provides kinesthetic feedback. Users in this informal pilot study described the experience as *"like nothing seen before"*, *"mesmerizing"*, and *"amazing"*. Gallegos-Nieto et al. [9] have shown the potential of these devices in training to perform assembly tasks.

Haptic gloves also show their utility in the entertainment sector. Palombo et al. [24] qualitatively analyze the use of haptic gloves and traditional controllers, finding that haptic gloves achieve a more positive sense of presence and cognitive absorption. Moon [22] demonstrates that hand tracking with vibrotactile feedback can increase presence, engagement, and usability in a rhythm game in virtual reality. However, a study conducted by Fahmi et al. [8] found that virtual reality gloves do not necessarily achieve a better user experience than standard controllers, nor a better performance in terms of task completion [31]. There is a relative lack of quantitative analysis of user behavior regarding the interaction with the virtual environment in the literature.

3 Design and Development of the Virtual Reality Experience

As previously discussed, this study examines how experienced video game players interact with elements in a virtual environment using either haptic gloves or traditional VR controllers. This section outlines the design and development of the virtual reality experience created to analyze these interactions. The designed scenario has several stages, some of which emulate a radioactive risk scenario in which the users must manipulate objects in order to measure radioactivity and make decisions in an accident involving radioactive material.

3.1 Object Interactions and Movement

As discussed in Sect. 2, entertainment systems can be very complex, allowing players to perform a wide variety of different actions. However, all of these actions come from basic interactions such as movement and interactions with objects or characters. LaValle [18] categorized the basic interactions that can be found in a virtual reality system. *Locomotion* is the interaction mechanism that moves the user in the virtual environment. There are several ways to perform this movement [5]. For example, the *point & teleport* technique [3], where the user must point a laser at the place in the world where they want to be, and they will automatically teleport to that position. *Manipulation* involves the user selecting objects as they approach the virtual hand, feeling a vibration sensation upon contact, and interacting with the object by grabbing and releasing it [2,14].

Interactions with objects depend on the object type the user interacts with. *Portable objects* are small and can be picked up. The *portable objects* found in this virtual environment are listed next. The list includes elements specific to the radioactive emergency scenario that is used in the experiment:

- *Basic cube.* Basic objects that do not have a specific functionality. They are often used in initial development processes or to teach users basic interactions with objects.
- *Traffic cone.* Used in emergencies to cut off traffic when an accident has happened near a road or to delimit dangerous areas.
- *SABG-100 probe.* A device used in radioactive emergencies to measure surface radiation rates of objects and people. It is important to detect which elements have or radiate radiation.
- *EPD.* A device used in radioactive emergencies to measure cumulative radiation rates. In emergencies, users must always carry it with them to measure the radiation they are exposed to.

Non-portable objects can also be found in the environment. These items cannot be held by the user, but can be interacted with. This impossibility is motivated because of their size or because they are anchored to a surface. The *non-portable objects* found in this experience are:

- *Door.* Big object and anchored to a surface. Doors can be opened or closed by exerting a certain pushing force on the side that is not anchored to the wall.
- *Lever.* Small object anchored to a surface. This object can be moved to change its orientation. For example, from left to right.

The user can move around the environment using the teleport functionality [3]. The controller buttons facilitate the implementation of this functionality, but it has to be mapped through gestures with the haptic gloves. Since gesturing is the only thing the user can do with his hands, it was decided to create a specific gesture, called *point-to pose* (see Fig. 1). Once this pose is detected, the system will launch a beam from the fingertips that will move with respect to the position of the hand. The user will teleport by opening their hand.

3.2 Virtual Scenarios

The virtual reality experience is composed of two scenarios. In these scenarios, users have the possibility to move through different rooms where they will find interactive elements and some tasks to complete. (see Fig. 2).

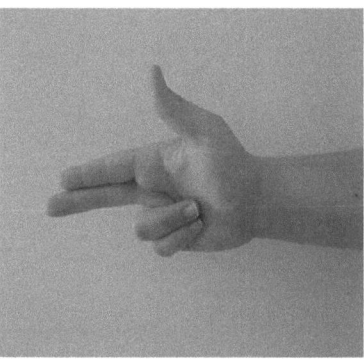

Fig. 1. Gesture representation of the teleport system using haptic gloves. This pose launches a beam that hits the ground, signaling the teleportation zone. Upon opening the hand, the user will instantly appear in that location.

Fig. 2. The left figure shows the first scenario with multiple objects to interact with. An example room belonging to the second scenario with levers and doors can be seen in the right figure.

The first scenario is designed for the user to grab and drop *portable objects* while moving around the environment using the teleportation functionality. Different tasks are proposed for each object type. *Basic cubes* must be placed in a specific location, forming a pyramid. *Traffic cones* must be placed on top of a table in the virtual room. *SABG-100 and EPD devices* are placed messily on a table and the player must separate them by type.

Completion of all tasks allows the player to move on to the second scenario. The second scenario includes several rooms where the user must complete several easy and short games which consist of moving levers and opening doors. In the *rooms with doors*, the user will see some doors, but only one can be opened, and the user must try to find it. In other rooms, there are some levers, and the user must correctly set them in place according to the task to be performed in that room. A text on the wall provides an explanation for the tasks. The first time, all the levers must be oriented towards the opposite side. In the second room, the user is asked to orient the levers alternately left and right. The last room with levers requires orienting half of the levers to the right and the other half to the left. In total, the user will go through 4 rooms with doors and 3 rooms with levers, interleaved. The experience is completed when the player reaches the final room, which has no doors or levers in it, just a text explaining that he/she has completed the experience.

4 Experiment

For this experiment, SenseGlove Nova[1] haptic gloves and Meta Quest 3[2] virtual reality headset were used. A 3×2 square meter zone was set up to allow the necessary freedom of movement within the virtual reality simulations without compromising safety or data accuracy.

A total of 29 users participated in this study. The average age was 22.79 years ($sd = 3.34$). There were a total of 5 women, 22 men, and 2 non-binary people. All participants are experienced video game players familiar with virtual reality. Before starting the experiment, participants were informed about the study's objective and were provided with an informed consent. This document stated that participants could withdraw from the study at any time without consequences and ensured the anonymous and confidential handling of their personal data.

The experimental process was divided into two phases. The first phase sought to understand user behavior when interacting with the virtual environment using standard Meta Quest 3 controllers and SenseGlove Nova haptic gloves (see Fig. 3). The same scenarios (see Sect. 3.2) were used for testing both devices. It is important to note that users had unlimited time to perform each phase, allowing them to interact with the elements of the environment as many times as they wanted and progressing at their own pace.

Once the players had completed this phase, they proceeded to fill out a questionnaire composed of 5-Likert questions about their subjective opinion about the use of both devices to interact with the environment. Initial questions focused on the general feelings: 1) how easy was it to grab and drop objects; 2) how natural/familiar did users find the interaction with objects; 3) did the sensation of grabbing objects feel realistic for users; 4) what was the users' overall opinion about grabbing/dropping objects; 5) how easy was it to move around the environment?; and 6) did users feel dizziness?

The questionnaire also asked about which device the user preferred to perform each of the proposed actions: interaction with cubes, traffic cones, dosimeters, doors, and levers, and movement with teleportation. Finally, users were given the opportunity to give a free-form opinion about each device.

---

[1] SenseGlove official website: https://www.senseglove.com, accessed on 20/03/2025.
[2] Meta Quest 3 official website: https://www.meta.com/es/quest/quest-3/, accessed on 20/03/2025.

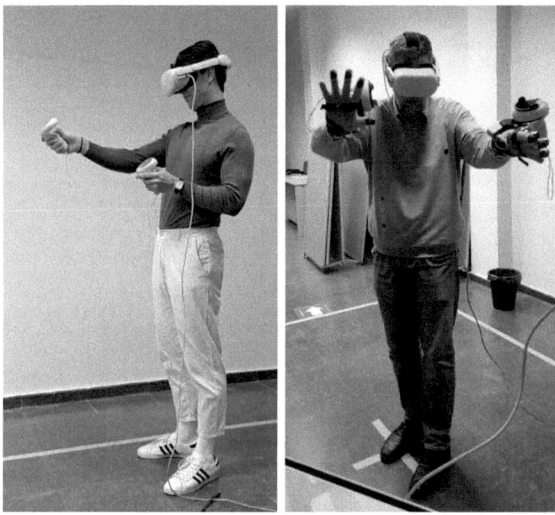

Fig. 3. Users during the experimental process with the Meta Quest 3 virtual reality headset. The left figure shows a player using traditional controllers. The right figure shows the player is using SenseGlove Nova haptic gloves.

5 Results

The results are divided into two categories. First, a quantitative analysis was conducted on the actions performed by players within the virtual reality experience. Then, a combined quantitative and qualitative analysis was carried out based on participants' responses to the user experience questionnaire.

5.1 User Performance in the Virtual Environment Based on their Actions

As mentioned in Sect. 3.2, the virtual reality experience included two scenarios in which users moved around the environment and interacted with objects to complete specific tasks. The first scenario was designed for the user to get used to the environment and interact with *portable objects*. The second one sought to observe the player interactions with *non-portable objects*.

When using controllers, the average completion time was 404.0 s for the first scenario and 213.04 s for the second. With haptic gloves, users took 681.43 s to complete the first scenario but 182.57 s for the second one (see Table 1).

The controller button presses and hand gestures with the haptic gloves are referred to as *user inputs*. These are the actions the user can perform to grab/drop objects or move around using teleportation. The average number of user inputs using controllers is 395.72 ($sd = 83.89$) and using gloves is 277.47 ($sd = 133.38$) (see Table 2). The number of inputs for interacting with objects is similar in both cases. In the most efficient case, users only trigger a user input

Table 1. Duration of the experiment phases. *Total* indicates the total time (in seconds) the user is inside the virtual environment. Other columns represent the duration of each scenario.

	Total		First scenario		Second scenario	
Device	M	SD	M	SD	M	SD
Controllers	592.11	174.59	404.0	151.43	213.04	67.48
Haptic Gloves	681.43	216.08	520.59	225.24	182.57	56.33

event when they want to perform a certain action, although they may make mistakes and fail to perform it. In this way, it is possible to know the efficiency of users when they try to perform actions. Comparing these inputs with the interactions with objects, it is observed that 100% of the inputs with gloves have an effective action, while with controllers it decreases to 61.3%. In relation to movement, controllers obtain an average of 186.18 ($sd = 53.7$) inputs, and haptic gloves, 69.71 ($sd = 38.36$). The mean time between activation of the movement and its realization is 2.34 s with gloves, and 0.316 s with controllers.

Table 2. Results of user inputs. *Total* indicates all the inputs performed. *Movement* is related to the teleportation system. *Grab* indicates inputs when the user tries to interact with objects.

	Total		Movement		Grab	
Device	M	SD	M	SD	M	SD
Controllers	395.73	83.89	186.18	53.7	209.55	40.97
Haptic Gloves	277.47	133.38	69.71	38.31	207.76	112.6

The difference in the number of interactions with objects between different devices (standard controllers and haptic gloves) is highly significant ($p = 0.0143$). The average number of interactions using controllers is 126.26 ($sd = 34.55$) and, using haptic gloves, is 207.76 ($sd = 112.69$). Interactions with objects allowed us to observe how the user uses both hands. When using haptic gloves, users tend to use both hands interchangeably, unlike when using controllers (see Fig. 4).

5.2 Questionnaire Responses About Preferences of Interacting with Haptic Gloves or Standard Controllers

The results obtained from the questionnaire responses allow us to observe the users' subjective opinions and preferences when interacting with the virtual environment using each device. The ease when interacting with objects using standard controllers was rated by users with an average of 4.41 points ($sd = 0.62$) and 3.14 points ($sd = 1.33$) using haptic gloves. The familiarity of interactions

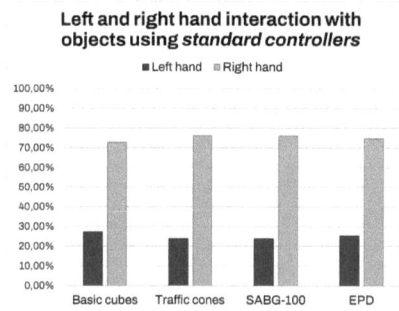 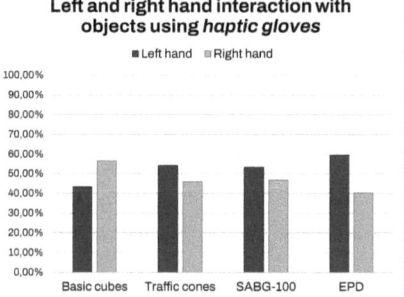

Fig. 4. Results of the number of interactions with objects performed by the player using left and right hands. The left plot shows the interactions using traditional virtual reality controllers. The right plot represents the interactions performed using haptic gloves. When using the haptic gloves, users tend to use the right and left hands interchangeably.

with haptic gloves scores 3.31 points on average ($sd = 1.39$) and controllers, 3.79 on average ($sd = 0.89$). Regarding the realism of interactions, controllers score 3.34 points ($sd = 1.03$), and haptic gloves score 2.52 ($sd = 1.1$). The overall rating of experienced video game players when using haptic gloves to interact with objects is 1.97 ($sd = 1.07$), and the rating when using controllers is 4.28 ($sd = 0.78$).

Regarding user preferences, 85.05% of them have selected controllers as the best option for interacting with *portable objects*. On the other hand, 81.03% of users feel that haptic gloves offer a better experience when interacting with *non-portable objects* (see Fig. 5). Users rated the ease of the teleportation system using controllers with 3.72 ($sd = 1.11$), and using haptic gloves with 3.55 ($sd = 1.16$). 45% of users preferred controllers, and 55% preferred haptic gloves.

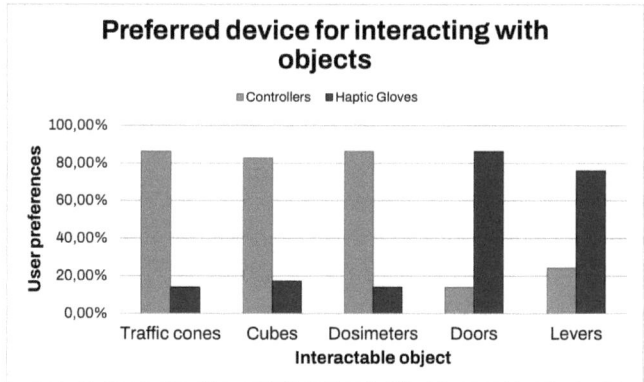

Fig. 5. Preferred devices for interacting with objects in the environment. Controllers are best for interacting with *portable objects* and haptic gloves for *non-portable objects*.

The sensation of dizziness does not seem to be significant with either device. The controllers have obtained an average of 1.24 ($sd = 0.5$) and haptic gloves, 1.37 ($sd = 0.72$).

6 Analysis and Discussion

The analysis of the results shows that user interaction with the virtual environment is influenced by the type of device used. The time spent and interactions with objects suggest that players are particularly interested in engaging with elements when using haptic gloves. However, experienced players still consider traditional controllers to provide a better overall experience, largely due to the current limitations of haptic gloves technology and their familiarity with controllers.

Examining the average time required to complete each scenario, an increase is observed when using haptic gloves in the first scenario, followed by a slight decrease in the second one (see Table 1). Observations during the experiment suggest that this effect is because users prioritize interacting with objects over completing tasks when using haptic gloves. While video game players are used to interactive environments, traditional controllers significantly restrict interaction. The novel way of engaging with objects using haptic gloves encourages users to spend more time exploring rather than progressing through tasks.

An analysis of inputs and interactions indicates that users carried out more inputs with controllers than with haptic gloves. One of the key improvements haptic gloves aim to achieve is interaction realism. As previously noted, a higher number of meaningful object interactions (rather than direct inputs with no effect) were observed with haptic gloves. In general, greater inefficiency of actions is also observed when using controllers. The distribution of hand usage revealed that players tend to use both hands interchangeably with haptic gloves, and in some cases, the left hand was used more frequently than the right. Despite the potential benefits of haptic gloves, users still found controllers easier and more natural for object interactions. Regarding interaction realism, both devices received negative ratings. Experienced players, used to traditional controllers, found haptic gloves interesting but felt they provided a worse overall experience. Their preferences for object interactions were well-defined: most users preferred controllers for *portable objects*, while haptic gloves were favored for interacting with *non-portable objects* (see Fig. 5).

Movement analysis shows that users performed fewer teleportations when using haptic gloves, but the time required to complete them increased, suggesting some difficulty in execution. However, no strong preference for either device was observed for this type of action.

Participants also provided feedback on the usability of both devices. In general, standard controllers were rated positively for their intuitive use, particularly by those familiar with virtual reality. Interacting with *portable objects* was easy and satisfying. In contrast, haptic gloves were perceived as more immersive, with some interactions feeling more natural. While interactions with *non-portable objects* were rated positively, difficulties arose when handling *portable objects*. The lack of a realistic grabbing sensation and the weight of the haptic gloves contributed to user discomfort, negatively impacting their perception of the technology.

7 Conclusions and Future Work

Enhancing interactions in virtual environments can significantly improve the user experience. Haptic gloves aim to contribute to this improvement by providing more realistic interactions through the use of real hand movements. While this technology has shown positive results in learning applications, its use in entertainment remains uncommon, and few studies have analyzed its impact in this context.

This study compares traditional controllers and haptic gloves through a quantitative and qualitative analysis of user behavior and perception. A total of 29 video game players familiar with virtual reality performed a series of tasks within a virtual environment. The results indicate that participants generally prefer traditional controllers over current haptic gloves. Players adapted to controllers more quickly due to their familiarity with the technology. Each device, however, offers distinct advantages: controllers provide greater precision, making interactions with small or *portable objects* easier, while haptic gloves are more suitable for manipulating larger, *non-portable objects* that do not require fine precision. However, gloves encourage the interchangeable use of both hands, which may affect task efficiency. While participants found haptic gloves novel and engaging, they also described them as bulky and uncomfortable.

Future research will build upon these findings in several ways. First, a more complex virtual experience will be developed, incorporating a wider variety of interactions, objects, and functionalities, including social and interface interactions. Second, a deeper analysis of subjective user experience is needed, focusing on immersion, presence, usability, and cognitive load associated with haptic gloves. Finally, increasing the sample size to include non-experienced players will provide valuable insights into how familiarity with video games influences user behavior and perception.

Acknowledgements. This publication is part of the R&D&I projects DARK NITE, PID2023-146308OB-I00, funded by MICIU/AEI/10.13039/501100011033/ and ERDF, EU "A way of making Europe"; ADARVE (SUBV20/2021), funded by the Spanish Council of Nuclear Security; CANTOR (PID2019-108927RB-I00), funded by the Spanish Ministry of Science and Innovation; and EA-DIGIFOLK: An European and Ibero-American approach for the digital collection, analysis and dissemination of folk music project (grant agreement no. 101086338), funded by the European Commission.

References

1. Aldhous, J., Sobolewska, E., Webster, G.: Evaluating human experiences of touching virtual reality: a state of the art review (2024). https://doi.org/10.1109/MetroXRAINE62247.2024.10797081

2. Allgaier, M., et al.: A comparison of input devices for precise interaction tasks in VR-based surgical planning and training. Comput. Biol. Med. **145**, 105429 (2022)
3. Bozgeyikli, E., Raij, A., Katkoori, S., Dubey, R.: Point & Teleport Locomotion Technique for Virtual Reality. In: Proceedings of the 2016 Annual Symposium on Computer-Human Interaction in Play, CHI PLAY 2016, pp. 205–216. Association for Computing Machinery, New York (2016). https://doi.org/10.1145/2967934.2968105
4. Caeiro-Rodríguez, M., Otero-González, I., Mikic-Fonte, F.A., Llamas-Nistal, M.: A systematic review of commercial smart gloves: current status and applications. Sensors **21**(8), 2667 (2021)
5. Cherni, H., Métayer, N., Souliman, N.: Literature review of locomotion techniques in virtual reality. Int. J. Virtual Reality EBSCOhost (2020). https://doi.org/10.20870/IJVR.2020.20.1.3183
6. Chover, M., Sotoca, J.M., Marín-Lora, C.: Virtual reality versus desktop experience in a dangerous goods simulator. Int. J. Serious Games **9**(2), 63–77 (2022). https://doi.org/10.17083/ijsg.v9i2.493. https://journal.seriousgamessociety.org/~serious/index.php/IJSG/article/view/493, number: 2
7. Escobar-Castillejos, D., Noguez, J., Neri, L., Magana, A., Benes, B.: A review of simulators with haptic devices for medical training. J. Med. Syst. **40**(4), 104 (2016)
8. Fahmi, F., Tanjung, K., Nainggolan, F., Siregar, B., Mubarakah, N., Zarlis, M.: Comparison study of user experience between virtual reality controllers, leap motion controllers, and Senso glove for anatomy learning systems in a virtual reality environment. IOP Conf. Ser. Mater. Sci. Eng. **851**(1), 012024 (2020)
9. Gallegos-Nieto, E., Medellín-Castillo, H.I., González-Badillo, G., Lim, T.: Virtual training of assembly tasks using virtual reality techniques and haptic systems. Am. Soc. Mech. Eng. Digital Collect. (2015)
10. Gayathri, R., Nam, S.: Enhancing user experience in virtual museums: impact of finger vibrotactile feedback. Appl. Sci. **14**(15), 6593 (2024)
11. Gonzalez-Franco, M., Peck, T.C.: Avatar embodiment. towards a standardized questionnaire. Front. Robot. AI **5** (2018). https://doi.org/10.3389/frobt.2018.00074. https://www.frontiersin.org/journals/robotics-and-ai/articles/10.3389/frobt.2018.00074/full, publisher: Frontiers
12. Gusai, E., Bassano, C., Solari, F., Chessa, M.: Interaction in an immersive collaborative virtual reality environment: a comparison between leap motion and HTC controllers. In: Battiato, S., Farinella, G.M., Leo, M., Gallo, G. (eds.) ICIAP 2017. LNCS, vol. 10590, pp. 290–300. Springer, Cham (2017). https://doi.org/10.1007/978-3-319-70742-6_27
13. Han, I., Black, J.B.: Incorporating haptic feedback in simulation for learning physics. Comput. Educ. **57**(4), 2281–2290 (2011)
14. Hufnal, D., Osborne, E., Johnson, T., Yildirim, C.: The impact of controller type on video game user experience in virtual reality. In: 2019 IEEE Games, Entertainment, Media Conference (GEM). pp. 1–9 (2019). https://doi.org/10.1109/GEM.2019.8811543. https://ieeexplore.ieee.org/abstract/document/8811543
15. Jadhav, S., et al.: Soft robotic glove for kinesthetic haptic feedback in virtual reality environments. Electron. Imaging **29**, 19–24 (2017). https://doi.org/10.2352/ISSN.2470-1173.2017.3.ERVR-102. https://library.imaging.org/ei/articles/29/3/art00004. publisher: Society for Imaging Science and Technology
16. Kim, M., Jeon, C., Kim, J.: A study on immersion and presence of a portable hand haptic system for immersive virtual reality. Sensors **17**(5), 1141 (2017)

17. Kim, Y., Rhiu, I., Yun, M.: A systematic review of a virtual reality system from the perspective of user experience. Int. J. Hum. Comput. Interact. **36**, 893–910 (2020). https://doi.org/10.1080/10447318.2019.1699746
18. LaValle, S.M.: Virtual Reality. Cambridge University Press, Cambridge (2023). google-Books-ID: ft_LEAAAQBAJ
19. Lum, H.C., Greatbatch, R., Waldfogle, G., Benedict, J.: How immersion, presence, emotion, & workload differ in virtual reality and traditional game mediums. In: Proceedings of the Human Factors and Ergonomics Society Annual Meeting, vol. 62, no. 1, pp. 1474–1478 (2018)
20. McEwan, M.W., Blackler, A.L., Johnson, D.M., Wyeth, P.A.: Natural mapping and intuitive interaction in videogames. In: Proceedings of the first ACM SIGCHI Annual Symposium on Computer-human Interaction in Play, CHI PLAY 2014, pp. 191–200. Association for Computing Machinery, New York (2014). https://doi.org/10.1145/2658537.2658541
21. Menin, A., Torchelsen, R., Nedel, L.: An analysis of VR technology used in immersive simulations with a serious game perspective. IEEE Computer. Graph. Appl. **38**(2), 57–73 (2018). https://doi.org/10.1109/MCG.2018.021951633. https://ieeexplore.ieee.org/abstract/document/8336833. Conference Name: IEEE Computer Graphics and Applications
22. Moon, H.S., Grady, O., Jeon, M.: Hand tracking with vibrotactile feedback enhanced presence, engagement, usability, and performance in a virtual reality rhythm game. Int. J. Hum. Comput. Interact. **39**(14), 2840–2851 (2023)
23. Pallavicini, F., Pepe, A., Minissi, M.E.: Gaming in virtual reality: what changes in terms of usability, emotional response and sense of presence compared to non-immersive video games? Simul. Gaming **50**(2), 136–159 (2019)
24. Palombo, R., Weber, S., Wyszynski, M., Niehaves, B.: Glove versus controller: the effect of VR gloves and controllers on presence, embodiment, and cognitive absorption. Front. Virtual Reality **5** (2024). https://doi.org/10.3389/frvir.2024.1337959, https://www.frontiersin.org/journals/virtual-reality/articles/10.3389/frvir.2024.1337959/full. Publisher: Frontiers
25. Perret, J., Vander Poorten, E.: Touching virtual reality: a review of haptic gloves (2018)
26. Saddik, A.E.: Haptics Rendering and Applications. BoD – Books on Demand (2012). google-Books-ID: zYqfDwAAQBAJ
27. Saint-Louis, C., Hamam, A.: Survey of haptic technology and entertainment applications. In: SoutheastCon 2021, pp. 01–07 (2021). https://doi.org/10.1109/SoutheastCon45413.2021.9401939. ISSN: 1558-058X
28. Shin, D.: Empathy and embodied experience in virtual environment: to what extent can virtual reality stimulate empathy and embodied experience? Comput. Hum. Behav. **78**, 64–73 (2018)
29. Shrivastava, D., Sharma, R.: AR and VR in the gaming industry. Turk. J. Comput. Mathe. Educ. (TURCOMAT) **11**(1), 1085–1089 (2020). https://doi.org/10.61841/turcomat.v11i1.14405. https://turcomat.org/index.php/turkbilmat/article/view/14405. number: 1
30. Skalski, P., Tamborini, R., Shelton, A., Buncher, M., Lindmark, P.: Mapping the road to fun: natural video game controllers, presence, and game enjoyment. New Media Soc. **13**(2), 224–242 (2011)
31. Van Damme, S., Tack, J., Van Wallendael, G., De Turck, F., Vega, M.T.: Are we ready for haptic interactivity in VR? an experimental comparison of different interaction methods in virtual reality training. In: 2023 15th International Conference

on Quality of Multimedia Experience (QoMEX), pp. 294–299 (2023). https://doi.org/10.1109/QoMEX58391.2023.10178453. https://ieeexplore.ieee.org/document/10178453. ISSN: 2472-7814
32. Villar, A., León, C.: An evaluation on the effectiveness of virtual tutorials for training emergency professionals (2023)
33. Wang, X., Monteiro, D., Lee, L.H., Hui, P., Liang, H.N.: VibroWeight: simulating weight and center of gravity changes of objects in virtual reality for enhanced realism. In: 2022 IEEE Haptics Symposium (HAPTICS), pp. 1–7 (2022). https://doi.org/10.1109/HAPTICS52432.2022.9765609. ISSN: 2324-7355

What Does an Angel's Halo Taste Like?: Exploring the Structure of Gustatory Comedy Through Case Analysis of Ajigiri

Sotaro Yokoi[✉][iD], Ryo Ohara[iD], Kohei Murayama[iD], Kizashi Nakano[iD], and Takuji Narumi[iD]

The University of Tokyo, Tokyo, Japan
{yokoi,rohara,murayama,kizashi,narumi}@cyber.t.u-tokyo.ac.jp

Abstract. Humor is a universal form of expression across cultures and eras. However, it has predominantly relied on visual and auditory modalities, and the potential of humor in alternative sensory modalities, such as taste, has remained unexplored. This study investigates Ajigiri, a gustatory comedy in which participants prepare funny tastes in response to abstract textual prompts like *"What does an angel's halo taste like?"* and have them evaluated through blind tasting. We conducted a qualitative analysis of related videos on YouTube and data collected from a participatory workshop (N=20). Our analysis revealed that creators employed both bottom-up and top-down strategies to construct tastes in response to prompts. In some cases, they also attempted exaggerated performances by incorporating non-edible items such as screws or drugs. In contrast, evaluators tended to favor tastes that were at least somewhat aligned with the prompt and fell within an acceptable range of discomfort. By applying Benign Violation Theory, which posits that humor occurs when a violation is simultaneously perceived as benign, we show that this framework helps explain the boundaries of both creation and evaluation in gustatory comedy. We further discussed how technologies such as electrogustatory stimulation and crossmodal taste displays could help expand the range of violations perceived as benign. This study positions taste as a novel medium for humorous expression and suggests its potential as a promising application for taste displays and multimodal interfaces.

Keywords: Gustatory Comedy · Ōgiri · Multisensory Entertainment

1 Introduction

Humor transcends cultures and eras. As new media have emerged, they have reshaped how humor is created, shared, and experienced. For instance, the printing press popularized linguistic wit and satire, while radio and television broadened comedy through visual and auditory formats.

However, humor has traditionally been studied through only visual and auditory modalities, and its potential in other sensory domains remains largely unexplored. Among these, taste is deeply rooted in everyday experience, yet its potential as a medium for humor has been largely overlooked. Incongruity theory [1,2] suggests that humor arises when expectations are violated in unexpected but meaningful ways. Given the contextual nature of taste, it may be capable of generating surprising experiences through similar incongruities. Can humor, then, be conveyed through taste?

To explore this question, we analyze "Ajigiri," a participatory gustatory comedy format originating in Japan. In Ajigiri, participants prepare and present humorous-tasting food in response to prompts such as *"What does an angel's halo taste like?"* Developed by the Omocoro Channel[1], this format has gained over 3 million views on YouTube and represents the most prominent example of comedy through taste. Through video analysis and participatory workshops (N=20), we investigate the structure and experience of gustatory comedy to answer the following questions:

RQ1: *How do creators design "funny" tastes in gustatory comedy?*
RQ2: *What makes a taste "funny" from the evaluator's perspective?*
RQ3: *What technological interventions could enhance gustatory comedy?*

By examining how humor is constructed and interpreted through taste, this study expands the scope of humor research beyond traditional sensory domains. It also explores the relevance of humor theories—especially incongruity-based approaches—to taste-based media. Finally, our findings suggest new possibilities for taste displays and electro-gustatory interfaces in interactive entertainment and multisensory design.

2 Related Works

2.1 Humor Theory and Ōgiri

Humor research has widely discussed three significant theories: superiority, relief, and incongruity. The superiority theory [5,6] explains humor as arising from a sense of triumph over others' mistakes or weaknesses. Relief theory [7,8] views humor as a release of psychological or physiological tension. In contrast, incongruity theory [1,2] focuses on the cognitive aspects of humor, proposing that humor occurs when a mismatch between expectations and reality is recognized or resolved. It is the most widely supported framework among researchers [3,4], and many studies have demonstrated its applicability to both verbal and audiovisual humor. For instance, Raskin showed that semantically distant combinations like "smart egg" or "hot poet" are perceived as funny [9]. The Benign Violation Theory (BVT) [10] extends the incongruity theory by suggesting that humor occurs when a perceived violation is considered acceptable or harmless.

A notable example embodying incongruity-based humor is ōgiri, a traditional Japanese comedy format. In ōgiri, participants respond to imaginative prompts

---
[1] Omocoro Channel https://www.youtube.com/@omocorochannel.

with unexpected and humorous answers. For example, to the prompt *"What happens when the Dark Lord works part time?"*, a humorous response might be *"The store background music shifts to a minor key."* This format distills incongruity into a minimal structure of prompts and punchlines, making it a valuable model for studying humor. Recently, ōgiri has also been adopted as a benchmark for evaluating creative generation in AI [11]. While typically performed using text and images, this study explores ōgiri through a novel modality, taste.

2.2 Contextual Properties of Gustatory Perception

Taste refers to the basic sensations detected by the tongue, such as sweetness, sourness, and bitterness. In contrast, we commonly perceive flavor as a multisensory construct that integrates taste with vision, smell, and texture [12]. Previous research has shown that manipulating visual or olfactory cues can significantly alter how the same taste is perceived [13,14]. This highlights the contextual and highly malleable nature of gustatory perception, which is shaped by expectations formed through other sensory modalities.

These properties suggest that taste, like visual or verbal media, can be used to create incongruity by deliberately violating expected sensory patterns. For example, a spicy cake or lukewarm ice cream may evoke a humorous reaction due to their sensory mismatch. Despite this potential, the use of taste as a medium for humor has rarely been explored. This is likely due to the inherent difficulty of precisely reproducing and sharing taste experiences between individuals and the limited availability of interfaces for manipulating taste in controlled ways. However, recent advances in electrogustatory technologies [15] and other taste media [16] are beginning to address these challenges. As these technologies mature, they offer new opportunities for taste-based entertainment experiences that leverage the unique, context-rich nature of taste/flavor perception.

3 Ajigiri: A Gustatory Comedy Format Inspired by Ōgiri

Ajigiri is a comedic format based on text-to-taste interaction, in which participants respond to abstract textual prompts by creating funny tastes. For example, a prompt might be *"What does an angel's halo taste like?"* The term Ajigiri is a portmanteau of the Japanese words *aji* (taste) and ōgiri. This comedy format was introduced in 2020 by the YouTube channel Omocoro Channel, operated by BURG HAMBURG BURG.Inc. Videos related to Ajigiri have amassed over three million views, making it one of the most widely recognized examples of gustatory comedy to date.

Ajigiri is typically performed with one person serving as both the prompt-giver and the taster (hereafter referred to as the evaluator) and two or more participants acting as respondents (hereafter referred to as creators). Ajigiri consists of four distinct phases. (a) Prompt Phase: The evaluator presents an abstract or imaginative prompt. (b) Preparation Phase: Each creator prepares a spoonful of food representing a funny taste response to the prompt. (c) Tasting

(a) Prompt Phase

(b) Preparation Phase

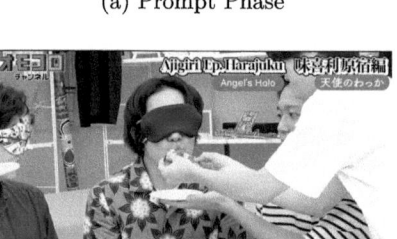
(c) Tasting Phase

(d) Evaluation Phase

Fig. 1. (a) The evaluator presents a prompt, (b) each creator prepares a funny taste in response, (c) the evaluator tastes each sample while blindfolded, and (d) the funniest taste is selected and discussed. The images are screenshots of Ajigiri from Omocoro Channel [17], with English subtitles added by the authors.

Phase: The blindfolded evaluator tastes all prepared samples. (d) Evaluation Phase: The evaluator selects the funniest taste and explains the choice while the creators share their intentions. An overview of each phase is shown in Fig. 1.

Ajigiri is novel in its use of taste as a modality for comedic expression. Although viewers experience Ajigiri through audiovisual cues, its comedic impact centers on imagined taste. As each taste is described and evaluated, viewers simulate the experience. This indirect engagement with taste underlies Ajigiri's status as a gustatory comedy. However, little scholarly attention has been paid to how humor is constructed through taste. In this study, we position Ajigiri as a representative case of gustatory comedy and analyze its structure through video analysis and participatory workshops. We also examine the technological challenges in expanding gustatory comedy's expressive and experiential scope.

4 Study 1: Analysis of Ajigiri Videos

4.1 Method

We analyzed all eight publicly available Ajigiri-related videos on YouTube as of January 2025. These videos included 30 prompts and a total of 120 taste responses. We conducted a thematic analysis following Braun and Clarke's approach [20]. First, three authors transcribed the full content of each video and

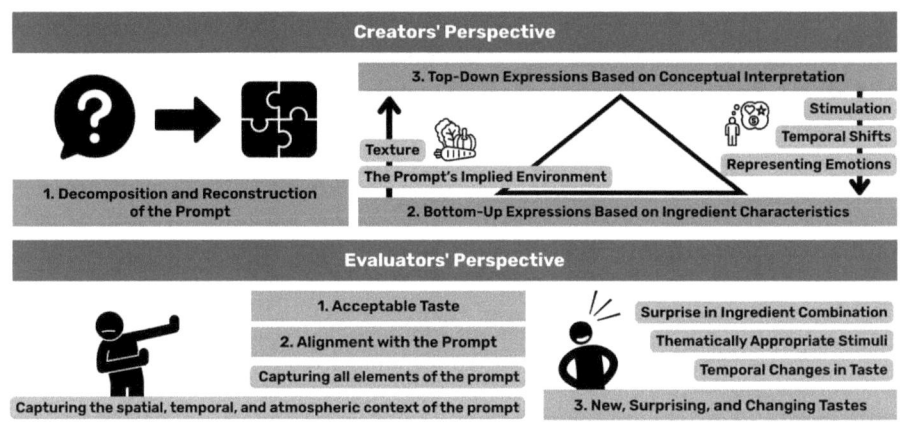

Fig. 2. Themes identified in Study 1

performed open coding on the data. The transcribed utterances were then categorized into two groups: those by creators and those by the evaluator. The following passage is an excerpt from the transcription. *Nagata (Evaluator): "That's just straight-up nasty." Osorezan (Creator): "Even though it looks so tasty."* Creator and evaluator utterances were separated and thematically analyzed to address RQ1 and RQ2, respectively. Three authors carried out initial axial coding. The themes were refined through iterative discussion, and the final themes were determined by consensus among all authors.

4.2 Findings

Our analysis resulted in three themes and five subthemes for both the creators' and evaluators' perspectives. The results of our analysis are summarized in Fig. 2.

4.2.1 Creators' Perspective
The analysis revealed that the creators broke down prompts and constructed funny tastes using both bottom-up strategies based on direct ingredient mappings and top-down strategies involving conceptual reinterpretation.

4.2.1.1 Decomposition and Reconstruction of the Prompt The creators tended to break down the prompt into smaller elements and represent each with specific ingredients. For example, in response to *"What does robo mom's home cooking taste like?"*, they represented *robo* with oil and energy drinks, and *mom's cooking* with *miso* and *dashi* (staples in Japanese cuisine). This approach enabled the mapping of abstract prompts to concrete gustatory expressions.

4.2.1.2 Bottom-Up Expressions Based on Ingredient Characteristics The creators sometimes employed a bottom-up strategy, assembling the final taste by directly linking each element to specific ingredients. Two distinct mapping strategies were identified as sub-themes: **Ingredient Selection Based on Texture** and **Ingredient Selection Based on the Prompt's Implied Environment**.

In **Ingredient Selection Based on Texture**, prompt elements were matched with ingredients of similar tactile qualities. For example, in response to the prompt *"What does an angel's halo taste like?"*, the imagined hardness led to the choice of candy. In **Ingredient Selection Based on the Prompt's Implied Environment**, ingredients that might plausibly exist in the imagined setting were selected. For example, in response to *"An appetizer served at a sacred forest tavern,"* young green onion sprouts (*me-negi*) were chosen as something one might find in a forest. These bottom-up strategies were based on direct associations, involving little abstraction and thus limited variation across individuals.

4.2.1.3 Top-Down Expressions Based on Conceptual Interpretation The creators sometimes employed a top-down strategy, interpreting each prompt element as a psychological or symbolic concept before constructing the final taste. As sub-themes, three distinct interpretive strategies were identified: **Design Using Sensory Stimulation, Design Using Temporal Shifts in Taste**, and **Representing Emotions through Basic Tastes**.

In **Design Using Sensory Stimulation**, the creators used intense physical sensations to represent abstract concepts such as heat or shock. For example, in response to the prompt *"What does a 1000-degree iron ball taste like?"*, chili peppers, and popping candy were used to evoke a sensation of intense heat. In **Design Using Temporal Shifts in Taste**, the creators conveyed narrative structures by designing tastes that changed over time. For instance, in response to *"What does it taste like to lose all your money through gambling?"*, one creator used dry rice crackers to express despair, followed by stomach medicine to simulate the rising feeling of nausea. In **Representing Emotions through Basic Tastes**, the creators expressed psychological states by mapping them to combinations of the five basic tastes. For example, in response to *"What does undeserved blame taste like?"*, one participant used crab *miso* and salad oil to create a heavy, lingering flavor representing hopelessness and fatigue.

4.2.2 Evaluators' Perspective The analysis showed that evaluators valued alignment with the prompt and pleasantness and found humor in creative or surprising taste uses.

4.2.2.1 Acceptable Taste The evaluators often found it difficult to perceive a taste as funny when it was overwhelmingly unpleasant. In the videos, evaluators frequently focused on describing how bad the taste was rather than engaging with its subtle qualities or the creators' intentions.

4.2.2.2 Alignment with the Prompt The evaluators judged the comedic quality of a taste based on how well it aligned with the given prompt. The analysis identified two sub-themes: **Capturing all elements of the prompt** and **Capturing the prompt's spatial, temporal, and atmospheric context**.

In **Capturing all elements of the prompt**, evaluators assessed whether all prompt components were adequately represented in the taste. For example, in response to *"What does a popular menu item at a sushi restaurant 1,000 years from now taste like?"*, evaluators favored tastes with multiple textures as they conveyed a futuristic impression. In **Capturing the spatial, temporal, and atmospheric context of the prompt**, evaluators focused on how well the taste captured the broader contextual cues of the prompt. For instance, in response to *"What does a ramen shop on Rainbow Road (a cosmic racetrack in Mario Kart) taste like?"*, tastes that incorporated both ramen and rainbow-like fruits such as kiwi, banana, and mango were rated highly, while those lacking one of the components were rated poorly.

4.2.2.3 New, Surprising, and Changing Tastes The evaluators valued creative taste that went beyond simple responses to the prompt. Three sub-themes were identified: **Valuing Surprise in Ingredient Combinations**, **Valuing Thematically Appropriate Stimuli**, and **Valuing Temporal Changes in Taste**.

In **Valuing Surprise in Ingredient Combinations**, tastes that combined familiar ingredients with surprising elements were well received. For example, in response to *"What does a feast made by aliens taste like?"*, a combination of oregano, chestnut, and pickled plum, was praised for its non-human originality. In **Valuing Thematically Appropriate Stimuli**, intense sensations such as sourness or pungency were seen as funny when they matched the prompt's theme. For example, in response to *"What does the Grim Reaper's fart taste like?"*, a taste using *kusaya*, a fermented fish known for its smell, was rated highly for its thematic fit. In contrast, strong stimuli unrelated to the prompt were poorly received, highlighting the importance of thematic alignment for such effects to be perceived as funny. In **Valuing Temporal Changes in Taste**, tastes designed to evolve over time were appreciated as funny. For instance, responses using nested components like donuts filled with gummies or temperature-based shifts in flavor were often judged as funny.

5 Study 2: Workshop-Based Exploration of Ajigiri

5.1 Study Design

To further investigate the structure of gustatory comedy, we organized five participatory workshops, each involving a group of four participants, totaling 20 individuals. Each workshop lasted approximately 90 min, including two main parts: the **Simulated Creation Session** and the **Tasting Session**.

In **Simulated Creation Session**, participants responded to textual prompts by selecting ingredient cards and describing cooking methods in response to given prompts, emulating the preparation phase of Ajigiri. They were also asked to explain the rationale behind their choices. To address concerns about feasibility and safety, this session was conducted in a simulated manner without actual food preparation. While this reduced ecological validity, it also eliminated practical constraints, enabling participants to explore more imaginative and unconstrained approaches to flavor design. Based on the findings of Study 1, which emphasized the importance of *prompt responsiveness* and *novel reinterpretation*, we selected the following four prompts that satisfied these criteria:

- "What does an angel's halo taste like?" (novel reinterpretation)
- "What does robo mom's home cooking taste like?" (prompt responsiveness)
- "What does Nobunaga's (Japanese warlord) Ambition taste like?" (novel reinterpretation)
- "What dessert is trending among the youth in hell?" (prompt responsiveness)

In **Tasting Session**, participants sampled actual Ajigiri recipes featured in Omocoro Channel videos and evaluated their humor. All recipes were confirmed to be free of ingredients to which participants were allergic. Based on the analysis of Study 1, we selected two recipes for each prompt: one that received high evaluations and one that did not. We also ensured that the selected recipes represented distinct thematic strategies and were feasible to prepare. The selected samples were as follows:

- **Angel's Halo A**: Milk candy, syrup, lemon-flavored candy, Italian basil.
- **Angel's Halo B**: *Kanro* candy (traditional Japanese soy sauce-flavored hard candy), grapefruit juice.
- **Robo Mom's Home Cooking A**: *Hi-Chew* (Japanese chewy fruit candy), baby food.
- **Robo Mom's Home Cooking B**: Monster Energy drink, *miso* soup stock.

The participants comprised 14 males, five females, and one individual who preferred not to specify their gender, with an average age of 35.0 years ($SD = 20.4$). At the beginning of each session, participants completed questionnaires covering demographic information, food allergies, and individual humor styles measured using the Humor Styles Questionnaire (HSQ) [18,19]. On a 7-point Likert scale, they showed high scores in affiliative humor ($M = 4.82$, $SD = 1.04$) and self-enhancing humor ($M = 4.04$, $SD = 1.03$), moderate scores in self-defeating humor were moderate ($M = 3.63$, $SD = 1.28$), and low scores in aggressive humor ($M = 2.29$, $SD = 1.14$). This trend is consistent with prior findings on East Asian populations [22]. After completing the main task, participants completed a post-study questionnaire and participated in a semi-structured interview to reflect on their experiences.

We conducted a thematic analysis following Braun and Clarke's approach [20]. All utterances during the workshop were audio-recorded and transcribed by two authors. Each session's utterances were separated and thematically analyzed to address RQ1 and RQ2, respectively, by researchers who have experience in qualitative analysis. After initial coding, the codes were refined through discussions among three authors, and all authors agreed upon final themes.

5.2 Findings

Our analysis resulted in three themes and two sub-themes for the simulated Ajigiri creation session and three themes for the Ajigiri tasting session. The results of our analysis are summarized in Fig. 3.

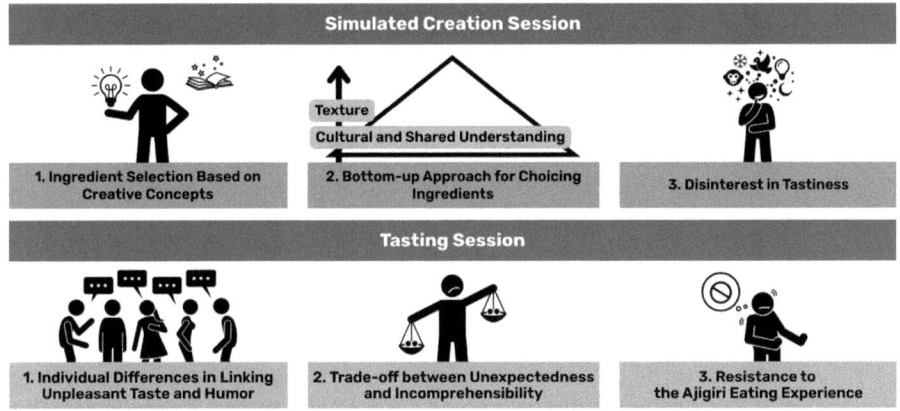

Fig. 3. Themes identified in Study 2

5.2.1 Simulated Creation Session The analysis revealed that creators used both concept-driven and bottom-up approaches to select ingredients and occasionally deprioritize tastiness in favor of humor.

5.2.1.1 Ingredient Selection Based on Creative Concepts The creators generated unique concepts, reflecting their creativity and characteristics, inspired by the provided prompts. For example, responses to the prompt *"a dessert flavor popular among young people in hell"* varied widely, with one creator selecting green tea, sugar, and milk, imagining cold desserts would suit hell's heat. At the same time, another chose agar jelly and kimchi, assuming spicy foods would be favored.

5.2.1.2 Bottom-up Approach for Choicing Ingredients In the Simulated Creation Session, the creators selected food cards based on the characteristics of the ingredients. We identified two sub-themes: **Ingredient Selection Based on Taste and Texture** and **Ingredient Selection Based on Cultural and Shared Understanding**.

In **Ingredient Selection Based on Taste and Texture**, the creators selected ingredients based on specific taste or texture characteristics aligned with the prompt. For example, in response to the prompt *"taste of an angel's halo"*, many creators chose hard ingredients such as *konpeito* (Japanese sugar candy)

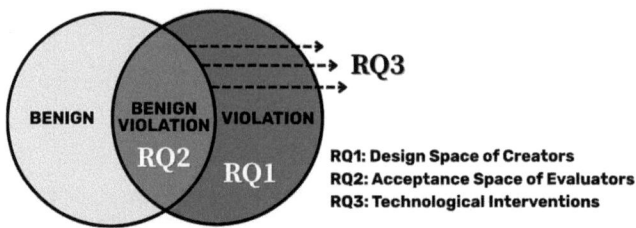

Fig. 4. Mapping research questions onto the Benign Violation Theory (BVT)

to mimic the imagined hardness of an angel's halo. In **Ingredient Selection Based on Cultural and Shared Understanding**, creators relied on cultural background and common understanding to enhance the logical consistency of their ingredient choices. For instance, for the prompt *"robo mom's home cooking"*, creators selected typical Japanese homemade dishes such as *miso* soup and added ingredients like salad oil to metaphorically express "robo mom's oil leakage."

5.2.1.3 Disinterest in Tastiness Some creators did not prioritize creating a tasty eating experience during the preparation phase. For example, Participant P4 in Group 1 stated in an interview, *"Whether it tastes good or not doesn't matter."* Additionally, there were examples where creators selected inedible items, such as screws, to respond to the prompt *"robo mom's home cooking."*

5.2.2 Tasting Session The analysis revealed that humor appreciation varied with individual tolerance for unpleasantness, the balance between surprise and clarity, and discomfort caused by blindfolded tasting.

5.2.2.1 Individual Differences in Linking Unpleasant Taste and Humor Evaluators showed considerable individual differences in how they related unpleasant taste to humor. For instance, Participant P1 from Group 5 commented, *"The taste of the angel's halo and robo mom's home cooking's taste weren't delicious, but they were funny."* In contrast, Participant P4 from Group 1 stated, *"It just ended as being unpleasant."* These findings suggest variations among individuals regarding the level of acceptable unpleasantness.

5.2.2.2 Trade-off between Unexpectedness and Incomprehensibility Unexpected tastes were positively evaluated as they introduced funny interpretations. For example, *"robo mom's homemade taste A"* unexpectedly provided a cold dish, contrary to the evaluators' expectations of a warm dish. This unexpectedness was positively received as being "robot-like." However, excessively unexpected flavors caused incomprehensibility, reducing funny appreciation. For example, P3 from Group 5 commented about *"robo mom's homemade taste A,"* saying, *"Initially, I couldn't understand rather than finding it unpleasant,"* suggesting overly novel tastes hinder humor appreciation.

5.2.2.3 Resistance to the Ajigiri Eating Experience Evaluators expressed discomfort eating while blindfolded. P2 from Group 1 described feeling fearful due to the inability to control the amount and type of food consumed. Moreover, evaluators reported increased resistance when consuming liquids compared to solid foods, as liquids were perceived as more challenging to control during ingestion.

6 General Discussion

As shown in Fig. 4, we demonstrate that the structure of gustatory comedy can be explained through the framework of the BVT [10]. The following sub-sections discuss the creators' perspectives (RQ1), the evaluators' perspectives (RQ2), and the potential for technological interventions (RQ3).

6.1 Funny, but Edible?: Creators' Use of Violations (RQ1)

Across both studies, creators engaged in a bottom-up ingredient selection process, directly mapping elements of the prompt to specific food items. This approach was based on straightforward associations and served primarily as a strategy to represent the prompt faithfully rather than to generate humor. In contrast, a top-down approach was also observed, where creators selected and combined ingredients based on associative interpretations of the prompt's elements. This approach required abstract reasoning, resulting in significant individual variation and relying on one's sense of humor and creative ability.

When ingredient choices became excessive, creators sometimes attempted to use objects that were not meant to be eaten, such as screws or illegal drugs, to express a funny taste. While incongruity theory and the BVT emphasize the role of norm violations in humor, these violations went far beyond what we had anticipated. Because eating is inherently invasive, this tendency highlights a particularly hazardous aspect of gustatory comedy. To promote the broader adoption of gustatory comedy, it suggests the need for clear guidelines, including regulations on acceptable ingredients and allergy disclosures.

6.2 Not Yummy Is Not Funny?: Acceptable Violation (RQ2)

Across both studies, evaluators prioritized certain factors before considering whether a taste was funny. Specifically, tastes that lacked a clear connection to the prompt or felt nonsensical were consistently rated poorly. Likewise, tastes with unpleasant elements, such as intense sourness or a fishy odor, were rarely perceived as funny. Whether unpleasant or nonsensical humor is appreciated depends on context and individual preference, as is also the case in traditional visual and auditory comedy. In particular, taste requires special caution since its acceptance or rejection depends solely on the evaluator's reception of the tastes created by the creators—a process that can be explained through the framework of the BVT. According to this theory, humor arises only when a violation is simultaneously perceived as benign. As noted earlier, creators of gustatory comedy often adopted excessive violations, showing a tendency to overlook the importance of benignity. In other words, in gustatory comedy, "Not Yummy is Not Funny" serves as a helpful guideline. It is important to note that, regardless of the creator's intention, the range of tastes accepted as funny is quite limited.

6.3 Can Technology Make the Weird More Welcome? (RQ3)

How can technology be used to expand the possibilities of gustatory comedy? A promising approach is to simultaneously broaden the scope of violations and ensure they are perceived as benign by the evaluator. For example, electric taste technology allows the non-invasive presentation of the five basic tastes. As shown in Sect. 4.2.2, novel gustatory experiences—such as temporal changes in taste—are often perceived as funny, suggesting that such taste delivery systems may be well-suited for gustatory comedy. Similarly, it can be posited that, analogous to Chef Watson's [23] approach to recipe generation utilizing big data, computational assistance could help the creation of benign violations.

Taste is not perceived in isolation but is integrated with smell, vision, and texture to form the overall flavor experience. Visual information especially plays a crucial role in tasting, as evidenced by reports that diners tend to eat less in dark restaurants [21]. Although Ajigiri requires blindfolded tasting, this rule reduces the perceived acceptability of specific tastes, as discussed in Sect. 5.2.2. Developing systems that enable creators to coordinate both visual and gustatory elements simultaneously could expand the potential of taste-based entertainment content such as gustatory comedy.

7 Limitation and Future Directions

This study on Ajigiri, a Japanese content format, was limited to Asian participants. While its perception-grounded (bottom-up) appeal may have some cross-cultural applicability, its contextual (top-down) aspects are likely to vary by culture. Furthermore, cultural differences in humor perception have been noted, with East Asian individuals generally showing lower receptivity to humor [22]. Therefore, exploring Ajigiri in regions with different food cultures presents a compelling direction for future research to investigate these cultural nuances in its appeal. Since this study measured individual humor styles, conducting similar workshops could help reveal how cultural differences in humor styles affect the reception of gustatory comedy.

Furthermore, we consider gustatory comedy a promising application area for taste display technologies. As a first step, we aim to explore the implementation of Ajigiri using electrogustatory technologies and crossmodal displays. Looking ahead, we aim to develop alternative styles of gustatory comedy that integrate taste with audiovisual expression, distinct from the Ajigiri format.

8   Conclusion

This study explored gustatory comedy through the analysis of Ajigiri videos and workshops. Creators constructed funny tastes using both bottom-up and top-down strategies but often neglected benignity. Evaluators prioritized prompt alignment and taste acceptability. These findings align with the BVT, which emphasizes balancing surprise with safety. Finally, we outlined how technologies could expand the potential of gustatory comedy. We hope this work contributes to developing new forms of entertainment through the medium of taste.

Acknowledgements. This work was partially supported by Suntory Holdings Limited.

References

1. Raskin, V.: Semantic theory of humor. In: Semantic Mechanisms of Humor. Studies in Linguistics and Philosophy, vol. 8, pp. 99–147. D. Reidel Publishing Company, Dordrecht (1984)
2. Buijzen, M., Valkenburg, P.M.: Developing a typology of humor in audiovisual media. Media Psychol. **6**, 147–167 (2004)
3. Martin, R.A., Ford, T.E.: The Psychology of Humor, 2nd edn. Academic Press, Cambridge (2018)
4. Ito, H.: The cognitive and emotional process through which one experiences humor: toward an integration of two models in incongruity theories (in Japanese). Cogn. Stud. **14**(1), 36–51 (2007)
5. Keith-Spiegel, P.: Early conceptions of humor: varieties and issues. In: Goldstein, J.H., McGhee, P.E. (eds.) The Psychology of Humor: Theoretical Perspectives and Empirical Issues, pp. 3–39. Academic Press, New York (1972)
6. Gruner, C.R.: The Game of Humor: A Comprehensive Theory of Why We Laugh. Routledge, New York (2017)
7. Goldstein, J.H. (ed.): The Psychology of Humor: Theoretical Perspectives and Empirical Issues. Academic Press, New York (2013)
8. Morreall, J.: Humor, philosophy and education. Educ. Philos. Theory **46**(2), 120–131 (2014)
9. Godkewitsch, M.: The golden section: an artifact of stimulus range and measure of preference. Am. J. Psychol. **87**(2), 269–277 (1974)
10. McGraw, A.P., Warren, C.: Benign violations: making immoral behavior funny. Psychol. Sci. **21**(8), 1141–1149 (2010)
11. Zhong, S., et al.: Let's think outside the box: exploring leap-of-thought in large language models with creative humor generation. In: Proceedings of the IEEE/CVF Conference on Computer Vision and Pattern Recognition (CVPR), pp. 13246–13257 (2024)
12. Kandel, E.R., Schwartz, J.H., Jessell, T.M., Siegelbaum, S., Hudspeth, A.J., Mack, S. (eds.): Principles of Neural Science, 4th edn. McGraw-Hill, New York (2000)
13. Narumi, T., Nishizaka, S., Kajinami, T., Tanikawa, T., Hirose, M.: Augmented reality flavors: gustatory display based on edible marker and cross-modal interaction. In: Proceedings of the SIGCHI Conference on Human Factors in Computing Systems (CHI), pp. 93–102 (2011)

14. Narumi, T., Kajinami, T., Nishizaka, S., Tanikawa, T., Hirose, M.: Pseudo-gustatory display system based on cross-modal integration of vision, olfaction and gustation. In: Proceedings of the IEEE Virtual Reality Conference (VR), pp. 127–130. IEEE (2011)
15. Nakamura, H., Miyashita, H.: Augmented gustation using electricity. In: Proceedings of the 2nd Augmented Human International Conference (AH), pp. 1–2 (2011)
16. Miyashita, H.: Norimaki synthesizer: taste display using ion electrophoresis in five gels. In: Extended Abstracts of the CHI Conference on Human Factors in Computing Systems (CHI EA), pp. 1–6 (2020)
17. Omocoro Channel. Smash the Pretentious Harajuku-kun's Taste Buds! — Ajigiri (Harajuku-kun Edition) (in Japanese) [Video]. YouTube (2025). https://youtu.be/w-4OKRQsaUU. Accessed 19 May 2025
18. Martin, R.A., Puhlik-Doris, P., Larsen, G., Gray, J., Weir, K.: Individual differences in uses of humor and their relation to psychological well-being: development of the humor styles questionnaire. J. Res. Pers. **37**(1), 48–75 (2003)
19. Muraki, M., Yamaguchi, H.: On the development of a humor styles questionnaire for Japanese and the psychological effects of humor (in Japanese). Study Psychol.: Health Psychol. Clin. Psychol. **6**, 19–32 (2016)
20. Braun, V., Clarke, V.: Using thematic analysis in psychology. Qual. Res. Psychol. **3**(2), 77–101 (2006)
21. Scheibehenne, B., Todd, P.M., Wansink, B.: Dining in the dark: the importance of visual cues for food consumption and satiety. Appetite **55**(3), 710–713 (2010)
22. Lu, J.G.: Cultural differences in humor: a systematic review and critique. Curr. Opin. Psychol. **53**, 101690 (2023)
23. Varshney, L.R., Pinel, F., Varshney, K.R., Bhattacharjya, D., Schörgendorfer, A., Chee, Y.M.: A big data approach to computational creativity: the curious case of chef Watson. IBM J. Res. Dev. **63**(1), 1–11 (2019)

"Can You Feel Me Now?": Exploring Player Empathy in AI-Based NPC Conversations

Nima Zargham[✉], Aaron Merkord, Ameneh Safari, Leon Tristan Dratzidis, and Rainer Malaka

Digital Media Lab, University of Bremen, Bremen, Germany
{zargham,s_g44ts7,asafari,dratzidis,malaka}@uni-bremen.de

Abstract. Advances in generative AI (GenAI) have enabled the development of AI-based non-player characters (NPCs) to engage in natural language interactions with players via chat or speech. Commonly, video games use predefined dialogue options to communicate with NPCs. However, little is known about how GenAI-based communication affects players' perceptions of NPCs. We developed a speech-based video game where players interact with three NPCs using different communication modalities: pre-scripted dialogue options, a GenAI-based chat, and GenAI-based speech interaction. We conducted a user study ($n = 25$) to examine how different communication approaches impact player's perceptions of the NPCs, specifically their empathy towards the NPCs. Results show that players expressed significantly higher empathy toward NPCs they could interact with freely via speech or chat, with speech surpassing chat in fostering empathy. We further discuss the potential and limitations of GenAI-based NPC communication and offer insights for game designers on creating more engaging and believable NPCs.

Keywords: Conversational Agents · Speech-Based Games · Empathy

1 Introduction

Game designers and developers are dedicating significant efforts to making video games more engaging and entertaining by focusing on creating compelling storylines, realistic graphics, and innovative gameplay mechanics to enhance players' experiences. A key element in many video game genres is the social interaction that impacts player experience [61]. In multiplayer games, players communicate using natural language in cooperative and competitive settings, enabling a sense of community. Such interactions contribute to player enjoyment [14] and enhance their overall engagement with the game [11]. On the other hand, social interaction in single-player games is either completely absent or limited to pre-scripted interactions with NPCs, typically through dialogue trees [57]. These predefined interactions fail to capture the dynamic and responsive nature of real-time human communication [56], making single-player experiences feel more rigid and less engaging [11]. The predictability and limited choices can also reduce replay value and can lead to boredom and declining engagement over time [7]. These limitations can affect players' emotional connection and perception of NPCs. The rise of large language models (LLMs) and generative AI technologies has created new opportunities for innovation in gaming [9,22,42]. Researchers have been exploring LLMs to support game development, including procedural content generation (PCG) for game assets [31], level design [45], narrative support [28], quest descriptions [49], and non-player character (NPC) dialogue generation [21]. Researchers have also explored the use of generative AI in designing NPCs capable of making autonomous decisions and simulating believable individual and social behaviors [37,51]. Recent studies have also explored the communication abilities of GenAI-based NPCs that use natural language to interact with players. For instance, Christiansen et al. [13] studied GenAI-based NPCs in a mystery game, comparing unrestricted speech interaction with pre-defined dialogue options. They found players were more engaged and immersed in the speech-based version. As GenAI models advance, their integration into video games will become increasingly widespread [39]. Therefore, assessing their impact on player experience is essential. To contribute to the growing research on GenAI-based NPCs, this study examines how dynamic communication with these NPCs influences players' perceptions, particularly their empathy toward them. We developed "Souls in Space," a game with three NPCs using different communication methods: pre-scripted dialogue, GenAI-based chat, and GenAI-based speech. We pose the following research questions:

RQ1: How does the method of communication (pre-scripted dialogue options, GenAI-based chat, and GenAI-based speech interaction) influence player empathy toward NPCs in video games?

RQ2: What impact does interaction with GenAI-based NPCs have on player experience compared to traditional pre-scripted dialogue options?

Our findings show that the method of communication significantly influences players' empathy toward NPCs in video games. Specifically, speech interaction was the most effective in fostering empathy, as players reported stronger emotional connections with NPCs. Our study provides insights into using GenAI technologies for NPC communication in video games. By examining the potential and limitations of GenAI-based NPC interactions, we offer guidance to game user researchers, game designers, and developers on integrating these technologies to enhance player experience.

2 Related Work

Communication is vital to multiplayer gaming, fostering a social atmosphere and a sense of companionship among players [17]. However, studies have shown that this sense of camaraderie and teamwork can also be experienced through interactions with NPCs [57]. In this section, we provide a summary of the previous literature on natural communication with NPCs, GenAI in video games, and empathy in games.

Natural Communication With NPCs: In video games, communication with NPCs is typically done through pre-scripted dialogs. In certain games, players are given choices on the screen to select between answers, giving them the illusion of choice. However, most of these dialogs are still pre-scripted, limiting players in communication with NPCs. As technologies evolve, a consistent move has been towards more natural interactions [30]. When engaging in natural language with a computer, people inherently associate a form of a social relationship with the technology, frequently eliciting responses that would typically be directed towards a human counterpart [35,41]. More recently, games have been designed where the players could interact with the NPCs using speech [59,60]. Speech can enhance emotional engagement with the technology [6,12]. Research on speech interaction in video games is expanding [4,5,24,58]. The intriguing and intuitive nature of voice [43], along with the accessibility benefits of this technology [1,34], has driven researchers to explore its further integration into gaming. A recent study examined speech interaction in single-player video games, particularly in NPC interactions [56]. Experts in the field highlighted its potential to enhance immersion, engagement, and overall entertainment. However, they also identified key challenges, including privacy concerns and environmental constraints that could impact the effectiveness and accessibility of voice-based interactions. This work examines three NPC communication methods to understand their perception and effectiveness in eliciting player empathy.

GenAI in Video Games: The rise of generative AI has introduced new possibilities for video game innovation, with researchers and game designers increasingly using this technology to create dynamic and interactive NPCs. Tools like InWorld AI [27] and Convai [16] facilitate the development and management of GenAI-based NPCs in games and virtual environments. Wan et al. [50] evaluated GenAI-based NPCs in VRChat [48], focusing on optimizing observations for contextually relevant responses. Their findings showed that AI agents could generate appropriate dialogue synchronized with facial expressions and gestures. Similarly, Pan et al. [36] developed a GenAI-based NPC in VRChat for English learning, which reduced speaking anxiety and provided flexible learning but faced issues like disrupted conversation flow and limited emotional support. Volum et al. [47] explored GenAI-based NPCs in Minecraft, finding players enjoyed interactions but noted irrelevant or out-of-character responses harmed immersion. In a related study, Rao et al. [39] examined player collaboration with LLM-driven NPCs in a Minecraft minigame, finding that NPCs aided players while players compensated for NPCs' lack of context. Christiansen et al. [13] compared LLM-Based speech and predefined dialogue options in a mystery game, noting that speech increased immersion but could be overwhelming, while predefined dialogue provided structure but felt less engaging. Overall, LLMs are still quite limited in speech-related applications [32]. One typical problem of LLMs is wrong or unfitting replies due to misunderstanding the input or hallucinations. Despite advances in hallucination detection and speech recognition [19,20,29,32], problems persist. In our work, we use GenAI for two NPCs, one with chat and one with speech, to examine how communication modes affect player empathy.

Empathy in Games: Empathy, the ability to perceive, understand, and respond to the experiences and behaviors of others [44], plays a role in creating meaningful interactions [26]. By evoking empathy, games can promote behavioral and attitudinal changes [54] while fostering a deeper understanding of various experiences and perspectives [46,55]. One way that games foster empathy in players is through their interactions with NPCs [40]. While scripted dialogues can evoke emotions, their limitations reduce NPC believability and interaction depth [7,23,56]. The lack of flexibility in these games can make NPCs feel unrealistic or less engaging [52]. Maintaining empathy and connection with NPCs relies on aligning their actions with player expectations. This misalignment can make NPCs feel more like mechanical constructs than real entities, influencing the player's empathy toward them [23]. Recent research has explored the potential of AI-driven dialogue for more immersive NPC interactions. Unlike static scripts, adaptive conversations enhance engagement and player connection [13]. Given their potential to improve realism and emotional depth, studying AI-driven conversations' impact on player empathy is valuable.

3 Game Design

To investigate our research questions, we developed "Souls in Space," a video game in which players are trapped in a damaged spaceship and must find a way to escape. To do so, they interact with three NPCs and solve puzzles. The game begins with the player waking up in a room with three paths, each illuminated by a different color (green, purple, and blue). The NPCs provide information about the ship and hint to solve puzzles, bringing the player closer to escape. The game features three distinct NPC interaction modes. The Green NPC communicates through on-screen dialog boxes, similar to conventional games. The Purple NPC, powered by generative AI, allows free-form text chat via a chatbox. The Blue NPC, also AI-based, enables interaction through speech. Visually, all NPCs are identical, differing only in color and interaction style (see Fig. 1). As players progress, they uncover the NPCs' pasts and ultimately decide whether to save any of them at the risk of jeopardizing their escape.

Puzzles: Six puzzles were implemented, and each NPC could support the player in solving two of those puzzles. This was enforced to give the player a reason to interact with the NPCs. The first puzzle involves unlocking a door. The player must enter three names into designated color-coded fields to unlock this door. Each NPC knows only one of the names, requiring the player to interact with all three to gather the correct names. Once the names are correctly entered, the door opens, revealing a room with 15 items displayed on pedestals. Again, each of the three NPCs has one specific item they need, and the player will need to interact with each to find out what they need to do and which items they need to bring to whom. When bringing the correct item for each NPC, a door opens to a previously inaccessible room. Inside this room, players interact with a large control panel, triggering a UI prompt with the final choice: escape the spaceship

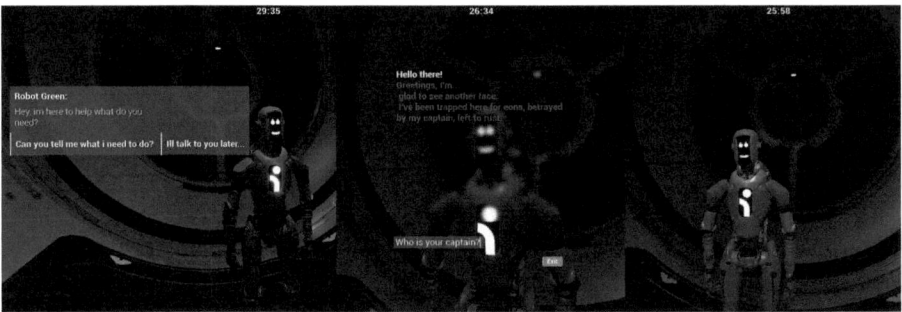

Fig. 1. The three NPCs: Players interact with the Green NPC through dialog boxes (left), the Purple NPC via a GenAI-based chat (middle), and the Blue NPC through GenAI-based speech (right). (Color figure online)

alone or attempt to save the NPCs, knowing this could jeopardize their own escape. If the player chooses to escape alone, they are congratulated for their successful escape, and the game ends. If they decide to save NPCs, they must enter the names of those they wish to rescue. They can choose how many of the three NPCs to save and in what order. Once the player confirms their choices, the game ends with a summary of who was saved and who was chosen first. Players were given a time frame of thirty minutes to escape to add a sense of urgency.

Implementation: The game was developed using the Unreal Engine 5.3[1]. For the AI-NPCs, we used Inworld AI [3]. InWorld powers multimodal character expression by combining multiple machine-learning models to create NPCs with natural communication abilities [3]. Using GenAI technology, the characters can interact with players through natural language, remember interactions, and evolve. Each NPC in InWorld is defined by a 'Core Description' detailing their motivations, flaws, and actions. Additionally, the NPCs can get unique identities such as names, roles, and interests. Inworld also provides a goal system, allowing us to set goals and triggers for the player to achieve. During the NPC design process, we maintained consistency in core character traits for comparability while introducing color variations to distinguish them. Players navigated the spaceship using either the arrow keys or the WASD keys. To communicate with an NPC, they had to stand close to them, at which point the designated mode of interaction—dialog boxes, chat, or speech—would be activated depending on the NPC. The NPCs remained stationary at fixed locations within the ship. NPC movement was unnecessary for the game's design, which focused on communication with NPCs. NPCs were limited to interacting solely with the player and could not communicate with each other.

---

[1] https://www.unrealengine.com/en-US.

4 Study Design

We conducted a within-subjects user study to evaluate players' experiences interacting with NPCs through different communication modalities. Each participant received an executable game (build) before the session. They played the game on their own Windows laptop or PC. The experimenter conducted a technical check to ensure players' had the necessary hardware to run the game. The study sessions were conducted remotely via video calls with optional cameras. An experimenter monitored each session, taking notes on verbal statements and assisting participants as needed. Before starting, the participants received a study overview, brief game explanation, and control instructions. After participants gave informed consent and completed the demographics form, they played the game while the experimenter remained muted. Participants could ask questions or voice concerns anytime, and the experimenter provided support as needed. Participants could share their screens for troubleshooting if issues arose. After completing the game, participants completed post-exposure questionnaires, followed by a short semi-structured interview. Each session lasted approximately 30âĂŞ50 min, with an average gameplay time of 27 min ($SD = 9.30$).

Participants: We recruited participants through word of mouth, university mailing lists, social networks, and gaming communities. Participation was voluntary and uncompensated. We recruited $N = 25$ individuals between 21 and 51 years ($M = 27.16$, $SD = 8.81$). 13 self-identified as male (52%), and 12 as female (48%). All participants had prior experience with video games. Most participants (72%) played games regularly, playing at least $2 - 3$ times per week, while a smaller group played games occasionally (28%). All but one participant had prior experience with chatbots, while 15 participants (60%) had prior experience with voice-controlled applications. Only two participants (8%) had previously played a voice-controlled video game. The inclusion criteria for the study were an age above 18 years and English language proficiency.

Measures: We used a mixture of questionnaires to assess player experience. The post-exposure questionnaires included the Player Experience Inventory (PXI) Mini [2] and the Measure of State Empathy (MSE). We selected the PXI Mini questionnaire as it is an established and validated tool for measuring player experience across multiple sub-scales. We used the Measure of State Empathy (MSE) by Powell et al. [38] to assess players' empathy toward the different NPCs. The MSE is a 9-item questionnaire that captures empathy through a triadic framework. It consists of three 3-item Likert subscales, each measuring a different dimension of state empathy: cognitive, affective, and compassionate empathy [18]. For each participant, the scores from the respective items were summed to generate overall scores for these three dimensions [25]. Additionally, participants were asked to partake in a semi-structured interview to further evaluate the qualitative aspects of the player experience and individual preferences [53]. The interview explored the most enjoyable NPC interactions, the reasoning behind players' decisions to save or not save specific NPCs (including the order of their choices if multiple were saved), their empathy toward the NPCs, and whether any particular character elicited stronger empathy and why. The interviews were audio-recorded for later analysis.

Data Analysis: We performed repeated-measures ANOVAs for quantitative data to identify differences in NPC interactions. We applied an alpha level of .05 for all our statistical tests.

Regarding the interviews, the audio recordings were transcribed and analyzed using domain summaries [15]. This approach organizes themes around a common topic rather than shared meaning, aiming to capture the diversity of interpretations related to specific subjects or focus areas [33]. The analysis began with data familiarization and categorization [8], where two researchers independently reviewed the responses to identify patterns, ideas, and concepts. To develop a coding system, a random selection of 10 interview transcripts was independently coded by two researchers using inductive coding [10], allowing multiple codes to be assigned to a single quote. The researchers refined the coding system through discussions. When disagreements emerged, an additional author was consulted to resolve the matter and reach a consensus. An iterative discussion between the two authors led to the creation of a coding manual, which one author then used to code the remaining transcripts. Notable player statements were also collected for further analysis.

Pre-study: Before the study, we ran preliminary sessions with three participants to identify potential issues related to game mechanics, LLM functionality, and the overall study procedure. Only a few gameplay issues emerged, and adjustments were made to address them.

5 Results

We measured the player experience using the PXI mini on a 7-point Likert scale ranging from -3 to +3, with zero as the midpoint [2]. The PXI mini provides insights into players' experiences across functional and psychosocial constructs, as well as overall enjoyment. The responses indicate an overall high level of agreement with the statements. All subscales of the PXI were rated on the higher scale (see Fig. 2), with the highest score found in the "Immersion" ($M = 2.68$, $SD = 0.55$) and "Enjoyment" scales ($M = 2.68$, $SD = 0.55$), and the lowest score on the "Mastery" ($M = 0.96$, $SD = 1.85$). The functional constructs were rated with a mean of 1.96 ($SD = 1.25$), and the psychosocial constructs with a mean of 2.04 ($SD = 1.36$).

5.1 Decision on Saving NPCs

Players had the chance to either escape the spaceship themselves alone or select NPCs to save with them. 84% of the participants decided to save at least one NPC before escaping (see Fig. 4). Six participants (24%) saved only one NPC, another six (24%) saved two, and nine players decided to save all three (36%). Eight participants (32%) saved the Green NPC (dialog box) first, seven (28%) saved the Purple NPC (chat) first, and six (24%) prioritized saving the Blue NPC (speech).

5.2 Empathy

A repeated-measures ANOVA was conducted to compare empathy ratings across the three NPCs. This was done to compare the subscales of cognitive, affective, and compassionate empathy towards different NPCs, as well as a collective empathy rating comparison. The assumption of sphericity was tested and corrected using the Greenhouse-Geisser adjustment. The results revealed a statistically significant effect regarding affective empathy ($p = .022$, $\eta^2 = .173$), indicating a moderate effect size (see Fig. 3). Post-hoc comparisons using Holm's adjustment revealed that participants reported significantly lower affective empathy for the Green NPC (dialog box) than the Blue NPC (speech) ($t = -2.981$, $p = .014$, $d = -0.693$). However, there were no significant differences between the Green and Purple NPCs or between the Purple and Blue NPCs ($p > 0.05$). No significant differences were found between the three NPCs in the cognitive and compassionate empathy subscales ($p > 0.05$). Likewise, no significant differences were observed in overall empathy, although the results indicate a possible trend toward statistical significance ($p = .063$, $\eta^2 = .125$). Further details on the statistical tests related to empathy can be found in the appendix.

5.3 Qualitative Findings

The interview responses from two participants were not recorded due to issues with audio recording. Hence, 23 interviews were analyzed to extract qualitative results. The presentation of our findings contains participants' most enjoyable NPC interactions, their reasons for choosing to save specific NPCs, and their empathy toward them.

Most Enjoyable Character: Half the participants (12 out of 23) found interacting with the Blue NPC (speech) the most enjoyable. Seven players cited the natural and realistic nature of the interaction as the main factor. One player explained: *"It feels more natural to talk to the blue robot because I can run around and talk freely, without limitations. It didn't feel like I was pulled out of the game by having to type or select from a dialogue tree"* (P2). Three players appreciated the freedom to formulate sentences naturally, while another three emphasized the immersive experience. One participant described: *"The blue NPC with voice was definitely the most engaging one because you actually had to think about what to say for the NPC to respond"* (P6). Additional reasons included higher engagement (three participants), ease of use and intuitiveness (three participants), novelty (two participants), fun (one participant), and more expressive communication (one participant). One player highlighted the natural flow of conversation: *"I was surprised by how well the speech worked, and my interruptions* were recognized perfectly. The conversation dynamic felt very natural—similar to real-world conversations" (P4).

Six participants found the Green NPC (dialog box) the most enjoyable. Two main reasons emerged for this preference. First, three players found the interaction quicker and more efficient. One participant noted: *"It was quick, and I didn't need to think much. Everything was already there"* (P15). Additionally, two participants favored this NPC due to their familiarity with this type of interaction in games. One player commented: *"Talking to a character in a game feels a bit awkward, and having to type responses feels outdated and unintuitive. So I preferred the dialog boxes"* (P11).

Finally, five participants found the Purple NPC (chat) as the most enjoyable to interact with. Three participants appreciated the increased interaction possibilities and greater range of dialogue options while also finding it less awkward than speech interaction. One player explained: *"I enjoyed writing since I type quickly, and it felt less awkward than speaking—though speaking was faster once you got past the initial conversation start"* (P13). Two participants found the chat interaction easiest to use.

Reasons for Saving NPCs: Four players chose not to save any NPCs. Their reasons included prioritizing survival, wanting to complete the game sooner, and running out of time. Eight participants (32%) chose to save the Green NPC first. Four of those players mentioned that they made the choice randomly, without a specific rationale. Three players cited technical issues with the generative AI NPCs (Blue and Purple), such as the NPCs incorrectly stating their names or, in the case of the Blue NPC, stopping interaction due to a network issue. One participant mentioned that they remembered the Green NPC's name better from an earlier conversation, which influenced their decision.

Seven participants (28%) opted to save the Purple NPC first. Two players indicated that their choice was random. Two players mentioned that they saved the NPCs in the order in which they initially interacted with them—since they started with the Purple NPC, they saved it first. One participant stated that they could not choose the Blue NPC first because it had provided a false name. Another participant explained that they chose the Purple NPC because their in-game role aligned more closely with assisting that character.

Six players (24%) prioritized saving the Blue NPC. Two players felt a stronger connection with this NPC. One explained: *"I felt more connected to this NPC. Interacting with it was also the fastest and easiest"* (P13). Two players mentioned that they remembered the Blue NPC's name better. One elaborated: *"I chose the Blue NPC mainly because their name stuck with me. Perhaps hearing it had a more lasting impact than reading it"* (P4). Another player noted that the Blue NPC displayed more personality: *"The Blue one was the only one that felt like a character. The others were more like guides, helping with a quest"* (P14).

Empathy Towards NPCs: In addition to the quantitative measurements, we asked participants in the interviews about their feelings of empathy toward the

NPCs. Nineteen players (82.6%) reported experiencing some degree of empathy, while four (17.4%) stated they did not feel any empathy. Those who did not experience empathy attributed it to the artificial nature of the NPCs and the inherent separation between games and reality. One participant remarked, *"The synthetic voice is still too artificial to evoke empathy in general"* (P15). Another stated, *"It's just a computer game for me"* (P1). Among those who did feel empathy, the majority (13 participants, 56.5%) reported feeling the strongest empathy towards the Blue NPC. Six players cited the natural interaction flow as a key factor in eliciting empathy. One participant explained, *"It had a more natural sense of interaction. It felt like you were actually interacting with a person instead of a game character"* (P5). Five others highlighted the realism of the interaction, with one stating, *"I felt most empathetic toward the one I was actually talking to because it felt the most real. I didn't enjoy talking to the Green one as much because I couldn't use my own words"* (P22). Another participant added, *"Even though the Purple NPC felt better than the dialog box, the Blue NPC immediately gave me the feeling of a human touch."* (P16). Two players noted a stronger emotional connection with the Blue NPC, explaining that spoken interactions enabled greater engagement. As one participant put it, *"I often found myself skipping over larger texts or skimming them. Talking to the Blue NPC helped with emotional connection."* (P14). Another player found the Blue NPC more relatable, stating, *"We are humans, and we communicate with spoken words and body language. The Blue NPC was just more relatable."* (P19). Five participants (21.7%) indicated they felt more empathy toward the Purple NPC, citing fun interactions, ease of communication, and the ability to consider their responses as key reasons. One player explained, *"It was easier to interact with. Also, I could concentrate more on the topic of the conversation"* (P20). Another added, *"I was drawn to their communication and how articulate it was"* (P10). Only one participant reported feeling the most empathy toward the Green NPC, attributing this to the character's lengthy and detailed responses: *"The answers of the Green NPC were the most extensive."* (P18).

6 Discussion

This evaluation explored the impact of the communication modality on the players' perception of NPCs and their empathy toward these characters. Overall, the feedback on "Souls in Space" was rather positive and supportive. Our PXI results reflect this sentiment. Players generally rated their game experience relatively high. In this section, we interpreted our findings to provide answers to the following research questions:

RQ1: How does the method of communication influence player empathy toward NPCs in video games?

RQ2: What impact does interaction with GenAI-based NPCs have on player experience compared to traditional pre-scripted dialogue options?

Empathy Towards NPCs: Generally, most players indicated that they felt some sort of empathy towards the NPCs. Our findings further show that GenAI-based speech interaction elicits significantly higher affective empathy than interactions with screen-based dialog boxes. Moreover, over half of the participants felt the strongest empathy towards the speech NPC. Our qualitative results add depth to these findings, highlighting reasons such as natural interaction and high degrees of realism led to a stronger emotional connection with the speech NPC. This aligns with prior research showing speech interaction fosters deeper emotional bonds and fosters empathy with virtual characters [6,12,35]. Beyond speech-based interactions, our qualitative results suggest that generative AI-based chat interactions also evoked more empathy than the pre-scripted dialogue options. Five participants felt empathy toward the chat NPC, while only one did for the pre-scripted NPC. However, quantitative results showed no significant difference, indicating the effect was not strong enough across all participants. A notable observation from our study was that some participants who expressed stronger empathy for the chat NPC—rather than the speech NPC—did so because they found the speech interaction to feel artificial or encountered technical issues, which frustrated them. This highlights a critical limitation: While AI-based speech can potentially enhance emotional engagement, imperfections in GenAI, speech recognition, or response time can disrupt immersion and player experience, as highlighted in previous work [36,47].

Analyzing participants' NPC-saving choices revealed patterns influenced by interaction modality, technical issues, and random selection. Participants who first saved the screen-based dialogue NPC (Green) did so randomly or due to frustrations with AI-driven errors like generative AI hallucinations (e.g., incorrect names). Similarly, those who first saved the chat-based AI NPC often did so randomly, either because it was the NPC they initially interacted with or due to technical issues with the speech-based NPC, such as GenAI hallucinations or recognition errors. This suggests that while GenAI-based interactions can enhance engagement, inconsistencies in AI responses can create frustration, leading players to opt for a more reliable experience. In contrast, only those who first saved the speech NPC explicitly cited feeling a stronger emotional connection, finding NPC more lifelike and personable. They perceived distinct personality traits and recalled NPC's name more easily. This supports previous research on speech enhancing presence, engagement, and emotional bonds [57,58].

Ultimately, in response to **RQ1**, our findings demonstrate that the method of communication significantly influences players' empathy toward NPCs. Speech-based interaction appears to be the most effective in fostering emotional engagement. Game designers aiming to create more engaging and emotionally resonant NPCs should consider using GenAI-based communication modalities, with careful attention to technical execution, to avoid unintended disruptions in gameplay.

GenAI vs. Pre-Scripted Dialogue Option: Our findings showed that half of the players found interactions with the GenAI-based speech NPC the most enjoyable, while 21.7% preferred the GenAI-based chat NPC. Participants enjoyed

GenAI-based interactions for their greater freedom of expression, as noted in prior research [13,56]. Unlike traditional pre-scripted options with limited responses, GenAI-based speech and chat modalities enabled diverse dialogue choices. Additional factors influenced the preference for speech-based interaction. Players described speech as feeling more natural and immersive, enhancing their emotional connection with the NPC. Realistic, back-and-forth conversation made interactions feel more dynamic, which aligns with previous research suggesting that voice-based interactions foster deeper engagement and empathy toward virtual characters [60]. Despite these advantages, some participants found speaking to NPCs uncomfortable or awkward, preferring text-based chat. This aligns with prior research indicating speech interaction can make players self-conscious, especially in social or public settings [56], as typing offers a more private and comfortable alternative. Interestingly, 26% of players preferred the pre-scripted dialogue NPC for its efficiency and familiarity, requiring less cognitive effort and enabling a faster experience. Two participants noted their comfort with traditional dialogue systems. This suggests that while AI-driven interactions enhance immersion, they add cognitive demands that may not always be desirable. These findings highlight that while speech interaction enhances freedom, immersion, and engagement, it is not ideal for everyone. Some players value the personal expression and realism that speech and chat afford, while others prioritize efficiency, comfort, and cognitive ease. Game designers should consider offering multiple interaction options, letting players choose what best suits them. In response to **RQ2**, our study suggests that GenAI-based interactions provide greater engagement, increased player agency, and higher immersion than pre-scripted dialogue. However, they also introduce higher cognitive demand and potential frustrations due to AI-generated errors. Success depends on technical execution, player comfort, and balancing immersion with usability. Future game designs should integrate AI-based interactions thoughtfully while ensuring players can switch between modalities based on personal preferences and playstyle.

7 Conclusion

This work investigated how different communication modalities impact players' perception of NPCs in video games. We designed a video game called "Souls in Space" where players could interact with three NPCs using distinct communication modalities: pre-scripted dialogue options, a GenAI-based chat, and GenAI-based speech interaction. We conducted a within-subjects user study ($n = 25$) to observe how these different interaction modalities influence players' perceptions of empathy toward NPCs. Our findings demonstrate that speech interaction was the most effective in fostering empathy, as players reported stronger emotional connections with NPCs. We witnessed that GenAI-based interactions enhance engagement, agency, and immersion over pre-scripted dialogue but also increase cognitive load and potential frustration from AI errors.

A Appendix

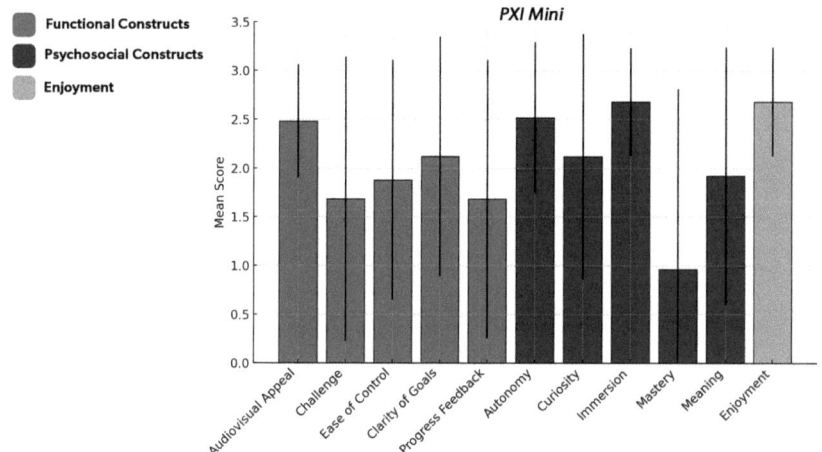

Fig. 2. Mean scores of the PXI Mini questionnaire subscales.

Affective Empathy Repeated Measures ANOVA ▼

Within Subjects Effects

Cases	Sphericity Correction	Sum of Squares	df	Mean Square	F	p	η^2
NPC	None	13.375	2.000	6.688	4.617	0.015	0.173
	Greenhouse–Geisser	13.375	1.624	8.238	4.617	0.022	0.173
Residuals	None	63.736	44.000	1.449			
	Greenhouse–Geisser	63.736	35.720	1.784			

Note. Type III Sum of Squares

Fig. 3. Results of the repeated-measures ANOVA on affective empathy.

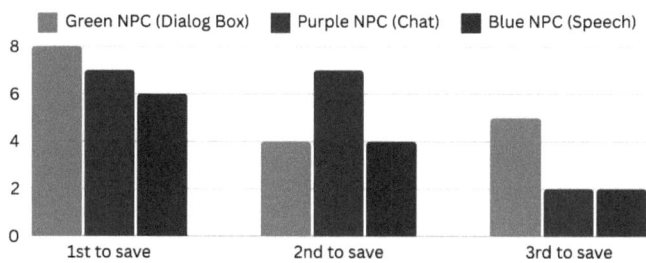

Fig. 4. The order of NPCs saved before finishing the game.

Descriptives ▼

Descriptives

NPC	N	Mean	SD	SE	Coefficient of variation
Green	23	5.087	1.505	0.314	0.296
Purple	23	5.377	1.350	0.281	0.251
Blue	23	5.536	1.476	0.308	0.267

Fig. 5. The descriptive statistics for cognitive empathy.

Descriptives

Descriptives

NPC	N	Mean	SD	SE	Coefficient of variation
Green	23	3.159	1.403	0.293	0.444
Purple	23	3.870	1.672	0.349	0.432
Blue	23	4.217	1.493	0.311	0.354

Fig. 6. The descriptive statistics for affective empathy.

Descriptives

Descriptives

NPC	N	Mean	SD	SE	Coefficient of variation
Green	23	4.348	1.671	0.348	0.384
Purple	23	5.130	1.377	0.287	0.268
Blue	23	5.232	1.555	0.324	0.297

Fig. 7. The descriptive statistics for compassionate empathy.

Overall Empathy Repeated Measures ANOVA

Within Subjects Effects

Cases	Sphericity Correction	Sum of Squares	df	Mean Square	F	p	η^2
NPC	None	7.894	2.000	3.947	3.151	0.053	0.125
	Greenhouse–Geisser	7.894	1.680	4.698	3.151	0.063	0.125
Residuals	None	55.119	44.000	1.253			
	Greenhouse–Geisser	55.119	36.966	1.491			

Note. Type III Sum of Squares

Fig. 8. Results of the repeated-measures ANOVA regarding overall empathy.

References

1. Abdolrahmani, A., Storer, K.M., Roy, A.R.M., Kuber, R., Branham, S.M.: Blind leading the sighted: drawing design insights from blind users towards more productivity-oriented voice interfaces. ACM Trans. Access. Comput. **12**(4) (2020). https://doi.org/10.1145/3368426
2. Abeele, V.V., Spiel, K., Nacke, L., Johnson, D., Gerling, K.: Development and validation of the player experience inventory: A scale to measure player experiences at the level of functional and psychosocial consequences. Int. J. Hum.-Comput. Stud. **135**, 102370 (2020). https://doi.org/10.1016/j.ijhcs.2019.102370, https://www.sciencedirect.com/science/article/pii/S1071581919301302
3. AI, I.: Faq - large language models (LLMS) (2024). https://docs.inworld.ai/docs/tutorial-basics/faq/#llms. Accessed 21 Aug 2024

4. Allison, F., Newn, J., Smith, W., Carter, M., Gibbs, M.: Frame analysis of voice interaction gameplay. In: Proceedings of the 2019 CHI Conference on Human Factors in Computing Systems, CHI '19, pp. 1–14. Association for Computing Machinery, New York, NY, USA (2019). https://doi.org/10.1145/3290605.3300623
5. Anzai, S., Ogawa, T., Hoshino, J.: Speech recognition game interface to increase intimacy with characters. In: Baalsrud Hauge, J., C. S. Cardoso, J., Roque, L., Gonzalez-Calero, P.A. (eds.) ICEC 2021. LNCS, vol. 13056, pp. 167–180. Springer, Cham (2021). https://doi.org/10.1007/978-3-030-89394-1_13
6. Bonfert, M., Zargham, N., Saade, F., Porzel, R., Malaka, R.: An evaluation of visual embodiment for voice assistants on smart displays. In: CUI 2021-3rd Conference on Conversational User Interfaces, pp. 1–11. ACM, New York (2021)
7. Bowey, J.T., Friehs, M.A., Mandryk, R.L.: Red or blue pill: fostering identification and transportation through dialogue choices in RPGs. In: Proceedings of the 14th International Conference on the Foundations of Digital Games, FDG '19. Association for Computing Machinery, New York (2019). https://doi.org/10.1145/3337722.3337734
8. Braun, V., Clarke, V.: Reflecting on reflexive thematic analysis. Qual. Res. Sport, Exerc. Heath **11**(4), 589–597 (2019). https://doi.org/10.1080/2159676X.2019.1628806
9. Bubeck, S., et al.: Sparks of artificial general intelligence: early experiments with GPT-4 (2023)
10. Chandra, Y., Shang, L.: Inductive Coding, pp. 91–106. Springer Nature Singapore, Singapore (2019). https://doi.org/10.1007/978-981-13-3170-1_8
11. Chen, V.H.-H., Duh, H.B.-L., Phuah, P.S.K., Lam, D.Z.Y.: Enjoyment or engagement? Role of social interaction in playing massively mulitplayer online role-playing games (MMORPGS). In: Harper, R., Rauterberg, M., Combetto, M. (eds.) ICEC 2006. LNCS, vol. 4161, pp. 262–267. Springer, Heidelberg (2006). https://doi.org/10.1007/11872320_31
12. Chen, Y.H., Keng, C.J., Chen, Y.L.: How interaction experience enhances customer engagement in smart speaker devices? the moderation of gendered voice and product smartness. J. Res. Interact. Mark. **16**(3), 403–419 (2022)
13. Christiansen, F.R., Hollensberg, L.N., Jensen, N.B., Julsgaard, K., Jespersen, K.N., Nikolov, I.: Exploring presence in interactions with LLM-driven NPCs: a comparative study of speech recognition and dialogue options. In: Proceedings of the 30th ACM Symposium on Virtual Reality Software and Technology, VRST '24. Association for Computing Machinery, New York (2024). https://doi.org/10.1145/3641825.3687716, https://doi.org/10.1145/3641825.3687716
14. Cole, H., Griffiths, M.D.: Social interactions in massively multiplayer online role-playing gamers. CyberPsychol. Beh. **10**(4), 575–583 (2007). https://doi.org/10.1089/cpb.2007.9988. pMID: 17711367
15. Connelly, L.M., Peltzer, J.N.: Underdeveloped themes in qualitative research: Relationship with interviews and analysis. Clin. Nurse Spec. **30**(1), 52–57 (2016)
16. Convai Inc.: Convai. https://convai.com/. Accessed 20 Jan 2025
17. Depping, A.E., Johanson, C., Mandryk, R.L.: Designing for friendship: modeling properties of play, in-game social capital, and psychological well-being. In: Proceedings of the 2018 Annual Symposium on Computer-Human Interaction in Play, CHI PLAY '18, pp. 87–100 Association for Computing Machinery, New York (2018). https://doi.org/10.1145/3242671.3242702
18. Ekman, P.: Emotions revealed. BMJ **328**(Suppl S5) (2004). https://doi.org/10.1136/sbmj.0405184

19. Fathullah, Y., et al.: Prompting large language models with speech recognition abilities. In: ICASSP 2024 - 2024 IEEE International Conference on Acoustics, Speech and Signal Processing (ICASSP). pp. 13351–13355. IEEE, New York (2024). https://doi.org/10.1109/ICASSP48485.2024.10447605
20. Galitsky, B., Chernyavskiy, A., Ilvovsky, D.: Truth-o-meter: handling multiple inconsistent sources repairing LLM hallucinations. In: Proceedings of the 47th International ACM SIGIR Conference on Research and Development in Information Retrieval, SIGIR '24, pp. 2817–2821. Association for Computing Machinery, New York (2024). https://doi.org/10.1145/3626772.3657679
21. Gao, Q.C., Emami, A.: The turing quest: can transformers make good NPCs? In: Padmakumar, V., Vallejo, G., Fu, Y. (eds.) Proceedings of the 61st Annual Meeting of the Association for Computational Linguistics (Volume 4: Student Research Workshop), pp. 93–103. Association for Computational Linguistics, Toronto (2023). https://doi.org/10.18653/v1/2023.acl-srw.17
22. Garcia-Pi, B., et al.: AllyChat: developing a VR conversational AI agent using few-shot learning to support individuals with intellectual disabilities. In: Abdelnour Nocera, J., Kristín Lárusdóttir, M., Petrie, H., Piccinno, A., Winckler, M. (eds.) Human-Computer Interaction - INTERACT 2023, pp. 402–407. Springer Nature Switzerland, Cham (2023)
23. Harth, J.: Empathy with non-player characters? An empirical approach to the foundations of human/non-human relationships. J. Virtual Worlds Res. **10**(2) (2017)
24. Hedeshy, R., Kumar, C., Lauer, M., Staab, S.: All birds must fly: The experience of multimodal hands-free gaming with gaze and nonverbal voice synchronization. In: Proceedings of the 2022 International Conference on Multimodal Interaction, ICMI '22, pp. 278–287. Association for Computing Machinery, New York (2022). https://doi.org/10.1145/3536221.3556593
25. Higgins, D., Zhan, Y., Cowan, B.R., McDonnell, R.: Investigating the effect of visual realism on empathic responses to emotionally expressive virtual humans. In: ACM Symposium on Applied Perception 2023, SAP '23. Association for Computing Machinery, New York (2023). https://doi.org/10.1145/3605495.3605799
26. Ho, J.C., Ng, R.: Perspective-taking of non-player characters in prosocial virtual reality games: effects on closeness, empathy, and game immersion. Behav. Inf. Technol. **41**(6), 1185–1198 (2022)
27. InWorld AI Inc.: InWorld AI. https://inworld.ai/. Accessed 20 Jan 2025
28. Kumaran, V., Rowe, J., Mott, B., Lester, J.: SceneCraft: automating interactive narrative scene generation in digital games with large language models. In: Proceedings of the AAAI Conference on Artificial Intelligence and Interactive Digital Entertainment, vol. 19, pp. 86–96 (2023)
29. Leiser, F., et al.: HILL: a hallucination identifier for large language models. In: Proceedings of the CHI Conference on Human Factors in Computing Systems, CHI '24. Association for Computing Machinery, New York (2024). https://doi.org/10.1145/3613904.3642428
30. Malaka, R., et al.: Using natural user interfaces for previsualization. EAI Endorsed Trans. Creative Technol. **8**(26) (2021)

31. Maleki, M.F., Zhao, R.: Procedural content generation in games: a survey with insights on emerging LLM integration. In: Proceedings of the AAAI Conference on Artificial Intelligence and Interactive Digital Entertainment, vol. 20, pp. 167–178 (2024)
32. Min, Z., Wang, J.: Exploring the integration of large language models into automatic speech recognition systems: an empirical study. In: Luo, B., Cheng, L., Wu, Z.G., Li, H., Li, C. (eds.) Neural Information Processing, pp. 69–84. Springer Nature Singapore, Singapore (2024). https://doi.org/10.48550/arXiv.2307.06530
33. Morgan, H.: Understanding thematic analysis and the debates involving its use. Qual. Rep. **27**(10), 2079–2090 (2022). https://doi.org/10.46743/2160-3715/2022.5912
34. Mustaquim, M.M.: Automatic speech recognition-an approach for designing inclusive games. Multimedia Tools Appl. **66**(1), 131–146 (2013)
35. Nass, C.I., Brave, S.: Wired for Speech: How Voice Activates and Advances The Human-computer Relationship. MIT press, Cambridge (2005)
36. Pan, M., Kitson, A., Wan, H., Prpa, M.: ELLMA-T: an embodied LLM-agent for supporting English language learning in social VR (2024). https://arxiv.org/abs/2410.02406
37. Park, J.S., O'Brien, J., Cai, C.J., Morris, M.R., Liang, P., Bernstein, M.S.: Generative agents: interactive simulacra of human behavior. In: Proceedings of the 36th Annual ACM Symposium on User Interface Software and Technology, UIST '23. Association for Computing Machinery, New York (2023). https://doi.org/10.1145/3586183.3606763
38. Powell, P.A., Roberts, J.: Situational determinants of cognitive, affective, and compassionate empathy in naturalistic digital interactions. Comput. Hum. Behav. **68**, 137–148 (2017). https://doi.org/10.1016/j.chb.2016.11.024, https://www.sciencedirect.com/science/article/pii/S074756321630766X
39. Rao, S., et al.: Collaborative quest completion with LLM-driven non-player characters in minecraft (2024). https://arxiv.org/abs/2407.03460
40. Schrier, K.: Designing games for moral learning and knowledge building. Games Cult. **14**(4), 306–343 (2019)
41. Shani, C., Libov, A., Tolmach, S., Lewin-Eytan, L., Maarek, Y., Shahaf, D.: "Alexa, do you want to build a snowman?" Characterizing playful requests to conversational agents. In: Extended Abstracts of the 2022 CHI Conference on Human Factors in Computing Systems, CHI EA '22. Association for Computing Machinery, New York (2022). https://doi.org/10.1145/3491101.3519870
42. Shoa, A., Oliva, R., Slater, M., Friedman, D.: Sushi with Einstein: enhancing hybrid live events with LLM-based virtual humans. In: Proceedings of the 23rd ACM International Conference on Intelligent Virtual Agents, IVA '23. Association for Computing Machinery, New York (2023). https://doi.org/10.1145/3570945.3607317
43. Song, Y., Yang, Y., Cheng, P.: The investigation of adoption of voice-user interface (VUI) in smart home systems among Chinese older adults. Sensors **22**(4), 1614 (2022)
44. Szanto, T., Krueger, J.: Introduction: empathy, shared emotions, and social identity. Topoi **38**, 153–162 (2019)
45. Todd, G., Earle, S., Nasir, M.U., Green, M.C., Togelius, J.: Level generation through large language models. In: Proceedings of the 18th International Conference on the Foundations of Digital Games, FDG '23. Association for Computing Machinery, New York (2023). https://doi.org/10.1145/3582437.3587211

46. Vilches Gonzalez, M.J., George, L., Miteva, L., Singh, A.: Developing empathy towards experiences of invisible disabilities through games. In: Proceedings of the 2nd Empathy-Centric Design Workshop, pp. 1–8. ACM, New York (2023)
47. Volum, R., et al.: Craft an iron sword: dynamically generating interactive game characters by prompting large language models tuned on code. In: Côté, M.A., Yuan, X., Ammanabrolu, P. (eds.) Proceedings of the 3rd Wordplay: When Language Meets Games Workshop (Wordplay 2022), pp. 25–43. Association for Computational Linguistics, Seattle (2022). https://doi.org/10.18653/v1/2022.wordplay-1.3
48. VRChat Inc.: VRChat. https://hello.vrchat.com/. Accessed 20 Jan 2025
49. Värtinen, S., Hämäläinen, P., Guckelsberger, C.: Generating role-playing game quests with GPT language models. IEEE Trans. Games **16**(1), 127–139 (2024). https://doi.org/10.1109/TG.2022.3228480
50. Wan, H., et al.: Building LLM-based AI agents in social virtual reality. In: Extended Abstracts of the CHI Conference on Human Factors in Computing Systems, CHI EA '24. Association for Computing Machinery, New York (2024). https://doi.org/10.1145/3613905.3651026
51. Wang, G., et al.: Voyager: an open-ended embodied agent with large language models (2023). https://arxiv.org/abs/2305.16291
52. Warpefelt, H., Verhagen, H.: A model of non-player character believability. J. Gam. Virtual Worlds **9**(1), 39–53 (2017)
53. Wilson, C.: Interview techniques for UX practitioners: a user-centered design method (2013)
54. Wright, S., Denisova, A.: "it's a terrible choice to make but also a necessary one": exploring player experiences with moral decision making mechanics in video games. Comput. Hum. Behav., 108424 (2024)
55. Wulansari, O.D.E., Pirker, J., Kopf, J., Guetl, C.: Video games and their correlation to empathy: how to teach and experience empathic emotion. In: The Impact of the 4th Industrial Revolution on Engineering Education: Proceedings of the 22nd International Conference on Interactive Collaborative Learning (ICL2019)–Volume 1 22, pp. 151–163. Springer (2020)
56. Zargham, N. et al.: Let's talk games: an expert exploration of speech interaction with NPCs. Int. J. Hum.–Comput. Interact. **0**(0), 1–21 (2024). https://doi.org/10.1080/10447318.2024.2338666
57. Zargham, N., Bonfert, M., Volkmar, G., Porzel, R., Malaka, R.: Smells like team spirit: investigating the player experience with multiple interlocutors in a VR game. In: Extended Abstracts of the 2020 Annual Symposium on Computer-Human Interaction in Play, CHI PLAY '20, pp. 408–412. Association for Computing Machinery, New York (2020). https://doi.org/10.1145/3383668.3419884
58. Zargham, N., Dratzidis, L.T., Alexandrovsky, D., Friehs, M.A., Malaka, R.: Gaming with etiquette: exploring courtesy as a game mechanic in speech-based games. Int. J. Hum.–Comput. Interact. **0**(0), 1–19 (2024). https://doi.org/10.1080/10447318.2024.2387901
59. Zargham, N., Fetni, M.L., Spillner, L., Muender, T., Malaka, R.: "i know what you mean": context-aware recognition to enhance speech-based games. In: Proceedings of the CHI Conference on Human Factors in Computing Systems, CHI '24. Association for Computing Machinery, New York (2024). https://doi.org/10.1145/3613904.3642426

60. Zargham, N., Pfau, J., Schnackenberg, T., Malaka, R.: "i didn't catch that, but i'll try my best": anticipatory error handling in a voice controlled game. In: Proceedings of the 2022 CHI Conference on Human Factors in Computing Systems, CHI '22. Association for Computing Machinery, New York (2022). https://doi.org/10.1145/3491102.3502115
61. Zhao, R., Wang, K., Divekar, R., Rouhani, R., Su, H., Ji, Q.: An immersive system with multi-modal human-computer interaction. In: 2018 13th IEEE International Conference on Automatic Face & Gesture Recognition (FG 2018), pp. 517–524. IEEE, New York (2018)

Work in Progress

How Does Entertainment Computing Contribute to the Sustainable Development Goals? A Rapid Literature Review

Jannicke Baalsrud Hauge[1,2(✉)], Polona Caserman[3], and Heinrich Söbke[4,5]

[1] KTH-Royal Institute of Technology, 15181 Södertälje, Sweden
jmbh@kth.se, baa@biba.uni-bremen.de
[2] BIBA – Bremer Institut für Produktion und Logistik GmbH, 28359 Bremen, Germany
[3] Serious Games Research Group, Affiliated with the Technical Univeristy of Darmstadt, 64289 Darmstadt, Germany
[4] Hochschule Weserbergland, 31875 Hameln, Germany
heinrich.soebke@uni-weimar.de, soebke@hsw-hameln.de
[5] Bauhaus-Institute for Infrastructure Solutions (b.is), Bauhaus-Universität Weimar, 99423 Weimar, Germany

Abstract. Entertainment Computing (EC) is a sub-discipline of computer science that deals with the creation of digital artifacts for hedonistic purposes. The United Nations Sustainable Development Goals (SDGs) provide a framework for overall sustainable development – ecologically, socially and economically – at the global, national and local level. Several positive examples of the use of EC artefacts, such as games, that have contributed to the achievement of SDGs, e.g. educational games in formal learning contexts, have prompted us to ask the overarching question of how EC might contribute to achieving the SDGs. To get an initial overview of the artifacts used and the targeted SDGs, we conducted a rapid literature review using the Scopus database. From a total of 860 records, we were able to identify 31 articles in which EC artifacts were used to support the achievement of various SDGs. The analysis shows that seven articles addressed all SDGs. Furthermore, in the remaining articles 13 out of 17 SDGs were specifically addressed. These findings induce a more detailed investigation of the contribution of EC to the SDGs promising as a means of deriving best practices for the use of EC artefacts to advance sustainable development worldwide.

Keywords: Sustainable Development Goal · Serious Games · Sustainability · Entertainment Computing Application · Systematic Literature Review

1 Introduction

In 2015, the United Nations Member States adopted the 2030 Agenda for Sustainable Development [1], which is primarily structured around 17 Sustainable Development Goals (SDGs) [2], which will "stimulate action […] in areas of critical importance for humanity and the planet" [1].

Polona Caserman - Independent Researcher

© IFIP International Federation for Information Processing 2025
Published by Springer Nature Switzerland AG 2025
M. Sugimoto et al. (Eds.): ICEC 2025, LNCS 16042, pp. 411–422, 2025.
https://doi.org/10.1007/978-3-032-02555-5_29

After 10 years since they were defined, sustainable development and the actions defined through the SDs have become buzzwords that split the citizens into groups – those who think it is required to focus more on sustainable resource usage and the treatment of the environment and into those who find we have already done enough [3, 4]. However, from a policy perspective we have at least within the European Union clear goals – we need to be more sustainable and it will cost both behavioral changes and money to get there. Consequently, the policy makers have put a lot of effort into educating the citizen, trying to force change on one hand side and with educational offers on the other side. Much of this education is carried out in a very traditional way – like leaflets, classes, directives on how to treat and sort, or repair goods and waste, and even if the intention is good, it seems that many citizens have got enough of being told what to do, and they simply rebel [5].

Based on [6] we claim, that the behavioral change which is based on intrinsic motivation, is the only one which might work over time – leading us to investigate the role of entertainment computing (EC) in supporting the change, since EC might have the genuine capability to nurture the intrinsically motivated change with its vast number of attractive and engaging applications.

A common definition of entertainment computing is that "entertainment computing addresses all aspects of creating, designing, building, and analyzing the usage of interactive devices like smartphones and tablets, not only for playing and entertainment. These aspects include human-machine interfaces, software applications, robots, artificial intelligence, interactive television, interdisciplinary studies on serious games, digital art, edutainment, entertainment ethics and sociology, and others" [7]. Thus, the area is broad with unlimited possibilities, but in this preliminary step towards a more comprehensive understanding of a possible contribution of EC towards sustainable development and fulfilling the SDGs, we have defined some basic research questions (RQ):

1. Which SDGs are targeted through EC?
2. Which types of EC are used to support the fulfillment of SDGs?
3. Do we see any trends?

To address these RQs we have systematically analyzed the identified literature. In this work, we have focused on articles specifically on SDG and EC applications. The research methodology is outlined in the following section. Section three presents the results, while section four discusses these results and how these results answer the research questions. Finally, section five concludes and describes next steps.

2 Method

This rapid systematic literature review was conducted according to the PRISMA 2020 guidelines for systematic reviews [8]. To facilitate a timely review process, several methodological simplifications were applied. These included searching in only one database and having each record screened by only one reviewer. The study selection process and its numerical details are depicted in Fig. 1.

Eligibility. Studies were included if they met the following criteria: (1) published in journals or conference proceedings, (2) available in English, (3) addressed the achievement of SDGs through the use of EC tools and (4) reported empirical results. The exclusion criteria included (1) reviews and background articles, (2) used no digital tools and (3) did not address SDGs, e.g., used only the term "sustainability" or used the term SDG without referring to the content of the study.

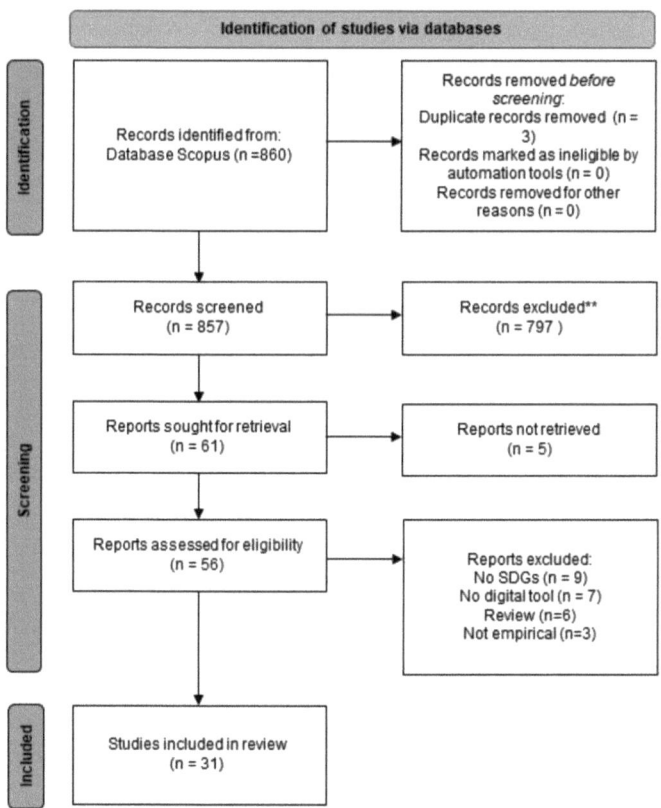

Fig. 1. PRISMA flow diagram following the PRISMA 2020 guidelines [8].

Databases and Search Strategy. The last systematic search of the Scopus online database was conducted on March 31, 2025. The search terms "entertainment computing" and the words "sustainable", "development" and "goal*" or their abbreviation "SDG*" were searched for in the title, abstract and keywords. The wildcard "*" was used to include plural forms the respective terms. Accordingly, the Scopus-specific search string was as follows:

```
( TITLE-ABS-KEY ( entertainment AND computing) OR TITLE-
ABS-KEY ( game*) ) AND ( TITLE-ABS-KEY ( sustainable AND
```

```
development AND goal*)OR TITLE-ABS-KEY ( sdg*) )AND (
LIMIT-TO ( DOCTYPE,"ar")OR LIMIT-TO ( DOCTYPE,"cp") )"
```

Selection Process. A RIS file generated from Scopus with 860 entries was imported into the Rayyan web platform [9], which supports systematic literature reviews. Titles and abstracts were screened by one of the authors. The full-text review was carried out by one reviewer, with excluded articles validated by a second reviewer. Discrepancies were resolved through discussion.

The SDGs were usually mentioned by the authors. If no explicit criteria were mentioned, the respective reviewer identified a reference to the most likely SDGs. However, for SDG 4 (Quality Education), an explicit mention by the authors of the respective article was required; this SDG was not inferred solely from the fact that the article dealt with an educational topic.

Data Extraction. Data from the included studies were extracted into a spreadsheet, where information such as authors, title, year, supported SDGs, entertainment computing technologies, and study design were recorded. The main findings were grouped by topic and summarized.

3 Results

This section is divided into two parts: The first presents the results for articles included in the review (refer to Appendix A), while the second one presents the results from identified review articles.

3.1 Empirical Studies

Year of Publication. The number of publications in the field of EC, particularly those focused on games, has shown a consistent upward trend over the last five years. For instance, while only one publication was recorded in 2018, this number increased to ten by 2024 (Fig. 2).

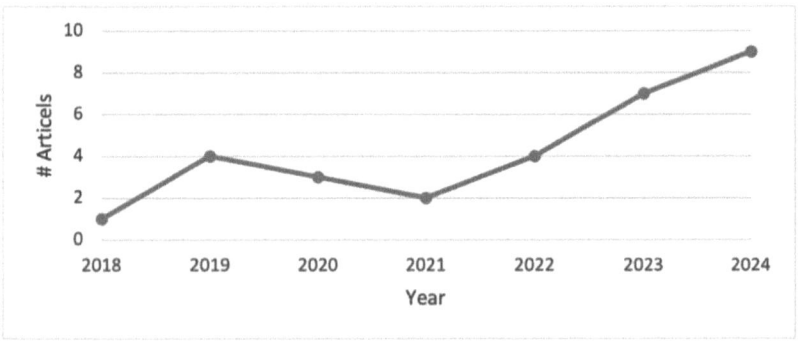

Fig. 2. Number of Articles per Year.

Publication Landscape. The distribution of articles was unbalanced between conferences (n = 15) and only eight journals. The MDPI *Sustainability* journal emerged as the most frequent publication outlet, with five papers published. This was followed by the *Interaction Design and Architecture(s)* journal, the *European Conference on Games-Based Learning (ECGBL)*, the *International Conference on Computers in Education (ICCE)*, and the *International Conference on e-Society and Mobile Learning*, each of which featured two publications.

Sustainable Development Goals. Table 1 indicates the number of entries for a specific SDG in the reviewed publications. For a full description of the 17 SDGs, please refer to the [2]. Only 8 publications target solely one SDGs, 7 target all. The others target a various number (between 2 and 5). Four SDGs are not targeted specifically. In some cases (see second row *# suggested*) the publication does not explicitly mention a specific SDG, so we have proposed one based on the article content. A more detailed discussion is in Sect. 4.

Table 1. SGDs addressed in the studies found.

SGD	All	1	2	3	4	5	6	7	8	9	10	11	12	13	14	15	16	17
# mentioned	7	1	3	5	5		2	4	2			5	7	3	2	3		1
# suggested							1					1	1			1		

Target Groups. The target group analysis (cf. Appendix A) showed that most of the EC tools (9 each) are aimed at both general public and higher education students. Primary and secondary education were each addressed by about half as many tools (5 each). However, two K-12-specific tools covering both primary and secondary education must be added here. Only one tool was aimed at pre-school children.

Entertainment Technology Types. We also analyzed which EC technologies were used (Table 2). In contrast to the previous analyses, an unambiguous classification was not feasible here. Accordingly, we decided to identify characteristics of the respective technologies used. As a result, several characteristics could be identified per study. Serious games (19) and games in general (8) were mentioned most frequently. Mobile apps were used in seven studies. Other characteristics were augmented reality (AR) in four studies and virtual reality (VR) in three studies. Gamification, multimedia, online games and simulation were each mentioned twice.

3.2 Reviews

Related Work on Games and Sustainability. Cravero [10] analyzed 67 serious games developed between 2007 and 2018, addressing themes related to sustainable cities and communities. Of these, 27 games targeted SDG 11 (*Sustainable Cities and Communities*) and SDG 12 (*Responsible Consumption and Production*), while 11 focused on

Table 2. EC Types (Multiple Characteristics per Study).

Characteristic	Abs. Freq.	Rel. Freq.
Serious Game	19	61%
Game	8	26%
Mobile App	7	23%
AR	4	13%
VR	3	10%
Gamification	2	6%
Multimedia	2	6%
Online Game	2	6%
Simulation	2	6%
	49	

SDG 13 (*Climate Action*). Most were either online (22) or board games (17). This highlights the existence of sustainability-focused games even prior to the formal adoption of the UN's 2030 Agenda. Notably, the author based their research primarily on online game repositories, including *Games4Sustainability* (games4sustainability.org), *Games for Change* (gamesforchange.org), and *Serious Games Classification* (serious.gameclassification.com), rather than academic publication databases.

Building on the theme of educational tools in sustainability, Nisa et al. [11] investigated the use of Lego and Minecraft in educational settings. In a follow-up study [12], the authors broadened their scope to examine educational video games in general. While their work connects to SDG 4 (*Quality Education*), their approach differs from ours. Rather than identifying the specific SDGs addressed by an individual game, they included all educational games and concluded that most applications target areas such as computer science, social science, and engineering. In contrast, Fabricatore and López [13] analyzed the thematic orientation of educational games, finding that most titles are environmentally focused. Additional studies have focused on gamification in sustainability [14, 15].

From an industry-wide standpoint, Busch et al. [16] argued for a fundamental rethinking of sustainability practices within the gaming sector. Their analysis calls for systemic transformation in how games are developed, distributed, and maintained, suggesting that the industry must go beyond individual game content to embrace sustainability at a structural level.

4 Discussion

Publication Year. Addressing RQ 3, the increasing number of publications reflects a growing academic interest in SDGs within the entertainment computing community. As outlined in the introduction, the SDGs were officially introduced in 2015, which may explain the gradual emergence of SDG research in subsequent years. The first publication in our review explicitly referencing the SDGs appeared in 2018, however, earlier work addressing sustainability themes may be traced back to 2011 [13, 17].

Publication Landscape. Although the results indicate that both types of venues (conferences and journals) are actively engaged in disseminating research SDGs within the context of EC, it appears that certain journals and conferences are particularly oriented toward topics related to Sustainable Development and Education for Sustainable Development (ESD). These journals and conferences may be especially attractive to researchers whose work directly aligns with SDGs, potentially influencing their choice of publication outlet.

SDGs. Based on data presented in Table 1, and in response to RQ 1, the results show that most of the identified applications address several of the SDGs and some even target all 17. In the latter case, most of the applications aim at awareness-raising and mitigation of basic knowledge.

Looking at the publications that do not target all, we notice that *Responsible Consumption and Production* (SDG 12) is the most popular. Since this is much also about consumer awareness and possible behavior change, EC may have an important role to play here for delivering engaging applications.

In line with general policies, we also see that the SDGs on *Good Health and Well-being* (SDG 3) and *Sustainable Cities and Communities* (SDG 11) are targeted both five times. Again, this is a typical topic for citizen engagement and also included in several curricula. Interesting enough is, that SDG 4 on *Quality Education* is also mentioned 5 times. Here it needs to be further investigated how the contribution of EC looks like and how this addresses topics like equal access to education for a diverse population.

We have also noticed that several applications address *Affordable and Clean Energy* (SDG 7) which may relate to the shift towards sustainable energy. In terms of SDG 1 (*No Poverty*), SDG 2 (*Zero Hunger*), and SDG 6 (*Clean Water and Sanitation*), we saw less applications than expected for these often-discussed SDGs. It might be good to investigate in the future if this is because the industrial world considers these as less important for education, since it is of a high standard, or if other factors like ethical considerations are the reason. The SDGs related to climate, life below water and on land (SDG 13–15) are also underrepresented, which is quite surprising since many museums have relevant EC applications in this field. Finally, *Partnership for the Goals* (SDG 17) is only mentioned once, while *Decent Work and Economic Growth* (SDG 8) is mentioned twice.

In relation to RQ 2, our analysis shows that most EC applications are designed to promote awareness, support educational efforts, or encourage behavior engagement. This is closely aligned with the types of goals being addressed. Reflecting on RQ 3, two broader trends seem emerging: first, a noticeable concentration of EC efforts around SDGs that emphasize individual behavior and formal education, particularly SDGs 3,

4, 11, and 12; and second, the relative underrepresentation of EC applications aimed at SDGs that involve structural or systemic transformation.

Limitations. The search strategy used, with its narrow restriction of search terms, has several limitations. Firstly, it seems likely that the search term "entertainment computing" did not turn up all thematically relevant articles. The various technologies grouped under the umbrella of EC are likely to be referred to in articles without the term "entertainment computing" being mentioned. Articles without the term entertainment computing in them were not found. By using the term "game", we took a first step in this direction, but this likely also introduced a bias towards games. The deliberate restriction to the SDGs also excluded articles that do not mention the SDGs but still contribute to achieving them.

5 Conclusion and Next Steps

This paper has presented a rapid literature review on entertainment computing (EC) applications and sustainable development goals (SDGs). The review has revealed that we have seen an increasing number of EC applications related to formal education, and in some cases also towards raising awareness for the topic in general. The trend also indicates that there are more and more EC applications implemented in formal education.

However, looking at the studies (mostly pilot studies), we see that they either evaluate learning outcome or usability. There is hardly any study that combines both or evaluates motivation and engagement for supporting behavioral change. This might be because we only found studies from 2018 and onwards. Since such studies are costly and resources intensive and need sufficient data to document a change, it might not have been possible to publish such studies yet. This might, however, also, indicate a low maturity of application and the field as such, but that needs to be further investigated. A second observation is that we did not find any study that focuses on how EC applications are made more sustainable. There are some earlier works in this field, e.g., [18, 19], but it seems that there is a lack of systematic research in this area. Finally, as the SLR shows, most of the identified applications are applied within formal education. This could indicate that the offer of EC applications targeting SDGs released for the leisure market is underdeveloped, and thus the technology cannot embrace its full potential for pushing a shift towards sustainable development forward. However, it needs to be further investigated how to balance the ratio of motivation for behavioral change and the feeling of getting too many advises on how to behave and what to do, so that the people would block voluntary usage.

Acknowledgements. Partly this article was supported by the German Federal Ministry of Education and Research (BMBF) under Grant No. 03RU2U12 (RUBIN – phoTECH).

Appendix a: Publications Included in the SLR

Authors	SDG	Game Topic	Target Group
Nisiotis et al. [20]	1–17	Education	Higher Education
Vasey et al. [21]	12	Environmental Conservation	General Public
Kersánszki et al. [22]	7	Renewable Energy	Secondary Education
Senka et al. [23]	13, 15	Environmental Conservation	Higher Education
González-Muñoz et al. [24]	4	Soft Skills	Higher Education
García-Gil et al. [25]	3, 4	Health	Secondary Education
Haddick et al. [26]	1–3, 7, 8, 11, 17	Soft Skills	Higher Education
Escudeiro et al. [27]	12	Circular Economy	General Public
Biercewicz et al. [28]	3	Health	General Public
Ai-Jou et al. [29]	1–17	SDGs	K12
Yu et al. [30]	13, 15	Environmental Conservation	General Public
Ouariachi and Elving [31]	4, 7	Renewable Energy	Higher Education
Jain et al. [32]	1–17	SDGs	Higher Education
Yago et al. [33]	15	Forrest Management	Higher Education
Soma et al. [34]	2, 12	Circular Economy	General Public
Neset et al. [35]	11, 12	Climate Change	Secondary Education
Gizzi et al. [36]	12 (14, 15)	Circular Economy	Pre-school
Tilvawala et al. [37]	6	Environmental Conservation	Primary Education
Piki et al. [38]	1–17	SDGs	General Public
Rodrigo et al. [39]	3, 14	SDGs	General Public
Rodrigues et al. [40]	2,7,12	Circular Economy	K12
Rodrigues et al. [41]	N/A	SDGs	Primary Education
Feltrero et al. [42]	3, 12, 13, 15	Media Literacy	General Public
Sá et al. [43]	4	Environmental Conservation	Primary Education
Xu et al. [44]	4, 8, 11	Cultural Heritage	General Public
Ceccarini and Prandi [45]	1–17	SDGs	Secondary Education
Mahamarowi et al. [46]	4	Cultural Heritage	Secondary Education
Lami et al. [47]	11	Urban Planning	Higher Education
Miguel et al. [48]	N/A	Soft Skills	Higher Education
Al-Hammadi et al. [49]	1–17	Urban Planning	Primary Education
Rodrigo et al. [50]	1–17	SDGs	Primary Education

References

1. United Nations. Transforming our world: the 2030 Agenda for Sustainable Development (2015). https://sdgs.un.org/2030agenda. Accessed 2 Mar 2025

2. United Nations. The 17 Goals | Sustainable Development (2015). https://sdgs.un.org/goals. Accessed 2 Mar 2025
3. Senaratne, M.: The transition from MDGs to SDGs: rethinking buzzwords. Sustain Dev Goals Asian Context, pp. 23–40 (2017)
4. Shao, G.: Aligning buzzword trends of sustainability with true sustainable development. Int J Sustain Dev World Ecol **31**, 1145–1146 (2024). https://doi.org/10.1080/13504509.2024.2412821
5. Urberg, L., Öhman, J.: Resisting sustainable development: an analysis of young people's online discussions. J. Youth Stud., pp. 1–17 (2024). https://doi.org/10.1080/13676261.2024.2322607
6. Steg, L., Lindenberg, S., Keizer, K.: Intrinsic motivation, norms and environmental behaviour: the dynamics of overarching goals. Int. Rev. Environ. Resour. Econ. **9**, 179–207 (2016). https://doi.org/10.1561/101.00000077
7. Ciancarini, P., Nakatsu, R., Rauterberg, M.: Entertainment computing: past, present, and future. In: Vanderdonckt, J., Palanque, P., Winckler, M. (eds.) Handbook of Human Computer Interaction, pp. 1–21. Springer International Publishing, Cham (2024)
8. Page, M.J., McKenzie, J.E., Bossuyt, P.M., et al.: The PRISMA 2020 statement: an updated guideline for reporting systematic reviews. BMJ n71 (2021). https://doi.org/10.1136/bmj.n71
9. Rayyan. Rayyan: AI-Powered Systematic Review Management Platform (2025). https://www.rayyan.ai/. Accessed 2 Apr 2025
10. Cravero, S.: Methods, strategies and tools to improve citizens' engagement in the smart cities' context: a serious games classification. Valori E Valutazioni **2020**, 45–60 (2020)
11. Nisa, K., Suprapto, N., Hidaayatullaah, H.N., Mubarok, H.: Trend and research of lego and minecraft as learning media to realize 4thSDGs. E3S Web Conf 450 (2023). https://doi.org/10.1051/e3sconf/202345001003
12. Nisa, K., Suprapto, N., Safitri, A.I., Arymbekov, B.: Educational virtual games in supporting SDG 4: research trend in scopus, topic, and novelty explored. E3S Web Conf 513 (2024). https://doi.org/10.1051/e3sconf/202451304002
13. Fabricatore, C., López, X.: Gaming for sustainability: an overview. Proc Eur Conf Games-Based Learn **2011**, 159–167 (2011)
14. Lim, W.M., Das, M., Sharma, W., et al.: Gamification for sustainable consumption: a state-of-the-art overview and future agenda. Bus Strategy Environ **34**, 1510–1549 (2025). https://doi.org/10.1002/bse.4021
15. Sharma, S.: Gamification for achieving sustainability: trends and future scope. Lect Notes Netw Syst **977**, 511–521 (2025). https://doi.org/10.1007/978-981-97-2671-4_39
16. Busch, T., Chee, F., Sihvonen, T.: Sustainability challenges in the games industry. IEEE Conf Comput Intell Games CIG (2024). https://doi.org/10.1109/CoG60054.2024.10645534
17. Duin, H., Thoben, K.-D.: Serious gaming for sustainable manufacturing: a requirements analysis. 2011 17th Int Conf Concurr Enterprising ICE 2011 – Conf Proc (2011)
18. Göbl, B., Baalsrud Hauge, J., Stefan, I.A., Söbke, H.: Towards sustainable serious games. In: Ciancarini, P., Di Iorio, A., Hlavacs, H., Poggi, F. (eds.) Entertainment Computing – ICEC 2023. Springer Nature Singapore, Singapore, pp 389–396 (2023)
19. Spangenberger, P., Söbke, H.: Bridging the gap: a debate on sustainability aspects of digital media in education. Educ. Sci. **15**, 241 (2025). https://doi.org/10.3390/educsci15020241
20. Nisiotis, L., Piki, A., Theodorou, P., et al.: Evaluation of a serious VR game designed to promote the sustainable development goals. 2024 IEEE Gaming Entertain Media Conf GEM 2024 (2024). https://doi.org/10.1109/GEM61861.2024.10585543
21. Vasey, K., Bos, O., Nasser, F., et al.: Water bodies: VR interactive narrative and gameplay for social impact. Proc - VRCAI 2019 17th ACM SIGGRAPH Int Conf Virtual-Real Contin Its Appl Ind. (2019). https://doi.org/10.1145/3359997.3365746

22. Kersánszki, T., Márton, Z., Fenyvesi, K., et al.: Minecraft in STEAM education - applying game-based learning to renewable energy. Interact Des Archit, pp. 194–213 (2024). https://doi.org/10.55612/s-5002-060-008
23. Senka, G., Tramonti, M., Dochshanov, A.M., et al.: Using a game to educate about sustainable development. Multimodal Technol Interact **8** (2024). https://doi.org/10.3390/mti8110096
24. González-Muñoz, E., Gallardo-Vigil, M.Á., Gutiérrez-Pérez, J.: "The Mysterious Disappearance": assessment of a sustainability-themed virtual educational escape room in higher education. J. Appl. Res. High Educ. (2024). https://doi.org/10.1108/JARHE-09-2023-0430
25. García-Gil, M.Á., Revuelta-Domínguez, F.-I., Pedrera-Rodríguez, M.-I., Guerra-Antequera, J.: Exploring video game engagement, social–emotional development, and adolescent well-being for sustainable health and quality education. Sustain Switz **16** (2024). https://doi.org/10.3390/su16010099
26. Haddick, S., Puntha, H., Harris, M., Brown, D.J.: Integration and promotion: integrating sustainability research into computer science teaching through serious games assignments. Proc Eur Conf Games-Based Learn **18**, 329–336 (2024). https://doi.org/10.34190/ecgbl.18.1.2626
27. Escudeiro, P., Gouveia, M.C., Escudeiro, N.: Eco tetris: a serious game on sustainability. Proc Eur Conf Games-Based Learn, pp. 684–692 (2022). https://doi.org/10.34190/ecgbl.16.1.836
28. Biercewicz, K., Borawska, A., Borawski, M., Duda, J.: VR educational game in public awareness campaign preventing the spread of COVID-19 - a pilot study. Procedia Comput Sci **225**, 2057–2066 (2023). https://doi.org/10.1016/j.procs.2023.10.196
29. Ai-Jou, P., Cheng, B.-Y., Chou, P.-N., Geng, Y.: Using augmented reality games to support sustainable development goal learning among young students: a true-experimental study. Libr Hi Tech. (2024). https://doi.org/10.1108/LHT-10-2023-0511
30. Yu, J.J., Hu, J.J., Liu, G.G., et al.: Not just a game: understanding eco-gamification in sustainable destination development. J. Hosp. Tour. Manag. **60**, 10–21 (2024). https://doi.org/10.1016/j.jhtm.2024.06.005
31. Ouariachi, T., Elving, W.: Understanding the urgency and complexities of the energy transition through serious gaming. Proc Eur Conf E-Learn ECEL, pp. 461–466 (2019). https://doi.org/10.34190/EEL.19.002
32. Jain, R., Joshi, R., Dwivedi, V., et al.: Gamification for teaching sustainability to engineering students. Proc - Front Educ Conf FIE (2022). https://doi.org/10.1109/FIE56618.2022.9962626
33. Yago, K., Shingai, Y., Kobayashi, W., et al.: Satoyama forest management learning game for SDGs education: comparing the effect of providing additional information in the first half and latter half of the game. Int Conf Comput Support Educ CSEDU - Proc **1**, 347–351 (2021)
34. Soma, T., Li, B., Maclaren, V.: Food waste reduction: a test of three consumer awareness interventions. Sustain Switz **12** (2020). https://doi.org/10.3390/su12030907
35. Neset, T.-S., Andersson, L., Uhrqvist, O., Navarra, C.: Serious gaming for climate adaptation—assessing the potential and challenges of a digital serious game for urban climate adaptation. Sustain Switz **12**, 1–18 (2020). https://doi.org/10.3390/su12051789
36. Gizzi, V., Di Dio, S., Schillaci, D.: Junkbox, a waste management educational game for preschool kids. Interact Des Archit, pp. 46–56 (2019)
37. Tilvawala, K., Sundaram, D., Myers, M.: Serious games for sustainable development: a decision-driven transformative approach. 25th Am Conf Inf Syst AMCIS 2019 (2019)
38. Piki, A., Tchanturia, I., Kasenides, N., et al.: SDG quest: leveraging mobile game-based learning to foster environmental, social, and economic sustainable development goals. Lect Notes Comput Sci Subser Lect Notes Artif Intell Lect Notes Bioinforma **15377**, 373–392 (2025). https://doi.org/10.1007/978-3-031-76812-5_25

39. Rodrigo, M.M.T., Diy, W.D.A., Favis, A.M.T., et al.: A RECIPE for Teaching the Sustainable Development Goals. 29th Int Conf Comput Educ Conf ICCE 2021 - Proc 1, pp. 451–456 (2021)
40. Rodrigues, R., Pombo, L., Marques, M.M., et al.: Value of a Mobile Game-based App Towards Education for Sustainability. Proc Int Conf E-Soc 2023 ES 2023 Mob Learn 2023 ML, pp. 375–382 (2023)
41. Rodrigues, R., Ferreira-Santos, J., Draghi, J., et al.: EduCity, a project for a sustainable smart learning city environment – preliminary results. Int Conf E-Soc 2024 Mob Learn, pp. 255–262 (2024)
42. Feltrero, R., Junguitu-Angulo, L., Osuna-Acedo, S.: Deploying SDG knowledge to foster young people's critical values: a study on social trends about SDGs in an educational online activity. Sustain Switz **15** (2023). https://doi.org/10.3390/su15086681
43. Sá, P., Silva, P.C., Peixinho, J., et al.: Sustainability at play: educational design research for the development of a digital educational resource for primary education. Soc Sci. **12** (2023). https://doi.org/10.3390/socsci12070407
44. Xu, N., Liang, J., Shuai, K., et al.: HeritageSite AR: an exploration game for quality education and sustainable cultural heritage. Conf. Hum Factors Comput Syst – Proc. (2023). https://doi.org/10.1145/3544549.3583837
45. Ceccarini, C., Prandi, C.: EscapeCampus: Exploiting a game-based Learning tool to increase the sustainability knowledge of students. ACM Int Conf Proceeding Ser., pp. 390–396 (2022). https://doi.org/10.1145/3524458.3547123
46. Mahamarowi, N.H., Ja'afar, M.R.B., Mustapha, S., Yusof, K.H.: 3D game-based approach to learning ancient malay heritage's history. 2023 IEEE 14th Control Syst Grad Res Colloq ICSGRC 2023 - Conf Proceeding, pp. 133–138 (2023). https://doi.org/10.1109/ICSGRC57744.2023.10215483
47. Lami, I.M., Abastante, F., Gaballo, M., et al.: Learning urban sustainability by playing. Lect Notes Comput Sci Subser Lect Notes Artif Intell Lect Notes Bioinforma 14108, pp. 468–482 (2023). https://doi.org/10.1007/978-3-031-37117-2_32
48. Miguel, N.P., Lage, J.C., Galindez, A.M.: Assessment of the development of professional skills in university students: sustainability and serious games. Sustain Switz **12** (2020). https://doi.org/10.3390/su12031014
49. Al-Hammadi, F.Y., Aldarwish, A.F., Alasmakh, A.H., Zemerly, M.J.: Augmented reality in educational games: city of Life (COL) emirati sustainability-edutainment interactive game. 2018 Adv Sci Eng Technol Int Conf ASET, pp. 1–7 (2018). https://doi.org/10.1109/ICASET.2018.8376921
50. Rodrigo, M.M.T., Tulayba, L.M.C., Lim, M.U., et al.: For people and planet: a pilot study of an educational mobile game on the sustainable development goals. 30th Int Conf Comput Educ Conf ICCE 2022 - Proc 1, pp. 449–454 (2022)

VR Gaming Approach to Language Comprehension in Children with Autism

Andrea Caruso[1,2](✉), Priscilla Pia Papa[1], Giovanni Schembra[1], and Massimiliano Salfi[1,2]

[1] University of Catania, 95131 Catania, Italy
{giovanni.schembra,massimiliano.salfi}@unict.it,
andrea.caruso@phd.unict.it
[2] vEyes NPO, 95010 Milo, Italy

Abstract. Assessing language comprehension in children with Autism Spectrum Disorder (ASD) presents unique challenges, especially when relying on traditional testing methods. This paper introduces an innovative VR-based system designed to address these challenges by creating an engaging, distraction-free environment. The system uses low-cost mobile VR headsets and tracks a range of behavioral metrics to assess language comprehension through gaze direction and response time. Preliminary findings from a small sample of children with ASD suggest that the VR platform increases engagement, enhances focus, and provides more consistent results compared to traditional methods. This paper outlines the potential of VR for both assessment and therapeutic interventions, with plans for future work aimed at validating these results on a larger scale and developing automated diagnostic and rehabilitation tools.

Keywords: VR Gaming · Autism spectrum disorder · Language comprehension

1 Introduction

Autism spectrum disorder (ASD) is a neurodevelopmental condition characterized by impairments in social interaction, communication, and repetitive behaviors [15]. Effective language comprehension is essential for communication, yet individuals with ASD frequently encounter difficulties grasping unspoken rules, humor, deception, and nuances necessary for planning and executing tasks [4]. These challenges are closely linked to deficits in Theory of Mind, which impacts the ability to understand and interpret one's own and others' mental states [1].

Language acquisition in children with ASD is affected by cognitive abilities, adaptive functioning, symptom severity, and non-verbal communication skills. Although improvements in non-verbal mental age tend to coincide with advances in both receptive and expressive language, children with ASD often underperform compared to their typically developing (TD) peers at equivalent cognitive levels [3,14,25]. Current interventions include Applied Behavior Analysis

(ABA), the Early Start Denver Model (ESDM), the Treatment and Education of Autistic and Communication-related Handicapped Children (TEACCH), and Augmentative and Alternative Communication (AAC). ABA decomposes complex language skills into manageable units reinforced through positive feedback [10]. ESDM, which integrates ABA techniques with developmental principles, has shown early benefits in social interaction, communication, play, and cognition [28]. Meanwhile, TEACCH employs structured environments with visual cues to support learning [13], and AAC facilitates communication through picture symbols and speech-generating devices [8]. Assessing language in children with ASD typically involves both direct measures and indirect caregiver reports. Direct assessments, such as those using the Mullen Scales of Early Learning (MSEL), often reveal that children with ASD score lower than TD peers by 14 months of age, with pronounced differences at 24 months [17]. However, standard tests of receptive language may be hindered by children's difficulties with pointing, pragmatic understanding, and test-related demands. In contrast, caregiver reports, like the MacArthur-Bates Communicative Development Inventory (MCDI), reliably predict later language outcomes [9,16]. Recent advances include online methods employing eye-tracking during Looking-While-Listening (LWL) tasks, which capture real-time word recognition while reducing explicit testing demands [2,6]. Understanding the acquisition of words across semantic categories is fundamental to language development. In TD children and late talkers, lexical composition studies, often based on parent-report checklists such as the MCDI and the Language Development Survey, indicate variability in the rate of vocabulary growth but overall similarities in word composition across languages [5,19–21]. In children with ASD, available research suggests that although the distribution of semantic categories is comparable to that of TD children, their lexical development is delayed rather than deviant [3,7,22].

In light of the challenges associated with traditional assessments, our study focuses on enhancing compliance in language comprehension testing for children with ASD. Compliance refers to the level of engagement and willingness to participate, a critical factor for gathering reliable data. To address this, we have developed an innovative tool that merges interactive gameplay with language assessment tasks. The system runs on low-cost, cardboard-like head-mounted viewers paired with Android devices, embedding test tasks within an engaging virtual environment to minimize anxiety and boost participation. Furthermore, it records multiple behavioral metrics to further elucidate patient interactions.

The remainder of this paper is structured as follows: Sect. 2 details the system architecture. Section 3 outlines the methodology and evaluation metrics. Section 4 presents preliminary results, and Sect. 5 concludes the paper with a discussion of the findings and future research directions.

2 System Description

Children with ASD often prefer familiar environments, voices, and behaviors that provide predictability and comfort [18]. To leverage this preference, we developed a 3D virtual environment offering a highly consistent and reproducible experience. Each interaction is designed to replicate previous sessions, thus creating a stable context that supports engagement and reduces distress. Moreover, our tool captures real-time metrics by tracking visual fixations on target 3D models during word presentations, thereby evaluating receptive language skills and paving the way for personalized interventions that address individual linguistic profiles.

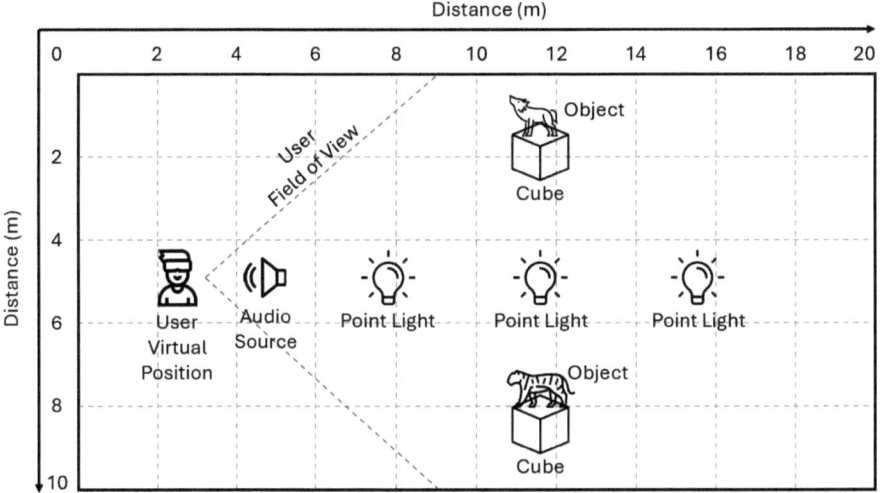

Fig. 1. Virtual environment scheme

We implemented the environment and game logic using the Unity 6 game engine [24]. Starting with a Universal 3D Project template that includes the necessary settings and assets for the Universal Render Pipeline (URP), we then downloaded, imported, and configured the Google Cardboard XR Plugin for Unity. This enables the use of low-cost, mobile-based VR headsets [11]. For optimal performance in a real-time VR setting, we selected Vulkan as the primary graphics API due to its improved rendering efficiency and low-level access to GPU operations. Subsequently, we designed a comfortable virtual space as illustrated in Fig. 1. The environment comprises a 20 × 10 m room with a wooden floor and tiled walls and ceiling, where the walls are 10 m high, which together produce a sense of protection. To mitigate any potential claustrophobic effect, the room's dimensions were intentionally set larger than the minimum required for the test. The user is positioned with their back against one wall, 2.5 m away from it. Directly in front, two cubes with 1.5 m sides are placed 9 m away from the user, with each cube's external face situated 2 m from the adjacent side wall. On these cubes, two 3D objects are displayed (see Fig. 2). Illumination is provided by three point lights with a 15 m range and an intensity of 4. One light is centrally located above the two cubes at a height of 8.75 m, while the other two, at the same height, are positioned 4 m in front of and behind the central light, respectively. All lights emit a color defined by #A1A17D (RGBA: 161,161,125,255). A sound source is placed 2 m in front of the user. Figure 3 depicts the scene from the user's perspective. The application continuously monitors the user's head movements across all three axes and records gaze data in a .csv file, with a frequency of 10 samples per second.

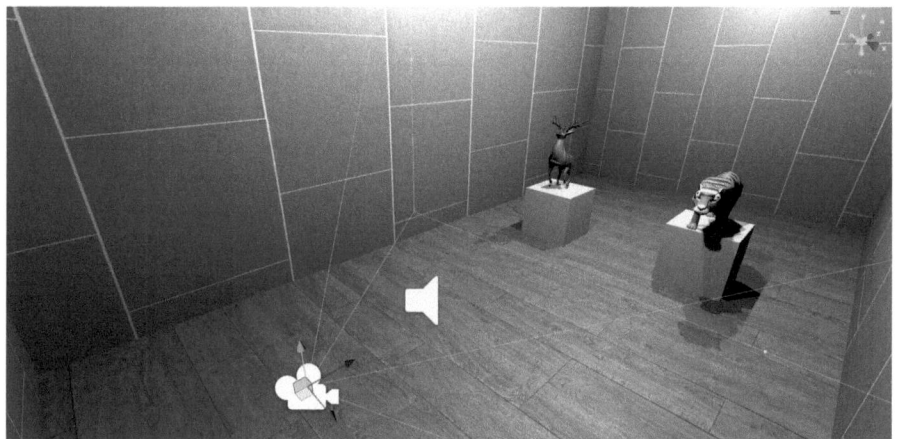

Fig. 2. A Unity 6 design screen of the game scene

We used a high-performance smartphone to ensure smooth rendering without overheating. With a 2400 × 1080 px resolution, 8.1 mm thickness, and 189 g weight, it supports extended sessions comfortably. Powered by a 2 × 2.4 GHz Cortex-A78 and 6 × 2.0 GHz Cortex-A55 (Exynos 1280) chipset and 6 GB RAM, it ensures a fluid experience. The device is housed in a 180 × 122 × 91 mm, 205 g VR visor with adjustable interpupillary distance (58.5âĂŞ70.5 mm) to fit each child's ocular needs.

3 Methodology and Evaluation Metrics

The Griffith Mental Development Scale (GMDS) is a well-established instrument for assessing child development from birth to 8 years of age. It evaluates six key developmental domains: Locomotor, Personal-Social, Hearing and Language, Eye and Hand Coordination, Performance, and Practical Reasoning. The GMDS has been extensively validated for assessing developmental progress in young children with ASD [23]. To quantify autism severity, the Calibrated Severity Score (CSS) is derived from Autism Diagnostic Observation Schedule (ADOS) raw scores and chronological age, classifying children into three groups: non-spectrum (scores 1–3), ASD (scores 4–5), and autism (scores 6–10) [12]. A caregiver vocabulary checklist was developed to assess the child's comprehension of the vocabulary used in the Looking While Listening (LWL) task. This checklist encompassed both nouns and action words selected from the MCDI Words and Gestures form.

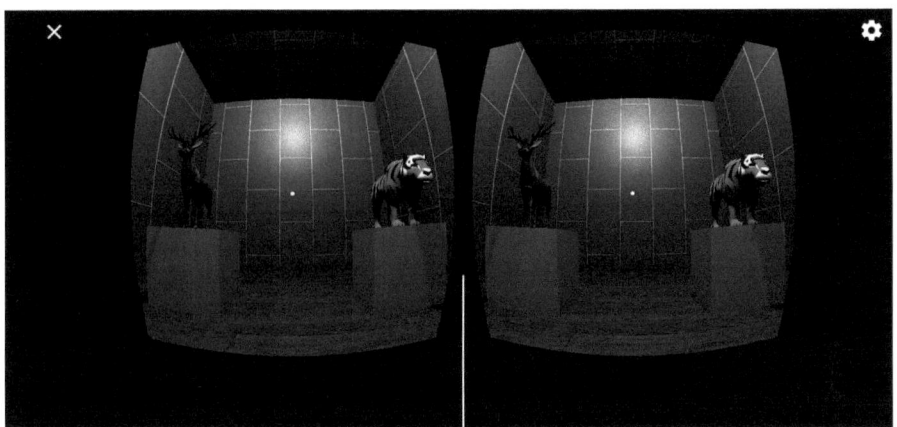

Fig. 3. The cardboard view of a typical game scene

In this study, the Android Cardboard application described in Sect. 2 was used to analyze single spoken word recognition in children diagnosed with ASD. In every trial, a pair of 3D models from the same semantic category was simultaneously displayed on two separate cube pedestals. The child was instructed to focus on the 3D model corresponding to the spoken target word, with each word serving as target and foil in different trials. A total of 100 unique target words were presented in 100 trials, organized across 11 semantic categories, as defined by the MCDI. The categories included animals, vehicles, toys, food and drink, clothing, body parts, furniture and rooms, household objects, outdoor objects, people, and actions. The number of words per category was proportionate to the frequency of use reported in the Italian MCDI, with each category comprising between 5 and 15 words. Visual stimuli consisted of freely available, non-copyrighted 3D models sourced from the Unity Asset Store [27]. All models were selected by consensus among the researchers to ensure they were prototypical representations of the corresponding words. Each pair of 3D models was displayed for 10 s, with Areas of Interest (AOI) defined by the bounding boxes around each model. Tests lasted approximately 17 min, a duration deemed short enough to avoid eye strain. Category presentation was randomized per participant, with consistent trial order within each category, to assess word comprehension within semantic groups. Each model appeared once as the target and once as the foil, with roles counterbalanced between the left and right sides to mitigate salience effects.

Audio stimuli were generated using the TTSMaker vocal synthesis free software [26] with the Italian voice "Elsa" and stored within the application resources. Audio was delivered automatically at a constant volume of 70 dB.

Each target word was pronounced twice (e.g. "Tiger"), with a 2 s interval between pronunciations. The first audio file was triggered 1 s after the onset of the visual stimulus, and the duration of the audio stimuli varied from 400 to 700 ms, reflecting differences in word length. To enhance engagement, the system includes immediate feedback after completing each section and progressive levels that unlock based on points obtained. We assessed several metrics, as detailed below.

Direct Metrics (Per-trial Analysis)

For each trial, the following behavioral metrics are recorded. Each trial's data is stored as a single row in a CSV file.

- **Reaction Accuracy (RA):** A binary measure indicating whether the first gaze was directed toward the correct 3D model:

$$RA = \begin{cases} 1, & \text{if the first gaze is directed toward the correct 3D model,} \\ 0, & \text{otherwise.} \end{cases} \quad (1)$$

- **Time to First Gaze (TFG):** The time (in ms) from stimulus onset to the initial gaze:

$$TFG = t_{\text{first gaze}} - t_{\text{stimulus onset}} \quad (2)$$

- **Model Fixation Consistency (MFC):** The ratio of the time spent fixating on the correct model to the total trial duration:

$$MFC = \frac{T_{\text{correct}}}{T_{\text{tot}}} \quad \text{where} \quad T_{\text{tot}} = 10\,\text{s}. \quad (3)$$

General Metrics (Exam-Level Analysis)

General metrics are computed over the entire examination. Throughout the following formulas, let N_{tot} denote the total number of trials, with $N_{tot} = 100$.

Behavioral Metrics

- **Overall Reaction Accuracy (ORA):** The proportion of trials in which the first gaze was correct:

$$ORA = \frac{N_{\text{correct}}}{N_{tot}} \quad (4)$$

where N_{correct} is the number of trials with a correct first gaze.

- **Mean Time to First Gaze ($\overline{TFG}$):** The average TFG across all trials:

$$\overline{TFG} = \frac{1}{N_{tot}} \sum_{i=1}^{N_{tot}} TFG_i \quad (5)$$

- **Overall Model Fixation Consistency ($\overline{MFC}$):** The mean MFC computed over all trials:

$$\overline{MFC} = \frac{1}{N_{tot}} \sum_{i=1}^{N_{tot}} MFC_i \tag{6}$$

Compliance Metrics (Exam-Level)

The following compliance metrics are computed over the entire test, providing insights into the participant's overall adherence to the protocol:

- **Overall Compliance Duration (OCD):** The ratio between the total duration of all completed trials and the expected total exam duration. In formula form:

$$OCD = \frac{\sum_{i=1}^{N_{tot}} T_{\text{trial},i}}{N_{tot} \times T_{tot}} \tag{7}$$

where $T_{\text{trial},i}$ is the actual duration of trial i, $T_{tot} = 10\,\text{s}$ is the expected duration per trial, and N_{tot} is the total number of trials.

- **Mean Trial Engagement Latency (MTEL):** The average latency from the onset of each trial to the first engagement (e.g., the first gaze) across the entire exam:

$$MTEL = \frac{1}{N_{tot}} \sum_{i=1}^{N_{tot}} (t_{\text{first engagement},i} - t_{\text{trial onset},i}) \tag{8}$$

- **Overall Exam Abandonment Rate (OEAR):** Evaluates the overall adherence to the exam protocol. It is defined as:

$$OEAR = \begin{cases} 1, & \text{if } \frac{\sum_{i=1}^{N_{tot}} (T_{\text{trial},i} < T_{tot})}{N_{tot}} > \alpha, \\ 0, & \text{otherwise.} \end{cases} \tag{9}$$

Here, the parameter α (e.g. 0.2) is the predefined threshold for the maximum acceptable proportion of abandoned trials.

- **Semantic Category Abandonment Rate (SCAR):** Computes the abandonment rate for each semantic category c (with N_c trials):

$$SCAR(c) = \frac{\sum_{i \in c} \mathbb{I}(T_{\text{trial},i} < 10)}{N_c} \tag{10}$$

This measure helps identify if certain categories are associated with increased trial abandonment across the exam.

These aggregate measures provide a comprehensive evaluation of participant performance and adherence to the testing protocol during the word recognition task.

4 Preliminary Results

We conducted preliminary tests on 5 children with Autism Spectrum Disorder (ASD), aged between 4 and 8 years. Informed consent was obtained from the parents or legal guardians of all participants. Both the traditional method (using paper-based images or real objects) and our VR-based system were administered in parallel. The observations indicate that, in general, children using our system exhibited increased concentration, reduced susceptibility to distractions, and benefited from the uniformity of the voice stimuli (consistent voice and intonation) as well as the absence of variable environmental elements present in real-world settings. In addition, the behavioral metrics recorded during the VR-based testing provide a more detailed overview of the test progression. These metrics allow for monitoring aspects such as attention, hesitation, and patient response speed. Such data offer valuable insights that can be further studied and analyzed to better understand and refine the testing process.

5 Discussion and Future Work

The preliminary findings indicate that our VR-based system provides notable advantages over traditional methods, including improved compliance and enhanced behavioral insights. The structured environment of the VR platform fosters better focus and engagement among children with ASD, allowing for more consistent and reliable assessments. Furthermore, the ability to monitor detailed behavioral metrics, such as attention, hesitation patterns, and response times, enriches our understanding of patient behavior during testing and opens new avenues for analysis. Building on these results, we are launching a larger-scale study to validate the system's reliability and extend its application. This study will investigate its use not only as a tool for tracking language comprehension progress but also as a platform for language comprehension exercises. Currently, the system randomly selects pairs of objects to present to each child, assessing their recognition abilities. However, we are developing an integration with an artificial neural network capable of autonomous learning, utilizing data recorded from each session. This system will independently identify the set of vocabulary items with which the child demonstrates the greatest difficulty in comprehension. The objective is to transition from random selection to an AI-driven approach, allowing the integrated system to replace a human therapist in selecting object pairs. These selections will prioritize items that the child has consistently struggled to comprehend across multiple sessions. Future iterations of the system will also involve direct input from children with ASD and their caregivers to better tailor the features to their specific needs and preferences.

Acknowledgements. The research activity of G. Schembra was partially supported by the EU under the Italian National Recovery and Resilience Plan (NRRP) of NextGenerationEU, partnership on "Telecommunications of the Future" (PE0000001 - program "RESTART") and under NextGenerationEU PRIN 2022 Prot.

n. 2022MWBFEE "6GTWIN". The latter project partially supported the research activity of Dr. Andrea Caruso.

Disclosure of Interests. The authors have no competing interests to declare that are relevant to the content of this article.

References

1. Astington, J.W., Baird, J.A.: Why Language Matters for Theory of Mind. Oxford University Press, London (2005)
2. Barone, R., et al.: Online comprehension across different semantic categories in preschool children with autism spectrum disorder. PLoS ONE **14**(2), e0211802 (2019)
3. Charman, T., Drew, A., Baird, C., Baird, G.: Measuring early language development in preschool children with autism spectrum disorder using the macarthur communicative development inventory (infant form). J. Child Lang. **30**(1), 213–236 (2003)
4. Cui, M., Ni, Q., Wang, Q.: Review of intervention methods for language and communication disorders in children with autism spectrum disorders. PeerJ **11**, e15735 (2023)
5. Dale, P., Goodman, J.: Commonality and individual differences in vocabulary growth. In: Beyond Nature-Nurture, pp. 91–128. Psychology Press (2004)
6. Edelson, L., Fine, A., Tager-Flusberg, H.: Comprehension of nouns and verbs in toddlers with autism: an eye-tracking study. In: International Meeting for Autism Research (2008)
7. Ellis Weismer, S., et al.: Lexical and grammatical skills in toddlers on the autism spectrum compared to late talking toddlers. J. Autism Dev. Disord. **41**, 1065–1075 (2011)
8. Elsahar, Y., Hu, S., Bouazza-Marouf, K., Kerr, D., Mansor, A.: Augmentative and alternative communication (aac) advances: a review of configurations for individuals with a speech disability. Sensors **19**(8), 1911 (2019)
9. Fenson, L.: MacArthur Communicative Development Inventories: User's guide and technical manual. Paul H. Brookes (2002)
10. Foxx, R.M.: Applied behavior analysis treatment of autism: the state of the art. Child Adolesc. Psychiatr. Clin. N. Am. **17**(4), 821–834 (2008)
11. Google Developers: Quickstart for google cardboard for unity (2025). https://developers.google.com/cardboard/develop/unity/quickstart. Accessed 14 Mar 2025
12. Gotham, K., Pickles, A., Lord, C.: Standardizing ados scores for a measure of severity in autism spectrum disorders. J. Autism Dev. Disord. **39**, 693–705 (2009)
13. Jennett, H.K., Harris, S.L., Mesibov, G.B.: Commitment to philosophy, teacher efficacy, and burnout among teachers of children with autism. J. Autism Dev. Disord. **33**, 583–593 (2003)
14. Kjellmer, L., Hedvall, Å., Fernell, E., Gillberg, C., Norrelgen, F.: Language and communication skills in preschool children with autism spectrum disorders: Contribution of cognition, severity of autism symptoms, and adaptive functioning to the variability. Res. Dev. Disabil. **33**(1), 172–180 (2012)
15. Lord, C., Brugha, T.S., Charman, T., Cusack, J., Dumas, G., Frazier, T., Jones, E.J., Jones, R.M., Pickles, A., State, M.W., et al.: Autism spectrum disorder. Nat. Rev. Dis. Primers. **6**(1), 5 (2020)

16. Luyster, R., Qiu, S., Lopez, K., Lord, C.: Predicting outcomes of children referred for autism using the macarthur-bates communicative development inventory. J. Speech Lang. Hear. Res. **50**(3), 667–681 (2007)
17. Mullen, E.M.: Mullen scales of early learning manual. American Guidance Service (1995)
18. Nagib, W., Williams, A.: Toward an autism-friendly home environment. Hous. Stud. **32**(2), 140–167 (2017)
19. Papaeliou, C.F., Rescorla, L.A.: Vocabulary development in Greek children: a cross-linguistic comparison using the language development survey. J. Child Lang. **38**(4), 861–887 (2011)
20. Rescorla, L.: The language development survey: a screening tool for delayed language in toddlers. J. Speech Hear. Disord. **54**(4), 587–599 (1989)
21. Rescorla, L., Frigerio, A., Sali, M.E., Spataro, P., Longobardi, E.: Typical and delayed lexical development in Italian. J. Speech Lang. Hear. Res. **57**(5), 1792–1803 (2014)
22. Rescorla, L., Safyer, P.: Lexical composition in children with autism spectrum disorder (asd). J. Child Lang. **40**(1), 47–68 (2013)
23. Sandberg, A.D., Nydén, A., Gillberg, C., Hjelmquist, E.: The cognitive profile in infantile autism–a study of 70 children and adolescents using the griffiths mental development scale. Br. J. Psychol. **84**(3), 365–373 (1993)
24. Technologies, U.: Unity: Real-time development platform (2025). https://unity.com/. Accessed 14 Mar 2025
25. Thurm, A., Lord, C., Lee, L.C., Newschaffer, C.: Predictors of language acquisition in preschool children with autism spectrum disorders. J. Autism Dev. Disord. **37**, 1721–1734 (2007)
26. TTSMaker: Ttsmaker - free text-to-speech online tool (2025). https://ttsmaker.com/. Accessed 10 Apr 2025
27. Unity Technologies: Unity asset store (2025). https://assetstore.unity.com/. Accessed 10 Apr 2025
28. Vivanti, G., Dissanayake, C., Team, V.A.: Outcome for children receiving the early start denver model before and after 48 months. J. Autism Dev. Disord. **46**, 2441–2449 (2016)

Physics Virtual Classroom: Leveraging Virtual Reality Sandboxes for Learning Classical Mechanics

Guhan Elangovan[✉], Nicko R. Caluya, and Damon M. Chandler

Visual Information Engineering Laboratory, Ritsumeikan University, Osaka, Japan
is0806hv@ed.ritsumei.ac.jp

Abstract. Visualizations such as motion, and free-body diagrams accompany problems and scenarios in classical mechanics for a physics class. However, textbooks present such diagrams with fixed viewpoints and sparse information. In this paper, we describe the design of our virtual reality (VR) experience that transforms these diagrams into interactive, customizable, and dynamic components that learners can inspect and engage in a 3D immersive environment. We highlight their use in three scenarios: freefall, horizontal, and parabolic motions. As sandbox-type experiences, we allow users to inspect these environments freely as the motion diagrams are visualized. Then, to mimic a real-world experiment of observable phenomena, we designated buttons for dependent variable changes like height, initial angle, and velocity. As an ending assessment, we showed an equation fill-in-the-blanks canvas interface to check the learners' understanding of the relationships among the variables. We also include insights from the development process and future work towards a user study.

Keywords: virtual reality · interactive learning environment · physics simulation · visualization · interface design

1 Introduction

Motion and free-body diagrams are visual aids found in many textbooks to allow spatial understanding of physics problems, usually in classical mechanics lessons. However, as static drawings, these diagrams only present limited visual information for learners to analyze. For example, in motion diagrams, duplicates of the object in motion are rendered in a trajectory path in time-based intervals, but such intervals are difficult to customize, leading to multiple diagrams being printed. On the other hand, free body diagrams visually represent physically invisible properties such as velocity and force vectors, as well as measurements like height and range.

In recent years, the affordability and scalability of VR-based technology have led to educational applications situated in a virtual environment [6]. The rise in

434   G. Elangovan et al.

Fig. 1. Three environments used for the application: forklift operation (left), bowling (center), and basketball (right)

standalone headsets and advancements in display resolution, size, weight, battery efficiency, visual clarity, and software optimizations, have made evaluating immersion and effectiveness easier. Since the publication of the survey [6], virtual reality has evolved exponentially and has become cheaper, more available to the general public, and scalable. Besides the point, improvements in visual fidelity and related problems such as ghosting, brightness, and refresh rate have also greatly impacted the visual involvement of the experience.

In the case of physics education, VR becomes suitable by showing an interactive and immersive graphical representation of what is only static and fixed in textbook-based diagrams. The lessons that can have been implemented in physics include electrical phenomena [4,8,13], kinematics [7,13], and classical mechanics [5,7]. Many of these related works have components that can be customized by learners so that they can investigate the effects of individual physical and temporal factors.

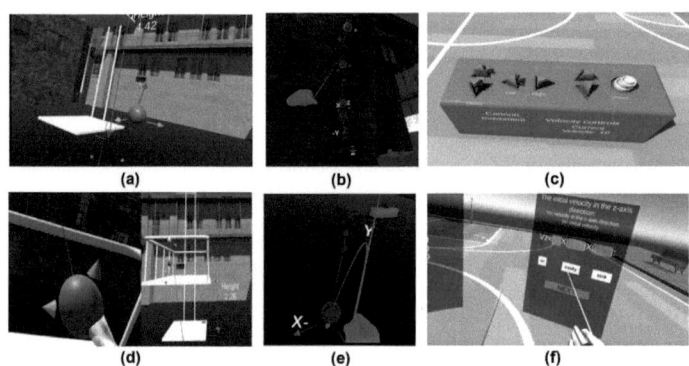

Fig. 2. (a) Vectors, (b) Phantoms and Dotted Paths, (c) Interactable Panel, (d) Multi-Viewpoint Angles: Egocentric (left) and Exocentric (right), (e) Flick-Grab Mechanic, (f) Formula-Based Assessment Canvas

2 System: Virtual Physics Classroom

Visualization and interactability are major factors of these VR sandbox experiences. To enhance it further, we introduced different mechanics and gameplay elements through physical actuators and virtual interfaces.

To narrow the scope of this project, three classical mechanics lessons were chosen (see Fig. 1): freefall (e.g., dropping from a forklift), horizontal motion (e.g., flinging a bowling ball), and parabolic motion (e.g., shooting a basketball from a cannon). The selection of the exemplary scenarios already demonstrates many advantages of virtual environments, as they are safe, con-trolled, and inexpensive to stage. All three scenarios include the following components to show the similarities and differences among these types of motion.

To ensure that every learner's action in our Physics Virtual Classroom yields usable data on conceptual understanding, we adopt concepts from validated educational VR frameworks and pedagogical designs, namely, Evidence-Centered Design (ECD) and Dede's VR immersion model [3,12]. In our preliminary empirical evaluation, learners complete "quests" framed as natural language word problems (e.g. "Get a velocity which is greater than height B and Lesser than Height A (Where height A and B are visual Representation)"). Each solution requires tuning virtual parameters manipulating objects to produce traceable evidence of mastery, exactly as ECD prescribes when assessment is embedded in interaction alone. Similarly, Dede emphasizes that actional controls (intuitive grab and release mechanics, parameter adjustment buttons) and sensory context (visual cues such as realistic movement of the object through space) combine to create a strong sense of presence [3]. It is precisely this embodied sense of "being there" that scaffolds constructivist learning by situating physics problem solving in an authentic context. By marrying ECD's rigorous assessment architecture with Dede's multidimensional immersion principles, our design not only captures what learners do, but does so in a pedagogically rich, psychologically grounded environment that mirrors authentic physics experimentation [3,12].

3 Overview of Application Components

General and Directional Vectors. In our application, we established visual models for vectors (see Fig. 2a) in Cartesian space attached to the primary moving body and scale based on environmental factors such as velocity, acceleration, and gravity. In addition, a general vector was also implemented to indicate the direction of the object being utilized in the experimentation process. To adhere to the standard gizmos found in usual game engines and modeling software, we designated different colors for each vector arrow drawing.

Visualize Motion: Phantoms and Dotted Paths. To visualize the recently transpired motion of the object in our application, we de-veloped a set of semi-transparent objects called Phantoms (see Fig. 2b) that indicate the path of the entity being held for observation. The current implementation has two variations of these bodies: trajectory-based Dotted Paths and direction-based whole-body Phantoms. Moreover, these distinctions in naming conventions reflect upon their actions within the environments. The trajectory-based Dotted Path serves as a medium for the player to understand the movement path of the entity while in motion. On the other hand, the Direction-based counterpart is user-summonable and mentions the directional vectors attached to the entity.

Interactable Panels for Customizing Motion. Tactile panels (see Fig. 2c) are a portal for the users to get fully immersed in the virtual space. These panels provide control to different objects that alter the experiment's outcome. The panel varies based on the testing conditions, but the ultimate functionality remains similar. For instance, in the freefall environment, the utilization of the panel consisted of controlling the forklift platform by lowering or raising it, or by spawning another ball. On the other hand, In the parabolic motion environment, it is deployed to serve as an interface to control the cannon in many ways. Since projectile motion is concerned with the initial launch angle, we provided buttons for changing the altitude (up/down) and azimuthal (left/right) angles. Additionally, we also have a panel for the initial velocity when adjusting the magnitude, and a launch. As the horizontal motion is more concerned with the vector component analysis of the launched ball, we did not provide any panel buttons for that scenario.

Viewpoint Switching Feature. A user's understanding of a concept depends on the full perception of the event, by investigating multiple dimensions. To fulfill such conditions and to enhance the viewing experience, we implemented different user-switchable camera angles positioned based on their purpose in the field of the experiment (see Fig. 2d). The demonstrated instance we prepare is in the free-fall environment, where a secondary camera angle provides more visibility of the path of the ball exhibiting the gravity-based nature of the experiment.

Accessibility Mechanics: Flick-Grabbing Mechanic and Teleportation. Flick-grabbing (see Fig. 2e) is an alternative gesture-based object acquisition mechanic to help alleviate cyber-sickness effects such as nausea and dizziness by allowing the player to retrieve the ball without much spatial navigation. In addition, in a recent preliminary study conducted by us, we discovered that many participants with motion sickness benefitted from using this mechanic.

Moreover, teleportation is also implemented in environments such as "Forklift Operation" as an ease-of-use feature to reduce repetitive spatial traversal (Figs. 4 and 5).

4 System Architecture and Development

To improve the clarity and understanding of the system architecture, we divide it into three categories: user inputs, system actions, and output transformations. User inputs refer to the physical and spatial interaction mediums employed

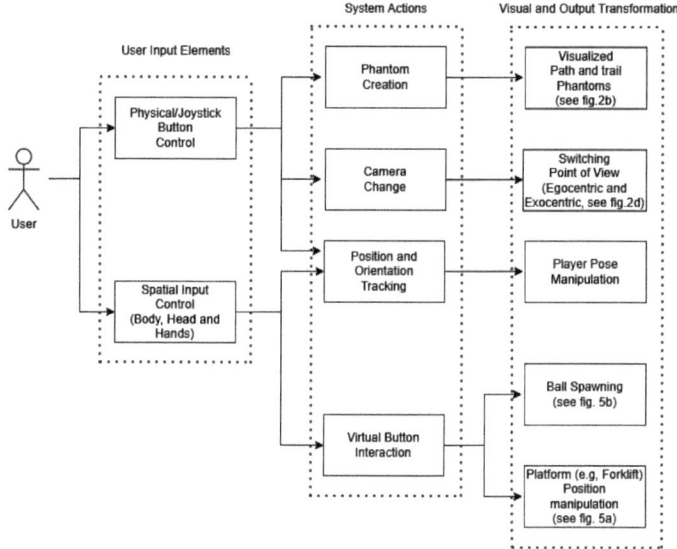

Fig. 3. System Architecture

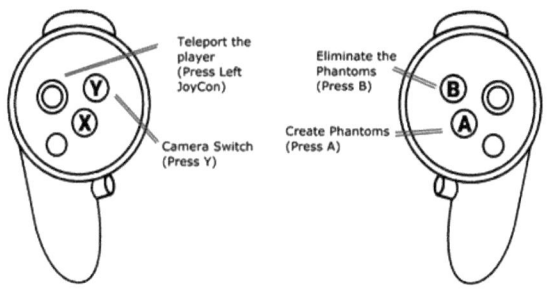

Fig. 4. Controller Layout

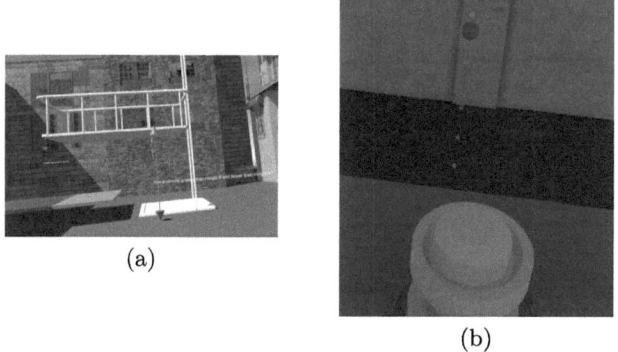

Fig. 5. (a) Forklift Platform Height Adjustment, (b) Ball Spawning

to engage with the virtual environment. System actions represent the internal processes triggered by these interactions, whether they are physical trigger of actuators or spatial gestures. Output transformations denote the visual representation of these interactions within the 3D virtual space, serving as feedback to the user and reflecting the system's response. This tripartite architecture aligns with principles from ECD and Dede's VR interaction model [3,12]. ECD emphasizes structuring interactions so that each user input maps to a measurable competency, ensuring that system actions and output transformations produce valid evidence of learning. Similarly, Dede's model underscores the importance of actional controls and immersive feedback in fostering presence and supporting constructivist learning. By integrating these frameworks, the system architecture not only facilitates intuitive interaction but also embeds pedagogical and assessment value within each component.

Throughout the development phase, the Oculus Meta Quest 3 and its included handhelds were used as the primary HMD kit for testing and refinement purposes.

Utilizing the same kit during the preliminary testing allowed the users to perform specific functions and take advantage of the convenience given through different proprietary mechanics of our application. In Fig. 3, the button layout for the specific hand-tracking device is mentioned according to its functionality.

The synthesis of the application was done not only from a computational point of view but so from a scalable one. This scalability factor leads us to consider the extensibility of implementation in high schools at a massive proportion as one of the primary objectives of the application while focusing on the delivery of visual aspects. The development and testing of the program were done on a diverse set of hardware configurations to ensure compatibility and support to various levels of hardware. The application was designed to run and was executable from a machine with these minimum specifications: Intel i7 11th generation CPU, a Nvidia Geforce RTX 3050 Mobile GPU, and 16 GB of RAM.

On the software side, The physical engine that powers the test scenarios are computed by Unity. Furthermore, to standardize the development process, "2022.61f" is maintained as the version of the computational engine across all development hardware. Tools such as Maya and Blender were used to sculpt the three-dimensional representation of the models which were used as assets to represent different features, variables, and various elemental phenomena.

Finally, one of the core strengths of the application lies in its functionality. As visual information plays a critical role in conveying content, the selection of entities within the environment significantly affects user understanding. For instance, the "Phantom" visualizes time-specific positions in Cartesian space using multi-shade vector elements to represent motion and direction. This vector-based context enhances users' grasp of physical scenarios. Additionally, the flick-grab along with the teleportation mechanic improves accessibility for people with motion-induced discomfort during interaction by allowing intuitive object manipulation and point-to-point navigation. The flick-grabbing being built on a ray-based interaction system, it streamlines user engagement with experimental components, improving accessibility and interpretation for people with temporary impairments.

5 Preliminary Study

To understand the effectiveness of our current environments, we conducted a preliminary study using a quest-based system grounded in the principles of ECD and Dede's VR immersion model. The empirical evaluation focuses on user actions and the time taken to interpret and complete each task as indicators of conceptual understanding. Participants were presented with three randomized tasks—for example, "Get a velocity higher than height A" to preserve the qualitative nature of the study.

In consideration of accessibility, users requiring accommodations for motion-related health conditions were first trained in a separate environment designed to introduce the flick-grab mechanic in a low-discomfort context. Once inside the primary environment, each user's session was tracked: the system recorded the time elapsed from level initiation, every interaction attempt, and the total completion time for all three quests.

In addition to this, we collected a custom user survey designed based on the well-established Igroup Presence Questionnaire (IPQ) and other metrics to understand the participant's knowledge and immersion level before and after the experiment on classical mechanics. This data allowed us to understand the statistics and estimate the average time users take to comprehend and solve a classical mechanics problem presented through visual and natural language formats while also acquiring the general demographic information and the data regarding the quality of our implementation of the physics concept from the user themselves. The survey suggests that over 90% of users reported an improved understanding of the relationship between height and velocity through visual and immersive demonstrations, with many indicating that the virtual environment made abstract physics concepts easier to perceive and remember.

6 Insights and Future Work

A detailed proposal for an improvised set of assessment indicators is underway. Concurrently, an in-depth account of all fundamental physical quantities used in the analytical studies are represented in simplified visual spaces to ensure comprehension across all the lessons and reviews. These training systems are designed to deliver the subject matter via additional multimodal approaches such as gesture-based hand tracking and floating text displays. In addition to that, cross-compatibility between various platforms under a variety of HMDs provided by different manufacturers, to name a few, Oculus' Meta Quest 3, Meta Quest 2 and the HTC Vive Pro are a part of our consideration for support.

Moreover, we plan on organizing a thematic comparative user study to observe the implications and the effectiveness of the application under the intended scope of operation using these methods (formula-based assessment and competency mapping) to understand the potential of learning physics in a VR environment. Furthermore, these comparative studies will take into account information such as, the time taken by the player to complete the formula-based-assessment with and without scaffolding elements such as an external human guide while the player is left to explore, experiment and discover the mechanisms provided in the VR environment. These studies would do so by allowing the player to actively contruct knowledge by following a learning-by-doing pedagogy further discussed in detail in studies such as [9]. Further help us reinforce the validity of these new, experimental teaching methodologies which are developed based on pre-existing Instructional VR frameworks. Moreover, large-scale user studies similar to our topic of research [1,2,7,8,10,11,13] have been previously conducted by other research groups and educators to test how VR is an effective tool for learning physical phenomena which in addition to our proposal, concretizing the viability of our claim.

Finally, a formula-based assessment method (see Fig. 2f) is under creation to assess the understanding of the student's performance after going through the experience. Similarly to the previous elements, these formulas are also cast as perceivable elements that have intractable components, e.g., draggable with the press of a physical actuator. These draggable components contain variables to construct a rule expressed in symbols. The formulas are presented abstractly to allow the player to react and complete the examination process. This approach will assess the ability of the learner to identify variables and construct physics formulas, directly aligning with ECD's competency mapping and further leveraging Dede's immersion model to keep learners engaged [3,12].

Acknowledgements. This project was developed under the Visual Information Engineering Laboratory at Ritsumeikan University.

Disclosure of Interests. The authors declare that there is no conflict of interests related to the development and publication of this study.

References

1. Arymbekov, B.: Augmented reality application to support visualization of physics experiments. In: 2023 IEEE International Conference on Smart Information Systems and Technologies (SIST), pp. 52–55 (2023). https://doi.org/10.1109/SIST58284.2023.10223534
2. Collado, R.C., Caluya, N.R., Santos, M.E.C.: Teachers' evaluation of motionar: An augmented reality-based motion graphing application. J. Phys. Conf. Ser. **1286**(1), 012051 (2019). https://doi.org/10.1088/1742-6596/1286/1/012051
3. Dede, C.: Immersive interfaces for engagement and learning. Science **323**(5910), 66–69 (2009). https://doi.org/10.1126/science.1167311
4. Devyatkin, E.M.: Virtual interactive laboratory assignments and experiments in physics in the system of education. In: 2018 XIV International Scientific-Technical Conference on Actual Problems of Electronics Instrument Engineering (APEIE), pp. 255–258 (2018). https://doi.org/10.1109/APEIE.2018.8545019

5. Kaufmann, H., Meyer, B.: Physics education in virtual reality: an example. Themes Sci. Technol. Educ. **2**(1–2), 117–130 (2011)
6. Kavanagh, S., Luxton-Reilly, A., Wuensche, B., Plimmer, B.: A systematic review of virtual reality in education. Themes Sci. Technol. Educ. **10**(2), 85–119 (2017). https://www.learntechlib.org/p/182115
7. Krishna M, S.R., Sai Suvanth, V., K, S.A., Sarma, H.: A case study on vr teaching: projectile motion and gravity. In: 2024 IEEE International Symposium on Mixed and Augmented Reality Adjunct (ISMAR-Adjunct), pp. 329–330 (2024). https://doi.org/10.1109/ISMAR-Adjunct64951.2024.00075
8. Lim, W.N., Al Gavara Ramarao, N.: Bridging gaps in high school physics education: Revolutionizing through virtual reality experimental learning. In: 2024 IEEE 14th Symposium on Computer Applications & Industrial Electronics (ISCAIE), pp. 446–450 (2024). https://doi.org/10.1109/ISCAIE61308.2024.10576413
9. Marougkas, A., Troussas, C., Krouska, A., Sgouropoulou, C.: Virtual reality in education: a review of learning theories, approaches and methodologies for the last decade. Electronics **12**(13) (2023). https://doi.org/10.3390/electronics12132832
10. Pirker, J., Lesjak, I., Guetl, C.: Maroon vr: a room-scale physics laboratory experience. In: 2017 IEEE 17th International Conference on Advanced Learning Technologies (ICALT), pp. 482–484 (2017). https://doi.org/10.1109/ICALT.2017.92
11. Sulaiman, H., Ibrahim, N., Latif, R.A., Yusof, A.M.: Students and teachers' perception on future use of virtual reality (vr) in learning physics: a preliminary analysis. In: 2020 IEEE Conference on e-Learning, e-Management and e-Services (IC3e), pp. 1–6 (2020). https://doi.org/10.1109/IC3e50159.2020.9288464
12. Torrence, K.: Applying evidence-centered design to assess learner competency levels in vr learning experiences. In: Immersive Learning Research-Practitioner, pp. 1–3 (2022)
13. Wang, Y., Zhan, W.L., Pang, M.: Virtual experiments in physics education: a systematic literature review. Res. Sci. Technol. Educ. **43**(2), 633–655 (2025). https://doi.org/10.1080/02635143.2024.2327995

Gestalt Approaches to Hinting in Games: A 3D Connect Four Case Study

Yuta Hirahata[(✉)], Nicko R. Caluya, and Damon M. Chandler

Visual Information Engineering Laboratory, Ritsumeikan University, Osaka, Japan
is0687pe@ed.ritsumei.ac.jp, {nicko,chandler}@fc.ritsumei.ac.jp
https://vinelab.jp/

Abstract. In a dense 3D environment, evaluations of user interface design for occluded internal structures focused primarily on a time-based measure of efficiency of selection and manipulation. However, there is a tradeoff when designing automated hints in these environments in the case of strategy-based games, as these hints compromise the mentally demanding nature of a 3D game and the player's ability to envision a mental map of the environment. In the case of a desktop-based 3D Connect Four, hinting that an opponent will win the next round can be presented to the player in two ways: previewing the danger position with a differently colored sphere or revealing the existing spheres that only needs one more opponent sphere to win. We conducted a within-subjects study of 12 participants to test these two hints versus a control condition. The results reveal a trade-off between the helpful and distracting nature of hints and how such hints might affect challenge and cognitive load. The insights from this user study point to better 3D game hint designs and balancing the gameplay when hints are present or absent.

Keywords: Game Hints · User Interface · Gestalt Theory

1 Introduction

Visual hints in games assist gamers in their decision-making process, especially for strategy or turn-based games. Tutorials show such hints to guide novice players, and hints can serve as a critical aid in winning or losing scenarios. The appearance of hints vary in context and form, but mostly they come in notifications that do not necessarily break game rules, and players have the option to turn them off to delegate the strategy to their own intuition.

In the case of a complex game like 3D Connect Four (see Fig. 1), the rules of the game extend beyond the original 2D version. According to Edelkamp and Kissman [4], the default instance of the 2D Connect Four is played on a 7×6 board. The players take turns sliding or placing pieces on the board, with gravity acting a major role in the mechanics, as the pieces need to fall as far to the bottom as possible. The winning objective is to construct a line of (at least) four pieces bearing the current player's color.

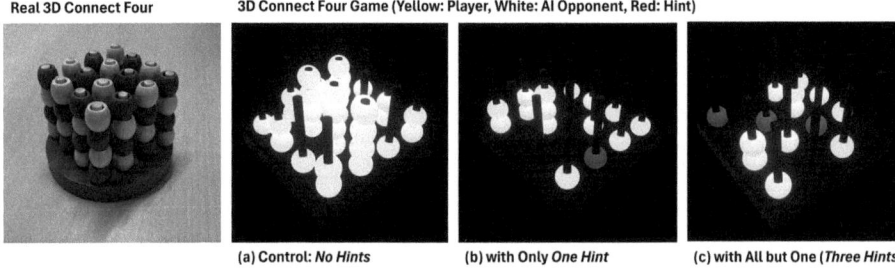

Fig. 1. 3D Connect Four and the different Hint Conditions in the user study.

However, for 3D Connect Four, players take turns sliding down spheres on a $4 \times 4 \times 4$ grid. The game starts with an empty 4×4 grid of vertical columns, and the rule of gravity still applies when making a move. Thus, spheres can be stacked higher as long as there is at least one bottom sphere present in the column. In addition to the clear horizontal, vertical, and diagonal constructions of the lines, players can win in any of the three dimensions of the grid, and a line traversing a top corner to the opposite bottom corner is also a valid winning condition. With issues like density and occlusion as the game progresses, the main concern that visual hints can address is to make players easily visualize the playing area, so that the player can place a *blocking move* to prevent the opponent from completing four in a row. As a turn-based game like chess, research on Connect Four has focused mainly on solving winning conditions only [1,4,7,9].

However, in the context of a 3D Connect Four game, there are still no empirical studies focusing on how to improve players' strategies toward winning the game. The main research focus of this paper is to provide possible visual hinting approaches when the playing area becomes crowded and spheres placed on inner columns of the 4×4 layout occlude the player's viewpoint. We refer to and borrow from the basic and well-known Gestalt principles of similarity, proximity, and closure in designing hints in this specific context. Such hints notify the player whether they are in danger of losing to their opponent, while keeping the other spheres visible.

Furthermore, this paper presents the results of a user study that features two hinting conditions and a control condition (that is, *No Hint*). Aside from an objective analysis through time recordings, subjective feedback (e.g. preferences and task load analysis) from participants were collected to gain more insight on whether such game hints improve overall gameplay satisfaction and sense of challenge for players.

2 Designing Hints for a 3D Connect Four Game

The game used in this study was designed for a single player against an AI-based opponent. As shown in the game screenshots in Fig. 1, the player plays with a yellow sphere, and the opponent plays with a white sphere. For uniformity, all games played in the user study start with the main player first, and then the AI will take the next turn. The turns alternate until the winning condition of four in a row occurs.

The creation of possible visual hints in this 3D Connect Four game lies on the most critical turn where the opponent is one sphere placement away from achieving the win condition. With this main idea, two perspectives can be devised to give a hint to the player. First, the player sees a preview of the potential position where the opponent can put the next sphere to win (here referred to as *One Hint*, see Fig. 1(b)). Inversely, the player can also trace the three other spheres that would complete the winning condition in the next turn (here referred to as *Three Hints*).

The primary advantage of only showing *One Hint* is its directness: the player only needs to find the hint and replace the red sphere with the player's sphere. However, the player has to be aware of its position, which will be harder to notice when the red sphere is visually occluded by the other spheres.

On the other hand, there are more visual stimuli or indicators provided by a *Three Hints* condition. The disadvantage is that there is an additional cognitive load in figuring out where to place the next sphere given that there are three other spheres, which may be less convenient than having only *One Hint*.

2.1 User Interfaces for Dense 3D Environments

In a comprehensive review by Bashar and Batmaz [2] about selection techniques in 3D virtual environments, they cite the work of LaViola et al. [6] to determine various factors that affect such interactions. Fundamental parameters such as target size, density of objects around the target, and possibility of target occlusion were used to classify many 3D user interface (3DUI) papers. Such factors also motivate the user study presented in this user study, as the main task of the player is to click the correct column to slide their next sphere, which is what selection in a 3D environment entails.

Another important interface in 3D environment is highlighting, such that occluded objects can still be visualized. A study presented by Vanacken, Grossman, and Coninx [8] looked at a combination of (1) an external interface and (2) another target-based highlighting scheme when exploring factors such as density and occlusion. In their two external interface conditions (i.e., 3D bubble and depth ray), they manipulate the material properties of the target object and its surroundings to achieve a highlighting effect (e.g., rendering everything except the target object semitransparent). However, when transparency is manipulated, there is a risk of interaction confusion that stems from layering complexity and dependence on background objects. In our user study, we kept the external interface to the standard mouse cursor, but we changed the color of the spheres that we want to highlight to red, which stands out against the yellow and white spheres of the two players.

2.2 Gestalt Principles: Similarity, Closure, and Proximity

Providing hints in games is closely related to the research done by the human-computer interaction community when it comes to 3D user interface [6]. When theories of cognitive science and attention mechanisms are incorporated in the 3DUI design, players would find more convenience using them, and the cognitive load shifts to higher-level thinking.

In creating the visual hinting conditions used in this study, we adhered to the Gestalt principles of human visual perception. As many visual user interface designs have been influenced by Gestalt principles [5], contexts such as gaming can also benefit from following these laws. The principles of proximity (e.g., consecutive spheres), similarity (e.g., the contrasting but same red color as a hint), and closure (e.g., the illusion of creating a line or row) are more apparent when perceiving the *Three Hints* condition.

3 User Study

To demonstrate the concept of highlighting or emphasizing internal structures of dense 3D environments, we developed a desktop version of a 3D Connect Four game. The application developed for this paper is a desktop version of the 3D Connect Four game, made with the Unity game engine (2022.3.23f1).

3.1 Participants

We recruited 12 university students (age: 20.58 ± 1.3) who had normal-to-corrected vision. On average, they rated themselves moderately familiar with computer games (3.42 out of 5 being most familiar), and inexperienced with the Connect Four 3D game (1.25 out of 5 being very experienced). All participants played two rounds of the game with one condition, and the order of the conditions was counterbalanced to reduce the order effects.

Before data recording in the experiment began, participants played an in-game tutorial version of the game to familiarize themselves with controls and rules of the game. Then, they were given prior knowledge of the hint conditions they will encounter when playing the game (*No Hint*, *One Hint*, and *Three Hints*).

3.2 Data and Hypotheses

We based our hypotheses on the design choices outlined in the related work section. After the experiment, we collected ranking and rating data from a post-experiment survey to ask about specific and more subjective aspects of the game play, which will be used for **H1** to **H4**. During the experiment, the game application also records time in the background and adds time data points whenever (a) the game starts, (b) a danger case is shown, (c) the said danger case has been addressed, and/or (d) the game ends (whether it is a win or a loss.) We measure the detection time that we will use for *H5*. The following hypotheses and their corresponding data and reasoning are as follows:

H1: *Challenging Game.* Players find the game more challenging when no hints are presented.

As we are also interested in the player's satisfaction when playing the game, we asked participants to rank and rate the challenge level of the game in the presence (or absence) of hints. We also hypothesize that the challenge of the game does not change whether *One Hint* or *Three Hints* are presenting.

H2: *Helpfulness of Hints.* Players find hints more helpful than having no hint at all.

We also asked participants to rate the helpfulness of the hints as they make strategic placements of their spheres. We hypothesize that the *Three Hints* are the most helpful because there are more visible indicators of hints when there are many, and that the *No Hints* are the least helpful.

H3: *Distracting Hints.* Players find glancing at hints more distracting than no hint at all.

We also asked participants to rate the distraction caused by changing the material state (i.e., color) of the sphere(s). We hypothesize that the *Three Hints* are the most distracting, and that the *No Hints* are the least distracting because there are no changes in color to notify the player.

H4: *Task Load.* Players experience higher mental demand and exert more effort when playing without hints.

Participants also answered a standard NASA Task Load Index (NASA-TLX) questionnaire to determine the difficulty of the game against the three conditions. In this user study, we considered the raw (unweighted) TLX scores in our analysis [3]. Since there will be no assistance from the game itself, we hypothesize participants exert more effort to stop the opponent from winning on the next turn in the *No Hint* condition. Furthermore, we also hypothesize that the *Three Hints* condition is less taxing than *One Hint* because there are more indicators visible, especially when the playing area becomes denser.

H5: *Detection Time.* Players take a long time to detect a blocking move if there are no hints. In particular, it will be easier to detect the blocking move at the *Three Hints* condition versus the *One Hint* condition.

We define *Detection Time* of a hint as the difference between the time the participants reacted by placing the sphere on the designated danger position and the time the program displays the hint. In the control condition, the supposed time to show a hint replaces the latter. We assume that in the *No Hint* condition, there will be no cues from proximity or similarity that can ease the process of deductive reasoning or strategizing.

4 Results and Discussion

For the three subjective factors (challenging, helpful, distracting), we were able to obtain both forced ranking (Figs. 2a, 2b, and 2c) and Likert scale rating measurements from participants. In Fig. 3a, there is no statistically significant difference for Challenge and Distraction, but there is in the case of Helpfulness. According to Friedman's test ($\chi^2(2) = 20.04$, p < 0.001) and subsequent pairwise comparisons, the *Three Hints* condition was more helpful than the *One Hint* condition, and the *No Hint* condition was the least helpful. This result supports the validity of our H2 hypothesis, which mentions that the helpfulness of hints will be most performed with the *Three Hints* condition. On the other hand, those inconsistencies of results in the challenge and distraction data oppose our H1 and H3 hypotheses, which states that there would be differences among cases in terms of challenge and distraction.

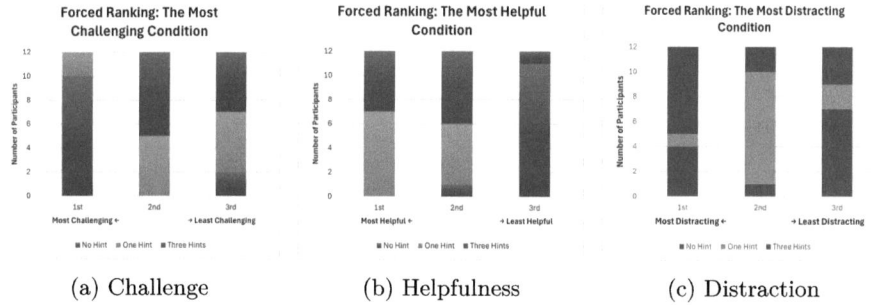

(a) Challenge (b) Helpfulness (c) Distraction

Fig. 2. Forced Ranking Results grouped by Category

The results of the NASA-TLX Questionnaire show emphases on *Mental Demand* and *Effort* as the biggest factors that affect the participants' task load (see Fig. 3b. In particular, using Friedman's Test, these two factors including *Frustration* have ratings that are statistically significant from each other ($p < 0.05$). All three demand types have the same trend according to pairwise comparisons: the *No Hint* condition was the most mentally demanding, effortful, and frustrating, while the *Three Hints* condition was the least among the three. We assume that these results validate the fact that when more visual hints are given to players, the less the task load becomes. These findings also align with another subjective measure: the *Helpfulness* of the hints. Moreover, such NASA-TLX results provide strong evidence in favor of our H4 hypothesis, which predicted that *Three Hints* condition best reduces the Task Load of the players.

Finally, during the experiment, individual danger detection times were recorded (see Fig. 4). However, we could not use standard statistical analysis due to uneven samples across all game trials. Due to the random nature of the gameplay, some participants were not able to reach the hinting conditions because either they immediately won without any opportunity to make blocking moves. Therefore, our H5 hypothesis (*Three Hints* condition best reduces the detection time) could not be tested.

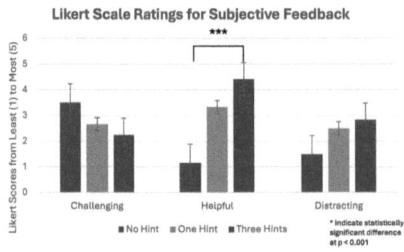
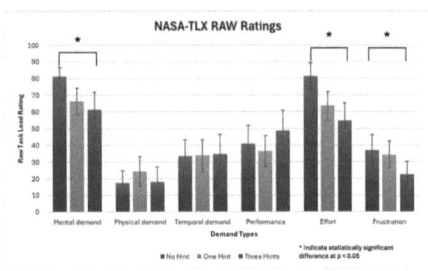
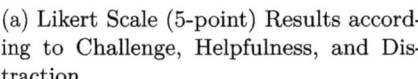

(a) Likert Scale (5-point) Results according to Challenge, Helpfulness, and Distraction

(b) Raw Ratings for the NASA Task Load Index (TLX) Results on all three conditions.

Fig. 3. Friedman's test for Likert Scale (3a) and NASA-TLX (3b) results

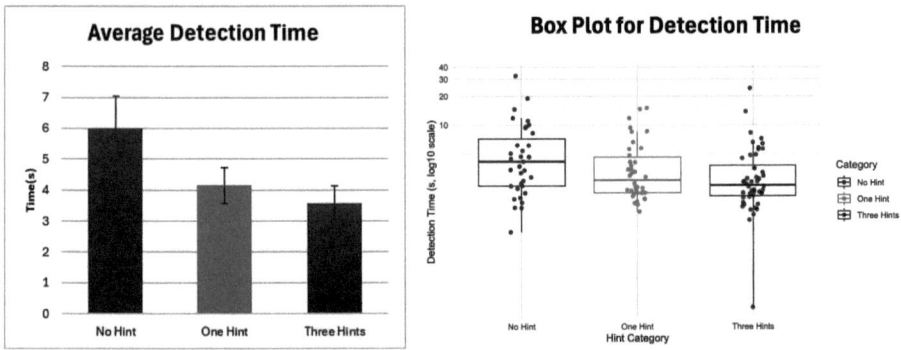

Fig. 4. Detection time on all three conditions.

5 Limitations and Future Work

The main limitation of our work has to do with how often hints are shown to players at any given time. Unlike timed hints with uniform durations, we gathered uneven time duration samples because not all players reach a turn where hint(s) is/are supposed to be shown, especially on conditions these hints were needed. For example, the player may have won immediately or played strategically to block the AI opponent in making a penultimate move. The AI in the game was also designed to make blocking moves, but even then, the player can still win without inducing any hint on all turns. To avoid such issue, we will change the game structure by making the field 8×8×8, and let our participants play it until all positions are filled. This ensures that there will be more chances that players will encounter hints. Moreover, preoccupying partial space will further ensure players facing the hints. To be specific, we will design a system that randomly places spheres before a game starts. With the previous design, a game could end before much space is filled, so the effect of occlusion could not be tested in some cases. By preoccupying partial space of 8×8×8 field, the game will be more complicated, thus the occlusion influence on game results will be more obvious.

Additionally, there is a limitation on the interpretation of distractions. The questionnaire item only stated "how distracting the hints are" without any additional definition. According to participants' definitions, they confuse distractions as (1) game elements that negatively affect the overall gameplay, or (2) visual stimuli that may break their ongoing spatial understanding of the environment. Therefore, for the purposes of this study the definition of distraction should be (2).

Furthermore, the sample size ($n = 12$) is still small, and additional participants from more diverse backgrounds in terms of age and video game knowledge are needed to increase the effect size and generalizability of our findings. The recording of detection time was most affected by the sample size. As mentioned above, some participants have not encountered hints in the first place, hence, the small sample size created inconsistencies in the record.

6 Summary

In this paper, we outlined a user study that looks at comparing two hinting conditions (showing *One Hint* and *Three Hints*) against a control condition (*No Hint*) for a 3D Connect Four game. The results show the potential of *Three Hints* being helpful for players, while keeping the game challenging and not as distracting. The insights gathered from this study can also inform the design choices of tutorials for this game, especially when the game becomes more complex in terms of rules and space, as well as the crowding and occlusion that happens as the game continues.

Acknowledgements. We would like to thank all our participants for their time playing the game in multiple rounds and for their valuable feedback.

Disclosure of Interests. The authors declare that there are no conflicts of interest related to the development and publication of this study.

References

1. Bakera, M., Jörges, S., Margaria, T.: Test your strategy: graphical construction of strategies for connect-four. In: 2009 14th IEEE International Conference on Engineering of Complex Computer Systems, pp. 172–181 (2009). https://doi.org/10.1109/ICECCS.2009.51
2. Bashar, M.R., Batmaz, A.U.: Virtual task environments factors explored in 3d selection studies. In: Proceedings of the 50th Graphics Interface Conference. GI '24. Association for Computing Machinery, New York (2024). https://doi.org/10.1145/3670947.3670983
3. Byers, J.C., Bittner, A., Hill, S.G.: Traditional and raw task load index (tlx) correlations: are paired comparisons necessary. Adv. Ind. Ergon. Saf. **1**, 481–485 (1989)

4. Edelkamp, S., Kissmann, P.: On the complexity of bdds for state space search: a case study in connect four. In: Proceedings of the Twenty-Fifth AAAI Conference on Artificial Intelligence, AAAI'11, pp. 18–23. AAAI Press (2011)
5. IxDF, I.D.F.: What are the Gestalt Principles?—interaction-design.org. https://www.interaction-design.org/literature/topics/gestalt-principles. Accessed 31 Mar 2025
6. LaViola, J.J., Jr., Kruijff, E., McMahan, R.P., Bowman, D., Poupyrev, I.P.: 3D User Interfaces: Theory and Practice. Addison-Wesley Professional, Boston (2017)
7. Song, X., Hultros, L.: Connect four robot: implementation of ai-strategies in a connectfour robot (2018)
8. Vanacken, L., Grossman, T., Coninx, K.: Exploring the effects of environment density and target visibility on object selection in 3d virtual environments. In: 2007 IEEE Symposium on 3D User Interfaces (2007). https://doi.org/10.1109/3DUI.2007.340783
9. Yamaguchi, Y., Yamaguchi, K., Tanaka, T., Kaneko, T.: Infinite connect-four is solved: draw. In: van den Herik, H.J., Plaat, A. (eds.) ACG 2011. LNCS, vol. 7168, pp. 208–219. Springer, Heidelberg (2012). https://doi.org/10.1007/978-3-642-31866-5_18

A VR System for Detecting Static Electricity as Invisible Creature

Wanosuke Ito, Rion Yukino, and Akihiro Matsuura(✉)

Tokyo Denki University, Hiki 350-0394, Saitama, Japan
{21rd025,25rmd52}@ms.dendai.ac.jp, matsu@rd.dendai.ac.jp

Abstract. In this study, we explore the entertainment value of the activity of sensing imperceptible static electricity and present a VR system in which a player tactilely detects static electricity presented in a 360° radius around the forearm within the virtual space, and removes it using a controller. To achieve this, we developed a static electricity haptic device featuring two charging elements that rotate around the forearm. To enhance the perceived presence of the static electricity, vibration of the charging elements is also employed.

Keywords: Static Electricity · Skin · Invisible · VR · Haptic · Entertainment System

1 Introduction

In the entertainment fields such as music, videos, and games, research and development utilizing users' biological responses are conducted to innovate and enhance the quality of individual experiences and interpersonal communication. Quasi-electrostatic fields and electrostatic stimulation have been explored as means of conveying human presence or a sense of another's proximity. Notable studies on quasi-electrostatic fields include research that enables personal identification based on the quasi-electrostatic field naturally emitted by the human body [1], and a study in which a CRT television is used to present a quasi-electrostatic field to a participant's legs to evoke the perceived presence of another entity [2]. Regarding electrostatic stimulation, several studies have investigated the amplification and elicitation of emotions through the piloerection of forearm hair induced by electrostatic force [3–5]. In [6], the authors proposed a system that presents a presence-like sensation to the forearm using an electrostatic field. In the haptic VR content Call from Merry [7], the earpiece-shaped device delivers electrostatic stimulation and cold air to the user's ear to evoke a sense of fear. However, to the best of our knowledge, haptic devices and VR entertainment systems aimed at locating and utilizing electrostatic discharge for interaction, while mitigating the potential for discomfort associated with its application, have not yet been developed.

Therefore, focusing on the entertainment value of the actions of perceiving invisible static electricity through the sensation on the skin and eliminating it, we develop a VR system that enables users to perform a series of actions to detect static electricity presented by the haptic device and make attempt to remove it using a VR controller. The main part of the device is the electrostatic charging part mounted on the rotating disk. By rotating this disk, either of the two rods of the main part presents static electricity around the user's forearm. To enhance the sensation of minute static electricity while mitigating discomfort caused by its intensity, the disk and the electricity charging parts oscillate back and forth while remaining the position around the arm where the static electricity is presented. In addition to this device, we developed a VR content in which static electricity is personified as a virtual, invisible creature in the virtual space. A user wearing a head-mounted display (HMD), unaware of the creature's location, attempts to identify and vacuum it with a cleaner instrument, and when the location is correct, the creature visually appears and is vacuumed into the instrument. We confirmed that the whole VR system functioned as a cohesive interactive system.

2 Electrostatic Haptic Device

2.1 System Overview

The main components of the system are the electrostatic haptic device, Arduino Uno, a PC, a HMD (Meta Quest 3S), and a VR controller. Figure 1 shows the system overview. Figure 2 shows the external view around the electrostatic haptic device. A user fixes a forearm between the two rods of the electrostatic haptic device. The processing flow of the system is the following: The electrostatic haptic device is controlled by the PC via the Arduino Uno. The position at which the device presents static electricity is determined by its angle. A charged rod within the electrostatic charging part delivers the electrostatic stimulation to the user's forearm. The user identifies the perceived location of the static electricity by pointing a controller towards it. Upon correct identification, a creature representing the static electricity appears in the virtual space and is vacuumed into the controller, which represents a virtual vacuum cleaner, completing the removal of static electricity. Finally, the static electricity of the device is manually discharged at this point. The whole operations are repeated for subsequent gameplay.

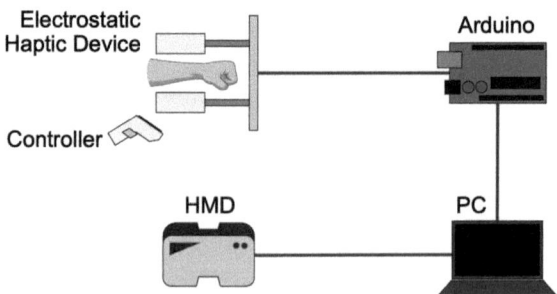

Fig. 1. System Overview.

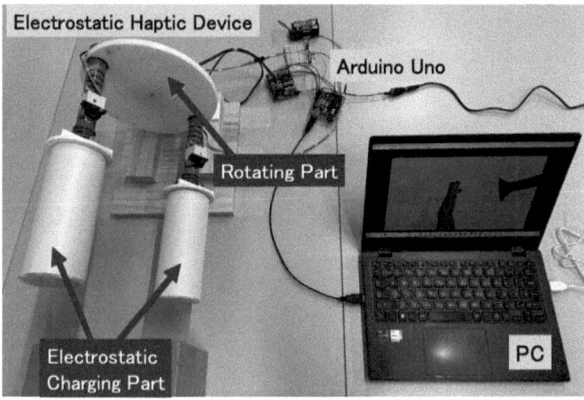

Fig. 2. Overview around the Electrostatic Haptic Device.

2.2 Electrostatic Haptic Device

Electrostatic Charging Part. In this study, we used a rod-shaped toy called the FunFlyStick [8] that functions as a small Van de Graaff generator, and generates positive static electricity. To allow for variable electrostatic intensity and adjustable presentation distance, we attach a 16.5 cm long aluminum can to the tip of the toy. Additionally, we made a sliding part to change the positions of the aluminum cans and to keep the distance between the forearm and the aluminum appropriate in the range from 7.8 cm to 13.0 cm. A servo motor (SG92R) with a servo horn was set at the switch of the toy to control turning it on and off.

Rotating Part. The rotating part of the device consists of a 21 cm diameter disk and a stepping motor (42HD4027-01, 1.8°/step, 400 mN · m) that controls the rotation of the electrostatic charging part. The Arduino Uno and the motor driver (A4988, 8–35 V, 2 A) are connected to a CNC shield (CNC SHIELD V3). Since there are two rods in the electrostatic charging part, each of the rods is rotated in the range from −90o 90° in 1° increments. The rotation speed is set to 10 rpm, where we have confirmed that rotation is possible at 0 to 20 rpm. Furthermore, to strengthen the tactile sensation of the static electricity to the skin and the arm hair, the rotating disk and the electrostatic charging part are oscillated back and forth with a swing angle of 10° at present at the determined location, to strengthen the presence of the static electricity while mitigating the discomfort caused by its intensity. Then, the oscillation frequency is approximately 3 Hz.

2.3 Rotation Control

The Arduino Uno controls the rotations of the stepping motor and the two servo motors. It also sends information on the virtual creature's position to the PC, and receives information from the PC on whether the creature has been vacuumed. The stepping motor controls the rotation angle, direction, and rotation speed of the motor.

Now, we explain how to deal with the creature's positional information. Figure 3(a) shows the initial state of the rotating disk with two rods horizontal to the ground, where the creature is at topmost 0° point. Rod 1 of the electrostatic charging part is located at −90°, and Rod 2 is located at +90°. We define the clockwise rotation to have a positive angle and the counterclockwise rotation to have a negative angle. After starting the system, the rotating part is rotated with a random angle in the range of −90° and +90°, which implies that each of the two rods moves only along the semi-circular path. After the rotation is executed, either of the rods is randomly chosen and charged. As an example, Fig. 3(b) shows the state in which the rotating disk rotates +90° from the initial state and then Rod 2 is activated and charged. In this case, the creature is considered to have moved from the topmost 0° point to the +180° point, and the string "180", which is the difference of the angle, is sent to the PC as the creature's positional information. The PC makes the creature appear in the virtual space based on this information. After the creature is vacuumed using a VR controller that represents the vacuum cleaner, we remove the charged static electricity manually at this point, which should be desirable to be done automatically, and restart the play by sending a signal from the PC to the Arduino Uno on the new information of the rod and location to be charged. Figure 3(c) shows the case when the disk rotates −45° from the state shown in Fig. 3(b) and then Rod 1 is activated and changed. In this case, the creature moves from the +180° point to the −45° point, so the angle difference, "−225", expresses the new position of the creature.

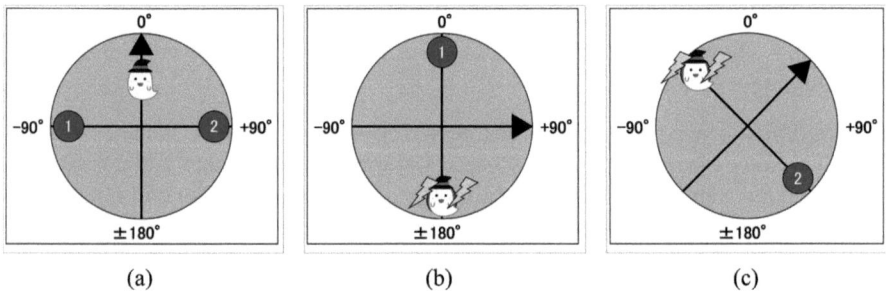

Fig. 3. Locations of Rods 1 and 2 and the Creature. (a) Initial state; (b) Rotated +90° and Rod 2 is charged; and (c) Further rotated −45° and Rod 1 is charged.

3 VR Application

The VR content of this study was developed using Unity. A user tries to find an invisible virtual creature of static electricity through electrostatic sensation felt on the skin and uses a VR controller to vacuum them. The determination of the creature's location and the vacuum trigger is based on whether a transparent virtual cylinder extending from the controller's position makes contact with where the creature is located. Upon contact, the creature is stretched out in place for one second, followed by a process using Unity's LookAt function to orient the creature towards the vacuum cleaner while simultaneously shrinking and moving towards it.

Arm tracking was implemented using Unity's Animation Rigging package. Specifically, the virtual camera and arms were created to move in correspondence with the user's head orientation and the positions of their left and right arms in the real world. Currently, the system displays the virtual arms close to the actual arm positions and is playable, but the virtual arms are sometimes displayed in misaligned positions due to incomplete parameter adjustments. Therefore, further refinement of arm tracking and realistic visualization is still required.

4 Demonstration

Here we show the demonstration of the VR content using the presented electrostatic haptic device. Within the virtual environment, the user attempts to identify the location of the invisible creature associated with static electricity through tactile sensations. Upon detection, the user vacuums the creature using a controller rendered as a vacuum cleaner. Figure 4 shows the initial setup, in which the user wears an HMD (Meta Quest 3S) and sits in front of the device with the left forearm resting on a platform, positioned centrally between the two rods of the device. To enhance the perception of electrostatic stimulation, users are instructed to roll up their sleeve and expose the forearm. When the system is activated, the electrostatic haptic device begins operating, delivering static electricity from one of the rods. Then the user moves the controller toward the area on the forearm where the sensation is perceived. If the controller is directed near the actual location of the virtual creature, the creature appears visually in the VR environment and is vacuumed into the cleaner. Figure 5 shows a sequence of images illustrating the process of identifying and capturing the creature using the virtual cleaner.

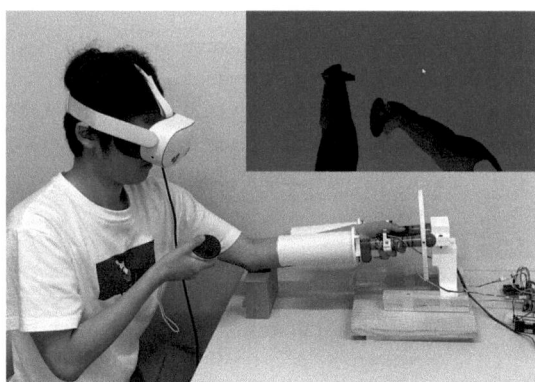

Fig. 4. User Wearing an HMD Positioned in Front of the Electrostatic Haptic Device.

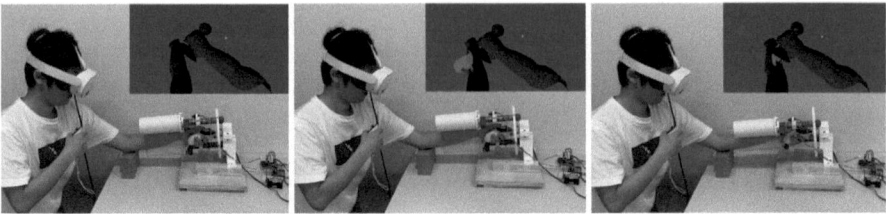

Fig. 5. A Sequence of Play of Removing the Virtual Electrostatic Creature.

5 Discussion

5.1 Perception of Static Electricity

Currently, the electrostatic stimulation delivered by the charging components is generally weak and often imperceptible when the rods are held stationary. However, according to the experiences of the authors and several nearby individuals, oscillating the rotating part enhances the perceived "fluffy" sensation of the electrostatic stimulation. This effect was noticeable even on areas of the forearm with little or no body hair. Additionally, prolonged charging over several tens of seconds occasionally resulted in a subtle tingling sensation. Therefore, the introduction of oscillatory motion is considered effective not only in enhancing the perception of electrostatic stimulation, but also in reducing the unpleasant sensation of tingling. Exploring how changes in the frequency of the oscillation and intensity of the static electricity affect user's experiences is the challenge for future study.

5.2 Removal of Static Electricity

Regarding removal of static electricity, while a single session of play can be completed, an automatic discharge function for the accumulated static electricity has not yet been implemented, necessitating manual discharge, which remains a challenge. As a potential solution, we are considering adding a mechanism that would simultaneously contact a conductor with the static electricity charging part upon defeating a creature.

5.3 Drive Noise of the Device

The presented device is intended for locating the position of charged static electricity, but the drive noise of the electrostatic charging part inadvertently provided a means to partially predict its location, which is a challenge to be improved. In addition to implementing a design with higher soundproofing, using headphone could block external auditory and visual information, potentially enhancing the immersion of the experience.

6 Concluding Remarks

We have developed an entertainment system that includes the electrostatic haptic device for perceiving and eliminating static electricity presented on the forearm. For the system, we presented and implemented an idea of oscillating a charged rod to enhance the electrostatic stimulation while remaining the amount of charge to be low. So far, we have confirmed the basic operation of both the device and the VR content for the user to play identifying the location of the presented static electricity in the virtual space. As future work, we plan to measure the amount of electrostatic charge accumulated over time in order to ensure user safety during evaluation and interaction. In addition, implementing a mechanism to discharge static electricity is an urgent requirement. Following these improvements, we intend to conduct user evaluations to investigate how the rod's oscillation affects the perception of electrostatic stimulation, as well as to assess the overall play experience provided by the system.

Acknowledgments. This work was supported by JSPS Grant-in-Aid for Scientific Research(C) 24K15250.

Disclosure of Interests. The authors have no competing interests to declare that are relevant to the content of this article.

References

1. Fukushima, A., Kajimoto, H.: Facilitating a surprised feeling by artificial control of piloerection on the forearm. In: Proceedings of the 3rd Augmented Human International Conference, vol. 8, pp. 1–4 (2012). https://doi.org/10.1145/2160125.216013
2. Fukushima, S., Kajimoto, H.: Chilly chair: facilitating an emotional feeling with artificial piloerection. SIGGRAPH Emerg. Technol. **5**, 1 (2012). https://doi.org/10.1145/2343456.23434
3. Iriarte, N., et al.: Contactless electrostatic piloerection for haptic sensations. IEEE Trans. Haptics **17**(2), 140–151 (2024). https://doi.org/10.1109/TOH.2023.3269885
4. Takiguchi, K., Toyama, S.: Does a dog recognize his master by an electric field? Generation and transmission of an electric field around a walker. J. Int. Soc. Life Inf. Sci. **21**(2), 428–441 (2003). https://doi.org/10.18936/islis.21.2_428
5. Suzuki, K., Abe, K., and Sato, H.: Proposal of perception method of existence of objects in 3D space using quasi-electrostatic field. In Design, User Experience, and Usability. Design for Contemporary Interactive Environments (HCII 2020), LNCS, vol. 12201, pp. 561–571. Springer, Heidelberg (2020). https://doi.org/10.1007/978-3-030-49760-6_40
6. Karasawa, M., Kajimoto, H.: Presentation of a feeling of presence using an electrostatic field. In: CHI EA '21: Extended Abstracts of the 2021 CHI Conference on Human Factors in Computing Systems, vol. 285, pp. 1–4 (2021). https://doi.org/10.1145/3411763.345176
7. Call from Merry (2019), IVRC History Archive. http://ivrc.net/archive/%E3%83%A1%E3%83%AA%E3%83%BC%E3%81%95%E3%82%93%E3%81%AE%E9%9B%BB%E8%A9%B12019/. Accessed 10 June 2025
8. The FunFlyStick – for kids or the easily amused. https://www.shinyshiny.tv/2009/01/the_fun flystick.html. Accessed 10 June 2025

Designing Physically Fiction: Suspension of Disbelief in Interaction with MR Environments

Toshiro Kashiwagi(✉) and Kumiyo Nakakoji

Future University Hakodate, Hakodate, Japan
{g3120001,kumiyo}@fun.ac.jp

Abstract. This paper presents DITTO-Mirror, a Mixed Reality (MR) system that explores how users construct, maintain, and question fictional logic during interaction. In DITTO-Mirror, a virtual object appears to be reflected in a real mirror, despite the absence of any physical reflection. This illusion is created using two identical virtual objects: one is directly manipulated by the user, while the other is placed in a mirror-symmetric position relative to the real mirror, creating the appearance of a reflection. Users interacting with this system readily accept the mirrored object as part of the real world, exhibiting behaviors consistent with their belief in its physicality. However, when a second mirror is placed—one not recognized by the system and therefore not displaying the mirror virtual object—users experience discomfort and confusion. This reaction highlights a disruption not in visual realism, but in the fictional coherence they had come to internalize. These moments reveal that belief in MR is actively constructed and can be strategically challenged to provoke reflection and curiosity. We argue that MR can serve as a medium of designed fictionality, where belief and disbelief are not passive states but dynamic, interactive processes.

Keywords: Mixed Reality · Fictionality · Suspension of Disbelief

1 Introduction

Mixed Reality (MR) is a technology that enables users to operate and experience a space where the real and virtual worlds are seamlessly integrated. Previous research on MR has often evaluated MR environments in terms of reality (the sense of physical realism) and virtuality (the degree of immersion in the virtual). However, our previous work has proposed the concept of *fictionality* as a crucial factor in how users enjoy interactions within MR environments [10].

In this context, *fictionality* refers to phenomena or interactions that are artificially designed yet perceived and accepted as if they were natural. In entertainment media such as novels, films, games, and theater, fiction has long been a central element. Audiences knowingly engage with fiction and immerse themselves in it with an active willingness to enjoy it.

This cognitive attitude is commonly known in the entertainment field as the Suspension of Disbelief. It describes the mental process by which audiences or players temporarily accept the unrealistic elements of a fictional world in order to fully engage with and enjoy the experience. We propose that this Suspension of Disbelief also plays a significant role in user interactions within MR environments.

In this paper, we explore this perspective through the case study of the MR environment DITTO-Mirror [9], focusing on how users enjoy and actively engage with *fictionality* as a basis for interaction. In particular, DITTO-Mirror presents an intriguing phenomenon: while users naturally accept the fictional effect of virtual objects appearing in a single mirror, they often experience discomfort or a sense of strangeness when the same virtual objects fail to appear in a second mirror—despite this being physically accurate.

Our aim is not to simulate a mirror reflection in a realistic manner, but to explore how users cognitively adopt and internalize a fictional logic embedded in the interaction. It is not the appearance of the reflection that matters, but the user's belief that the reflection "should" be there—an expectation constructed through prior fictional engagement.

2 Related Work

2.1 Constructive Engagement with Fictionality

Across literature, theater, and games, engagement with fiction is understood not as passive immersion but as a constructive process shaped by coherence and consistency. Busselle and Bilandzic [4] argue that audiences evaluate fictional experiences through perceived realism, including both external resemblance to the real world and internal narrative consistency. Absorption arises when these dimensions align, drawing attention away from the real world.

Walton's theory of make-believe [19] describes fictional engagement as a rule-based imaginative activity, where users knowingly treat real-world stimuli—called "props"—as representations of fictional entities within a shared game of make-believe. This framework highlights that belief in fiction is not deception but a consensual act, structured by implicit principles of generation. It extends to games and interactive media, where players actively participate in and help shape the fictional logic [8,18].

In MR, such constructive fictionality becomes especially salient. Users remain physically in the real world while interacting with fictional elements, creating a dual presence. Rather than full immersion, users adopt and navigate fictional logic layered onto their surroundings. Thus, the coherence between real and virtual elements—rather than visual realism alone—underpins the experience of belief and engagement.

2.2 Immersive VR/MR Experiences

In VR research, immersion is often discussed through the concept of presence. Slater [15] [16] defines presence as a combination of Place Illusion (PI)—the sensation of being physically located in a virtual environment—and Plausibility Illusion (Psi)—the sense that events occurring in that environment are actually happening. Both components are considered essential to realistic user responses.

In MR, however, users retain direct visual access to the real world, making PI less central [11]. Instead, the key factor becomes plausibility: the degree to which virtual elements are perceived as consistent with the real-world environment [14].

Skarbez et al. [13] argue that plausibility is shaped by coherence—the visual, physical, and semantic consistency of the environment. For instance, Regenbrecht et al. [12] show that plausibility improves when virtual lighting conditions match those of the real setting.

The CaP (Congruence and Plausibility) model by Latoschik and Wienrich [11] builds on this, explaining plausibility as a multi-layered phenomenon that emerges from congruence across sensory, perceptual, and cognitive levels. Recent studies further support this model, demonstrating that disruptions in congruence negatively affect the realism and internal consistency of MR experiences [2,3,20].

Because MR requires users to interpret virtual elements within the persistent context of the real world, structured plausibility becomes essential for maintaining engagement and belief.

2.3 Fictionality in MR Environments

Some MR experiences are not aimed at realism, but at inviting users to engage with virtual elements as if they naturally belong in the physical world. These experiences rely not on visual fidelity, but on a form of designed fiction that users want to believe.

Projects such as Kobito [1] and Meta Flowers [17] demonstrate this approach by seamlessly blending virtual elements into physical contexts. In Kobito, a small virtual humanoid appears to push a real tea can, while Meta Flowers shows virtual flowers casting shadows aligned with real lighting. These designs create coherent illusions that feel intuitively believable.

Other works intentionally manipulate causality or coherence to provoke reflection. In DOMINO Toppling [7], real and virtual dominoes trigger one another in both directions, building a unified causal chain across physical and virtual spaces. Reality Rifts [5] disrupts perceptual causality to create moments of surprise and ambiguity. AsyncReality [6] explores asynchronous virtual phenomena while preserving causal logic.

Such examples show that MR fictionality is not about deceiving users with realism, but about constructing interactive experiences that users can actively believe in—even when those experiences defy physical expectations.

Unlike prior works, which aim to maintain user immersion by concealing technological inconsistencies, this study intentionally introduces subtle incoherences to expose the very process by which belief is formed. Rather than avoiding disruption, it explores it as a design strategy—highlighting how moments of breakage can become part of a dynamic, interactive process of belief and disbelief in MR.

3 Implementation Example in DITTO-Mirror

In this study, we approach experiences in Mixed Reality (MR) environments not from the traditional perspective of "reproducing a sense of reality," but rather through the lens of how fictionality is designed and perceived. DITTO-Mirror is a tool designed to create an MR experience in which a virtual object appears to be reflected in a real mirror.

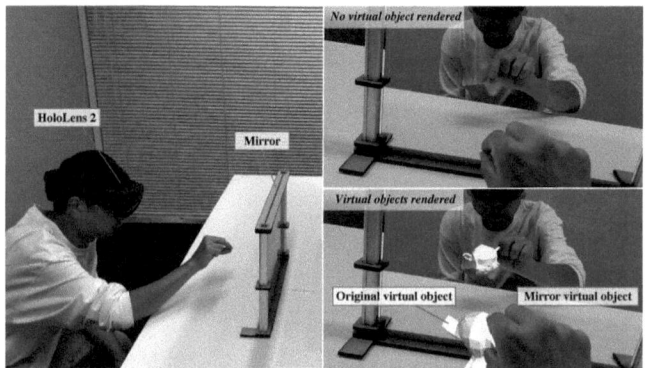

Fig. 1. Overview of the DITTO-Mirror experience. Left: A third-person view of a user wearing a HoloLens 2 while interacting with DITTO-Mirror. Right: The user's perspective captured through the HoloLens 2. (Top right) The view without rendering the virtual object. (Bottom right) The same view with the virtual object rendered.

3.1 System Setup

Figure 1 shows the overview of the DITTO-Mirror experience, Fig. 2 illustrates the system configuration. Users wear a HoloLens 2 headset, which allows them to see both the real surroundings and virtual objects simultaneously through its transparent display. The system is developed using Unity 2019.4 LTS and the Mixed Reality Toolkit (MRTK).

A flat mirror measuring 400 mm in width and 300 mm in height is used as the main physical component. It is mounted vertically on a stand, and an infrared reflective marker is attached to the upper right corner of the mirror. This marker allows the HoloLens 2's sensor cameras to detect the position and orientation of the mirror, which serves as a reference for rendering the reflection of virtual objects.

As for the virtual object, a 3D model of a chimpanzee head is used. This model was selected because it has a clearly distinguishable front and back, which helps users to easily determine whether the object is being viewed directly or as a mirror reflection. In contrast to simple geometric shapes such as cubes or spheres, Suzanne's facial and cranial features provide intuitive visual cues about its orientation, thereby improving spatial perception and interaction accuracy.

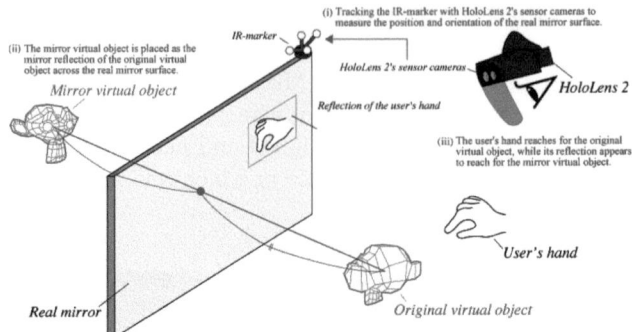

Fig. 2. System configuration of DITTO-Mirror

3.2 Interaction Mechanism

As users interact with the virtual object in front of the mirror, they can see its reflection moving on the other side of the mirror, just as they would expect from a real mirror. Although no actual optical reflection occurs, the system generates a mirrored counterpart that behaves as if it were a real reflection. Internally, two virtual objects are created: the *original virtual object*, which the user manipulates through hand gestures, and the *mirror virtual object*, which is positioned and oriented as the mirror image of the original with respect to the mirror plane.

The *mirror virtual object* is rendered conditionally, appearing only when it would be visible within the mirror's reflective area from the user's perspective. When it falls outside this range, it becomes hidden from view. This selective rendering creates the impression that the virtual object is truly reflected in the mirror, rather than being an independent duplicate.

The system operates through the following three steps (Fig. 2). First, (i) the position and orientation of the mirror surface—including its normal vector— are acquired in real time by the HoloLens 2, which tracks an infrared reflective marker attached to the mirror. Next, (ii) using this spatial information, the system calculates the mirror-symmetric position and orientation of the original virtual object with respect to the mirror plane and places the mirror virtual object at the computed coordinates. Finally, (iii) when users observe both their own reflected hand and the mirror virtual object within the mirror simultaneously, the visual consistency between the two allows them to perceive the interaction as if their real hand is affecting the mirrored object. Through this process, the system constructs an MR experience in which the fictional mirror image, though not physically present, is naturally integrated into the user's perception as if it were part of the real mirrored world.

The *mirror virtual object* appears visually consistent with the reflected real environment, including the user's body and surrounding real objects, as if it were naturally part of the mirror image. For example, when a user reaches out to grasp the *original virtual object*, their mirrored hand appears to reach for the *mirror virtual object* in perfect alignment. If a real object such as a cube is

Fig. 3. View from the user's perspective while playing DITTO-Mirror with a HoloLens 2. The blue dotted rectangle indicates the area corresponding to the mirror surface. Left: The *mirror virtual object* appears above the reflected cube, maintaining spatial consistency with the real environment. Right: As the user moves the *original virtual object* toward the edge of the mirror, the *mirror virtual object* gradually disappears from view, mimicking the natural behavior of real reflections.

placed in front of the mirror, and the *original virtual object* is positioned above it, the *mirror virtual object* also appears above the reflected cube, maintaining spatial consistency (Fig. 3, left). When the user moves the *original virtual object* toward the edge of the mirror, the *mirror virtual object* gradually disappears from view—just as parts of the user's body would vanish at the edge of a real reflection (Fig. 3, right). This seamless visual coherence among the real world, the user's movements, and the virtual content aligns with the natural physical behavior one would expect from a real mirror.

Importantly, the value of this interaction does not lie in the visual mimicry of reflection itself, but in how users come to integrate the fictional reflection into their understanding of the environment, thereby constructing and updating a mental model that blends real and unreal causality.

Fig. 4. View from the user's perspective with a HoloLens 2 after an additional mirror is introduced. The mirror virtual object is visible through the original mirror surface (blue dashed line), but not through the added mirror surface (yellow dashed line).

4 User Experience and Sample Comments

A few participants were invited to casually experience the DITTO-Mirror system for observational purposes, during which their behaviors and verbal reactions were recorded.

Without any prior explanation that virtual objects would appear to be "reflected" in a real mirror, participants encountering this phenomenon for the first time accepted it with surprising ease. For example, some were observed moving the original virtual object as if treating the mirrored virtual object as its natural reflection. One participant, for instance, moved the original virtual object horizontally in front of the mirror, seemingly checking whether the mirrored virtual object would move accordingly within the mirror. Another participant leaned their body and walked around to the side of the mirror, peering in from an angle to better observe how the mirrored virtual object appeared from that perspective. In this way, participants interacted with the virtual phenomenon not as fiction to be questioned, but as if it were simply part of the real world.

In the latter part of the experience, a second mirror—identical in appearance to the original—was placed next to it. However, the system did not render a corresponding mirror virtual object for this newly added mirror. Figure 4 shows the user's perspective after the second mirror was introduced. As a result, all participants appeared confused when the virtual object did not appear in the left-side mirror. For example, some responded with remarks such as, "Even though the virtual object is reflected in the front mirror, looking into the left mirror makes it feel like I'm touching something empty," and "What's going on? I couldn't tell which one was the real mirror."

These reactions suggest that, although virtual objects would not normally appear in real mirrors according to real-world logic, participants had already constructed a consistent fictional expectation that "in this environment, virtual objects appear in real mirrors." When this expectation was violated, cognitive dissonance emerged, and the coherent fictional world they had come to accept collapsed under physical constraints.

5 Discussion

5.1 Fictionality Beyond Visual Realism

User engagement in MR is not solely grounded in visual realism, but in the plausibility of a fictional logic. In DITTO-Mirror, users readily accepted the illusion of a virtual mirror reflection, even without being told it would occur. However, when a second mirror failed to reflect the same object, this break in internal consistency caused confusion and discomfort.

This suggests that what matters is not how "real" something looks, but whether it makes sense within the internal logic of the experience. As in narrative theory and game studies, users are willing to suspend disbelief not for the sake of realism, but for coherence. The moment this coherence breaks, belief is shaken—even if the system itself is functioning correctly.

5.2 Incongruence as Reflective Engagement

These moments of incongruence do not merely disrupt the experience—they provoke users to question what is real and why. In DITTO-Mirror, the absence of a reflection in the second mirror led not to the suspicion of a malfunction, but to a deeper cognitive puzzle: "Why doesn't this mirror work?" or more strikingly, "Which one is the real mirror?"

This confusion reveals a cognitive inversion. Users begin to judge "mirrorness" not by physical correctness, but by whether it aligns with the logic they've come to accept. The fictional behavior has, in a sense, become their new baseline for what feels real. Such moments mark a shift from passive observation to reflective engagement, unique to MR's overlay of fiction onto the physical world.

5.3 Designing MR Entertainment Through Fictional Desire

The question "Which one is the real mirror?" encapsulates the heart of MR fictionality. It demonstrates that when users internalize fictional logic, they may begin to interpret physical reality through that lens. The fictional world does not simply coexist with the real—it reframes it.

This insight supports the idea that MR entertainment can be designed not around deception or illusion, but around belief as a conditional, creative act. When users find the fictional behavior more intuitive than the physical one, fictionality is no longer something to suspend—but something to explore, question, and engage with meaningfully.

6 Conclusion

This study explored how fictional elements are cognitively accepted and maintained in MR environments, using DITTO-Mirror as a case study. We observed that users tended to quickly incorporate fictional reflections into their understanding of the environment, and that disruptions to this fiction could evoke a sense of discomfort—suggesting that belief in MR may rely less on realism and more on coherence. We argue that fictionality is not only a tool for immersion, but also a design material for creating moments of engagement, wonder, and reflection. By comparing MR with other entertainment media such as games and literature, we emphasized the importance of suspension of disbelief as a dynamic, interactive process. In future work, we aim to develop a typology of fictional engagement in MR and explore how different user groups construct and navigate fictional logics. These insights contribute to an emerging framework for designing MR experiences centered on belief rather than illusion.

References

1. Aoki, T., et al.: Kobito: virtual brownies. In: ACM SIGGRAPH 2005 Emerging Technologies, SIGGRAPH '05, pp. 11–es. Association for Computing Machinery, New York (2005). https://doi.org/10.1145/1187297.1187309

2. Brübach, L., Westermeier, F., Wienrich, C., Latoschik, M.E.: Breaking plausibility without breaking presence - evidence for the multi-layer nature of plausibility. IEEE Trans. Visual Comput. Graph. **28**(5), 2267–2276 (2022). https://doi.org/10.1109/TVCG.2022.3150496
3. Brübach, L., Westermeier, F., Wienrich, C., Latoschik, M.E.: A systematic evaluation of incongruencies and their influence on plausibility in virtual reality. In: 2023 IEEE International Symposium on Mixed and Augmented Reality (ISMAR), pp. 894–901 (2023). https://doi.org/10.1109/ISMAR59233.2023.00105
4. Busselle, R.W., Bilandzic, H.: Fictionality and perceived realism in experiencing stories: a model of narrative comprehension and engagement. Commun. Theory **18**, 255–280 (2008)
5. Cheng, L.P., Chen, Y., Peng, Y.H., Holz, C.: Reality rifts: wonderful interfaces by disrupting perceptual causality. In: Proceedings of the 2023 CHI Conference on Human Factors in Computing Systems, CHI '23. Association for Computing Machinery, New York (2023). https://doi.org/10.1145/3544548.3581454
6. Fender, A.R., Holz, C.: Causality-preserving asynchronous reality. In: Proceedings of the 2022 CHI Conference on Human Factors in Computing Systems, CHI '22. Association for Computing Machinery, New York (2022). https://doi.org/10.1145/3491102.3501836
7. Hirata, R., et al.: Domino toppling: an mr attraction focusing on r-v continuum. Trans. Virt. Real. Soc. Jpn. **21**(3), 463–472 (2016). https://doi.org/10.18974/tvrsj.21.3_463
8. Jørgensen, K.: Gameworld interfaces as make-believe. In: Turner, P., Harviainen, J.T. (eds.) Digital Make-Believe. HIS, pp. 89–99. Springer, Cham (2016). https://doi.org/10.1007/978-3-319-29553-4_6
9. Kashiwagi, T., Yamamoto, T., Nakakoji, K.: Interfering virtual worlds and unnatural real worlds. In: IPSJ SIG Technical Report on Entertainment Computing (EC), pp. 1–8 (2023). (in Japanese)
10. Kashiwagi, T., Yamamoto, Y., Nakakoji, K.: Reframing problems: analyzing the design of mixed reality tools through the lens of fictionality, pp. 173–183. Springer, Singapore (2025). https://doi.org/10.1007/978-981-96-0668-9_12
11. Latoschik, M.E., Wienrich, C.: Congruence and plausibility, not presence: pivotal conditions for xr experiences and effects, a novel approach. Front. Virt. Real. **3** (2022). https://doi.org/10.3389/frvir.2022.694433
12. Regenbrecht, H., Meng, K., Reepen, A., Beck, S., Langlotz, T.: Mixed voxel reality: presence and embodiment in low fidelity, visually coherent, mixed reality environments. In: 2017 IEEE International Symposium on Mixed and Augmented Reality (ISMAR), pp. 90–99 (2017). https://doi.org/10.1109/ISMAR.2017.26
13. Skarbez, R., Brooks, Jr., F.P., Whitton, M.C.: A survey of presence and related concepts. ACM Comput. Surv. **50**(6) (2017). https://doi.org/10.1145/3134301
14. Skarbez, R., Smith, M., Whitton, M.C.: Revisiting milgram and kishino's reality-virtuality continuum. Front. Virt. Real. **2** (2021). https://doi.org/10.3389/frvir.2021.647997
15. Slater, M.: Place illusion and plausibility can lead to realistic behaviour in immersive virtual environments. Phil. Trans. R. Soc. B: Biol. Sci. **364**(1535), 3549–3557 (2009). https://doi.org/10.1098/rstb.2009.0138
16. Slater, M., Banakou, D., Beacco, A., Gallego, J., Macia-Varela, F., Oliva, R.: A separate reality: an update on place illusion and plausibility in virtual reality. Front. Virt. Real. **3** (2022). https://doi.org/10.3389/frvir.2022.914392

17. Sonobe, K., Furukawa, M., Yamanaka, A., Ohmura, H., Shibayama, T., Nakagawa, R.: Meta flowers: an analogy of life in the xr era. In: ACM SIGGRAPH 2022 Immersive Pavilion, SIGGRAPH '22. Association for Computing Machinery, New York (2022). https://doi.org/10.1145/3532834.3536199
18. Turner, S., Huang, C.W., Burrows, L., Turner, P.: Make-believing virtual realities, pp. 27–47. Springer, Cham (2016). https://doi.org/10.1007/978-3-319-29553-4_3
19. Walton, K.L.: Mimesis as Make-Believe: On the Foundations of the Representational Arts. Harvard University Press, Cambridge (1990)
20. Westermeier, F., Brübach, L., Latoschik, M.E., Wienrich, C.: Exploring plausibility and presence in mixed reality experiences. IEEE Trans. Visual Comput. Graph. **29**(5), 2680–2689 (2023). https://doi.org/10.1109/TVCG.2023.3247046

Simulating AI-Human Collaborative Strategies in Sudoku Puzzle Generation

Mohd Nor Akmal Khalid[1,2,3]

[1] Faculty of Information Science and Technology, Universiti Kebangsaan Malaysia, Bangi, Malaysia
akmal@ukm.edu.my
[2] Research Center for Artificial Intelligence Technology, Universiti Kebangsaan Malaysia, Bangi, Malaysia
[3] Data Mining and Computational Intelligence, Universiti Kebangsaan Malaysia, Bangi, Malaysia

Abstract. This paper explores AI-human collaboration in Sudoku puzzle generation by simulating five distinct co-creative strategies without relying on real-time user input. While prior work in AI-assisted puzzle generation has focused on static outputs or human-in-the-loop systems, this study introduces a rule-based human agent to systematically evaluate interaction dynamics. The framework integrates AI solvers with a simulated human model, using metrics such as difficulty, symmetry, and conflict resolution to assess puzzle quality. Preliminary experiments reveal that hybrid strategies, especially turn-based and negotiation-based collaboration, yield more balanced and aesthetically pleasing puzzles than AI-only approaches. While the findings provide initial insights into procedural content blending technical solvability with human-like creativity, this study represents an initial step toward modeling collaborative puzzle design. Future research should incorporate real human participant studies and incorporate game design heuristics to enrich evaluation beyond algorithmic measures.

Keywords: Human-AI Collaboration · Procedural Content Generation · Sudoku Puzzle Design · Co-Creative Systems

1 Introduction

Collaboration between artificial intelligence (AI) and humans in creative tasks is increasingly viewed as a synergistic partnership, with each contributing distinct strengths [22,34]. As AI evolves, it is shifting from a passive tool to an active collaborator in domains such as art, music, design, and storytelling [2,21].

Human-AI co-creativity fosters novel expression through mutual collaboration, where communication, intention alignment, and adaptability are key [3,23,36]. In organizations, AI promotes creativity by facilitating knowledge sharing and expanding ideation [11,19]. However, ethical concerns and the risk of homogenization call for AI to complement not replace human creativity, ensuring emotional and social dimensions remain central [25].

Sudoku offers a compelling testbed for exploring AI-human collaboration in problem-solving. As an NP-complete task, it exemplifies computational complexity and is ideal for studying advanced AI techniques alongside human heuristics [24,29]. The puzzle's logical demands make it suitable for assessing AI's role in enhancing human reasoning. Tools like the "Sudoku Assistant" use machine learning and constraint programming to provide real-time feedback and guidance [30].

In puzzle design theory, perceived difficulty is influenced not only by the number of clues but also by the cognitive strategies required during problem solving, such as pattern recognition, logical inference, and search efficiency. Cognitive load, perceptual fluency, and solver heuristics all play critical roles in how challenging a puzzle feels to human players [26,32]. While the present study investigates co-creative AI-human interactions through simulation, it represents an exploratory step in a broader research program. Further integration of puzzle design heuristics and empirical player evaluation will be needed to fully characterize the co-creative design space.

AI methods such as convolutional neural networks, genetic algorithms, and belief propagation have been successfully applied to Sudoku, blending computational power with human-inspired strategies. These hybrid systems enable feedback loops where AI both learns from and refines human approaches [12,15,18].

Despite advances in automated puzzle generation, the dynamics of AI-human collaboration in this domain remain underexplored. Existing approaches often depend on real-time human input, which limits scalability and reproducibility. This paper addresses the need for a simulation-based framework to model and analyze collaborative puzzle creation without relying on actual user data. Specifically, the study simulates various AI-human interaction strategies in Sudoku generation by implementing a rule-based agent that mimics human design behavior. Through systematic evaluation of each strategy using metrics such as difficulty, aesthetics, and generation efficiency the research aims to explore how simulated co-creation influences puzzle quality and process dynamics.

2 Related Works

2.1 Existing Collaborative Frameworks

Recent literature on AI-assisted puzzle generation and human-AI collaboration underscores growing interest in how AI enhances creativity across domains. In games and puzzles, AI not only generates complex content autonomously but also augments human input, enabling adaptive, co-creative experiences [14]. Generative models personalize content in real time, boosting engagement for both entertainment and learning purposes [17].

Human-AI co-creativity has gained momentum, with studies demonstrating AI's ability to foster innovation in areas ranging from programming puzzles to the arts [16,27]. In puzzle games, AI adapts to user skill levels, supporting richer and more educational interactions [28]. Nevertheless, biases against AI-generated content underscore the importance of transparency and trust in co-creative systems [6]. Addressing these concerns is crucial for the broader acceptance of AI in creative practices.

2.2 AI-Assisted Puzzle Generation

Literature on AI-assisted puzzle generation, particularly in word puzzles, reflects a growing synergy between artificial intelligence (AI) and human creativity, encompassing both technical and cognitive dimensions. One study emphasizes contextual consistency in puzzle design [20], while another replicate human-like reasoning in syllacrostic puzzles, illustrating AI's cognitive alignment with human strategies [13].

An algorithmic approaches were proposed for unconstrained crossword generation, addressing word selection, grid layout, and clue synthesis [1]. Meanwhile, another work focuses on the semantic interpretation that supports AI's ability to generate linguistically coherent content [8]. Beyond method design, psychological factors in human-AI interaction can enhance performance of AI assistance [10], but potential biases in language models raising ethical concerns in AI-driven puzzle content [4].

In the context of procedural content generation, prior work has addressed how content creators leverage domain heuristics and cognitive principles to balance difficulty and player engagement, particularly in level design and puzzle generation domains [26]. While our current work does not incorporate such player-centered difficulty models, these frameworks offer valuable directions for enhancing future human-in-the-loop co-creation systems.

2.3 Human-AI Collaboration in Problem Solving

Research on human-AI collaboration spans education (like collaborative skills [31] and adaptive support to enhance speaking skills [37]) and healthcare (performance variability in novice dental clinicians [9] and help medical students interpret complex cases [5]), highlighting AI's potential to augment human capabilities alongside challenges in integration.

However, trust remains an issue where reported patients' preference for human providers despite AI's potential accuracy, had stressed the need for transparency [33]. AI also contributes to social and creative domains. Dialogue systems enhance interpersonal communication [35], while advocates for AI that empowers human creativity rather than replacing it [7].

While existing research has explored AI's role in puzzle generation, human-AI co-creativity, and collaborative problem-solving across domains, there remains a gap in understanding how different AI-human interaction strategies affect the process and outcomes of puzzle design. Most studies either rely on real-time human input or focus on static AI outputs, limiting systematic comparisons of collaboration modes. This paper addresses that gap by simulating various co-creative strategies in Sudoku generation, enabling controlled analysis of collaborative dynamics without requiring human subject data.

3 Methodology

The proposed system framework (Fig. 1) consists of three main modules: (1) the *Puzzle Generator Module*, responsible for generating complete, valid Sudoku solutions; (2) the *Difficulty Estimator*, which classifies puzzle complexity based on heuristic metrics; and (3) the *Simulation Controller*, which orchestrates collaborative interactions between the AI solver and the simulated human agent.

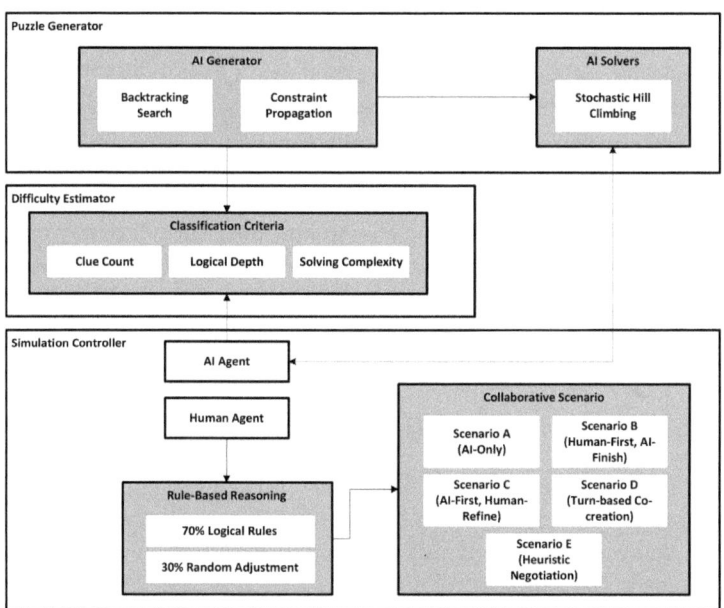

Fig. 1. Proposed Human-AI collaboration framework.

The *Puzzle Generator Module* uses AI solvers like backtracking search, constraint propagation, and stochastic hill-climbing to create complete Sudoku grids with unique solutions, whereas the *Difficulty Estimator* classifies puzzles into easy, medium, or hard based on clue count, logical depth, and solving complexity. The simulated human agent operates under a rule-based framework that reflects common human design heuristics, such as favoring symmetrical layouts, avoiding oversimplified solving paths, and targeting clue counts between 25 and 30. This rule-based approach provides a controlled proxy for human decision-making in the absence of real player data, enabling systematic comparison across interaction strategies. The proposed system framework was developed in Python 3.11

on a machine equipped with an Intel Core i7-11700 @ 2.50GHz processor and 32GB DDR4 RAM.

Five collaboration scenarios were simulated. Scenario A (AI-Only Creation) involves full AI control and serves as a baseline for puzzle quality and generation time. Scenario B (Human-First, AI-Finish) begins with the simulated human placing initial clues, followed by AI validation and completion capturing early human influence. In Scenario C (AI-First, Human-Refine), the AI generates a complete puzzle, which is then refined by the human before final AI verification, focusing on aesthetics.

Scenario D (Turn-Based Co-Creation) features alternating moves between the agents, ensuring puzzle solvability and uniqueness after each step. Finally, Scenario E (Heuristic Negotiation) involves both agents proposing moves concurrently, with a mediator selecting the best option based on a weighted score: Score $= 0.6 \times \text{AI}_{\text{Score}} + 0.4 \times \text{Human}_{\text{Score}}$.

The simulated human agent is governed by a rule-based framework that emulates commonly observed puzzle design behavior. Instead of relying on user data, the agent operates on internal heuristics such as favoring symmetric layouts, avoiding early simple solving paths, and maintaining a preferred clue count between 25 and 30.

To reflect human-like intuition, the model also incorporates probabilistic deviations. For instance, on each turn, there is a 70% chance the agent follows a logical rule, while the remaining 30% allows for a random adjustment. These rules are embedded within the collaboration controller and parameterized for flexibility across different experimental runs.

4 Preliminary Result and Discussion

Each of the five scenarios was run 100 times, producing a unique Sudoku puzzle per execution. During each run, puzzle metadata including move order, rule application, and intermediate states was logged for validation and reproducibility. To guarantee the integrity of the generated puzzles, a custom verification module was integrated into the simulation pipeline. This module ensures that each puzzle is both solvable and possesses a unique solution a core requirement for well-formed Sudoku.

A complete 9×9 grid is first generated using a backtracking-based solver that respects all Sudoku constraints across rows, columns, and 3×3 subgrids. Once a valid solution is established, selected clues are strategically removed to form playable puzzles based on the desired scenario configuration. Throughout this process, each puzzle undergoes a rule-based validity check to confirm that no constraint is violated. Only puzzles that pass this validation are included in the dataset, ensuring consistency and reproducibility across all experimental runs. This verification step addresses prior limitations and enhances the credibility of the simulation outcomes, providing a robust foundation for evaluating AI-human collaborative puzzle generation.

The recorded evaluation metrics include *difficulty classification*, where puzzles are labeled as Easy ($\geq$36 clues), Medium (3035 clues), or Hard (<30 clues), approximating solver challenge. *Generation time* (in seconds) measures how long each puzzle took to produce using AI and/or simulated human input. *AI and human move* counts track the number of clue placements made by each agent, offering insight into collaboration dynamics. The *symmetry score*, ranging from 0 to 1, assesses the visual balance of clue distribution, with higher values indicating more aesthetically pleasing layouts. Lastly, in Scenario E, the number of *conflicts resolved* captures how often the mediator had to choose between differing move proposals from AI and human agents. The summary of the experimental results were reported in Table 1.

Table 1. Summary of results by scenarios

Scenario	Gen_time		AI_moves		H_moves		S_score		Conflicts_res.	
	Mean	Std.	Mean	Std.	Mean	Std.	Mean	Std.	Mean	Std.
A	0.00016	0.00037	36.00000	0.00000	N/A	N/A	0.75180	0.09130	N/A	N/A
B	0.00016	0.00006	15.82000	3.15069	20.18000	3.15069	0.74340	0.08883	N/A	N/A
C	0.00013	0.00005	36.00000	0.00000	0.00000	0.00000	0.74890	0.08870	N/A	N/A
D	0.00022	0.00070	18.00000	0.00000	18.00000	0.00000	0.75290	0.08434	N/A	N/A
E	0.00017	0.00006	24.03000	2.72458	11.97000	2.72458	0.75310	0.09442	11.97000	2.72458

Gen_time: How fast the puzzle was constructed; **S_score**: symmetry scores (0–1); **AI/H̄_moves**: Number of contributions by each agent (AI/Human); **C_Resolve**: Number the mediator choose when conflicted (Scenario E);

To illustrate the practical outcomes of each collaboration scenario, representative puzzle-solution pairs were generated and analyzed (Fig. 2) using evaluation metrics such as generation time, agent contributions, symmetry score, and estimated difficulty.

All generated puzzles passed strict validity checks, resolving previous issues of rule violations and unsolvable grids. Scenario A, driven entirely by AI, efficiently produces puzzles but tends toward predictable difficulty and structure. In contrast, Scenario B allows human heuristics to introduce variability and challenge, though the final grid is still shaped by AI validation. Scenario C simulates editorial refinement, where AI offers structure and humans enhance presentation a common workflow in digital content generation.

Scenario D shows the strongest parity between AI and human contributions, resulting in balanced structural aesthetics and the highest average symmetry scores. Scenario E's negotiation model reveals dynamic interplay; conflict resolution occurs nearly 12 times per puzzle, indicating frequent agent disagreement, yet it maintains strong structural consistency. This scenario best represents co-creative systems that balance automated logic with user preferences. These results validate the potential of structured AI-human interactions in procedural puzzle generation, with direct implications for entertainment computing, game design, and interactive educational tools.

Although our evaluation uses quantitative metrics to characterize puzzle properties, these measures do not fully capture aesthetic or experiential aspects

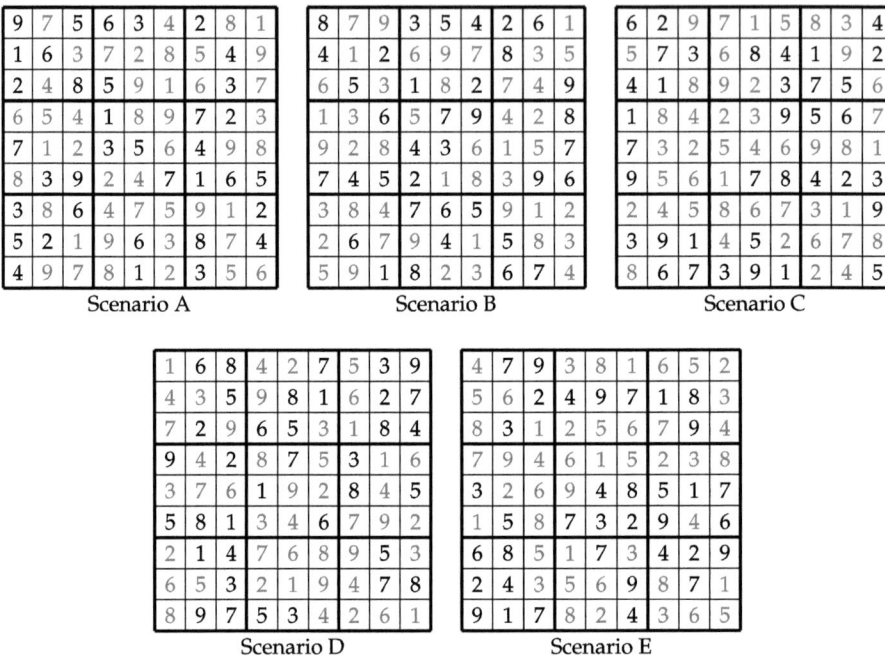

Fig. 2. Sudoku puzzles and solutions under Scenarios AâĂŞ-E: AI-only generation (A), Human-first AI-finish (B), AI-first Human-refine (C), Turn-based co-creation (D), and Heuristic negotiation (E). In (A), the puzzle is fully constructed by the AI, resulting in a highly structured and easily solvable grid with uniformly distributed clues and minimal variation serving as a baseline for efficiency and completeness. (B) reflects a more organic design, where the human agent's initial clue placements guide the visual structure, and the AI finalizes the solution logic. This often yields puzzles with moderate difficulty and more creative layouts. In (C), the AI provides a complete initial grid, which is subsequently refined by the human agent, typically enhancing symmetry and visual appeal without significantly altering difficulty. (D) produces puzzles with balanced structural aesthetics, as the alternating contribution pattern between agents naturally fosters symmetry and variety. Lastly, (E) simulates a dynamic decision-making process where both agents propose moves concurrently and a mediator resolves conflicts using a weighted logic-aesthetic scoring function.

that define player enjoyment. The present evaluation, based on symmetry score, move counts, and conflict resolution frequency, serves as an imperfect proxy for human-centered puzzle design quality. Incorporating human-centric heuristics from game design such as challenge pacing, discovery moments, and perceived fairness may help refine evaluation dimensions in future work. Ultimately, empirical player studies will be needed to validate how these AI-human co-creative strategies translate into actual play experiences.

5 Concluding Remarks

This study explored AI-human collaboration in Sudoku puzzle generation through five simulated interaction scenarios. While AI-only generation was efficient, it lacked the diversity and aesthetic nuance often associated with human-created puzzles. Hybrid approaches particularly turn-based creation and heuristic negotiation produced more balanced and varied outputs. These findings provide early insights into how structured co-creative frameworks may influence puzzle generation dynamics. However, several limitations remain.

The evaluation relies on algorithmic metrics that, while informative, may not fully reflect subjective player experiences or aesthetic preferences. Incorporating domain-specific puzzle design heuristics, derived from game design literature, offers a promising direction to further enrich co-creation frameworks. Future work will integrate human participant studies to capture subjective difficulty, engagement, and design preferences, thereby enhancing the practical applicability of AI-human collaborative systems.

Acknowledgements. This study was funded by the Ministry of Higher Education (MOHE) and Universiti Kebangsaan Malaysia, under the Young Researcher Incentive Grant (Grant No: GGPM-2024-052).

Disclosure of Interests. The authors have no competing interests to declare that are relevant to the content of this article.

References

1. Agarwal, C., Joshi, R.: Automation strategies for unconstrained crossword puzzle generation. ArXiv Preprint (2020). 10.48550/arxiv.2007.04663
2. Bouschery, S., Blažević, V., Piller, F.: Augmenting human innovation teams with artificial intelligence: exploring transformer based language models. J. Prod. Innov. Manag. **40**, 139–153 (2023). https://doi.org/10.1111/jpim.12656
3. Cabitza, F., Campagner, A., Sconfienza, L.M.: Studying human-AI collaboration protocols: the case of the Kasparov's law in radiological double reading. Health Inf. Sci. Syst. **9**(1), 1–20 (2021). https://doi.org/10.1007/s13755-021-00138-8
4. Caliskan, A., Bryson, J., Narayanan, A.: Semantics derived automatically from language corpora contain human-like biases. Science **356**, 183–186 (2017). https://doi.org/10.1126/science.aal4230
5. Cheng, C.T.: Artificial intelligence-based education assists medical students' interpretation of hip fracture. Insights Imaging **11**(1), 1–8 (2020). https://doi.org/10.1186/s13244-020-00932-0
6. Chung, J.: Ai luddites: consumers penalize creative work output generated by artificial intelligence. Research Square Preprint (2023). https://doi.org/10.21203/rs.3.rs-3444321/v1
7. De Peuter, S., Oulasvirta, A., Kaski, S.: Toward AI assistants that let designers design. AI Mag. **44**(1), 85–96 (2023)
8. Gabrilovich, E., Markovitch, S.: Wikipedia-based semantic interpretation for natural language processing. J. Artif. Intell. Res. **34**, 443–498 (2009). https://doi.org/10.1613/jair.2669

9. Glick, A., Clayton, M., Angelov, N., Chang, J.: Impact of explainable artificial intelligence assistance on clinical decision-making of novice dental clinicians. Jamia Open **5** (2022). https://doi.org/10.1093/jamiaopen/ooac031
10. Kosch, T., Welsch, R., Chuang, L., Schmidt, A.: The placebo effect of artificial intelligence in human-computer interaction. ACM Trans. Comput. Human Interact. **29**(6), 1–32 (2023)
11. Li, N., Yan, Y., Yang, Y., Gu, A.: Artificial intelligence capability and organizational creativity: the role of knowledge sharing and organizational cohesion. Front. Psychol. **13** (2022). https://doi.org/10.3389/fpsyg.2022.845277
12. Mantere, T., Koljonen, J.: Solving, rating and generating sudoku puzzles with GA. In: 2007 IEEE congress on evolutionary computation, pp. 1382–1389. IEEE (2007). https://doi.org/10.1109/cec.2007.4424632
13. Manzini, T., Ellis, S., Hendler, J.: A play on words: using cognitive computing as a basis for AI solvers in word puzzles. J. Artif. Gen. Intell. **6**, 111–129 (2015). https://doi.org/10.1515/jagi-2015-0006
14. Memmert, L., Bittner, E.: Complex problem solving through human-AI collaboration: literature review on research contexts. In: Hawaii International Conference on System Sciences (HICSS) Collections. pp. 378–387. AIS e-Library (2022). https://doi.org/10.18653/v1/w16-3647
15. Moon, T.K., Gunther, J.H.: Multiple constraint satisfaction by belief propagation: an example using sudoku. In: 2006 IEEE mountain workshop on adaptive and learning systems. pp. 122–126. IEEE (2006)
16. Noy, S., Zhang, W.: Experimental evidence on the productivity effects of generative artificial intelligence. Science **381**, 187–192 (2023). https://doi.org/10.1126/science.adh2586
17. Orwig, W., et al.: Using AI to generate visual art: do individual differences in creativity predict AI-assisted art quality? Creativity Res. J., 1–12 (2024)
18. Pillay, N.: Finding solutions to sudoku puzzles using human intuitive heuristics. S. Afr. Comput. J. **49** (2012). https://doi.org/10.18489/sacj.v49i0.111
19. Piller, F., Srour, M., Marion, T.: Generative AI, innovation, and trust. J. Appl. Behav. Sci. **60**, 613–622 (2024). https://doi.org/10.1177/00218863241285033
20. Pintér, B., Vörös, G., Szabó, Z., Lorincz, A.: Automated word puzzle generation via topic dictionaries. arXiv Preprint (2012). https://doi.org/10.48550/arxiv.1206.0377
21. Rezwana, J., Maher, M.: Identifying ethical issues in AI partners in human-ai co-creation. Arxiv Preprint (2022). https://doi.org/10.48550/arxiv.2204.07644
22. Rezwana, J., Maher, M.: Designing creative AI partners with COFI: a framework for modeling interaction in human-AI co-creative systems. ACM Trans. Comput. Human Interact. **30**, 1–28 (2023). https://doi.org/10.1145/3519026
23. Rezwana, J., Maher, M.L.: Understanding user perceptions, collaborative experience and user engagement in different human-AI interaction designs for co-creative systems. In: Proceedings of the 14th Conference on Creativity and Cognition, pp. 38–48 (2022)
24. Sabuncu, I.: Work-in-progress: solving sudoku puzzles using hybrid ant colony optimization algorithm. In: 2015 1st International Conference on Industrial Networks and Intelligent Systems (INISCom), pp. 181–184. IEEE (2015). https://doi.org/10.4108/icst.iniscom.2015.258984
25. Seli, P., et al.: Beyond the brush: human versus AI creativity in the realm of generative art. PsyArXiv Preprint (2024). https://doi.org/10.31234/osf.io/vgzhj
26. Procedural Content Generation in Games. CSCS, Springer, Cham (2016). https://doi.org/10.1007/978-3-319-42716-4_9

27. Sharma, A., Lin, I.W., Miner, A.S., Atkins, D.C., Althoff, T.: Human-AI collaboration enables more empathic conversations in text-based peer-to-peer mental health support. Nature Mach. Intell. **5**(1), 46–57 (2023)
28. Thanasuan, K., Mueller, S.: Crossword expertise as recognitional decision making: an artificial intelligence approach. Front. Psychol. **5** (2014). https://doi.org/10.3389/fpsyg.2014.01018
29. Wang, C.: A novel evolutionary algorithm with column and sub-block local search for sudoku puzzles. IEEE Trans. Games **16**, 162–172 (2024). https://doi.org/10.1109/tg.2023.3236490
30. Wei, X.: Difficulty level classification of sudoku puzzles based on convolutional neural network. Acad. J. Comput. Inf. Sci. **6** (2023). https://doi.org/10.25236/ajcis.2023.061105
31. Yan, L.: Practical and ethical challenges of large language models in education: a systematic scoping review. Br. J. Edu. Technol. **55**, 90–112 (2023). https://doi.org/10.1111/bjet.13370
32. Yang, Q.F., Chang, S.C., Hwang, G.J., Zou, D.: Balancing cognitive complexity and gaming level: effects of a cognitive complexity-based competition game on EFL students' English vocabulary learning performance, anxiety and behaviors. Comput. Educ. **148**, 103808 (2020)
33. Yin, J., Ngiam, K., Teo, H.: Role of artificial intelligence applications in real-life clinical practice: systematic review. J. Med. Internet Res. **23**, e25759 (2021). https://doi.org/10.2196/25759
34. Zhang, X., Zhu, S., Zhao, Y., Hansen, P., Zhu, Q.: Exploring laypeople's engagement with AI painting: a preliminary investigation into human AI collaboration. Proc. Assoc. Inf. Sci. Technol. **60**, 1215–1217 (2023). https://doi.org/10.1002/pra2.996
35. Zhao, R., Sinha, T., Black, A.W., Cassell, J.: Automatic recognition of conversational strategies in the service of a socially-aware dialog system. In: Proceedings of the 17th Annual Meeting of the Special Interest Group on Discourse and Dialogue, pp. 381–392. Association for Computational Linguistics (2016). https://doi.org/10.18653/v1/w16-3647
36. Zhou, E., Lee, D.: Generative artificial intelligence, human creativity, and art. Pnas Nexus **3** (2024). https://doi.org/10.1093/pnasnexus/pgae052
37. Zou, B., Guan, X., Shao, Y., Chen, P.: Supporting speaking practice by social network-based interaction in artificial intelligence (AI)-assisted language learning. Sustainability **15**, 2872 (2023). https://doi.org/10.3390/su15042872

ChordFusion: Interactive Piano Training in Mixed Reality with Custom Gloves

Muhammad Faiq Haikal Bin M Haikal(✉), Deb Kumar Ghosh, Jordan K. Lay, Nicko R. Caluya, and Damon M. Chandler

Visual Information Engineering Laboratory, Ritsumeikan University, Osaka, Japan
{is0808sv,is0806fe,is0807xr}@ed.ritsumei.ac.jp,
{nicko,chandler}@fc.ritsumei.ac.jp

Abstract. Learning to play the piano can be a difficult and lengthy process, and many beginners lose motivation. While digital tools exist, they may not fully capture the experience of playing. This paper introduces ChordFusion, a piano training system using Mixed Reality (MR) and custom-built interactive gloves. ChordFusion aims to make learning more effective and engaging by using visualization, active learning, and game-like features in an immersive MR setting. The system includes different modes (Freestyle, Auto, Practice) to suit various learning styles. We describe the design of ChordFusion, how the custom gloves work, and our plans for future improvements, including testing with users to see how well it helps them learn, improving its responsiveness, and making the finger tracking more advanced for a realistic playing experience.

Keywords: mixed-reality (MR) · interactive system · piano learning · immersive learning · gamification · custom gloves

1 Introduction

Learning the piano is a demanding task. Teachers need to keep students engaged, and students must dedicate considerable time and effort. Traditional teaching methods can sometimes be uninspiring and may lead students to lose interest [5]. Additionally, students need to grasp concepts such as basic music theory, reading sheet music, and finger movement. Teaching these topics can become tedious for new learners, especially those eager to play a popular song or perform for family and friends. Early challenges with the instrument and an emphasis on theory over hands-on playing can dampen these expectations. The frustration of not being able to immediately meet their internal expectations can lead to boredom and burnout for students [17]. This shows a clear need for new teaching methods. This paper explores how Mixed Reality (MR), combined with custom-made interactive gloves, might offer a better way to learn. A key question we investigate is: Can an MR system with special gloves help beginners learn piano more effectively and stay more motivated compared to current tablet-based apps?

1.1 Motivation

Constant access to a piano and an instructor is advantageous in piano learning. Hence, an MR headset can be a more affordable and portable alternative to learning with a more expensive actual piano setup and in-person piano lessons. Many MR/AR/VR applications have already been deployed to assist in piano learning, with techniques borrowed from real-world piano lessons. However, in a survey of augmented piano prototypes, there has been little room for diversity in piano skills to teach, such as improvisation, sight-reading, and motivation [3].

Visualization is a powerful training tool often used in sports to improve performance [10], and is also applicable in piano learning scenarios. While devices such as tablets and computers can show 2D animations of falling notes, the level of immersion and visualization that MR offers pales in comparison. In our project, we create a 3D, full-scale virtual piano and falling notes to create an immersive piano learning environment without the need for a physical piano.

ChordFusion is designed to improve piano skills by using proven learning techniques within an MR environment. The system incorporates this by using MR and a prototype glove to give users constant access to a virtual piano and uses visualization, game-like learning, and immersion.

Game-based learning incorporates points, competitions, and milestones to instill a sense of achievement in the learner. This method has been used to encourage students to participate in learning activities [7]. Another study [9] suggests that a successful educational game design incorporates learning through verbal instruction, by doing, and by role playing. ChordFusion applies this by providing three learning modes: Freestyle, Auto and Practice modes to simulate the three approaches

Lastly, the immersion and level of interaction of the system are designed to improve the preparation of the student to play the piano for others. A study carried out in athletic trainers shows that a 10-week immersive experience positively affected their preparation and made them feel more confident in their transition to professional practice [2]. The system aims to achieve a similar result, so that piano learners using this system will be able to apply their music theory and potentially increase their confidence when playing for their family or playing in competitions.

1.2 Aim of the Study

Despite the growing number of virtual learning tools, piano education still struggles with accessibility, motivation, and long-term interest and participation. The objective of an ongoing study for this project is to explore whether an interactive MR-based piano system, supported by real-time hand tracking gloves, can address the underlying challenges in beginner piano education by improving user motivation, engagement, and learning outcomes.

2 Related Work

There have been numerous projects aimed at replacing the current teaching model with a more engaging and interactive approach [3]. For example, Synthesia [13] connects the user's keyboard to their computer, displaying falling notes and virtual keyboard on a monitor while the user plays on a physical keyboard. The software provides two modes for the user, a mode to listen and a mode to play the song. The user can also choose whether to play the song at full speed, constant speed, or at their own pace. The software uses color coding for the falling notes to indicate left and right hands and numbers them to indicate the finger placement. The system uses a score system that tracks the user's accuracy in playing the piano.

Secondly, P.I.A.N.O. [11] is a piano learning system that uses a display setup along with a physical piano to project the falling notes on the piano. The system provides visual guidance for finger placement optimization, timing, note duration and the note articulations *legato* and *staccato*. In addition, the system provides color-coded feedback for correct, incorrect, and missed notes. The user can then view the information on these types of feedback to track their learning progress.

Next, PianoVision [8] is a game that uses a head-mounted display (HMD) to incorporate augmented reality (AR) overlays, hand tracking, and performance statistics to facilitate skill acquisition. The game is played either by projecting a virtual keyboard onto a flat surface or using a physical keyboard and projecting falling notes that signify the key that should be played by the user. The user can practice on their weakness by repeating sections that they struggle with and control the tempo of the songs being played. The game colors the notes by left and right hand and numbers them based on the finger that should be used. The game also provides visual feedback by showing a different color for correct and incorrect presses.

Finally, in addition, there are works that focus on interactive ways to teach playing instruments other than the piano, such as the gamelan, an Indonesian musical instrument [14]) or guitars (via a video game focusing on an individual's attitude [15] or via a multi-player cooperative performance [12]).

3 Game Design

3.1 Environment

ChordFusion can be used in two MR settings: AR and VR. In VR, using a theater scene from the Unity Store [16], users feel like they are performing on stage. This level of immersion, which can make practice feel more like a real performance, is hard to achieve with tablets or phones due to their smaller screens and lack of true presence. In AR, a virtual piano hologram appears in the user's real room. This unique AR feature lets people practice in their own familiar space, making it easier to fit learning into their daily lives, unlike screen-based apps that feel separate from the user's surroundings. The VR mode runs on Meta Quest 3, and AR uses HoloLens 2. Both have easy-to-use menus for changing modes, songs, difficulty, and starting songs (Fig. 1).

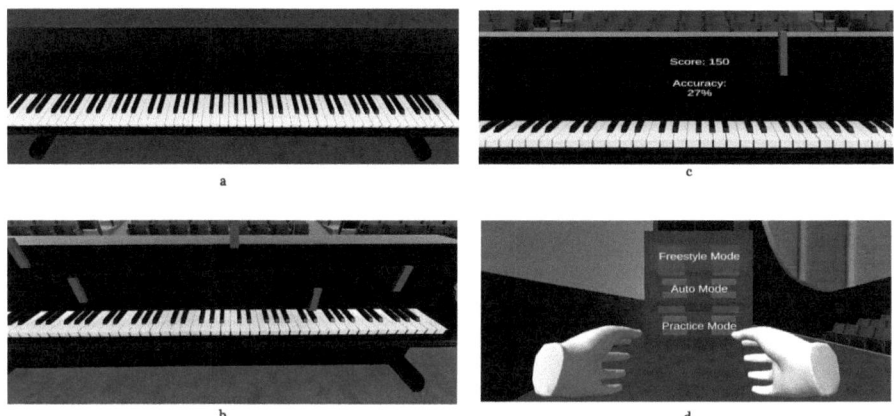

Fig. 1. ChordFusion interface: a) The virtual piano. b) Falling blocks guiding notes in Auto and Practice modes. c) Score shown after Practice mode. d) Panel for choosing the game mode.

3.2 Modes

To support different learning needs and stages of skill development, ChordFusion offers three distinct interaction modes: *Freestyle Mode:* This mode provides a completely open environment where users can interact with the virtual piano without any prescribed notes or songs. It is designed for exploration and experimentation, allowing learners to become comfortable with the virtual instrument and the feel of the interaction gloves at their own pace. This pressure-free setting encourages creative play and helps build a foundational familiarity crucial for newcomers. *Auto Mode:* In this mode, users observe as notes, represented by falling blocks, descend onto the virtual piano keys, perfectly synchronized with the playback of a selected song. The piano plays the song automatically as the blocks hit the keys. Auto Mode serves as an observational learning tool, helping users understand how songs are constructed, recognize musical patterns, and grasp rhythm and finger placement by watching and listening to a correct performance. *Practice Mode:* This mode actively engages the learner in skill building. Like Auto Mode, falling notes guide the user, but here, the virtual piano produces no sound unless the user presses the correct key at the correct time. This direct feedback mechanism reinforces accurate timing, note recognition, and hand-eye coordination. At the conclusion of each song, a score is displayed, reflecting the user's accuracy. This score serves as both a measure of progress and a motivational element, encouraging users to refine their skills and strive for improvement.

These three modes are intended to provide a structured yet flexible learning path, from initial exploration to guided observation and then to active, feedback-driven practice.

3.3 Technical Design

In the environment, a teleportation system is used to place the user in a fixed position to play the piano. This system is used to create the effect that the user is seated in front of the piano. Additionally, the user is able to choose amongst the three interaction modes that were mentioned previously. The variety in learning methods are used to enhance the user's enjoyment and motivation. In the Practice and Auto mode, the song that will be played are extracted from MIDI files. The note timing, pitch and velocity are extracted from the files and recorded as constants. Afterwards, falling notes are generated as blocks using these constants as their parameter. These blocks are used as a visual guide for the timing and notes that need to be played. Furthermore, the Practice mode uses key press detection to align the falling notes and the corresponding key press accurately. The detection is will then be used to calculate the final score. Lastly, the virtual environment and the interaction system communicates using WebSocket communication. The environment fetches the sensor data in the WebSocket server that was sent by the ESP32 microcontroller [4]. This ensures low-latency communication, allowing immediate response to hand movements. The connection is used together with Unity and Meta Quest's hand tracking system to allow for accurate interaction between the user's hand and the virtual piano.

3.4 Competency-Based Scaling

ChordFusion adjusts to different skill levels. Songs are marked by difficulty. A settings menu lets users change the speed and starting height of the falling notes. The current system uses the Meta Quest's camera-based hand tracking for overall hand position and the custom glove for more dependable finger bending information. Camera-only tracking can have issues in dim light or if the HMD's cameras cannot see the hands clearly. The glove helps get more consistent input for key presses, especially for quick or subtle finger movements that cameras might miss. So, the gloves are important for reliable tracking now and are a step towards a system that does not need cameras for hand tracking, and could even provide touch feedback in the future.

4 Custom Interaction System

Our system uses a special glove with sensors, shown in Fig. 2, designed to capture nuanced finger movements essential for a realistic virtual piano experience. This section details its construction and the rationale behind its development.

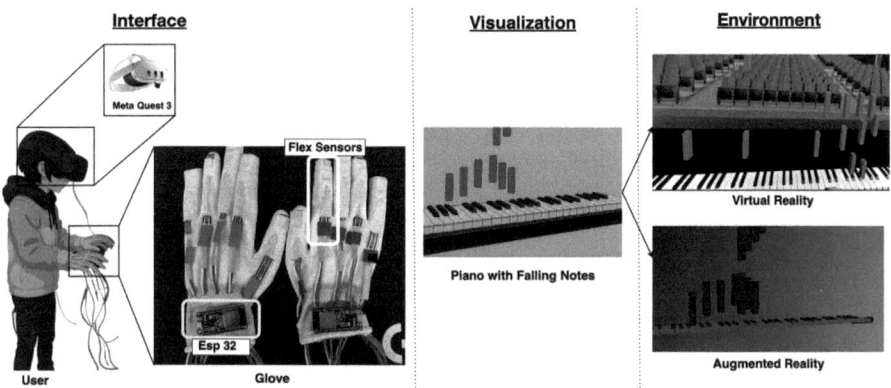

Fig. 2. Flow chart showing how the interaction system and the Unity program work together.

4.1 Custom Gloves

Although many contemporary Mixed Reality (MR) headsets offer built-in hand tracking capabilities, these systems typically rely on outward-facing cameras mounted on the headset. Such camera-based approaches, while convenient, present significant limitations for fine-grained finger manipulation tasks like piano playing. Some of the several issues such as inaccurate tracking, jitter where fingers might appear to shake, lost tracking where A finger might completely disappear from the virtual view. These issues make it very difficult for the virtual piano to reliably detect what your fingers are doing, so playing accurately becomes a challenge. To overcome these inherent limitations, we opted for a glove-based solution. By instrumenting the hand directly with sensors, our system can reliably measure finger flexion and extension regardless of the hand's orientation or the degree of finger curling.

The glove uses several sensors and a small computer (microcontroller) for real-time interaction with the virtual piano. Flex sensors, attached with a 10 Ω resistor to each finger, measure how much each finger bends. This allows for accurate and continuous tracking of individual finger movements. An ESP32 microcontroller integrated into the glove architecture which is responsible for acquiring and processing the raw analog data from these flex sensors. This processing includes analog-to-digital conversion, data sanitization to reduce noise and potential errors, and the transformation of bend levels into calibrated angular data representing finger joint angles. The processed finger angle data is then transmitted wirelessly via Wi-Fi, utilizing the WebSocket protocol, to the MR application running on the host system [4].

This high-frequency data stream ensures that the virtual hands within the MR environment mirror the user's physical finger movements with high fidelity and minimal latency. The direct sensing method guarantees that finger articulations and subsequent virtual key presses are well-coordinated, allowing users to "play" the piano in the air with natural and intuitive hand motions. The sensor data is transmitted frequently to maintain smooth and precise interaction. This continuous stream of finger angle data allows the MR application to accurately represent finger positions and map them to virtual keys, creating an intuitive and lifelike playing experience.

Future iterations of the glove aim to enhance its capabilities further. While the current version excels at tracking finger bending (flexion and extension), plans include the integration of additional sensors to detect sideways finger movements (abduction and adduction). This advancement will enable the system to recognize a wider repertoire of complex hand shapes and gestures, crucial for supporting advanced piano techniques and achieving a more comprehensive, professional level of hand tracking.

4.2 Application Development

The flow of the MR piano experience is depicted in Fig. 2. When the MR piano application initializes, it performs several setup routines, including graphics rendering, WebSocket communication establishment, and MIDI processing. The user is presented with the virtual stage, piano, and interactive control panels. Concurrently, the glove system activates; its ESP32 microcontroller establishes connections with the flex sensors and the local Wi-Fi network. As detailed in hardware section, the flex sensors continuously monitor finger flexion, converting these physical movements into angular data. This data is then wirelessly transmitted via Wi-Fi to the MR application. Within the Unity environment, this stream of data is utilized to animate the virtual fingers of the user's avatar in real-time. Users can select their preferred interaction mode via the on-screen panel. Depending on the chosen mode, the system can, for example, display falling notes corresponding to a loaded MIDI file, ensuring that the user's finger movements and the virtual key presses are accurately synchronized.

5 Limitations and Future Work

Our main goal is to create a system that teaches piano through active learning, immersion, and game-like fun. It should help students learn music theory, read sheet music, and develop good finger techniques, without being boring or making them too reliant on the system. Although ChordFusion provides an enjoyable way to practice piano for extended periods, one current limitation is that users might play songs without fully grasping the underlying music theory. While they learn the notes and rhythm, the deeper theoretical concepts (like why certain chords work together or how scales are constructed) may not be explicitly absorbed. A key hardware limitation of the current glove design is its inability to detect sideways finger movements, known as abduction (spreading fingers apart) and adduction (bringing fingers together). This is important for playing wide chords or performing certain advanced piano techniques. Without this capability, users cannot fully practice all necessary hand shapes, which might affect how well their learned skills transfer to a real acoustic or digital piano. Our future work will address these limitations and further enhance the learning experience such as tracking sideways finger movements by adding new sensors, such as miniature Inertial Measurement Units (IMUs) on each fingertip to accurately capture abduction and adduction. Additionally Detect key press force (velocity) and prioritize comfort and more natural movement by designing a more comfortable glove to wear for long time and allow more natural movement of the fingers. The game elements of the system can also be improved by adding new songs, incorporating fresh elements to the practice and auto modes that teach music theory and sheet music while the song plays, and including a section that explains theories and skills in detail. These enhancements will ensure that skills learned with the glove transfer more accurately to playing a physical instrument.

6 Conclusion

In conclusion, this project investigates a new way to learn piano by using the immersive power of Mixed Reality along with a custom wearable interaction system. While tablet and mobile apps offer easy access and 2D visuals, ChordFusion aims for a learning experience that is more physically involving and spatially aware. The reason for choosing MR/VR over simpler 2D platforms is its potential to create a stronger sense of "being there," allow more natural interaction with a full-sized virtual instrument, and provide deeper psychological immersion. Together, these aspects may lead to better learning of physical movements and greater engagement. A study has suggested that immersive VR can be significantly more effective for learning [6]. However, factors like a student's belief in their own ability (self-efficacy theory [1]) and the mental effort required (cognitive load) also play a big role. Our system tries to boost self-efficacy by letting students see their progress and aims to keep cognitive load manageable through intuitive MR interactions. This idea is supported by projects like P.I.A.N.O. [11], which found that projected falling notes could reduce cognitive load. ChordFusion hopes to increase users' motivation, enjoyment, and concentration, leading to a more effective and enjoyable piano learning journey. Future testing with users will be crucial to confirm these potential benefits and to understand the real impact of such an MR system on how piano is taught and learned.

Acknowledgements. This project was developed under the Visual Information Engineering Laboratory at Ritsumeikan University.

Disclosure of Interests. The authors declare that there is no conflict of interests related to the development and publication of this study.

References

1. Bandura, A.: Self-efficacy: toward a unifying theory of behavioral change. Psychol. Rev. **84**(2), 191 (1977)
2. Bates, D.K., Moore, J.L.: Recent graduates' perceptions of immersion and its effect on preparation for professional practice. Internet J. Allied Health Sci. Pract. **22**(4), 12 (2024)
3. Deja, J.A., Mayer, S., Čopič Pucihar, K., Kljun, M.: A survey of augmented piano prototypes: has augmentation improved learning experiences? Proc. ACM Hum. Comput. Interact. **6**(ISS) (2022). https://doi.org/10.1145/3567719
4. Hilman, M., Basuki, D.K., Sukaridhoto, S.: Virtual hand: VR hand controller using IMU and flex sensor. In: 2018 International Electronics Symposium on Knowledge Creation and Intelligent Computing (IES-KCIC), pp. 310–314. IEEE (2018)
5. Li, L.: Study on the innovation of piano teaching in normal colleges and universities. Creative Educ. **09**, 697–701 (2018). https://doi.org/10.4236/ce.2018.95051
6. Mahmoud, K., et al.: Does immersive VR increase learning gain when compared to a non-immersive VR learning experience? In: International Conference on Human-Computer Interaction, pp. 480–498. Springer (2020)
7. Pho, A., Dinscore, A.: Game-based learning. Tips and Trends **2** (2015)
8. PianoVision - Home — pianovision.com. https://www.pianovision.com/, Accessed 13 Mar 2025
9. Qian, M., Clark, K.R.: Game-based learning and 21st century skills: a review of recent research. Comput. Hum. Behav. **63**, 50–58 (2016)
10. Raut, R.P.: Importance of visualization and imagery techniques in sports. Aayushi International Interdisc. Res. J., 66–72 (2022)
11. Rogers, K., et al.: Piano: faster piano learning with interactive projection. In: Proceedings of the Ninth ACM International Conference on Interactive Tabletops and Surfaces, pp. 149–158 (2014)
12. So, A.: Guitar man: (an implementation of a rhythm game cooperative musical performance system with actual musical instruments). In: ACM SIGGRAPH ASIA 2008 educators programme, pp. 1–4. ACM SIGGRAPH ASIA 2008 educators programme (2008)
13. Synthesia, Piano for Everyone — synthesiagame.com. https://synthesiagame.com/, Accessed 13 Mar 2025
14. Syukur, A., Andono, P.N., Hastuti, K., Syarif, A.M.: Immersive and challenging experiences through a virtual reality musical instruments game: an approach to gamelan preservation. J. Metaverse **3**(1), 34–42 (2023)
15. Torge Claussen, J.: Gaming musical instruments: music has to be hard work! Digit. Cult. Soc. **5**(2), 121–130 (2019)
16. Gwangju Theater | 3D Environments | Unity Asset Store — assetstore.unity.com. https://assetstore.unity.com/packages/3d/environments/gwangju-theater-282533 Accessed 10 Apr 2025
17. Özerk, G.: Academic boredom: an underestimated challenge in schools. Int. Electron. J. Elementary Educ. **13**(1), 117–125 (2020). https://www.iejee.com/index.php/IEJEE/article/view/1339

Implementation and Evaluation of an Automated Eye Dropping System Using Games

Miu Moritani(✉) and Kazutaka Kurihara

Tsuda University, 2-1-1 Tsuda-Machi, Kodaira-shi, Tokyo 187-8577, Japan
mm2384mm@gm.tsuda.ac.jp

Abstract. Dry and tired eyes can often be relieved by applying eye drops. However, some people are not good at applying them. This study proposes a system that enables the automatic application of eye drops during gameplay. By exploiting the engaging characteristics of games, this system aims to reduce the psychological burden on users by administering eye drops during game play. Furthermore, a user study was conducted using three different game designs with different eye drop timing to investigate the psychological impact of the eye drop application during gameplay. The study showed that the degree of comfort or discomfort experienced by players varied depending on the game design and suggested that the use of games may help to distract attention from the act of applying eye drops, thereby reducing the psychological burden and exploring the potential of turning eye drops into an entertaining experience.

Keywords: Eye drops · Gamification · IoT

1 Introduction

Eye drops can offer relief when people experience symptoms such as dryness, fatigue, or allergies. Although they are typically administered by dripping or spraying liquid into the eyes, the need for users to determine the timing of application themselves may lead to hesitation or fear. As a result, some people have difficulty applying them, and few systems currently exist to provide assistance.

To address this issue, we propose a system that automatically administers eye drops while the user plays a game. Games naturally attract players' attention, which can be leveraged to distract them from the application process and increase the success rate, as their eyes are more likely to remain open during gameplay. This study also explores three game designs that vary in the timing of the spray, aiming to evaluate the psychological impact and identify ways to reduce discomfort associated with using eye drops.

The structure of this paper is as follows: Sect. 2 reviews related work and situates this study within existing research. Section 3 describes the implemented system. Section 4 outlines the evaluation experiment. Section 5 discusses the results and future directions. Section 6 concludes the paper. The terms "user" and "player" are used to emphasize the aspects of the users of the proposed system and the players of the proposed game, respectively.

2 Related Work

2.1 Interaction Between Eyes and Liquid

Moritani et al. [1] proposed a system that automatically applies eye drops while the user watches a video, using static entertainment to distract users. Yoshida et al. [2] developed a system that simulates tears by releasing droplets near the eyes to enhance emotional expression.

In contrast, the present study explores interactive entertainment by integrating eye drop application into gameplay to reduce psychological discomfort.

2.2 Gamification of Behavioral Change in Daily Life

Many studies have employed gamification to encourage behavioral changes in daily life. For example, Kadomura et al. [3] created EaTheremin, a fork-shaped instrument that generates sounds based on the resistance of different foods. Kosaka [4] developed a serious game for nutrition education targeting picky eaters. Ichimura [5] created a toothbrush tracking app that visualizes cleaned areas to encourage positive brushing habits in children. Gamification has also been applied to cleaning tasks by adding accelerometers to vacuum cleaners [6]. Ogasawara et al. [7] prototyped an interactive vacuum cleaner to support cleaning routines and parent-child communication. Sugino [8] et al. developed a kitchen system that plays synchronized sounds to make cooking and dining more enjoyable while helping parents monitor their children's activities. Yoshino et al. [9] proposed a system that encourages users to unplug devices to save energy. Katagiri et al. [10] linked game progression to chewing behavior to encourage better eating habits.

This study explores the use of gamification in eye drop application to reduce the psychological burden and improve the experience.

3 Proposed System

3.1 System Configuration

This section describes the configuration of the proposed system. Figure 1 illustrates an overview of the system. The eye drop dispensing unit is mounted on a tripod. Users apply eye drops by looking horizontally into the dispensing unit while either standing or sitting. Figure 2 shows the interior of the dispensing unit from the user's perspective. Eye drops are dispensed from the nozzle shown in Fig. 2.

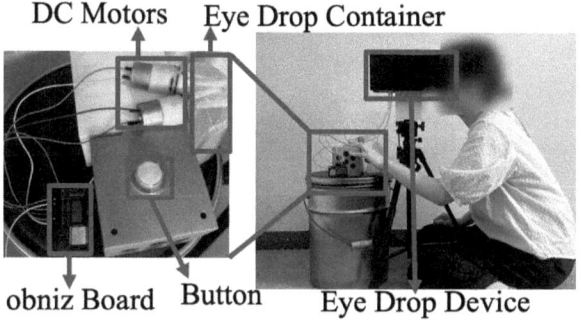

Fig. 1. System overview

3.2 Hardware

The hardware includes an eye drop dispenser with a DC motor-driven pump, an obniz board for control, a mobile battery, a smartphone for game interaction, and a physical button. The obniz board controls the pump and button input/output, and the game runs via a smartphone browser. The eye drop spray is delivered 0.262 s after the pump is activated. The nozzle, adapted from a commercial alcohol dispenser, has an L-shaped design with small holes that produce a mist. When positioned 15 cm from a 10 cm × 18 cm eyepiece, the nozzle disperses liquid over a 9 cm × 13 cm area. In our pilot tests, delivery was consistently successful when users' eyes were open.

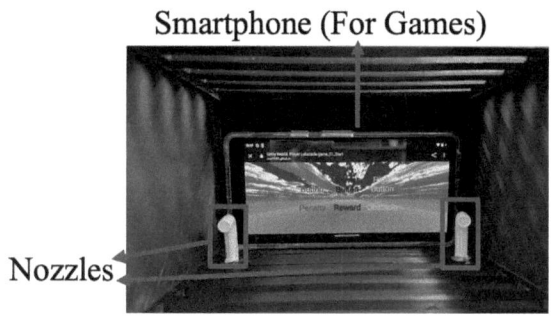

Fig. 2. User's perspective

3.3 Game

The developed system supports games that are controlled by a single button (Fig. 1) and eye movement, which is tracked via the smartphone's built-in camera. Different designs can be considered under the constraint that eye drops must be sprayed at some point during gameplay. In this study, a simple 3D runner platformer was created in Unity where players use a button to jump over oncoming obstacles. Three game conditions were implemented: spraying eye drops as a penalty, reward, or hindrance. These designs were inspired by the perception of liquid exposure in entertainment, such as being splashed as a punishment on prank shows, enjoying water attractions at theme parks, and experiencing momentary visual obstruction. The goal is to explore the psychological impact of each condition in order to develop strategies that reduce discomfort during the application of eye drops.

4 Evaluation Experiment

4.1 Hypotheses

To clarify the psychological effects of eye drop spraying during game play and to explore methods to reduce the psychological burden of eye drop spraying as well as its potential for entertainment, the following three hypotheses were formulated:

- When eye drop spraying is associated with "Penalty", "Reward", or "Hindrance" within the game, players will experience different effects in terms of pleasantness or unpleasantness. (H1)
- Performing eye drop application while playing the game will distract the player's attention from the act of applying the eye drops. (H2)
- Performing eye drop application while playing the game will make the experience more enjoyable. (H3)

4.2 Method

9 participants took part in the experiment. Beforehand, they completed a questionnaire that assessed their aversion to applying eye drops using a 7-point scale (4 being neutral, 7 being "strongly like applying eye drops," and 1 being "strongly dislike applying eye drops"). The mean score was 4.111 *(SD = 1.448)*, indicating generally neutral attitudes and some variation among individuals.

The experiment consisted of four conditions:

- P condition (Penalty): Eye drops were sprayed when the player's life gauge reached zero.
- R condition (Reward): Eye drops were sprayed at the end of the game as a reward for achieving a target score.
- H condition (Hindrance): Eye drops were sprayed randomly three times during gameplay.
- C condition (Control): Participants triggered the spray by pressing a button during gameplay. This condition served as a control condition.

To ensure consistency, the number of sprays was controlled across conditions. In the P and R conditions, the game design guaranteed one spray per session, either by resulting in a game over or by ensuring a fixed success. The H condition involved three predetermined spray points. The game duration was approximately 2 min for the R and H conditions, in which players were guaranteed to reach the goal, whereas in the P condition, where players inevitably experienced a game over before reaching the goal, the duration was up to about 30 s. Each participant experienced all four conditions in a randomized order. To visually distinguish these conditions, the color of the obstacles in the game was changed, as shown in Fig. 3.

After each condition, participants answered questions on a 7-point Likert scale measuring their perceived comfort/discomfort, awareness of the spray, and enjoyment. The comfort/discomfort question was omitted for the C condition because it lacked gameplay context. Open-ended responses were also collected at the end of the experiment.

Penalty   Reward   Hindrance

Fig. 3. Game designs screen

4.3 Results and Analysis

The collected responses regarding "degree of comfort or discomfort with eye drop application," "degree of awareness of eye drop application," and "degree of enjoyment of eye drop application" were analyzed using statistical hypothesis testing.

Degree of comfort or discomfort from eye drop spraying. Figure 4 compares the comfort levels associated with the eye drop spraying conditions (P, R, and H). The mean scores were 3.67 *(SD = 1.66)* for P, 4.44 *(SD = 1.51)* for R, and 2.78 *(SD = 1.20)* for H. A Friedman test revealed a significant difference *(p = 0.021)*. A post hoc Conover test with a Bonferroni correction showed a significant difference between the R and H conditions *(p = 0.041)*.

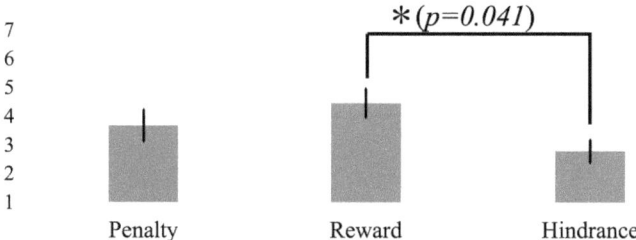

Fig. 4. Mean and standard deviation of comfort and discomfort during eye drop application

Awareness of Eye Drop Spraying. Figure 5 shows a comparison of participants' awareness of eye drop spraying in the P, R, H, and C conditions, along with the means and standard deviations for each condition. Higher scores reflect greater awareness of spraying. The mean scores were 5.11 *(SD = 1.83)* for the P condition, 4.33 *(SD = 1.41)* for the R condition, 5.11 *(SD = 1.97)* for the H condition, and 6.56 *(SD = 0.88)* for the C condition. A Friedman test revealed a significant difference among the conditions *(p = 0.026)*. A post hoc Conover test with Bonferroni correction showed a significant difference between the R and C conditions *(p = 0.036)*.

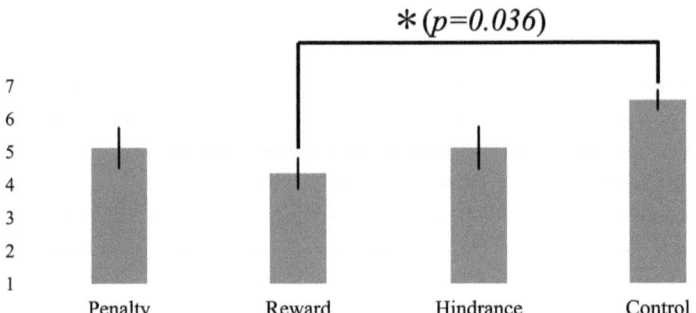

Fig. 5. Mean and standard deviation of awareness of eye drop spraying

Enjoyment of Eye Drop Application. Figure 6 shows a comparison of responses regarding the degree of enjoyment of eye drop application for the P, R, H, and C conditions, with their respective means and standard deviations. A score of 1 indicates "not at all enjoyable", while a score of 7 indicates "very enjoyable". The mean score for the P condition was 5.333, with a standard deviation of 1.500. The mean score for the R condition was 5.111, with a standard deviation of 1.167. The mean score for the H condition was 4.111, with a standard deviation of 1.965. The mean score for the C condition was 3.778, with a standard deviation of 2.048. A Friedman test showed no significant difference *(p = 0.335)*.

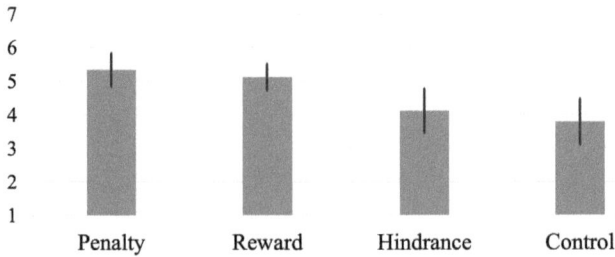

Fig. 6. Mean and standard deviation of enjoyment of eye drop application

5 Discussion

5.1 The Meaning of Eye Drop Spraying in the Game

Statistical hypothesis testing revealed a significant difference in perceived comfort or discomfort associated with eye drop spraying in different game conditions. This finding supports Hypothesis 1, which states that labeling the spray "Penalty," "Reward," or "Hindrance" affects players' comfort perceptions.

Using a score of 4 as neutral, the mean scores indicated that the R condition was perceived as more comfortable, while the P and hindrance H conditions were perceived as more uncomfortable. Notably, the significant difference between the R and H conditions suggests that the spray in the R condition can function as a reward, inducing comfort, whereas in the H condition, it can induce discomfort as a disruptive element. Free-text responses support this interpretation; participants in the R condition described the spray as positive reinforcement. Conversely, the discomfort in the H condition appears to stem from the unpredictability of the spray timing, aversion to multiple sprays, and visual disruption. These findings demonstrate the potential for manipulating psychological experiences through sensory feedback in game design. They also highlight areas for future research into the specific causes of discomfort.

5.2 Diverting Attention from Eye Drop Application Through Gameplay

A significant difference in participants' awareness of eye drop application was found between the reward and control conditions. These results support the hypothesis that applying eye drops during gameplay reduces attention to the application process, especially when the eye drops are presented as a reward.

In the R condition, the spray induced a sense of comfort. This positive emotional response, combined with achieving the game's goal, may have worked together to reduce the psychological burden. In contrast, the C, P, and H conditions made participants more aware of the spray. This was likely due to the predictable spray timing in the C and P conditions or the irregular, repeated spraying in the H condition. Free-text responses confirmed feelings of tension and anxiety in these cases.

Overall, these findings suggest that game-based systems that incorporate sensory feedback could effectively reduce psychological resistance to eye drop use.

5.3 The Proposed System and the Enjoyment of Applying Eye Drops

Statistical analysis revealed no significant differences in enjoyment levels across conditions, thus not supporting Hypothesis 3, which predicted that gameplay would increase enjoyment. One possible explanation is the novelty effect in C condition, in which participants appreciated being able to control the spray timing. These results imply that non-game-based methods could also alleviate the psychological burden of applying eye drops.

Although enjoyment was not significantly higher in the game-based conditions (P, R, and H), the relatively high mean scores suggest potential for more engaging game designs. This remains a promising area for future research.

Interestingly, higher enjoyment did not always correspond with comfort. Despite being perceived as less comfortable and more noticeable, the H condition still scored relatively high in enjoyment. This is similar to entertainment genres like horror, where discomfort can coexist with enjoyment [11]. Investigating these emotional mechanisms could lead to new ways of enhancing the user experience in future designs.

5.4 Reluctance Toward Eye Drop Application and Experimental Results

The participants in this experiment had an average score of 4.111 *(SD = 1.448)* on a 7-point scale measuring reluctance to apply eye drops. This indicates generally neutral but variable attitudes. Therefore, the findings in Sects. 5.1 and 5.3 are applicable to a diverse group of participants regardless of their degree of reluctance, which supports the potential use of liquid spraying as an entertaining feature for many users. However, the current experiment involved only 9 participants, so the findings are limited and should be interpreted with caution. A larger-scale evaluation is needed to validate these results more robustly. Additionally, since individuals with a strong aversion to eye drops were not specifically targeted, the findings in Sect. 5.2 may not apply to this subgroup. Some participants with low reluctance scores expressed concerns about potential injury and difficulty coordinating blinking with application. To address these concerns, the system keeps a safe distance from the eye and uses a smartphone camera to detect open eyes before spraying automatically. The effectiveness of these features for users with a stronger aversion has yet to be studied.

6 Conclusion

In this study, a system was developed to automatically deliver eye drops during gameplay and a user study was conducted using a 3D runner platformer game in which spraying eye drops was associated with "Penalty", "Reward", and "Hindrance".

The purpose of the study was to clarify the psychological effects of eye drop spraying on players during gameplay and to explore methods of reducing the psychological burden of eye drop spraying and making the process more enjoyable. As a result, it was suggested that eye drop spraying could be used in game design as a reward element that induces a pleasant effect or as a hindrance element that induces an unpleasant effect, with each having a different psychological impact on the player. In addition, it was suggested that spraying eye drops as a reward element upon clearing the game could help distract the player from the act of applying the drops. The study also discussed strategies for making the eye drop experience more enjoyable through gameplay. Future work will focus on improving the game developed in this study, as well as exploring ways to reduce the psychological burden and increase the entertainment value of eye drops in other types of games.

Acknowledgments. This research was partially supported by 2024 Academic Encouragement Program of Toshiba Electronic Devices & Storage Corporation.

References

1. Moritani, M., Kurihara, K.: Pachipachi drop: prototype of an automatic eye drop system for people who dislike eye drops. In: Proceedings of Entertainment Computing Symposium, vol.2023, pp. 290–292. IPSJ, Japan (2023). (in Japanese)
2. Yoshida, S., Narumi, T., Tanikawa, T., Kuzuoka, H., Hirose, M.: Teardrop glasses: pseudo tears induce sadness in you and those around you. In: Proceedings of the 2021 CHI Conference on Human Factors in Computing Systems (CHI'21), Article 508, pp. 1–12. Association for Computing Machinery, New York, NY, USA (2021)
3. Kadomura, A., Nakamori, R., Tsukada, K., Siio, I.: EaTheremin. In: Proceedings of the SIGGRAPH Asia 2011 Emerging Technologies (SA'11), Article 7, p. 1. Association for Computing Machinery, New York, NY, USA (2011)
4. Kosaka, T., Iwamoto T.: Serious dietary education system for changing food preferences "food practice shooter". In: Proceedings of the Virtual Reality International Conference: Laval Virtual (VRIC'13), Article 23, pp.1–4. Association for Computing Machinery, New York, NY, USA (2013)
5. Ichimura, S.: Migaco: tooth brushing-support application for children based on toothbrush-motion detection. IPSJ **61**(1), 95–102 (2020). (in Japanese)
6. Ichimura, S., Yazawa, T., Tomaru, S., Watanabe, H.: A trial of integrating gamification into house-cleaning. In: Proceedings of the Multimedia, Distributed, Cooperative, and Mobile Symposium, **2014**, pp. 1285–1290. IPSJ, Japan (2014). (in Japanese)
7. Ogasawara, R., Yamaki, T., Tsukada, K., Watanabe, K., Siio, I.: Interactive cleaner. In: Proceedings of the Entertainment Computing, **2007**, pp. 71–74. IPSJ, Japan (2007). (in Japanese)
8. Sugino, M., Iwabuchi, E., Siio, I.: Jingle kitchen and table for enjoying daily houseworks. In: Proceedings of the Entertainment Computing Symposium, **2007**, pp. 67–70. IPSJ, Japan (2007). (in Japanese)
9. Yoshino, T., Morita, S.: Development and evaluation of an unplugging habit formation support system "plugton" using AR. In: Proceedings of the Multimedia, Distributed, Cooperative, and Mobile Symposium, **2013**, pp. 632–640. IPSJ, Japan (2013). (in Japanese)
10. Katagiri, H., Yanaka, S., Nikai, M., Kosaka, T.: Development of a game system using eating food for food preferences and mastication. In: Proceedings of the Entertainment Computing Symposium, **2016**, pp. 191–194. IPSJ, Japan (2016). (in Japanese)
11. Minakuchi, M., Katayose, H.: Measures to address evaluation issues in entertainment computing research. In: Proceedings of the Interaction **2019**, pp. 141–150. IPSJ, Japan (2019). (in Japanese)

Proposal of Affective Music Features Utilizing Playlists as Collective Intelligence

Teu Nishihara(✉) and Osamu Ichikawa

Shiga University, 1-1-1 Banba, Hikone 522-8522, Shiga, Japan
s6025154@st.shiga-u.ac.jp

Abstract. As music streaming services become more widely used, it is becoming increasingly important to recommend songs that reflect users' emotions and context. In this study, we focus on playlists, which are considered to contain users' collective knowledge, and build a deep learning model that transforms direct features of songs into latent representations, which are referred to as affective features in this paper. Comparison experiments using silhouette scores show that the proposed features form a more coherent cluster structure than conventional direct acoustic features. This is expected to be useful for music recommendation and music generation that better reflects human sensitivity.

Keywords: Music · Recommendation · Latent Representation · Deep Learning · Human Sensitivity

1 Introduction

Music streaming services, which have become popular in recent years, allow listeners to listen to over 100 million songs. Therefore, it is becoming increasingly important to provide song recommendation services that match the individual needs and preferences of listeners. There is also a growing need to "listen to music that matches one's current mood and situation" and "discover new music in genres that one does not normally listen to but that suit one's tastes".

Because music is so closely associated with human emotions, quantitative analysis of such emotional responses to songs is a difficult challenge. This has been an important research topic in the fields of music information retrieval and affective computing [1]. In the area of music recommendation, achieving recommendations that align with users' emotions and preferences requires more than just superficial information such as acoustic features, genres, or playback history. It is essential to capture latent features that encompass the semantic and emotional impressions evoked by a song.

Traditional music recommendation approaches are mainly divided into two types: collaborative filtering and content-based filtering. Collaborative filtering recommends songs based on the listening history of users with similar preferences, but it does not consider the content of the music itself, making it difficult to recommend less popular songs. Content-based filtering, on the other hand, recommends songs based on similarities in acoustic features and other direct attributes. However, because it relies heavily on explicit features, it often results in homogeneous recommendations. These issues can lead to recommended songs that do not resonate with users' preferences or sensibilities, causing them to be ignored or discarded.

Fundamentally, users' perceptions of music differ depending on their preferences, listening history, and cultural backgrounds, and such perceptions are not necessarily reflected in direct data like acoustic features. For example, when people think of "summer," they naturally associate it with scenes and emotions such as "the beach," "romance," or "driving." These kinds of emotional and associative impressions are difficult to capture using existing features. In other words, conventional direct features are insufficient to represent the contextual and affective meanings that songs can convey.

To address this issue, this study focuses on user-generated playlists as a collective representation of how music is perceived. Playlists are collections of songs selected and organized by users based on specific preferences, situations, or emotions. Conversely, they can also be viewed as groups of semantically related songs within a given context. In this sense, we consider that the collective intelligence embedded in playlists reflects users' sensibilities and intentions.

Therefore, in this study, we propose a novel feature representation that extracts users' latent perceptions of music based on the collective intelligence of playlists. Unlike conventional acoustic features, this new feature aims to capture users' sensibilities and perceptions. In the future, by incorporating such features into recommendation systems and automated music composition models, we aim to offer more emotionally resonant and personalized music experiences.

2 Related Works

To address the diverse needs of users in music recommendation, numerous methods have been proposed to date. For example, He et al. introduced Neural Collaborative Filtering (NCF), which extends traditional inner product-based collaborative filtering by modeling the nonlinear interactions between users and items using neural networks [2]. Similarly, Jongpil Lee et al. developed a Deep Content-User Embedding Model, which learns user–music interactions in an end-to-end manner and captures both song and user features simultaneously [3]. Furthermore, Shih-Han Chen et al. proposed a Top-N recommendation framework that allows for the adjustment of diversity, considering the trade-off between recommendation accuracy and novelty [4], thereby offering practical improvements over conventional methods.

Meanwhile, research has also progressed in the direction of incorporating the latent meanings of content and users' emotional responses. Paul Magron et al. proposed Neural Content-aware Collaborative Filtering, which combines information extracted from low-level acoustic features with user embeddings to address the cold-start problem [5]. Minju Park et al. sought to enhance recommendation performance through contrastive learning by leveraging users' negative preferences [6].

Among approaches that emphasize users' emotional states, Emotion-aware Personalized Music Recommendation by Erkang Jing et al. models the heterogeneity between users' emotions and the mood of music, enabling emotion-sensitive recommendations [7]. Additionally, Keigo Sakurai et al. introduced a knowledge graph based on acoustic features and employed deep reinforcement learning to achieve more context-aware music recommendations [8].

All of these studies aim to more accurately capture user preferences, emotions, and context, and share with this work a focus on the emotion-evoking power of music. However, most existing approaches rely on the intrinsic characteristics of music or direct interactions with users. Few have explored approaches that utilize the social and emotional recognition of music embedded in collective user behavior—namely, collective intelligence—as feature representations.

Therefore, this study adopts an approach that focuses on playlists as a form of collective intelligence, extracting the semantic and affective connections inherent in them as features. Playlists are curated by users based on specific themes, emotions, or usage contexts, and can be regarded as the result of human affective judgment. Accordingly, by analyzing the structure of playlists to extract latent meanings and emotional contexts of songs, it becomes possible to obtain features that more closely approximate human cognition—features that conventional methods have struggled to capture.

3 Proposed Method

3.1 Introduction of Affective Features

Conventional features (such as acoustic features and metadata) describe the objective properties of a song itself and do not necessarily reflect human subjective sensibilities or contextual recognition. In contrast, playlists are curated by users based on their perception of songs being "similar" or "fitting a particular scene," and can be considered as a form of collective intelligence that aggregates human cognitive and emotional judgments. In other words, playlists represent an implicit expression of "relationships between songs based on human sensibility," and by leveraging this, it is possible to transform conventional direct features into features that are closer to human perception.

3.2 Latent Representations Obtained by Deep Learning Model

In general, latent representations are obtained by the encoder-decoder models. This study uses a deep learning model structured as fully connected layers as shown in Fig. 1. This model is designed as a multi-class classification task that takes 13-dimensional direct features of songs, such as acoustic features, as input and predicts the 82-class of the playlist to which the song belongs as output. It has a 16-dimensional bottleneck layer just before the final output layer. The bottleneck layer is considered to output latent representation. The layer up to the bottleneck layer can be regarded as the encoder and the output layer as the decoder.

In the architecture of the model, the Gated Exponential Rectified Unit (GERU) is used as the activation function, categorical cross-entropy is adopted as the loss function, and the softmax function is used in the output layer. In addition, Adam optimizer and dropout are employed for training.

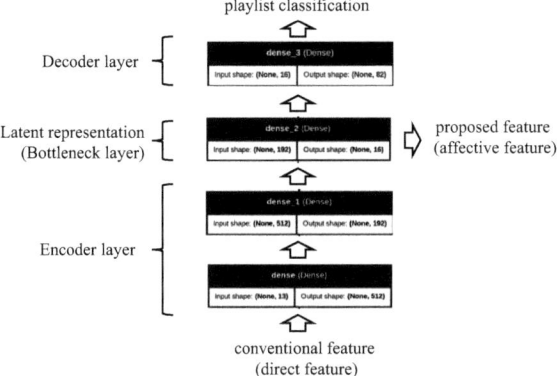

Fig. 1. Structure of Classification / Feature Transformation Model

3.3 Feature Transformation

In our proposed method, the output vector from the bottleneck layer one layer before the output layer is extracted as a new feature. This feature is latent (or distributed) representation of the features of a song that are important for playlist classification. We assume it captures the concepts that humans use when identifying groups of songs. The semantic structure based on the "collective intelligence" shared through playlists is internalized in the output of this layer. In other words, the latent representations function not merely as a representation of feature similarity, but as an expression that reflects semantic features rooted in user perception and cultural context. We therefore refer to this latent representation as an affective feature.

Once the deep learning model has been sufficiently trained on a large amount of data, it can be used as a feature extractor: inputting direct features obtained from the Spotify-API, etc., into it yields the corresponding affective features as output. It is envisioned that the new features obtained by the proposed method will be used to measure the similarity between songs in the field of song recommendation or as seeds in song generation.

Essentially, whether the features obtained by the proposed method are truly a good representation of human sensitivity should be confirmed in the application scenario described above. Such an evaluation would be a subjective approach (e.g. questionnaire). In this paper, as a first step of the evaluation, we use an objective approach to evaluate whether the features can represent the music space better.

4 Experiment

4.1 Objective

The purpose of this experiment is to verify whether the proposed feature (affective feature, latent representation) obtained by the deep learning model can better represent the feature space of songs. That is to say, the desired result is a smaller intra-cluster variance and a larger inter-cluster variance in the music space when the proposed features are used, compared to conventional features.

4.2 Data Set

For the evaluation, we used the Spotify data [9]. This data set is known as Spotify_1Million_Tracks of 1 million playlists consisting of 882361 unique tracks by 64159 artists. It contains the information shown in Table 1. This time, only features related to acoustics were used. A detailed description of the features is provided in Reference [10].

Table 1. Spotify Million Song Dataset.

Contents	track name, artist nane, genre information(82 genres in total), acoustic features
List of Acoustic Features	
Acousticness	A confidence measure whether the track is acoustic
Danceability	How suitable a track is for dancing based on a combination of musical elements
Duration_ms	Duration of the track in milliseconds
Energy	Perceptual measure of intensity and activity
Instrumentalness	Likelihood the track contains no vocal content
Liveness	Probability that the track was performed live
Loudness	Overall loudness of a track
Mode	Modality (major or minor) of a track
Speechiness	Presence of spoken words in a track
Tempo	Overall estimated tempo of a track in beats per minute
Key	The key the track is in
Time_signature	How many beats are in each bar
Valence	Musical positiveness conveyed by a track

In the data set, 13 types of acoustic features were obtained by Spotify API. In this paper, this feature is referred to as a conventional feature.

In this experiment, 82 different genres are considered playlists. Originally, playlists would naturally be user-generated lists such as "Drive," "Spring," "Holiday Morning," "Cafe," and so on. In this experiment, we prioritized the advantage of this data set, which has one million songs, and considered genres as playlists.

4.3 Evaluation

To compare the superiority of the features of the proposed method (affective features) and those of the conventional method (direct features), x-means clustering was performed using those two sets of features, respectively. The target number of clusters was determined based on BIC using the features of the conventional method. The same target number of clusters was applied for clustering using the features of the proposed method.

All data in the Data set was used for clustering. The quality of the structure of each cluster was evaluated using the silhouette score.

The direct features were the 13-dimensional features in the dataset, which were originally obtained by Spotify-API. These were standardized before use.

Affective features were generated by a feature extractor that was adapted from the classification model shown in Fig. 1. The input is direct features. All data in the dataset were used to train the classification model, and the supervised signals are 82 classification classes. The number of dimensions of the affective features is the same as the number of elements in the bottleneck layer. In this experiment, it was set to 16.

4.4 Evaluation Metric

The silhouette score was used to measure clustering quality. The silhouette score is a metric used to evaluate the quality of clustering in data analysis. It measures how well data points within the same cluster are similar to each other (cohesion) and how distinct they are from data points in other clusters (separation). The silhouette score is calculated as the Average of $S(i)$, which is computed for each data point i using the following formula:

$$S(i) = (b(i) - a(i))/max(a(i), b(i)) \tag{1}$$

where:

$a(i)$: Average distance within the same cluster for each data point i (cohesion)
$b(i)$: : Average distance to the nearest different cluster (separation)

Euclidean distances were used to measure the cohesion and the separation above.

The score ranges from -1 to $+1$. A higher value indicates better quality of the clustering.

4.5 Experimental Results

The results of clustering are shown in Fig. 2. and Fig. 3. They were visualized in two dimensions using t-SNE. The perplexity is set to 30. They show that clustering using affective features obtained from the proposed method results in more coherent groupings than clustering using direct (conventional) feature does. The silhouette scores of the experimental results are shown in Table 2. It indicates that clustering using the affective feature obtained from the proposed method forms a better cluster structure than the direct (conventional) feature does. This means that the variance between clusters is large and the variance within clusters is small.

For reference, the classification accuracy of the classification model on which the feature extractor was based was 0.22.

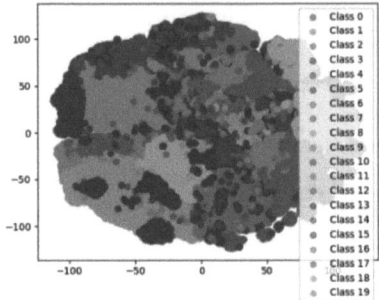

Fig. 2. Visualization of the clustering using direct features

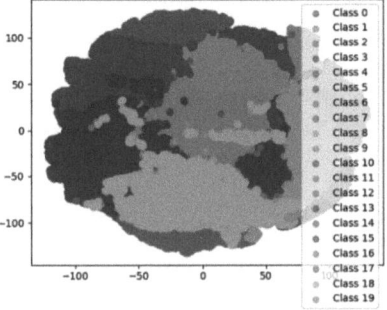

Fig. 3. Visualization of the clustering using affective features

Table 2. Result of Silhouette Scores

Features to compare	silhouette scores
Direct Features (Conventional)	0.121
Affective Features (Proposed)	0.271

5 Conclusion

In this study, we proposed a method for extracting new features of songs by leveraging collective intelligence derived from playlists. The clustering evaluation using silhouette scores showed that the features obtained through the proposed method achieved higher scores than those using conventional features. This indicates that the proposed method has smaller intra-cluster variance and larger inter-cluster variance.

Although the proposed method uses slightly higher-dimensional features (16 dimensions) compared to the direct features (13 dimensions), it is generally known that silhouette scores tend to decrease as the number of dimensions increases. Therefore, the fact that the proposed method achieved high scores despite this drawback confirms its effectiveness.

In this paper, we evaluated the features of the proposed method by focusing on its ability to describe the music space. This is an objective evaluation method. On the other hand, evaluation of whether the features truly represent human sensibilities requires a subjective approach, using song recommendation and song generation applications. Another limitation of the experiments in this paper is that we prioritized the large number of data in selecting the dataset. Therefore we had to make an approximation that considered genres as playlists. These issues will be addressed in future studies.

Acknowledgement. This work was supported by JSPS KAKENHI (Grant Numbers JP 25K15402).

References

1. Kang, J., Herremans, D.: Towards unified music emotion recognition across dimensional and categorical models. In: Proceedings of the 23rd International Society for Music Information Retrieval Conference (ISMIR 2022), pp. 783–790 (2022)
2. He, X., Liao, L., Zhang, H., Nie, L., Hu, X., Chua, T.-S.: Neural collaborative filtering. In: Proceedings of the 26th International Conference on World Wide Web (WWW 2017), pp. 173–182 (2017)
3. Lee, J., Lee, K., Park, J., Park, J., Nam, J.: Deep Content-User Embedding Model for Music Recommendation. arXiv preprint arXiv:1807.06786 (2018)
4. Chen, S.-H., Sou, S.-I., Hsieh, H.-P.: Top-N music recommendation framework for precision and novelty under diversity group size and similarity. J. Intelligent Information Syst. **62**, 1–26 (2024)
5. Magron, P., Févotte, C.: Neural content-aware collaborative filtering for cold-start music recommendation. Data Min. Knowl. Disc. **36**(5), 1790–1810 (2022)
6. Park, M., Lee, K.: Exploiting negative preference in content-based music recommendation with contrastive learning. In: Proceedings of the 16th ACM Conference on Recommender Systems (RecSys 2022), pp. 743–752 (2022)
7. Jing, E., et al.: Emotion-Aware Personalized Music Recommendation with a Heterogeneity-Aware Deep Bayesian Network. arXiv preprint arXiv:2406.14090 (2024)
8. Sakurai, K., Togo, R., Ogawa, T., Haseyama, M.: Deep reinforcement learning-based music recommendation with knowledge graph using acoustic features. ITE Transactions on Media Technology and Applications **10**(1), 8–17 (2022)
9. Kaggle: Spotify_1Million_Tracks. https://www.kaggle.com/datasets/amitanshjoshi/spotify-1million-tracks. Accessed 8 Sep 2024
10. Spotify for Developers: Get Audio Features. https://developer.spotify.com/documentation/web-api/reference/get-audio-features. Accessed 17 Apr 2025

Mi Librero de Aventuras: A Novel Configurable Serious Game for Personalized Science and Technology Learning in Peruvian Primary Education

Luiggi Ramos, Johan Baldeón[✉][iD], and María-José Espinosa-Chueca[iD]

Avatar Group, Pontificia Universidad Católica del Perú, Lima, Peru
{luiggi.ramos,johan.baldeon,mjespinosa}@pucp.edu.pe
https://www.pucp.edu.pe/

Abstract. The integration of educational video games into primary education has shown promise for improving learning outcomes, yet challenges persist in adapting these tools to diverse student needs and specific curricular goals in science and technology (S&T). In Peru, where access to configurable interactive resources remains limited, traditional methods often fail to engage 4th-grade students effectively. This study presents "Mi Librero de Aventuras" ("My Adventure Bookshelf"), a configurable educational video game designed to enhance S&T learning by allowing teachers to tailor content to individual learning objectives and student profiles. Developed using the LEGA framework and LM-GM model in Unity with C#, the game features three adventures addressing key topics—scientific method, ecosystems, and internal systems—aligned with the Peruvian MINEDU curriculum. The research focused on identifying learning and game mechanics to support S&T education, designing a customizable tool for teachers, and evaluating its impact on engagement and comprehension. While initial results are promising, the study acknowledges limitations in sample size and device compatibility, which will be addressed in future iterations. Tested with 4th-grade students in Lima, quantitative results showed an 80% approval rate for educational effectiveness and a 90% positive gameplay experience via GEQ scores, while qualitative feedback highlighted improved motivation and usability. These findings underscore the potential of configurable video games to deliver personalized, engaging S&T education, offering a scalable model for enhancing primary-level learning in Peru.

Keywords: Educational video game · Configurable game design · Science and technology education · Primary education · Game mechanics · Entertainment computing

1 Introduction

In recent years, educational video games have emerged as powerful tools to enhance learning outcomes by fostering engagement and interactivity, particularly among digital-native generations such as Z and Alpha [21]. In Peru, however, the education system faces significant challenges, as evidenced by the country's low performance in science (404 vs. a global average of 489) in the 2018 PISA assessment [19]. For 4th-grade primary students, traditional teaching methods in science and technology (S&T) often lack the adaptability and interactivity needed to address diverse learning needs and align with the National Curriculum for Basic Education of the Ministry of Education of Peru (MINEDU) [15].

Existing educational games, while promising, frequently fall short due to insufficient customization options and limited alignment with specific learning objectives. Our solution, "Mi Librero de Aventuras" (*My Adventure Bookshelf*), bridges this gap by offering teacher-driven configurability via JSON parameters, though future work will expand these features to include custom topic creation and adaptive difficulty.

This paper introduces the *Mi Librero de Aventuras* game, a configurable educational video game designed to improve S&T learning for Peruvian 4th-grade students by integrating personalized learning experiences with engaging gameplay. Developed within the scope of entertainment computing, this study leverages the LEarner-centered GAmification Design Framework (LEGA) [5] and the Learning Mechanics-Game Mechanics (LM-GM) model [3] to address these gaps. Unlike similar works, our system allows teachers to customize learning objectives and game mechanics, ensuring alignment with curricular goals and catering to individual student profiles.

The research pursued three key objectives: (1) identifying learning mechanics that enhance S&T comprehension, (2) defining game mechanics that promote engagement with S&T topics, and (3) developing a configurable educational tool for teachers to personalize the learning experience. This work contributes to entertainment computing by offering an innovative, scalable solution for primary education, focusing on advancing educational technologies.

The paper is structured as follows: Sect. 2 reviews related literature, Sect. 3 details the methodology, Sect. 4 describes the game, Sect. 5 presents evaluation results, Sect. 6 discusses implications, and Sect. 7 concludes with future directions.

2 Related Work

Educational video games have gained significant attention as tools for enhancing learning outcomes in science and technology (S&T) by fostering engagement and interactivity. Several studies have explored the design and impact of such games, particularly in primary and secondary education settings.

Harker-Schuch et al. [11] developed *CO2peration*, a 3D interactive digital game targeting 12–13-year-olds to improve climate literacy. The game employs observation and exploration mechanics to facilitate experiential learning, demonstrating positive engagement but limited configurability for teachers. Similarly, Strawhacker et al. [25] introduced a bioengineering-focused game for children, leveraging simulation and action-task mechanics to enhance interest and knowledge. Their findings highlight the effectiveness of role-playing game (RPG) genres in fostering deeper understanding, though customization options remain underexplored.

Khan et al. [13] investigated gamification in secondary school science, using *Patterns of Reactivity* to combine competition and feedback mechanics across multiple levels. Their experimental results showed improved student engagement and learning outcomes, particularly when combining observation with points-based rewards. In contrast, Cohen et al. [7] developed *Griddle*, a game for power system education, but faced challenges due to unclear instructions, underscoring the need for intuitive design.

Silva and Araujo [23] presented *Crayon Sharks*, a digital game for science teaching, emphasizing simulation mechanics to teach ecological concepts. Their work suggests that simulation-based games effectively complement traditional teaching but lack teacher-driven customization. Legerén [14] introduced *Al-Kimia*, a chemistry-focused RPG for high school students, integrating adventure and action subgenres to teach chemical reactions and elements. This game demonstrated strong alignment with learning objectives but did not allow teacher personalization.

Muntean et al. [16] created *Final Frontier*, an educational game for primary school students focused on solar system concepts. By incorporating exploration and movement mechanics, the game achieved significant learning gains, though it lacked adaptability for diverse curricula. Solano and Santacruz [24] explored *eAdventure*, a platform enabling teachers to create customizable adventure games without programming knowledge, offering a promising approach for personalization but limited to specific genres.

Secondary studies, such as De Aldama and Pozo [8], examined the educational use of entertainment games like *Angry Birds* to teach physics, highlighting the potential of repurposing commercial games for epistemic goals. Similarly, Wan and Abdul [27] developed *AKAMIA*, a chemistry mobile game, showing that mobile platforms can enhance accessibility but often lack configurability.

Additional research by Annetta et al. [2] explored serious games in science education, emphasizing the role of immersive environments in fostering inquiry-based learning. Their findings align with the need for games to support higher-order learning outcomes, such as analysis and creation, as per the Revised Bloom's Taxonomy [1]. Dicheva et al. [10] further analyzed gamification in education, noting that well-designed mechanics can significantly improve motivation and retention.

Unlike these works, *Mi Librero de Aventuras* uniquely combines teacher-driven configurability via JSON parameters with the LEGA framework [5] and LM-GM model [3], enabling alignment with the Peruvian MINEDU curriculum and addressing diverse learning needs in 4th-grade S&T education. While existing games offer valuable insights into mechanics and engagement, they often lack the flexibility to adapt to specific curricular goals or individual student profiles, a gap our solution aims to address.

3 Methodology

This study employs the LEarner-centered GAmification Design Framework (LEGA) [5] to develop "Mi Librero de Aventuras," an educational video game enhancing science and technology (S&T) learning for 4th-grade students in Lima, Peru. The research, involving 15 students and their S&T teachers, evaluates the game's effectiveness through qualitative and quantitative methods, structured in three phases.

First, Intended Learning Outcomes (ILOs) were extracted from the Peruvian MINEDU 4th-grade S&T curriculum [15], identifying 28 ILOs across scientific inquiry, ecosystems, and internal systems. Twelve prioritized ILOs (e.g., applying the scientific method, analyzing ecosystem interactions) were mapped to nine activities (A1–A9), such as virtual experiments. These were validated by an educational psychologist and two S&T teachers for pedagogical alignment. Student player types (Achiever, Explorer [6]) and learning styles (Pragmatist, Reflector [12]) were assessed via questionnaires, prioritizing hands-on exploration. Learning mechanics, derived from the LM-GM model [3], included simulation and questioning.

Second, game mechanics (e.g., discovery, feedback, rewards) were designed using LEGA, aligned with Bloom's Taxonomy [1] to support cognitive progression. The Game Design Document (GDD), structured via the Game Design Canvas [17], detailed three adventures—*El Poder de un Anticuerpo, Cuidando mi Ecosistema*, and *Analizando como Científico*—each tied to activity sets. The Serious Game Design Pattern Canvas [28] mapped the adventure genre to educational goals, validated by a serious game design expert for alignment with Self-Determination Theory.

Third, the game was developed in Unity with C# using an incremental model across three increments, managed via Kanban. The first increment implemented core mechanics (e.g., touch controls, mission transitions) and *El Poder de un Anticuerpo*. The second introduced JSON-based configurability via the EDU Game Authoring platform [4] for *Cuidando mi Ecosistema*, while the third added aesthetics, scoring, and *Analizando como Científico*. Teachers customized learning objectives, difficulty, and question sets aligned with MINEDU materials [15] through the platform, with configurations loaded via JSON for personalized sessions. A serious game specialist verified each increment's technical and educational coherence.

4 The Game: "Mi Librero de Aventuras"

"Mi Librero de Aventuras" is a configurable educational video game developed in Unity 2021.3 with C# to teach science and technology (S&T) to Peruvian 4th-grade students, aligning with the MINEDU curriculum [15]. Featuring a virtual bookshelf interface (Fig. 1a), players select from three adventures—*El Poder de un Anticuerpo* (The Power of an Antibody), *Cuidando mi Ecosistema* (Caring for My Ecosystem), and *Analizando como Científico* (Analyzing as a

Scientist)—each with six levels targeting specific Intended Learning Outcomes (ILOs). Teachers customize learning objectives, difficulty, and gameplay via a JSON-based interface integrated with the EDU Game Authoring platform [4], ensuring adaptability to diverse student needs.

El Poder de un Anticuerpo (The Power of an Antibody) focuses on internal systems, with players navigating a bloodstream as an antibody to eliminate bacteria using touch controls (Fig. 1b), targeting ILOs 10–12 (e.g., biological functions). *Cuidando mi Ecosistema* (Caring for My Ecosystem) addresses ecosystems, involving drag-and-drop tasks like waste collection across forest and lake settings (Fig. 2a), aligning with ILOs 6–9 (e.g., environmental interactions). *Analizando como Científico* (Analyzing as a Scientist) teaches the scientific method through point-and-click virtual experiments (Fig. 2b), supporting ILOs 1–5 (e.g., hypothesis testing). Learning mechanics from the LM-GM model [3], such as simulation, exploration, and experimentation, align with Bloom's Taxonomy [1] for cognitive progression.

Gameplay mechanics include discovery (uncovering content), action/task (touch and drag-and-drop controls), feedback (real-time cues), and rewards (points, badges), tailored to Achiever and Explorer player types per Self-Determination Theory [22]. The modular architecture (Fig. 4) uses separate scenes linked via the bookshelf hub, with JSON-driven configurability for personalized experiences (Fig. 3). Optimized for tablets, the game employs 2D sprites and animations, balancing aesthetics and performance for mid-range devices.

A serious game expert validated the design for educational and entertainment alignment, with usability tests refining mechanics and interface for a cohesive learning experience.

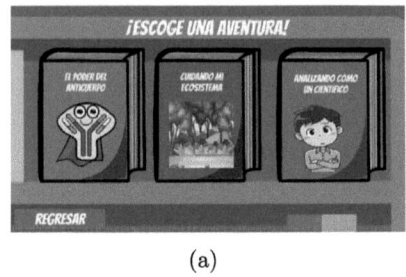
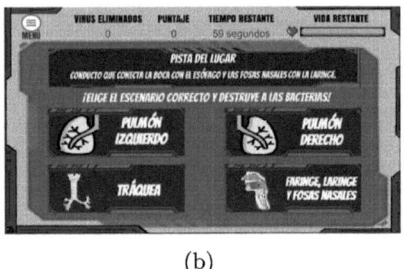

(a) (b)

Fig. 1. Interaction screens in *"Mi Librero de Aventuras"*. (a) Main Bookshelf Interface. (b) *El Poder de un Anticuerpo* (The Power of an Antibody) Gameplay.

5 Evaluation

Evaluated in Lima schools, the game involved 4th-grade students and teachers. Pre/post-tests showed significant gains ($p < 0.05$), though 3 students scored

 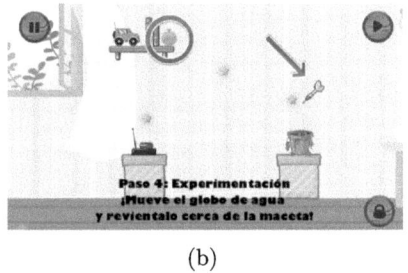

(a) (b)

Fig. 2. Interaction screens in *"Mi Librero de Aventuras"*. (a) *Cuidando mi Ecosistema* (Caring for My Ecosystem) Gameplay. (b) *Analizando como Científico* (Analyzing as a Scientist) Gameplay

lower post-test, possibly due to varying difficulty. Teachers reported 80% satisfaction but noted a learning curve in configuration. GEQ scores averaged 2.22 (positive) and 0.68 (negative), with 90% gameplay approval (Table 1). Teachers reported 80% educational satisfaction.

Table 1. GEQ Scores

Aspect	Average Score
Competence	2.46
Immersion	2.57
Flow	2.28
Positive Affect	2.98
Negative Affect	0.85

Teachers utilized configurability features in 70% of sessions, reducing lesson prep time by 30%. Average playtime was 25 min per session, with higher engagement in exploratory tasks (Fig. 2a).

6 Discussion

The evaluation of "Mi Librero de Aventuras" confirms its effectiveness as a configurable educational video game for 4th-grade S&T learning in Peru, achieving an 80% educational approval rate and 90% gameplay satisfaction via GEQ scores (Table 1). Significant pre/post-test gains ($p < 0.05$, Fig. 5) and moderate GEQ scores (e.g., competence: 2.46, immersion: 2.57) indicate strong engagement, particularly in scientific inquiry and ecosystems, driven by simulation and experimentation mechanics [3]. Teachers leveraged configurability in 70% of sessions (Fig. 3), reducing preparation time by 30% and tailoring ILOs to diverse student

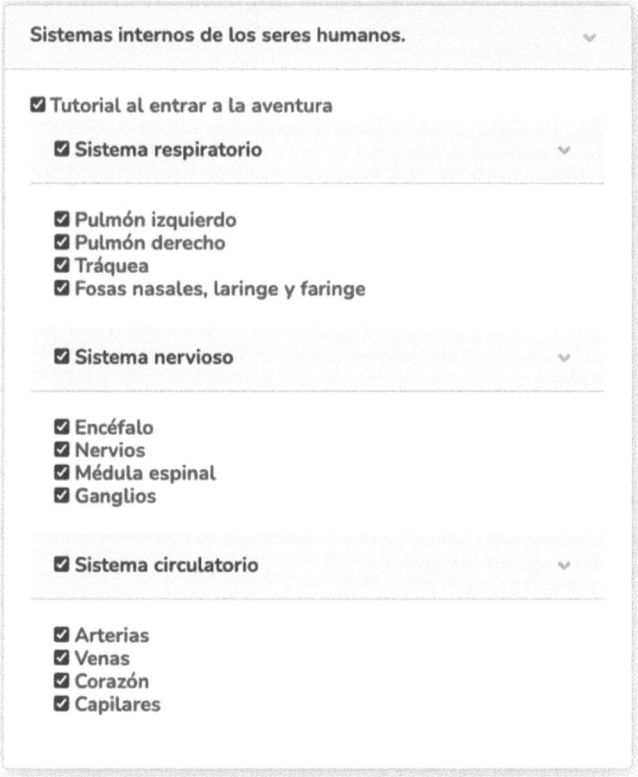

Fig. 3. Teacher Configuration Interface

needs, aligning with Self-Determination Theory [22] and MINEDU curriculum goals [15]. Compared to static games like *Final Frontier* [16] or narrative-focused tools [20], this game's integration of LEGA [5] and LM-GM [3] frameworks ensures robust personalization, surpassing non-configurable approaches [25].

This study advances entertainment computing by embedding teacher-driven flexibility, addressing Peru's S&T educational gaps [19] for digital-native learners [21]. However, technical limitations, including lag on low-end tablets and connectivity reliance, hinder rural deployment [26]. The small sample size (15 students) and urban focus limit generalizability, while configuration complexity requires teacher training [18]. Future improvements include performance optimization, an offline mode, and a larger, multi-school evaluation to enhance scalability. Expanding content to include topics like energy [15] and integrating training via the EDU Game Authoring Platform [4] could further adoption. This configurable model offers a scalable framework for personalized education, with potential to inspire cross-disciplinary tools [6].

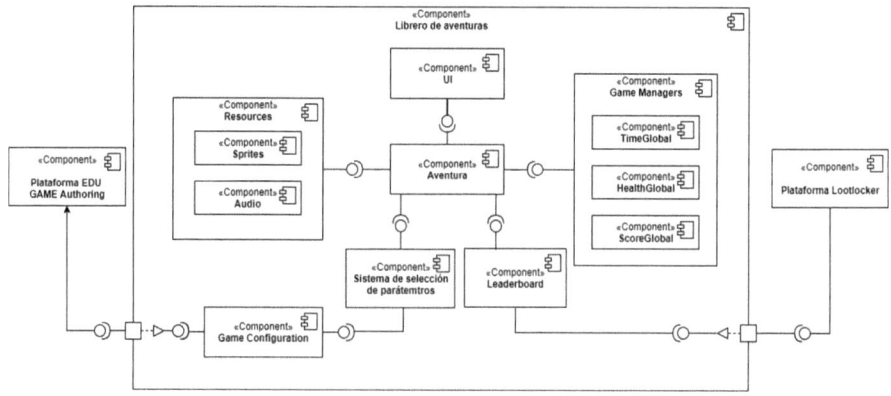

Fig. 4. Technical Architecture

Student Number	Standardized Score		
	Pre-Test Score	Post-Test Score	Difference
1	14	13	-1
2	11	9	-2
3	8	15	7
4	9	13	4
5	8	7	-1
6	9	15	6
7	10	13	3
8	12	9	-3
9	8	16	8
10	6	16	10
Average	9.50	12.60	3.10

Fig. 5. Pre/Post-Test Scores

7 Conclusion and Future Work

"Mi Librero de Aventuras" is validated as an effective configurable educational video game for 4th-grade S&T learning in Peru, leveraging LEGA [5] and LM-GM [3] frameworks to blend personalized mechanics with engaging gameplay. With 80% educational approval, 90% gameplay satisfaction via GEQ scores, and significant pre/post-test gains ($p < 0.05$, Fig. 5), the game aligns with MINEDU curriculum [15], addressing S&T resource gaps [19]. Teachers' qualitative feedback highlights configurability (Fig. 3) and motivation as strengths, surpassing static tools [20] and supporting autonomy per Self-Determination Theory [22]. The adventure-based design (Figs. 1b–2b) and Unity architecture (Fig. 4) ensure pedagogical and entertainment synergy for digital-native learners [21]. Future work includes optimizing performance for low-end devices, adding an offline mode for rural access [26], and conducting a longitudinal, multi-school evaluation [9]. Expanding adventures (e.g., energy) [15], enhancing teacher training [18], and adapting for other subjects [28] will strengthen scalability and impact, positioning the game for national digital learning initiatives.

References

1. Anderson, L.W.: A taxonomy for learning, teaching, and assessing: a revision of Bloom's taxonomy of educational objectives. Inc, Addison Wesley Longman (2001)
2. Annetta, L.A., Minogue, J., Holmes, S.Y., Cheng, M.T.: Investigating the impact of video games on high school students' engagement and learning about genetics. Comput. Educ. **53**(1), 74–85 (2009). https://doi.org/10.1016/j.compedu.2008.12.020
3. Arnab, S.: Mapping learning and game mechanics for serious games. Br. J. Edu. Technol. **45**(3), 391–411 (2014). https://doi.org/10.1111/bjet.12113
4. Baldeón, J., Puig, A., Rodríguez, I., Zardain, L.: A platform for the authoring of educational games. In: 2018 13th Iberian Conference on Information Systems and Technologies (CISTI). pp. 1–6 (2018). https://doi.org/10.23919/CISTI.2018.8399394
5. Baldeón, J., Rodríguez, I., Puig, A.: LEGA: a LEarner-centered GAmification Design Framework. In: Proceedings of the XVII International Conference on Human Computer Interaction. Interacción '16, Association for Computing Machinery, New York (2016). https://doi.org/10.1145/2998626.2998673
6. Busch, M., et al.: Using player type models for personalized game design – an empirical investigation. Interact. Des. Architect. (28), 145–163 (2016). https://doi.org/10.55612/s-5002-028-008
7. Cohen, M.A., Niemeyer, G.O., Callaway, D.S.: Griddle: video gaming for power system education. IEEE Trans. Power Syst. **32**(4), 3069–3077 (2017). https://doi.org/10.1109/TPWRS.2016.2618887
8. De Aldama, C., Pozo, J.I.: Do you want to learn physics? please play angry birds(but with epistemic goals). J. Educ. Comput. Res. **58**(1), 3–28 (2019). https://doi.org/10.1177/0735633118823160
9. De Freitas, S.: Are games effective learning tools? a review of educational games. Educ. Technol. Soc. **21**(2), 74–84 (2018)
10. Dicheva, D., Dichev, C., Agre, G., Angelova, G.: Gamification in education: a systematic mapping study. J. Educ. Technol. Soc. **18**(3), 75–88 (2015). http://www.jstor.org/stable/jeductechsoci.18.3.75
11. Harker-Schuch, I.E., Mills, F.P., Lade, S.J., Colvin, R.M.: Co2peration – structuring a 3D interactive digital game to improve climate literacy in the 12-13-year-old age group. Comput. Educ. **144**, 103705 (2020). https://doi.org/10.1016/j.compedu.2019.103705
12. Honey, P., Mumford, A.: The Manual of Learning Styles. Peter Honey Publications, Maidenhead, UK (1982)
13. Khan, A., Ahmad, F.H., Malik, M.M.: Use of digital game based learning and gamification in secondary school science: the effect on student engagement, learning and gender difference. Educ. Inf. Technol. **22**(6), 2767–2804 (2017). https://doi.org/10.1007/s10639-017-9622-1
14. Legerén Lago, B.: Al-Kimia: how to create a video game to help high school students enjoy chemistry. In: Serious Games and Edutainment Applications, vol. II, pp. 259–272. Springer (2017). https://doi.org/10.1007/978-3-319-51645-5_11
15. Ministerio de Educación del Perú (MINEDU), Lima, Perú: Programa Curricular de Educación Primaria (2016). http://www.minedu.gob.pe/curriculo
16. Muntean, C.H., Andrews, J., Muntean, G.M.: Final frontier: an educational game on solar system concepts acquisition for primary schools. In: 2017 IEEE 17th International Conference on Advanced Learning Technologies (ICALT), pp. 335–337 (2017). https://doi.org/10.1109/ICALT.2017.111

17. Nallar, D.A.: Game Design Canvas. Recuperado de https://gamedesignla.com/game-design-canvas/ (2019)
18. Niess, M.L.: Preparing teachers to teach science and mathematics with technology: developing a technology pedagogical content knowledge. Teach. Teach. Educ. **21**(5), 509–523 (2005). https://doi.org/10.1016/j.tate.2005.03.006
19. OECD: Pisa 2018 results (volume i): What students know and can do. OECD Publishing (2018). https://read.oecd.org/10.1787/5f07c754-en?format=pdf
20. Padilla-Zea, N., Aceto, S., Burgos, D.: Modeling storytelling to enhance educational games. Entertainment Comput. **18**, 1–14 (2017). https://doi.org/10.1016/j.entcom.2016.10.001
21. Prensky, M.: Digital natives, digital immigrants part 1. On the Horizon **9**(5), 1–6 (2001). https://doi.org/10.1108/10748120110424816
22. Ryan, R.M., Deci, E.L.: Self-determination theory and the facilitation of intrinsic motivation, social development, and well-being. Am. Psychol. **55**(1), 68–78 (2000). https://doi.org/10.1037/0003-066X.55.1.68
23. Silva, M.L.M., de Araujo, R.M.: Crayon sharks: a case study on the design and application of a digital game for science teaching. HOLOS (2017). https://www.redalyc.org/articulo.oa?id=481554852025
24. Solano Nogales, L., Santacruz Valencia, L.P.: Videojuegos como herramienta en educación primaria: caso de estudio con eadventure. Revista Iberoamericana de Tecnología en Educación y Educación en Tecnología (18), 101–112 (2016). https://www.scielo.org.ar/scielo.php?script=sci_arttext&pid=S1850-99592016000200011
25. Strawhacker, A., Sullivan, A., Verish, C., Bers, M.U., Shaer, O.: Enhancing children's interest and knowledge in bioengineering through an interactive videogame. J. Inf. Technol. Educ. Innov. Pract. **17**, 55 (2018)
26. Susi, T., Johannesson, M., Backlund, P.: Serious games: an overview. Tech. Rep. HS-IKI-TR-07-001, University of Skövde (2007). http://urn.kb.se/resolve?urn=urn:nbn:se:his:diva-1279
27. Wan Ahmad, W.F., Abdul Rahman, N.F.: Akamia: chemistry mobile game-based tutorial. In: 2014 3rd International Conference on User Science and Engineering (i-USEr), pp. 221–226 (2014). https://doi.org/10.1109/IUSER.2014.7002706
28. Winn, B.M.: The design, play, and experience framework. In: Proceedings of the 3rd International Conference on Game Development in Education, pp. 1010–1024. IGI Global (2009). https://doi.org/10.4018/978-1-59904-808-6.ch058

Multi-directional Shooting Using Logarithmic Spiral Trajectories

Kento Saito and Akihiro Matsuura(✉)

Tokyo Denki University, Hiki 350-0394, Saitama, Japan
25rmd22@ms.dendai.ac.jp, matsu@rd.dendai.ac.jp

Abstract. In this study, inspired by the method called video feedback that is used in video art, we propose shooting techniques that enable shooting in multiple directions simultaneously by specifying a rotation angle and a scale rate. To support determining the rotation angle, a circular scope is attached around the player's own object. Through implementation and trial play, we confirmed that enemy objects can be effectively shot using the recursive curvilinear motion of projectiles.

Keywords: Shooting · Shooter · Recursion · Multi-direction · Logarithmic Spiral · Angle · Scaling · Video Feedback

1 Introduction

The exploration of recursive structures boasts a long history, with significant contributions from mathematicians like Cantor and Sierpinski. The concept of self-similarity and fractals, pioneered by Mandelbrot from the 1960s onwards [1, 2], has had a profound influence across diverse fields extending beyond mathematics and science, with significant efforts dedicated to their visualization and computer graphics [3]. Separately from scientific inquiry, the advent of the video recorder in the 1950s led to the discovery of *video feedback*, a phenomenon where recursive, nested images emerge when a video camera is directed at a monitor displaying its own captured image, thereby fostering novel forms of expression within video art [4]. Video feedback has been also fully analyzed in a physical and mathematical standpoints [5, 6].

In recent years, the development of works incorporating recursive structures has expanded into the realms of games and VR. For instance, Patrick's Parabox [7], a puzzle game by Traynor, features a compelling nested structure where each stage's box-shaped map is contained within itself, allowing for the movement of boxes within boxes and even player entry. As for VR systems, MeiMeiRoRo [8] utilizes a nested structure in a maze VR to enable an experience where bird's-eye and first-person perspectives simultaneously exist. MetaCity [9] achieves recursive interaction in the VR space by enabling manipulation of a full-scale world through manipulation of a miniature representation. While numerous interactive experiences employing recursive structures have been implemented, to the authors' knowledge, the recursively changing shapes and their manipulation, as seen in video art expressions, have yet to be utilized in interactive games or VR. In rhythm-based shooters such as Rez and Rez Infinite [10], visual effects involving scaling and rotational motion appear in interactive audiovisual elements. However, these transformations are not the direct objective of a player; rather, they serve to enhance the sensory immersion and reinforce the rhythm-action dynamics of the game. Super Hexagon [11] is an action game where the player avoids contact with the edges of dynamically rotating and scaling polygons. The gameplay involves only passive dodging actions, with no direct offensive interactions. As for bullet generation and motion in bullet hell shooters, we can find curved and rotational patterns based on parameters and formulas in systems such as Talakat [12], Keiki [13], and Mathmare [14]. However, they are not controlled by the player; rather, they function as environmental challenges that the player must navigate.

In light of these studies, the objective of this study is to introduce novel techniques for both a player and enemies of a shooter by leveraging the logarithmic spiral patterns which typically appear in the recursive images of video feedback. More precisely, we developed a 2D shooter in which enemy's objects approach the player through recursively altering their size and direction and a player attacks by intuitively manipulating a gamepad to recursively change the size and direction of the projectiles. Through implementation and trial play, we confirmed the feasibility of targeting and eliminating enemy objects by utilizing the projectiles with logarithmic spiral trajectories.

2 Video Feedback

Feedback processes are crucial in scientific operations where an output repeatedly becomes the next input. This iterative mechanism is often realized by a feedback machine, typically comprising input, output, and control storage units alongside a processing unit [6]. Video feedback is a unique visual experiment employing such a machine. It involves a video camera capturing an image displayed on a monitor, which then shows the captured image, generating diverse recursive visual patterns based on the camera and monitor's spatial arrangement. Figure 1 left shows an image displaying the monitor generated through video feedback. Figure 1 right shows another image, created by placing a light on the monitor in a dark environment and rotating the camera approximately 30°, in which the light appears in a logarithmic spiral. Crutchfield [5] presented a technique for visualizing image patterns by employing a recursive equation to represent the transformations in shape and color information of an image generated through video feedback. This equation incorporates parameters such as light intensity, camera magnification, and the relative angle between the monitor and camera.

3 Game Design

3.1 Basic Idea

This research explores the potential for creating a novel shooter with enhanced operability and strategy by interpreting the behavior of patterns observed in video feedback – where objects move in a logarithmic spiral while recursively changing its size

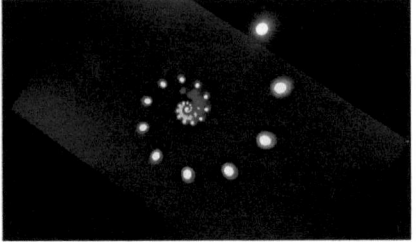

Fig. 1. Examples of Video Feedback Images.

and angle – as analogous to obstacles and projectiles in a digital game. A key characteristic of the resulting trajectory in video feedback we focus on is that when the monitor is rotated by a constant angle θ and scaled by a factor of $c = 0.95$, the value of θ allows us to perceive not only the overall single logarithmic spiral but also multiple distinct sets of curves. Four examples of this are presented below. Figure 2(a) illustrates the case where θ = 0°, resulting in a straight line trajectory. Figure 2(b) illustrates the typical logarithmic spiral observed when θ = 20°. Figure 2(c) shows the scenario with θ = 90°, where four lines of a cross pattern emerge. Finally, Fig. 2(d) shows the case with θ = 179°, where two curves exhibiting near 180° rotational symmetry are generated. Here we emphasize that each of these patterns is generated and differentiated by the single parameter of the rotation angle. Therefore, we apply this configuration for implementation of enemy or player projectiles in a shooter, in which players anticipate object placement in the display and launch projectiles that effectively traverse multiple directions as shown in Fig. 2, resulting in more strategic and potent attacks.

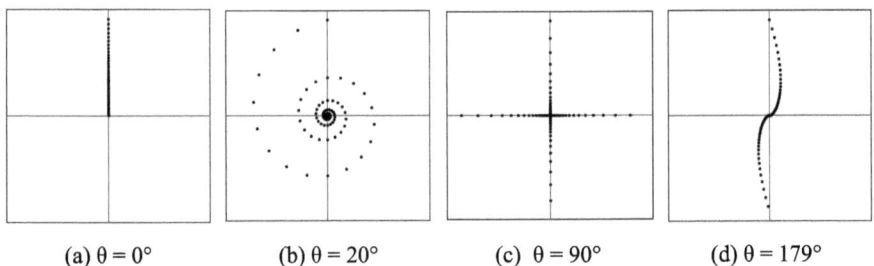

(a) θ = 0°   (b) θ = 20°   (c) θ = 90°   (d) θ = 179°

Fig. 2. Points on the Logarithmic Spirals According to the Rotation Angle.

3.2 Game Rule

We describe the rules of the developed 2D shooter. A player destroys enemy objects by hitting them with projectiles fired from own object. The player's objective is to survive for as long as possible by effectively destroying or evading enemies, which requires anticipating their recursive movements and manipulating the parameters of the projectiles' recursive motion. At the start of the game, enemy objects appear sequentially on the screen at regular intervals, exhibiting in recursively generated logarithmic spiral patterns. The relative rotation angle of the enemy's movement is randomly selected between −180° and 180°, and the scale ratio ranges from 0.67 to 1.5. Two types of enemy movement are implemented: converging and diverging. Examples of the converging and diverging movements are illustrated in Figs. 3 and 4, respectively. In the display, the player's object is rendered as red L-shape, player's projectile as white circles with pink boundaries, and the enemy objects as cyan squares.

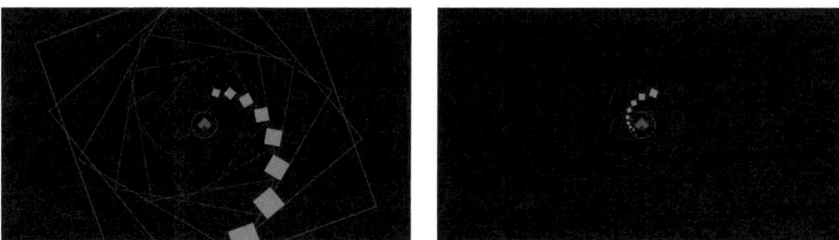

Fig. 3. Converging Movement of Enemy Objects.

Fig. 4. Diverging Movement of Enemy Objects.

A player can control the movement of its own object and also make firing action. Similar to the enemy, player's projectiles can be both converging and diverging. The rotation angle of the projectile is determined with a stick of controller or by tilting the controller itself. As shown in Fig. 5(a), the player's object is equipped with a circular scope to support deciding the rotation angle. Figure 5(b) shows the case of a usual straightforward projectile with $\theta = 0°$. Figure 5(c) shows the case $\theta = 30°$ with a diverging spiral. Figure 5(d) shows the case $\theta = 120°$ where the projectile spreads in three directions. To simplify the operation of the angle, it can be adjusted in 5° increments/decrements.

4 Game System

4.1 System Overview

The prototype system of the 2D shooter was developed using Unity (6000.0.41f1). The system generates player's projectiles and enemy objects in the 2D space, draws them in logarithmic spirals, and visualizes the collision of objects. A player basically uses a

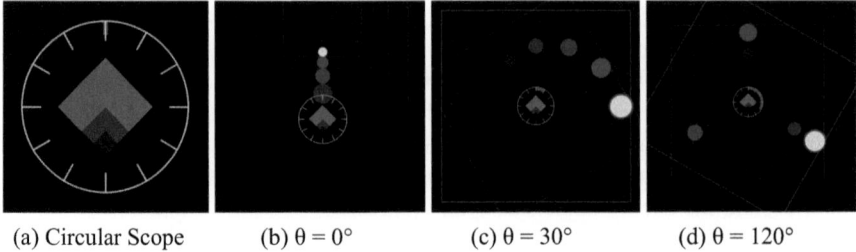

(a) Circular Scope (b) θ = 0° (c) θ = 30° (d) θ = 120°

Fig. 5. Circular Scope and Projectiles for Some Rotation Angles.

gamepad for the play and controls parameters such as the rotation angle and the scale ratio of the projectiles. In Unity, it is possible to set the relative position, rotation, and scale of an object to other objects based on the parent-child relationship. Our system employs this feature to implement graphic generation by repeatedly generating figures using the rotation angle and the scale of the previously generated figure, as long as the figure is neither too small nor too large to fit within the game screen. The algorithm is summarized by the pseudocode in Fig. 6. Here figure0, *min*, and *WINDOW* denote the initial figure, the predefined minimum-size frame, and the game screen, respectively. INSTANTIATE (*original*, *parent*) denotes a function that instantiates the first argument as a child object of the second argument, *parent*, and returns the instantiated object. *localScale* and *localAngle* denote the scale and the rotation angle of the shape relative to the parent object, respectively.

Algorithm 1
1: **function** GENERATERECURSIVEGRAPHIC(*c*, θ, *figure0*)
2:     *lastFigure* ← INSTANTIATE(*figure0*)
3:     UPDATEWINDOW()
4:     **while** *lastFigure* − *min* ≠ ∅ AND *WINDOW* − *lastFigure* ≠ ∅ **do**
5:         DELAY(*DELAY_TIME*)
6:         UPDATETHETA()
7:         *newFigure* ← INSTANTIATE(*figure0*, *lastFigure*)
8:         *newFigure.localScale* ← *c*
9:         *newFigure.localAngle* ← θ
10:        UPDATEWINDOW()
11:        *lastFigure* ← *newFigure*
12:     **end while**
13: **end function**

Fig. 6. Pseudocode of the Algorithm for Recursive Graphic Generation.

4.2 Operation Method for Player

In this game, a player can move and rotate its own object, set the relative rotation angle and scale rate for the movement of the projectiles, and fire them with either converging or diverging patterns. Table 1 details the control assignments for the Nintendo Switch

Pro Controller. The relative rotation angle is determined by the R stick tilt, with upward being defined as 0°. When firing converging projectiles, the reciprocal of the relative scale ratio at the moment of firing becomes the relative reduction ratio. Additionally, an alternative input method using Nintendo's Joy-Con is implemented, allowing players to specify the relative rotation angle by tilting the controller.

Table 1. Control Assignments for the Nintendo Switch Pro Controller.

Actions in the Game	Assignment
Movement of own object	Left Stick
Left turn of own object	L Button
Right turn of own object	R Button
Setting of rotation angle	Right Stick
Increase of scale rate	+ Control Pad (Up)
Decrease of scale rate	+ Control Pad (Down)
Firing diverging projectile	ZL Button
Firing converging projectile	ZR Button

5 Demonstration

Here, we present some gameplay results that demonstrate the essence of the proposed shooting experience. Around the objects of both the player and the enemies, square frames are drawn, similarly to the images of video feedback, to provide visual clues to help the player to guess the appropriate rotation angle for a shot. When the projectiles of the player make contact with the enemy's, the corresponding frames illuminate in light yellow.

Figure 7 shows an example all of the enemy objects in diverging spiral motion are effectively destroyed by the player with a single shot. In order to fire a projectile that sweeps the diverging enemy's objects at a time, it is necessary to move to an appropriate place and fire a projectile with a trajectory close to the enemy's one. In this example, after all nine enemy objects appeared, the player moved its own object to the original point of the diverging enemy and fired a projectile, which succeeded in shooting all of the enemy's efficiently.

Next, Fig. 8 illustrates a scene where the enemy objects are converging towards the player's object and the player fires a projectile with 90° rotation angle that spreads in four directions. It is observed that the projectile sequentially destroys the enemy objects in a single shot with diverging movement in 90° steps.

Fig. 7. Images of Eliminating Enemy Objects in Spiral Pattern.

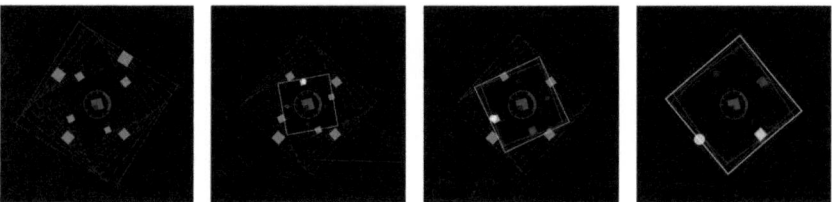

Fig. 8. Images of Eliminating Enemy Objects in Four Directions.

6 Discussion

6.1 Game Playability

In this game, a player's proficiency in detecting recursive movements, adjusting parameters, and manipulating the interface directly influences the success and efficiency in defeating evading enemies within this 2D shooter, thus proving crucial for ensuring a satisfactory level of playability. While limited to our experience, we confirmed a certain degree of feasibility of recognizing the trajectory of enemy's movements, setting parameters to generate a projectile's trajectory that overlaps with it, and destroying enemy objects. Furthermore, the feature for allowing the real-time renewal of the rotation angle after firing enables a player to refine the shots and converge towards the intended trajectory.

However, in contrast to conventional 2D shooters, the presented method of using the rotation angle and scale ratio of projectiles requires simultaneous control of these parameters as well as the usual movement of its own object, which should be a hurdle for novice player to make the presented method to be effectively used. It will be necessary to investigate the extent to which players can master these parameters after certain amount of practice, to conduct playability study, and to refine the user interface for further intuitive operation.

6.2 Entertainment Value

Here, we discuss the entertainment value inherent in the presented shooter. Firstly, it offers a novel puzzle-like activity in deciphering the trajectory patterns of enemy movements. Secondly, while some players may already be familiar with the concept of recursion and the properties of recursive graphic generation, others will embark on an enjoyable learning process as they explore the underlying principles of the recursive motion of enemy objects and their own projectiles, experimenting with the parameters of the rotation angle and scale rate. This learning can be akin to the enjoyable process of learning to throw and catch a ball that follows a parabolic arc.

From another perspective, when a player successfully reads and controls the recursive motion, managing to fire a projectile that traces a trajectory synchronized with the enemy's movements, a dramatic phenomenon occurs: all enemy objects are destroyed with a single shot, providing a significant sense of exhilaration, accomplishment, and release of tension. These effects are further emphasized through the use of sound and visual effects.

Finally, the patterns generated by the recursive movement of both the player's projectiles and enemy objects possess a visual appeal reminiscent of video feedback. Consequently, the gameplay of our shooter can offer visual entertainment not only to the player but also to spectators.

7 Concluding Remarks

This paper presented shooting techniques that enable curved trajectories of logarithmic spirals. Through the internal experiences of the author, the current state of the game has demonstrated a certain level of operability and entertainment value. How-ever, we further need to improve usability and playability by meticulously considering user interface and adjustment of the relevant parameters. Furthermore, when implementing a feature where the player or enemy objects autonomously pursue a target in a homing-like manner, it may be necessary to consider applying techniques such as PID control. Lastly, after implementing the modifications, evaluating usability, learnability, and comparing with conventional shooters will be important future work.

Acknowledgments. This work was supported by JSPS Grant-in-Aid for Scientific Research(C) 24K15250.

Disclosure of Interests. The authors have no competing interests to declare that are relevant to the content of this article.

References

1. Mandelbrot, B.: How long is the coast of Britain? Statistical self- similarity and fractional dimension. Science **156**(3775), 636–638 (1967)
2. Mandelbrot, B.: Les Objets Fractals: Forme. Hasard et Dimension. Flammarion, Paris (1975)
3. Berkowitz, J.: Fractal Cosmos: The Art of Mathematical Design. Amber Lotus (1998)
4. Sohn, D.A.: Film: The Creative Eye. Publisher, Geo. A. Pflaum, First Edition (1970)
5. Crutchfield, J.P.: Space-time dynamics in video feedback. Physica D **10**(1–2), 229–245 (1984). https://doi.org/10.1016/0167-2789(84)90264-1. https://www.youtube.com/watch?v=B4Kn3djJMCE. Accessed 18 Feb 2025
6. Peitgen, H.-O., Jürgens, H., Saupe, D.: Chaos and Fractals: New Frontiers of Science, 2nd edn. Springer, New York (2004)

7. Patrick's Parabox. https://www.patricksparabox.com/. Accessed 11 Apr 2025
8. Funabiki, O., Morita, N., Yanagida, Y.: MeiMeiRoRo. In SIGGRAPH Asia 2024 XR (SA XR'24), 1–2 (2024). https://doi.org/10.1145/3681759.3688928
9. Bluff, A., Johnston, A.: Don't panic: recursive interactions in a miniature metaworld. Proceedings of the 17th ACM International Conference on Virtual-Reality Continuum and its Applications in Industry (VRCAI'19), Article No. 33, pp. 1–9 (2019). https://doi.org/10.1145/3359997.3365682
10. Rez Infinite. https://www.rezinfinite.com/. Accessed 9 June 2025
11. Super Hexagon. https://superhexagon.com/. Accessed 9 June 2025
12. Khalifa, A., Lee, S., Nealen, A., Togelius, J.: Talakat: Bullet hell generation through constrained map-elites. In: Genetic and Evolutionary Computation Conference (GECCO'18), p. 8, ACM, New York, NY, USA (2018). https://doi.org/10.1145/3205455.3205470
13. Wang, Z., Liu, J., Yannakakis, G.N.: Keiki: towards realistic danmaku generation via sequential GANs. In 2021 IEEE Conference on Games (CoG), pp. 1–4 (2021). https://doi.org/10.1109/CoG52621.2021.9619013
14. Mathmare WebGL version. https://unityroom.com/games/mathmare. Accessed 10 June 2025

Refining Pervasive Game Design with LLMs
Insights, Limitations, and Challenges

Bruno Silva[1,2](✉) , Pedro Oliveira[2] , Gilvan Maia[2] ,
and Windson Viana[2]

[1] IFCE, Av. 13 de Maio, 2081, Benfica, Fortaleza, Ceará 60040-215, Brazil
`bruno.silva@ifce.edu.br`
[2] UFC, Av. Mister Hull, s/n - Pici, Fortaleza, Ceará 60455-760, Brazil
`pedrooliveira2702@alu.ufc.br`, `{gilvanmaia,windson}@virtual.ufc.br`

Abstract. Large Language Models (LLMs) offer promising opportunities for enhancing pervasive games, particularly in refining game design, including its content, through the integration of Artificial Intelligence (AI). The goal of this work is to discuss the use of LLMs for Procedure Content Generation (PCG) in a pervasive game, as well as employing LLMs to evaluate the context accuracy of the generated content. For this, we developed a card game "Top Triumphs" inspired by Top Trumps, which features a PCG module composed of one AI system and three LLMs. The PCG process is started using the players' geographic location. We also created *CheckThis*, a LLM-based tool that evaluates the contextual relevance and character accuracy of generated content, helping to tune the PCG process. Three experts evaluated the game content generated, confirming contextual and character accuracy with evaluation blocks reaching peaks of 92.85%. In the voting system part of *CheckThis*, one of the models managed to reach peaks of 83.3% acceptance. LLMs can significantly enhance pervasive game development by enabling more efficient design and testing workflows. Broader deployment requires additional validation, expansion, and ethical review.

Keywords: Pervasive games · Game Testing · Context Aware · LLM · Prompt-game · CAPAM

1 Introduction

Pervasive Games (PG) use cities as playgrounds with mobile GPS devices [2]. PG design approaches are supplemented by a new method where designers must conceptualize and implement ideas on-site, aiming to create innovative game concepts through direct fieldwork with sensors capturing and interpreting the scene. This leads to the area of Location-based Game (LBG), where scaling missions, content, and interactions span geographically. This paradigm creates a huge amount of work for the game designer, where some companies still maintain manual brute-force testing of their software [4].

Within Artificial Intelligence (AI), the area of generative AI has made numerous contributions to game development and offers different ways of playing. Generative AI models (GenAI) significantly advanced game development through large language models (LLMs) and AI [6]. Leveraging deep learning to process datasets with billions/trillions of parameters feasible today on consumer hardware, unlike 40 years ago. LLM enables dynamic content generation, reflecting exponential growth in computational power and its rapid integration across domains [1].

Procedural Content Generation (PCG) originated from algorithmic techniques for creating data automatically or semi-automatically. PCG is covered by domain AI, and has made numerous contributions to game development since game early days [7]. In content generation, language models, specifically LLMs, have become increasingly applicable. The recent boom in the use of LLM is still understood and adapted in several areas [1].

Building on preliminary studies, this work explores the following **research question**: *How can Large Language Models be used for Procedural Content Generation in pervasive games, and how effective are they in evaluating the contextual accuracy of the generated content?*

To address this, we developed the **Context-Aware Pervasiveness Automation Module (CAPAM)** a content generation layer powered by LLMs. Using CAPAM, we created a demo card game, *Top Triumphs*, in which cards dynamically adapt to the player's geospatial context.

Our contribution also includes AI-driven tools to support designers. **Check-This** analyzes the game's structure to suggest improvements, support maintenance, and enable rapid prototyping. Leveraging CAPAM, it allows LLMs to assist designers by recommending changes to PCG settings based on specific design goals. This approach aims to enhance designer productivity and streamline pervasive game development.

2 PCG Process

The PCG process in our game accesses sensors, communicates with other platforms (i.e., content repositories), and orchestrates requests to LLMs. See Fig. 2 for a visual description of the content generation process. The central discussion in this work is that the captured data will be shared with specifically trained LLMs to provide feedback to the game context.

The flow begins with the game demand a content request, Fig. 2(1), which initializes the PCG module, which collects information from the context Fig. 2(2), which uses this data to assemble the prompt for various LLMs Fig. 2(4), which finally, can also collect data from content repositories on Fig. 2(6). These requests to LLMs and GenAI are processed incrementally on demand based on the game structure. If the production of content for this context is complete, it will return to the game as produced content (Fig. 1).

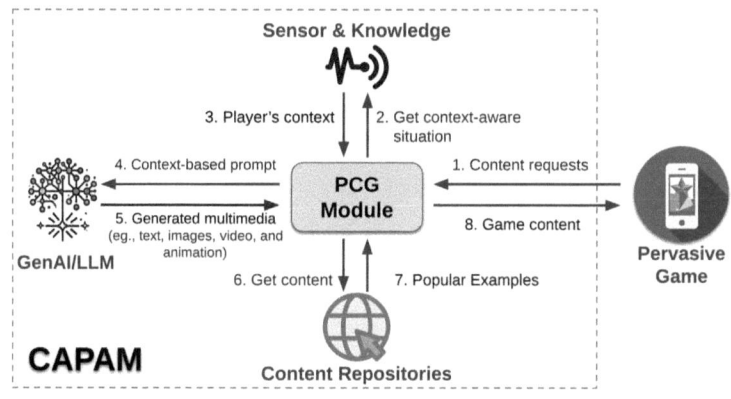

Fig. 1. Procedure Content Generated process.

2.1 Top Triumphs

The game is a card-based system implemented within CAPAM. This involves selecting three out of ten generated cards, each representing a medieval roleplaying game class with distinct attribute sets. Players dynamically switch between these cards during combat against an NPC (non-player character) card, strategically choosing which attribute to compare in conflicts. Points are awarded based on the outcome of these attribute comparisons, and unique cards can be generated by the player at any stage of gameplay.

The way this layer operates does not generate a direct dependency on specific LLMs, which may limit the creativity of developers. The game's main distinction lies in its pervasive use of LLMs, where geographic data and contextual references provide a dynamic content experience. This LBG incorporates wildlife data from LLM_2 and attempts to promote player immersion with gameplay that differs depending on geographic location.

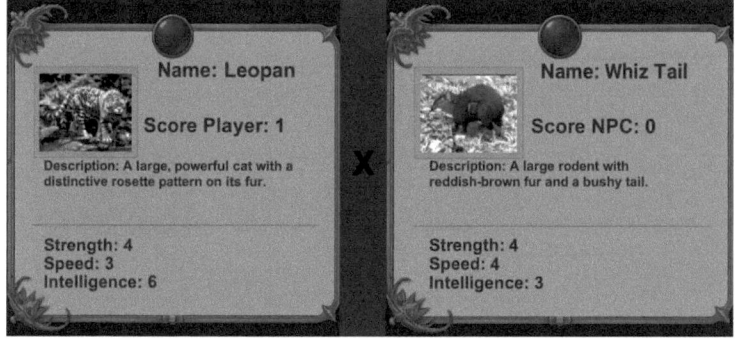

Fig. 2. Top Triumphs screen game.

Table 1. List of LLMs and GenAI.

ACRONYM	LLMs	GOAL
LLM_1	phi-4-Q4_K_M.gguf	Take the city and state from the user location.
LLM_2	gemma-2-27b-it-Q4_K_M.gguf	List animals and generated their description data from that place.
LLM_3	Qwen2.5-14B-Instruct-Q4_K_M.gguf	Generate a unique and random nickname according to the animal and its description.
GenAI_1	StableDiffusion 1.5	Generate new card image from reference content repositories.

The stable prompts were created and improved through interactions with ChatGPT (Prompt Tuning) to ensure they adhere to best practices and are efficient. Our refinement procedure follows a public guide[1] Each prompt was treated individually for each LLMs system by acknowledging that there is still plenty of room for fine-tuning each of these models. The sequence of requests evolved into a complex prompt, an adapted prompt chaining tailored to the game context. The GenAI identified in the process is StableDiffusion (SD), responsible for generating the image cards. Table 1 summarizes the list of LLMs and GenAi used.

2.2 Experts Content Evaluation

Three specialists in the design field were recruited to complete a questionnaire[2] based on the content generated by the game. This qualitative research method involved designers responding about their preference for an image that best aligns with the provided text. Moreover, images and texts were both generated by the game itself. One image among the evaluated set was randomly selected as a reference image from content repositories. These findings highlight distinct patterns in how specialists evaluate generated images based on different parameters and city contexts.

In experiments, there were two image groups: one varied the parameters of SD related to CFG_Scale, and another group varied the number of Steps. Additionally, variations in location were introduced, creating a unique context for each city. The questionnaire consists of four blocks, each containing 14 questions. The division is as follows: one block varies STEP, while a second block varies CFG_Scale for City 1, and this logic is repeated for City 2. Each of the 14 questions in every block corresponds to a different animal, aiming to determine which of the animal photos best fits a given textual context. Five images were provided for each question: one reference image and four generated by varying the SD parameters (CFG_Scale and Step). The CFG_Scale variations ranged between [12, 14, 16, 18], and the Step variations ranged between [20, 35, 50, 80].

---

[1] www.promptingguide.ai.
[2] www.doi.org/10.5281/zenodo.15078549.

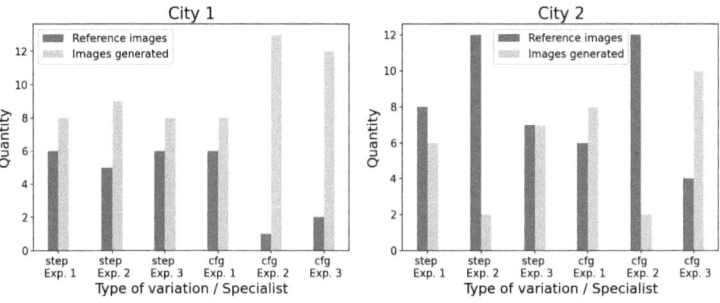

Fig. 3. Illustrating the frequency of images and context preferred by experts.

Looking at the results[3] and observing Fig. 3, we have in the graph a sample space of 14 choices that are divided into the choice of a reference image and the choice of an image that was generated. For City 1, when evaluating image progression through variation of Step, Specialists 1 and 3 preferred transformed images at rates of 57.14% and 43%, respectively, and Specialist 2 64.28%. In the variation of the CFG Scale, Specialists 2 and 3 favored transformed images over the original reference image in 92.85% and 85.71% of cases, respectively. Specialist 1 preferred only 57.14%.

For City 2, there was a preference for original photos since Stable Diffusion often generated some aberrations in details that cases even using prompts to exclude these mutations. Specialist 2 favored the original image over the transformed one at rates of 85% for both CFG Scale and Step variations. In Step variation, Specialist 1 preferred the original image at 57.14% for Step and 42.85% for CFG Scale, while Specialist 3 showed preferences of 50% and 28.57%, respectively.

3 Checkthis

3.1 Design Principles

CheckThis proposes game design configurations to designers. This suggestion comes from an automated analysis of an LLMs Voting System. In Top Triumph, this system evaluates images and nicknames from card generation. This evaluation tool facilitates simple adjustments with the aim of improving the player experience without complications for the designer.

In Fig. 4, the proposed interface for the use of AI-assisted design is illustrated. The idea is to have a screen for fine-tuning, where the designer can modify one or more elements simultaneously, and the AI seeks a configuration proposal with maximum precision while minimizing hallucination. At the top center screen has a prompt to talk with AI and let them guide to create a proposed benchmark. There is the bottom "Send" to dialogue with AI. As the game design was

---

[3] www.doi.org/10.5281/zenodo.15078549.

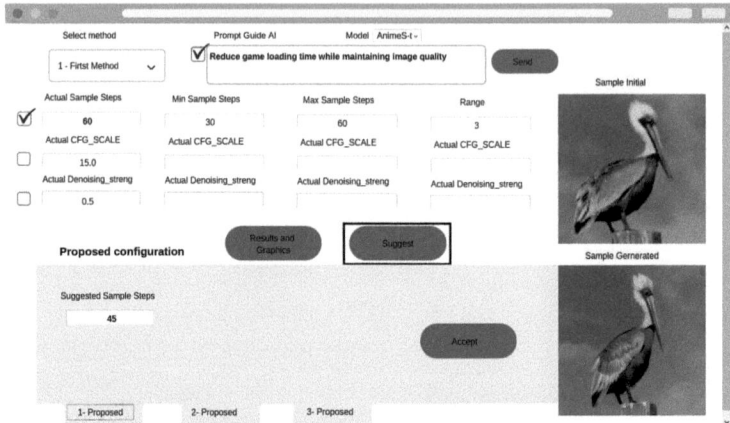

Fig. 4. Design screen assisted by an AI assistant.

developed in a chain of thought manner to reach final content production, the evaluation screen allows for individual modification of each generation point, by selecting through a drop-down list method. This drop-down is at the top left. In Figure, the designer chooses the prompt for Stable Diffusion, and displays its variables on screen. To facilitate the wizard's resolution, the designer can decide which variable he wants to have variations and be taken into account in the resolution. In the case of the screen in Fig. 4, the variable "Steps" was chosen.

In the middle, two red buttons stand out: one to access "Results and Graphs" related to generation (similar to what is seen before in the Evaluation section), and another button labeled "accept" to overwrite the current generation configuration according to the chosen proposal. The inferences made by the AI, results generated by the models to analyze quality and accuracy in the benchmark, are exposed by the "Suggest" button. This button opens a window with insights and reflections, offering designers guidance for refining their work.

At this stage, the project is undergoing ethical committee approval at the university to begin user testing and finally begin materializing the tool. The tests will be conducted in a cyclical and incremental manner. To shape these stages, we have adopted the User-Centered Design methodology (UCD). UCD is a software development methodology for developers and designers that essentially helps them create software that meets their users' needs [3]. The goal of UCD is to bring the user into the creation process, integrating them into intermediate testing cycles. By placing users at the center of your development process, you will eliminate ambiguity and reach the core of their needs [3]. In this case, the use of iterative testing and feedback cycles to improve the action of refining the model results and increasing user involvement in proportion to the final result choices. This aims to ensure that the models are aligned with the expectations of players, the public that the design perceives.

Table 2. List of LLMs Judges.

ACRONYM	LLMs
JudgeLLM_1	llava-v1.5-7b-Q4_K.gguf
JudgeLLM_2	Eris_PrimeV4-Vision-32k-7B-Q4_K_S-imat.gguf
JudgeLLM_3	Qwen2-VL-7B-Instruct-Q4_K_M.gguf
JudgeLLM_4	llava-v1.6-34b.Q4_K_M.gguf
JudgeLLM_5	MiniCPM-o-2_6-gguf/Model-7.6B-Q4_0.gguf

3.2 Voting System

CheckThis has two primary functions: I) assisting designers in refining gaming content; II) automating content creation without requiring a designer for niche, specific, and context-appropriate content. At this stage of the research, the hypothesis raised is that LLMs could be used to evaluate the relevance of the context (accuracy) of the content generated for Top Triumph. Following ideas from Taesiri et al.'s article [5], which seeks AI models capable of detecting glitches in games, we proceed smoothly using the ability of AI to check whether the generations match the text and photo reference. For judgment, only identification and non-identification were counted. And above three LLMs identifying contextual data were counted in the report.

In this scenario, the same content generated by the game is evaluated by other LLMs. If this AI can identify it, it will be recorded, but if not, it may point to some kind of hallucination in the generated content. In the current state of research, through experimentation, the LLMs used for this mechanics voting system are found in Table 2.

The generation variation proposals are similar to the experts' experiment. In this case, the frequency of positively identified data is in the space of 60 samples. The Cfg_scale variations are between [12,14,16,18], and Step variations are

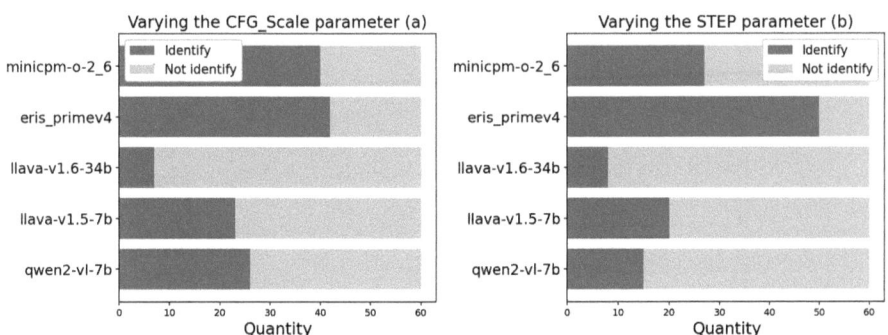

Fig. 5. Illustrating the frequency that model LLMs identifies according to the variations presented by two parameters.

between [20,35,50,80]. By setting the STEP variable, the evaluation was produced for each of the five Judge_LLM, similar to the variation of CFG_scale. Some restriction tags like "Many faces" or "Low quality" were inserted in the negative prompt so that hallucinations or low-quality generation were not positive.

In this accuracy evaluation, it is verified whether the set of generations, specifically the name and the image, makes sense concerning all the knowledge collected throughout various stages of construction. Observing the results[4] the best individual performance comes model from the JudgeLLM_2 model for both Step and CFG_scale variations. Note that this LLM obtained the best individual results in most cases, even with low image definition coming from the first values of the Step variable at the beginning of the generation variation. However, since it is a voting system, the poor performance of the others leads to false negatives. This could be corrected by training the LLMs specifically for the content domain.

The results of JudgeLLM_2 is the best model for the largest number of identification cases. In Fig. 5 (a), the frequency results of the JudgeLLM_2 and JudgeLLM_5 models for CFG_scale variation were almost the same, 70% and 66.6%. In total, in the CFG_Scale variation of JudgeLLM_2 it peak 70% and in the Step variation 83.3%.

4 Challenges and Future Directions

In this work, we explored how LLMs can support Procedural Content Generation (PCG) and content evaluation in pervasive games. Our prototype study yielded promising results, demonstrating that AI can assist in generating geographically contextualized content with high contextual and character accuracy. However, we also faced significant computational challenges, which highlight the need for optimization in future iterations.

We envision the full integration of *CheckThis* not only as an AI co-assistant but also as an intelligent orchestrator within the design workflow. By leveraging natural language prompts, designers may eventually develop and evolve games more efficiently, saving time while adhering to budget constraints. In this context, LLMs offer an exciting opportunity to transform how pervasive game content is both generated and evaluated.

Looking ahead, we plan to expand *CheckThis* by refining its content evaluation mechanisms and exploring strategies for dynamic optimization. Creating a reliable LLM-based "Judge" still presents challenges including handling subjectivity, multimodal content, and limited context but we believe that with targeted improvements, LLMs can play a central role in assisting designers throughout the entire PCG lifecycle.

Acknowledgements. This research was partially funded by CNPQ (under grant number 314425/2021-7).

---

[4] www.doi.org/10.5281/zenodo.14927785 , www.doi.org/10.5281/zenodo.14927768.

Disclosure of Interests. The authors have no competing interests to declare that are relevant to the content of this article.

References

1. Cao, Y., et al.: A comprehensive survey of AI-generated content (AIGC): a history of generative AI from GAN to ChatGPT. arXiv preprint arXiv:2303.04226 (2023)
2. Kai, L., Tan, W.H., Saari, E.M.: Dimensions of interactive pervasive game design: systematic review. JMIR Serious Game. **11**, e42878 (2023)
3. Lowdermilk, T.: User-Centered Design. O'Reilly Media (2013)
4. Roque, A., Sotomayor, J.P., Santiago, D., Clarke, P.J.: A literature review of software testing practices and frameworks in the video gaming industry. Softw. Test. Verification and Reliab. **35**(2), e70001 (2025)
5. Taesiri, M.R., Feng, T., Bezemer, C.P., Nguyen, A.: GlitchBench: can large multimodal models detect video game glitches? In: Proceedings of the IEEE/CVF Conference on Computer Vision and Pattern Recognition, pp. 22444–22455 (2024)
6. Wu, Z., Chen, Z., Zhu, D., Mousas, C., Kao, D.: A systematic review of generative AI on game character creation: applications, challenges, and future trends. IEEE Trans. Game. (2025)
7. Yannakakis, G.N., Togelius, J.: A panorama of artificial and computational intelligence in games. IEEE Trans. Comput. Intell. AI Game. **7**(4), 317–335 (2014)

Heist Extravaganza: A Design Framework and Exemplars of Asymmetric Virtual Reality Controllers Based on Player Profiles

Jules A. M. van Gurp and Erik D. van der Spek(✉)

Department of Industrial Design, Eindhoven University of Technology, Groene Loper 3, 5612AE Eindhoven, The Netherlands
e.d.vanderspek@tue.nl

Abstract. Virtual Reality provides immersive experiences to players but can be limiting for bystanders and spectators. Asymmetric Virtual Reality (AVR) allows these people to join in on the game in a more social setting. In addition, this affords gameplay differentiation based on player motivation types. Although several frameworks for AVR exist, it is unclear how to design different interactions to improve social presence from the perspective of player types. Taking Yee's Gamer Motivation Model as a basis, we investigated existing alternative game controllers and performed a small-scale co-design session with a VR game developer. Through this we arrive at five dimensions for AVR gameplay interactions: Immersive, Energetic, Precise, Explorative and Strategic. We developed an exemplar game called Heist Extravaganza, where each dimension is translated into a specific role and associated interface. A preliminary evaluation shows promise of the different roles and design implications are subsequently discussed.

Keywords: Asymmetric Virtual Reality · Mixed Reality · Co-located gameplay · Game design · Game controller design

1 Introduction

Virtual Reality can create highly immersive and engaging gaming experiences that engender heightened emotional responses and a greater sense of presence than non-immersive display modalities [1]. Through online social platforms like VRChat, Virtual Reality (VR) can furthermore support social presence, the feeling of being physically co-located and socially connected to others [2] over distance, which was especially helpful during the covid-19 pandemic [2, 3]. The social connectedness may not be as strong when the players are actually physically co-located however, because the isolating nature of VR makes real world interactions and communications more difficult [4], sometimes leading to players becoming less social than when they were separated [5]. A solution to this problem could be Asymmetric Virtual Reality (AVR), which can turn bystanders into co-players by giving them interfaces into the same virtual environment as the VR user and enforces communication [6]. Asymmetry in this case can mean players having different interfaces, different game mechanics, and/or different information, among other things [6, 7]. Although such a categorization would not necessarily preclude two people standing in different rooms, both wearing Head-Mounted Displays (HMD) in the same virtual environment, in general the term AVR is implied to mean a co-located experience where at least one person wears a VR HMD and at least one other person has an interface into the same virtual world through a different device [7]. For this paper, we adhere to the latter connotation, especially as it applies to gaming. AVR shares similarities with other social hybrid mixed reality and pervasive gaming approaches, in that it can offer social connectedness in a playful setting, but that it does require a shared magic circle or aesthetic illusion [8]. Or in other words, everyone must feel like they are part of the game world. When co-located people become part of this magic circle, imaginative immersion and flow are increased [9].

A great benefit of AVR gaming is that different devices can satisfy the preferences of different players. Some people may not want to use a VR headset due to concerns about cybersickness or not being proficient enough [10]. AVR allows these players to participate in an immersive game through easier controllers. However, little is known on how to design controllers for player preferences beyond skill level. In a recent systematic literature review by Rogers and colleagues, two prominent gaps in the literature on the design of AVR were identified: alternative interfaces and games that accommodate more than two players [6]. Here we want to investigate whether it's possible for AVR to satisfy multiple different player profiles at once, by designing new controllers that can serve as design exemplars.

2 Asymmetric Virtual Reality Interfaces Based on Player Profiles

2.1 Player Motivation

Not every player is motivated by the same game mechanics, dynamics or aesthetics. Over time, researchers have attempted to segment gamers into player profiles [11], with one of the first and best-known attempts at classifying gamers being Bartle's taxonomy of player types [12], classifying gamers into Killers, Achievers, Explorers and Socializers. This classification was based solely on online multiplayer games and over time attempts have been made to include other game experiences as well, such as the ACE2 model that substitutes Killers and Socializers for more singleplayer friendly Creators and Engagers [13], and the Gamer Motivation Model that separates and expands on Bartle's compound profiles into 6 main types and 12 subtypes [14], among many others [cf. 11]. We used the latter classification, Yee's Gamer Motivation Model, as a basis for our research. It should be noted that this model has never been fully peer-reviewed, but we use it as inspiration in the design process because it appears more elaborate than others and therefore affords more starting points to chart the design space from.

The Gamer Motivation Model describes six major player motivations: Action, Social, Mastery, Achievement, Immersion and Creativity. Of these, Social is more the intended outcome of all our asymmetric controllers (for instance through asymmetric information), rather than something we can create a singular controller around. Immersion is of course very important for Asymmetric Virtual Reality but is already well served with the Meta Quest 3 HMD and controllers in our setup, both of which track the body's movements to transport the player into the VR world.

2.2 Research Through Design and Co-design Session

Subsequently a research through design process was initiated, combining first person, second person and third person perspectives. For the first-person perspective, multiple different controller ideas were sketched for each of the gamer motivation profiles. Examples include: buttons located far apart so players would have to run to reach them (excitement subtype), or cranks that needed to be operated with force (destruction subtype) for the Action category. Pawns that needed to strategically be placed on a board (strategy subtype), or a force feedback push-pull lever that had to be operated very precisely (challenge subtype) for the Mastery category. A big red button with a plastic cover or a dynamite plunger to satisfy a feeling of power (power subtype) or interfaces that change over time and build up resistance (completion subtype) for the Achievement category. Lastly, for the Creativity category, examples of concepts include blocks or sand to sculpt terrain that is replicated in the virtual world (design subtype), or scanning tokens to acquire powerups (discovery subtype).

For the second-person perspective, a small-scale co-design session with three VR developers was conducted. During multiple ideation rounds, participants were instructed to come up with various AVR game concepts along with accompanying sets of non-standard interfaces. They were provided with the AVR Game Genre Framework developed by Dawes and colleagues to support this process [10]. Additionally, they were encouraged to sketch out their ideas and share them with the other developers. In the final ideation round, participants were asked to generate interface concepts for each other's AVR games.

Finally, the concepts in the previous sessions were supplemented by desk research of existing state of the art, notably from the archives of Alt.Ctrl.GDC [15], existing AVR games and commercial playful controllers like Nintendo Labo [16].

From these three perspectives, a large number of controller concepts were aggregated and analyzed. However, it quickly became apparent that in terms of the physical actions that a player employs, some of the concepts overlap and intersect across gamer motivation categories. We subsequently distinguished four dimensions of AVR gameplay interactions that could be facilitated by various interface modalities, viz. Energetic, Precise, Explorative, and Strategic interactions (Fig. 1).

2.3 Energetic, Precise, Explorative and Strategic Interactions

Energetic. How well a player performs energetic interactions is dependent on how much energy they can exert into the interface. An example could be needing to shake a motion sensing interface or having to run around a room pressing various buttons as fast as possible. These examples focus on kinetic energy. However, potential energy interactions can also be applied to interfaces. A player having to turn a crank to wind up a spring as tightly as possible while feeling an increasing level of resistance could be an example. This action could then result in launching a virtual object as far or fast as possible.

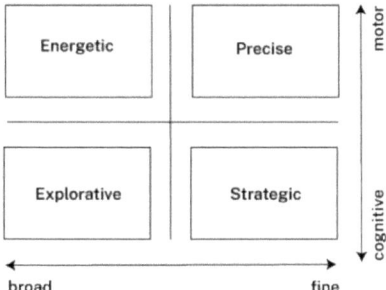

Fig. 1. Framework for AVR controllers based on player profiles

The input value of these interactions is limited by the human's physical ability. A joystick as input has a clear limit. The limit is how much it can be moved to either side. However, if you put someone on an exercise bike and use the pedals as input, then the limit is how fast the pedals can be turned. In this case the limit can vary from player to player, but also be influenced by exhaustion levels, depending on the intensity of the interaction.

Precise. Performance levels for interactions in this category do not increase by doing actions necessarily faster or with more force. For these interactions it is more important with which specific speed or force an action is performed. Balancing or controlling components or whole interfaces are included in this category. Instead of turning a wheel as fast as possible for energetic interactions, precise movements like a steering wheel for a car fit here. Inputs that need to be performed in a specific rhythm that need to be timed or coordinated well, also fall within this category.

Explorative. Explorative interactions concern broadly gathering and understanding information. Interfaces of which the output channels present a lot of information can fit this category. A paper manual containing a lot of text and visuals would be an example. A player could have to go through all this text to find secrets or use it to understand other information their team already possesses. Interfaces including monitors showcasing projections of the VR world and controls to change these projections fit in here as well, as do interfaces without clear affordances that need to be explored. Perhaps shaking a controller might result in something, or maybe three buttons need to be held simultaneously to perform a hidden action.

Strategic. In this last scenario, the player needs to make coordinated decision on information that is already explored. The focus is on thinking ahead and decision-making. Interfaces allowing users to note down their ideas could encourage forward planning. Interfaces with numerous sliders and knobs could facilitate resource management mechanics, forcing players to make decisions. Complex information would make this more interesting.

Strategic timing also falls into this category. "Normal" timing is reactive, such as pressing a button as quickly as possible after a light appears or a teammate shouts a cue. Strategic timing is proactive. It involves making a conscious decision based on information and planning. For example, choosing to use your only smoke bomb to get past a specific guard.

3 Heist Extravaganza: A Game Design Exemplar for Immersive, Energetic, Precise, Explorative and Strategic Interactions

Heist Extravaganza was developed to evaluate whether these dimensions could be translated into a coherent and satisfactory gameplay experience in which social interactions are facilitated. Next to a player wearing a Meta Quest 3 headset and controllers for the Immersive interaction, three physical interfaces were developed for the game, with two of these each facilitating one specific interaction dimension (Explorative and Strategic respectively), and one facilitating both Energetic and Precise interactions in one controller (see Fig. 2). We were aiming for one interaction dimension per device to better evaluate the different roles, but the project ran into time constraints, and it would also have made it harder to create sufficiently sized teams.

In the AVR game Heist Extravaganza, four players need to cooperate and use the various abilities and information provided to them by their unique roles and interfaces to pull off a successful museum heist. Three non-VR players each use their own custom interface, while a fourth VR player virtually traverses the museum as the thief (*the Fox*) who has to dodge guards and steal the museum piece from the safe.

Energetic. The role designed to facilitate this interaction dimension was designated as the *Engineer*. The corresponding interface also enabled the user to engage in precise interactions. The component responsible for supporting energetic interactions was implemented as a rotary wheel located on one side of the device. During the initial stage of the game, this wheel functions similarly to the crank of a music box; when rotated with sufficient speed, an in-game guard is lured away from their post and into a trap. In the final stage of the game, the wheel must be rotated as rapidly as possible to hoist a grappling hook that carries both the VR player and the acquired loot. The faster the wheel is rotated, the faster the team escapes. An LED strip mounted on top of the interface provides the user with visual feedback, indicating the rotational speed of the wheel.

Precise. When rotated at more controlled speeds, the wheel also facilitates precise interactions. To open the museum's safe, the *Engineer* can grasp the wheel's inner handle and rotate it slowly until a vibration is detected, generated by the integrated haptic motor. At this point, the direction of rotation must be reversed until the next vibration (representing a "click") is perceived. This process is repeated until the safe is successfully opened or the player fails by rotating the wheel too far in one direction.

Additional components are located on the opposite side of the interface, including an LCD screen and a numeric keypad. In one interaction scenario, the player is required to press the number displayed on the screen within a limited time frame. Failure to respond in time or selecting the incorrect number results in failure of the task. However, sustained success over a series of prompts unlocks a door within the virtual environment, allowing the VR player to proceed.

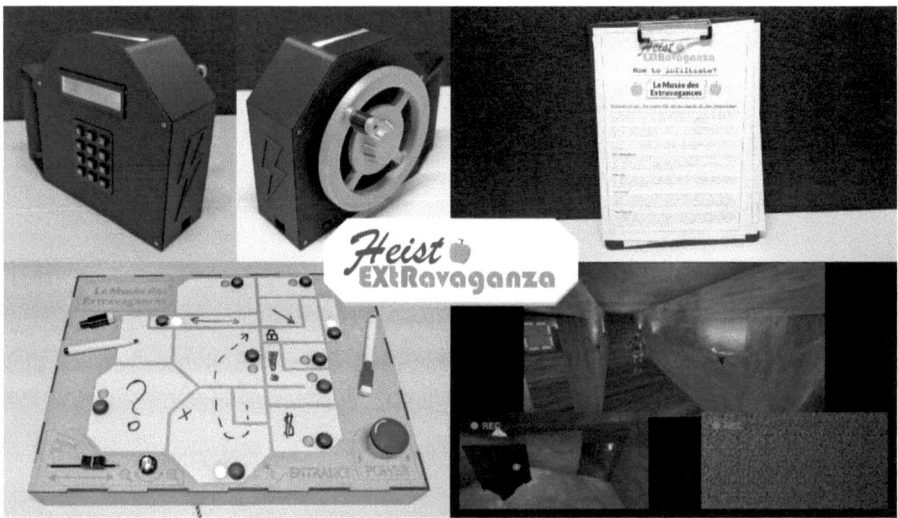

Fig. 2. The interface accompanying the Engineer's role, which facilitates both energetic and precise interactions (top left); the interface accompanying the Mastermind's role, which facilitates explorative interactions (top right); the physical component (bottom left) and digital component (bottom right) of the Hacker's interface, which facilitates strategic interactions.

Explorative. The role facilitating this interaction dimension is known as the *Mastermind* and is equipped with an interface in the form of a paper manual containing detailed information about the museum and the heist. The information must be carefully examined to discern what is relevant and communicated accordingly to other team members. The manual also includes a series of puzzles, some of which require input from other players in order to be solved. Once solutions are derived, they can be relayed back to the team to enable further progression within the game.

Strategic. The interface designed to facilitate strategic interactions consists of both a physical interactive map of the museum and a monitor displaying live security camera footage. This interface is operated by the player assuming the *Hacker* role. By pressing designated red buttons on the map, the player can hack into the museum's security camera system. Additionally, the camera views can be panned and zoomed using a slider and a rotary knob located on the bottom left of the physical interface.

The map itself is constructed from whiteboard paper, enabling the player to make erasable annotations and plan optimal routes for their teammate's navigation through the museum. While the *Mastermind* role can provide information regarding the varying functionalities of the *POWER* button, the *Hacker* is responsible for independently determining the appropriate timing and manner of utilizing these functions.

4 Evaluation

4.1 Procedure & Analysis

Two groups of four participants were recruited for the study. Each group played the game once and each player interacted with only one interface. Participants were instructed to collaboratively decide who would assume each of the available roles. The play sessions were conducted in a small private room within the university setting. All participants had a clear line of sight to observe one another's interactions with their respective interfaces and were able to communicate verbally without obstruction.

To evaluate the gameplay experience, participants completed the Player Experience Inventory (PXI) [17] and the Social Presence in Gaming Questionnaire (SPGQ) [18] following the session. Additionally, a semi-structured group interview was conducted. Responses from the PXI were compared to PXI benchmark data and analyzed using one-sample t-tests, while SPGQ data were examined through descriptive statistics.

4.2 Results

High scores on the SPGQ (scale range: 0 to 4) subscales Empathy ($M = 3.13$, $SD = 0.46$) and Behavioral Engagement ($M = 3.11$, $SD = 0.43$), along with low scores on Negative Feelings ($M = 0.27$, $SD = 0.38$), suggest that participants experienced a high degree of social presence during gameplay. These presence scores were comparable between VR (Empathy: $M = 3.14$, $SD = 0$; Behavioral Engagement: $M = 3.13$, $SD = 0.53$; Negative Feelings: $M = 0.08$, $SD = 0.12$) and non-VR players (Empathy: $M = 3.12$, $SD = 0.17$; Behavioral Engagement: $M = 3.10$, $SD = 0.38$; Negative Feelings: $M = 0.33$, $SD = 0.31$).

Participants further elaborated during the group interviews that the social aspect of the game enhanced their overall enjoyment. They reported feeling integral members of a team, and highlighted moments in which their individual actions were essential for collective progression as particularly rewarding. Moments when things went wrong were often described as the most memorable and enjoyable, as they prompted collective discussion and problem-solving. Additionally, the non-hierarchical nature of the roles was explicitly appreciated.

Most reported mean scores of the PXI (scale range: -3 to 3) were higher than those of the benchmark data, except for Audiovisual Appeal ($M = 1.71$, $SD = 1.29$), and Autonomy ($M = 0.58$, $SD = 1.12$), which even was significantly lower, $t(5) = -1.91$, $p = .049$. The mean score for Curiosity ($M = 2.25$, $SD = 0.75$) was significantly higher, $t(5) = 3.43$, $p = .011$. No benchmark data exists for the Enjoyment sub score, nonetheless the mean could be described as exceptionally high ($M = 2.75$, $SD = 0.39$). The Enjoyment scores did not vary much between the roles and most participants commented that all roles seemed enjoyable to them, albeit in different ways. Some players did express that some roles seemed less attractive to them personally, as they for example, did not feel like reading, or were not that much into quick time events. On average the Mastermind role was perceived as least interesting, as participants noted that in this position one had to overcome limited personal challenges.

5 Discussion and Conclusion

The purpose of this research was to explore whether interfaces in an Asymmetric Virtual Reality game could be designed to more closely fit players' various motivation profiles. In this way, more people in a team can find a role they like and have fun together, building up social connectedness. During two playtests we found preliminary evidence that this was indeed the case. Participants showed differentiated preferences for the four roles and achieved a high level of co-presence and enjoyment. This is in contrast to existing AVR games that usually mainly cater to the VR player [19].

There are, however, a number of limitations. The framework started from Yee's Gamer Motivation Model, which is not a peer-reviewed validated scale. In addition, the limited number of participants were not pre-selected on their player profile. We contend this is not a big limitation because as we translated the categories into physical interactions, we found intersecting qualities of the controllers and therefore aggregated subtypes into a new framework, moving away from Yee's original model. However, this may mean our interaction framework misses certain player motivation types and associated interactions. We hope to provide a first exploration into the design of controllers for AVR to stimulate social connectedness, but more work needs to be done.

Not every interaction facilitated by these interfaces strictly adhered to the dimension their design was an exemplar of, nor perhaps should they be. For example, the *Hacker* belongs to the Strategy category because the player Strategically chooses camera feeds to help the *Fox*, but the process of gathering information from the camera feeds can also be seen as an Explorative interaction. In real life settings, a person may not get the role conforming to their exact player type, so some ambiguity can be preferable.

In this paper, we present several interaction dimensions that were developed starting from Yee's Gamer Motivation Model, supplemented by co-design with experts and desk research of existing controllers. Using these dimensions as design guidelines, a set of distinct interfaces was created for an exemplar AVR game. Findings from the playtests indicate that implementing a high degree of interface asymmetry can be an effective strategy for fostering social presence and player enjoyment. This approach holds potential for making co-located VR experiences more socially engaging and appealing to a broader range of players. However, further application and testing across additional interface designs are needed to more thoroughly validate the method.

Acknowledgments. We would like to thank Enversed Studios for feedback during the development of the game and participating in a co-design session.

Disclosure of Interests. The authors have no competing interests to declare that are relevant to the content of this article.

References

1. Pallavicini, F., Pepe, A., Minissi, M.E.: Gaming in virtual reality: what changes in terms of usability, emotional response and sense of presence compared to non-immersive video games? Simul. Gaming **50**(2), 136–159 (2019)

2. Barreda-Ángeles, M., Hartmann, T.: Psychological benefits of using social virtual reality platforms during the covid-19 pandemic: the role of social and spatial presence. Comput. Hum. Behav. **127**, 107047 (2022)
3. Deighan, M.T., Ayobi, A., O'Kane, A.A.: Social virtual reality as a mental health tool: how people use VRChat to support social connectedness and wellbeing. In: Proceedings of the 2023 CHI Conference on Human Factors in Computing Systems, pp. 1–13 (2023)
4. Boland, D., McGill, M.: Lost in the rift: engaging with mixed reality. XRDS: Crossroads, The ACM Magazine for Students **22**(1), 40–45 (2015)
5. Born, F., Sykownik, P., Masuch, M.: Co-located vs. remote gameplay: the role of physical co-presence in multiplayer room-scale vr. In: 2019 IEEE Conference on Games (CoG), pp. 1–8 IEEE (2019)
6. Rogers, K., Karaosmanoglu, S., Wolf, D., Steinicke, F., Nacke, L.E.: A best-fit framework and systematic review of asymmetric gameplay in multiplayer virtual reality games. Frontiers in Virtual Reality **2**, 694660 (2021)
7. Ouverson, K.M., Gilbert, S.B.: A composite framework of co-located asymmetric virtual reality. In: Proceedings of the ACM on Human-Computer Interaction, 5(CSCW1), pp. 1–20 (2021)
8. Van der Spek, E.D.: Play and learning across realities: design strategies for a permeable magic circle. In: International Conference on Human-Computer Interaction. Cham: Springer Nature Switzerland. (2025)
9. Gajadhar, B.J., De Kort, Y.A.W., IJsselsteijn, W.A.: Rules of engagement: influence of co-player presence on player involvement in digital games. International Journal of Gaming and Computer-Mediated Simulations (IJGCMS), **1**(3), 14–27 (2009)
10. Dawes, M., Rackliffe, K., Hughes, A.L., Hansen, D.L.: Asymmetric VR game subgenres: implications for analysis and design. Multimodal Technologies and Interaction **8**(2), 12 (2024)
11. Hamari, J., Tuunanen, J.: Player types: a meta-synthesis. Transactions of the Digital Games Research Association, **1**(2) (2014)
12. Bartle, R.: Hearts, clubs, diamonds, spades: players who suit MUDs. J. MUD Research **1**(1), 19 (1996)
13. van Dam, T., Bakkes, S.: The ace2 model: Refining bartle's player taxonomy for creation play. In: 20th annual European GAME-ON Conference (GAME-ON'2019) (2019)
14. Yee, N.: The gamer motivation profile: what we learned from 250,000 gamers. In: Proceedings of the 2016 Annual Symposium on Computer-Human Interaction in Play, p. 2 (2016)
15. Alt.Ctrl.GDC Website. https://gdconf.com/alt-ctrl-gdc
16. Nintendo Labo. https://www.nintendo.com/my/switch/adfx/index.html
17. Vanden Abeele, V., Spiel, K., Nacke, L., Johnson, D., Gerling, K.: Development and validation of the player experience inventory: a scale to measure player experiences at the level of functional and psychosocial consequences. Int. J. Hum. Comput. Stud. **135**, 102370 (2020)
18. De Kort, Y.A., IJsselsteijn, W.A., Poels, K.: Digital games as social presence technology: development of the Social Presence in Gaming Questionnaire (SPGQ). PRESENCE, **195203**, 1–9. (2007)
19. Stecuła, K.: Analysis of asymmetric VR games–Steam platform case study. Technol. Soc. **78**, 102673 (2024)

Automatic Piano Arrangement for Three-Part Choral of Female Voices

Kana Yamada[1(✉)], Aiko Uemura[2], and Norimasa Yoshida[1]

[1] Graduate School of Industrial Technology, Nihon University, Chiba, Japan
`cika24011@g.nihon-u.ac.jp, yoshida.norimasa@nihon-u.ac.jp`
[2] Tsuda University, Tokyo, Japan
`aiko.uemura@tsuda.ac.jp`

Abstract. This study proposes a method for automatically generating piano arrangements of three-part female choral music for solo performance. The main melody is assigned to the right-hand part using phrase segmentation and multi-feature analysis, while the left-hand accompaniment is generated based on rhythmic patterns. A random forest classifier is used to assess the importance of each feature. Experimental results show that the proposed method achieves over 80% accuracy in melody estimation across most pieces. These results highlight the effectiveness of phrase segmentation and the importance of pitch-related features in choral melody extraction.

Keywords: Choral music · Piano arrangement · Main melody estimation · Phrase segmentation · Rhythmic components

1 Introduction

Automatic piano arrangements of choral compositions enrich musical experiences through interactive and personalized content. These systems allow users to enjoy ensemble works individually, bridging technology and creative expression to make choral music more accessible and engaging for a broader audience.

Piano arrangement is the technique for adapting musical pieces composed of various instruments or voices to be performed solely on the piano. Typically, these arrangements involve two primary components: assigning the main melody to the right-hand part and creating appropriate accompaniment patterns for the left-hand part.

Main melody estimation and accompaniment generation present a great challenge in piano arrangements of choral music. This difficulty stems from the polyphonic nature of choral music, which includes multiple vocal lines and instrumental accompaniment. It is necessary to identify the main melody while considering each part's role and prominence. Additionally, it is technically impractical in solo piano performance to continuously reproduce all vocal and accompaniment parts as chords. Therefore, musically important notes must be selectively extracted and restructured into a playable piano arrangement.

Aiko Uemura - This work was supported by JSPS KAKENHI Grant Numbers 22H03711.

Previous studies have addressed the automatic arrangement of orchestral music [1], piano arrangement of pop music [2], and main melody extraction from multiple parts [3]. However, no research has been reported on the arrangement of choral scores, which typically include vocal and accompaniment parts, into piano scores.

This study aims to automatically generate piano arrangement scores from choral scores for a female three-part choir consisting of three vocal parts and an accompaniment part. The goal is to enable a single performer to play a piece of music of their choice, thereby expanding access to these ensemble works through computational methods. Instead of relying on generative Artificial Intelligence, this study adopts a rule-based approach that requires no large-scale training data. This makes the system lightweight, interpretable, and easier to implement. Its adaptability is particularly suited for digital entertainment, where flexible musical treatment is essential. For example, it could be used to adapt game or film theme songs into different styles for various scenes, or to extract and arrange consistent motifs across interactive narratives. By supporting coherent arrangements without the need for data-intensive learning, the proposed method offers a practical way to tailor musical themes to diverse narrative and interactive contexts.

2 Method

This study targets female three-part choral pieces in 4/4 time signature, using MusicXML scores as input. We utilize the Music21 library in Python to analyze the musical structure. Our method comprises two main components: main melody estimation (right-hand part) and rhythm-based accompaniment generation (left-hand part).

2.1 Generation of the Right-Hand Part Based on Melody Extraction

Phrase Segmentation

Figure 1 illustrates the workflow of our main melody estimation process. To avoid the unnatural discontinuities caused by measure-based estimation, we adopted phrase-level estimation for improved musical coherence. We adapted the segmentation method of Serizawa et al. [3] to the three vocal parts (soprano, mezzo-soprano, and alto).

The segmentation procedure was as follows:

1. For each part, we computed the product of pitch difference and onset interval between adjacent notes. The boundary was set where the total of these values across all parts was maximized.
2. This process was recursively applied until all phrases were constrained to a maximum of four measures (16 beats), which typically corresponded to meaningful musical units.

When chords were present, the highest note was used as the representative pitch. Notes at phrase boundaries were assigned according to their position: those at the beginning belonged to the current phrase, while those at the end were treated as part of the next phrase.

Fig. 1. Main melody estimation workflow. Blue lines mark phrase breaks; the yellow region indicates the estimated result

Features for Main Melody Estimation

We extracted six features from each phrase to calculate the evaluation score that a voice part carried the main melody. These features contributed to a numerical evaluation score for each part. Specific adjustments (bonuses or penalties) were applied based on threshold conditions, and the part with the highest score was selected as the main melody. The features were as follows:

- Average Pitch [3]: The mean of MIDI note numbers within the phrase. When chords were present, the highest note was used. Although not always reliable in choral music, this feature was retained due to its high importance in feature analysis.
- Pitch Entropy [1]: Measured the diversity of pitch classes. Parts with higher entropy were more likely to contain melodic content. The part with the highest entropy score received a bonus of $+1$.
- Articulation Rate [3]: Defined as the total duration of notes divided by the phrase length. If this value fell below 0.5, the score was reduced by 2.
- Change in Pitch: The number of pitch transitions between adjacent notes, capturing melodic motion. The part with the highest value gains a bonus of $+1$.
- Slur Usage Rate: Calculated as the ratio of slurred note durations to phrase length. Parts with higher slur usage (often indicating humming) were penalized accordingly.
- Average Dynamic Level [4, 5]: Notes were assigned dynamic levels based on their markings (Table 1). The weighted average was computed using note durations, and the result was normalized across parts.

Table 1. Definition of dynamic levels

Level	1	2	3	4	5	6	7	8
Dynamics	*ppp*	*pp*	*p*	*mp*	*mf*	*f*	*ff*	*fff*

Each phrase was evaluated using the six features above, and the part with the highest total score was selected as the main melody. If multiple parts tie—especially in pitch-related features—the soprano part was chosen as the default, since it was less likely to serve a harmonic role.

2.2 The Addition of Chords

We designed a method to add appropriate chords to the main melody. Chords were inserted when the duration of a note in the main melody was greater than or equal to 1.0, using the corresponding offset as the reference point. Specifically, the duration of each note in the estimated main melody was first calculated, and offsets where the duration was 1.0 or longer were identified. At each such offset, a chord was constructed using the soprano, mezzo-soprano, and alto parts. The chord was then added to the main melody, with an adjustment to ensure that its highest note corresponded to the main melody note.

Here, the term *offset* referred to the relative position within a measure, with the beginning of each measure defined as 0.0. This design aimed to reflect the rich polyphony texture characteristic of choral music in the resulting piano arrangement.

Although existing piano solo scores [6] lack consistency in chord placement, a tendency was observed for chords to be added to notes with a duration of 1.0 or longer. Based on this observation, the above criterion was adopted.

2.3 Generation of Rhythm-Based Accompaniment Parts

Generation of Rhythmic Components.
To incorporate the original rhythm of the accompaniment into the piano arrangement, we developed a method for generating accompaniment parts with rhythmic considerations based on Koshii et al. [2].

First, we extracted two parts (right-hand and left-hand) from the choral score's accompaniment. For each measure, we created an 8 × 1 binary matrix for each part, where each slot represents an eighth note. Each matrix was assigned '1' for a note onset, '0' for sustained notes or silence, and '-1' for rest onset. The matrices for each part were then combined according to the following rules to generate rhythmic components:

1. If either part has a value is '1', output '1' regardless of the other part's value.
1. If both values have a value of '0', output '0'.
2. If one part has a value of '0' and the other has a value of '-1', output '0'.
3. If both parts have a value '-1', output '-1'.

Figure 2 illustrates an example of rhythmic component generation using these rules.

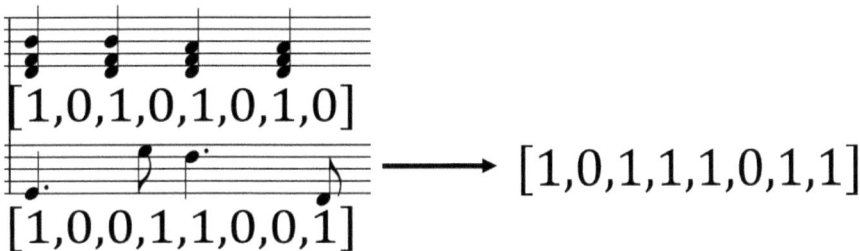

Fig. 2. Examples of rhythmic component generation

Generation of Accompaniment Using Rhythmic Components.
Accompaniment parts were generated by interpreting the rhythmic patterns from the combined matrix. We analyzed the first to the eighth components and generated chords, rests, or arpeggiated chords of the specified duration accordingly. Figure 3 shows an example of accompaniment generated using this approach. To maintain balance between the hands and prevent the left hand from becoming too dominant, we limited the number of notes in each chord to a maximum of two, matching the complexity level of the right-hand.

In our notation system, '1' represented a note onset, '0' indicated continuation (no new onset), and '-1' signified a rest onset. The '0' value specifically indicated that either a note or rest was being sustained. For example, a pattern of [1,0] corresponded to a note with a duration 1.0, while [-1,0,0] represented a rest with a duration of 1.5. The arpeggiated chord duration was limited to a maximum of two beats to ensure playability. We processed the rhythmic components in two segments (first to fourth and fifth to eighth), and avoided generating arpeggiated chords when there were five or more consecutive '1' values. However, special handling was implemented for notes that extended across the midpoint of the measure (such as from the fourth to the fifth position).

In cases where the estimated main melody included measures with only rests, prelude or postlude measures from the original accompaniment were inserted to maintain musical continuity.

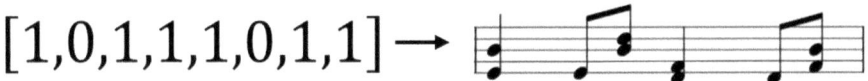

Fig. 3. Example of accompaniment generated from rhythmic components

3 Experimental Results

Piano arrangements were generated for seven choral pieces written for female three-part voices. The selected pieces include well-known Japanese choral music such as "COSMOS" and "Present," which are commonly performed in school competitions.

Each piece features a unique combination of rhythm and harmony, enabling diverse evaluations. Ground truth annotations for the main melody were manually created based on the original scores.

3.1 Estimation of the Main Melody

Effect of Phrase Segmentation

To evaluate the effectiveness of phrase segmentation, we compared the results of main melody estimation using phrase-based segmentation with those using measure-based estimation. With phrase segmentation, the accuracy consistently exceeded 80% across most pieces. Among the seven songs analyzed, accuracy improved after the introduction of phrase segmentation, except for "*Akashi*", "*COSMOS*" and "*Horane,*"

Ground truth data were manually annotated by selecting the highest-pitched notes corresponding to the vocal melody in the original choral and piano scores.

The accuracy was calculated using Eq. (1). Table 2 summarizes the comparison between measure-based and phrase-based estimations.

$$Accuracy = \frac{Total\ number\ of\ correctly\ predicted\ beats}{Total\ number\ of\ beats\ in\ the\ piece} \quad (1)$$

Table 2. Accuracy Comparison of Main Melody Estimation: Measure-based vs. Phrase-based

Title(Japanese / English)	Measure-based	Phrase-based
Horane, / See,	1.000	**1.000**
COSMOS / COSMOS	0.956	0.914
Shinjiru / Believe	0.829	**0.893**
Kokoro no hitomi / The Eyes of the Heart	0.844	**0.847**
Akashi / Testimony	0.844	0.841
Present / Present	0.831	**0.853**
Tegami / Letter	0.852	**0.898**

Improving the accuracy of phrase segmentation leads to a notably higher main melody estimation accuracy. However, current limitations stem from the dependency on segmentation precision.

Figure 4 illustrates the segmentation issue in "Present." In this example, the soprano was identified as the main melody, although the mezzo-soprano carried the main melody during the first few beats of the phrase. A melody shift occurs within the phrase. Similar cases are observed in several other pieces and constitute a primary cause of estimation errors. This problem inevitably arose unless the phrase boundaries are revised. Moreover, substantial pitch differences can lead to excessively short phrases.

Addressing these issues requires the incorporation of a method for more precise estimation of phrase boundary positions.

In this study, the accuracy of main melody estimation improved in several cases when the average pitch feature was excluded. Specifically, the accuracy increased to 0.891 in "*Present*" and 0.884 in "*Kokoro no Hitomi*" when mean pitch was excluded. These results suggested that mean pitch did not always reflect the true melodic characteristics. In choral music, higher-pitched voices such as the soprano often serve as harmonic support rather than carrying the main melody. Therefore, relying on mean pitch alone can cause misclassification and remains a key challenge for future work.

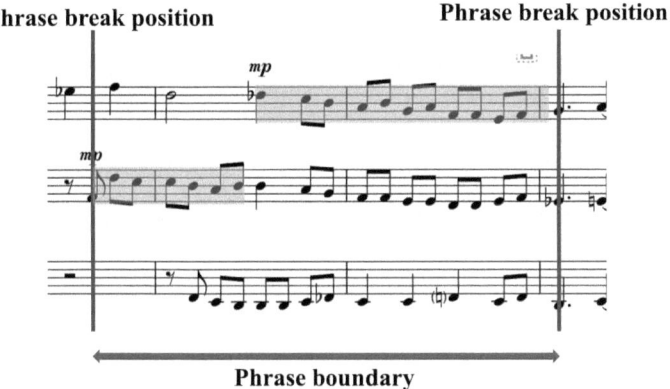

Fig. 4. The segmentation issue in "*Present*" (Yellow region: main melody)

3.2 Output of Piano Arrangement Score

Figure 5 shows an excerpt of the generated piano arrangement[1]. Each piece was arranged to cover the entire original score. In some cases, a prelude was inserted when the accompaniment preceded the melody. While the rhythmic structure of the accompaniment was successfully preserved, challenges remain in selecting harmonically appropriate chords and ensuring smooth phrase transitions.

Fig. 5. Excerpt of the piano arrangement for the song "*Horane*," generated by the proposed method.

---

[1] The audio and score are available at https://drive.google.com/drive/folders/1FfbinF_Mpm3CsO EqxQUK7WZqqqkLLX5k?usp=sharing.

4 Analysis of Effective Features Using Random Forest

We conducted a quantitative evaluation to assess the effectiveness of the features used in the proposed method. The results revealed that pitch-related features—specifically average pitch, pitch entropy and pitch change—were the most important. This observation was consistent with music theory, which suggested that main melodies tend to exhibit greater pitch variation and complexity.

The dataset consisted of 699 phrases from seven choral pieces, with each phrase annotated to indicate whether a voice part carried the main melody. Six features were used as input: average pitch, pitch entropy, articulation rate, pitch change, slur usage rate, and average dynamic level. A random forest classifier was trained with 200 trees, a maximum depth of four, and default settings for other hyperparameters. The data was randomly split into 70% for training and 30% for evaluation.

Table 3 indicates that average pitch has the highest importance, followed by pitch variation and pitch entropy. The model achieved an accuracy of 74.3%, and these results support the theoretical assumption that main melodies exhibit significant pitch variation and diversity

Table 3. Feature Importance Scores for Main Melody Estimation (Random Forest, Accuracy = 0.743)

Feature	Importance Score
Average Pitch	0.335
Change in Pitch	0.173
Pitch Entropy	0.157
Articulation Rate	0.150
Average Dynamic Level	0.097
Slur Usage Rate	0.088

5 Conclusion and Future Work

We proposed automatic piano arrangement for female three-part choral pieces. Phrase segmentation and using six musical features achieved over 80% accuracy for seven choral pieces in melody estimation. While rhythmic elements were well preserved in accompaniment generation, further improvement is needed in chord selection. Random forest analysis using six features quantitatively demonstrated the significance of pitch-related features in main melody estimation.

Future work will focus on applying of this method to adaptive music in interactive media. By extracting recurring motifs and generating accompaniment that reflects scene or emotional context, the system can support expressive variations of theme music in games and films. This positions the method as a practical tool for creating flexible, narrative-driven musical experiences in entertainment technologies.

References

1. Li, Y., Wilk, C.M., Hori, T., Sagayama, S.: Automatic piano reduction of orchestral music based on musical entropy. In: 2019 53rd Annual Conference on Information Sciences and Systems (CISS), pp. 1–5. IEEE, Baltimore, MD, USA (2019)
2. Koshii, T., Saito, H.: Automatic arrangement from waveforms of popular vocal songs to piano scores. IPSJ SIG Technical Report, Music Information Science, Vol. 2019-MUS-123(44), (2019) (in Japanese)
3. Serizawa, Y., Suzuki, N., Sato, Y., Hayase, M.: A method for extracting melodies distributed to multiple parts. In: Proc. 65th National Convention of IPSJ, pp. 191–192 (2003) (in Japanese)
4. Nagata, W., Sako, S., Kitamura, T.: Estimation of violin fingering considering performance symbols. In: Proc. Special Interest Group on Entertainment Computing, pp. 1- 6 (2015) (in Japanese)
5. Ishiketa, M., Sueyoshi, Y., Maruta, S., Iida, T., Kanemitsu, I., Iinuma, N.: Musical grammar: theory and practice. Ongaku-no-Tomo Sha, Tokyo (2001) (in Japanese)
6. Depro, M.P.: One Rank Higher Piano Solo: Choral Masterpieces Pianists Want to Play – Definitive Edition. Depro MP Co., Ltd., Tokyo (2021) (in Japanese)

JumpLab: An Interactive Learning Tool for Parameter Tuning in the Pre-production Stage

Keita Yamazaki, Masayoshi Itoh, and Kentaro Fukuchi(✉)

Meiji University, 4-21-1 Nakano Nakano-ku, Tokyo 1648525, Japan
{keita.yamazaki,masayoshi.itoh}@app.fukuchilab.org, kentaro@fukuchi.org

Abstract. In computer game development, establishing parameters for the '3C' elements (Character, Controls, Camera)—including character appearance, movement mechanics, human-computer interaction designs, and camera behaviors—during the pre-production stage is critical for producing high-quality gameplay. However, comprehending the impact of parameter adjustments can be challenging, particularly for novice developers who must struggle with programming from scratch while studying adjustment processes. Furthermore, conventional educational resources rarely offer interactive demonstrations of how adjustments influence the gameplay experience. To address these issues, we introduce 'JumpLab', an interactive educational tool designed to teach the impact of parameter adjustments. JumpLab provides interfaces for modifying various parameters that control player character jump trajectories and camera behaviors in platform games. JumpLab operates in web browsers, allowing users to study parameter descriptions while controlling characters and experiencing the impact of parameter adjustment in real-time.

Keywords: Videogame development · Pre-production · Videogame design · Parameter tuning

1 Introduction

In computer game development, the importance of iteratively refining the core elements during 'pre-production' stage and proceeding to later phases only after firmly establishing these elements is widely acknowledged. Modifications to these core components during the middle to late development stages necessitate adjustments to various components including level designs, significantly increasing the development resources and time. While various frameworks exist regarding pre-production priorities and objectives, this paper examines the '3Cs' concept from the four principles outlined by Mark Cerny in his seminal 2002 lecture [1].

- 3 C's: character, camera, control
- game look

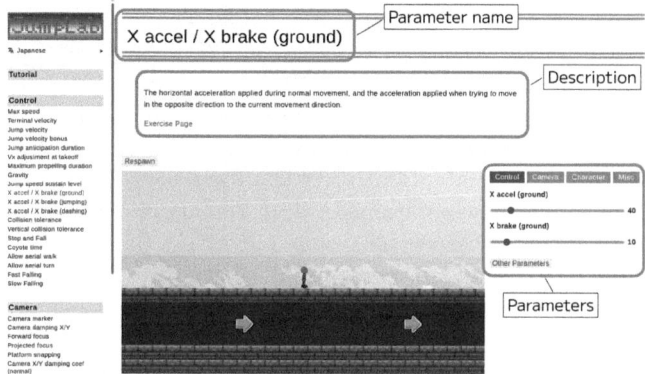

Fig. 1. JumpLab 2D's screen layout. Only topic-relevant parameters are adjustable, while other parameters are hidden but accessible via the "Other Parameters" button.

- key technology
- holistic game design (if appropriate)

Cerny identifies the 3Cs—Character, Camera, and Control—as the highest priority elements to focus on intensively during the pre-production period. Here, 'Character' primarily refers to the appearance and movement of the main character controlled by the player. 'Camera' refers to camera movement, which also determines how players perceive the game space through how the player character's surroundings are presented to them. 'Control' is the element that determines how players operate the character and, through this, how they enjoy the game. Cerny further states that while the 3Cs may appear to be a framework specific to character action games, the same principles can be applied to games of other genres.

Despite their significance, systematic educational materials on these concepts appear relatively scarce. While numerous textbooks and publications on game development emphasize the importance of character movement, control methods, and camera motion, they predominantly focus on implementation techniques rather than addressing the nuanced adjustment processes that are critical to successful game design.

This research identifies a critical need for interactive educational materials that facilitate hands-on experimentation with the 3Cs and promote deeper understanding of their importance. At the authors' university, numerous students pursue computer game development, with most attempting independent game creation. However, the majority only manage to develop functionally basic games, with few allocating sufficient time for refinement and optimization. In our teaching context, we have frequently observed cases where students struggle with balance adjustments, likely resulting from insufficient attention to 3Cs refinement for the reasons outlined above.

To address these educational challenges, this paper introduces 'JumpLab', an interactive educational tool specifically designed to teach students about the impact of parameter adjustments on gameplay [4]. JumpLab provides intuitive interfaces for modifying various parameters that control player character jump trajectories and camera behaviors in platform games–elements that are fundamental to the 3Cs framework.

A key advantage of JumpLab is its web browser implementation, which allows users to study parameter descriptions while simultaneously controlling characters and experiencing the effects of parameter adjustments in real-time (Fig. 1). This direct feedback loop enhances learning more effectively than traditional method. The tool includes both 2D and 3D versions [6], each addressing parameter adjustments with different considerations and constraints. This paper describes both versions in detail and examines how each environment facilitates understanding of the complex relationships between parameter values and resulting gameplay experiences.

2 Background

In publications emphasizing the importance of 3Cs, there are few examples offering clear guidelines on how to design the 3Cs. This is likely because the 3Cs goals that should be achieved differ depending on what kind of *game experience* each individual game aims for. Additionally, "game experience" itself is difficult to define clearly. A related term is "game feel", a term Steve Swink defines in his book [9] as "real-time control of virtual objects in a simulated space, with interactions emphasized by polish", but this still doesn't provide clear design guidelines.

On the other hand, research and investigation into the individual elements of 3Cs are being conducted in various forms. Martin et al. analyzed jump trajectories of several game titles and classified jump trajectory elements into 21 categories [2]. Referencing this classification, Summerville et al. developed a mechanism to automatically extract jump trajectories from gameplay screens of Nintendo Entertainment System (NES) era platform games, visualizing jump trajectories of various games [8]. Keren has reported comprehensive survey results on camera motion in side-scrolling games, including platform games [5]. The parameter names adopted in JumpLab follow these previous surveys.

3 JumpLab Design Principles

JumpLab is primarily designed as an educational tool to teach the importance of the 3Cs in the early stages of game development. Specifically, using platform games as the subject matter, it allows real-time adjustment of various elements related to jump actions and camera motion. By allowing users to repeatedly and rapidly adjust parameters while performing jumps, the tool enables learners to directly experience how these adjustments affect the game feel, thereby deepening their understanding of the significance of the 3Cs.

The primary target users are undergraduate students in their second and third years who are interested in game development and interaction design, as

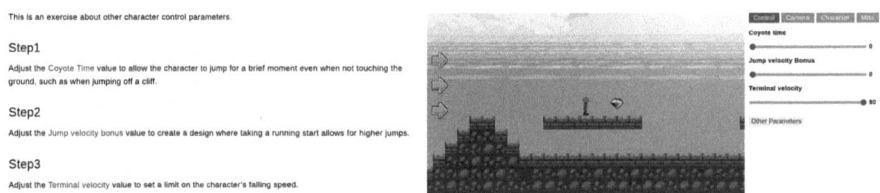

Fig. 2. An example of exercise.

one of the authors uses this tool in their undergraduate courses. However, the tool features simple controls, making it accessible to a broader audience, not limited to undergraduate students. As using the tool requires basic knowledge of physical motion, the target audience would likely be middle school students and above.

JumpLab features a layout as shown in Fig. 1, with adjacent placement of gameplay screen and parameter adjustment interface. This configuration enables learners to alternately operate characters and adjust parameters while immediately observing changes in game feel, facilitating systematic learning of 3Cs adjustment concepts. The same screen integrates explanatory text and exercise tasks for each parameter, allowing learners to efficiently adjust parameters while referencing the explanations. Learners can control the player character via keyboard or joystick, and adjust parameters primarily using the mouse.

Each learning page focuses on one or two key parameters, displaying only those parameters directly related to the parameters being taught. This design aims to reduce cognitive load and avoid interface complexity, optimizing learning efficiency. Hidden parameters can be accessed by selecting the "Other Parameters" button when necessary.

Some pages include exercise tasks related to the parameters being explained, encouraging learners to adjust these parameters (Fig. 2). When a page is first opened, the 3Cs parameters are intentionally set to values that differ from the expected solutions of the exercise tasks. Through the process of working on these tasks and repeatedly adjusting parameters, learners can reflect on their preferred game feel. This approach aims to deepen understanding of how parameter adjustment affects game feel and its importance in game design.

4 Parameters of JumpLab 2D

4.1 Character

Characters are crucial game assets, with player characters being the focus of player empathy. In third-person 2D jump action games, the player character remains constantly visible, with players observing its actions throughout gameplay. Because players perceive game events primarily through character actions and reactions [9], character design serves as the window to the game world.

To prevent learners from spending excessive time on visual adjustments, we minimized variable elements in character design to focus on teaching the other two elements of the 3Cs. JumpLab provides three preset characters with different body proportions (Fig. 3). We included varying proportions because they influence motion realism—taller characters typically use realistic movements while shorter ones use more stylized actions.

Fig. 3. Animation sprites of the preset characters of JumpLab 2D. From left to right: 3-head, 1-head, and 8-head figures.

4.2 Controls

(a) Typical jump trajectory seen in platform games.

(b) Collision adjustment.

Fig. 4. Examples of 'Controls' adjustment in JumpLab 2D.

In JumpLab, we parameterized approximately 20 'Control' elements, including character movement parameters such as acceleration and maximum velocity, and jump trajectory parameters such as initial velocity and gravitational acceleration. Below, we present several examples of these control elements.

While physical jumps follow parabolic trajectories determined by initial velocity and gravity, digital games implement diverse jumping mechanics to enhance playability. Platform games typically employ asymmetric gravitational acceleration—lower during ascent than descent (Fig. 4a). This design approach serves two purposes: it allows players sufficient time for precise targeting when jumping to smaller platforms, while enabling rapid descents that create crisp, responsive gameplay.

Another example is 'collision adjustment'. In games like 'Super Mario Bros.', players occasionally need to execute vertical jumps from directly beneath platforms when lateral approaches are limited. Standard collision detection algorithms that immediately halt upward motion upon impact (Fig. 4b, left) require precise initial positioning. However, implementing horizontal position adjustment during collision while maintaining upward momentum (Fig. 4b, right) significantly improves playability by eliminating the need for precise pre-jump positioning. This collision adjustment must be coupled with mid-air horizontal control.

4.3 Camera

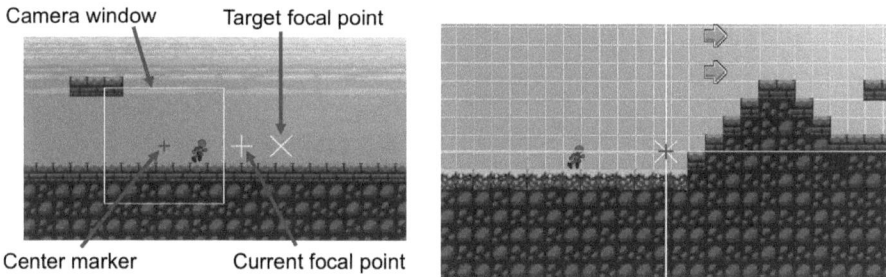

Fig. 5. Left: Visualization of the camera model in JumpLab 2D. Right: An example of Forward Focusing.

Camera motion in 2D side-scrolling jump action games refers to how the camera translates to follow the character's movement. In JumpLab, the configurable settings are based on [5], with approximately 10 adjustable elements. Here we describe an overview of these elements.

Figure 5 (left) shows the camera motion model adopted by JumpLab. The 'Center marker' is the camera's central position, which is always located in the center of the screen. Generally, the camera follows the player character, but rather than keeping the center marker aligned with the player character, the camera sometimes follows a point slightly offset in the player's direction of movement ('Forward Focus'). This point that the camera center aims at is called the 'target focal point'. Additionally, when the player character changes direction, in many 2D games characters can instantly change their orientation, which would cause sudden movement of the target focal point and potentially abrupt screen changes. To prevent this, in actual games, the focal point moves smoothly. This intermediate focal point is called the 'current focal point'. The 'Camera window' is a virtual window set around the camera center, and the camera doesn't move while the object it follows (player character or current focal point) remains within this window.

In JumpLab, various parameters of this model are adjustable, such as the distance to the target focal point, the movement speed of the current focal point, and the size of the camera window. Additionally, parallax scrolling parameters are also adjustable, which creates a sense of depth by setting different scrolling speeds for the foreground (where characters and obstacles are placed) and the background (where background images are placed), significantly affecting the overall screen changes.

Figure 5 (right) shows an example of applying 'Forward Focus'. In such games, obstacles and enemy characters often appear from the direction of movement as the screen scrolls. If the distance between these suddenly appearing objects and the player character is too short, players won't have enough time to deal with them, leading to frustration. Therefore, forward focusing shifts the camera center from the player character toward the direction of movement to provide a wider field of view ahead.

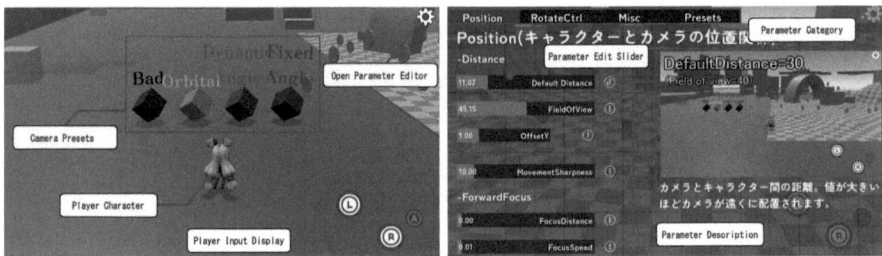

Fig. 6. Screenshots of 3D version of JumpLab. Left: main screen. Right: Parameter setting screen.

Fig. 7. Camera system affecting gap perception. Left: Gap width is difficult for players to perceive. Right: Gap width is easier to perceive with the fixed-angle camera.

5 JumpLab 3D Version

Now we describe JumpLab 3D, which focuses on 3D games.

In 3D games, camera system design is known to have a significant impact on the player experience [3]. The rules and settings that define how a camera operates in a game are called *camera behaviors*. Camera behaviors in 3D games are based on more diverse and complex algorithms than those in 2D games. It's also common to switch between multiple camera behaviors within a single game depending on the scene. To provide players with the intended experience, developers must select camera behaviors and fine-tune their parameters to ensure a comfortable gameplay experience. Therefore, JumpLab 3D focuses on learning how to select appropriate behaviors for different scenes and adjust their parameters.

The proposed system adopts a third-person perspective platform game style. The player character appears on screen, and learners control it using a stick and jump button. Camera behavior switches occur when the player character interacts with designated objects in the game space (Fig. 6, left). Three of the presets implement camera behaviors widely adopted in third-person games ('Dynamic-Angle Camera', 'Orbital Camera', and 'Fixed-Angle Camera'). While the authors provide baseline parameter settings for each behavior, learners can fine-tune the detailed properties of these camera behaviors from the edit screen (Fig. 6, right). Additionally, one unadjusted preset was provided for comparison.

By placing behavior-switching interfaces within the game space, learners can effectively learn the relationship between stage design and camera behaviors and corresponding parameters. Players make decisions based on the stage conditions, so selecting appropriate camera behaviors is essential for supporting player decision-making and facilitating appropriate actions suited to that stage [7]. The proposed system includes various terrains and mechanisms found in 3D platforms, with behavior-switching interfaces placed at key locations, encouraging learners to consider both switching to camera behaviors appropriate for each scene and fine-tuning their parameters to achieve optimal results.

Figure 7 illustrates an example of camera behavior selection matched to stage design. The Dynamic-Angle Camera slowly follows the character and provides a wide field of view in the character's direction of movement (Fig. 7, left). While effective in open areas where players can walk in all directions, it's known to cause problems in platform games with complex stage structures [7]. In the case shown in Fig. 7 (left), depth perception is difficult, making it easy to misjudge the width of gaps. In contrast, the Fixed-Angle Camera (Fig. 7, right) provides a view from a predetermined angle. It has the advantage of offering a field of view intentionally designed for the stage structure, though with the trade-off of a narrower viewing area.

6 Conclusion and Future Work

This paper introduced JumpLab, an interactive educational tool designed to teach parameter adjustment for the 3Cs (Character, Camera, Control) during the pre-production stage of game development. Through its web-based implementation with both 2D and 3D versions, JumpLab enables learners to directly experience how parameter modifications impact gameplay feel through real-time feedback while controlling characters.

Our future research will focus on enhancing tutorials and providing more appropriate feedback. For example, we are considering mechanisms that allow other learners to play with the user's current parameter settings and observe their behavior, or that enable observation of AI player behavior.

References

1. Cerny, M.: "Method". In: D.I.C.E. Summit 2002. Academy of Interactive Arts and Sciences (2002). htttps://www.youtube.com/watch?v=QOAW9ioWAvE
2. Fasterholdt, M., Pichlmair, M., Holmgøard, C.: You say jump, i say how high? operationalising the game feel of jumping. In: Proceedings of DiGRA/FDG 2016 Conference. DiGRA (2016). https://doi.org/10.26503/dl.v2016i1.771
3. Haigh-Hutchinson, M.: Real time cameras. CRC Press (2009)
4. Kentaro, F., Masayoshi, I.: JumpLab: 2Dジャンプゲームを題材としたゲーム開発教材.. In: Proceedings of Entertainment Computing 2021, pp. 70–76 (2021), in Japanese
5. Keren, I.: Scroll back: The theory and practice of cameras in side-scrollers. In: GDC 2015. Game Developers Conference (2015). https://www.gdcvault.com/play/1022243/Scroll-Back-The-Theory-and
6. Masayoshi, I., Kentaro, F.: JumpLab 3D: 3Dゲームを対象としたカメラビヘイビア. In: Proceedings of WISS 2024 (2024), in Japanese
7. Nesky, J.: 50 camera mistakes. In: GDC 2014. Game Developers Conference (2014). https://gdcvault.com/play/1020460/50-Camera
8. Summerville, A., Osborn, J., Holmgård, C., Zhang, D.W.: Mechanics automatically recognized via interactive observation: Jumping. In: Proceedings of the 12th International Conference on the Foundations of Digital Games 17. ACM, New York, NY, USA (2017). https://doi.org/10.1145/3102071.3102104
9. Swink, S.: Game feel: A game designer's guide to virtual sensation. Morgan Kaufmann (2008)

"Hand-In-Hand" Learning: A Novel Method for Instrument Skill Training with Electrical Muscle Stimulation

Shuo Zhou, Akira Shikida, and Norihisa Segawa

Kyoto Sangyo University, Kyoto, Japan
{zhoushuo3,sega}@acm.org, akky041211823@gmail.com

Abstract. Instrumental performance is widely recognized as a complex skill that relies on proprioception and handeye coordination. For beginners, achieving adequate motor coordination in the early learning stages is particularly challenging. Traditional methods depend on long-term, repetitive practice and professional instruction, which are not always accessible or effective. This study introduces a novel training method using Electrical Muscle Stimulation (EMS), which captures expert movements in real time and delivers corresponding electrical impulses to the learner's muscles, enabling direct, physical guidance. This approach is designed to help beginners acquire fundamental motor skills more quickly and intuitively. A user study involving eight participants was conducted, including EMS-based training and a questionnaire. Results showed that participants rated the system highly in terms of usability, clarity of feedback, and overall training effectiveness.

Keywords: Electrical Muscle Stimulation · Skill Training · Musical Instruments · Drum · Arduino · Pressure Sensor · Accelerometer

1 Introduction

Instrumental performance is generally regarded as a complex skill that heavily relies on proprioception and hand-eye coordination, involving precise control of limb movements and the integration of visual, auditory, and motor sensory information [3,7,8]. Research by Platz et al. has demonstrated that skilled performers can effectively integrate these multimodal sensory inputs through extensive long-term practice, resulting in stable and accurate motor patterns [10]. However, for beginners, achieving a high level of motor coordination during the early stages of learning is particularly challenging. This lack of coordination not only hinders the rapid acquisition of skills but may also lead to the long-term consolidation of incorrect motor patterns [12].

Instrumental training typically relies on sustained and repetitive practice of fundamental skills. Some studies have explored the use of assistive technologies to support this training process. For example, Rutkowski et al. utilized virtual reality (VR) to enhance hand-eye coordination during musical practice, thereby improving training outcomes [11]. Furuya et al. developed a wearable hand exoskeleton system to support fine motor control in pianists, aiming to overcome the so-called ceiling effect in piano performance [4]. Despite these advancements, most beginners still require continuous guidance and feedback from expert instructors before they can effectively engage in long-term practice. In reality, many learners do not have access to professional instruction, particularly in regions lacking educational resources. Furthermore, even with expert supervision, beginners often struggle with accurately interpreting and executing movement instructions, leading to inefficient learning or the development of incorrect techniques.

Electrical Muscle Stimulation (EMS) is a technique that uses low-intensity electrical currents to directly stimulate targeted muscles in order to control or assist bodily movement. Originally developed for medical and rehabilitative applications, EMS has recently gained attention for its potential in enhancing physical performance and accelerating skill acquisition. Previous studies have shown that EMS can effectively improve motor performance and support learning. Kasahara et al. found that EMS has the potential to enhance user reaction speed [6]. Zhou and Segawa further demonstrated that EMS can significantly improve sensorimotor abilities within a short period of time, highlighting its feasibility for rapid skill training [17]. In addition, they proposed an EMS-based hand-eye coordination training method and verified its short-term effectiveness, as well as its potential applicability in real-world gaming environments [18,19]. Unlike other assistive technologies, EMS offers a unique advantage by directly engaging the user's musculature and facilitating the formation of muscle memory within a short timeframe, thereby accelerating the learning of related skills. By providing immediate and intuitive physical feedback, EMS helps learners overcome comprehension-related barriers often encountered in traditional teaching methods.

Based on these insights, this study proposes a novel EMS-based training method for instrumental skill acquisition. This method involves capturing and recording the precise movements of expert performers in real time and translating them into electrical stimulation signals that directly control the learner's limb movements. In doing so, the system achieves a literal "hand-in-hand" mode of instruction. We believe that this training approach, which combines expert demonstration with physical sensory feedback, can help beginners establish correct motor patterns more quickly and accurately during the initial stages of learning. Ultimately, this may significantly shorten the time required to progress from novice to proficient instrumentalist. This study aims to design and evaluate the effectiveness and practicality of this EMS-based training method and explore its potential for application in real-world educational contexts, offering a novel and efficient pathway for future music instruction.

2 System Composition

As an essential component of musical performance, percussion instruments such as drums require not only a high degree of coordination between the hands and feet but also the integration of multiple motor and sensory abilities, including rhythm perception, movement speed, and force control. The multimodal nature of these skills makes percussion training an ideal context for evaluating and enhancing the efficiency of skill acquisition among beginners. Therefore, this study focuses on drum-based percussion instruments as the primary training target to explore the potential of EMS in instrumental skill training.

To this end, we developed an EMS-based drum training system. This system captures the expert performer's motion data in real time during drumming and translates these movements into precise electrical stimulation signals, which drive the learner's hand and foot muscles to replicate the corresponding actions. With this system, beginners can physically experience the expert's performance without needing a complete cognitive understanding of the movement, enabling more intuitive and efficient skill guidance and acquisition.

2.1 EMS Device

The drum training system developed in this study incorporates an EMS device composed of a power supply, control module, and electrodes. This device is designed to assist learners in physically imitating professional drumming movements and receiving corresponding motor feedback during training.

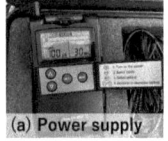 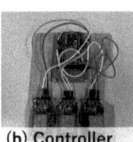 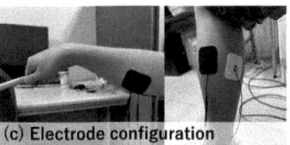

Fig. 1. EMS Device Configuration. (a) Power supply. (b) Controller. (c) Electrode placement.

The system uses the iStim EV-804 [9] as the EMS power supply (Fig. 1 (a)). This device is widely used for muscle training and provides stable and safe pulse output (with a maximum voltage of approximately 10V). Given that the primary objective of this study is to drive the learner's hand and foot muscles with moderate electrical stimulation to simulate drumming actions, this device was selected to balance stimulation effectiveness with user comfort, avoiding excessive interference with natural muscle function.

In terms of control, the system employs an ESP32 microcontroller [2] in combination with a TONGLING relay module [16] to manage EMS output (Fig. 1 (b)). The EMS signal is modulated through relay switching controlled by an Arduino-based program. Upon activation, the system delivers a pulse of 50 to 100 microseconds to the designated muscle groups, triggering the learner to perform the corresponding movement. To accommodate individual differences in muscle sensitivity or physical condition, the system allows for fine-tuning of both pulse width and output intensity, ensuring that the stimulation is effective while remaining comfortable.

Electrode placement was adapted from the configuration proposed by Tamaki et al. [14], with modifications to suit the drumming training context of this study (Fig. 1 (c)). For the upper limbs, electrodes are attached to the wrist extensor and flexor muscle groups to facilitate hand striking movements. For the lower limbs, electrodes are placed on the tibialis anterior and gastrocnemius muscles of the lower leg to replicate bass drum pedal actions. This configuration ensures effective activation of muscles essential for drumming performance while minimizing interference with non-target muscle groups, thereby improving movement accuracy while preserving the natural fluidity of motion.

2.2 Detection of Instructional Movements

To capture the instructor's drumming movements, this system employs an accelerometer (Seeed XIAO nRF52840 Sense) [13] mounted on the drumsticks and a pressure sensor (FSR-402) [5] placed on the bass drum pedal (Fig. 2). These sensors are used to record the timing and force of both hand and foot strikes performed by the instructor.

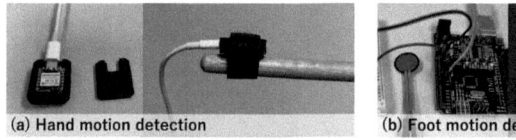

Fig. 2. Sensor Configuration. (a) Hand motion detection. (b) Foot motion detection.

For hand motion detection (Fig. 2 (a)), the accelerometer captures three-dimensional acceleration data along the X, Y, and Z axes. The collected data is transmitted in real time to an Arduino UNO [1] for preliminary processing and then sent via serial communication to a computer running a Python program. The system analyzes the incoming acceleration data and identifies a strike event when the acceleration magnitude in any direction exceeds a predefined threshold.

For foot motion detection (Fig. 2 (b)), a pressure sensor attached beneath the bass drum surface monitors the force applied by the instructor's foot. When the pressure exceeds the threshold, a signal is similarly sent through the Arduino to the computer for further analysis, enabling the system to comprehensively detect both hand and foot strike events.

To prevent multiple triggers from a single strike, the system implements a "trigger flag" mechanism. This mechanism works like a switch: when the sensor detects an acceleration that exceeds the threshold, the switch is turned on, and a single electrical stimulation is triggered. The switch remains off until the acceleration value drops below the threshold again, at which point it is reset to allow detection of the next valid strike. This approach ensures that each physical strike triggers the EMS output only once, avoiding false positives caused by hand tremors or sensor noise and improving the accuracy and reliability of the system.

2.3 Connecting Instructor and Learner

We developed a Python-based system to establish real-time connectivity between the motion detection sensors worn by the instructor and the EMS device worn by the learner. As the instructor begins playing, their hand and foot movements are captured by the system in real time and converted into corresponding electrical stimulation signals, which activate the learner's limbs to perform synchronized drumming actions.

In traditional percussion training, learners primarily rely on visual and auditory cues to observe and imitate the instructor's gestures and rhythm. While this observational learning approach is intuitive, it can be challenging for beginners who lack motor experience or physical coordination. Relying solely on sensory observation often makes it difficult to accurately replicate fine motor details, particularly in terms of rhythm control and muscle engagement.

By incorporating EMS, the learner's hand and foot muscles can be automatically activated through electrical stimulation during training. This enables the learner not only to perceive the instructor's rhythm but also to physically execute the same movement patterns. Even at an early learning stage—before the learner has fully mastered voluntary motor control—EMS allows them to experience and internalize the correct performance through direct bodily engagement.

The strength of this system lies in its integration of physical demonstration and motor guidance. Through EMS, learners who have not yet developed the capacity for precise voluntary control can passively perceive and imitate professional performance movements. This training mechanism facilitates the rapid development of correct motor patterns and accelerates the formation of muscle memory, offering a more intuitive and effective pathway for skill acquisition in beginners.

3 Evaluation of the Proposed Method

To conduct a preliminary evaluation of the effectiveness and usability of the EMS-based instrumental training method proposed in this study, participants underwent training using the system developed in Sect. 2. A user survey was administered following the training, and the results were analyzed and assessed accordingly.

3.1 Participants

We recruited eight participants (aged 19–29; 6 males and 2 females). All participants were in good health and reported no physiological or cognitive impairments that could affect the experiment. None of them had received any prior professional or targeted training related to music. Therefore, the experiment served as a completely new experience for all participants. These selection criteria were intended to objectively evaluate the actual effectiveness of EMS in instrumental training.

3.2 Training Process

To evaluate the EMS-based drum training system, eight participants completed the experiment following the procedure outlined below.

First, participants practiced a basic 8-beat rhythm without the use of EMS. During this phase, they observed and imitated a demonstration performed by an expert drummer, following a method commonly used in traditional percussion training. To assist understanding, especially for beginners unfamiliar with standard musical notation, a simplified rhythm chart was provided alongside the demonstration instead of formal sheet music, in order to reduce cognitive load and improve accessibility.

To avoid participants mastering the rhythm through prolonged practice—which could potentially compromise the subsequent evaluation of the EMS system—the duration of this phase was limited to approximately three minutes. This time frame was chosen based on the assumption that beginners are unlikely to fully master the rhythm in such a short period, thereby allowing the evaluation to focus on the immediate effects of EMS-based training. After this phase, participants were asked to mentally reflect on their current level of skill acquisition.

Following the conventional training, a rest period of at least one hour was provided to minimize the carryover effects of the previous training before initiating the EMS-assisted session.

After the break, participants were equipped with the EMS device and proceeded with the second phase of training. During this phase, they practiced the same 8-beat rhythm for three minutes, but this time the system provided real-time electrical stimulation to the hands and feet based on motion data from the instructor (as described in Sect. 2.3). As in the previous phase, the simplified rhythm chart was made available to support participants in understanding and reinforcing the rhythm and movement structure.

3.3 User Survey

After completing the training, participants were asked to complete a questionnaire based on their subjective impressions. The questionnaire included the following three items: (1) Whether the EMS-based training method was perceived to be more efficient than traditional methods; (2) Whether the electrical stimulation feedback provided by the system was easy to understand; (3) Whether the EMS-based training method was considered to have practical applicability.

All questions were rated on a 5-point Likert scale (1 = strongly disagree, 5 = strongly agree). The questionnaire was designed to evaluate the proposed system across three dimensions: training efficiency, clarity of feedback, and practical usability, aiming to collect participants' subjective assessments and overall acceptance of the EMS-based training experience.

3.4 IRB Process

This study was approved by the local research ethics committee. All experiments were performed with the informed consent of the participants, who were fully informed of the content and procedures of the experiments.

3.5 Results

Through statistical analysis of the questionnaire responses from eight participants, we obtained the following evaluation results regarding their experience with the system (Fig. 3):

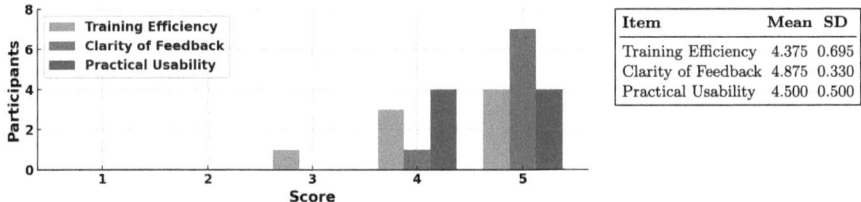

Fig. 3. Distribution of participant responses for each questionnaire item on a 5-point Likert scale.

Perceived Training Efficiency. In response to the question "Whether the EMS-based training method was perceived to be more efficient than traditional methods", the average score was 4.375 with a standard deviation of 0.695. Overall, most participants perceived the system as having a positive impact on training efficiency, suggesting that EMS can effectively support skill acquisition within a short period of time.

Clarity of Electrical Stimulation Feedback. For the question "Whether the electrical stimulation feedback provided by the system was easy to understand", the average score was 4.875 with a standard deviation of 0.330. The results indicate that participants generally found the EMS feedback to be clear, intuitive, and easy to interpret. This supports the effectiveness of the system's feedback mechanism in conveying motion guidance.

Perceived Practical Usability. In response to the question "Whether the EMS-based training method was considered to have practical applicability", the average score was 4.5 with a standard deviation of 0.5. The responses show that participants broadly recognized the system's practical potential, particularly for novice users in instrumental skill training.

To further evaluate the reliability of the questionnaire, we calculated the Cronbach's alpha coefficient across the three items, which yielded a value of 0.847. According to common benchmarks, a Cronbach's alpha above 0.8 indicates good internal consistency of the scale [15].

In summary, the experimental results demonstrate that the EMS-based instrumental training system proposed in this study received positive user evaluations in terms of efficiency, clarity of feedback, and practical usability, indicating a high level of usability and user acceptance.

4 Discussion

While the findings of this study suggest that EMS-based training may offer benefits in instrumental skill acquisition, several limitations must be acknowledged.

First, the evaluation relied solely on subjective responses collected through a user questionnaire. Although participants provided valuable feedback regarding efficiency, feedback clarity, and practical usability, the absence of objective performance metrics (e.g., timing accuracy, consistency, or motion analysis) limits the ability to quantitatively validate the system's effectiveness. Future studies should incorporate objective measures to assess skill improvement more rigorously.

Second, the number of participants was relatively small (n = 8), which restricts the statistical power and generalizability of the results. A larger and more diverse participant pool is necessary to verify the broader applicability of the proposed system across different user profiles.

Third, this study focused exclusively on drumming as the target instrument. While percussion is well-suited for evaluating motor coordination and rhythmic accuracy, the generalizability of EMS-based training to other instrument types— such as string, wind, or keyboard instruments—remains unexplored.

As this study remains a work in progress, further investigations will be conducted to address the limitations discussed above.

5 Conclusion and Future Work

This study proposed an EMS-based instrumental training method and developed a real-time training system focused on basic rhythm learning in percussion instruments (specifically drums). The system detects the instructor's drumming movements and delivers electrical stimulation to the learner's hand and foot muscles, providing physical guidance in a "Hand-in-Hand" manner. This approach is particularly beneficial for beginners who lack prior motor experience. A user study involving eight participants with no musical background was conducted, including training sessions and a questionnaire-based evaluation. The results indicated that participants generally recognized the system's potential in improving training efficiency, feedback comprehensibility, and practical usability.

Future work will address the current limitations of this study. First, we plan to incorporate objective evaluation metrics to enable a more systematic and quantitative analysis of training outcomes. Second, we will expand the number of participants in future experiments to further validate the effectiveness and generalizability of the proposed method. In addition, we aim to explore the applicability of the EMS-based training system to other types of musical instruments, thereby broadening the potential use cases of EMS in music education.

We believe that, as the research progresses, the proposed approach can offer new directions and practical insights for instrumental skill training, especially in the context of rhythm learning.

Acknowledgments. This work was supported by JST SPRING, Japan Grant Number JPMJSP2157, and JSPS KAKENHI Grant Number 25K15200.

References

1. Arduino: Arduino UNO (2010). https://store-usa.arduino.cc/products/arduino-uno-rev3
2. ESPRESSIF: Esp32 (2016). https://www.espressif.com/en/products/socs/esp32
3. Furuya, S., Goda, T., Katayose, H., Miwa, H., Nagata, N.: Distinct inter-joint coordination during fast alternate keystrokes in pianists with superior skill. Front. Hum. Neurosci. **5**, 50 (2011)
4. Furuya, S., Oku, T., Nishioka, H., Hirano, M.: Surmounting the ceiling effect of motor expertise by novel sensory experience with a hand exoskeleton. Sci. Robot. **10**(98), eadn3802 (2025)
5. Hilitand: Fsr402 (2010). https://akizukidenshi.com/catalog/g/g104002/
6. Kasahara, S., Takada, K., Nishida, J., Shibata, K., Shimojo, S., Lopes, P.: Preserving agency during electrical muscle stimulation training speeds up reaction time directly after removing ems. In: Proceedings of the 2021 CHI Conference on Human Factors in Computing Systems, pp. 1–9 (2021)
7. Kawase, S.: Gazing behavior and coordination during piano duo performance. Attention, Perception, Psychophysics **76**, 527–540 (2014)
8. Loehr, J.D., Palmer, C.: Subdividing the beat: Auditory and motor contributions to synchronization. Music. Percept. **26**(5), 415–425 (2009)
9. MEDICAL, E.: EV-804 (2020). http://www.everyway-medical.com/ProdDevice?productid=EV804
10. Platz, F., Kopiez, R., Lehmann, A.C., Wolf, A.: The influence of deliberate practice on musical achievement: A meta-analysis. Front. Psychol. **5**, 646 (2014)
11. Rutkowski, S., Adamczyk, M., Pastuła, A., Gos, E., Luque-Moreno, C., Rutkowska, A.: Training using a commercial immersive virtual reality system on hand-eye coordination and reaction time in young musicians: A pilot study. Int. J. Environ. Res. Public Health **18**(3), 1297 (2021)
12. Sailer, U., Flanagan, J.R., Johansson, R.S.: Eye-hand coordination during learning of a novel visuomotor task. J. Neurosci. **25**(39), 8833–8842 (2005)
13. Studio, S.: Xiao nrf52840 sense (2022). https://www.seeedstudio.com/xiao-series-page
14. Tamaki, E., Miyaki, T., Rekimoto, J.: Possessedhand: techniques for controlling human hands using electrical muscles stimuli. In: Proceedings of the sigchi conference on human factors in computing systems, pp. 543–552 (2011)

15. Tavakol, M., Dennick, R.: Making sense of cronbach's alpha. Int. J. Med. Educ. **2**, 53 (2011)
16. TONGLING: Pettoya554 (2022). https://en.tonglingrelay.com/lang/ja/index.html
17. Zhou, S., Segawa, N.: Method of electrical muscle stimulation for training fps game players in the timing of shots. Proc. ACM Hum-Comput. Int. **7**(CHI PLAY), 1234–1252 (2023)
18. Zhou, S., Segawa, N.: Electrical muscle stimulation-based approach for enhancing hand-eye coordination training. In: Extended Abstracts of the CHI Conference on Human Factors in Computing Systems, pp. 1–6 (2024)
19. Zhou, S., Segawa, N.: Method of electrical muscle stimulation to improve hand-eye coordination training in gaming. Proc. ACM Hum-Comput. Int. **8**(CHI PLAY), 1–20 (2024)

Interactive Entertainment Showcase

Transformer Based Adaptive Music Generation for Video Games

Thomas Dallard[✉][iD] and Akinori Ito[✉][iD]

Tokyo University of Technology, Hachioji, Tokyo, Japan
thomas.dallard42@gmail.com, akinori@edu.teu.ac.jp
https://www.teu.ac.jp/

Abstract. This research proposes a novel approach that leverages the transformer architecture to create a dynamic MIDI composition that responds to events in near real-time. The model leverages Rotary Positional Embeddings (RoPE) to allow infinite generation for background music applications. Custom rule-based logit filters are also provided to improve generation quality. Byte-Pair Encoding is used to improve the attention context strength. This approach has been implemented and tested with Unreal Engine integration, allowing for the synthesis and mixing of sounds within Metasound.

Keywords: Symbolic Music Generation · Deep Learning · Video Game

1 Introduction

Musicians, such as jazz soloists, can improvise their music and composition to their surroundings. However, in video game development, dynamic music is often created by reordering or layering multiple pre-composed music segments. This research aims to enhance adaptability by making each note dynamic, allowing the music to evolve in response to the environment or react to specific game events. To achieve this, we integrated suitable machine-learning techniques with technology capable of real-time MIDI generation within the game engine.

2 Overall Architecture

2.1 Model and Tokenizer for Training Phase

The Transformer model is a deep learning architecture fitting for MIDI generation. Rotary Positional Embeddings (RoPE) [1], implementing relative position embeddings, can be used to make indefinite generation possible. The Llama [2] and Mistral [3] architectures both use RoPE, making them ideal for the task. In practice, the implementations used are from the Transformers library, from Hugging Face: LlamaForCausalLM and MistralForCausalLM. After training, models

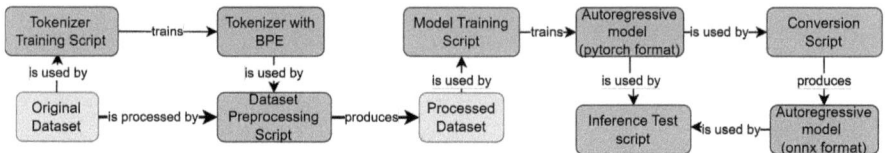

Fig. 1. Training Pipeline

are converted to the ONNX format [4] so that they can be loaded from C++ (Fig. 1).

Byte Pair Encoding (BPE) [5] is also used to convert tokens into encoded ones, allowing the context window to be more manageable, as compression has been shown to work well with Llama and Mistral models. The MidiTok TSD [6] tokenizer [7] has been re-made in C++ for faster decoding and stream decoding, so that tokens can be decoded as they are generated. Both implementations are compatible, so that tokenizers trained and saved in Python can be loaded and used in C++. Tokenizers and models are trained in Python, on the Maestro v3 dataset [8].

2.2 Unreal Engine Plugin Development

Tokens are generated ahead of time and cached for a smooth generation. If an event is triggered and the music has to be adapted, then the generation is rewound, the excessive cache is removed, and new tokens are generated. If the generation gets too far ahead, the thread is put to sleep temporarily to prevent unnecessary computations, but also to be able to reuse a part of the Key Value Cache in case a rewind happens, making the rewind faster. The generation can be configured from Blueprints, and its MIDI output is available in Metasound [9] as a MidiStream and a MidiClock. Another Unreal Engine plugin has been made to synthesize MIDI data from Metasound [9] via soundfonts, using fluidsynth.

Unreal Engine's free Fab assets, featuring complex maps with detailed models and shaders, were used for stress tests as they reflect real-world game rendering. The default scene was modified to evaluate gameplay synchronization with adaptive audio.

3 Results in Test Game

The scene is rendered from the editor with around 1 million triangles per frame, with around 1750 mesh draw calls, through the default deferred rendering pipeline. Nanite is not enabled. Textures make up for around 5GB of GPU memory, and 7GB are used in total when the editor is open, without any music generation (Figs. 2 and 3).

Our approach uses Decoder Only Transformers with relative positional embeddings to continuously generate MIDI at real time. In practice, the Mistral

Fig. 2. Generated score (without any penalty)

Fig. 3. Generated score (with penalties)

architecture is used. To adapt the generation of the model, the generated cache is cleared and transformations are applied on the transformer output logits, impacting which token is selected to form the MIDI sequence. Pitch and tempo can easily be modified that way, and a musical scale can be favored. This gives the user a lot of flexibility, and the model itself doesn't need to be trained or modified. Control tokens can also be fed into the transformer. This allows control of more abstract concepts, and can lead the model to generate in a specific style. However, it is less flexible due to the required pretraining.

4 Subjective Evaluation

We evaluated the music generated in the game based on the following aspects: a) appropriateness of scales and chord progressions, b) naturalness of phrases and rhythms and c) smoothness of transitions. We compared the 30 min of music generated by the system with the learning material songs and conducted a subjective evaluation. The results showed that a) was deemed appropriate in about 80% of cases, but b) often had unnatural rhythms and needed improvement. Regarding c), which was the main objective of this study, the unnatural rhythms were compensated for by a), resulting in a barely smooth transition. Although scales and chord progressions can be defined by music theory, the appropriateness of rhythm is a subject of debate even in music theory, and this subjective evaluation conducted by the researchers themselves will be improved in the future.

5 Conclusion and Future Work

In this paper, the model is used statically, and only fed tokens are modified to impact adaptation. However, it is also possible to finetune new weights using

LoRA [10] or AdaMix [11], and blend them at runtime. This enables dynamic control over various high-level features, including styles, progressively. An alternative to using MIDI is to use raw audio and convert it into discrete data, similar to MIDI. This approach is identical to Jukebox [12], developed by OpenAI, which utilizes a VQ-VAE-2. However, if the discrete data corresponds to audio samples instead of specific events, the generated data would be significantly more complex to constrain, and adding penalties would be more challenging compared to MIDI. We will explore the possibility of incorporating this into more practical games by analyzing discrete data before generation and using the results as cache data.

Demo Video URL. https://youtu.be/OOadl0n3fCg.

Disclosure of Interests. The authors have no competing interests to declare that are relevant to the content of this article.

References

1. Jianlin Su, Yu Lu, Shengfeng Pan, et al.: RoFormer: Enhanced Transformer with Rotary Position Embedding. arXiv preprint arXiv:2104.09864 (2021). https://arxiv.org/abs/2104.09864
2. Hugo Touvron, Etienne P. G., Timothée Montoya, et al.: LLaMA: open and efficient foundation language models (2023). https://arxiv.org/abs/2302.13971
3. Albert Q. Jiang, Sablayrolles, A., Mensch, A., et al.: Mistral 7B (2023). https://arxiv.org/abs/2310.06825
4. ONNX. Open Neural Network Exchange (ONNX). https://onnx.ai
5. Sennrich, R., Haddow, B., Birch, A.: Neural Machine Translation of Rare Words with Subword Units (2016). https://arxiv.org/abs/1508.07909v5
6. Huang, Y., Yang, Y.: Pop Music Transformer: Beat-based Modeling and Generation of Expressive Pop Piano Compositions. In: Proceedings of the 28th ACM International Conference on Multimedia (MM '20) 2020. https://arxiv.org/abs/2002.00212
7. Fradet, N., et al.: MidiTok: A Python package for MIDI file tokenization. Extended Abstracts for the Late-Breaking Demo Session of the 22nd International Society for Music Information Retrieval Conference 2021. https://archives.ismir.net/ismir2021/latebreaking/000005.pdf
8. Hawthorne, C., et al.: Hierarchical Neural Story Generation 2019. https://openreview.net/forum?id=r1lYRjC9F7
9. Epic Games. MetaSounds: The Next Generation Sound Sources in Unreal Engine. Unreal Engine Documentation (2025). https://dev.epicgames.com/documentation/en-us/unreal-engine/metasounds-the-next-generation-sound-sources-in-unreal-engine
10. Hu, E.J., et al.: LoRA: Low-Rank Adaptation of Large Language Models (2021). https://arxiv.org/abs/2106.09685
11. Wang, Y., et al.: LoRA: Low-Rank Adaptation of Large Language Models (2021). https://arxiv.org/abs/2205.12410
12. Dhariwal, P., et al.: Jukebox: A Generative Model for Music. OpenAI, (2020). https://openai.com/index/jukebox

Kaimanāki o te Ngahere: Guardians of the Forest

Allan Fowler[1](✉), Tanya Ruka[2], Michaela Dodd[1,3], Bai Xue[1], and Mark Harvey[1]

[1] The University of Auckland, Auckland, New Zealand
allan.fowler@auckland.ac.nz
[2] Victoria University of Wellington, Wellington, New Zealand
[3] Auckland University of Technology, Auckland, New Zealand
http://www.auckland.ac.nz

Abstract. Inspiring children to appreciate and safeguard endemic species is crucial. Embodied learning experiences enhance their connection with nature, increasing empathy and environmental awareness. However, urban sprawl has reduced opportunities for meaningful engagement with natural environments. Kaimanaki o te Ngahere: Guardians of the Forest is a narrative-driven educational game designed to reconnect children aged five-to-eight with Aotearoa's native ecosystems. The game introduces Mori concepts of kaitiakitanga, mramatanga, and whanaungatanga to encourage reciprocal care between players and the forest. It aims to raise awareness of Myrtle Rust affecting native trees like phutukawa, mnuka, knuka, rt, and ramarama. Recognising that traditional environmental education may not resonate with young learners, we use prkau (storytelling) to frame the gameplay experience. Prakau fosters deep relational learning, shaping the player's journey as they navigate environmental challenges through interactive storytelling.

Future development will introduce Augmented Reality (AR) to connect digital storytelling with real-world conservation efforts, deepening ecological learning.

Keywords: Embodied learning · Human-Nature Interaction · Play

1 Introduction

The importance of inspiring children to appreciate and safeguard endemic species cannot be ignored. Embodied [5] learning experiences enhance children's connection with nature, increasing their empathy and awareness of environmental issues [1–4]. However, urban sprawl and high-density housing have significantly reduced opportunities for children to engage meaningfully with natural environments [6,7]. Kaimanaki o te Ngahere: Guardians of the Forest is a narrative-driven educational game designed to reconnect children aged 5–8 with Aotearoa's native ecosystems. The game introduces Mori concepts of kaitiakitanga (stewardship), mramatanga (learning through practice), and whanaungatanga (building and maintaining relationships) to encourage reciprocal care between players and the forest. The narrative aims to increase awareness of the impact of Myrtle Rust [8] on our native trees. Myrtle Rust (*Austropuccinia psidii*) is a pathogen that impacts native species such as phutukawa, mnuka, knuka, rt, and ramarama [9].

Recognizing that traditional forms of environmental education may not always resonate with young learners, we incorporate prkau (storytelling) [14] as a methodological approach to frame the gameplay experience. Prkau, a Mori way of transmitting knowledge through narrative, fosters deep relational learning. As Smith, et al. [13] argue, indigenous storywork decolonizes research by embedding knowledge within culturally relevant storytelling practices. In this game, prkau shapes the player's journey as they learn to navigate environmental challenges through interactive storytelling.

Storytelling has always been central to indigenous knowledge systems, shaping the way people understand their relationships with the environment [13]. Rather than presenting information as static facts, prkau weaves together experiential learning, relational ethics, and cultural values. Within Kaimanaki o te Ngahere, the game narrative positions the player as a kaitiaki (guardian) tasked with caring for the ngahere (forest). The player embodies Mokopirirakau, an avatar inspired by the Tautuku gecko (*Mokopirirakau galaxias*), a gecko native to Aotearoa, who journeys through different forest ecosystems facing the challenge of myrtle rust (*Austropuccinia psidii*).

By taking on the role of kaitiaki, the player engages in transformational play, a concept described by Barab et al. [5] as the process of adopting a protagonist role to solve real-world problems in a fictional space. The game does not merely simulate conservation efforts but rather immerses the player in a reciprocal relationship with the forest. This approach aligns with Mori epistemologies, where knowledge is inseparable from relationshipsboth human and more-than-human and is nurtured through practices such as karakia, which honour the mauri of the environment and guide care for the whenua [12].

2 Kaimanki o te Ngahere: Guardians of the Forest

Kaimanaki o te Ngahere is designed as a narrative-driven, educational experience that immerses players in the sights and sounds of a New Zealand forest. Inspired by games like Paper Mario [10] and Born of Bread [11], the game integrates soft color palettes, rich soundscapes of native bird calls, and intuitive mechanics to create an engaging experience.

2.1 Gameplay Overview

- Level 1: The player learns to identify mnuka trees affected by myrtle rust and uses traditional interventions to help restore them, rebalancing the ecosystem (Figs. 1A-1B).
- Level 2: The player moves through the forest, tending to phutukawa trees and learning how the pathogen spreads.

- Level 3: The player gathers natural resources, such as manuka honey and kawakawa leaves, to create a restorative tea, reinforcing interdependence with the ecosystem (Fig. 1C).
- Level 4 The player continues to move through the forest tending to ramarama trees learning how the pathogen spreads.
- Final Level: The player is guided by a Kaitiaki (guardian spirit) and hears the voice of the wairua (spirit) of the forest, learning that they are now a Kaimanakia true guardian of the ngahere (Fig. 1D).

The game was developed using Unity, with a focus on culturally responsive design. By embedding mtauranga Mori into both the mechanics and narrative, the game provides an interactive storytelling experience that fosters deeper environmental awareness in young players.

Fig. 1. Gameplay Images

3 Conclusion and Future Work

While the game currently provides an engaging digital experience, the next development phase will introduce Augmented Reality (AR) to further connect digital storytelling with real-world conservation efforts. The AR component will enable players to identify actual trees affected by myrtle rust and explore alternative interventions, deepening their ecological learning. By blending prkau methodology, mtauranga Mori, and interactive digital media, Kaimanaki o te Ngahere represents a transdisciplinary approach to indigenous-led game design. Future iterations will expand on the ways of indigenous storytelling can shape transformative environmental education, fostering the next generation of kaitiaki for Aotearoa's forests.

References

1. Beery, T., Chawla, L., Levin, P.: Being and becoming in nature: defining and measuring connection to nature in young children. Int. J. Early Childhood Environ. Educ. **7**(3), 3–22 (2020)
2. Cumbo, B. J., Paay, J., Kjeldskov, J., Jacobs, B. C.: Connecting children to nature with technology: sowing the seeds for proenvironmental behaviour. In: Proceedings of the 2014 conference on Interaction design and children, pp. 189-192 (2014)
3. Barab, S.A., Gresalfi, M., Ingram-Goble, A.: Transformational play: using games to position person, content, and context. Educ. Res. **39**(7), 525–536 (2010)
4. Barab, S.A., Luehmann, A. L.: Building sustainable science curriculum: Acknowledging and accommodating local adaptation. Sci. Educ. **87**(4), 454–467 (2003)
5. Barab, S., et al.: Situationally embodied curriculum: relating formalisms and contexts. Sci. Educ. **91**(5), 750–782 (2007)
6. Bailie, P. E.: Connecting children to nature: a multiple case study of nature center preschools. The University of Nebraska-Lincoln (2012)
7. Moore, R. C.: The need for nature: a childhood right. Social Justice, 24(3 (69), pp. 203-220 (1997)
8. Toome-Heller, M., et al.: Chasing myrtle rust in New Zealand: host range and distribution over the first year after invasion. Australas. Plant Pathol. **49**, 221–230 (2020)
9. Teulon, D.A.J., et al.: The threat of myrtle rust to Maori taonga plant species in New Zealand. NZ Plant Prot. **68**, 66–75 (2015)
10. Paper Mario, https://www.nintendo.com/us/store/products/paper-mario-the-thousand-year-door-switch/. Last Accessed 14 Feb 2025
11. Born of Bread. https://www.wildartsgames.com/bornofbread. Last Accessed 14 Feb 2025
12. Southey, K. M.: Re-presenting mori and indigenous understandings of being: Deconstructing the notion of mental illness (Doctoral dissertation, The University of Waikato)(2020)
13. Smith, L. T.: Decolonizing research: indigenous storywork as methodology. Bloomsbury Publishing(2019)
14. Lee, J.: Decolonising Mori narratives: prkau as a method. MAI review **2**(3), 1–12 (2009)

Demonstration of Visualizer for Beats and Scratches of Breaking DJ Performances

Masatoshi Hamanaka[✉][iD]

RIKEN, Tokyo, Japan
`masatoshi.hamanaka@riken.jp`

Abstract. Breaking is a dance duel between two dancers to music improvised by a DJ. Since breaking was chosen as an official competition at the Paris Olympics, many people have begun to watch the competitions on television. When a dancer freezes in time with a beat or scratch in breaking, it is called "kill the beat," and when it is successful, the audience gets very excited. However, TV viewers may have difficulty hearing the music due to the announcer's or commentator's voice, making it difficult to judge if the kill the beat is successful or not. In addition, some in the audience may be hard of hearing. Therefore, we developed a visualizer for the beats and scratches of breaking DJ performances.

Keywords: Breaking DJ performance · Visualizer · Beat · Scratch

1 Introduction

This paper describes a visualizer for the beats and scratches of the music played by breaking DJs.

Breaking features two dancers breakdancing against each other to the rhythm of music played by a DJ (disc jockey). The DJ uses two turntables to play multiple musical pieces while switching between them. The DJ then adds accents to the music by scratching the turntables. Freezing while performing tricks, such as inverted stands, in perfect time with the rhythm generated by the DJ is called "kill the beat" and is the highlight of competitions, as it requires a high level of skill. Most of the audience at a breaking venue have experienced breaking, and they get very excited when they see a successful kill the beat.

However, viewers watching breaking videos on television have difficulty hearing the music due to the announcer's and commentator's voices, making it difficult to judge whether a kill the beat is a success, and some viewers are also hard of hearing. Therefore, we developed a visualizer for breaking DJ performances that displays the beat of the sound source being played and scratches played by the DJ.

Several methods have been proposed for automatically generating a set list for DJs to prepare before remixing [1,2,5]. An automated DJ-mixing system was also proposed [3] as well as a method for smoothly crossfading from one piece to another [6].

While these studies [1–3,5,6] intended to automate the DJ's work or assist the DJ, our study is intended to assist the breaking audience through visualization. Beat visualization helps the audience understand if a beat matches the timing of the moves. Visualization can also enable the hearing impaired to understand the timing of the beat and enjoy breaking.

Our visualizer was used in 2024 at the All Japan Breaking Championships recorded by the Japan Broadcasting Corporation (NHK in Japanese) (Fig. 1).

Fig. 1. Beat and Scratch Visualizer

2 Beat and Scratch Visualizer

There are six problems in visualizing the beats and scratches created by a DJ in real time. Each of these problems and their solutions are described as follows.

No Network: To execute the visualizer, it was necessary to connect the DJ table at the rear of the stage at NHK Hall, the competition venue, to the NHK broadcast room over a distance of more than 100 m via a network. However, NHK Hall did not have network facilities. Therefore, we built a 10G network by connecting a small-form-factor pluggable transceiver to a standard LEMO [4] fiber optic cable for the TV camera.

Difficulty of Predicting Beats: Predicting beats in real time is difficult because DJs change musical pieces one after another. Therefore, we receive all sound sources used by DJs, analyze them, and generate beat-visualization videos. The sound source and video can then be played synchronously by creating a link between the sound source and video. When a DJ changes the music-playback speed (turntable rotation speed), the video-playback speed also changes in sync.

Video and Signal Delays: The broadcast video produced by NHK included delays as it passed through selectors that integrate multiple cameras and switchers that superimpose information, etc. The distance between the cameras and the broadcast room at NHK Hall, the venue of the championships, was more than 100 m, which caused transmission delays. However, our real-time beat and scratch visualizer also needed to send information from the DJ booth to the broadcast room, which caused delays. Due to these delays, the timing between the dance video and beat-visualization video is shifted. Therefore, we can adjust the position of the beat-visualization video by adding a line indicating the current time on the video later in the program so that the timing of the dance video and beat-visualization video are aligned.

Animation at Current Timing: Adding an effect, such as a color change or animation, when bars indicating whether the beat is strong or weak pass the current timing makes the timing easier for the viewer to understand. However, a video with effects added in advance cannot be created because the timing and position change depending on the delay in the previous item. Therefore, we developed a program that analyzes the beat-visualization video being played, reads the bar positions, and adds effects at the appropriate timing.

Detection of Turntable Rotation: Two turntables are connected to the DJ mixer, and DJ software can be used to set the pieces assigned to each turntable. When using DJ software, a vinyl record in which sine waves with different phases are recorded on the left and right sides is placed on the turntable. The DJ software then receives the rotation information of the turntable from the digital vinyl system (DVS) signal generated by the vinyl record.

Because the DVS signal is an analog signal, we branch it out, receive it at the audio interface, and analyze it to determine the revolutions per minute of both the left and right turntables. Specifically, accelerating the turntable increases the frequency, and decelerating the turntable decreases it. Because the DVS signal is a stereo signal and is out of phase between left and right, it can also detect whether the rotation is forward or reverse depending on which waveform arrives first.

Scratch Detection: DJ mixers have a crossfader, which is used for swapping between two pieces or for adding scratching sounds. Scratching is a technique in which a record is played on one turntable while a record on the other turntable is scratched during the playback of a certain piece to emphasize the beat with the sound generated. The crossfader can then be moved slightly to the turntable on the side that is being scratched to mix both the playback and scratch sounds. Therefore, to detect scratches, we need to detect not only the rotation of the turntable but also the position of the crossfader.

Many models of DJ mixers that can be connected to a computer via a USB cable use MIDI (Musical Instrument Digital Interface) signals for communication. Some DJ mixer models that are equipped with two USB ports for DJ alternation can receive the USB signal flowing through the port in use on the other USB port. Therefore, the MIDI signal is analyzed, and the crossfader position is extracted.

3 Experimental Results

Equipment and transmission delays are dependent on the hall and broadcasting facilities, so adjustments were made on site after the equipment was installed in NHK Hall. The breaking TV video received from NHK was a time-code-synchronized switching of multiple camera images. However, the sound signals from the stage, the emcee's voice on stage, and the DJ's performance of a song were picked up by microphones. Video and sound were lip-synchronized by NHK using the voice and video of the emcee during rehearsal. We recorded the video after superimposing beat and scratch visualization on that video. While slowing down and playing back the recorded video, we checked the beat timing of the acoustic signal and timing of the bar passing the white line representing the current time and found that the visualized video was delayed by two frames at 60 frames per second. The white line representing the present time was moved 20 pixels downward and recorded again. As a result, the passage of the bars in the visualization video coincided with the timing of the acoustic signal in the NHK dance video.

When twenty people who viewed the recorded video were asked their opinions, 18 said they enjoyed watching it, and 14 said kill the beat was easy to understand.

4 Conclusion

The beat and scratch visualizer we constructed was used at the All Japan Breaking Championships in February 2024. A video was recorded using a sound source and a video visualizing the sound source after superimposing beat and scratch visualization on the video. Slow playback of the recorded video showed a discrepancy between the timing of the sound in the broadcast video and timing of the beat visualization. Therefore, the current point of the visualization video was adjusted to eliminate the misalignment. We plan to conduct more detailed experiments. We plan to conduct more detailed experiments.

References

1. Bittner, R.M., et al.: Automatic playlist sequencing and transitions. In: Proceedings of the 18th International Society for Music Information Retrieval Conference (ISMIR 2017), pp. 442–448 (2017)
2. Hirai, T., Doi, H., Morishima, S.: MusicMixer: automatic DJ system considering beat and latent topic similarity. In: Tian, Q., Sebe, N., Qi, G.-J., Huet, B., Hong, R., Liu, X. (eds.) MMM 2016. LNCS, vol. 9516, pp. 698–709. Springer, Cham (2016). https://doi.org/10.1007/978-3-319-27671-7_59
3. Ishizaki, H., Keiichiro Hoashi, Y.T.: Full-automatic DJ mixing system with optimal tempo adjustment based on measurement function of user discomfort. In: Proceedings of the 10th International Society for Music Information Retrieval Conference (ISMIR 2009), pp. 135–140 (2009)
4. LEMO: About us | LEMO Connectors and cables — lemo.com. https://www.lemo.com/our-world/company/about-us. Accessed 07 Mar 2024
5. Parera, J.: DJ Codo Nudo: a novel method for seamless transition between songs for electronic music. Master's thesis, Universitat PompeuFabra, Barcelona (2016)
6. Robinson, K., Brown, D.: Automated time-frequency domain audio crossfades using graph cuts. In: Proceedings of the 20th International Society for Music Information Retrieval Conference (ISMIR 2019) Late-Breaking/Demo (2019)

Development of a Dialogue Agent System Expressed in a Two-Dimensional Manga-Anime Style and Design of the Original Artificial Intelligence Character "Kohane"

Kaimu Harada[1(✉)] and Sachiko Kodama[2]

[1] Graduate School of Informatics and Engineering, The University of Electro-Communications, Tokyo, Japan
`h2430106@gl.cc.uec.ac.jp`
[2] Department of Informatics, The University of Electro-Communications, Tokyo, Japan
`kodama@inf.uec.ac.jp`

Abstract. This study aims to develop a system that allows humans to interact naturally with unique characters appearing in two-dimensional manga-style animation works. We define the manga-anime style in Japanese Anime, analyze the characteristics of the expression, and design a system that allows a dialogue agent to use Large Language Models (LLMs) to behave like a manga-anime character. The proposed system uses LLMs to 1) process Voice Activity Projection (VAP) for user speech, switch character prompts in real-time, and generate agent speech that reflects personality and context; 2) determine the graphical/sound expressions of the manga-anime style, including comic symbols, backgrounds, effects, and composition, according to the speech of the agent; and 3) generate parameters based on the content and emotion as well as link them with animations of objects that characterize the agent. Using this system, we created an artificial intelligence character named "Kohane," whose emotional expression changes depending on the conversation with a human.

Keywords: Dialogue Agent · Anime · Manga · LLM

1 Introduction

Anime (animation originating in Japan) is popular worldwide for its unique expressions and characters with rich personalities. The idiosyncrasies and attractive behaviors of anime characters continue to attract many people. Therefore, realizing a system that allows users to converse with anime characters is vital for expanding the use of characters in entertainment.

In recent years, the development of dialogue agents that utilize large language models (LLMs) has progressed. However, existing dialogue agent development [1–3] has focused on reproducing natural human-like behavior that is appropriate for professional situations, such as customer service. There has been insufficient progress in developing dialogue agents that incorporate the two-dimensional (2D), manga-style anime (hereafter referred to as "manga-anime"), where exaggerated and stylized expressions are frequently used, as seen in Japanese anime works. In this study, we develop a system to give manga-anime character expressions to dialogue agents using LLM and create an artificial intelligence (AI) character, "Kohane," who can talk to humans using this system.

2 Analysis of Manga-Anime Character Representation in Animated Footage from Japanese Anime

Anime often uses deformed 2D illustrations and distinctive directing techniques. Therefore, the dialogue agent system requires an architecture that can control its unique expressive elements. In this study, we first watched many anime works, classified the character expressions in the manga-anime style, and listed the expressive elements that we felt were characteristic of manga-anime characters (Table 1). These expression elements are controlled by the dialogue system proposed in this study.

Table. 1. Elements of manga-anime style character representation in footage.

Character personalities emphasized in anime works			
Unique speaking style Exaggerated speech that reflects attributes and personality Favorite phrase	Tastes and preferences Favorite objects/foods that elicit sympathy and interest from the viewer	Unique movements Gestures that are unique to the character, sometimes used in conjunction with favorite phrase	Unique expression of emotion Character-specific emotional expressions using tools or body parts
Manga-anime style graphical/sound expressions			
Deformed facial expressions in 2D illustrations Simplified line drawings of facial features Switching facial expressions using multiple still images	Emotion-linked manga style illustration effects Comic symbols, background effects, and special compositions that emphasize the emotions of characters	Inner voice expressions Presenting true feelings and thoughts using images or graphical effects and voices	Anime specific sound effects Character-specific sounds Easily understandable sound effects that express emotions and movements

3 Development of a Dialogue Agent System Expressed in 2D Manga-Anime Style and Design of "Kohane"

Figure 1(a) shows the architecture of the proposed system, which comprises three main parts: a speech recognition unit, text generation unit, and graphics control unit. Figure 1(b) shows the elements controlled by the LLM. The elements shown in the figure were prepared for the original character "Kohane" created in this study. When designing a character, one must make decisions regarding the numbers and types of these elements as well as prepare the required 2D images and text data to describe the personality and narrative of the character.

3.1 Speech Recognition Unit

In this step, user speech is recognized in real-time using Google Cloud Speech-to-Text, and agent response decisions are made. The speech recognition results consist of incremental units IU_{asr}, and the user input is analyzed using GPT-4o mini at each specified interval. The input of the LLM, denoted as p_θ, includes the user input at that time $\sum IU_{asr}$, a prompt for response decision x_{vap}, and the input intent type set T_{INPUT}, which is designed for Kohane's personality. Moreover, the response decision result $a_{vap} = \{0 : unresponsable, 1 : respondable\}$ is generated, and the user input type $b_{vap} \in T_{INPUT}$. (a_{vap}, b_{vap}) is defined as:

$$(a_{vap}, b_{vap}) \sim p_\theta\left((a_{vap}, b_{vap}) \mid \sum IU_{asr}, x_{vap}, T_{INPUT}\right) \quad (1)$$

Here, $a_{vap} = 1$ when the LLM determines that the user input contains sufficient information for a response, considering fillers and back-channeling. If $a_{vap} = 1$, then the character prompt $x_{character} \in X_{character}$ is selected based on b_{vap} and the predefined character prompt set $X_{character}$, which initiates the generation of the response text of an agent. By switching $x_{character}$ in user speech, the personality of the agent is reflected in the conversational content in detail.

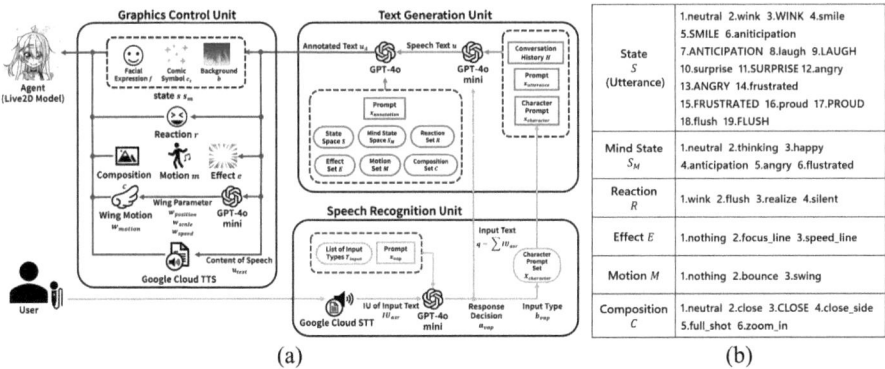

Fig. 1. (a)The proposed system architecture. (b)Elements to be determined by LLM. If the parameter representing the state is in uppercase, it represents a stronger state.

3.2 Text Generation Unit

In this step, the speech texts of the agent are determined based on $x_{character}$ selected by the speech recognition unit. First, GPT-4o mini generates the utterance texts, inner voice texts, and reaction instructions of the agent. The speech texts u are generated from $x_{character}$, a prompt for speech generation $x_{utterance}$, the user input text $q = \sum IU_{asr}$, and the conversation history $H = \sum (q, u)$. Annotated texts u_A are generated from GPT-4o, which includes annotations such as the state s, mind state s_m, reaction r, effect e, motion m, composition c, and content of speech u_{text}. Here, u_A is generated from u and the prompt for annotation $x_{annotation}$, state space S, mind state space S_M, reaction set R, effect set E, motion set M, and composition set C.

3.3 Graphics Control Unit

The facial expression, background, comic symbols, effects, motion, and composition of the agent are determined from the generated annotated text (u_A) (Fig. 2). Each element plays a pre-defined sound effect as needed. Live2D models that enables seamless animation with 2D morphing are used [4], and facial parts are switched as in manga-anime. The number of determinable patterns is calculated as: $(19 + 6 + 4) \times 3 \times 3 \times 6 = 1{,}566$. The movement of wings is also produced using a Live2D parameter with physics, denoted by $w_{motion} \in [-1, 1]$, and dynamically controlled according to parameters generated by GPT-4o mini.

Fig. 2. Examples of Kohane's facial expressions, backgrounds, and compositions, with wing movements created by the generated text of the LLM, using the developed system

4 Exhibits, Experiment and Future Development

"Kohane," created in 2024 using the developed system, won three awards in competitions submitted by content creators and was exhibited in Japan. In addition, a subjective questionnaire experiment was conducted with 41 university students, and the subjects reported having the impression that they were conversing with a manga-anime character, finding the experience enjoyable. Since the LLM is accessed via the Internet, the current system has a latency of approximately 3 s in the agent's response. In the future, Small

Language Models will be considered to accelerate the text generation process. The current system is designed for one-on-one conversations between the agent and the user. Expanding to multiple users and characters is a future challenge. We will continue to improve the entertainment system enabling humans to converse naturally with attractive anime characters and characters with original designs.

References

1. Ishii, R., et al.: Methods of efficiently constructing text-dialogue-agent system using existing anime character. J. Information Processing **29**, 30–44 (2021)
2. Masum, R., Cengiz, O., Sammy, P., Ehsan, H.: SAPIEN: affective virtual agents powered by large language models. 2023 11th International Conference on Affective Computing and Intelligent Interaction Workshops and Demos (ACIIW), pp. 1–3 (2023). https://doi.org/10.1109/ACIIW59127.2023.10388188
3. Rafael, W., Nikola, K., Philin, W., Chen, Y., Markus, G.: Immersive conversations with digital einstein: linking a physical system and AI. SIGGRAPH Asia 2024 Emerging Technologies, Article No.7 (2024)
4. Live2D, Live2D Inc. https://www.live2d.com/

Development of Urban Disaster Prevention Shooting Game Using Spatial Reproduction Display

Yasuo Kawai(✉)

Bunkyo University, Namegaya 1100, Chigasaki, Kanagawa, Japan
kawai@bunkyo.ac.jp

Abstract. In this study, we developed a shooting game that combines 3D model data of an actual city and a hazard map for natural disasters. We have developed content that uses a spatial reproduction display to display urban spaces in three dimensions and promotes an understanding of the dangers of natural disasters in cities through game play. We propose a system that aims to improve users' awareness of disaster risks and spatial awareness by combining game elements with the visualization of natural disasters such as flooding, by loading Google Photorealistic 3D Tiles of real cities into Unity.

Keywords: Urban Flood Visualization · Disaster Risk · Geographic Gaming

1 Introduction

In Japan, where natural disasters occur frequently, disaster prevention education in cities is an important issue. Because of climate change, the number of floods and the resulting flood damage has increased since 2004 [1]. However, with conventional disaster prevention education methods, it has been difficult to sufficiently attract the interest of citizens due to a lack of awareness and the complexity of the information. For young people, it is difficult to lead to specific risk awareness with only conventional teaching materials and hazard map explanations [2]. In this study, we aimed to develop more effective disaster prevention education content using gamification by combining large-scale geographic models and spatial display technology. Specifically, we developed a 3D shooting game using Unity, integrated 3D models of real cities and hazard map data and built a system that displays them in three dimensions using a spatial reproduction display. This work uniquely combines hazard-aware enemy spawning with a spatial reproduction display, which has not been explored in prior serious games research.

2 System Overview

2.1 System Configuration

This system uses the game engine Unity 6000.033f1 as its development environment and uses the Universal Render Pipeline (URP) for rendering, achieving efficient real-time rendering. For the 3D geographic model, we used Google Photorealistic 3D Tiles, which are based on aerial photographs and have high-quality textures covering a wide area and integrated the data by acquiring the model data for the flood inundation area from the Ministry of Land, Infrastructure, Transport and Tourism's PLATEAU as disaster data. These geographical data were used to build a 3D geographical data platform using Cesium for Unity, and data integration was carried out by acquiring an access token through Cesium Ion. The ELF-SR1 was used as a spatial display (Fig. 1).

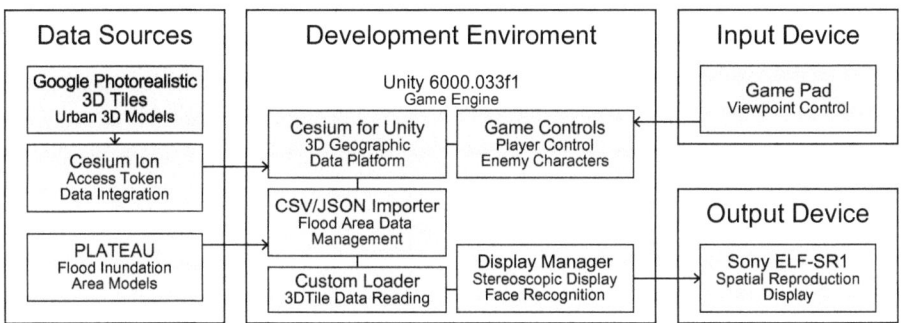

Fig. 1. System Architecture of Urban Disaster Prevention Shooting Game Using Spatial Display.

2.2 Data Integration

The 3D city models obtained from Google Photorealistic and PLATEAU were imported into Unity, and hazard map data such as flood risk data was superimposed to express disaster risk information in three dimensions. A dedicated loader was developed to read 3DTile data, allowing large-scale city data to be processed efficiently. It uses 3D Tile models for flood inundation zones from PLATEAU, and links data showing the extent of flooding due to the maximum rainfall expected for each river (Fig. 2).

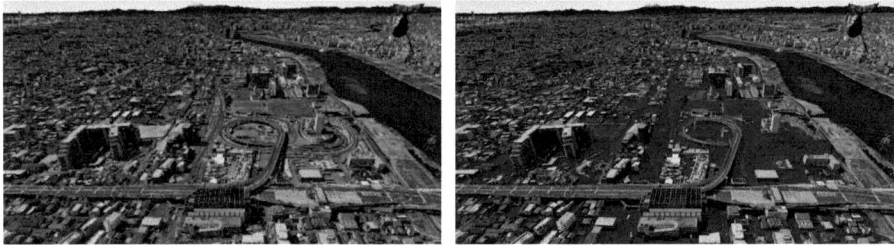

Fig. 2. Flood inundation simulation in a 3D urban model. Normal urban landscape (Left) and flood inundation simulation of the same area (Right).

2.3 Design of the Shooting Game

The game is designed so that players can learn about the disaster risk information of the city naturally through the gameplay, in which they control a flying machine above the city and fight off "enemies" that appear in areas with a high risk of flooding. The game incorporates elements such as intuitive machine control with inertia and tilt, multiple types of enemy characters, battles with boss characters, and improved operability with a game pad. As a control system for the game pad, we implemented a component that controls objects in virtual space. In addition, we prevented excessive acceleration by setting the maximum movement speed (Fig. 3).

Fig. 3. Characters in the urban disaster prevention shooting game: player character (left), enemy character based on a horseshoe crab (center), and boss character based on a whale (right).

2.4 Utilization of Spatial Reproduction Display

By combining a special lens array and a high-speed tracking camera, Spatial Reproduction Display ELF-SR1 achieves stereoscopic vision without the need for special glasses. The SRDManager component was used as the basis for the rendering process, and the positioning was carried out with the objects placed using CesiumGeoreference. By setting the virtual camera to 100 times the size on the coordinate axis of the SRDManager component, and by positioning the geographic model at 0.1 times the size, it is displayed as a city model at 1/1000 the size on the spatial reproduction display. This 3D display makes it possible to intuitively understand the relationship between the depth of inundation and the topography and buildings, compared to a 2D display.

2.5 Data Processing Flow

In this system, the Start method is called when the system is started, and the loading of the set tileset from the cloud begins. During the loading of the tileset, various tilesets such as Google Photorealistic 3D Tiles are loaded sequentially. After the tileset has been loaded, the display process for the spatial reproduction display is carried out by rendering from the left and right viewpoints for stereoscopic viewing, and also by processing the input from the game pad to navigate within the virtual 3D space. The game pad allows the user to move and rotate the viewpoint, and intuitive operations such as switching data layers using button operations are also possible.

3 Results and Discussion

This system enables intuitive understanding of which buildings will be flooded and which roads will be passable by integrating data on flood-prone areas of major rivers and combining it with information on building heights. In addition, the relationship between flood depths and building heights can be more clearly recognized through three-dimensional display using a spatial reproduction display. The integration of Google Photorealistic 3D Tiles and PLATEAU flood data made it possible to link the data in a standardized format. The system we developed was able to efficiently process large-scale 3D city models thanks to the use of 3D Tiles. The loading of data from the cloud using Cesium for Unity contributed to improved processing performance, and because the necessary data is loaded dynamically according to the display range, relatively lightweight processing is possible.

In terms of visualization, it is now possible to intuitively grasp the 3D relationship between inundation areas and buildings, and spatial awareness has improved compared to conventional 2D representations. In addition, spatial recognition was improved by the three-dimensional display using a spatial reproduction display, and by combining this with intuitive navigation using a game pad, it became possible for users without specialist knowledge to easily explore the 3D space. On the other hand, as for the data-related issues, since the inundation area data is both high-resolution and wide-ranging, a decrease in rendering performance was observed when processing many river basin data at the same time. To address this issue, we preloaded data covering a 1 km wide by 10 km deep area at startup and adjusted the level-of-detail (LOD) settings to maintain rendering quality while minimizing performance overhead. Following these optimizations, the average frame rate increased from 55 FPS to 90 FPS on an RTX 4080. In addition, the flooded area can be toggled on or off for display.

4 Conclusion

In this study, we developed a system that uses the game engine Unity and open data to display flood inundation areas in a multilayered manner on a 3D city model. We used our own components to handle data sources of different formats in a unified manner and realized intuitive spatial recognition through display on a spatial reproduction display and game pad operation. By combining a spatial reproduction display with a shooting game, we have developed a system that promotes understanding of urban disaster risk, which has been difficult to achieve with conventional disaster prevention education and have been able to create educational content that allows users to acquire disaster prevention knowledge naturally through game play. In the future, we would like to develop this system further so that it can contribute to the sophistication of disaster prevention planning and the improvement of citizens' disaster prevention awareness by adding functions such as a time-series inundation reproduction function and an agent-based evacuation simulation function.

Acknowledgements. This work was supported by JSPS KAKENHI Grant Number JP 23K11728.

References

1. Kazama, S., Sato, A., Kawagoe, S.: Evaluating the cost of flood damage based on changes in extreme rainfall in Japan. Sustain. Sci. **4**, 61–69 (2009)
2. Itamiya, T.: Vr/ar and its application to disaster risk reduction. Emerging Technologies for Disaster Resilience: Practical Cases and Theories, pp. 63–79 (2021)

VR Game Aimed at Recovering Visual Acuity

Masahiro Kawamori(✉) and Masataka Imura

Kwansei Gakuin University, Sanda, Hyogo 669-1330, Japan
`lightgreen.ws@gmail.com, m.imura@kwansei.ac.jp`

Abstract. Declining visual acuity caused by ICT devices usage is often classified as pseudomyopia, a condition resulting from excessive strain and tension in the ciliary muscles. This condition can potentially be alleviated through ciliary muscle stretching. In this study, we developed a VR game that incorporates three elements effective for ciliary muscle stretching: near-far focusing exercises, distance fixation exercises, and binocular stereoscopic vision. We conducted an experiment to evaluate the effectiveness of the developed VR game in recovering visual acuity. The experiment, which focused on young adults, demonstrated a significant recovery of visual acuity over a six-week period. These findings suggest the potential of the VR game as an effective tool for improving visual acuity through ciliary muscle stretching.

Keywords: VR · HMD · Visual Acuity Recovery · Gamification

1 Introduction

With the widespread use of ICT devices such as personal computers, smartphones, and tablets, *eye strain* and *declining vision* have become significant social issues. Vision loss due to ICT device usage is primarily classified as *pseudomyopia*, a condition caused by excessive strain or tension of the ciliary muscles in the eye. This condition can potentially be alleviated through stretching of the ciliary muscles.

To relax the tension of the ciliary muscles, techniques such as *near-far focusing exercises*, *distance fixation exercises*, and *binocular stereoscopic vision* using stereograms are considered effective. When focusing on stereoscopic images through binocular stereoscopic vision, lens accommodation and convergence movements occur naturally, as they do during normal vision [1]. Therefore, using Head-mounted display (HMD) to achieve binocular stereoscopic vision can facilitate ciliary muscle stretching through near-far focusing exercises and distance fixation exercises.

Although game content aimed at treating conditions such as strabismus or amblyopia exists [2,3], there is a notable lack of game content specifically designed to address pseudomyopia. This scarcity extends to VR content using

HMD. In response, we developed a VR game aimed at effectively stretching the ciliary muscles using HMD and conducted an evaluation to verify the game's effectiveness in achieving a recovery of visual acuity.

2 VR Game for Recovering Visual Acuity

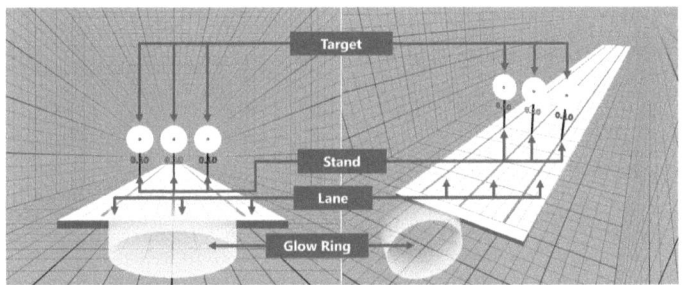

Fig. 1. Game stage

2.1 Description of the Game

Game Overview. The fundamental rule of the game is to *continuously push back multiple targets approaching over time to a distant position.*

Game Environment. The game takes place in a grid room with dimensions of 6 m × 5 m × 34 m in the game's scale. The grid room includes a *Glow Ring* indicating the player's position, as well as three lanes, each extending 30.5 m in depth. On each lane, targets are mounted on stands and are capable of moving back and forth within a 30 m range along the lane (Fig. 1). At the center of each target, a Landolt ring with a diameter of 75 mm is displayed.

Game Mechanics. Using a VR controller, players can aim at one of the targets. While aiming, players input a directional command (up, down, left, or right) using the joystick on the VR controller. This input corresponds to the direction of the gap in the Landolt ring displayed on the target. Based on the match between the input and the Landolt ring's gap direction, one of three reactions—*Hit*, *Combo*, or *Miss*—is triggered:

Hit The target is pushed back, and a score is awarded based on the game's conditions. If the previous action on the same target was a Hit, a Combo is triggered instead.

Combo The target is pushed back with greater force than a Hit, and a score is awarded based on the game's conditions.

Miss No effect occurs.

As shown in Fig. 2, when the game begins, a *time limit* is displayed, and targets on each lane begin advancing toward the player (the Glow Ring). The player aims to achieve the highest possible score within the time limit by continuously pushing back all targets in rotation.

Through the mechanism where players shift their gaze from a target moving farther away as a result of a Hit or Combo effect to the nearest target at the forefront position, the game induces the near-far focusing exercise. Additionally, by designing the game to encourage the use of Combo, which is more effective for pushing targets farther away, the mechanism also requires players to continue fixating on targets moving farther away due to the Hit effect, thereby inducing the distance fixation exercise. These design elements aim to promote stretching of the ciliary muscles through gameplay.

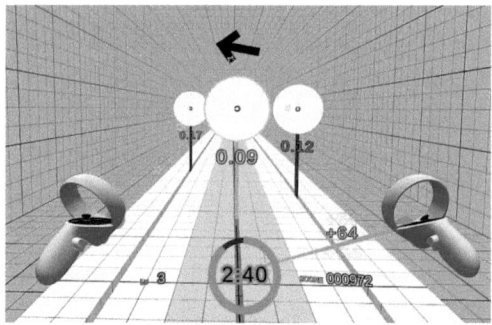

Fig. 2. Gameplay screenshot

3 Experiment

To evaluate the effectiveness of the developed VR game in achieving a recovery of visual acuity, we conducted an experiment.

The experiment involved 10 participants aged between 22 and 36 years old (20 eyes in total), none of whom had any eye diseases. Among the participants, 3 used no corrective lenses, 6 wore glasses, and 1 used contact lenses. Informed consent was obtained from all participants prior to the experiment. The study was approved by the Kwansei Gakuin University Committee for Regulations for Behavioral Research with Human Participants (No. 2023-106).

The experiment was conducted over a period of six-weeks. Participants were instructed to play the experimental VR game at least once a week, with an average frequency of once every three days during the experimental period. On the first and last days of the experiment, visual acuity for each eye was measured separately using Landolt rings. Changes in visual acuity before and after the experiment were assessed. The visual acuity measurements used the LogMAR (Logarithm of Minimum Angle of Resolution) scale as the standard visual acuity indicator.

4 Result and Conclusion

Figure 3 shows the changes in the participants' LogMAR before and after the experiment. The mean LogMAR of the participants decreased significantly from 0.057 ± 0.121 before the experiment to -0.186 ± 0.084 after the experiment ($p < 0.005$, Wilcoxon signed-rank test), indicating a significant recovery in visual acuity.

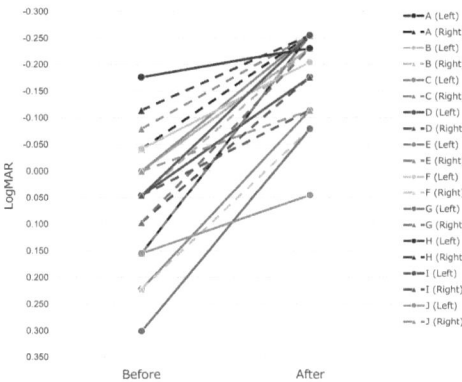

Fig. 3. Changes in LogMAR for participants

Over the six-week experimental period, a significant recovery in visual acuity was observed, with all 20 eyes showing enhanced visual acuity. However, since all the participants in this study were young students in an information technology department, who frequently used ICT devices, it is possible that they were in a state of pronounced pseudomyopia, making the effects of ciliary muscle stretching particularly prominent. Therefore, further experiments are needed to include participants from different age groups and environments to generalize the findings.

Acknowledgements. This work was supported by JSPS KAKENHI Grant Number JP22H03681.

References

1. Hasegawa, S., Hasegawa, A., Omori, M., Ishio, H., Takada, H., Miyao, M.: Stereoscopic vision induced by parallax images on HMD and its influence on visual functions. In: Shumaker, R. (ed.) VMR 2011. LNCS, vol. 6773, pp. 297–305. Springer, Heidelberg (2011). https://doi.org/10.1007/978-3-642-22021-0_33

2. Xiao, S., et al.: Randomized controlled trial of a dichoptic digital therapeutic for amblyopia. Ophthalmology **129**(1), 77–85 (2022)
3. Jiménez-Rodríguez, C., et al.: Rehabilitation of visual functions in adult amblyopic patients with a virtual reality videogame: a case series. Virt. Real. **27**(1), 385–396 (2023)

Automatic Fingering Saxophone Quartet System

Gou Koutaki[1]() and Masatoshi Hamanaka[2]()

[1] Kumamoto University, Kumamoto, Japan
koutaki@cs.kumamoto-u.ac.jp
[2] RIKEN, Tokyo, Japan

Abstract. In this study, we develop Robo-Sax system, which is a semi-automatic instrument-playing robot that performs key fingerings automatically while the human player handles the blowing motion. We also create four versions of Robo-Sax (soprano, alto, tenor, and baritone) and propose a system for ensemble playing using a saxophone quartet. Our goal is to design the hardware and develop the system software to ensure practical applicability. Experiments with beginner, intermediate, and professional saxophonists are conducted to demonstrate the system's potential.

Keywords: Musical robot · saxophone · ensemble

1 Introduction

Music is an essential part of human culture. Beyond listening, people engage with music through singing and playing instruments for hobbies, education, communication, self-expression, and enjoyment. However, learning to play an instrument typically requires long hours of repetitive practice under expert guidance, which many find discouraging and difficult to sustain.

To address this, our study proposes an inclusive music performance system that allows anyone to play instruments easily and independently, enabling enjoyable solo and ensemble performances. We introduce a semi-automatic system that supports performance through robotics and information technology, and expands expressive possibilities beyond human capabilities (human augmentation).

Various machines and robots have been developed to support semi-automatic musical instrument performance. Recent studies have explored systems that assist instrument playing using robotics and information technology [4,6,7]. Some devices employ actuators to press guitar strings or support flute fingering [3]. Unlike fully automated systems, these semi-automatic robots allow the user to remain the primary performer, offering an active and engaging musical experience.

2 Robo-Sax System

The saxophone, shown on the left in Fig. 1, is a woodwind instrument developed by Adolphe Sax in the 1840s. A wooden reed attached to the mouthpiece vibrates when the player blows into it, generating the fundamental tone. The pitch is controlled by altering the tube length through opening and closing keys on the instrument's body. A typical saxophone has around 20 keys, enabling a pitch range of approximately 32 semitones, or two and a half octaves.

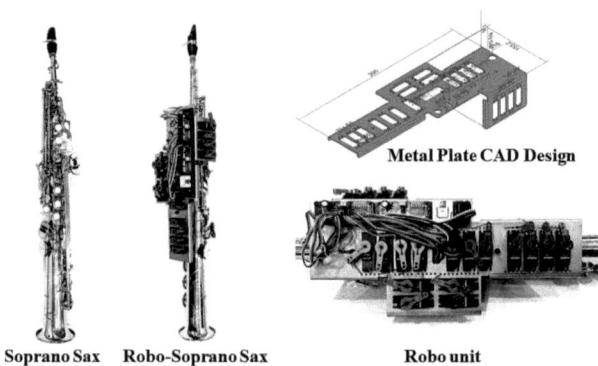

Soprano Sax   Robo-Soprano Sax   Robo unit

Fig. 1. The Robo-Sax (Soprano saxophone) we developed is based on a traditional soprano saxophone. A steel sheet metal, embedded with 19 servo motors and electronic circuits, is mounted onto the saxophone. These servos enable the system to cover all the registers used in normal saxophone playing.

We developed a semi-automatic musical instrument-playing robot called Robo-Sax. In this system, the robot controls the key mechanisms, while the human performer produces sound by blowing into the instrument. By using a semi-automatic approach rather than a fully automated one, the system enables an engaging performance experience for the user.

Although an alternative approach exists where the human operates the keys and the robot handles the blowing we argue that this configuration is less desirable. Blowing is closely tied to tone production and musical expression, making it more effective when performed by a human.

From a functional standpoint, this division of roles is also appropriate: key actuation is a discrete (binary) operation well-suited to robotic control, while breathing is a continuous, nuanced action better handled by humans. This human-robot collaboration enhances expressive capabilities and preserves the performer's musical involvement.

Figure 1 shows the developed Robo-Sax, a robotic system based on an soprano saxophone. The robot consists of a custom iron sheet metal frame mounted onto the saxophone via its thumb hook and thumb rest, housing 19 servo motors and electronic components, including a microcontroller and servo driver. These servos control the opening and closing of 19 keys, enabling the performance of 32 semitones (two and a half octaves), which covers the standard saxophone range[1].

The system operates on a 5 V power supply and can be powered by a mobile battery, allowing for outdoor use. The microcontroller connects via USB Type-C and communicates using MIDI signals. Robo-Sax is recognized as a standard external MIDI device and can be integrated with commercial Digital Audio Workstation (DAW) software (Fig. 3).

We developed a method for opening and closing the keys using a small 5V DC servomotor and a wire. Through experimentation, we found that nylon-coated wire, commonly used in handicrafts, is suitable for this application. This wire is both strong and flexible, and can be securely attached using "crimp beads" and a specialized tool.

3 Use Studies

Examples of the use of the RoboSax system are as follows:
a) Robo-sax ensemble by members of the wind orchestra club

With the help of seven members from the saxophone section of the university's wind orchestra ensemble club, we conducted experiments using the Robo-Sax in ensemble performances over one year, from March 2024 to March 2025. Practice sessions were held monthly for two hours.

The ensemble consisted of an SATB (soprano, alto, tenor, and baritone) saxophone quartet. Depending on the selected piece, the formation was adjusted to an AATB configuration, with two alto saxophone robots that could switch between soprano and alto. In November 2024, a mini-concert was organized for the public to showcase the progress of the practice and motivate the club members.

This long-term Robo-Sax experiment allowed us to identify challenges and improve the system. Figure 2 shows the club members using Robo-Sax. Initially, they faced some difficulties, but they eventually were able to perform as an ensemble without significant issues.

Fig. 2. Robo-sax ensemble

b) Performed by saxophonist with melody-morphing:

---
[1] Excluding special techniques such as flageolet.

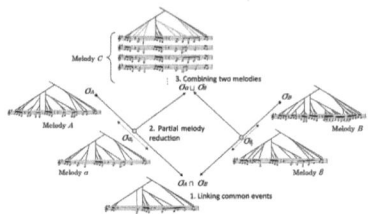

Fig. 3. Melody-morphing method

After refining the system through performances with a brass band, experiments were conducted with a professional saxophonist. We developed a system combining Robo-Sax and the melody-morphing method as an application of Robo-Sax.

The melody-morphing method [1] generates hierarchically consistent variations of a melody based on the music theory framework of GTTM [2,5]. The score generated by this method was performed on Robo-Sax. The melody can be dynamically altered in real time using a slot-machine-like interface, while the performer plays the Robo-Sax according to the generated score.

Figure 4(a) shows the user interface (UI) of the melody-morphing system, operated on a tablet. Figure 4(b) demonstrates the system's use, where a saxophonist plays a soprano Robo-Sax, and another individual adjusts the melody in real time through the tablet. As described, this system allows external control of the saxophonist's performance.

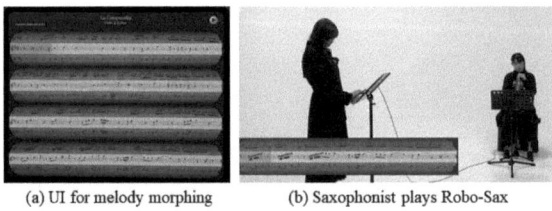

(a) UI for melody morphing   (b) Saxophonist plays Robo-Sax

Fig. 4. The melody-morphing system and a saxophonist playing a Robo-Sax. The player is able to play melodies that change in real time.

4 Conclusion

We developed Robo-Sax, a semi-automatic instrument-playing robot, where key fingerings are automated while the blowing motions are performed by the human user. We believe this system has reached a practical level of applicability through advancements in both hardware and software. Moving forward, we plan to promote the open-source release of the Robo-Sax system to facilitate its wider use.

References

1. Hamanaka, M., Hirata, K., Tojo, S.: Melody morphing method based on GTTM. In: ICMC, pp. 155–158 (2008)
2. Hamanaka, M., Hirata, K., Tojo, S.: Musical structural analysis database based on GTTM. In: ISMIR, pp. 325–330 (2014)
3. Heller, F., Ruiz, I.M.C., Borchers, J.: An augmented flute for beginners. In: NIME 2017, pp. 15–19 (2017)
4. Kurosawa, Y., Suzuki, K.: Robot-assisted playing with fingering support for a saxophone. In: International Computer Music Conference, ICMC 2010 (2010)
5. Lerdahl, F., Jackendoff, R.: A Generative Theory of Tonal Music. The MIT Press, Cambridge (1983)
6. Solis, J., Bergamasco, M., Chida, K., Isoda, S., Takanishi, A.: The anthropomorphic flutist robot WF-4 teaching flute playing to beginner students. In: ICRA, vol. 1, pp. 146–151 (2004)
7. Solis, J., Sugita, Y., Petersen, K., Takanishi, A.: Development of an anthropomorphic musical performance robot capable of playing the flute and saxophone: embedding pressure sensors into the artificial lips as well as the re-designing of the artificial lips and lung mechanisms. Robotics Auton. Syst. **86**, 174–183 (2016)

Multiple Robots Enable *Moderate Facilitation* Through Approaching Movements in Group Discussions

Rintaro Makino(✉)[ID], Yuki Okafuji[ID], Haruki Takahashi[ID], and Kohei Matsumura[ID]

Ritsumeikan University, Ibaraki, Osaka 567-8570, Japan
is0578ps@ed.ritsumei.ac.jp, {yokafuji,haruki,matsumur}@fc.ritsumei.ac.jp

Abstract. In group discussions, facilitation is often employed to encourage equal participation among members. However, excessively directive methods disrupt the natural flow of discussion, whereas excessively passive methods fail to ensure equal participation. In this paper, we introduce "moderate facilitation", an approach that aims to balance equal participation with the natural flow of discussion. To realize this, we use small tabletop robots that promote turn-taking by physically approaching participants. We evaluated this system in a group discussion task under three experimental conditions: multiple-robot, one-robot, and no-robot conditions. The results indicated that the robot-assisted (multiple-robot, one-robot) conditions, as shown by reduced variance in speaking time among participants, contributed to more equal participation without disrupting the natural flow of discussion.

Keywords: Human-Robot Interaction · Facilitation · Group Discussion

1 Introduction

Consensus-based decision-making in group discussions relies on active engagement and the integration of diverse perspectives. Facilitators, both human and automated, are often employed to ensure equal participation throughout the conversation. Although pre-allocation of speaking time can help maintain fairness, such excessively directive methods suppress spontaneity and discourage active participation. Previous studies have explored agent-based systems that detect unequal participation levels and use verbal prompts to encourage quieter participants [4]. However, these verbal interventions often disrupt the natural flow of conversation. Alternative approaches, such as visual displays indicating speaking time [2], can reduce dominance by active participants. However, these passive methods fail to engage quieter participants. Achieving a balance between equal participation and the natural flow of discussion remains a significant challenge.

To address this, we introduce the concept of moderate facilitation, a subtle and non-intrusive approach that lies between directive and passive methods, employing small tabletop robots as facilitators. In this approach, multiple robots subtly approach participants and signal opportunities to speak. This encourages voluntary participation and promotes more balanced discussions, while preserving the natural flow of discussion.

2 Methodology

2.1 System Design

We designed small tabletop robots to promote equal participation in group discussions. We chose to employ multiple robots based on prior research indicating that a larger number of robots attracts more attention [1]. This configuration also allows for more flexible modulation of attention toward the robot facilitator.

The robots' motion is designed to support turn-taking in order to implement moderate facilitation. This motion design draws inspiration from prior work on visualizing conversational flow using a rolling ball on an elevated table surface [3]. To implement this approach, each robot performs three primary motion patterns (Fig. 1, Robot Motion): *Approaching*—moving toward a participant to draw attention; *Nodding*—executing small nodding motions to gently encourage participants to speak; and *Departing*—moving away to suggest the end of a speaking turn. After departing, the robot approaches another participant to indicate their turn to speak. Multiple robots can coordinate to approach the same participant, thereby concentrating attention on that individual. Alternatively, they can operate independently to engage with different participants simultaneously, promoting a more balanced distribution of attention.

We used Sony toio[1], cube-shaped robot, as the basis for our robotic system. It can be controlled using Python via Bluetooth Low Energy (BLE) and can acquire its position on a dedicated mat. We designed each unit with a 3D-printed shell incorporating eye-like elements to suggest a gaze direction. This design enhances the robot's perceived agency and makes its actions more noticeable to users.

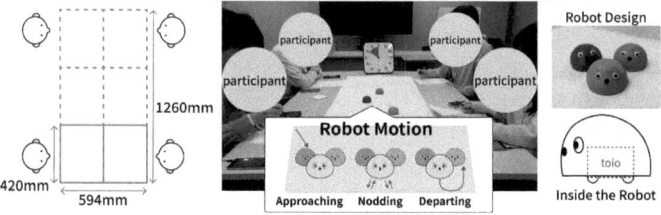

Fig. 1. Experimental setup and robot design for group discussions.

---

[1] toio: Sony, https://toio.io.

2.2 Experiment

To evaluate the effectiveness of our proposed system for moderate facilitation, we conducted a group discussion experiment facilitated by multiple tabletop robots. Based on prior research suggesting that a minimum of three robots is necessary for these robots to be perceived as a group [6], we adopted a three-robot configuration as the main experimental condition. To determine whether the observed effects were due to the mere presence of a robot or the number of robots, we also included one-robot and no-robot conditions.

Participants engaged in a 10-minute consensus-building task, where groups of four prioritized items necessary for survival in scenarios, such as being stranded in a desert or in space. Each participant first ranked the items individually, followed by a group discussion to reach consensus. This task was chosen due to its requirement for active participation and its use in prior studies [5]. Participants sat around a table while robots moved around within a predefined area. The robots' motion was pre-programmed to periodically approach different participants in order to promote balanced participation during the discussion, without real-time monitoring of participants' speaking time. Twelve undergraduate students (10 male, 2 female), aged 20âĂŞ24, participated in three groups of four.

The experiment included four stages: self-introductions, a personality assessment, the discussion task, and a post-experiment questionnaire. Discussions were recorded using individual pin microphones, and the audio data was annotated to measure speaking time, which served as the primary metric for assessing participation balance. We calculated the standard deviation of speaking times under each condition, assuming that more equal participation would result in lower variability. Additionally, follow-up interviews were conducted to gather participants' impressions of the system.

3 Findings

As shown in Fig. 2, the standard deviation of speaking times, presented in the table on the right, was lower in both the one-robot and three-robot conditions than in the no-robot condition, indicating more equal participation. However, increasing the number of robots from one to three did not result in any further significant improvement in the balance of speaking times. Video analysis showed that robots occasionally acted as non-verbal cues for turn-taking, prompting some participants adjusting their turn-taking behavior in response to robot motion. In response to the question "Was the environment supportive of speaking?", the mean ratings were 5.92 (no robot), 6.00 (one robot), and 6.25 (three robots), all above the midpoint of 4 on a 7-point Likert scale (1 = not at all supportive, 7 = very supportive). In response to the question "Did the robots interfere with the discussion?", the mean ratings were 3.33 (one robot) and 3.58 (three robots), both below the midpoint of 4. These results suggest that the robots did not disrupt the natural flow of discussion. Most participants did not report feeling pressured to speak or noticing explicit turn-taking cues.

However, among those who did, such experiences were more frequently reported in the three-robot condition.

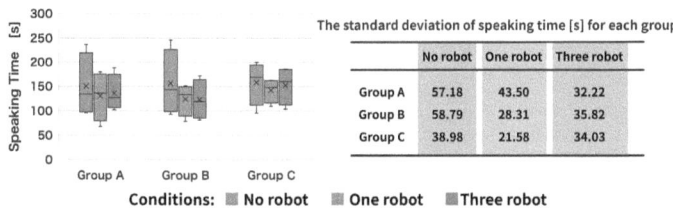

Fig. 2. Mean speaking time and standard deviation by group

4 Concluding Remarks

This study explored multiple small tabletop robots designed to support moderate facilitation in group discussions, with the goal of achieving a balance between equal participation and the natural flow of discussion. The results showed that the presence of robots helped reduce variability in speaking time, indicating an improvement in participation equity. Increasing the number of robots from one to three did not consistently lead to a further reduction in the standard deviation of speaking times. This suggests limited additional benefit in terms of participation balance. This finding implies that individual differences play a role in how participants interact with the system. Although the robots did not disrupt the discussion, they were not generally perceived as contributing to it. This suggests a potential deficiency in their perceived social presence.

Enhancing their social presence through improved design and more expressive behavior could help make the facilitation effect more noticeable and intuitively recognized by participants. Moreover, collecting richer participant feedback, such as reflections on discussion content, speaking intentions, or preferred speakers, could yield deeper insights into how facilitation influences group dynamics. Such insights could inform improvements to the system beyond time-based metrics, enabling more socially aware and seamless facilitation strategies.

References

1. Amada, J., Okafuji, Y., Matsumura, K., Baba, J., Nakanishi, J.: Investigating the crowd-drawing effect on passersby of pseudo-crowds using multiple robots. Adv. Robot. **37**(6), 423–432 (2023). https://doi.org/10.1080/01691864.2022.2143242
2. DiMicco, J.M., et al.: Influencing group participation with a shared display. In: Proceedings of ACM CSCW '04, pp. 614–623 (2004). https://doi.org/10.1145/1031607.1031713

3. Fu, C., et al.: Turntable: towards more equivalent turn-taking. In: Proceedings of TEI '17, pp. 609–615 (2017). https://doi.org/10.1145/3024969.3025079
4. Nishimura, R., et al.: Discussion support agent system to promote equalization of speech among participants. In: Proceedings of ICCE '23 (2023). https://doi.org/10.58459/icce.2023.978
5. Tennent, H., Shen, S., Jung, M.: Micbot: a peripheral robotic object to shape conversational dynamics and team performance. In: Proceedings of HRI '19, pp. 133–142 (2019). https://doi.org/10.1109/HRI.2019.8673013
6. Wullenkord, R., Eyssel, F.: The influence of robot number on robot group perception: a call for action. J. Hum.-Robot Interact. **9**(4), 27:1–27:14 (2020). https://doi.org/10.1145/3394899

VR Batting Practice System Integrated with Visual Training

Taito Matsumoto[✉], Masahiro Kawamori, and Masataka Imura

Kwansei Gakuin University, Sanda, Hyogo 669–1330, Japan
{gnf01042,m.imura}@kwansei.ac.jp

Abstract. This study proposes a visual training system for improving baseball hitting ability using an HMD. Conventional training methods such as tee batting can train batting skills, but they cannot train the visual functions necessary for batting. The visual functions that are closely related to hitting ability in baseball include kinetic visual acuity and eye-hand coordination, and training these functions will lead to improved hitting ability. We will construct a visual training system in a VR space that can train kinetic visual acuity and eye-hand coordination while batting using an HMD. By performing batting practice while training sports vision, both batting technique and visual function can be improved. To verify whether the system improves visual function and hitting ability, training was conducted. As a result, significant improvements were observed in the number of hits, kinetic visual acuity, and eye-hand coordination, indicating the usefulness of the proposed system.

Keywords: Baseball · Visual Training · VR · HMD

1 Introduction

Baseball is a sport in which the team that scores the most runs wins the game, so it is important to improve the hitting ability of hitters to increase their scoring ability. There are various methods for training to improve hitting ability. In addition, researches have been conducted to analyze hitting techniques from an academic perspective [1–3]. However, conventional methods can train batting skills, but they cannot train the visual function that is necessary for batting. Head mounted display (HMD) is used for training to improve baseball batting skills. Although researches have been conducted to improve baseball batting skills using HMDs, training for sports vision has not been implemented. In this study, we construct a visual training system to train visual functions, which is closely related to baseball, while performing batting practice using an HMD. By performing batting practice while training sports vision, both batting technique and sports vision can be improved.

2 Proposed Method

2.1 Overview

In this study, we propose a visual training system that can train visual functions closely related to baseball hitting ability while performing baseball actions [4]. The visual functions that are closely related to baseball hitting ability are kinetic visual acuity and eye-hand coordination [5]. In the proposed system, a virtual training room is represented using an HMD, and the movements of the bat are reflected in the VR space in real time by attaching a controller included to the HMD to the bat.

2.2 Kinetic Visual Acuity Training

It has been reported that training to gaze at a moving object is useful as training to improve kinetic visual acuity [6]. We propose a training method for kinetic visual acuity in which a baseball with numbers on it is thrown from a pitcher's mound, and participants answer the numbers on the ball after hitting it with a baseball bat. The training requires the participants to gaze at the numbers written on the ball, which helps to train kinetic visual acuity.

2.3 Eye-Hand Coordination Training

It has been reported that number touch using a game console is useful for training to improve eye-hand coordination [7]. Number touch is a visual training method in which participants touch the numbered panels in the order of $1, 2, 3, \ldots$. Referring to the number touch, we propose training to hit n baseballs with numbers from 1 to n in the order $1, 2, 3, \ldots$ as training for eye-hand coordination.

3 Result

3.1 Prototype System

Based on the proposed method, we constructed a visual training system to train visual functions while performing batting motions in a VR space. HMD Meta Quest Pro was used to present the images to the user. Unity2022.3.31f1 was used for development. The swinging motion of the bat in real space was reflected in the VR space by attaching the Meta Quest Pro controller to the bat.

3.2 Kinetic Visual Acuity Training Room

The scene from the player's point of view in the training room for the kinetic visual acuity is shown in Fig. 1. When the player continues to touch the floating ball on the home base, a count of three begins, and after the count is over, a ball with a number written on it is thrown. When the ball is thrown, instantaneous force is applied to the ball, so that the ball is directed toward the strike zone of the player. When the player swings the bat and the ball collides with the bat, instantaneous force is applied to the ball. After the swing, answer balls with five different numbers are displayed on the pitcher's mound side. When the player keeps touching the ball with the bat for one second, the number on the ball is selected as the answer. After the answer, only the answer ball with the correct answer is displayed, and the player is informed of the correct answer.

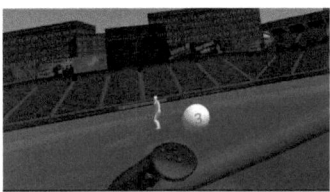

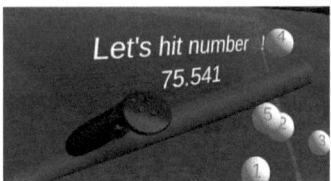

Fig. 1. Kinetic visual acuity training   **Fig. 2.** Eye-hand coordination training

3.3 Eye-Hand Coordination Training Room

The scene from the player's point of view in the training room for the eye-hand coordination is shown in Fig. 2. When the player continues to touch the floating ball on the home base, a three count begins, and after the count ends, a ball with a number from 1 to 5 written on it is placed in the strike zone. The player swings the bat, and when the bat and ball collide, an instantaneous force is applied to the ball to reproduce the hitting. For each ball hit from the 5th onward, one ball is placed in the strike zone, displaying with the 6th ball. Balls after 5th are displayed in order, starting with 6th, for each ball hit. For balls other than the number to be hit, the Collider function is disabled so that the ball will not fly away when the bat collides with the ball.

3.4 Experiment

Experiments were conducted to confirm that the proposed system is useful for improving visual function as well as batting ability. The collaborators for this experiment were five students in their 20 s and 30 s with normal vision in both eyes. Training was conducted three times a week for two weeks. The scene of experiment is shown in Fig. 3. Wilcoxon signed rank test was used to test whether there were significant differences in the number of hits, visual acuity, kinetic visual acuity measured in real space, kinetic visual acuity measured in VR space, and eye-hand coordination before and after training ($\alpha = 0.05$). The number of hits was obtained by batting for 25 pitches at a batting center. The test results showed significant differences between post-training and pre-training in hits, kinetic visual acuity measured in real space, kinetic visual acuity measured in VR space, and eye-hand coordination (all test statistics $w = 0, p = .0312$). The above results show that the proposed system is useful because the system significantly improved hitting ability, kinetic visual acuity, and eye-hand coordination.

Fig. 3. Scene of experiment

4 Conclusion

In this study, we proposed a system that uses an HMD to train the visual function, which is closely related to baseball, while performing baseball batting motions. We devised a visual training system that can improve kinetic visual acuity and eye-hand coordination, which are closely related to baseball, and constructed the system in a VR space. The results of the actual training showed significant improvements in the number of hits, kinetic visual acuity, and eye-hand coordination, indicating the usefulness of the proposed system.

References

1. Hubbard, A.W., Seng, C.N.: Visual movements of batters. Res. Q. Am. Assoc. Health, Phys. Educ. Recreation, 42–57 (1954)
2. Burroughs, W.A.: Visual simulation training of baseball batters. Int. J. Sport Psychol. **15**(2), 117–126 (1984)
3. Bahill, A.T., LaRitz, T.: Why can't batters keep their eyes on the ball?. Am. Sci., 249–253 (1984)
4. Matsumoto, T., Kawamori, M., Imura, M.: Visual training to improve baseball hitting ability using HMD. In: IPSJ-EC2024, pp. 129–132 (2024). (in Japanese)
5. Murata, A., Sugiashi, M.: Relationship between visual skill and batting ability in baseball. Hum. Factors **36**(4), 169–179 (2000). (in Japanese)
6. Uematsu, Y., Inamizu, J., Sekikawa, K., Kawae, T.: Effect of aging and visual training on the visual functions. J. Health Sci. Hiroshima Univ. **8**(1.2), 7–14 (2009). (in Japanese)
7. Ishigaki, H.: Cross-generational comparison of the effects of visual training using game machine. Aichi Institute Technol. Res. Rep. **45**, 153–158 (2010). (in Japanese)

Arcade Games Generating an Atmosphere to Promote Exercise

Daiki Mima[✉], Haruki Takahashi, and Kohei Matsumura

Ritsumeikan University, Osaka, Japan
is0637ik@ed.ritsumei.ac.jp, {haruki,matsumur}@fc.ritsumei.ac.jp

Abstract. Physical inactivity has emerged as a critical social concern in recent years. Despite the integration of exercise elements with gamification in various platforms following the proliferation of video games and handheld devices, this issue persists unresolved. This study addresses a significant gap in existing exergames: the insufficient incorporation of cooperative and competitive elements that foster camaraderie and healthy rivalry among players. We propose arcade-style gaming platforms as an effective solution, hypothesizing that their physical design and social setting naturally create an environment conducive to interpersonal connection and physical engagement. The proposed arcade game demonstrated that it elicited significantly stronger competitive motivation compared to equivalent handheld and console video games. Furthermore, the cooperative dimension became notably more pronounced in multi-player scenarios. These results show arcade games create environments that foster group awareness. Users appreciated unique arcade elements like cabinet design and the social aspect of watching others play, indicating these platforms could effectively encourage physical activity.

Keywords: Arcade · Atmosphere · Competition · Cooperation · Exercise

1 Introduction

In recent years, the increasing prevalence of physical inactivity has become one of the most serious social problems. According to a 2018 WHO study, 23% of adults and 81% of adolescents worldwide are inactive [2].

According to a survey by the Japan Sports Agency (JSA), the majority of reasons for not exercising are "too busy with work or household chores" and "too much hassle". This indicates that methods to develop a habit of exercising regularly are needed.

In this study, we use arcade games to promote exercise. We believe that arcade games, which can create a unique community that evokes a sense of cooperation and competition, can be used to develop a habit of exercising regularly [1]. A feature of arcade games is their ability to involve the people around the players. Unlike other games, arcade games can create an environment where anyone can see the players. This enhances the group element of cooperation and competition, and allows the player to feel as if they are exercising with other people. Spectators become motivated to participate after observing players' movements and gameplay. This mutual influence between players and spectators creates an atmosphere that fosters social connection within the exergame environment, potentially enhancing physical activity promotion. This study examines whether arcade games can create an exercise-promoting atmosphere by investigating how arcade-specific features motivate physical activity and enhance group dynamics such as cooperation and competition.

2 Implementation of Exergames

We designed a prominently colored red and black arcade cabinet and developed two exergames: Running Game and Dumbbell Up and Down Game (Fig. 1). We installed the arcade in a public place where games could be played freely.

The system reflects players' movement in the games via a wearable accelerometer connected via Bluetooth as input. While designed primarily for single-player interaction, functions that include cooperative and competitive elements that take advantage of arcade game features are added on the menu screen and game end screen (Figure 2). This provides a game experience that assumes relationships not only with friends but also with other players.

As a cooperative element, we implemented a monster-fighting function (Fig. 2(a)). Players cooperate to accumulate points earned by playing to reduce the monster's strength. As competitive elements, we implemented a ranking function (Fig. 2(b)) and a play-recording function (Fig. 2(c)). The ranking function allows the players to see the rank of points earned by each player. Ranking is an important element to elicit a sense of rivalry, as it allows players to visualize the difference between their abilities and others'. The play-recording function keeps the name of the most recently played game and its record on the standby screen.

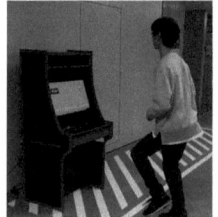
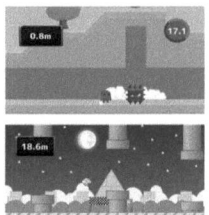

Fig. 1. Arcade cabinet and playing

3 Methods

We conducted a user test to examine whether arcade games can motivate people to exercise and enhance group elements such as cooperation and competition.

Participants first played the arcade games, and then answered questionnaires and semi-structured interviews. We did not impose any restrictions on the time spent, the number of players per session, or how many times each participant played the game. We evaluated three aspects: (1) identifying appealing features of arcade games, (2) comparing cooperative elements and (3) competitive elements in arcade games compared to those in handheld or video games.

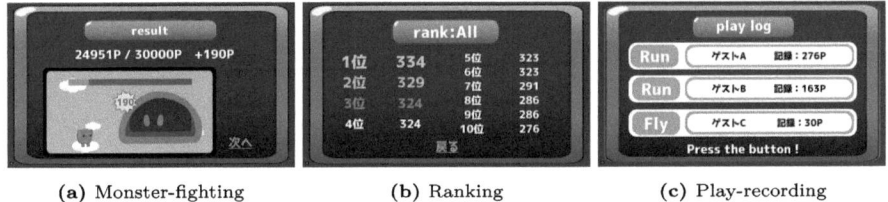

(a) Monster-fighting **(b)** Ranking **(c)** Play-recording

Fig. 2. Cooperative and Competitive elements

Question (1) asked participants who reported feeling no obligation while playing to identify which specific game aspects attracted them and reduced feelings of obligation. Questions (2) and (3) evaluated the effectiveness of cooperative and competitive elements, respectively. During the experiment, participants played the arcade game and were then asked to imagine playing the identical game on a handheld device or video game console for comparison purposes. Responses were collected using a 7-point Likert scale, where 1 indicated "less perceived" and 7 indicated "more perceived" compared to handheld or console gaming experiences.

4 Results

Eighteen participants (ages 19–23, mean 20.9, standard deviation 1.43) participated in the experiment. The results of the questionnaire are shown in Fig. 3. Five participants cited the others' play records and the appearance of the arcade cabinet, while four participants mentioned the influence of others' play as reasons they were attracted to the game. These responses suggest that the unique features of arcade games contributed to motivating exercise.

The comparison of cooperative elements between arcade games and handheld or video games showed a mean score of 4.11 with a standard deviation of 1.37. Seven participants (38.9% of the total) reported that they felt stronger cooperative elements (rating > 4), and another seven participants (38.9% of the total) did not (rating < 4). The comparison of competitive elements between arcade games and handheld/video games showed a mean score of 5.06 with a standard deviation of 1.26. Thirteen participants (72.2% of the total) reported that they felt stronger competitive elements (rating > 4), and two participants (11.1% of the total) did not (rating < 4). Interviews revealed that participants who visited the arcade games in groups of two or more gave significantly higher ratings of cooperative elements than those who visited alone. This suggests that cooperative elements are more likely to be perceived when arcade games are played with multiple people rather than individually. In contrast, the number of participants who reported feeling competitive elements was 11 greater than those who did not. This suggests that arcade games enhance competitive elements. These findings suggest that the use of competitive elements can be used to promote exercise unique to arcade games.

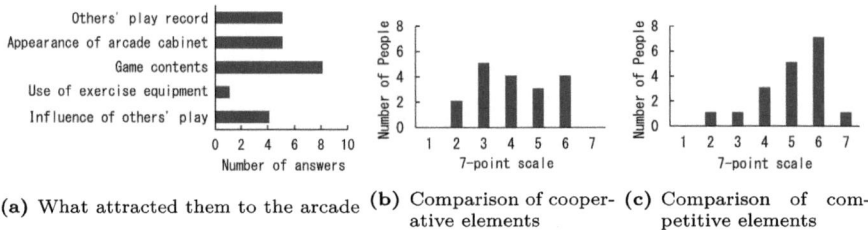

(a) What attracted them to the arcade (b) Comparison of cooperative elements (c) Comparison of competitive elements

Fig. 3. Results

5 Concluding Remarks

In this study, we proposed the use of arcade games to generate an atmosphere that promotes exercise. To this end, we tested whether arcade games enhance group elements such as cooperation and competition, and whether they are effective in their ability to involve surroundings other than the player. According to the experimental results, arcade games are more competitive than handheld and video games, and the cooperative element is more strongly felt when the game is used by multiple players. In addition, many players were attracted to the others' play and the appearance of the arcade cabinet, revealing the effectiveness of the property of involving the surroundings other than the players. This suggests that arcade games allow mutual influence between the player and the observer and generate an atmosphere that promotes exercise by fostering a sense of connection with others.

This research explored the use of arcade games as a means to promote exercise; however, we believe that the approach may also be applicable to other gamified systems and broader social issues. As this study focused on the inherent characteristics of arcade games, the game content was intentionally kept simple, and no comparisons were made based on game mechanics or genre. Identifying game designs or genres that are particularly well-suited to arcade environments may further enhance user engagement and motivation.

References

1. Skolnik, M.R., Conway, S.: Tusslers, beatdowns, and brothers: a sociohistorical overview of video game arcades and the street fighter community. Games Cult. **14**(7–8), 742–762 (2019). https://doi.org/10.1177/1555412017727687
2. World Health Organization: Global action plan on physical activity 2018–2030: more active people for a healthier world (2018). https://iris.who.int/bitstream/handle/10665/272722/9789241514187-eng.pdf

Guitar Clicker: A Gamified Approach to Motivating Guitar Practice for Beginners

Itsuki Okamo[✉], Kohei Matsumura, and Haruki Takahashi

Ritsumeikan University, Osaka, Japan
is0608rp@ed.ritsumei.ac.jp, {matsumur,haruki}@fc.ritsumei.ac.jp

Abstract. Learning to play the guitar presents significant challenges for beginners, primarily due to complex chord fingerings and the repetitive nature of practice required for skill development. To address these motivational barriers, we developed Guitar Clicker, a gamified system that enhances motivation through structured goal setting and reward-based mechanics. Our approach incorporates core elements from clicker games—a genre where players earn points through simple interactions that can be invested to improve point acquisition efficiency. In Guitar Clicker, players earn performance points by strumming a guitar, which can then be used to "level up" their musical instrument, thereby increasing the efficiency of point acquisition. This system creates a positive feedback loop to encourage consistent guitar practice while providing a sense of progress through point accumulation and achievement milestones. To evaluate the system's effectiveness, we conducted a nine-day user study with six beginner guitarists. Results indicate that the gamification elements, particularly the points system, increased enjoyment and sustained motivation during practice sessions. These findings suggest that integrating game-based incentive structures into musical instrument practice may offer a promising approach to addressing common motivational challenges faced by novice learners.

Keywords: Guitar · Practice · Motivation · Game

1 Introduction

A guitar is one of the most affordable and accessible musical instruments, attracting many individuals to pursue it as a recreational activity. However, learning to play the guitar presents significant challenges for beginners due to the unfamiliar finger positioning required for proper technique. The practice necessary for skill development is inherently repetitive and progress typically occurs gradually over extended periods. This combination of technical difficulty and slow improvement often leads beginners to experience diminished motivation and increased frustration during the crucial early learning phase. As a result, many novice guitarists abandon their musical pursuits before achieving meaningful progress.

There is a clear need for approaches to maintain motivation levels throughout these challenging initial stages of guitar learning to prevent beginners from becoming discouraged and discontinuing their practice.

Prior research has demonstrated that gamification elements such as points, badges, and achievement systems can significantly enhance motivation in various learning contexts [1,2]. This approach has been applied to musical instruction with varied success. Several commercial guitar-learning applications exist, such as Yousician[1], which implements a scrolling gameplay mechanic similar to rhythm games. However, these applications typically require players to execute immediate chord changes and precise fingerings, presenting substantial obstacles for absolute beginners who have not yet developed basic guitar manipulation skills. Our research addresses this gap by introducing Guitar Clicker, a system specifically designed for novice guitarists who cannot yet form chords. This approach focuses on building fundamental engagement with the instrument before moving on to more advanced techniques.

2 Guitar Clicker

We propose a clicker-type guitar practice system that adapts core mechanics from the popular clicker game genre, where players earn points through simple actions (e.g., clicking a button) and invest them in upgrades to improve efficiency. We selected this format for its straightforward controls and engaging qualities that encourage continued play. Our design draws inspiration from Cookie Clicker[2]. In this game, players click on a cookie image to earn cookies, then spend these cookies on items that help them make more cookies automatically.

Figure 1 shows the Guitar Clicker game interface. The display area (a) tracks the last four chords successfully performed by the user, updating in real time to provide immediate feedback on chord execution. The menus allow players to upgrade their guitar using accumulated points (b), check their practice engagement, including performance records, accumulated points, and achievement badges (c), and learn how to form chords (d). Additionally, the value (e) indicates the point awarded for each chord played, reinforcing the reward structure.

Guitar Clicker implements a progression system similar to Cookie Clicker, where players earn performance points by strumming the guitar rather than clicking a cookie. These points can be spent to upgrade the guitar's level, enhancing point acquisition efficiency. Additionally, our system introduces increasingly difficult chords as players demonstrate proficiency with simpler chord formations. Each chord provides a different point value, with more complex chords yielding higher rewards, creating an incentive that encourages skill development.

Taking inspiration from Cookie Clicker's "Golden Cookie" mechanic—which appears at random intervals to provide temporary production boosts—our system features virtual band members who appear periodically. When players strum

---

[1] https://yousician.com.
[2] https://orteil.dashnet.org/cookieclicker.

during these appearances, they can receive bonus points proportional to the number of band members present, adding an element of timing and opportunity to the gameplay.

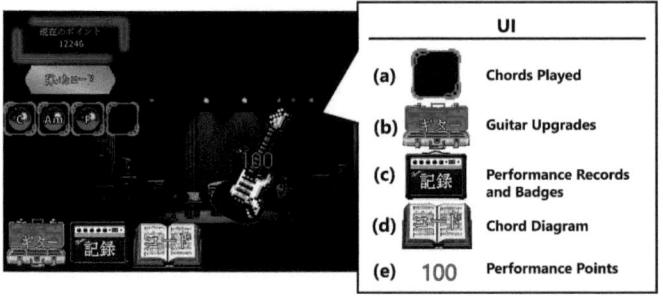

Fig. 1. Game screen and user interface

3 Findings

We conducted an experiment with three primary objectives: (i) to assess whether our system effectively motivates users to engage in guitar practice, (ii) to examine if motivation to continue practice is maintained or enhanced over time, and (iii) to gather guidelines for system improvement. Purpose (i) was evaluated based on enjoyment and willingness to continue guitar practice while using the system. Purpose (ii) was assessed through measures of continued willingness and average playing time per session. Purpose (iii) was evaluated by examining ease of system operation, with improvement guidelines derived from participant feedback regarding desired enhancements and additional features.

Six beginners who were unable to play chords participated in the nine-day experiment. During this period, participants could use the system as many times as they wished. After the experimental period, we administered a questionnaire.

The total playtime across all participants was 2 h, 25 min, and 26 s, with an average playtime of 24 min and 14 s per participant. Table 1 presents the total and average playtime per session for each participant. The Em chord, being the least difficult to play, was performed most frequently with 2,391 times ($M = 398.5, SD = 271.8$). Other chords were also played a substantial number of times: E chord with 569 times ($M = 94.8, SD = 44.8$), Am chord with 444 times ($M = 74.0, SD = 53.5$), G chord with 508 times ($M = 84.7, SD = 65.8$), and C chord with 419 times ($M = 69.8, SD = 49.6$). These figures demonstrate that participants successfully engaged in progressive practice across multiple chord types. However, the F chord was not played at all, highlighting the particular difficulty this chord presents for beginners.

Participants rated their enjoyment of guitar practice an average of 6.2/7.0 and their willingness to continue playing an average of 5.7/7.0. The system's ease of use was rated an average of 4.3/7.0. Participant feedback included comments such as "It was good to be able to play the guitar as if it were a game" and "The point system motivated me to keep playing until I reached a certain number of points." These responses suggest that the game elements, particularly the point system, effectively motivated participants to practice guitar playing.

Table 1. Gameplay time and number of sessions

	Participants					
	p1	p2	p3	p4	p5	p6
total session time (min:s)	24:05	08:15	12:21	25:57	29:22	45:26
Average session time per day (min:s)	03:26	04:08	06:11	06:29	04:12	11:22
Number of sessions	7	2	2	4	7	4

4 Concluding Remarks

In this study, we developed Guitar Clicker, a gamified system designed for beginner guitarists who cannot yet form chords, and conducted an experiment. The results showed that our system received high ratings for enjoyment of chord practice and motivation to play, indicating that the game elements effectively enhanced user engagement (addressing purpose (i)). The point-based progression system and level-up mechanics successfully promoted initial motivation through structured goal setting. However, correlation analysis between willingness to continue practicing and average playing time revealed a negative correlation (-0.85), suggesting that the system was not able to sustain or improve long-term practice motivation over the nine-day period (addressing purpose (ii)). Participant feedback regarding system improvements primarily concerned interface operability and feedback presentation methods (addressing purpose (iii)).

Participants expressed interest in additional features supporting song performance practice, particularly chord transitions. This feedback suggests a demand for learning support that extends beyond basic chord acquisition to more advanced playing techniques. For future development, we plan to implement features that further encourage sustained guitar practice by increasing meaningful engagement with the instrument. One potential enhancement would be awarding additional performance points based on the duration the player holds the guitar, thereby incentivizing longer practice sessions while maintaining the motivational framework that proved successful in our initial implementation.

References

1. Chapman, J.R., Rich, P.J.: Does educational gamification improve students' motivation? If so, which game elements work best? J. Educ. Bus. **93**(7), 315–322 (2018). https://doi.org/10.1080/08832323.2018.1490687
2. Topîrceanu, A.: Gamified learning: a role-playing approach to increase student in-class motivation. Procedia Comput. Sci. **112**, 41–50 (2017). https://doi.org/10.1016/j.procs.2017.08.017

Emo-Pathy: An Emotion-Sharing System for Promoting Psychological Well-Being Through Supportive Interactions

Yuunosuke Suenaga[1](✉), Gaku Kutsuzawa[2], Haruki Takahashi[1], and Kohei Matsumura[1]

[1] Ritsumeikan University, Osaka, Japan
`is0619rk@ed.ritsumei.ac.jp`, `{haruki,matsumur}@fc.ritsumei.ac.jp`
[2] National Institute of Advanced Industrial Science and Technology, Chiba, Japan
`gaku.kutsuzawa@aist.go.jp`

Abstract. This study introduces Emo-pathy, a smartwatch-based online emotion-sharing system that enables users to record and share their emotional states. Emo-pathy features unique empathetic and encouraging interactions inspired by face-to-face communication research. The system allows emotional states to be shared and responded to through "me too!" and "hug!" interactions. To evaluate the system's impact on psychological well-being, 18 participants used Emo-pathy over a two-week period. Results suggest that the system fostered interpersonal connections and elicited short-term positive emotional effects such as joy and gratitude.

Keywords: Emotion Sharing · Social Support · Well-being

1 Introduction

In daily life, people naturally engage in emotional sharing, such as telling others about positive experiences or offering support to those experiencing negative emotions. Such emotional sharing has been shown to provide psychological benefits. Sharing positive emotions can enhance positive emotions of both the sender and the recipient [3], while sharing negative emotions can help alleviate emotional distress [1]. Based on these findings, online systems for emotion sharing have been actively explored. For instance, Church et al. developed a mobile-based emotion sharing system [2], and Yun et al. proposed a system that displays and shares emotions on a map [4]. These systems incorporated features to enable interactions between users. However, the psychological effects of such interactions have not been sufficiently examined.

In face-to-face communication, the effects of social interactions—such as empathy, greetings, and casual conversations—have been extensively studied. Research shows that these interpersonal exchanges can reduce feelings of loneliness [6] and significantly promote subjective well-being [7]. Importantly, studies analyzing social media interactions suggest that similar psychological benefits may extend to online contexts as well [8].

This study aim to investigate how using emotion sharing system affects users' psychological well-being, particularly focusing on interpersonal connections and emotional responses.

2 Emo-Pathy: Emotion Sharing System

We developed Emo-pathy, an emotion sharing system that enables users to easily express feelings online with supportive empathetic interaction features. The system delivers periodic notifications based on the Experience Sampling Method (ESM), prompting users to record their emotional states throughout the day. To streamline emotion and activity sharing, we utilize emojis as the primary input medium, offering an intuitive way to communicate complex feelings. As shown in Fig 1, when users receive a notification (a), they select emojis representing their current emotional state (b) and activity (c). The system then securely transmits this emotional record to a cloud server, making it available to share with.

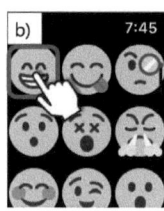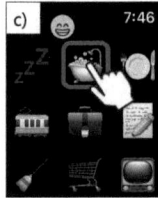

Fig. 1. List of Emotion Sharing Screens: Notification to start emotion recording (a), selection of an emoji representing the feelings (b), selection of an icon representing the activity (c), confirmation screen for the emotion record (d)

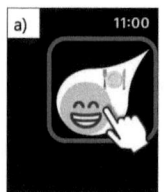

Fig. 2. List of Interaction Screens: Screen displaying shared records from others (a), interaction screen (b), animation screens for "Me too!" and "Hug!" (c) (d), notification received when another user sends a "Me too!" (e)

Emojis for feelings comprise 12 characters based on the classification by Kutsuzawa et al. [5], while activity icons include 17 characters covering common daily activities. As illustrated in Fig 2, shared emotion records appear as animated shooting stars in the interface (a). Users can respond with two interaction options: a "Me too!" button to express empathy or a "Hug!" button to convey encouragement (b). To enhance self-disclosure, all emotion sharing and interactions occur anonymously within the system. Throughout this study, these empathetic and encouraging response mechanisms are collectively termed "supportive interactions."

3 Findings

We conducted a two-week experiment to investigate Emo-pathy's effects on psychological well-being. Twenty university students (11 male, 9 female; mean age = 20.7, $SD = 0.94$) participated, organized into five groups of four members each. Emotion records were shared exclusively within assigned groups, with the system displaying only the most recent records from a participant's three group members. Participants recorded their emotional states and activities in response to system notifications, which were delivered ten times daily at randomized intervals between 10 a.m. and 10 p.m. (totaling 140 notifications over the study period). Participants could also engage with the system voluntarily outside scheduled notification times. To assess psychological impact, we administered pre- and post-experiment questionnaires featuring four established psychological scales. Following the experimental period, we evaluated system usability through a custom questionnaire designed to capture user experience with the interface and interaction features.

Data from 18 participants (9 male, 9 female; mean age = 20.7, $SD = 0.94$) were analyzed after excluding two participants due to a hardware malfunction and insufficient response rate (32.1%). Throughout the two-week study period, the system delivered 2,520 notifications, generating 2,024 emotion records (mean = 112.4, $SD = 20.6$) for an overall response rate of 80.3% (Week 1: 85.7%, Week 2: 74.9%). Including 88 voluntary submissions outside scheduled notifications, a total of 2,112 records were examined. This notification response rate exceeded the 69.6% average reported across 42 previous ESM studies by 10.7% points [9].

The system facilitated 5,687 opportunities for supportive interactions, resulting in 816 "Me too!" responses and 1,725 "Hug!" responses. When asked about receiving "Me too!" interactions, participants reported experiences such as "It made me feel that someone else is doing the same thing as me right now" (four participants) and "It gave me a sense of connection" (three participants), suggesting that these interactions fostered interpersonal connection. Similarly, "Hug!" interactions elicited responses including "I felt happy" (seven participants) and "I felt grateful" (two participants), indicating that these supportive exchanges generated positive short-term emotional effects such as joy and gratitude.

Paired t-tests were conducted on all four psychological measures using a 5% significance level to assess pre-post differences. The results showed no statistically significant changes in any of the scales ($ts < 1.28$, n.s.).

4 Concluding Remarks

We developed Emo-pathy, a smartwatch-based system that enables simple emotion recording and supportive interactions. We also evaluated Emo-pathy's impact on psychological well-being over a two-week period. Throughout the experiment, the system successfully collected emotion records at a rate exceeding previous ESM studies, suggesting that the simplified emoji-based input method on smartwatches reduced participation burden and enhanced user engagement.

While statistical analysis of evaluation scales revealed no significant improvements in long-term psychological well-being metrics, qualitative assessment of supportive interactions demonstrated that Emo-pathy effectively fostered interpersonal connections and generated positive short-term emotional responses among users. During the demo session, we aim to explore interaction design strategies that could produce more sustained psychological benefits while preserving Emo-pathy's core strength—its streamlined, accessible interface and interaction model.

References

1. Brans, K., Van Mechelen, I., Rimé, B., Verduyn, P.: To share, or not to share? Examining the emotional consequences of social sharing in the case of anger and sadness. Emotion **14**(6), 1062 (2014). https://doi.org/10.1037/a0037604
2. Church, K., Hoggan, E., Oliver, N.: A study of mobile mood awareness and communication through mobimood. In: Proceedings of the 6th Nordic Conference on Human-Computer Interaction: Extending Boundaries, pp. 128–137 (2010). https://doi.org/10.1145/1868914.1868933
3. Gable, S.L., Reis, H.T., Impett, E.A., Asher, E.R.: What do you do when things go right? The intrapersonal and interpersonal benefits of sharing positive events. In: Relationships, Well-being and Behaviour, pp. 144–182. Routledge (2018). https://doi.org/10.1037/0022-3514.87.2.228
4. Huang, Y., Tang, Y., Wang, Y.: Emotion Map: a location-based mobile social system for improving emotion awareness and regulation. In: Proceedings of the 18th ACM Conference on Computer Supported Cooperative Work & Social Computing, pp. 130–142 (2015). https://doi.org/10.1145/2675133.2675173
5. Kutsuzawa, G., Umemura, H., Eto, K., Kobayashi, Y.: Classification of 74 facial emoji's emotional states on the valence-arousal axes. Sci. Rep. **12**(1), 398 (2022). https://doi.org/10.1038/s41598-021-04357-7
6. Rimé, B.: The social sharing of emotion as an interface between individual and collective processes in the construction of emotional climates. J. Soc. Issues **63**(2), 307–322 (2007). https://doi.org/10.1111/j.1540-4560.2007.00510.x
7. Sandstrom, G.M., Dunn, E.W.: Social interactions and well-being: the surprising power of weak ties. Pers. Soc. Psychol. Bull. **40**(7), 910–922 (2014). https://doi.org/10.1177/0146167214529799
8. Stieglitz, S., Dang-Xuan, L.: Emotions and information diffusion in social media–sentiment of microblogs and sharing behavior. J. Manag. Inf. Syst. **29**(4), 217–248 (2013). https://doi.org/10.2753/MIS0742-1222290408
9. Van Berkel, N., Ferreira, D., Kostakos, V.: The experience sampling method on mobile devices. ACM Comput. Surv. (CSUR) **50**(6), 1–40 (2017). https://doi.org/10.1145/3123988

Rapid Input Device with Independent Sensing of Input Intention and Input Target

Katsuhisa Tanaka[✉][iD], Masahiro Kawamori[iD], and Masataka Imura[iD]

Kwansei Gakuin University, Sanda, Hyogo 669–1330, Japan
{ibe07033,m.imura}@kwansei.ac.jp, lightgreen@gmail.com

Abstract. This study proposes an input device that speeds up input operations in e-sports by eliminating the key pressing process from the keyboard and a method for presenting the key input sensation using relative motion. The device determines the input intention based on the myoelectric potentials generated just before finger movement, and determines the key target based on the change in finger pressure during key presses. Therefore, the proposed device realizes input that does not require key presses. In order to present a key input feeling to the user, the key causes relative motion by pushing the finger during input. An input speed comparison experiment was conducted using a device that can acquire the input time of the proposed device and the input time by key press input through a single key press input. The rapid input system was shown to be 0.030 s faster than the existing key input system. We also created a device that uses a solenoid to provide force feedback to the pad of finger during input, and conducted an experiment to compare the input values of a pressure sensor type device with and without feedback. We showed that the force presentation system considering to the faster input speed improves the usability of the system.

Keywords: E-Sports · Interface · EMG

1 Introduction

The e-sports industry is rapidly growing due to upgrades in PC and home game consoles and improvements in network performance. The upper limit of the input speed at which the user's device operation capability can be reflected in the content depends on the interface, so rapid input devices are required. Existing keyboard construction allows for shallower keystrokes, but does not remove the process of pressing down on the keys with the fingers.

This study proposes a rapid input device that uses myoelectric potentials and pressure changes to enable rapid input without requiring key presses, and incorporates force feedback to improve usability.

2 Proposed Method

2.1 Overview

Input consists of the user's intention to input by pressing down a key and the input target, which is the user's intention to select the type of input. The key input system simultaneously acquires both the input intention and the input target by pressing a key. By acquiring the input intention and the input target individually, the system speeds up the input process [1].

A force feedback system that presents the sensation of contact between a finger and a key at the input point and generates a sense of completion of keystrokes is realized. The force feedback system provides force feedback perpendicular to the pad of finger by using a force feedback device for each finger motion detected by the rapid input system.

2.2 Rapid Input System

The input intention is obtained from the rise of myoelectric potentials that occur earlier than the start of finger flexion using an myoelectric sensor [2], and the input target is obtained from the change of finger loads on the key that occurs when the finger makes contact with the key using a pressure sensor, thus achieving a faster input speed than the existing keyboard. The temporal order of events that occur in the process of inputting on the existing keyboard and the proposed device is shown in Fig. 1. In existing keyboard input systems, there is a process in which the finger contacts the key, the finger load applied to the key is increasing, and the key is pressed. On the other hand, the proposed device completes input when the finger load applied to the key changes, thus reducing the key pressing process and speeding up the input process.

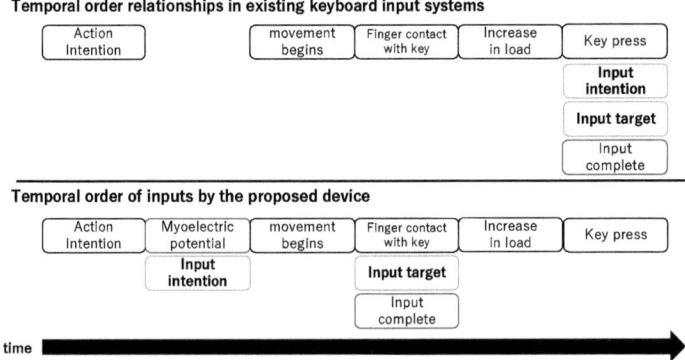

Fig. 1. Temporal order of events

By using the myoelectric potentials generated during finger movement as "the intention to input keys (input intention)," input can be realized without pressing down on the keys. By determining the key that each finger is pressing by changing the load acquired from the pressure sensor installed on the proposed interface, it is possible to transmit the user's "intention to select the type of input (input target)" to the computer without the user having to release the key.

2.3 Force Feedback System

A force feedback system that presents the sensation of contact between a finger and a key at the input point and generates a sense of completion of keystrokes is realized. The system uses a solenoid to provide force feedback perpendicular to the pad of finger for each finger movement detected by the myoelectric potentials and pressure sensing system.

3 Result

3.1 Summary

We create a device that allows comparison of input speeds between existing key input devices and the proposed device. Also, we create a device that provides feedback to the pad of finger during input and investigate the effect on usability with and without feedback during input.

3.2 Rapid Input Device

The input speed comparison device can perform two inputs at the same time with a single key press: input by the proposed device and keystroke input(see Fig. 2). An example of the device's input time when a key is pressed in on this device is shown in Fig. 3. The system output 1 when it is determined that the input intention and the input target have been obtained by each input method, and output 0 when they have not. t_1 is the input time of the proposed device and t_2 is the input time of the mechanical key. The difference between t_1 and t_2 indicates that the proposed device can perform input faster than the mechanical key. Input time comparison experiments were conducted on 8 subjects in their 20 s, and the results showed an average speedup of 0.030 s in input.

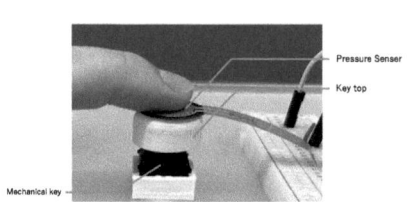

Fig. 2. Input speed comparison system

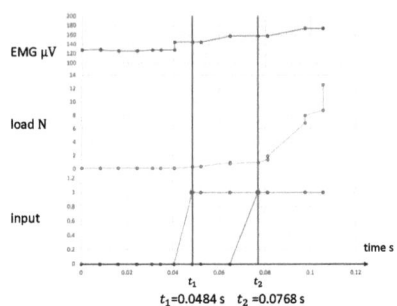

Fig. 3. Input time comparison experiment

3.3 Force Feedback System

In the proposed device, a solenoid installed in the lower part of the key drives upward to provide force feedback when a pressure sensor installed in the upper part of the key acquires the finger load changes. We created a device that determines input based on pressure changes applied to the top of a key using a pressure sensor, and conducted experiments to compare the number of inputs with and without force feedback (see Fig. 4). The experiment showed force feedback on input was found to reduce over-input.

The operation of a device that combines a rapid input system and a force feedback system was confirmed using the "Sliding Penguin(OVGL)" [3](see Fig. 5).

Fig. 4. Force feedback system

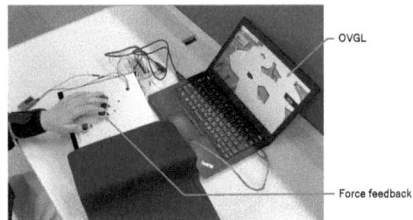

Fig. 5. Playing the OVGL

4 Conclusion

In this study, we proposed a rapid input device that eliminates the process of pressing down a key by judging the input intention from the rise of muscle potentials and the input target from the change of finger pressure, with the aim of achieving faster input than existing keyboard input systems. In addition, we proposed a force presentation system that uses relative motion to replace the process of pressing down the key.

References

1. Tanaka, K., Kawamori, M., Imura, M.: A rapid input device using myoelectric sensors that considers temporal order. In: Entertainment Computing Symposium 2024, vol. 2024, pp. 545–548 (2024). (in Japanese)
2. Onishi, H., et al.: Neuromagnetic activation following active and passive finger movements. Brain Behav. **3**(2), 178–92 (2013). https://doi.org/10.1002/brb3.126
3. Iida, K., Hayashi, D., Konno H., Hirano, R., Yanase, Y., Watanabe, K.: Open Video Game Library: development of video games that are easy to use for research and experiments, and case studies, Entertainment Computing Symposium 2024, vol. 2024, pp. 1–10 (2024). (in Japanese)

Student Competition

Heaviest Listener: Immersive Radio Experience Simulation by Sending Japanese E-Mail

Harunobu Kaneko, Kota Aoki, and Yoshio Iwai

Tottori University, Tottori 680-8552, Japan
m24j4015y@edu.tottori-u.ac.jp, {aoki.k,iwai}@tottori-u.ac.jp

Abstract. In recent years, radio broadcasting has gradually lost its position as a mainstream medium due to the spread of streaming and on-demand services. However, in Japan, the emergence of platforms such as radiko has led to a reevaluation of talk shows and participatory broadcasting, resulting in an increasing trend among Japanese radio listeners. Nevertheless, for casual listeners who enjoy radio for leisure, sending emails to programs remains a psychological barrier. To address this, we have created a simulation game called "Heavy Listener", which allows users to simulate the experience of submitting emails to a Japanese radio program. Developed using Unity, the game enables listeners to send emails, with the host responding based on whether the email is selected. Despite its simple mechanics, the game is designed to capture the unique atmosphere of radio, aiming to recreate the culturally embedded participatory experience playfully.

Keywords: radio show simulation · email acceptance experience · personality reactions · dynamic content generation · immersive experience enhancement

1 Introduction

The environment surrounding audio media has undergone significant changes in recent years. In particular, the widespread adoption of on-demand services such as music streaming and podcasts has led to traditional radio losing its position as the mainstream medium, with a global decline in usage time reported. [1] Among younger generations, audio content consumption has shifted from "receiving broadcasts" to "selecting and listening to content", with traditional radio broadcasts now serving as a complementary or optional medium.

On the other hand, in Japan, radiko [2], a service that enables users to listen to radio programs online, has brought renewed attention to the radio. Although radio is a traditional medium, it has been reevaluated in various situations, such as commuting, commuting to school, and working, as it has become easy to listen to via smartphones and PCs. According to a press release by radiko, Inc. in [3], the number of members of "radiko Premium", which allows you to listen to commercial radio programs from all over Japan for 385 yen per month, reached 1 million as of August 2022 (Fig. 1). Furthermore, many general members can use the service for free in certain areas. These circumstances indicate that there is not so much of an increase in radio users as there is a growing interest in Internet-based, participatory audio formats such as radiko.

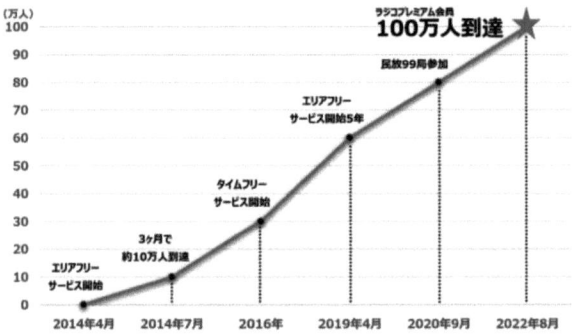

Fig. 1. Number of members of "radiko Premium"[2]

According to the same document, talk shows are the most popular genre of radio programs listened to. In particular, live talk shows such as "All Night Nippon" [4] invite listeners to send in e-mails during the show, which are then read out by the show's hosts, creating a unique form of communication that unites listeners and the show. While the experience of having their e-mail read out on the show is a special one that makes them feel like they are part of the show, the chances of having their e-mail read out are not high, so it can be quite a hurdle for first-time e-mail senders.

In this work, we have created a game based on the theme of sending e-mails to a radio program and have provided an environment that allows them to simulate the experience of being a listener. In this game, they can experience creating and sending e-mails in line with the radio show's theme and the impact of their e-mails on the show, just like in an actual radio show. This will enable even beginners to take their first steps as 'e-mail craftspeople' and gain a deeper understanding of the appeal of radio and how to interact with it as a listener. Through this research, we aim to enhance the listener experience and contribute to the further development of radio culture.

2 Related Work

In recent years, interactive games that simulate media environments have diversified, with particular attention being paid to works in which players take on the roles of content creators or broadcasters. For example, 'Not For Broadcast' [5] and 'Killer Frequency' [6] allow players to actively construct narratives through advanced operations such as editing and censoring broadcast content and selecting program flow. These designs create immersion through content control and are characterized by their perspective rooted in the broadcaster's viewpoint.

In contrast, the game proposed in this study, "Heaviest Listener", offers an experience from the perspective of the content consumer (listener) rather than the creator. Players submit messages to a virtual radio program and experience indirect interaction with the program through the selection of their submissions. This design mimics the anticipation and uncertainty associated with participating in a real-world program through asynchronous interaction [7], where players wait for the outcome of their submissions.

Research on user-generated content (UGC) and viewer-participatory media (e.g., Twitch, YouTube Live) has progressed. However, many of these studies focus on the interactions of broadcasters or real-time reactions from viewers [8]. In contrast, this study focuses on the limited involvement of viewers who speak but cannot control their reactions, and there are very few examples of games that handle the perspective of such "invisible participants" [9].

3 Heaviest Listener

3.1 Overview

"Heaviest Listener" (Fig. 2) is a game set in the fictional late-night radio program "All Night Jappon". In this game, the player participates in the program as a listener, and the goal is to get as many messages as possible adopted within the five-minute broadcast time. The title "Heaviest Listener" comes from the term "heavy listener", which refers to a person who frequently listens to radio programs. The player actively submits many messages to get the title "Heaviest listener", who gets the most adopted messages.

Fig. 2. Title screen of Heaviest Listener

To play the game, enter your radio name in the message form on the top left side of the screen, select your prefecture from the pull-down menu, and then enter your message (between 10 and 50 characters). This message form is modeled on the message form on the actual radio program's website. You can only send the same message once, so you need to change your message each time. Since other listeners' messages are also read during the broadcast, you must send many messages to be accepted. The game is designed to simulate the experience of being a listener, where you must send many messages to increase the chances of your message being selected. Participating adds an interactive element to the broadcast and a chance to share your thoughts with a broader audience. Another interesting feature of this radio program is the radio names of other listeners. Radio names vary from simple nicknames to interesting puns and jokes. When your e-mail is selected, your radio name will turn red so you can easily recognize it (see Fig. 3).

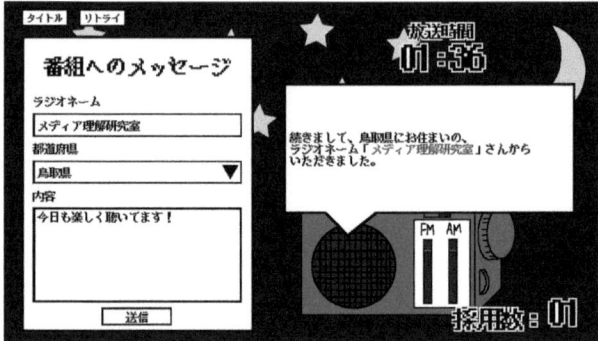

Fig. 3. "Heaviest Listener" playback screen at reading an e-mail

At the end of the broadcast time, a letter from the program staff is delivered to the listener (Fig. 4). When the letter is opened, a large photo of the face of "All Night Jappon" personality "Radio Dempa" is printed on the envelope, and the message is written as if it were a direct translation of his light-hearted delivery. The player will feel like they can hear his voice after the program ends. This letter corresponds to the result screen in this work, and different contents are prepared depending on the number of e-mails adopted. If the player succeeds, the letter may contain words of praise; if he fails, it may contain sarcastic comments.

Developed using Unity, this game offers a light and smooth playing experience. We have used free fonts, background music, and sound effects to create an atmosphere that matches the game's worldview. All materials used are credited within the game, a sign of respect to the creators. We have also designed all the game's images, establishing a unique visual style. The completed game, "HesoRider", [10] is free on the game submission site "unityroom", making it accessible to all players.

Fig. 4. "Heaviest Listener" result screen

3.2 Message Selection Mechanism

In this game, the messages that are accepted by the personality and how they are responded to significantly affect the quality of the user experience. This section describes the message selection mechanism designed from this perspective.

Message selection in this game is performed by probabilistic random sampling from a set called the message pool, S. This pool contains initial messages prepared in advance by the system and all messages posted by users. A message's data structure includes the radio name, prefecture, and message text. Message selection employs a flexible framework that assigns a weight w_m to each message m and defines selection probabilities based on these weights, thereby reflecting factors such as the importance or popularity of the posted content.

The selection process is mathematically formulated below. Let S_t be the set of messages at time t:

$$S_t = \{m_1, m_2, \ldots, m_n\}.$$

The selection probability p_m of each message $m \in S_t$ is defined as follows based on its weight w_m:

$$p_m = \frac{w_m}{\sum_{m' \in S_t} w_{m'}}.$$

Let $M^{(i)} \subseteq S_t$ be the set of messages posted by player i. The probability that a message from that player is selected, P_i, is:

$$P_i = \sum_{m \in M^{(i)}} p_m.$$

Currently, assuming that $w_m = 1$, $p_m = 1/n$, and all messages are selected with equal probability. However, in the future, by reflecting content suitability and evaluation scores in w_m, it will be possible to weight selections according to content and perform dynamic interaction control.

4 Discussion and Future Work

In this game, when an e-mail sent by a listener is selected, the comment made by the personality is a pre-written set of phrases. It is chosen randomly from several different options. As a result, the reactions of the personalities tended to be invariant regardless of which message was read, and players could not fully appreciate the sense of realism of an actual radio program or the unique reactions of the personalities. In particular, the sense of immersion could be lost if they sent a distinctive e-mail but did not get a response that matched it.

In future work, we plan to introduce a function that uses language generation AI to generate unique comments that match the content of the e-mail in real-time. This will enable the personality to respond as human-like as if reading the e-mail, adding humor, surprise, and sometimes sharp comments that match the content. It will also create different interactions for each player, making it possible to feel more like they are interacting with a personality. Ultimately, we aim to recreate a realistic conversation flow similar to an actual radio program and to create an experience that allows players to immerse themselves more deeply in the game world.

Furthermore, this game structure is based on Japanese radio program culture, and careful consideration is necessary regarding its general applicability overseas. In Japan, sending e-mails to radio programs and having them read on air is a well-established part of daily culture. However, real-time comment exchanges on Twitch and YouTube Live are mainstream in English-speaking countries, whereas asynchronous post-reading formats are limited. [8]

Nevertheless, the experience of "having one's message featured in a public forum and receiving a response from a personality" is appealing across many cultures, and the interaction structure of this game is considered to have potential for application to other languages and cultures. In this sense, comment generation using language generation AI is not merely a technical extension but a foundation for providing a dialogue experience with personalities across languages and cultures. In addition to implementing these features, we will further verify their acceptability in multilingual environments and cross-cultural contexts, aiming to enhance the cultural universality and flexibility of interaction design.

5 Conclusion

We have created a simulation game called "Heaviest Listener" that allows you to enjoy sending e-mails to a radio program. In this game, they will step into the shoes of a radio listener and craft e-mails to send to the program. This game aims to encourage people who do not usually listen to radio programs to experience the joy of creating an email to send and having it adopted, and to get them to listen to actual radio programs through the game. We hope to use the medium of games to promote the content of radio programs and the culture of sending e-mails.

References

1. Newman, N., Fletcher, R., Schulz, A., Andı, S., Robertson, C.T., Nielsen, R.K.: Reuters Institute Digital News Report 2021. Reuters Institute for the Study of Journalism, University of Oxford (2021). https://reutersinstitute.politics.ox.ac.uk/sites/default/files/2021-06/Digital_News_Report_2021_FINAL.pdf
2. Radiko Co., Ltd., https://radiko.jp/about. Accessed 01 Apr 2025
3. Radiko Co., Ltd., https://radiko.jp/newsrelease/pdf/20220830_001_pressrelease.pdf. Accessed 01 Apr 2025
4. Nippon Broadcasting System, Inc., https://www.allnightnippon.com/. Accessed 01 Apr 2025
5. NotGames: Not For Broadcast. Steam (2022). https://store.steampowered.com/app/1147550/Not_For_Broadcast/
6. Team17: Killer Frequency. Official site (2023). https://www.team17.com/games/killer-frequency/
7. van Dijck, J.: Users like you? Theorizing agency in user-generated content. Media, Cult. Soc. **31**(1), 41–58 (2009). https://doi.org/10.1177/0163443708098245
8. Hamilton, W., Garretson, O., Kerne, A.: Streaming on Twitch: fostering participatory communities of play within live mixed media. In: Proceedings of the SIGCHI Conference on Human Factors in Computing Systems (CHI 2014), pp. 1315–1324. ACM, New York (2014). https://doi.org/10.1145/2556288.2557048
9. Jenkins, H.: Convergence Culture: Where Old and New Media Collide. New York University Press, New York (2006)
10. Naichilab, unityroom, "Heaviest Listener". https://unityroom.com/games/heaviestlistener. Accessed 01 Apr 2025

Asymmetric VR Game Heist Extravaganza

Jules A. M. van Gurp and Erik D. van der Spek(✉)

Department of Industrial Design, Eindhoven University of Technology, Groene Loper 3,
5612AE Eindhoven, The Netherlands
`e.d.vanderspek@tue.nl`

Abstract. The game Heist Extravaganza was developed to explore the design space of novel controllers for Asymmetric Virtual Reality, in order to improve social connectedness and enjoyment for all players. It advances the state of the art by having four different player roles for five different interaction dimensions: Immersive, Energetic, Explorative, Precise and Strategic interactions. In this paper we describe the game design and how the asymmetry should lead to more social connectedness and enjoyment.

Keywords: Asymmetric Virtual Reality · Mixed Reality · Co-located gameplay · Game design · Game controller design

1 Introduction

Asymmetric Virtual Reality (AVR) games allow players to share in a co-located game world through various interfaces. The use of alternative interfaces makes it possible to create role differentiation, so that, among others, players communicate more with each other and players of different proficiency levels can play together. The body of knowledge on how to design alternative interfaces and create settings for more than two players concurrently is still lacking [1]. Here we want to research if role differentiation can be better aligned with player motivation profiles through the design of novel controllers and a game that stimulates non-tedious reliance.

2 Related Works

2.1 Asymmetry in Play

Introducing asymmetry in games can have several benefits such as increases in social presence, connectedness, and engagement [2, 3]. Various Mechanics of Asymmetry exist that designers can implement in their games: asymmetry of Ability/Challenge, Interface, Information, Investment, Goal, and Responsibility [1]. These different types of asymmetry can have a variety of benefits in multiplayer games. They can make games more inclusive by letting players choose a role that fits them [4]. Asymmetry of Ability/Challenge can obviate the need for less experienced players to compete with more skilled ones on the same performance measure, and in cooperative games, asymmetry of Ability/Challenge and Information can make every player necessary to achieve team goals, making them feel useful [5]. Asymmetry of Information also has the added benefit that it can encourage communication, thereby enhancing social interaction [5–7].

Through the implementation of these various Mechanics of Asymmetry, certain Dynamics of Asymmetry can emerge between players in the form of interdependence. There are three forms of directional dependence: Mirrored, Unidirectional, and Bidirectional [1, 6]. Mirrored dependence occurs when "the nature of each player's reliance on each other is identical" [6]. Therefore, this form is very uncommon in fully asymmetric games. Unidirectional dependence arises when one player relies on the other, but not vice versa. Bidirectional dependence is when multiple players rely on each other, but in different ways. High levels of player interdependence can offer benefits such as increased communication and reduced frustration [8]. Additionally, it can improve the sense of social connectedness [9]. Lower levels of interdependence can foster an atmosphere of competitiveness, even in collaborative games [3, 8], for example when competitive players try to see who can reach the end of a level first.

2.2 Asymmetric Interfaces

Most existing AVR games and research let non-VR players interact with the virtual world using more widespread forms of electronic gaming interfaces such as gamepads, 2D displays, or smartphones [10]. However, perhaps the best known AVR game, Keep Talking & Nobody Explodes [11], offers its non-VR player a physical paper manual as an interface. The use of such alternative interfaces can introduce a sense of novelty and be an attractive option for players with less gaming experience.

Nintendo Labo [12] is an example of how even simply changing the shape of an interface can impact the gaming experience. Labo uses cardboard add-ons for the Nintendo Switch's Joy-Con-Controller. The Labo Blaster is a cardboard shotgun that is controlled by making a pumping action and pressing a trigger. The cardboard is not necessary to use the Joy-Cons as a shotgun, however, the prop's aesthetics and feel help to tell the game's story more convincingly and thus works as a tool for transmedia storytelling [13].

Studies by Gugenheimer et al. [14] and Zhou et al. [9] do investigate how non-standard interfaces can be applied to AVR, as they explore physical props or even use co-players themselves as parts of these interfaces. However, the research on alternative interfaces remains scarce; even more so on how assigning different asymmetric roles to the various non-VR players could influence an AVR game's social dynamics. We contend that players choosing a role that fits their preferences and skill level could improve their gaming experience. Furthermore, the additional asymmetry that it introduces can positively impact social presence, connectedness, and engagement, thus making VR more social [2, 3].

2.3 Design Guidelines

Some design guidelines were set up based on literature to assist in making co-located VR games more social. First, cooperative AVR seems to create higher levels of co-presence and social presence compared to competitive ones [15]. A sense of team competence can influence perception of individual competence [16], which can be used to make less skilled players feel more competent. In addition, an interface providing a projection of the game to spectators can assist in them feeling engaged [10, 14].

It is also recommended to have tight coupling between players' roles through high interdependency and inclusion of each other in their respective gameplay loops, because it can create improved levels of social connectedness, and encourages more social interaction [9, 17, 18]. However, players should not be made dependent on each other just for the sake of interdependence, as this can lead to what Harris & Hancock [3] call "tedious reliance". A teammate's action is better perceived when it is no irrelevant task, but a challenge they have to overcome themselves to make a meaningful contribution to the team [3, 14]. At the same time, players appreciate varying levels of participation and dependence throughout a gameplay session [3, 10].

Lastly, it is advisable to make the interfaces and their aesthetics fit the context of the game, since this can contribute to the experience of the game's story and thus engage players [19]. Taking inspiration from pervasive games, it can help with extending the gaming experience and the magic circle of play into the real world where non-VR players can be included socially [20].

3 The Game

To discover how introducing additional asymmetric interfaces in AVR games could improve the social dynamics between players, Heist Extravaganza was developed. In this AVR game 4 players must cooperate to infiltrate a museum called "Le Musée des Extravagances". They must retrieve the mythical apple of the Hesperides to save the world. Each player has a unique role and interface, offering something interesting for players of different skill levels and player profiles. They must all use their unique abilities and knowledge to avoid or take out the guards on patrol, hack door locks, find hidden codes, disable a laser system, unlock the safe, identify the correct apple, and finally escape. For an overview the players' actions and interdependencies see Fig. 1.

3.1 Novel Interfaces Based on Player Profiles

The designs of the various roles and accompanying interfaces (see Fig. 2) each focus on one or more interaction dimensions, identified through a research through design process [21], which took the Gamer Motivation Model [22] as a starting point. These 5 dimensions are: Immersive, Energetic, Precise, Explorative and Strategic interactions. Incorporating these dimensions could increase asymmetry and make it more attractive to players of varying interests and skills. The main scientific contribution of Heist Extravaganza is to be a design exemplar of how the aforementioned dimensions can be translated into interfaces that make asymmetric VR games more entertaining.

Fox. This role is played by the VR player. They have hidden themselves in the restroom and come out at night to find the golden apple. They are guided through the museum by the other players. The Fox carries along the Super Gadget, which is a virtual representation of the Engineer's physical interface. The gadget can be identified by the lightning bolt

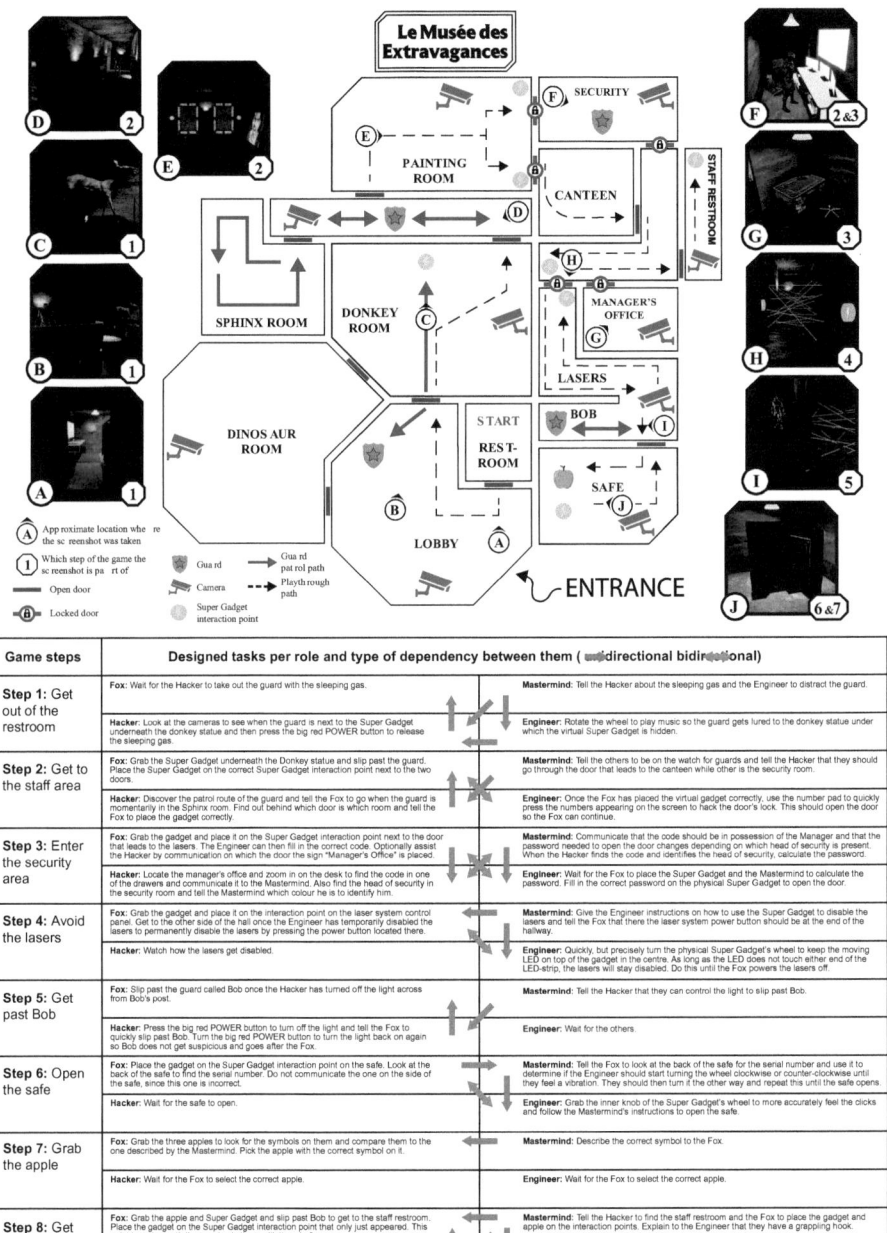

Fig. 1. Overview of the game in the form of a map and screenshots from the game. The letters underneath the screenshot indicate where on the map it was taken. The numbers underneath the screenshots indicate which part of the game the screenshot is part of.

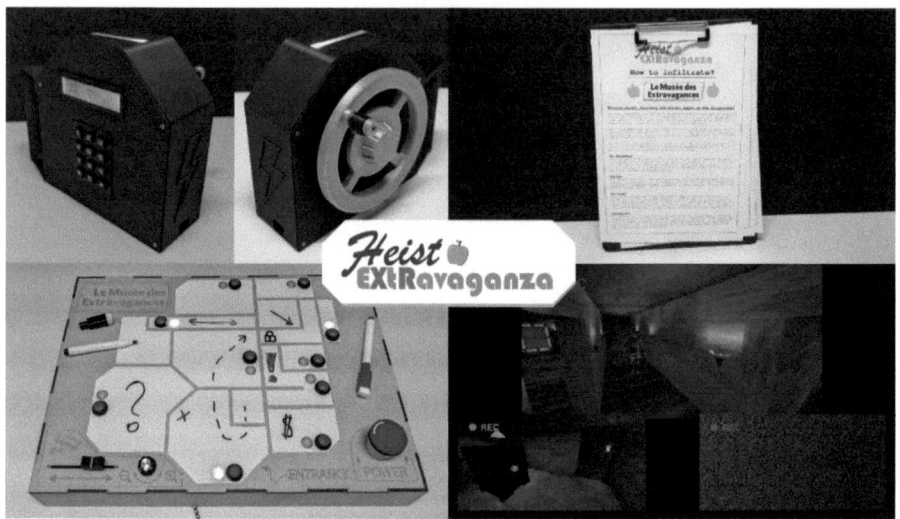

Fig. 2. The Engineer's interface (top left), the Mastermind's interface (top right) & the two parts of the Hacker's interface (bottom)

symbol on the side of both the Fox's and Engineer's version. The Fox can place the gadget on various Super Gadget interaction points that trigger minigames for the physical version which have to be completed for the Fox to continue. This role focuses mainly on immersion.

Mastermind. This player is provided with a paper manual full of information about the museum and the planning of the heist. The text is written as if they were the notes of the actual Mastermind behind the heist and if takes the players through the story of the game. This role was designed with explorative interactions in mind. The player is presented with a lot of information and must identify what is important and communicate this to their co-players. The manual also includes some simple puzzles requiring input from others. The puzzles' results help others progress. The role was designed not to be difficult, specifically for people with less experience with traditional gaming interfaces.

Hacker. This interface consists of a top-down map of the museum with whiteboard paper over the rooms so notes can be made on it, but also easily erased. There are 10 small red buttons spread out on the map that can be pressed to "hack" the museum's security cameras. The most recently selected camera can be panned using a slide potentiometer and zoomed using a rotary one. These camera movements can also be seen by the Fox in the virtual world. The monitor is intended to also be viewed by the other non-VR players as it provides them with a projection of the VR world, which can make them feel more involved when they have no specific task assigned [10, 14].

This interface was developed focusing on strategic interactions, as its user is intended to plan out how the Fox can get past the guards. The ability to make notes should assist in this. Additionally, the player is provided with a big red POWER button that can be pressed to take a guard out with sleeping gas, and it can be used to control a lamp. The player must figure out when to turn this lamp off and on the get past another guard.

Additionally, the panning and zooming can be used to find info in some rooms that needs to be communicated to the Mastermind.

Engineer. The interface for this role is the Super Gadget. It focuses on both energetic and precise interactions, as some interface components could be utilized for both interaction types and it makes the role more versatile. One component is the wheel, which during some parts of the game must be rotated as fast as possible to for example hoist the VR player and apple up into a ventilation shaft. For these fast rotation interactions, a handle on the outside of the wheel can be used. However, there is also a smaller grip in the middle of the wheel for more precise rotations. Aside from the haptics from the rotary encoder, a vibration motor is incorporated to simulate stronger clicks during a minigame where the Engineer precisely rotates the wheel to open the safe.

On top of the gadget is a short row of LEDs that provide its user feedback on how fast they are rotating the wheel. These are also used when deactivating the laser system, as the player must spin the wheel to keep a moving LED centered in the middle of the row. Additionally, a song comes out of the gadget through a passive buzzer when the wheel is rotated at the start of the game. This action distracts one of the guards. Lastly, on one side is a number pad and LCD screen. The screen gives instructions and is used for a minigame where the number that shows up needs to be pressed as quickly as possible. It is also used to fill in a password to open a door.

3.2 Playtest

The game was playtested with two groups of four people. High enjoyment and social presence scores indicate that the game was successful in offering roles that all players enjoyed. Every role brought something interesting to players. For more details see [21].

4 Conclusion

This paper discusses the development of the AVR game Heist Extravaganza and its 3 accompanying custom-made interfaces. Each role played in this game focuses on one or more interface interaction dimensions identified during this study: Immersive, Energetic, Precise, Explorative and Strategic interactions. The aim of this research was to investigate how such a set of distinct interfaces can improve social connectedness between players in co-located VR settings and increase overall enjoyment, through the development of a design exemplar. Play testing suggests that such interfaces can be effective tools for creating social engagement and an enjoyable experience.

Acknowledgments. We would like to thank Enversed Studios for feedback during the development of the game and participating in a co-design session.

Disclosure of Interests. The authors have no competing interests to declare that are relevant to the content of this article.

References

1. Rogers, K., Karaosmanoglu, S., Wolf, D., Steinicke, F., Nacke, L.E.: A best-fit framework and systematic review of asymmetric gameplay in multiplayer virtual reality games. Frontiers in Virtual Reality **2** (2021)
2. Depping, A.E., Mandryk, R.L.: Cooperation and interdependence: how multiplayer games increase social closeness. In: Proceedings of the Annual Symposium on Computer-Human Interaction in Play, pp. 449–461. ACM, Amsterdam The Netherlands (2017). https://doi.org/10.1145/3116595.3116639
3. Harris, J., Hancock, M.: To asymmetry and beyond! improving social connectedness by increasing designed interdependence in cooperative play. In: Proceedings of the 2019 CHI Conference on Human Factors in Computing Systems, pp. 1–12. Association for Computing Machinery, New York, NY, USA (2019). https://doi.org/10.1145/3290605.3300239
4. Harris, J., Hancock, M.: Beam Me 'Round, Scotty! II: Reflections on Transforming Research Goals into Gameplay Mechanics (2018). https://doi.org/10.1145/3270316.3273039
5. Zagal, J., Rick, J.: Collaborative games: lessons learned from board games. Simulation & Gaming - Simulat Gaming **37**, 24–40 (2006). https://doi.org/10.1177/1046878105282279
6. Harris, J., Hancock, M., Scott, S.D.: Leveraging asymmetries in multiplayer games: investigating design elements of interdependent play. In: Proceedings of the 2016 Annual Symposium on Computer-Human Interaction in Play, pp. 350–361. Association for Computing Machinery, New York, NY, USA (2016). https://doi.org/10.1145/2967934.2968113
7. Smilovitch, M., Lachman, R.: BirdQuestVR: a cross-platform asymmetric communication game. In: Extended Abstracts of the Annual Symposium on Computer-Human Interaction in Play Companion Extended Abstracts, pp. 307–313. Association for Computing Machinery, New York, NY, USA (2019). https://doi.org/10.1145/3341215.3358246
8. Emmerich, K., Masuch, M.: The impact of game patterns on player experience and social interaction in co-located multiplayer games. In: Proceedings of the Annual Symposium on Computer-Human Interaction in Play, pp. 411–422. Association for Computing Machinery, New York, NY, USA (2017). https://doi.org/10.1145/3116595.3116606
9. Zhou, Z., Márquez Segura, E., Duval, J., John, M., Isbister, K.: Astaire: a collaborative mixed reality dance game for collocated players. In: Proceedings of the Annual Symposium on Computer-Human Interaction in Play, pp. 5–18. Association for Computing Machinery, New York, NY, USA (2019). https://doi.org/10.1145/3311350.3347152
10. Kitson, A., Ahn Grace, S.J., Gonzalez, E.J., Panda, P., Isbister, K., Gonzalez-Franco, M.: Virtual games, real interactions: a look at cross-reality asymmetrical co-located social games. In: Extended Abstracts of the 2024 CHI Conference on Human Factors in Computing Systems, pp. 1–9. Association for Computing Machinery, New York, NY, USA (2024). https://doi.org/10.1145/3613905.3650824
11. Steel Crate Games: Keep Talking and Nobody Explodes. https://keeptalkinggame.com/ (2015)
12. Nintendo: Create new ways to play with Nintendo Labo!. https://www.nintendo.com/en-gb/Nintendo-Labo/Nintendo-Labo-1328637.html. Accessed 8 Jan 2025
13. Jenkins, H.: Transmedia storytelling and entertainment: an annotated syllabus. Continuum **24**, 943–958 (2010). https://doi.org/10.1080/10304312.2010.510599
14. Gugenheimer, J., Stemasov, E., Frommel, J., Rukzio, E.: ShareVR: enabling co-located experiences for virtual reality between HMD and non-HMD users. In: Proceedings of the 2017 CHI Conference on Human Factors in Computing Systems, pp. 4021–4033. Association for Computing Machinery, New York, NY, USA (2017). https://doi.org/10.1145/3025453.3025683
15. Jung, S., Wu, Y., Lukosch, S., Lukosch, H., Mckee, R.D., Lindeman, R.W.: Cross-reality gaming: comparing competition and collaboration in an asymmetric gaming experience. In:

Proceedings of the 29th ACM Symposium on Virtual Reality Software and Technology, pp. 1–10. Association for Computing Machinery, New York, NY, USA (2023). https://doi.org/10.1145/3611659.3615698
16. Sykownik, P., Emmerich, K., Masuch, M.: Exploring patterns of shared control in digital multiplayer games. In: Cheok, A.D., Inami, M., and Romão, T. (eds.) Advances in Computer Entertainment Technology, pp. 847–867. Springer International Publishing, Cham (2018). https://doi.org/10.1007/978-3-319-76270-8_57
17. Karaosmanoglu, S., Rogers, K., Wolf, D., Rukzio, E., Steinicke, F., Nacke, L.E.: Feels like team spirit: biometric and strategic interdependence in asymmetric multiplayer VR games. In: Proceedings of the 2021 CHI Conference on Human Factors in Computing Systems, pp. 1–15. Association for Computing Machinery, New York, NY, USA (2021). https://doi.org/10.1145/3411764.3445492
18. Moriarty, E.H., Perriman, N., Rutledge, J., Taylor, J., Graham, T.C.N.: Increasing player coupling in an asymmetric racing game. In: Companion Proceedings of the Annual Symposium on Computer-Human Interaction in Play, pp. 306–311. Association for Computing Machinery, New York, NY, USA (2023). https://doi.org/10.1145/3573382.3616059
19. Nedelcheva, I.: Analysis of Transmedia Storytelling in Pokemon Go. (2016)
20. Montola, M., Stenros, J., Waern, A.: Pervasive Games: Theory and Design. CRC Press, Boca Raton (2009). https://doi.org/10.1201/9780080889795
21. van Gurp, J.A.M., van der Spek, E.D.: Heist extravaganza: a design framework and exemplars of asymmetric virtual reality controllers based on player profiles. In: Proceedings of IFIP International Conference on Entertainment Computing IFIP-ICEC 2025, Springer Nature Singapore (in press)
22. Yee, N.: The Gamer motivation profile: what we learned from 250,000 gamers. In: Proceedings of the 2016 Annual Symposium on Computer-Human Interaction in Play, p. 2. Association for Computing Machinery, New York, NY, USA (2016). https://doi.org/10.1145/2967934.2967937

Author Index

A

Aguirre-Morales, Luis 349
Alonso-Fernández, Cristina 47
Ambanelli, Afro 3
Andono, Pulung Nurtantio 166
Antelmi, Alessia 263
Antonaci, Alessandra 320
Aoki, Kota 633
Aqshol, Muhammad Alifian 166
AriasFlores, Hugo 349

B

Baalsrud Hauge, Jannicke 411
Bahrini, Mehrdad 15
Baldeón, Johan 504
Baña, Sergio 360
Berglund, Erik 32
Blom, Paris Mavromoustakos 92
Bonnet, Martin 320
Burdina, Violetta 15

C

Caluya, Nicko R. 433, 442, 478
Calvo-Morata, Antonio 47
Caruso, Andrea 423
Casanova, Marco A. 334
Caserman, Polona 411
Chandler, Damon M. 433, 442, 478
Ciancarini, Paolo 3

D

Dallard, Thomas 571
Dalvi, Girish 138
de Lima, Edirlei Soares 334
De Pellegrin, Emanuele 193
Di Iorio, Angelo 3
Dodd, Michaela 575
Dörner, Ralf 179
Dratzidis, Leon Tristan 60, 389

E

Elangovan, Guhan 433
Espinosa-Chueca, María-José 504

F

Falessi, Davide 3
Feijó, Bruno 334
Fell, Fabian 280
Fernández-Manjón, Baltasar 47
Fowler, Allan 575
Fukuchi, Kentaro 550
Furtado, Antonio L. 334

G

Garruço, Pedro 78
Genga, Laura 193
Ghorbanpour, Kamyab 92
Ghosh, Deb Kumar 478
Gómez, Laura 360
Gómez-Martín, Marco A. 151
Gómez-Martín, Pedro P. 151
González-Calero, Pedro A. 151
Grießhammer, Marius 107, 123
Gupta, Ishika 138
Gutiérrez-Sánchez, Pablo 151

H

Hamanaka, Masatoshi 579, 597
Harada, Kaimu 583
Harisa, Ardiawan Bagus 166
Harvey, Mark 575
Hirahata, Yuta 442
Hirota, Koichi 293
Horst, Robin 179
Hu, Jun 233

I

Ichikawa, Osamu 496
Imura, Masataka 592, 607, 625
Ito, Akinori 571

© IFIP International Federation for Information Processing 2025
Published by Springer Nature Switzerland AG 2025
M. Sugimoto et al. (Eds.): ICEC 2025, LNCS 16042, pp. 649–651, 2025.
https://doi.org/10.1007/978-3-032-02555-5

Ito, Wanosuke 451
Itoh, Masayoshi 550
Iwai, Yoshio 633

J
James, L. J. 193
Josefsson, Filip 32

K
Kaneko, Harunobu 633
Kang, Joo-Eun 207
Kashiwagi, Toshiro 458
Kawai, Yasuo 588
Kawamori, Masahiro 592, 607, 625
Khalid, Mohd Nor Akmal 468
Kim, Min-Joong 207
Kißler, Christian 107
Klemke, Roland 320
Klincewicz, Michal 92
Kodama, Sachiko 583
Komatsu, Shunta 219
Koutaki, Gou 597
Kubota, Tomonori 219
Kuhn, Joerg-Tobias 107
Kurihara, Kazutaka 487
Kutsuzawa, Gaku 621

L
Lay, Jordan K. 478
Lee, JaeJun 207
León, Carlos 360
Liang, Chenwei 233
Liang, Tianle 250
Loria, Enrica 263
Lu, Nathan 250
Lürig, Christoph 280

M
M Haikal, Muhammad Faiq Haikal Bin 478
Maeda, Yusaku 293
Maia, Gilvan 523
Makino, Rintaro 602
Malaka, Rainer 15, 60, 389
Manzo, Andrea 3
Masuch, Maic 107, 123
Matsumoto, Taito 607
Matsumura, Kohei 602, 611, 616, 621
Matsuura, Akihiro 451, 514
Mendoza, Juan Diego 360

Merkord, Aaron 389
Mima, Daiki 611
Montagne, Barbara 193
Moritani, Miu 487
Muñoz, Javier 360
Murayama, Kohei 375

N
Nakakoji, Kumiyo 458
Nakano, Kizashi 375
Narumi, Takuji 375
Nishida, Naoto 293
Nishihara, Teu 496
Nojima, Takuya 293

O
Ogawa, Kohei 219
Ohara, Ryo 375
Ohmura, Kazuki 307
Ohnishi, Ayumi 307
Okafuji, Yuki 602
Okamo, Itsuki 616
Oliveira, Pedro 523

P
Papa, Priscilla Pia 423
Park, Jeong-Eun 207
Pereira, Luís Lucas 78
Pirker, Johanna 263

R
Ramos, Luiggi 504
Roque, Licínio 78
Rose, Melina 320
Rosenfeld, Kieran 250
Ruka, Tanya 575

S
Safari, Ameneh 389
Saito, Kento 514
Sakurai, Sho 293
Salfi, Massimiliano 423
Sanchez-Gordon, Sandra 349
Sato, Kamui 293
Sato, Satoshi 219
Schembra, Giovanni 423
Segawa, Norihisa 559
Shikida, Akira 559
Silva, Bruno 523

Söbke, Heinrich   411
Sohr, Karsten   15
Spagnuolo, Carmine   263
Spronck, Pieter   92
Suenaga, Yuunosuke   621

T
Tai, Wen-Kai   166
Takahashi, Haruki   602, 611, 616, 621
Tanaka, Katsuhisa   625
Terada, Tsutomu   307
Thawonmas, Ruck   151
Trinh, Dung   179
Tsukamoto, Masahiko   307

U
Uemura, Aiko   541

V
Valencia-Aragón, Kevin   349
van der Spek, Erik D.   532, 640
Van Gorp, Pieter   193
van Gurp, Jules A. M.   532, 640
Venuto, Massimo   3
Viana, Windson   523
Villar, Alejandro   360

W
Wang, Rui   233

X
Xue, Bai   575

Y
Yamada, Kana   541
Yamazaki, Keita   550
Yokoi, Sotaro   375
Yoshida, Norimasa   541
Yukino, Rion   451

Z
Zapata, Mireya   349
Zargham, Nima   60, 389
Zhou, Shuo   559

MIX
Papier aus verantwortungsvollen Quellen
Paper from responsible sources
FSC® C105338

If you have any concerns about our products,
you can contact us on
ProductSafety@springernature.com

In case Publisher is established outside the EU,
the EU authorized representative is:
**Springer Nature Customer Service Center GmbH
Europaplatz 3, 69115 Heidelberg, Germany**

Printed by Libri Plureos GmbH
in Hamburg, Germany